# LAW, JUSTICE, AND THE INDIVIDUAL IN SOCIETY
*Psychological and Legal Issues*

# LAW, JUSTICE, AND THE INDIVIDUAL IN SOCIETY
## Psychological and Legal Issues

*EDITED BY*

### JUNE LOUIN TAPP
*University of California, San Diego*

### FELICE J. LEVINE
*American Bar Foundation*

Published for the Society for the
Psychological Study of Social Issues

HOLT, RINEHART AND WINSTON
*New York   Chicago   San Francisco   Atlanta*
*Dallas   Montreal   Toronto   London   Sydney*

Library of Congress Cataloging in Publication Data

Main entry under title:

Law, justice, and the individual in society.

"Published for the Society for the Psychological
Study of Social Issues."
   Bibliography: p. 369
   Includes indexes.
   1. Sociological jurisprudence.   2. Law—
Psychology.   3. Justice.   I. Tapp, June Louin,
1929–     II. Levine, Felice J.   III. Society
for the Psychological Study of Social Issues.
K380.L39          340.1′15          77-24022
**ISBN 0-03-012156-6**

**From Generation . . .**

To Hannah Wacholder-Revier Louin (1901–1945) and Robert Louin (1896–1977) and to Ruth Drucker Levine and Benjamin Levine, who early on taught us the essence of the Kurt Lewin (1890–1947) tradition, in memory and in honor this SPSSI book is dedicated.

**. . . to Generation**

To Mara, Kami, Sarah, Julia, and all the world's children, whose inherent senses of justice are our present and our future, this book is dedicated as well with love, respect, and shared expectation.

# FOREWORDS

## The Society for the Psychological Study of Social Issues

The Society for the Psychological Study of Social Issues (SPSSI) is pleased to sponsor this major contribution to the understanding of law and justice in our society. One of the missions of SPSSI is the sponsorship of books that reflect the Society's goal of applying knowledge from social sciences to the analysis of social institutions.

The legal system, as such an institution, has been severely challenged and tested in the last decade. In response to this period of reflection and reassessment, the various chapters of this collection provide a data base and a number of stimuli for a scientific study of law. Readers will find the diversity of the contributions to be impressive and comprehensive—ranging from child abuse to jury behavior, from concerns with equity to the socialization of prison guards, from cross-national comparisons to developmental ones. Yet the collection of materials effectively hangs together, thanks to the thoughtful and creative efforts of the editors to provide interstitial materials that introduce each section, critically analyze the findings, generate questions, and identify applications.

No one discipline holds the one true perspective on the understanding of the legal system. Just as SPSSI encourages membership and contribution from persons of various professions and perspectives, so too does this book offer the wisdom and expertise of legal scholars as well as social scientists from a number of orientations. As the editors indicate, the union of law and psychology promotes justice and benefits the public interest through the exchange of these orientations and viewpoints.

In these days of a "knowledge explosion," it is rare to find a book that truly does break new ground. Yet *Law, Justice, and the Individual in Society* does so in providing an integrated outlook on a major social institution. The Society for the Psychological Study of Social Issues believes that this book will serve to define an area of knowledge and provide a resource for future policy and research decisions in our society.

Lawrence S. Wrightsman  
Professor of Psychology, University of Kansas  
Publications Chairperson, 1974–1976  
President, 1977–1978  
The Society for the Psychological Study of Social Issues

June 1977

# Psychology

There are a number of indications that we are entering a postindustrial era in many parts of the developed world. One of the characteristics of this era will be that we will have fewer resources, and that access to them will have to be regulated. Also, in the least economically developed parts of the world the focus of human activities will shift to survival. In an increasingly interdependent world, with instant communications, the relationships between the rich and the poor will have to be regulated, otherwise humankind will perish from this earth. Moreover, industrialization brings with it global pollution, which also needs regulation. Furthermore, as expectations for the good life mount, in both the developed and the less developed world, either increased use of systems for economic equalization or anarchy is the prospect. In short, the future is bound to include more and more regulation of interpersonal relationships by means of legal mechanisms as an alternative to anarchy and chaos. Already in our own lifetime we have witnessed an enormous increase in litigation, bureaucratization, and regulation. Though many of us dislike this, the postindustrial era is bound to accentuate these trends.

Psychology attempts to understand the determinants of human behavior and experience. Since a major set of determinants of human behavior will come from the legal system, psychologists are well advised to focus on the interface between law and psychology. In the preindustrial era a lot of human behavior was determined by norms, customs, moral obligations, interpersonal agreements, and roles. In a fast-changing world norms and customs are often unstable. In a secular society moral obligations are less powerful. The gap left from the weakening of these determinants is often filled by the operation of more formal—that is, legal —systems of interpersonal regulation. As this is happening, we are changing our conceptions of what causes human behavior and with such changes our notions of what to do when a person behaves "abnormally," "criminally," or "deviantly."

As a psychologist concerned with understanding social behavior, I am delighted to see a volume that probes in depth a variety of points of contact between psychology and law. A look at the table of contents is sufficient to increase one's understanding of the breadth of contact between the two fields. Reading the contributions themselves produces a much better understanding of many psychological phenomena, such as socialization, conceptual development, self-esteem and social behavior, the role of values in behavior, equity and social behavior, and the determinants of group decisions. Most psychologists will find reading this volume extremely rewarding.

Harry C. Triandis
Professor of Psychology, University of Illinois, Urbana-Champaign
President, 1975–1976
The Society for the Psychological Study of Social Issues

June 1977

# Law

It has been almost sixty years since (to use a phrase of the late Karl Llewellyn) the "first explosion" of interest in the relations of law and the social sciences occurred in U.S. Law schools. The movement to "integrate" law and other areas of knowledge did not proceed from triumph to triumph. On the contrary, there were diversions and retreats, and the intellectual pioneers who fostered the movement would no doubt have been dismayed had they anticipated how modestly their hopes were to be realized. To a large extent these failures of expectation were inherent in the assumptions underlying the movement in its earliest stages. Many lawyers had wholly unrealistic notions about the nature of behavioral science and how it might be employed to advance understanding of law and its processes. For some the movement became an intellectual fad, one to be abandoned whenever newer and more fashionable attractions came into view.

It is premature, of course, to engage in self-congratulation, but it can be said that the past half-century has brought with it increasing sophistication. This volume provides persuasive evidence of the fact. Some lawyers have discerned that cultivation of related bodies of knowledge is essential when responding to felt needs encountered in professional practice. Since World War II many law teachers and scholars have engaged in a remarkable effort of self-education beyond the traditional limits of their discipline, a phenomenon largely unnoticed in other parts of the university community. To paraphrase Holmes, many lawyers would now agree that familiarity with the findings and methods of psychology is not a duty; it is only a necessity.

Still, we have not traveled far. This book may perform its most vital function in demonstrating the importance of interdisciplinary inquiry to the resolution of some of the most pressing issues confronting the legal order in these times. We are only just emerging from a period of intense social stress when the very legitimacy of law received strong challenge. How can this legitimacy be enhanced without negating the values of individual autonomy that underlie our social and political aspirations? The findings of developmental psychology and its concerns with the processes of socialization have a relevance to this most encompassing of problems that is clearly demonstrated in these pages.

Again, a candid participant in the legal system is required to confess that in many critical areas of public policy we literally do not know what we are doing—and have not even begun to find out. Some of the contributions that follow indicate how we might go about obtaining this necessary knowledge.

This volume may also make another point. Perhaps the justification of behavioral inquiry in the areas of law and its institutions goes beyond a concern for law itself. At this moment the problems, frustrations, and dilemmas confronting the system of law are characteristic of our culture as a whole. Study of the law thus constitutes an important avenue for understanding much of broad social concern —in the family, our voluntary associations, our politics, and even in literature and the arts.

There is much offered here that is immediately useful to thought and action. More importantly, these papers delineate targets of opportunity for the generation ahead. In doing so this volume serves both law and psychology well.

Francis A. Allen
Edson R. Sunderland Professor of Law
University of Michigan
President, 1976
Association of American Law Schools

June 1977

# PREFACE

*Law, Justice, and the Individual in Society* represents an excursion for both psychology and law into the dynamics of human behavior in legal contexts. This book of 27 contributions is specifically designed as an interdisciplinary forum of exchange between these two fields. Undergirding this approach is the assumption that the union of social science and law promotes justice; that both are efforts in the public interest; that both use brands of empiricism; and that both need to communicate, if not collaborate, in order to broaden perspectives and policies

We have sought to incorporate diversity and depth in the array of issues addressed in this volume. The major substantive sections focus on the impact of law, the development of individuals' orientations toward law and legal institutions, socialization into legal systems, and decision making in civil and criminal, judicial and nonjudicial settings. While each chapter reflects the unique orientation of its authors, taken together the offerings map the scope of the field and reveal that multiple theories and methods may generate more robust hypotheses and yield greater clarity.

Many of the chapter contributions herein report on findings from field and experimental studies; further, research strategies including the use of questionnaires, in-depth interviews, observations, archival data, and simulation models are represented. Our coverage of the relation of the individual to legal systems is not intended to be exhaustive. By drawing from psychology and law we have sought to present different analytic models, theoretical conceptions, and methods of discourse, intending to convey the richness of the psychology-law interface and to engender an excitement for pursuing further inquiry.

This volume is prepared primarily as a textbook or handbook for advanced undergraduate and graduate students in the behavioral sciences and law as well as for scholars who in increasing numbers are specializing in problems of law and society. To enable the volume to function explicitly as a text, we have included interstitial materials before each major part and introductory and final chapters in order to provide integration and counterpoint. Courses for which this book might be appropriate as the primary text include Social Psychology and the Law, Legal Socialization, Political Psychology, and Law and Society. Our orientation in this book is to serve as a stimulus for critiquing old assumptions, appraising current perspectives, and advancing new ideas. Thus, what follows in these pages is intended not to impart facts but to initiate communication and conversation.

This dialogue has indeed been ongoing. The first forum of psychology-law exchange was a 1971 *Journal of Social Issues* symposium organized by Tapp. Chapters 2, 4–7, 9–13, 21, 24, 25 originally appeared as part of that symposium and are republished here with the permission of the Society for the Psychological Study of Social Issues (SPSSI). Each of these chapters has been revised, updated, and edited (at times rather extensively). Richard Schmuck, former Chair of SPSSI's Publication Committee, and Jacqueline Goodchilds, General Editor of *JSI*, provided help and substantive reviews as we moved from journal to book. Lawrence Wrightsman, also former Chair of the Publications Committee and President of SPSSI (1977–78), deserves special note for his availability and continuous counsel at each phase of creation. Other of our colleagues, Patricia Connelly, Barry Feld, Donna Fossum, and particularly Raymond Nimmer, were also responsive when additional reviews of certain manuscripts were necessary.

This book also evolved with the benefit of feedback from many students and research assistants over the past several years. We wish to thank Tapp's undergraduate and graduate students in the Department of Criminal Justice Studies and Institute of Child Development at the University of Minnesota, specifically students in "Law, Justice, and the Individual in Society" (CJS 5116–5117), "Children and Youth in Society" (CD 5339), "Ethnicity and Legality" (CD 8360), and "Legal Socialization" (CJS 8101). These students were exposed to many of the materials that now constitute our book; their reviews and critiques significantly shaped our work and provided invaluable inputs to our authors. Also we especially thank Kenneth Barry and Irene Sebastian, research associates at the American Bar Foundation, who likewise critiqued chapters and were a continuous source of help and support. Jennie Boulet at the Foundation and Ada Jane Akin, Billy Joe Shebo Van Zandt, and Gary Sawyers at the University of California, San Diego, helped to bring galleys and proofs as close to perfection as possible.

Such an enterprise, of course, could not have been completed if not for institutions that encourage excellence in scholarship. The American Bar Foundation, the University of California, San Diego, and the University of Minnesota admirably served this role. For constant secretarial support, we thank Glenda Hargrove, who kept track of us and our tasks. Several people at Holt, Rinehart and Winston also merit special acknowledgment: Deborah Doty for believing in the value of a psychology-law volume, Roger Williams for getting the presses finally rolling, and Kathy Nevils for bringing shared goals and standards.

In a task of this magnitude (36 authors, time constraints, space limitations), there are a few people who help make an impossible situation a possible dream. Katherine Rosich, Technical Services Director at the American Bar Foundation, has been friend and colleague to us throughout. Bette Sikes, Director of Publications at the Foundation, joined us to make what was otherwise too long . . . just long enough. To Robert Tapp and Judith Lichtman, we also extend our mutual and many thanks for hearing, supporting, and being. And, most importantly, we thank each other for wit, warmth, and wisdom.

Our final tribute, appropriately both ours and SPSSI's, is to Kurt Lewin. Throughout his professional life and as a SPSSI founder, he pressed for rigor and sensitivity in analyzing human behavior in all its complexity. His consciousness regarding social problems was fused with an equal commitment to use his competencies as a researcher and social scientist to pursue action. As Lewin himself emphasized: "Research that produces nothing but books will not suffice." In concluding this preface and introducing this book, we hope to stimulate books and more.

June Louin Tapp<br>Felice J. Levine

June 1977

# CONTENTS

# LAW, JUSTICE, AND THE INDIVIDUAL IN SOCIETY
*Psychological and Legal Issues*

# PART I

*Prologue for Science
and Society*

# CHAPTER 1

# Reflections and Redirections

*—JUNE LOUIN TAPP and FELICE J. LEVINE*

The years 1776, 1984, and 2001 are dates that shake ivory towers, challenge traditions, and forecast social change. Each symbolizes a turning point in the way society views the psyche and constructs the legal apparatus necessary to control or direct, guide or facilitate human behavior. The law viewed primarily as a mechanism for social control and coercion potentially fashions its role to those activities congruent with an instrument of repression. When viewed as a mechanism of facilitation, the law functions as an instrument to create opportunities as well as to promote expression and exchange. Whether the law becomes an instrument essentially of control and coercion *or* cooperation and communication in guiding human interaction is as much a problem for science as for social systems—for psychology as for law.

Both law and psychology are concerned with the configuration of normative human phenomena. Both disciplines feel responsible for establishing rule norms; both are involved in assessing established rule norms; and both deal with the "art" and "science" of human behavior. For example, any court case, any contractual agreement, any deviant expression, or any determination of criminal responsibility involves variables basic to both law and psychology. This identity of interest suggests that interdisciplinary communication and collaboration can yield rules more responsive to self and society.

The challenge then is whether 1984 or 2001 will look more like 1776 in its designs for achieving law and justice, choice and competence, peace and community for the individual in society. Fuller's counsel regarding the future and the formulation of law is sagacious:

If in the future [wo/man] succeeds in surviving his own powers of self-destruction, it will be because he can communicate and reach understanding with his fellows. . . . Communication is something more than a means of staying alive. It is a way of being alive. . . . [The] one central indisputable principle of . . . substantive natural law [is]: Open up, maintain, and preserve the integrity of the channels of communication by which men convey to one another what they perceive, feel, and desire [1969b, p. 186].

This is the essence and the basic mode of the enterprise of law *and* the enterprise of psychology. In their respective attention to human perceptions, values, anxieties, and conflicts, both fields can be instrumental in promoting communication and reducing coercion.

The present book is offered in the spirit of increased communication and collaboration. In a real sense, the future is now!

## ISSUES AND INDICATORS AT THE INTERFACE

### Research and Reform versus Reluctance and Responsibility

Historically, psychologists have investigated the processes of conflict, persuasion, control, authority, compliance, and morality (e.g., Asch, 1953; Bandura & McDonald, 1963; French & Raven, 1959; Kelman, 1958;

Milgram, 1963; Piaget, 1932). Psychologists traditionally have been interested in such topics as socialization, decision making, information processing, perception, memory, cognition, attitudes, group dynamics, and interpersonal relations, all of which are pertinent to the legal system (e.g., Allport, 1955; Bruner, 1958; Cartwright & Zander, 1960; Clausen, 1968; Festinger, 1957; Lewin, 1951; Tajfel, 1969). But with few exceptions (e.g., Freud, 1959; Healy, 1915; Moore & Callahan, 1943; Watson, 1913), until the 1970s, they rarely embarked on investigating the law—the oldest, most specialized authoritative rule system (see also Tapp, 1976). The reasons for this reluctance are multiple and complex (Tapp, 1969). During the first half of the twentieth century, much of psychology was dominated by a laboratory model of science. In addition to psychologists' refraining from field contexts, "perhaps," as Friedman conjectured, "lawyers and jurists have not been hospitable [1975, p. vii]."

Even in the 1960s—a period of social and political ferment—to many psychologists, the study of normal behavior in legal settings suggested a sellout. Many feared their findings would be used by the "enemy," namely the purveyors of an ideology of repression rather than an ideology of expression. They were concerned about the implicative taint of such words as "obedience," "control," and "punishment." Their reluctance to study situations of valuation seemed tied to the fear of being described as social planners, socialization engineers, or system advocates.

By the 1970s, the same issues erupted regarding "rehabilitative" work on deviant behavior in criminal justice settings. Doubts about the efficacy of the rehabilitative role, traditional therapies, and nonconsensual treatment caused many to question their place in the criminal justice system (Allen, 1959; Andenaes, 1975; Trotter, 1975; Wexler, 1973). Conflicted feelings about the role of psychologists surfaced further when, in several trials of national prominence (e.g.,

Camden 28, Ellsberg-Russo, Wounded Knee), the participation of psychologists evoked much debate on the ethical, legal, theoretical, and practical aspects of such psycholegal cooperation (e.g., Etzioni, 1974; Shapley, 1974). The cautions of a prominent judge captured the ambivalence of many psychologists:

[B]efore you respond with enthusiasm to our plea for help, you must ask yourselves whether your help is really needed or whether you are merely engaged as magicians to perform an intriguing side-show so that the spectators will not notice the crisis in the center ring . . . [Y]ou would do well to consider how much less expensive it is to hire a thousand psychologists than to make even a miniscule change in the social and economic structure [Bazelon, 1973, pp. 149–150, 152].

Researchers in law rightly must take care to insure that techniques and findings, particularly on the conditions of compliance, are not so used that the social scientist unknowingly becomes "an agent and mediator of dehumanizing forces [Kelman, 1965, p. 31]." New research contexts indeed raise serious issues about responsibility, whether the research is cross-cultural (e.g., Reynolds, 1975; Tapp, Kelman, Triandis, Coelho, & Wrightsman, 1974) or at the psychology–law interface (e.g., Boruch, 1974; Campbell, 1971; Schwitzgebel, 1970). For example, what are the investigator's responsibilities in research—to the recipients (i.e., the "subjects" or society) and/or to the sponsors? In establishing guidelines or regulations, what are the mutual rights of the scientist and of the subject—whether patient or prosecutor, prisoner or police? To address these questions, researchers must consider the welfare of groups and individuals as well as of individuals in groups. Moreover, developing professional guidelines *and* investigating research areas that comport with scientific and social values are essential if both justice and knowledge are to advance.

These considerations involve fundamental questions about the nature of social reforms based on psychological research. Whatever the source of support—local or state, public or private—psychologists must be as scrupulous about the use of their findings funded by "justice money" in the 1970s as they were (or should have been) about studies underwritten by "poverty money" in the 1960s. Clearly, no research is value-free; nor should it be controlled solely by economic demands or political whims. To safeguard the integrity of research and reform, psychologists and lawyers must be receptive not only to viewing both as experiments but also to accepting the innovative and interactive aspects of the scientific *and* social enterprise (Campbell, 1971, 1974).

The ethics of professional role and responsibility are much more than abstract philosophical problems for psychology and law. Fuller, in speaking to lawyers, discussed the ethics of their role (1969c), while Campbell did so for psychologists (1969, 1974); Wexler cautioned both (1973), and Boruch (1974), among others, analyzed the costs, benefits, and legal implications of social research (see also Campbell, Boruch, Schwartz, & Steinberg, 1975). The underlying theme in much of this discourse is that psychologists and lawyers must continuously evaluate their efforts to provide methodologically and ethically sound research that facilitates understanding the human capacity to function in and create a just legal order. To caution that the investigation of legal attitudes and behavior should be undertaken with awareness of ideological influences, ethical considerations, and policy implications is not to undermine the ideal of objectivity or acclaim the role of advocate. Rather, it is to assert that part of the scientist's legitimate role and responsibility is to study normative values in legal contexts, to adopt ethical guidelines, to court rational scientific and social laws, and to apply knowledge so gained for humane purposes.

However ambivalent or conflicted psychologists or lawyers have been about studying processes in the institution of law, both have come to recognize that "[t]he choice for society as a whole, as well as for social science, is between *capricious lawlessness* . . . and *rational law*. . . . Rational control is inevitable and the real test is which philosophy will guide its direction [Clark, 1965, pp. 18–19]." The philosophy that guides both psychologists and lawyers must have as its constitutive principle "justice" (see, e.g., Deutsch, 1975; Michelman, 1973; Thibaut & Walker, 1975). Only a society aimed toward ethical legality or reasoned justice (e.g., Fuller, 1969b; Rawls, 1971; Selznick, 1969) can implement criteria that distinguish between capricious lawlessness and rational law *and* can accommodate the association between the logical and the psychological, the legal and the moral. In essence, the ultimate purpose for uniting law and psychology is to promote justice and to assess the role of law in achieving a just social order.

## Evolving Roles and Rationales

In the early twentieth century, Pound, attempting to demythologize the law, cited the increasing "socialization of law." He described the necessity of a "legal revolution through the absorption into the laws of ideas developed in the social sciences [1959, p. 431]." This call to study the law as part of the larger process of social science investigation was renewed during the past decade by the plea to empiricize the study of law (Gibbs, 1968). By the 1970s, both law and psychology had been somewhat "socialized" (and "revolutionized") by each other's theories and techniques (cf. Kuhn, 1962) and by societal crises. As a result, changes have occurred in the ideas of both legal and behavioral science scholars.

Support for the proposition that scientific empirical research on legal phenomena (e.g., internalization of laws, efficacy of sanctions, content of legal norms) potentially affords more useful, definitive answers than does conceptual debate became increasingly evident in the late 1960s and early 1970s. For example, in 1969 both psychologist Ellsworth and lawyer Levy argued for the importance of psychological criteria in child custody cases, considered the psychological effects of courtroom decision making, and suggested a paradigm "to test the law's hypotheses while profiting from the methodological rigor possible with a scientific approach [p. 215]." In 1975 psychologist Thibaut and lawyer Walker, who were building on both social-psychological constructs (e.g., Kelley & Thibaut, 1969; Walster, Berscheid, & Walster, 1973) and jurisprudential-legal constructs (Fuller, 1969b; Rawls, 1971), experimentally studied the conditions that affect dispute settlement in adversary proceedings and proffered findings and field applications to stimulate communication and "facilitate the adoption of just procedures [p. 5]." Thus, psychologists and lawyers are now not merely talking the interdisciplinary game; they are actively engaged in mutual exploration of the dimensions of legal experiences.

Psychologists from diverse theoretical and methodological orientations (e.g., Campbell, 1971; Davis, Bray, & Holt, Chap. 26, this volume; Meehl, 1970c; Chap. 2, this volume) recognize that the documentation of multiple experiences is psychology's fundamental procedural contribution to the law. As psychologists move from investigating primarily *simulated* situations to acknowledging both laboratory and *in situ* research as appropriate ways of analyzing phenomena, they are more likely to advance the boundaries of science. Whatever the results of particular studies in the legal system, the existence of substantive gaps in psycholegal knowledge and a need for more systematic theory and diverse research methods has been clearly demonstrated. Although a major difficulty in "natural" settings is reduction of control, a major asset is that each research experience demands a re-evaluation of theory and technique, policy and procedure (cf. Lewin, 1948, 1951).

Lawyers as well must evaluate their propositions and analytic procedures aware that, although "[t]he people who make, apply, or use the law are human beings . . . the study of law has proceeded in relative isolation from other studies in the social sciences [Friedman, 1975, p. vii]." Part of the problem stems from the very definition of law itself—with many legal scholars analyzing the legal system solely in terms of its institutional character. The interactional process definition of law posited by Fuller (1969b), for example, yields a very different vantage on research and reform. To Fuller, "the word 'law' [is] to be construed very broadly . . . to include not only the legal systems of states and nations, but also the smaller systems—at least 'law-like' in structure and function [1969a, p. 1]." In contrast to a narrow definition of law, this approach is more productive and far reaching. A broader definition of law, like a broader definition of psychology, is likely to evoke increasing sophistication in the content and methods of psycholegal studies.

As an author-editor team, we heartily concur that the study of law and humankind's relations to the legal order can more readily be brought out of conceptual limbo by testing the questions of jurisprudence. Such inquiry is the domain of social scientists and legal scholars alike. However, such efforts must be undertaken with the knowledge that often traditional psychological methods are too limiting (see Buss, 1975; Elms, 1975; McGuire, 1973) and psychological insights directed too uncritically or quickly to the basic problems of justice and the legal process (see also Davis, Bray, & Holt, Chap. 26; Meehl, Chap. 2). Parallel problems may arise with the law as well. To deal with such limitations, researchers must broaden their constructs as well as their brands of "empiricism." To the extent that psychologists can array, use, and integrate their multiple methods with those of the lawyers, they can assist each other in describing and extending the limits of the law. To the extent that such integration does not occur, both the professions and society are the losers.

## Coming of Age

As the previous section suggests, the discussion of a rapprochement between psychology and the law is both old and recurrent (e.g., Burtt, 1931; Campbell, 1971; Frank, 1930; Hogan & Henley, 1970; Hutchins & Slesinger, 1929; Levine & Tapp, 1973; Marshall, 1966; Munsterberg, 1908; Shah, 1974; Singer, 1970; Tapp, 1969; Toch, 1961; Whipple, 1909). Although it appears that in the early 1900s there was interest in the relation of psychology and law (e.g., Freud, 1959; Stern, 1903), the scattered attempts from the 1920s to the early 1960s by psychologists (e.g., Burtt, 1931; McCarty, 1929) or lawyers (e.g., Frank, 1930; Riesman, 1951) reflected little move toward collaboration. The major empirical work on law from the 1940s through the mid-1960s was heavily anthropological (e.g., Llewellyn & Hoebel, 1941), sociological (e.g., Cohen, Robson, & Bates, 1958), or psychiatric (e.g., Szasz, 1963). There were few calls for advancing a legal psychology, despite psychologist Clark's contribution to the historic 1954 *Brown* v. *Board of Education* decision.

The psycholegal literature of the past 10 years reveals a new intellectual rapprochement. Particularly during the 1940s, 1950s, and early 1960s, research was comparatively trivial in terms of problem selection, contrived in terms of problem design, and often lacked a sound philosophical or psychological base. However, in the 1970s, researchers in psychology and in law have come to see that their union can promote justice and science.

Key indicators of this collaborative pattern are revealed in organizational responses, academic programs, educational materials, and scholarly writings. This book as well as the first topical chapter on psychology and the law in the *Annual Review of Psychology* (Tapp, 1976), and several symposia and papers in law reviews, in psychological journals, or at meetings (e.g., Bermant, Nemeth, & Vidmar, 1976; Chein, 1975; Pepitone, 1975; *Stanford Law Review*, 1974;

Tapp, 1975) attest to the trend. Another illustration of change is the recent growth, particularly in the past five years, in law and psychology courses and degree programs. Finally, and most strikingly, evidence of the coming of age of the psychology–law movement is provided by the substantial increase in relevant entries in the published indexes in both law (*Index to Legal Periodicals*) and psychology (*Psychological Abstracts*), especially since 1970.

Both law and psychology independently and in concert have been increasingly concerned with the individual in society. Each has been increasingly exposed to the other's discourse as a means for comprehending the role of norm, rule, or law and the socialization of such standards. Psychology can offer multiple methods for systematically documenting human interaction, while the law can provide more realistic settings; together, both fields can posit more discriminating hypotheses. In sum, the phenomena of psychology and law require more confident, responsible, and public views of science and society (Buss, 1975; Campbell, 1971, 1974; Clark, 1965; Elms, 1975; Fuller, 1969b; Rappoport & Kren, 1975; Rawls, 1971). To respond to such pressures, communication *between* and *within* both disciplines needs to occur, and is finally occurring, across levels (i.e., practitioners and researchers) and fields (Riesman, 1951; Scriven, 1971; Tapp, 1969). This book is a testament to—and hopefully a stimulus for—such exchange.

## FROM SOCIAL ISSUES TO SOCIAL ISSUE: A JOURNEY FROM JOURNAL TO BOOK

In 1971, Tapp organized the first interdisciplinary effort in which psychologists and lawyers attempted to frame theoretical, empirical, and policy responses to inquiries about the interrelations of law, society, and the individual. In that *Journal of Social Issues* symposium the focus was on legal socialization and the development of legal values in societal settings. Using the unique format of lawyers *and* psychologists analyzing the interactive aspects of normative legal phenomena, her volume aimed to explore the boundaries of "permissible" and "impermissible" behavior and to clarify the need for an appropriate individual and institutional balance between compliance and independence. Like the present book, that symposium was specifically designed:

1. to provide a forum for exchange and a channel of communication between law and psychology;
2. to stimulate theoretical and empirical inquiry in both disciplines on the paradoxes of compliance and independence, law and justice, crime and order;
3. to increase the body of knowledge on the acquisition of legal values and their effects on the operations of just rule systems; and
4. to suggest research alternatives to scholars and reform possibilities to policymakers in science and society.

The first endeavor showed the importance of interaction between psychological and legal experts. The initial 1971 product nourished communication and seeded the present undertaking. Furthermore, the articles were useful in refining the theories and data of psychologists, legal scholars, and policymakers who "educate" (i.e., socialize) and implement values in society's multiple rule systems.

The demand of the late 1960s for relevance in psychology and for more than educated guesses in law has not abated. Since the first interdisciplinary exposition, additional and recurrent patterns have emerged as pertinent, and a greater number of participants—again from both disciplines —wish to continue intellectual exchange (see also Tapp, 1976). This book is proffered to further such theoretical and empirical inquiry. While each chapter reflects the unique interests and orientations of its authors, taken together these interdiscipli-

nary offerings delineate the scope of the field; indicate the interests, activities, and methods in use in law and in psycholegal scholarship; and reveal mutual commitments to understanding individuals and their interactions in the sociolegal order.

In inviting contributors, we have not, however, sought to create a logical or perfect whole. To have done so might have conveyed a distorted view of the nature of law and of that subject matter appropriately within its realm. As Friedman so aptly stated:

There is of course no "true" definition of law. . . . One might picture the ideal definition as a large, perfect circle; the subsystems as little boxes and squares, each smaller than the circle. If we put together enough boxes of the right shape and size, we get something that adds up more or less to a circle. . . . Geometrically, the figure is rough and imperfect, but it is close enough to the circle for our use [1975, pp. 10–11].

Since, in undertaking the study of law, we embrace such a pluralistic, dynamic, and interactive view, this book is designed to reflect that diversity—across substantive areas (e.g., criminal vs. civil), forums (e.g., jury vs. arbitration), contexts (e.g., U.S. vs. U.S.S.R.), and methods (e.g., observational vs. experimental).

In the journey from journal to book, we have undertaken to provide a basic framework on the coterminality, relationship, and "fit" of psychology and law. Building on the tradition and format of the 1971 *Journal of Social Issues* symposium, the book has retained the joining of psychology and law while broadening the scope of inquiry beyond the legal socialization process. Through organization and content, the editors and contributors aim to highlight the scientific, scholarly, and societal value of addressing social issues from dual perspectives. In so doing, it is hoped that readers will come to appreciate the weddedness of the two fields as revealed in the development and operation of the law *and* in the development and functioning of the individual in legal society. To achieve this end and to avoid the pitfalls of earlier, "traditional" marriages (i.e., with forensic or clinical psychology, or any other social science), we brought to each chapter a substantial but not singular social-psychological perspective. Although activity at the psychology–law interface requires more than just one kind of psychologist—since more than one kind of problem is being addressed (Tapp, 1976)—the promise of social psychology lies in both its catholicity and its "mundaneness" (Weick, 1969).

Given our social-psychological bias and its very nature (i.e., catholic, interdisciplinary, mundane), we sought colleagues across the disciplines of psychology and law who saw the dilemmas, dreams, and designs of the legal order as scientific, social priorities and who queried the components of senses of justice, order, and efficacy. In essence, we were guided by a commitment to create a clime where commentators could evolve "a more meaningful contemporary relationship between psychology and social problems [Rappoport & Kren, 1975, p. 840]." Through our selection and ordering of topics we intend:

1. to foster an understanding of the meanings of law and the law in action;
2. to document the interactions of individuals and institutions as dependent and independent variables;
3. to increase knowledge about the acquisition and impact of legal values within and between rule and justice systems;

4. to retain the primacy of legal socialization as basic to research on law; and
5. to extend the theoretical and empirical boundaries of the psychological sciences and the legal structures by expanding research paradigms.

The chapters are arranged in the following topical areas: Part I, a prologue to the psychology and philosophy of science; Part II, the role and use of law as a socializer in society; Part III, the pattern of legal development and legal socialization through childhood; Part IV, the socialization of adults and the processes of legal socialization into the community and justice systems; and Part V, decision making in judicial and non-judicial legal contexts. In the final section, Part VI, we sketch some considerations about the health and wealth—the "art" and the "science"—of future psychology–law efforts.

Our purpose is to provide a data base and stimulus for psychologists, lawyers, and citizens to investigate a multiplicity of rule or authoritative "legal" systems. New questions are raised about making and maintaining "law." Beyond illuminating a crucial area for focus and inquiry, the chapters and interstitial materials that follow should be a valuable resource for practitioner and policy-maker, scholar and student—and the multitude of others—concerned with the nature of legality and justice. As editors and authors, we hope the total experience will evoke additional critical research, theory, and policy about and between psychology and law.

# CHAPTER 2

# Law and the Fireside Inductions
## Some Reflections of a Clinical Psychologist[1]

—PAUL E. MEEHL

Legislators and judges have relied upon the "fireside inductions" (common-sense, anecdotal, introspective, and culturally transmitted beliefs about human behavior) in making and enforcing law as a mode of social control. The behavioral sciences conflict at times with the fireside inductions. While the sources of error in "common knowledge" about behavior are considerable, the behavioral sciences are plagued with methodological problems that often render their generalized conclusions equally dubious. Legal applications of generalizations from experimental research on humans and animals in laboratory contexts often involve risky parametric and population extrapolations. Statistical analysis of file data suffers from inherent interpretative ambiguities as to causal inference from correlations. Quasi-experiments in the "real-life" setting may often be the methodologically optimal data source.

## PSYCHOLOGY OF THE FIRESIDE

The phrase "fireside equities" is legalese for what the legal layman feels intuitively or commonsensically would be a fair or just result (see, e.g., Llewellyn, 1960). Sometimes the law accords with the fireside equities, sometimes not, and lawyers use the phrase with derisive connotation. Analogously, by "fireside inductions" I mean those common-sense empirical generalizations about human behavior that we accept on the culture's authority plus introspection plus anecdotal evidence from ordinary life. Roughly, the phrase "fireside inductions" designates what people believe about human conduct, about how it is to be described, explained, predicted, and controlled.

One source of conflict between the social scientist and practitioner of law—especially the legislator—is the former's distrust of common knowledge concerning human conduct and the latter's reliance on it. Such reliance is often associated among lawyers with doubts about the value of generalizations arising from systematic behavioral science research involving quantification and experimental manipulation in artificial situations. Reliance on "what everyone knows" was hardly looked at critically before the experimental and statistical methods of contemporary social science were developed. This historical fact provides a built-in preference for the commonsense knowledge of human behavior embodied in positive law. But psychologists mistakenly suppose that lawyers' continued reliance on the psychology of the fireside is wholly attributable to inertia, and these misunder-

[1] I am indebted to the Carnegie Corporation for support of a summer appointment as Professor in the Minnesota Center for Philosophy of Science and to my Law School colleagues Carl A. Auerbach, John J. Cound, and Joseph M. Livermore for their critical readings of the manuscript.

standings warrant consideration. Without being honorific or pejorative, I shall use "fireside inductions" to refer broadly to those expectations and principles, largely inchoate although partially embodied in proverbs and maxims (e.g., "The burnt child dreads the fire," "Blood is thicker than water," "Power always corrupts") arising from some mixture of (1) personal anecdotal observations, (2) armchair speculation, (3) introspection, and (4) education in the received tradition of Western culture before the development of technical social science method.

With my fellow psychologists I share a considerable skepticism concerning the fireside inductions. Even universally held generalizations about the origins and control of human conduct should be subjected to (at least) *quantitative documentary* research and, where feasible, to systematic *experimental* testing. Obviously the degree of skepticism toward a dictum of commonsense psychology should increase in those areas of social control where our efforts are hardly crowned with spectacular success. For example, no known system for the prevention or cure of crime and delinquency is so strikingly successful that our techniques do not need to be called into question (Meehl, 1970c). That the psychological presuppositions underlying the criminal law should be subjected to merciless armchair scrutiny and quantitative research is not said *pro forma,* but expresses a sincere conviction.

## UNFAIR CONTROVERSIAL TACTICS SOMETIMES USED BY LAWYERS AND PSYCHOLOGISTS

Nor is this merely a platitude—"we need research"—that everyone accepts. One does come across rational, educated persons who disagree, at least in concrete instances. I know, for instance, a very able law professor whose ignorance of the behavioral sciences was systematic and deliberate and who made no secret that he thought most

scientific research on law, such as quantitative studies of jury behavior, had little point. He had a foolproof heads-I-win-tails-you-lose technique for dealing with intellectual threats from the social sciences: If I introduced a quantitative-documentary or experimental study of some behavioral generalization having relevance to the law, the findings either accorded with his fireside inductions, or they did not. If they did, he typically responded, "Well, I suppose it's all right to spend the taxpayer's money researching that, although anybody could have told you so beforehand." If the results were *not* in harmony with the fireside mind-model, he refused to believe them! When I called this kind of dirty pool to his attention, he cheerfully admitted this truth about his debating tactics.

Without defending such illegitimate, systematic resistance to the inroads of behavior science data on legal thinking, I direct my behavior sciences' colleagues to some considerations that may render my law colleague's tactics less unreasonable than they seem at first glance. Some behavioral scientists are extremely critical and skeptical about accepting, and applying in practical circumstances, fireside inductions but are willing to rely somewhat uncritically on equally shaky generalizations purporting to be rigorous deliverances of modern behavioral science. A shrewd lawyer, even though he might not know enough philosophy, logic of science, experimental method, or technical statistics to recognize just *what* is wrong with a particular scientific refutation of the fireside inductions, may nevertheless be right in holding to what he learned at his grandmother's knee or through practical experience, rather than abandoning it because, say, "Fisbee's definitive experiment on social conformity" allegedly shows the contrary.

Consider the threat of punishment as a deterrent, one of the most socially important and widely disputed issues relating behavioral science to law. The commonest reaction of psychologists on hearing of my interest in studying law and teaching in the law school is a surprised, "I have always thought of you as a hard-headed, dustbowl-empiricist, quantitatively-oriented psychologist—how can you be interested in that medieval subject matter?" When pressed for an explanation of why they consider law medieval, my behavioral science colleagues generally mention the outmoded and primitive (sometimes they say "moralistic") reliance of the criminal law on punishment, which "is out of harmony with the knowledge of modern social (or medical) science." This kind of rapid-fire sinking of the lawyer's ship quite understandably tends to irritate the legal mind. But the same psychologist who says punishment does not deter relies on deterrence in posting a sign in the department library stating that if a student removes a journal without permission, his privilege to use the room will be suspended but his use fee not returned. This same psychologist suspends his children's TV privileges when they fight over which channel to watch; tells the truth on his income tax form for fear of the legal consequences of lying; and drives his car well within the speed limit on a certain street, having been informed that the police have been conducting speed traps there. It will not do for this psychologist to say that as a citizen, parent, professor, taxpayer, automobile driver, he must make such judgments upon inadequate evidence, but, when contemplating the legal order, he must rely only on scientific information.

Psychologists and psychiatrists say strange things when pressed to document their statement that the criminal law cannot deter. They say, for example, that the only way to control behavior is to get at its source or origin, rather than penalizing it; that capital punishment has been shown not to deter murderers; that experimental research on the behavior of infrahuman animals has demonstrated that punishment is an ineffective mode of behavior control. These are the three commonest responses, along with a general overall flavor to think about crime "scientifically" instead of "in moralistic categories (e.g., *justice*)."

As a psychologist-citizen, I incline to agree with Spinoza (and our contemporary social critic Albert Ellis) that "blaming" behavior is one of the more useless human responses. Antisocial conduct should be approached as a problem of genetics, economics, and behavior engineering, because that orientation tends to minimize the intrusion of emotions into our problem solving, thereby fostering rationality. "Blame" words are emotion elicitors; their use tends to impair the cognitive functions of blamer, blamee, and interested third parties. Regrettably, practically all the words available to designate infractions of moral or legal rules, or persons disposed thereto, are blame laden, since society cannot articulate its legal processes without using the concept of a rule, of its violation, and of a rule violator. We could profitably dispense with words like heinous, dastardly, brutal, bloodthirsty, or wicked. But few would want a society whose legal system had no use for the words justice, fair, equal treatment, malicious intent, offender, obliged, or responsible. Avoiding affect-arousing "blame" words while retaining an axiological vocabulary adequate for the purposes of law is terribly difficult. But we can strive for consistency, and it is both inconsistent and unfair to forbid application of ethical descriptors to a burglar while freely applying condemnatory labels to society for our less-than-optimal treatment of his problem. Nor is such selective moralizing likely to induce the objective attitude that would facilitate rationality and flexibility in our approach to crime control. If a psychiatrist tells a frightened shopkeeper, whose friend has recently been murdered by an armed bandit, that the shopkeeper is wicked because he wrongly thinks of the bandit as wicked, his most probable reaction is to conclude that psychiatrists must be wicked, rather than to examine critically whether wickedness is a useful conceptual tool in thinking about law as a mode of social control.

A well-known sociologist actually objected to the criminal law's reliance on (threatened) punishment as a deterrent on the ground that it does not work, since we find persons in jail who knew they would go there if convicted of crime! One can hardly understand the committing of this low-level methodological mistake (pointed out repeatedly by criminologists and jurists, e.g., Andenaes, 1952, 1966) by a social scientist other than from ideological motives. That some persons commit crimes despite the criminal law, and that incarcerated burglars admit that they knew burglary was illegal, is as helpful in evaluating the deterrent effect of the criminal sanction as it would be to study the prophylactic effect of a drug by conversing with a sample of patients who had fallen ill despite its administration! When a law professor hears a psychologist, sociologist, or psychiatrist argue this way, it is hardly surprising that his regard for the logical incisiveness of social science thinking is not increased. The amazing thing is that monographs are written, lectures delivered, and press releases made by university professors in the social or medical sciences that rely on an argument whose structure is identical with the following: Medicine has always tried to prevent disease and death, but, since people still get sick and everybody dies, we can safely conclude that the medical sciences are a waste of time. Would anybody be impressed with this argument unless he had some sort of ideological axe to grind?

## LEVELS OF SOPHISTICATION IN SOCIAL SCIENCE METHOD

This levels-of-sophistication question is of great importance in interdisciplinary work and in legal education. Any lawyer knows that having the more meritorious case does not guarantee winning it, a main interfering factor being skill of counsel. Differing levels of sophistication in any technical domain, even possession of a special vocabulary, often lead to misleading impressions as to who has the better of a theoretical or practical dispute. Dialectical upmanship has been responsible for some of the friction between

lawyers and social scientists, especially when the social scientist tendentiously presents what purports to be the findings of modern social science but is expressing a particular theoretical (ideological) prejudice. Undergraduate sophistication sufficiently questions the efficacy of criminal law sanctions as a deterrent and recognizes the desirability of adequate statistics on comparable jurisdictions or within the same jurisdiction before and after a change in severity (or certainty) of penalty. However, to understand threshold effects, asymptotes, second-order interactions, nonlinear dependencies, rate changes at different points on a growth function already takes us beyond the sophistication of many social and medical writers who have addressed legal problems.

Consider the rapid dismissal of the general idea that increasing a penalty will be effective, on the ground that capital punishment is not effective (i.e., more effective than life imprisonment) as a general deterrent to murder. To draw such a general conclusion from this instance is illegitimate, but the levels-of-expertise problem requires a certain amount of social science know-how even to talk about difficulties in choosing a murder-rate index and calculating a significance test. (It takes more technical know-how to handle the data when time changes in the same jurisdiction are relied on. See, e.g., Campbell, 1969; Campbell & Ross, 1968; Glass, 1968; Ross, Campbell, & Glass, 1969.) Just a bit more sophistication takes into account problems of extreme values, curvilinearity, and the like involved in such a far-out deviation from social norms as murder. You do not need a PhD in Axiology or Social Psychology to know that murder is a crime *malum in se* rather than *malum prohibitum;* that (allowing for varying definitions) it is forbidden in all known societies, literate and preliterate; that it is regularly attended by strong moral disapprobation and severe legal penalties; that it is explicitly forbidden by all known recorded moral codes; that it is a crime of high deviation threshold, having a very low incidence compared with crimes against property, sexual offenses, and so forth. Given these facts, it may be safely assumed that we deal largely with individuals who are aberrated socially or psychiatrically (I do not mean insane or even formally diagnosable; see Livermore, Malmquist, & Meehl, 1968; Livermore & Meehl, 1967) or who are responding to extreme and unusual stresses in low-probability contexts. Furthermore, the alternative to capital punishment is life imprisonment, a sufficiently extreme penalty that, assuming a Benthamite rational calculation model, a person would not take a chance on this consequence appreciably more than on the death penalty if the probabilities of detection and conviction were other than small. We are comparing the deterrent effects of two penalties both of which are sufficiently far out on the hedonic continuum that their difference is probably not very great at the Benthamite calculational stage, *even when* such calculation occurs—presumably rarely in this crime. Evidently, we cannot extrapolate, with any confidence at all, from "Capital punishment does not reduce murder rates" to "The notion of general deterrence in criminal law is empirically unsound."

Now the special-case question: Is capital punishment an efficacious general deterrent when operating (1) with less extreme personality deviates, and in a social context which (2) makes apprehension quasi-certain and (3) the penalty well publicized? That is, we inquire whether the threat of death as a sanction can be effective under conditions that come closer to the idealized Benthamite-calculus-user situation than is probably the case for most murderers or rapists. For an example, we have a fairly clear case in connection with the mass insubordination, defection, and mutiny of the French army during World War I. In 1917, following the collapse of the Nivelle offensive, morale in the French army was desperately low. The constant danger of death or horrible wounds, the obvious pointlessness of the attacks, and the overall conditions of daily existence must

have provided a set of psychological instigations whose pervasiveness, intensity, and duration were beyond anything found in civilian life. In some units, refusals to obey orders had the full character of a mass mutiny and over half of the French army's divisions experienced such mutinies. In the Ninth Division, all three regiments formed a protest march in which they sang the *Internationale* and shouted. "We won't go up the line!"

Petain, who had replaced Nivelle, understood the instigations to mutiny and took appropriate steps to see that some conditions (e.g., insufficient rest between attacks) did not occur. But he also recognized that the current emergency situation, in which half the army was mutinous, required drastic summary treatment. "I set about suppressing serious cases of indiscipline with utmost urgency [Barnett, 1965, p. 237]." Verdicts of guilty were passed on over 23,000 men, i.e., 1 in every 100 men in the field army on the Western front. Only 432 were sentenced to death and only 55 of these were actually shot, the remainder being sent to penal settlements. But, of course, every soldier and officer knew that the new commander was determined to punish mutineers, and the tiny number of executions were carefully dispersed and widely publicized. The general deterrence notion in criminal law presupposes knowledge or, more precisely, belief as to sanctions. As Petain wrote, "the High Command [must impress] on all ranks that it is resolved on the strictest discipline and obedience . . . It must ruthlessly make examples where necessary and bring them to the knowledge of the army [Barnett 1965, p. 226]."

As the fireside inductions would predict, the mutinies ceased entirely and immediately. Presumably the efficacy of Petain's approach lay in some near-optimal combination of (1) reduced instigations to mutiny, or the hope thereof, under new command, (2) severity of the penalty, and (3) near certainty of detection. As for (3), in 1764 the great Italian criminologist Beccaria (1963) noted that the certainty of punishment is more important than its severity. Severity and certainty combined would predict a high efficacy of general deterrence. Persuasive anecdotal support comes from narcotics law enforcement. Law enforcement officers cannot get into the higher echelons of the drug traffic because the small-fry peddlers cannot be effectively pressured by a prosecutor to tell anything about the next level of the higher-ups. Peddlers have a solid conviction, amounting to a subjective certainty, that if they are known or strongly suspected to have turned stool pigeon, they will be killed by the organized narcotics underworld (Lindsmith, 1965, p. 39). Why as a psychologist should I dismiss this kind of evidence as worthless because it is not "scientific" but merely anecdotal?

## INDIRECT EVIDENCE AS TO GENERAL DETERRENCE

Indirect evidence that persons not now engaged in criminal conduct might commit crimes if the general deterrent pressure of the criminal law were removed is the statistical finding that local crime rates rise dramatically when law enforcement functions are greatly reduced (Andenaes, 1952, 1966) and fall quickly when they are reinstated. Looting associated with natural catastrophes is expected; hence, National Guard troops are regularly called out in such emergencies. Conversations with ex-soldiers about the looting and raping that often occur when a town is occupied supports the fireside induction, "Many people will do illegal things if they know they can get away with it." A close friend, very law-abiding and moral in civilian life, recounted to me (with retrospective amazement) his stealing books from a bombed French bookshop during World War II, thinking "Everyone was doing it and nobody could stop us, so what the hell?" When law enforcement is ineffective, the crime rate often becomes intolerably high. Contrary to the connotation of "vigilante" as a riotous lynching mob, vigilante organiza-

tions were formed by reputable, law-abiding citizens, with their own courts and procedural rules, set up in desperation to enforce substantive law because the legitimate political authority could not or would not protect the community from predators (Bancroft, 1887; Brown, 1963; Newman, 1960; Valentine, 1956). They seem to have been fairly effective in deterrence.

In the recent past, the reactions of some social scientists to the problem of reducing campus violence was predicated on behavioral assumptions that there is no good reason to prefer over the fireside inductions. I heard it argued that punitive measures cannot have any effect because they do not get at the source of the unrest. Nobody ever proved this generalization. No scientific proof exists as to what the *source* was for most rioters. Neither psychological theory nor the fireside inductions suggest that the source of a student's seizing a building or manhandling a dean was the same from one participant to another. Suppose that photographs of law violators involved in campus disturbances were taken to clinch identification; that severe academic penalties and legal penalties for the felonies involved were imposed; that these consequences were widely publicized; and that these practices were uniform over all campuses. My prediction is that campus disturbances involving violence quickly would have been reduced to negligible incidence. A (nonpsychotic) college student who knows that he will be apprehended, thrown permanently out of school, and convicted of a felony carrying a three-year prison term is not appreciably more prone to commit a crime of violence than a looter is likely to steal the silverware from a wrecked house while a National Guardsman with an automatic rifle is observing him. Some of my fellow social scientists, actuated by their own identification with the offenders' cause, attempted to countervail the fireside inductions by invoking "modern behavioral science" as if they were talking about the well-established and highly-generalizable principles of mechanics.

I would not presume, *qua* psychologist, to instruct a government adviser with a PhD in economics on the adequacy of Keynesian theory in forestalling a major depression should a recession begin, relying upon Ayllon's beautiful studies of the "token economy" in a state hospital (Ayllon & Azrin, 1968) or Cowles' classic experiments (1937) concerning the efficacy of differently colored poker chips as token rewards for the chimpanzee. But some social scientists dared extrapolations equally dangerous as these.

When we generalize from laboratory research on punishment in infrahuman animals, the situation is extraordinarily complex, and few statements can be made unqualifiedly. Even before Skinner, behavioral scientists were aware that well-designed regimes of differential positive reinforcement were to be preferred over punishment (negative reinforcement, aversive control). Overreliance on aversive control can be counted as one respect in which the old fireside mind model was badly in error. I wish to state clearly that faith in more and tougher laws as the main way to reduce crime is unsound. The punitive technique combined inefficient behavior engineering with much needless human suffering (Skinner, 1948, 1953, 1961 especially Part I, 1968, 1969 especially Part I). But when we go on to quantitative details, necessary qualifications, and practical applications to influencing the adult human criminal offender (or deterring the rest of us potential offenders), matters become pretty complicated.

Consider the merits of severely punitive legislation against drunken driving. Advocates of a stiffer law may rely on fireside inductions. Psychologists may rely on the allegedly scientific generalization that "punishment doesn't prevent crime." Who makes the riskier extrapolation: The lawmaker, contrasting his own behavior and introspections about driving his car to a cocktail party in the United States and Copenhagen, or the psychologist, extrapolating from Estes's experiments on white rats (1944) and generalizing from what a severely disturbed juvenile delinquent told him in a therapeutic interview? Without denigrating these latter kinds of data, I cannot say that they are more persuasive than introspection and the (remarkably uniform) anecdotes about the Scandinavian drunk-driving sanctions. That it is often considered methodologically unsound to ask persons why they do things is one of the strange developments from behaviorism—here allied for a change with psychoanalysis.

## THE CONCEPTS EMPIRICAL, EXPERIMENTAL, QUANTITATIVE

Rational discussion of the law's reliance on the fireside inductions may be rendered needlessly difficult by an unfortunate semantic habit as to the honorific word "empirical." Since I have myself been fighting a running battle with my psychological associates for some years against this bad habit, I would dislike to see it accepted by legal scholars. The following methodological equation, often implicit and unquestioned, is being taken over by lawyers from behavioral science:

$$Empirical = Experimental\text{-}and\text{-}$$
$$Quantitative = Scientific$$

This equivalence is objectionable on several grounds. It is epistemologically inaccurate since there is a great deal of the empirical (i.e., arising in or supported by observations or experiences, including introspective experiences) that is neither experimental nor quantitative. Furthermore, the middle term assumes a false linkage because (1) not all experimental research is quantitative and (2) not all quantitative research is experimental. Third, several disciplines exhibit varying amounts of experimental manipulation conjoined with varying amounts of the qualitative/quantitative dimension, for example, astronomy, ecology, comparative anatomy, botany, genetics, paleontology, economics, meteorology, geography, historical geology, epidemiology, clinical medicine.

What is an experiment? I am not prepared to give an exact definition. Roughly, an experiment is a systematic, preplanned sequence of operations-cum-observations, the system of entities under study being relatively isolated from the influence of certain classes of causal factors; other causal factors being held quasi-constant by the experimenter; and still others manipulated by him, their values either being set for different individuals in the system or changed over time at the experimenter's will; and output is recorded at the time. Some would add (I would not) that remaining causally efficacious factors (known, guessed, or completely unidentified but assumed to exist) must be rendered noncorrelates of the manipulated variables by a randomizing procedure permitting their net influence to be estimated (statistical significance test).

This definition says nothing about apparatus, instruments, measurement, or even being in the laboratory. I disapprove of stretching the word "experiment" to include clinical or sociological research based upon ex post facto assessment processes, entering files of old data, naturalistic observations in the field or in public places, and so forth. But Campbell's "quasi-experiment" is useful to denote a subset of these possessing certain methodological features that render them relatively more interpretable (see Campbell, 1969). The word "experiment" has become invidious because biological and social scientists tend to denigrate nonexperimental sources of knowledge (such as clinical experience, file data, or the fireside inductions) by equating "experimental" with "empirical" with "scientific." But the fireside inductions *are empirical*. No logician would hesitate to say this. Their subject matter is the domain of empirical phenomena, and one who invokes a fireside induction will, when pressed to defend it, appeal to some kind of experience that he expects the critic will share with him, whether personally or vicariously.

Even the traditional law review article tracing, say, the development of a juridical concept like "substantive due process" through a sequence of appellate court opinions is empirical, since its subject matter is the verbal behavior, recorded in documents, of a class of organisms, and the researcher studies the changes in this behavior over time. The presence in the article of analytical discourse does not render it nonempirical, but to argue this is beyond the scope of the present paper (see Feigl & Meehl, 1974; Meehl, 1970b; Skinner 1969, Chap. 6).

There are important differences between the traditional law review and the kind of article we expect to find in *Law and Society Review*. But there are good words, more precise and less invidious, to characterize the difference. For a study of files or documents using the statistical techniques of behavioral science we can say simply "statistical." If structural statistics (such as factor analysis or multidimensional scaling; see Meehl, 1954, pp. 11–14) are used, we have the word "psychometric." Distinguishing the quantitative or statistical from the experimental dimension is particularly important in discussing methodology of research on law because—as in clinical psychology and personology—one research method is the application of statistical and psychometric techniques of analysis to documents (e.g., diaries, interview transcripts, jury protocols, Supreme Court opinions). It would be misleading to say that one "performs an experiment" if he plots a curve showing the incidence of concurring opinions over time in the behavior output of an appellate court, but it is equally misleading to say that an article that draws no graphs and fits no mathematical functions but traces through a set of opinions over time with reference to the incidence of split votes and dissents is not empirical. Research does not cease to be empirical, or even behavioral, when it analyzes behavior products instead of the ongoing behavior flux itself.

Since the control of variables influencing a dependent variable is a matter of degree, sometimes one wonders whether the word "experiment" is applicable. But this is merely the familiar problem of drawing an arbitrary cut whose location matters little. For research designs methodologically more powerful than studying a slice of cross-sectional file data because we have changes over time in relation to a societal manipulation (e.g., amendment of a penal statute), we have the expression "quasi-experiment" (Campbell, 1969).

## MENTAL TESTS AND SOCIAL CLASS: THE LEVELS-OF-SOPHISTICATION POINT EXEMPLIFIED

The sophistication-level effect is beautifully illustrated by the vexatious problem of interpreting socioeconomic differences on mental tests. I suppose the minimum sophistication level needed even to put the interesting questions is that of understanding why and how intelligence tests were built and validated, including basic concepts of correlation, content-domain sampling, reliability, validity, and developmental growth curves. Further, exposure to basic psychometric theory and multiple strands of validation data (Campbell & Fiske, 1959; Cronbach & Meehl, 1955; Jackson, 1969; Loevinger, 1957) should eliminate some common anti-test prejudices and excessive reliance upon anecdotal refutations.

This bottom level of psychometric sophistication would suffice for an employer using psychological tests in screening job applicants. At a higher level, one thinks about the social class bias in tests. If he relies on the class-score correlations as definitive proof of test bias, he will perhaps avoid using tests, either because he may "miss" some good candidates (a poor reason, statistically) or from considerations of fairness, justice, equal opportunity (a good reason, provided his psychometric premise concerning bias is substantially correct). Moving one step higher, we realize that the SES-IQ correlation is causally ambiguous, and that the limitations of statistical method for resolving this ambiguity are such that no analysis of file data can tell us what causes what. No one

knows and, worse, no one knows how to find out to what extent the SES-IQ correlation is attributable to environment or to genetics. This causal ambiguity, while rather obvious (and pointed out years ago in Burks & Kelley, 1928) is somewhat above the sophistication level of many sociologists and psychologists, who talk, write, and design experiments on the (implicit) assumption that social class is entirely on the causal input side of the equation.

I have treated the terrible complexity of this problem elsewhere (Meehl, 1969, 1970a, 1971). I can briefly concretize it by reference to the Coleman Report (Coleman, Campbell, & Hobson, 1966) on equality of educational opportunity. In an interdisciplinary discussion, a law professor argued: Since the Coleman Report showed that the psychological characteristics of a student's peer group were more closely correlated with his measured ability and achievement than either the school's physical plant or the characteristics of the teaching staff, these "empirical data of behavioral science" would indicate the way to achieve equal educational opportunity should be mandatory busing to provide disadvantaged pupils with the presumably better stimulation from abler peers. Whatever the legal merits of mandatory busing in relation to de facto segregation, the methodological point is important and requires a level of psychometric sophistication a notch above my law colleague's. It is possible that the higher statistical correlation between peer-group attributes and student's academic level is attributable mainly to geographic selective factors mediated by the family's social class. Parental intelligence, personality, and temperament factors are transmitted to the child in part genetically and in part through social learning. If physical plant characteristics and teacher characteristics are correlated with the biological and social inputs of the child's family only via the (indirect) economic-neighborhood-location and political (tax-use) factors, they will have a lower statistical relation with the child's cognitive level than is shown by indicators of the cognitive level of other children attending the same neighborhood school. Roughly, peer-group attributes happen to be a better (indirect) measure of average family and neighborhood causal factors—genetic and environmental—than teacher or physical plant attributes. The differential correlation would reflect more a psychometric fact (about the factor loadings and reliabilities of certain measures) than a causal fact (about peer-group influence).

No matter what statistical devices are used, we cannot infer whether social stimulation from other students is causally more efficacious than having better qualified teachers or a newer, better lighted, cleaner school building. The correlations with peer-group attributes cannot even tell us whether the impact on a lower-IQ child of being in a classroom with more bright, dominant, articulate, and intellectually self-confident children does more harm than good.

In the opinion of Judge Skelley Wright in *Hobson* v. *Hansen* (1967), one cannot find a single sentence indicating recognition of this methodological problem. Not that awareness of it would have led to a different result; but a single sentence obiter would surely occur somewhere in his careful, scholarly opinion of 109 pages had the judge thought of it or counsel argued it in connection with the Coleman Report's significance. One may feel, as I do, that the problems of racial discrimination and educational disadvantagement are so grave that the society should lean over backward—within limits set by principles of distributive justice to individuals—to change things. Under such pressing circumstances the adoption and implementation of policy cannot await definitive solution of difficult scientific questions, especially when the kind of controlled experiment or even semi-controlled quasi-experiment (Campbell, 1969) capable of yielding clear answers cannot be performed and statistical techniques are not adequate for the purpose of unscrambling causal influence. The Coleman Report shows

that minority-group children receive substandard educational treatment; I am willing to call that discriminatory, ipso facto. What concerns me here is the legal generalizability of a causal inference methodology. The kind of reliance on social science data found in *Hobson* v. *Hansen,* lacking adequate clarification of the concept "unfair discrimination" in relation to correlational findings, might produce some untoward results in other contexts where the interpretative principles would be difficult to distinguish. And if judges should become cynical about the trustworthiness of what psychologists and sociologists assert, we might be faced with a judicial backlash against the social sciences.

It is well recognized among psychologists concerned with the ex post facto design's deficiencies that the Coleman Report is dangerous reading for the nontechnically trained because of its pervasive use of causal-sounding terms: influence, affect, depend upon, account for, independent effect (sic). This causal atmosphere cannot be counteracted by the brief methodological sections, which contain the usual caveats. One wonders whether the report's authors were really clear about what regression analysis can and cannot do (Guttman, 1941, pp. 286–292). I am not arguing the merits, except to show that an unresolved scientific controversy exists that we psychologists have no right to sweep under the rug when we talk or write for lawyers and judges. If we present a distorted picture even in a good cause, implying that certain technical matters are settled when in fact they are obscure and controversial, the powerful forces of the lawyers' adversary system will sooner or later ferret out the secret. Could we then complain if the findings of social science were treated with less respect than those of chemistry, geology, or medicine by less tractable, more wised-up judges?

Consider a nonracial example that I predict will arise in the near future. There is some correlation between the vocational interests of fathers and sons (Forster, 1931; Strong, 1943, 1957), and part of this correlation has a genetic basis (Carter, 1932; Vandenberg & Kelly, 1964; Vandenberg & Stafford, 1967). Nichols (1966, Table 2) also presents persuasive data that he under-interprets through neglect of the statistical power function (Cohen, 1962). This ne-glect, combined with his disappointment in the heritability coefficient as a precise, stable, clearly interpretable measure (see Elston & Gottesman, 1968; Fuller & Thompson, 1960, pp. 62–68; Hirsch, 1967, p. 423; Roberts, 1967, pp. 233–242) and his following the traditional practice of simply sorting results into "significant" and "nonsignificant," leads him to be baffled by sex patterns that should not baffle him and that are probably theo-retically uninterpretable because they have no systematic meaning (except to a statistician interested in power functions). The "big-gest" fact in Nichols's Table 2 is that 23 out of 24 (MZ-DZ) correlation differences are in the expected direction and respectable in size. Even with his large samples, an (MZ-DZ) difference less than around .14 Pear-son $r$ units will have less than 50 percent power $(1 - \beta)$. We ought not be surprised by sex differences in the pattern of signifi-cant variables under such circumstances. A sophisticated consideration of the question would involve a currently unstable area of social science method, where matters are murky and the social science establishment is maintaining a conspiracy of silence (see Bakan, 1966; Hogben, 1958; Lykken, 1968; Meehl, 1967; also Rozeboom, 1960, and references cited therein). Whatever the merits, the point is that there exists a tech-nical controversy that an appellate court justice with an MA in psychology would have difficulty following, let alone adjudicat-ing. If the judge relies on expert testimony as to current accepted practice, he stands a good chance of being taken in by sincere diploma'd experts who will themselves be unaware how big a methodological storm is brewing. The discrepancy between Nichols's findings and the other twin studies provides a beautiful illustration of the levels-of-sophistication problem. Most law professors

are just now learning about the significance test. It will be 20 years or more before they learn what is wrong with it (Badia, Haber, & Runyon, 1970; Morrison & Henkel, 1970).

There is a sizable correlation between fa-thers' and sons' intelligence, the larger part of which is probably of biological origin (Burt, 1958, 1966, 1967; Erlenmeyer-Kimling & Jarvik, 1963; Fuller & Thomp-son, 1960, Chap. 7; Gottesman, 1963, 1968a, 1969b; Honzik, 1957; Jenkins & Paterson, 1961; Manosevitz, Lindzey, & Thiessen, 1969, Sections 5–6; Robinson, 1970; Shields, 1962; Thompson, 1967; Van-denberg, 1968; Waller, 1971; Whipple, 1940—still worth reading). Given these in-terest and ability correlations and other factors, the sons of physicians are more often admitted to medical schools than the sons of nonphysicians, and much more often than the sons of, say, unskilled laborers. Medical school selection committees alleg-edly have shown a preference for physicians' sons. To avoid this bias, some schools ex-clude father's occupation from the applica-tion blank, but a statistical association per-sists.

Suppose a WASP premedical student of proletarian origins brings an action against a state-supported medical school alleging occupational discrimination, offering in evi-dence the somewhat higher incidence of admission among physicians' sons. The school defends by showing that father's occupation does not appear on the applica-tion blank, and argues that selection is based on a combination of premedical grades, scores on the Strong Vocational Interest Blank, and the Medical Aptitude Test. The student replies that these instru-ments are biased in favor of physicians' sons and further generically biased against proletarians. If psychometric bias is defined ipso facto by tests yielding socio-demo-graphical differences (e.g., by parental oc-cupation, father's income, neighborhood, race, religion), all such tests are biased. Pushed to the limit, the position is that, whatever may be the social or biological origins of individual differences in intellectual capacity, vocational interest, study habits, or temperament, any selection variable reflecting these differences and shown to be a correlate of parental occupation is discriminatory (in the sense of unfair).

Nor could this consequence be avoided by relying solely on undergraduate grades, inasmuch as the latter also correlate with father's occupation, education, and income. *Point*: The problem of interpreting correlations and the influence of "nuisance variables" is not a hairsplitting academic exercise; it is a major methodological stomachache, arising in many legal contexts where social science findings are relevant to fair treatment or equal protection.

## AWAY FROM THE FIRESIDE AND BACK AGAIN

The levels-of-sophistication problem has a time component reflecting the stage of scientific knowledge. We psychologists should be cautious when an alleged principle of modern behavioral science appears to conflict with the fireside inductions. Some embarrassing instances of overconfident generalization and unjustified extrapolation were later corrected by movement back toward the fireside inductions. It would be worth knowing how often such back-to-the-fireside reversals have taken place, and whether there are features of subject matter or methodology that render the counter-fireside pronouncements of social science prone to reversal or modification. Sometimes psychologists seem to prefer negating the fireside inductions, especially those embedded in the received scholarly tradition.

Consider three examples relevant to law as a means of social control. Traditional reliance on punishment in socialization, both in suppressing antisocial conduct and in education, is horrifying to the contemporary mind. One reads Luther's description of his schooling, in which corporal punish-

ment was not even confined to infractions of discipline but was the standard procedure of instruction. Thirty years ago, I was taught that the useful role of punishment was to suppress undesirable responses sufficiently (in the short run) so that alternative competing behaviors could occur, and the latter could then be positively reinforced. This is still a fair statement of the practical situation.

Following the publication of Skinner's epoch-making *The Behavior of Organisms* (1938), his student Estes's doctoral dissertation (1944), and especially Skinner's *Science and Human Behavior* (1953) and his Utopian novel *Walden Two* (1948), aversive control fell into extreme disfavor. These writings, together with the gruesome stories told to us clinical psychologists by adult neurotics about their aversively controlled childhoods, combined to produce a rejection of both the general deterrent and rehabilitative functions of the criminal law. But this could be an illicit extrapolation, conflating the rehabilitative and general deterrent functions of the criminal law under the generic rubric "punishment." Supporters of general deterrence need not assume the same psychological process operates on deterrable persons as that involved when punishment is unsuccessful in reforming convicts. Only punishment as a reformer even approximates the laboratory model of an aversive consequence following emission of the undesired response. Furthermore, the criminal sanction is rather more like withholding positive reinforcement, both fines and imprisonment being deprivations. The distinction is becoming fuzzed up by experimental work with animals because manipulations such as "time out" (during which the instrumental act cannot be performed because the manipulandum is unavailable, or a stimulus signals that reinforcement will now be withheld) have aversive (punishing) properties. Having neither expertise nor space for the details, I refer the reader to Honig (1966), especially the chapter by Azrin and Holz, which should be read asking, "To what extent do the current experimental findings refute, confirm, or modify the fireside inductions concerning punishment?" How would the psychologist classify a statutory provision that threatens to deprive the citizen of, say, money that the citizen had never learned to expect, for example, the Agricultural Adjustment Act (see *U.S.* v. *Butler*, 1936, p. 81), where Mr. Justice Stone's dissent hinges partly on the semantics of coercion, which he argues must involve "threat of loss, not hope of gain." Can the experimental psychologist speak to this issue? I doubt it.

A second example concerns imitation. The folklore is that both humans and infrahumans learn by imitation. Our policy concerning TV and movie presentation of social models of aggression or forbidden sexual behavior is influenced by our beliefs about imitation. When I was a student the tendency in academic psychology was to minimize the concept of imitation to the point of skepticism as to whether there was any such process at all. I was taught that the classic experiments of E. L. Thorndike on the cat (*circa* 1900) had demonstrated that, for infrahuman organisms at least, there was no learning by imitation. This alleged laboratory refutation was presented as an example of how scientific research had overthrown part of folklore. The failure of Thorndike's cats to learn one particular problembox task was overgeneralized to the broad statement, "Infrahuman animals cannot learn by imitation." The received doctrine of scientific psychology became so well entrenched that a well-designed experiment by Herbert and Harsh (1944) was largely ignored by the profession (see Barber, 1961). But beginning slightly earlier with Miller and Dollard's *Social Learning and Imitation* (1941), a book that cautiously reintroduced the concept and made important conceptual distinctions as to kinds of imitation, the subject came to be restudied, especially by developmental psychologists in relation to aggressive behavior (see, e.g., Bandura & Walters, 1963; Megargee & Hokanson, 1970). In

1969, John, Chesler, Bartlett, and Victor suggested that Thorndike's negative dictum was just plain wrong, even for *Felis catus. Point:* A lawyer in 1930 might have lost a cocktail party debate with an animal psychologist, but the lawyer would have been closer to the truth.

A third area important in such legal contexts as presentence investigation is that of forecasting behavior probabilistically. The fireside inductions say that you should rely heavily upon the record of an individual's past conduct. As I have argued elsewhere (Meehl, 1970c), it may be that a naive judge will (over the long run) make better decisions than one who knows just enough psychology or psychiatry to rely on experts' making an intensive study of the offender. The efficiency of actuarial prediction is almost always at least equal to, and usually better than, prediction based on (purported) clinical understanding of the individual subject's personality (see references in Footnote 4 in Livermore, Malmquist, & Meehl, 1968; Footnote 8 in Meehl, 1970c). Second, behavioral science research itself shows that, by and large, the best predictor of anybody's behavior is his behavior in the past. Hence, the naive judge's reliance on the fireside inductions may yield better results than the intermediate-level sophistication that knows enough to ask a psychologist's or psychiatrist's opinion, but does not know enough to take what he says *cum grano salis.*

The subtle interaction between levels of sophistication and the developing state of scientific knowledge is nicely illustrated by the Supreme Court's attitude toward statutes postulating inherited tendencies to mental deficiency and criminalism. In *Buck* v. *Bell* (1927) the court upheld the constitutionality of an involuntary sterilization statute for mental defectives, in an opinion famous for Mr. Justice Holmes's "Three generations of imbeciles is enough." Without entering into technical issues in genetics, the court came to what I would regard as the right result (see Reed & Reed, 1965). In *Skinner*

v. *Oklahoma* (1942) involuntary sterilization of a habitual criminal was disallowed. The fireside inductions that underlay Oklahoma's statute are perhaps as strong and widespread for criminal or "immoral" tendencies as for mental deficiency. But the scientific data on inherited dispositions are much stronger in the one case than in the other, and *that* much social science knowledge the Court did possess. Suppose that a more refined taxonomy of delinquents and criminals should enable us to discover that some persons disposed to antisocial behavior get that way in part on a genetic basis (see Footnote 10 in Meehl, 1970c), although in most delinquents the etiology is social. A modified form of the fireside inductions underlying Oklahoma's unconstitutional statute would then be defensible, and a properly redrafted statute combining habitual criminality as a legal category with psychogenetic categories or dimensions could be upheld on the same grounds as Virginia's sterilization statute. But the court's new task would demand far more technical sophistication, especially given the ideological components that would saturate social scientists' opinions in the briefs, than was required for handling *Buck* v. *Bell* and *Skinner* v. *Oklahoma*.

## DIRECT APPLICATION OF EXPERIMENTAL RESULTS TO LEGAL PROBLEMS

### Some Rational Grounds for Caution

I sense a deep analogy between the problem faced by a judge or legislator in balancing the fireside inductions against purportedly scientific psychological or sociological findings, and the perennial problem of how far we clinicians are entitled to rely on our clinical experience, lacking (or apparently contradicting) experimental or quantitative research. I have not been able to resolve this dilemma in an intellectually responsible way, although I have been steadily conscious of it and engaged in theoretical and empir-

ical research on it for over a quarter century. So I am hardly prepared to clean up the analogous dilemma for lawyers. However, dwelling on this analogy may enable me to offer some tentative suggestions. There is a similarity in the pragmatic contexts of law and clinical practice in that something will be decided, with or without adequate evidence, good or bad, scientific or anecdotal. A judge cannot leave a case undecided—although a logician could point out that law, being an incomplete postulate set, renders some well-formed formulas undecidable.

Let us strip the concept "scientific experiment" to its essentials, as I have tried to do above in a rough meaning stipulation. Forget the usual images of glass tubing and electronic equipment operated by persons in white coats in a laboratory. What is the purpose of gadgetry? Scientific apparatus performs one of two functions. Either it plays a role on the input side, contributing to the physical isolation of the system under study and to the control or manipulation of the variables, or it facilitates the recording of observations (output side). We conceive a situation space whose dimensions are all physical and social dimensions having behavioral relevance. In research on human subjects, this set of dimensions will include such minor variables as the material of the experimenter's desk, since in our society the social stimulus value of an oak desk differs from that of pine.

If we are studying the impact of a psychoanalytic interpretation and we design an experiment to smuggle this real-life phenomenon into the laboratory, what happens? We move in the situation space from the ordinary-life context of psychotherapy to the experimental context. This movement is in the interest of locating the system studied more precisely, because in the ordinary-life, nonlaboratory situation, the values of certain variables known (or feared) to have an influence are neither assigned by the investigator nor measured by him (with the idea of their influence being removed statistically).

There is no mystery about this, no conflict between a scientific and nonscientific view of the subject matter. The problem presented is quite simple—it is the solution that presents complexities. By (1) eliminating, (2) fixing, (3) manipulating, or (4) measuring (and "correcting for") the input variables, we intend to test generalizations as to what influences what—generalizations we could not reach in the natural, field, nonexperimental situation. The price we pay is that these generalizations are only known to hold for the new region of the situation space; their application in the ordinary-life context is an extrapolation.

This untoward consequence of the experimental method does not flow from tendentious, polemic formulations polarizing a scientific against a nonscientific frame of reference (empirical versus armchair psychology). Such locutions are misleading, as they locate our methodological stomachache in the wrong place. The problem can be stated in general terms within the scientific frame of reference. To concretize it: Suppose I am interested in the behavior of tigers. If I rely uncritically on anecdotes told by missionaries, hunters, native guides, and so on, my evidence will suffer both on the input and output sides, that is, from indeterminacy of the input and inaccuracy of the output. If I have accurate output data (e.g., carefully screened independent, convergent testimony by skeptical, reliable, scientifically trained observers, use of telescopic camera recording, high-fidelity tapes of the tiger's vocalizations), I may be able by such means to take care of the recording-accuracy problem (although hardly the recording-completeness problem). But I will still be troubled by indeterminacy on the input side. I do not know all the inputs to this tiger when I am photographing him at a distance. I do not know his inputs an hour earlier, and I have reason to believe that those previous inputs alter his momentary state and change his behavioral dispositions.

Suppose, to get rid of this uncertainty on the stimulus side, I capture my tiger and put him in a zoo or bring him to my animal laboratory. I eliminate the influence of variations in the chirping of a certain bird as part of the tiger's surround. There is a sense in which I now do not have to be concerned about birds chirping, the only birds that chirp in a proper psychological laboratory being those that the experimenter himself introduces. But I *should* be worried about the influence of bird chirping. An average level of fluctuation of bird-chirps is part of the normal ecology of tigers in the wild. If I want to extrapolate my laboratory findings to the behavior of wild tigers, this extrapolation is problematic. The background of bird-chirps may have a quantitative impact on the tiger's behavioral dispositions, and perhaps on his second-order dispositions to acquire first-order dispositions (Broad, 1933; Meehl, 1972).

In research on human subjects, it is often found that the influence of variable $x$ on variable $y$ is dependent on values of variable $z$, called by statisticians an "interaction effect." Interaction effects regularly occur whenever the sensitivity of the experimental design suffices to detect them. It is not absurd to suppose that, in human social behavior, almost all interactions of all orders (for instance, the influence of variable $v$ on the interaction effect of the variable $z$ on the first-order influence of variable $x$ on variable $y$) would be detected if our experiments were sufficiently sensitive. When we liquidate the influence of a variable, either by eliminating it through physical isolation or holding it fixed, we are in danger of wrongly generalizing from our experimental results to the natural, real-life setting.

Law-trained readers unfamiliar with social science statistical methods may have found the preceding rather abstract. Suppose I am a developmental psychologist interested in the deterrent effects of punishment and I argue that the sanctions of the criminal law are inefficacious, relying on "Fisbee's classic ex-

**TABLE 1    Extrapolating from Fisbee to Real Life**

| EXPERIMENT | CRIMINAL SANCTION AGAINST LARCENY |
|---|---|
| Four-year-olds | Adults |
| Mostly upper-middle class | Mostly lower and lower-middle class |
| Mostly biologically normal | Numerous genetic deviates in group |
| Time-span: Minutes or hours | Time-span: Months or years |
| Social context: Subject alone | Social context: Criminal peer-group inputs |
| Reward: Candy | Rewards: Money, prestige, sex, autonomy, leisure, excitement |
| Punishment: Mild electric shock | Punishment: Deprivations of above rewards [Punishment more like nonreward or time-out than strictly aversive stimulus onset] |
| Punished response emitted; experimenter aims at reform | Punished response not emitted by most; law aims at general deterrence |
| Subject's perception of situation: Who knows? | Subject's perception of situation: Who knows? |

periments on punishment in nursery-school children." Table 1 lists differences that might be relevant in extrapolating from the laboratory study to the legal context.

One need hardly be obscurantist or antiscientific to be nervous about extrapolation from the left-hand column to the right as ground for repealing a statute penalizing larceny. In the foreseeable future, lawmakers will unavoidably rely on a judicious mixture of experimental research, quasi-experiments, informal field observations, statistical analyses of file data, *and* the fireside inductions. The legislator, prosecutor, judge, and public administrator—like the clinical psychologist —cannot adopt a scientistic/purist posture, "I will not decide or act until fully adequate standards of scientific proof are met by the evidence before me." In these matters, not doing anything or not changing anything we now do is itself a powerful form of action. When the fireside inductions are almost all we have to go on, or when they appear to conflict with the practical consequences of extrapolated experimental research or psychological theory, it would be nice to have some sort of touchstone as to pragmatic validity, some quick and easy objective basis for deciding where to place our bets. Unfortunately there is none.

## Are Some Classes of Fireside Inductions More Trustworthy than Others?

This problem is so important in a society that has become sophisticated and self-conscious as to its own modes of social control that one might reasonably argue in favor of support for second-level empirical research aimed at developing a taxonomy of fireside inductions, enabling us to sort them into categories having different average levels of accuracy. We do not even possess a corpus of the explicit fireside inductions on which our law relies. To ferret these out from statutes, appellate court opinions, the restatements, and so forth would be a monstrous and thankless task, although I suggest that a random sampling might be worth doing. One might inquire how many legal rules, principles, and practices accord even with the fireside inductions of contemporary men. Most law professors will readily agree that much of our law is predicated on notions about human conduct that hardly anybody would care to defend. *Example:* A lawyer will advise a testator to leave a dollar to one of his children whom he wishes to disinherit, because courts have held that, since a parent naturally tends to bequeath property to his child, failure to do so creates a legal presumption that the testator omitted him by inadvertence. I doubt that this presumption accords with the fireside inductions. Laymen agree with me that if a father is sufficiently *compos mentis* to write a valid will at all, his failure to mention a son is not attributable to forgetfulness. *Example:* One class of exceptions to the Hearsay Rule is "declarations against interest," when the declarant is unavailable as a witness. The unavailability creates a special need for hearsay, and the fireside induction is that the declaration's having been made against interest renders it more trustworthy. But the interest is required to be pecuniary, not penal (Livermore, 1968, pp. 76–78; Mc-Cormick, 1954, pp. 546–551). Surely our fireside inductions do not suppose that a man is more likely to be careless or mendacious in admitting rape than that he borrowed money! Similar oddities have been noted in the Hearsay exception for "Admissions of a party-opponent," where a litigant's predecessor or joint tenant falls under the exception, but not a tenant in common or a co-legatee (McCormick, 1954, pp. 523–525). I cannot imagine that the fireside inductions concerning motivations for accuracy would support these distinctions, which arose not from empirical considerations in the psychology of testimony but through formalistic intrusion of property-law metaphysics into the law of evidence.

A taxonomy of fireside inductions based upon their substantive, methodological, and psychological properties might permit a rough ordering of inductive types as to accuracy, comparing the fireside inductions in each category with social science generalizations. If strong taxonomic trends existed among researched cases, we would have some basis for judging the probable trustworthiness of those unresearched. We could inquire whether the following methodological features of a fireside induction are associated with a higher probability of its being scientifically corroborated:

Hardly anyone entertains serious doubts about the induction. Persons of different theoretical persuasions agree about the fireside induction almost as well as persons holding the same theoretical position. There is a consensus of the fireside that cuts across such demographic variables as education, occupation, social class, religious belief, and ethnic background. Within the legal profession prosecutors, defense lawyers, law professors, and judges are in substantial agreement. Personality traits (e.g., dominance, social introversion, hostility, rigidity) are not appreciably correlated with adherence to the induction. The particular fireside induction involves an observation of actions, persons, or effects that occur with sufficient frequency so that most qualified and competent observers will have had an extensive experience as a generalization basis. The fireside induction deals with relatively objective physical or behavioral facts rather than with complicated causal inferences. The policy implications of the induction are such that nobody's political, ethnic, religious, moral, or economic ideology or class interest would be appreciably threatened or mobilized by its general acceptance in the society or by lawmakers' or administrators' reliance on it in decision making. Sophisticated armchair considerations do not reveal a built-in observational or sampling bias that would operate in the collection of anecdotal support or refutation of the induction. The induction is qualitative rather than one that claims to make quantitative comparisons despite the lack of a reliable measuring device.

I do not profess to know the relative importance of items in this list, and I can think of exceptions to any of them as a touchstone. Thus, for example, the height of a person's forehead is a relatively simple physical fact. But judgments of forehead heights of prison inmates by their guards were shown[2] to be correlated with guards' estimates of their intelligence, whereas objectively measured forehead heights were not. (*Explanation:* The erroneous fireside induc-

---

[2] I cannot trace the reference, which is from the late Professor Donald G. Paterson's lectures.

tion that a low forehead—low-brow—indicates stupidity led guards' perceptions and/or memories of this simple physical feature to be infected with their behavior-based estimates of a prisoner's intellect.)

## And Are Some Experimental Findings Safer to Extrapolate?

One asks here about the comparability of two groups of organisms as to species, developmental period, and status. What motives, what rewards and punishments, what time relationships are shared between the experimental context and the natural setting? An indirect lead as to extrapolability can sometimes be picked up from the experimental literature itself, asking, "To what extent do the experimental findings replicate over a variety of species, drives, instrumental responses, rewards, and punishments?" If we cannot generalize within the laboratory, moving to the field is presumably risky. How sizable are the relationships? A social scientist who countervails a lawyer's fireside induction by extrapolating from psychological research yielding two correlation coefficients $r = .25$ with $r = .40$ is just plain silly; but an unsuspecting lawman, overly impressed with social science statistical methods, might be taken in. *Point:* Random sampling errors aside, this correlational difference represents an increment of less than 10 percent in variance accounted for, and could easily be liquidated by moving to a not very distant region of the situation space.

To have the best of both worlds, one would want accurate recording on the output side and proper statistical treatment, but with the situation being very similar to the one to which we wish to extrapolate. Accurate observations, accurate records (instead of memory and impressions), appropriate statistical analysis are all attainable in the field or natural life setting, lacking experimenter manipulation of the input. I am therefore inclined to view Campbell's "Reforms as Experiments" (1969) not as a second-best substitute for laboratory investi-

gation, but as often intrinsically preferable, because the situational-extrapolation problem is so grave that the scientific precision of laboratory experiments with college students or school children is largely illusory.

## THE LAWMAKER'S DILEMMA

The legislator's, judge's, or administrator's situation is most comfortable when there is a sizable and consistent body of research, experimental and nonexperimental (file data and field observation data), yielding about the same results as the fireside inductions. While one may be scientifically skeptical even in this harmonious situation, in the pragmatic context of decision making, rule writing, or policy adopting, such rigorous skepticism can hardly lead to pragmatic vacillation. Some sort of action is required, and all we have goes in the same direction. The methodologically unsatisfactory situations can be divided into three groups, differing in degree rather than kind: (1) No quantitative or experimental evidence is available or readily collectable before action must be taken. Here we rely upon the fireside inductions, these being all we have. A healthy skepticism concerning the fireside inductions, engendered by the study of social science, makes us nonetheless uncomfortable. (2) We have a large-scale, adequately conducted study in the field situation, supplemented by file data from jurisdictions varying in relevant parameters (e.g., offense rate, community socioeconomic indices); these field observation and file data results accord with theoretical concepts developed experimentally on humans and infrahumans; but the conclusion conflicts with the fireside. Such a massive, coherent body of information should countervail the fireside inductions, even those with admirable properties. It seems difficult to dispute this, since by including file data from the nonlaboratory setting to which we wish to extrapolate, we are in effect comparing two sets of anecdotal data, one with the methodological advantage of being based on records instead of relying on our memories of observations gathered nonsystematically as regards representativeness of persons and situations. *Example:* If statistics show that accuseds released without bail pending trial have such a low incidence of pretrial criminal offenses or failure to appear for trial that the bail system has negligible social utility (combined with its obvious inequity to the poor), our fireside inductions to the contrary should not countervail. But a nagging doubt persists, since other relevant statistics (e.g., ratio of reported felonies to arrests) tend to support the fireside induction that some fraction of these defendants have committed further crimes during their pretrial freedom, and we cannot accurately estimate this fraction (see Tribe, 1970). A lively sense of the lawmaker's dilemma can be had by reading the Senate debate on the District of Columbia crime bill (*Congressional Record*, 1970). (3) The most difficult situation is that in which there is a collision between a fireside induction having several of the good properties listed above, and a smattering of social science research that is strong enough to give us pause about the fireside inductions, but not strong enough to convince us. Thus, the research may not be entirely consistent; or it comes only from the experimental laboratory and conse-quently involves considerable extrapolation in the situation space; or, if a large-scale quantitative nonexperimental survey, it has the causal-ambiguity and variable-unscrambling difficulties intrinsic to such studies (Meehl, 1969, 1971). One hardly knows what to suggest in such collision situations except the social scientist's usual "more research is needed."

## CONCLUSION

Unavoidably the law will continue to rely on the fireside inductions. They should be viewed with that skepticism toward anecdotal evidence and the received belief system that training in the behavioral sciences fosters, but without intellectual arrogance or an animus against fireside inductions in favor of overvalued or overinterpreted scitific research. I can summarize my position in one sentence. In thinking about law as a mode of social control, adopt a healthy skepticism toward the fireside inductions, subjecting them to test by statistical methods applied to data collected in the field situation; but when a fireside induction is held nearly *semper, ubique, et ab omnibus* a similar skepticism should be maintained toward experimental research purporting, as generalized, to overthrow it.

# PART II

# The Role of Law as Socializer

## INTERSTITIAL BRIEF

*JUNE LOUIN TAPP*
*FELICE J. LEVINE*

The six chapters in Part II of this book consider the impact of law on the manifestation of various forms of legal behavior. As these contributions reveal, the role of law as a socializer is a complex phenomenon that is not uniform in its effects on human interaction. Although the law is only one among many "legal" socializers, it is the most visible embodiment of societal assumptions about the nature of humankind and the appropriate role relationships among individuals and between individuals and authoritative systems. Thus, to comprehend how individuals relate to their systems of law, we must identify the socializing functions of law as well as explore the law's potency when viewed as an independent variable.

To begin this examination, we present six chapters by lawyers that address the law's ability to regulate and facilitate human behavior. By considering the role of law cross-culturally, at different times, in various situations and rule contexts, and in terms of stability and change, these chapters vividly depict how the law can affect compliance and competence, criminal justice and civil justice. In addition to incorporating either research data or "fireside inductions," these legal scholars have prepared basic analytic pieces that ultimately generate questions for future hypothesis testing.

The chapters by Fuller and by Weyrauch deal with the role of law as socializer by examining the origins of law and certain of its dimensions. Fuller displays the complexity of the issues by analyzing the viability of three alternative models of socialization. He comparatively assesses socialization as a process whereby an individual either endorses the norms that a society imposes on its members, adheres to the constraints of state-made law, or participates in creating and maintaining laws. To Fuller, the third model most accurately reflects the essence of law. That definition derives from a view of the individual as an active force in shaping the nature of rules, not as a passive inculcator of either the social or legal "will" (both of which he implies are myths). In Fuller's view, human relationships across criminal and civil arenas are not based on a simple mastery of regulations that—when invoked—yield binary "yes–no" solutions. In whatever rule context, such variables as expectation, judgment, discretion, and interpretation are all part of the dynamic of law and ultimately at the core of what is dynamic about human interaction in the law.

Undertaking an empirical inquiry in the jurisprudential tradition of Fuller, Weyrauch analyzes the socializing role of law in terms of the development of law itself. Instead of viewing law in the context of state law, like Fuller, Weyrauch considers the broader "legal" or "rule" norms that regulate all forms of social interaction from dyadic exchanges to government processes. By observing volunteers isolated as part of a nutrition experiment, Weyrauch determines how group legal norms emerge to establish the limits of behavior. The behavioral "constitution" he abstracts represents an agreement based on shared ideals, sufficiently authoritative to engender compliance. The threat of the sanction of status degradation works to deter legal transgressions. Treating law as more than regulating what people can and cannot do, Weyrauch demonstrates how legal norms provide paths of action for various situations. Substantially influenced by Fuller's orientation, Weyrauch conceptualizes law as a "program for living together" and the group's legal system as reflecting a basic human need to organize perceptions into normative behavioral standards. He suggests that a broad perspective toward law—looking at the law as a set of decisional processes located in the interaction of various small groups (legal communities)—may offer new approaches for dispute settlement that traditional law and social science classifications (e.g., courts, police) could not accommodate.

While both Fuller and Weyrauch raise issues about the appropriate definition of law, their basic interest is not in esoteric conceptual debate about its nature. These scholars convey a pragmatic grasp of the implications of alternative conceptions of law for social control *and* social facilitation. It is clear from these chapters that such factors as cultural norms, individual morality, peer group influence, and sanctions may affect the structure and impact of law. Although psychologists have found repeatedly that an increase in punishment or the threat of it usually results in public compliance at least for the surveillance period, the crucial issue —given the complexity of human relations—centers on achieving an ongoing internalized standard about the limits of permissible and impermissible social behavior. The next chapters in Part II turn to specifying the variables that should relate to the socialization of such standards.

Andenaes, a foremost deterrence theorist, analyzes the general preventive effects of the threat of punishment. His primary concern is the development of long-term stable patterns. Instead of focusing on the deterrent effects of fear of unpleasant consequences, Andenaes explores the moral or educative influences emanating from criminal law. He hypothesizes six aspects as educative influences: The direct effects are based on respect for law, law as a moral eye-opener, punishment as authoritative statements about badness, and imprisonment as stigma; the indirect ones include punishment neutralizing the bad example and criminal law shaping the framework for moral education. While Andenaes emphasizes the attitude-shaping effect of the workings of the criminal law on such primary groups as family and school, he likewise sees variety in individual and societal inclinations to internalize specific laws. In critiquing psychological punishment research—with its heavy emphasis on animal psychology—Andenaes questions the utility of present findings to specific deterrence questions. It is only surmise that collaborative efforts by psychologists and legal scholars to apply extant social-psychological knowledge, for example, on socialization, social power, attitude change, and communication and persuasion to the realm of law would advance a more complete theory of legal behavior.

Zimring and Hawkins, within the tradition pioneered by Andenaes, develop a model on the socializing role of law for social change. They emphasize changing social customs and posit three kinds of conditions —variations in the nature of the custom, variations in the characteristics of those adhering to the custom, and variations in enforcement—that may facilitate or obstruct the introduction of social changes through legal threats. Aspects of each strikingly parallel the psychological analyses of attitude change, social influence, and forced compliance. For example, Zimring and Hawkins explain that the deterrent effects of threat may be reduced because belief in the legitimacy of a social custom may be of greater moral importance than belief in the legitimacy of law; thus sanctions only reinforce social support for the custom. In psychological research, this possibility has been labeled negative power, psychological reactance, or the boomerang effect. Not all customs, however, carry a moral commitment of greater magnitude than the commitment to law. In many instances, Zimring and Hawkins note, legal change results in changed expectations about social behavior, rendering the custom obsolete. Or if a group feels a sense of participation in the legal system and the larger society, it may experience greater pressure to comply. Among others, these variables may affect both public compliance and eventual private commitment to the new law.

As the chapter by Zimring and Hawkins reveals, the law can play a significant role in socializing attitudes and actions beyond simple compliance with established regulations. Friedman examines another, often neglected, part of that process: the socialization of rights consciousness. He explicates the critical function of claims of right to affect major social change. While Zimring and Hawkins present a model for social change through legal change, Friedman analyzes the potential power of individuals to obtain legal change by pressing just claims. His chapter underscores the possible consequences of denying rights and the value of this institutionalized, nonviolent mechanism for change as a legitimate avenue of participation and dissent. Friedman notes that conflict may stem from a gap between socialized values and social realities insofar as people might come to believe that all rights are absolute and limitless. While a high frequency of unexpected claims may precipitate drastic but necessary change, it also might indicate that socialization has failed to teach the true meaning of legal rights. Friedman, therefore, particularly attends to variations in the law's impact on rights consciousness. He calls for social science to broaden its scope to include socialization about the legitimacy of legal rights in various contexts and in various legal cultures.

Berman's chapter illustrates the effect of legal cultures on individuals' interactions in systems of law. His work provides the critical analysis that Zimring and Hawkins as well as Friedman see as requisite to understanding the role of law. In comparing the socializing role of law in the U.S.S.R. and U.S. settings, Berman demonstrates an appreciation of the relationship between social inputs and the natural "law-consciousness" of individuals. He cogently depicts, through appraising the courts and judicial procedures of both countries, how the two systems diverge in their "official" views of their respective socializing roles. In the U.S., when legal socialization occurs, it is considered to be a by-product of other regulatory and facilitative functions of law. In the U.S.S.R., there is explicit endorsement of the law's "nurturing role" and its educative responsibilities. Not directly compared, however, are the merits of the actual socializing goals adopted in these two cultures. More to the point, as Berman emphasizes, is that systems do contribute to shaping the "law-consciousness" of the people and that the value choices of what to do and how to do it cannot be intelligently addressed unless this teaching role is acknowledged (see Chaps. 14 and 15).

Berman's cross-cultural analysis recalls issues initially raised in Fuller's piece. Although there is greater acceptance of a socializing role in the U.S.S.R. than in the U.S., Soviet educative strategies demonstrate a more unidimensional view of persons as dependent children "to be guided and trained." Such an approach is markedly different from Fuller's conception of socialization as a collaborative enterprise among responsible, autonomous agents who are taking part in the creation of reciprocal expectations. Thus, across the chapters in Part II, a range of possibilities are considered about the limits of the law's impact. Among the underlying questions are the following:

1. What are the socializing goals of law, both implicit and explicit? What assumptions do they reflect about the nature of humankind?
2. What is the role of law in engendering critical compliance and independence?
3. How might the institution of law as a function of its symbolic legitimacy abuse its power? In the long haul, what type of legal system can provide the most stable basis for system support?

In subsequent sections of this book, these themes reappear.

# CHAPTER 3

# Some Presuppositions Shaping the Concept of "Socialization"[1]

## —LON L. FULLER

This chapter is not so much concerned with the process of socialization as it is with our perceptions of the processes—real or imagined—to which socialization itself is oriented. Three kinds of processes are examined: those by which a "society" is assumed to create and impose "norms" on its members; those by which rules of "law" are enacted, interpreted, and enforced; and those by which tacitly generated, reciprocal expectations serve to give order and predictability to human interactions. The underlying assumptions and implications of each conception are critically evaluated. The third view of law—as norms arising out of human interaction—suggests socialization approaches that encourage participation in rulemaking and sustaining activity.

The concept of socialization is complex. What one reads into it, or out of it, depends on a host of presuppositions—tacit or explicit—or a little of both. The object here is to express some assumptions that shape perspectives on "socialization." Examining these assumptions is vitally important to the development of an interactive view of law.

### SOCIALIZATION BY SOCIETAL IMPOSITION

The first of these assumptions, the one currently most influential at least among sociologists may be stated as follows: *"Socialization" is the process whereby a person comes to understand and accept the norms*

---

[1] This chapter expands upon and supplements some of the ideas I initially presented in "Human Interaction and the Law" published in the *American Journal of Jurisprudence* (1969a).

*of conduct that a society imposes on its members.* Behind this conception there is obviously a reification, or better, a personification of "society." Society is viewed as an entity capable of creating social norms or rules and imposing them on people.

There are many definitions and usages of the word "social," but none includes anything like the meaning conveyed by such modern phrases as "social norms" or "social standards," where the adjective "social" serves to designate the imputed origin of the role or norm in question. Over most of Western intellectual history "social norm" would convey a norm to be observed in social relations with others, not a norm imposed by an entity called "society." Instead of emanating from society, a social norm makes society possible in the sense of a fruitful association among persons.

Today this view has radically changed, and "social norm" would be taken to mean, at least in academic circles, a norm that in some way is imposed by society. How has

**33**

this change come about? It could be said that, in part, it had its origin with Durkheim and the pervasive influence of his thought on sociology and related academic disciplines.

The core of Durkheim's thought (1933, 1938) lay in the conception of a "collective consciousness" or "collective representations." This personification of society was for Durkheim indispensable in any theory entitled to be called a science for society. In his Preface to the second edition of *The Rules of the Sociological Method*, Durkheim reiterated "that social life is constituted wholly of collective 'representations' [1938, p. xli]." In the same work he stated what "socialization" meant to him:

[T]he aim of education is, precisely, the socialization of the human being; the process of education, therefore, gives us in a nutshell the historical fashion in which the social being is constituted. This unremitting pressure to which the child is subjected is the very pressure of the social milieu which tends to fashion him in its own image, and of which parents and teachers are merely the representatives and intermediaries [1938, p. 6].

While the concept of a group mind or a collective will has in modern sociology generally been reduced—quietly and tacitly—to the status of a metaphor, this conception is still, if anything, both more explicit and more potent than ever in some sociologists' thinking. A relatively recent treatise on the sociology of law, intended for the novice, emphasized:[2]

From what source does the law derive? For sociological theory . . . that question permits of only one answer . . . the law derives from the social group; legal rules express the way in which the group considers that social relations ought to be ordered. This point of view is quite different from that generally taught. The current doctrine . . . does not bring to clear articulation the question of

the origin of the force of law generally, though that question is basic and fundamental. Instead the current doctrine applies its efforts to the different modalities in which the law appears (legislation, custom, judicial decisions, expert opinion), thus giving the impression that these modalities are radically different from one another. On the contrary, from·a sociological point of view, these formal sources of law, which the jurists are concerned to distinguish, are simply different varieties of one single and unique source: the will of the social group. . . . Statutory law is not essentially different from custom: both are the expressions of the will of the group [Levy-Bruhl, 1964, pp. 39–40].

Reconciling a mystical "group will" with the highly formalized processes of parliamentary legislation is obviously difficult. Levy-Bruhl's position, however—at least verbally—seems fully equal to the· task. He writes, apropos of the problem of the constitutionality of laws:

The subordination of ordinary legal enactments to the laws of a constitution presents a somewhat perplexing problem. What results when a law regularly enacted is contrary to the letter or spirit of the constitution? . . . The truth is that no satisfactory solution for this problem has been offered. Some have considered that it is for the judiciary to determine the unconstitutionality of laws and to declare void any statutes tainted with this vice. . . . This system, which permits the judicial power to control the power of the legislature, cannot be accepted. It is contrary to the sociological principle by virtue of which a legal rule is an expression of the collective will [Levy-Bruhl, 1964, p. 60].

What would this writer say of a constitution that required every legislative enactment to be submitted to the populace? What if it were stipulated that legislative enactments must be approved by two-thirds of the electorate? If one wanted to preserve some reality for the concept of "the group will," this provision would seem to be deserving of any protection that was available, including the exercise of a power of annul-

---

[2] The translation of the excerpts from Henri Levy-Bruhl's book are my own.

ment by a supreme court if the statute did not receive the required endorsement.

The reader may object to devoting so much attention to the somewhat idiosyncratic directions suggested by the thinking of Durkheim. Few modern scholars take all his metaphors and his preachments literally. But are we immune to the lure of the attractive metaphor? After all, the word "socialization" is itself heavily infected with a metaphorical taint. In saying that socialization is the process whereby a person comes to perceive and to accept the norms of society, do we not suggest that an entity called society has a corporate capacity to create and impose rules of conduct on its members?

Socialization was once thought of as being accomplished, in large part, by exposing the oncoming generation to the prescriptions contained in some holy scripture, in the sayings of a revered sage, or in some other identifiable and awe-inspiring divine or human source. Catlin has suggested that behind Durkheim's reification of society there may have been a tacit and perhaps unconscious political motive. As a non-Catholic living in a Catholic community, Durkheim may have sought to "provide French anticlericals with as good a moral authority as that upheld by the Catholic church, with its appeal to a scholastic rationalism based on revelation [Durkheim, 1938, p. xxvi]." Are we sure that in our own skeptical age, lacking the authority of any generally accepted scripture, we too are not tempted to fill the vacuum with a metaphor that attributes to society itself the power of saying what is right and what is wrong? So much for socialization as coming to do the things that society wants us to do.

## SOCIALIZATION BY STATE-LAW CONSTRAINTS

I turn now to a second and, in many ways, very different conception of socialization: *"Socialization" is the process whereby a person becomes willing to accept and observe the constraints of state-made law.* In the transition to this perspective we seem to move out of a world of unreal simplicity to one distressingly and complicatedly real. The law is no longer something lurking in a mystical "group mind"; it presents itself tangibly in libraries full of fine print stipulating endlessly what we can and cannot do.

Durkheim speaks of "social norms" as having "'the power of crystallization." One way in which this crystallization can occur is when a standard of behavior imposed by the collective conscience is converted into a formal, explicit, and written rule of law. Attributing to written legal rules the quality that they "do not change with the diverse applications made of them," Durkheim goes on to say, "A legal regulation is what it is, and there are no two ways of looking at it [1938, p. 45]."

I would suggest that there are not two but many ways of looking at a "legal regulation." The factors bearing on the meaning of a written rule can vary in response to a great variety of circumstances. Let me set forth some factors that may affect—in some cases drastically—the apparent significance for human affairs of a written rule of law.

Nearly every law on the books carries with it a tacit footnote that, if expressed, would read something like this: "The above provision shall remain in effect so long as the basic conditions presupposed in its enactment do not undergo a radical change." For example, suppose A and B own tracts of land on either side of a river. The deed under which A claims title describes A's land as bounded on the east by the river; B's deed designates the river as setting the western boundary. As the result of a seismic disturbance the river suddenly changes course, taking 10 acres from A's land and adding 20 to B's. Now who owns what? Note that the shift in the course of the river may affect not only the established boundary line between the two owners, but also the accessibility and fertility of the land as well as its ease of cultivation. Needless to say, the courts have had great difficulty trying to find a satisfactory solution for cases like these.

The disasters that undermine the tacit assumptions on which law is based need not be those of nature: They may be manmade. Take, for example, drastic monetary inflation. A agrees to sell a house and lot to B for $50,000, delivery of the deed and payment being stipulated to take place two years after the contract is entered. During the two years, the purchasing power of the dollar drops 90 percent. Shall the court rewrite the contract by increasing the price to a figure commensurate with the land's value when the deed is to be delivered? Such situations occur again and again. One inherent difficulty is that, in reaching the agreement on the contractually stipulated price, each party may have been influenced by his own estimate of the value of money as it would be at the time of payment; thus some appraisal of the threat of inflation may have entered into the price term itself. Furthermore, if the court rewrites the contract by lifting the price, continuing inflation may make that price inappropriate before the decree goes into effect and the parties have a chance to comply with it.

To put a case more directly relevant to the problem of socialization, suppose that John Doe and his wife have just moved into a new house. They have for some time been without a car, and Doe's driver's license has expired. In the middle of the night Mrs. Doe suffers a heart attack. Doe attempts to call an ambulance but finds that his telephone is out of order. He tries to summon his neighbor but fails. Doe then takes a sledge hammer and breaks open the locked door of his neighbor's garage. He finds the car with the key in it, puts his wife in the car, and drives to the emergency room of the nearest hospital.

On the face of it, Doe has committed a number of crimes. Is he excused from criminal responsibility by the drastic necessities of the situation? There is generally nothing in the statutes covering this problem, though the courts have in a few cases developed a vague and very open-ended doctrine of "necessity" (Perkins, 1969, pp. 956–961). There are not many reported cases involving this doctrine, perhaps because it is usually applied outside the courtroom. The decision not to treat the act as a crime is likely, indeed, to occur on the police level or in the prosecutor's office.

Mention of the possibility that a case might be settled on "the police level" calls to mind at once a problem that is one of great embarrassment for the process—or agents—of socialization. This is the problem of the "selective enforcement" of the law. We like to depict the law as standing in majestic detachment from the petty complexities of human affairs, for "the law is no respector of persons." It judges those who infringe its mandates impartially and by the letter of the law without reference to their individual situations, their past behavior, or their own perceptions of what is right and wrong.

In fact, some degree of "selective enforcement" and "selective surveillance" is an ineluctable aspect of the police officer's job. Time is scarce, and must be allocated to the tasks that are most pressing. The significance of such an allocation was cogently expressed in action taken by a disgruntled group of New York City transit police who had been denied a pay increase given their colleagues, the city police. Barred from striking, the transit police resorted to spending their entire working day enforcing the law against littering. They engaged in a "rule-book slowdown"—simply going by the book, albeit one page. This conduct constituted selective enforcement of an intentionally "perverse" nature (*New York Times*, Oct. 24, 1972, p. 1).

We like to think of the criminal law as impersonal, directed toward carefully defined overt acts, and requiring an unconditional fidelity to its dictates. Any hint of discretion by the authorities or of selective tolerance seems contrary to the "rule of law." In fact, the actual administration of a legal system is permeated with what may be called "managerial discretion" (Fuller, 1969b, pp. 207–213) from the police officer on the beat to the robed judge. In the conduct of a trial there is, for example, no rule in the books specifying just how many minutes an attorney may devote to cross-examining a particular witness. But if the judge exercises no control over the length of cross-examination, the trial may drag on and on. A trial judge often at some point may say: "Counsel, I believe that you have pretty well exhausted that question; I suggest you move on to something else." An attorney who openly and persistently disregards such a politely phrased command might face contempt of court.

Like any joint human enterprise, the operation of a legal system is collaborative; it cannot be carried out by written rules alone. It demands an exercise of prudence and reasonableness by all who take part and—sometimes—firm managerial direction by those in authority. What may be posited as a goal of "legal socialization," therefore, is to encourage more than a mere willingness to go by the book (Tapp, 1970c; Tapp & Levine, 1974).

This discussion of state-made law does not deal with the problems involved in the judicial interpretation of written rules. That issue is addressed in the following section.

## SOCIALIZATION BY HUMAN INTERACTION

A third perspective presents the view that: *"Socialization" is the process whereby a person comes to perceive, respect, and participate in the creation of the reciprocal expectations that arise out of human interaction.* The social phenomenon that I describe as "the reciprocal expectations that arise out of human interaction" receives almost no attention in the literature of jurisprudence. Notwithstanding this neglect, it is basic to the process by which an ordering

of human relations is achieved (Fuller, 1969a). This interactional process is explicitly recognized in three seemingly disparate fields: (1) in relations among sovereign states, where the process enters into and helps to shape international law; (2) in relations among tribal peoples, especially tribes hostile to one another but wishing to avoid all-out warfare; and (3) in commercial practice and commercial law as interpreted and applied by the courts.

In international law silent adjustments in the relations of nations—adjustments that find their only expression in actions and forbearances—often take the place of agreements spelled out in words. International relations cannot be governed by explicit verbal standards. Differences of opinion within a nation may make treaty negotiations difficult; unexpected developments, such as the disruptive actions of a third nation, may overnight render inappropriate a previous verbal definition of the parties' relationship. Sometimes the need for some readjustment in reciprocal expectations may be so obvious that it cannot wait for incorporation in labored paragraphs.

Anthropology offers hundreds of illustrations of the wordless accommodations and meaningful but silent transactions that take place between tribes and members of different social groups. Often these processes of social interchange take ingenious forms, as in the much-discussed phenomenon of "silent trade" (see, e.g., Grierson, 1903; Hoyt, 1926). A similar ingenuity is often shown in the way discussions looking toward some settlement of differences are initiated. If the tribal leaders themselves approach the opposing party, their action may be mistaken for the onset of a hostile attack, and they may be set upon and killed. To avoid misunderstanding, it is customary in many parts of the world to send an advance delegation of aged women or young boys to begin discussions and arrange for a meeting of chieftains. Where this device has been used over the years and has become generally familiar, a departure from it would tend to take on a doubly sinister aspect. A small body of chieftains seen crossing the border without notice would be likely to be set upon at once, even though their intentions were in fact peaceful and their gestures showed they were unarmed. They would have made the fatal mistake of violating stable interactional expectancies.

"The reciprocal expectations that arise out of human interaction" receive their most explicit recognition in commercial law. For example, suppose two firms have over time engaged in a particular kind of transaction with one another. For some time all goes smoothly, but in one transaction a dispute arises concerning whether the seller's delivery of goods ordered by the buyer was timely or so tardy that the goods could properly be refused by their buyer. The Uniform Commercial Code, Section 1–205(1), provides that such a dispute may be decided by reference to the "previous course of dealing" between the parties. As the Code specifies, such a "course of dealing" may properly be treated by the court "as establishing a common basis of understanding for interpreting their expressions and other conduct." The "law" applicable to their relationship is derived directly from expectations that have arisen in their past interactions.

In the case just supposed, the interactional expectancies do not extend beyond a two-party relationship. It often happens, however, that a shared view of the expected conduct for a particular kind of transaction may be seen to cover a wider area. In this case the Uniform Commercial Code speaks of "a usage of trade." The definition offered of this term in Section 1–205(2) states:

A usage of trade is any practice or method of dealing having such regularity of observance in a place, vocation or trade as to justify an expectation that it will be observed with respect to [transactions of the kind in question].

The Code further specifies that in case of litigation a court may properly take such "a usage of trade" into account in deciding a case, where it arises in "a place, vocation or trade" within which the usage has become routine and tacitly accepted as setting the rights of the parties. (See generally U.C.C., 1968, pp. 53–54.)

Though the three fields just mentioned are those where one finds the most explicit recognition of the principle that reciprocal expectations can arise out of interaction, the phenomenon occurs everywhere in the affairs of those in interaction with one another and having occasion to guide their conduct by the expected conduct of others. For example, suppose that two retired women, A and B, occupy adjacent rooms in the same apartment house. Mail for the residents is delivered to marked boxes just inside the general entry. There have been frequent thefts from these boxes. A, knowing that B is away, finds a letter addressed to B, takes it from the box, and slips it under B's locked door. On another occasion this situation is reversed and B puts A's mail under A's door. This practice goes on for some time, though neither party has had a chance to comment on it to the other. Clearly, if either contemplates discontinuing this voluntary service, she should give the other adequate warning. This obligation, to continue a voluntary service until adequate notice of its discontinuance has been given, might arise where one party became invalid and unable to render a return service. In speaking of the reciprocal expectations that arise out of interaction, the term "interaction" must be interpreted to include foreseeable inaction or forbearance induced by the actions of another.

## INTERACTIONAL SOCIALIZATION IN THEORY AND PRACTICE

There remains for discussion the relation between the theoretical problems of socialization and the practical problems of individuals coming to understand the interactional processes of an ongoing society. Note, first, that there is no easy way of teaching the oncoming generation how and under what circumstances interactions will give rise to reciprocal expectations that reach the level of rights and duties. It is not easy to explain in words how to create reciprocal expectations that will set the pattern for an ordered social relationship. Any educative effort in that direction is rendered doubly difficult by the fact that the expectations arising out of interaction often are not consciously articulated until they have unexpectedly been disappointed.

In the area of law, socialization occurs primarily not from books or lectures but from actual participation in the processes of interaction that give rise to ordered social relations. Unfortunately, this experience is becoming increasingly attenuated in modern society. Take the business executive who moves with a family every two or three years. The children attend the first three grades of school in Fort Worth, the next two in Denver, and so on. Children who participate in this nomadic life have never really experienced membership in a stable interactive community. In like manner, the urban flight to the suburbs often means a move to what is at best a pseudo-community with houses far apart and an often-changing population. Increasing mobility thus has been destructive of the education—the socialization—that can only be derived from participation in a relatively stable, interacting community (see also Fuller, 1969c).

It may be thought that this loss of stability is in some measure offset by an increasing participation in games—a participation that itself affords a form of socialization. The child who attempts to play checkers or basketball soon comes to see that the game cannot be played without rules. This insight may help one to see that the Game of Life also depends on the existence of, and respect for, rules that govern and guide interaction.

But note that there is a significant difference between the lessons that can be learned from playing games and those that derive from taking part in interactions not yet structured by rules. Much of the interest and fascination of most games comes from the tactic of keeping one's opponent in doubt as to one's next move. The experienced player not only attempts to keep the opponent in doubt as to the next move, but also often uses ploys that deliberately mislead the opponent about intentions.

This attractive art of deception is utterly alien to any process of interaction that can give rise to reciprocal expectations that serve to give meaning and order to human relations. The participants in such interactions are both lawgivers and legal subjects; each participant in his or her role as lawgiver must make certain that his or her actions give clear signals. A little deception may provide innocent fun in a game played within a framework of established rules; it has no place in the social processes from which rules tacitly emerge.

## CONCLUSION

In closing I make a few general observations about some interrelations between formally enacted law and the informal "law" that may emerge tacitly from interactions. First, in interpreting a written statute a court may often—though not usually explicitly— take into account what effect a given interpretation would have on the interactional expectancies that have developed tacitly in the world beyond courts and law books. If these expectancies are innocent and beneficial, a judge familiar with them will incline, often unconsciously, toward an interpretation of legislative intent that will not needlessly disturb them.

Second, in the field of statutory law a practical realization of legislative intent through judicial action cannot be obtained without some stabilization of expectations between the legislature and the courts charged with interpreting and applying its enactments. If the courts of a given state have habitually adopted a severely restrictive and letter-bound attitude in interpreting statutes, the legislature will take this practice into account in its draftsmanship. But if the courts make a sudden and unexpected shift toward a more expansive and liberal interpretation, the legislature will obviously not attain its objective or, perhaps, will attain objectives it had no intention of achieving. So if the conception of "the reciprocal expectancies that arise out of human interaction" presented in this chapter seems at times a little fuzzy, this fuzziness invades the vital centers of legal power as well. I doubt whether anyone would suppose that this fuzziness could be removed by a constitutional provision to the effect that the courts must interpret statutes truly and avoid either a wooden literalness or a loose construction in terms of an assumed, but unarticulated, legislative purpose.

Finally and most fundamentally, the very existence of a functioning legal system depends on a certain reciprocity of expectations between the lawgiving authority and the populace it purports to govern. If the subjects of law, undeterred by the threat of sanctions, pay not the slightest heed to the enacted rules, a legal system will not be attained. After all, it is hardly possible to put the whole population in jail. Conversely, if the legal authority, in visiting penalties on the populace, pays no heed whatsoever to its own laws, if no discernable relation can be seen between the decisions of the courts and the law in the books, a legal system will exist in name only. These illustrations are extreme, perhaps, but we must remember that many points lie on the continuum between pure juristic perfection and the void of its total defeat.

# CHAPTER 4

# The "Basic Law" or "Constitution" of a Small Group

## —WALTER O. WEYRAUCH

Law can be viewed as a network of small-group interactions. Basic characteristics of legal systems govern the interactions and permeate each individual small group. The rule structure within a small group forms a kind of behavioral constitution containing provisions on fundamental policies, internal and external relations, sanctions to be imposed for breach of rules, and so on. The use of a legal frame of reference in small-group analysis expands the scope of inquiry and may furnish insights into current social problems. The constitution of a particular experimental group, confined for about three months in a penthouse on the Berkeley campus, is presented as illustration.

Several years ago I participated in a series of experiments involving nutrition at the University of California in Berkeley. Nine male volunteers between 21 and 30 years old were confined for about three months in a penthouse and fed varying diets under strictly controlled conditions. I took part in the observations as a law professor, being concerned with the rules that evolved within the small group.[1] The detailed findings are reported elsewhere (Weyrauch, 1967, 1968). This chapter uses the experiment to illustrate the way law comes into existence and how it operates. For greater clarity, it is confined to some of the most basic legal norms that emerged.

Law can be viewed as a network of small-group interactions. Basic characteristics of legal systems govern these interactions and permeate each small group, although the members' level of awareness of the dynamics is relatively low. A legal perspective can be helpful to the social sciences (Cowan, 1962) by viewing groups in terms of such legal concepts as jurisdiction, conflict of laws, procedure, due process, notice, presumptions, and sanctions.

## THE CONSTITUTIONAL DOCUMENT

The Appendix to this chapter sets forth a collection of fundamental rules observed in the penthouse group; specific rules are referred to in the text by number. The rules were abstracted from the day-to-day observations of normative behavior made by a number of persons. The need for cataloguing the data resulted in an index of norms that can be called the "basic law" or "constitution" of the small group. The de-

[1] My efforts were aided by the work of Thomas A. Cowan and Donald A. Strickland (1965). Also I appreciate the assistance of my associate, Suellen Huntington, a graduate student of sociology. Financial support by the University of California, Berkeley, Space Sciences Laboratory Social Sciences Project is gratefully acknowledged (NASA grant NSG-243).

tails of how the observations were made and their accuracy are matters for exploration at another time. What is important here was the ease of observing and stating rules operative in human groups (Llewellyn & Hoebel, 1941) and the close resemblance between these rules and what is commonly called law.

## THE SYSTEM AS A WHOLE

Fuller observed that it is somewhat unrealistic "to assume that any customary system can be reduced to a kind of code book of numbered paragraphs, each paragraph standing forth as a little law complete in itself [1969a, p. 11]." The law of a tribe or extended family, he points out, is really a program for living together supported by the basic logic of the system as a whole. The same is true of law based on the interactions within any small group. It is clear, for instance, that the appended "constitutional document" does not fully represent the reality of this particular small group; the wording and the order are not those of the group but of the professor.

To illustrate, the rule "Thou shall not kill" was probably part of the basic, high priority norms of the penthouse group, yet it does not appear in the Appendix. The reason is simple—no incident related to killing arose, thus the norm does not appear. On the other hand, basic concepts of equality were brought into the penthouse as part of United States cultural heritage and applied in various contexts and with many qualifications. Generally, the rules as restated reflect the logic of the system only imperfectly. They are ambiguous (e.g., what is "articulation" in rule 1?), overlap in part, and sometimes restate a similar matter from a slightly different angle. In these respects they are not too different from legal norms in the conventional sense, which are less clear than commonly assumed.

In regard to Fuller's observation, one may ask whether this effort was so different from what other law professors have done in restating the common law—for example,

the law of contracts. By their private and scholarly efforts these law professors have become quasi-legislators who sometimes intermingle their personal opinions with their observations of judicial behavior. Close accuracy in restating a specific norm was not important in their case either; they may have felt responsible to state the "better" rule from their knowledge as experts of the logic of the system as a whole. Yet, they too proceeded on the assumption that rules or patterns of rules were observable, even though different observers might have disagreed on details of content. Of course, the restaters of common law study behavior through written materials, while in the penthouse I studied behavior through observation.

## THE GENERALIZATION PROCESS

The basic law or constitution of a small group is probably as realistic as any generalization or law based on particular incidents. It is difficult, if not impossible, to restate the internal rules that govern a group without somewhat changing them. Take, for instance, the leading norm in the document, that rules are not to be articulated. Articulating this rule, certainly from the perspective of the penthouse inhabitants, seems to be a contradiction in itself as well as a contradiction of all rules articulated thereafter. Yet, would it have been more realistic and in conformity with the rule not to state the rule at all?[2]

## A BEHAVIORAL CONSTITUTION

The document, as the quotation marks in the title indicate, is not really a basic law or

---

[2] It might be said that I was not a member of the group and that the rule against articulation did not bind me. But my position was not that clear; to facilitate my observation of normative behavior, I established a close relationship with the inhabitants not dictated by the nutritional experiment. We have to be satisfied here with imperfection in the hope that we will reach a greater level of clarity at some later stage.

constitution in the sense of the Constitution of the United States. It is more in the nature of a behavioral constitution, a reflection of behavior within the group as observed and stated. For the penthouse inhabitants, it expresses some form of understanding based on shared ideals, which the inhabitants for whatever reason felt to be sufficiently authoritative to engender compliance. Many elements normally contained in constitutions are missing. For example, allocation of power is regulated only in rudimentary fashion (e.g., in rule 19). But the document is still a basic law or constitution because it contains more than a mere statement of ordinary law. Its content appears to be fundamental to the survival of this particular small group, and this crucial importance is best expressed by the term "constitution," which implies basic structure.

It might be possible to think of a behavioral constitution of the United States. Articulation of such an underlying constitution, including shared ideals, would be complex, probably beyond the capacities of any living person. Piecemeal articulation is attempted by the U.S. Supreme Court on a case-to-case basis. We can speculate that the underlying constitution reflecting the behavior and ideals of the people would probably be controversial in its specific content, just as the constitution of an experimental group is likely to be controversial to any reader, whether or not he has seen the data. Possibly articulation of social taboos causes dispute.

The reference to a behavioral constitution underlying the actual Constitution of the United States does not mean that there are two clearly dichotomous constitutions existing side by side. The underlying behavioral constitution is a multilevel body of complex normative behaviors changing over time. Without it, the real constitution would be lifeless and in fact could not operate.

## THE CONSTITUTION OF A SMALL GROUP

The title of this chapter indicates that the constitution is merely the reflection of basic rules in *a* small group. These rules as restated refer to this particular small group, the penthouse inhabitants, not to all small groups. Although it is impossible to articulate the universal law or constitution of *the* small group, some rules have rather general validity. For example, the basic norm that rules are not to be articulated (rule 1) has been observed in families (Fuller, 1969a), law firms (Smigel, 1969), and law faculties (Richard, 1964; Weyrauch, 1965). There may be occasional efforts to set down basic procedures, but this is often symptomatic of severe internal tensions that interfere with the healthy functioning of the group.

The document may also have some general validity in conveying the spirit of idealism and alienation of young people in the 1960s. The volunteers in the penthouse experiment were above average in intelligence and, though not students, were closely identified with their contemporaries in the universities and colleges (see Whittaker & Watts, 1969). Thus, the basic law of this small group acquires some elements of a manifesto of young people. It deviates from many tenets of the dominant U.S. culture, for example, in the emphasis on intellectuality, aesthetics, and individual self-development (rule 3); the disapproval of competition (rule 5); and the propagation of participatory democracy (rules 10–12). At the same time it reflects some contradictions that can also be observed in real life. Equality of all persons is espoused, but women are not really treated as equal (rules 5 and 7); racial and religious discriminations are outlawed, but if they occur the fact of their existence is to be denied (rule 9).[3]

## PROBLEMS OF COMPARISON AND TRANSLATION

When we speak of comparative law and of problems of translation, we normally re-

---

[3] Other information on ethnic tensions can be found in Weyrauch, 1968.

fer to law and modes of expression in different nations. Yet comparisons are possible between the cultures of law and of the social sciences.

Groups are governed by rule structures that resemble what lawyers commonly call law, although social scientists variously call them rules, norms (e.g., Sherif, 1966), behavior, patterns, structure (e.g., Deutsch, 1963; Lévi-Strauss, 1967), communication models, or decision systems (e.g., Deutsch, 1963). Since social scientists tend to avoid legal references, it is enough to realize that these terms are often used when law is described. The reasons are complex. Perhaps law as an intellectual discipline has succeeded in reserving knowledge for its own purposes that could have been used elsewhere. If so, a price was paid, because protective barriers may have slowed down information beneficial to law.

Using a legal frame of reference in a supposedly nonlegal context, for example in the penthouse experiment, expands the scope of both law and the social sciences. The proposition that behavioral rule structures in small groups are an essential element in the functioning of legal systems, as conventionally understood, suggests that it might be important to study small-group law in relation to such topics as the law of procedure (Murphy, 1966; Snyder, 1958; Strodtbeck & Hook, 1961; Strodtbeck & Mann, 1956), constitutional law, family law (Kay, 1965), labor law, contracts, corporations (Taubman, 1959), partnership, and land use (Karst & Clement, 1969). These areas of law, perhaps more visibly than others, regulate incidents of legal status, and status is involved in small-group interaction.

## LEGAL STATUS WITHIN A SMALL GROUP

We may think of status as an incident of small-group membership that tends to influence the substance of interactions, whether or not these interactions take place within the group or between members of the group and outsiders. More important, at least as

observed in the penthouse, may be the threat that a group member may impair or lose status if rulebreaking persists. Status thus becomes important in connection with sanctions for the rule violation.

The threat of sanctions is sometimes viewed as an essential element of legal systems (see, e.g., Llewellyn & Hoebel, 1941). Under this standard the basic law or constitution of the penthouse inhabitants *was* law. Rules 27 and 28, even though seemingly tolerant of internal violations, do provide for sanctions in the form of eventual degradation of status. Notice had to be given to the violator after fair warning, and due process had to be observed in an elaborate ritual.

The sanctions provided in the penthouse may strike us as mild compared to ordinary legal sanctions, but they were not perceived as mild by the inhabitants. Loss of status within the group appears to have been viewed by the members as a devastating defeat. The experiment set the stage for an internal system of pressures that made it mandatory in the minds of the inhabitants to maintain a position of respect. External pressures, such as those coming from the experimenters, appear to have been viewed as less significant.

## CONFLICT OF LAWS

Nevertheless we should not stop with a narrow examination of internal group law. The constitution also provides evidence of interactions between internal law and external law, for example, in rules 13–18 and 28. Most of the rules imply ways of solving conflicts between the self-given internal laws of the penthouse inhabitants and the laws of the experiment as legislated by the scientists' research design and execution. The main strategy of the penthouse inhabitants seems to have been to reconcile inconsistencies between external and internal law by interpreting the external law in a fashion that avoided conflict. One might compare this to the behavior of a judge who, reconciling foreign and local law in a process of interpretations, concludes that they really come to the same result. This may be pure fiction, of course, but a fiction that may go unchallenged. The rules regulating conflict between internal and external law clearly were themselves part of the internal law of the group in the sense that they were not acquiesced to by the experimenters.

In fact, the conflict rules were designed to maximize the comfort and local powers of the penthouse inhabitants, much as happens in real life when local decision-makers favor local interests over those of outsiders. Rule 28 includes, for instance, the well-known legal notion that foreign penal laws are not to be locally enforced. Mostly the conflict rules are of a frankness that under other conditions probably would be considered embarrassing. Legal rules do not ordinarily protect self-interest as openly as was attempted in the penthouse. These matters are usually adjusted by the courts in a discreet fashion. Yet we should recall that the constitution reflects behavioral law as restated by an outsider. The penthouse inhabitants themselves, following their main rule, would have refrained from any articulation of these norms.

More was involved than the interactions between the penthouse inhabitants and the experimenters. The penthouse, like most jurisdictions, was not a truly isolated society. It was subject to the rules of the university and to the laws of the city, the state, and the nation. These young men were also deeply committed to ideals of their country's culture and of humanity; even though they sometimes fell short of their aspirations, they provided for such shortcomings in their basic law or constitution. Also, interactions with other groups were not entirely cut off; telephone calls and mail were received and answered, and negotiations, some clearly legal in nature, took place.

## LAW AS SMALL-GROUP INTERACTION

It might be possible to look at law as it exists in nations as a conglomerate of small-group interactions that cut across traditional legal classifications. The constitution of this particular small group incorporated external law to some extent; the same is true of the constitution of any other small group. The penthouse inhabitants interacted with the outside world and were concurrently members of other small groups. These factors provide links between individual small groups, each one a legal system of its own, all in their aggregate operation constituting the law in its entirety.

This perspective may be helpful in understanding some contemporary problems that seem to defy traditional legal classifications. It may be relatively meaningless, for example, to look at a particular dispute between students and a university administration as a legal conflict between the state and individuals. This is the way the conflict may appear in a criminal prosecution against individual students, but for purposes of finding a solution to the dispute and of planning, other methods of legal analysis are needed. We may get closer to a realistic appraisal if we see the legal process as an interaction between identifiable small groups—the board of regents, the president of the university and other top administrators, certain faculty leaders, groups of politicians, a city council, members of student government, and certain student groups.

There are natural limits to perception and to the capacity of individuals to process and store information. Larger units, such as a nation, a major enterprise, a state, or a metropolitan center, may be too complex for full human comprehension. On the other hand, governance within institutions, business competition, adjudication, and legislative and executive processes can usually be broken down into small groups and interactions of individuals who act as members of small groups. These may be sufficiently limited in scope and complexity to be more comprehensible.

As is clear from the penthouse experiment, the boundaries between the individual groups are hazy. Was I one of the experimenters (I did not share the nutritional concern) or in any sense a member of the group? Many current social problems are related to such ambiguities, which can be viewed as boundary problems (Weyrauch, 1969). Who, for example, is the university? What groups participate in its governance? Are students insiders or outsiders (Study Commission, 1968)?

One special facet of the penthouse experiment was a formal nexus between the volunteers and the experimenters, namely individual contracts in the technical legal sense. This formal link may be missing in the interaction of other small groups. Interactions between a jury and other persons in the courtroom are governed by procedure (Erlanger, 1970; Kalven & Zeisel, 1966). Interactions between two competing street gangs are largely governed by environmental factors. Considering such interactions as well as the internal structure of groups to be legal in nature may be objectionable to those who require that law refer to governmental authority in a formal sense. But certain factors speak for use of a broader definition of law.

### LAW AS BASIC HUMAN NEED

The truth value of definitions may be limited by their social functions. Definitions, like exclusionary rules of law, tend to shut out whole areas from consideration. Calling the rules and interactions of a gang or revolutionary group "law" may be felt to give some form of recognition to outgroups and to detract from law as an expression of official authority. There seems to be an unsettling quality in the idea that any small group, no matter how worthy, is engaged in lawmaking. Yet we may really deal with law as an inherent human need that manifests itself whenever interactions take place, for instance, in somewhat stabilized patterns existing within small groups. This basic human need, which I choose to call law, is related to what in other contexts is referred to as the product of socialization (Hogan & Henley, 1970). People have a natural inclination to build laws governing their relationships; society reinforces this need through teaching that laws are essential to regulating interaction.

If what we encounter in small groups is a form of law or some basic phenomenon essential to the operation of legal systems, then one can see an infinite number of applications. If it is true that small-group law is essential for the operation of law as a whole, we may gain some measure of stability from an unexpected direction: Small groups, although individually vulnerable, are protected as legal institutions by their size, their often fleeting and casual nature, and their infinite multitude. These factors combined with ease of formation, change, and dissolution may help in the survival of societies. Narrower conceptions of law tied to the authority of particular governments may become eroded, as history has demonstrated; yet law as a basic human need, broadly defined, is really indestructible.

# APPENDIX

## THE "BASIC LAW" OR "CONSTITUTION" OF THE PENTHOUSE INHABITANTS

### MATTERS OF FORM

**1.** Rules are not to be articulated. In case of articulation they are to be discarded, regardless of whether such articulation was accidental or deliberate. If a substantial segment of the group has in fact talked about the rule, the level of articulation is reached and its existence acknowledged.

A rule that has become spurious by articulation and acknowledgment can be discarded by any form of behavior designed to destroy its effectiveness, for instance by deliberate disregard in a demonstrative fashion without the normal group sanctions that otherwise would have been imposed.

**2.** The closer a rule comes to a taboo area, the less articulate it should be. Minor administrative matters may be articulated.

The stringency of a rule is determined by the level of its articulation. The more articulate it is, the less it has to be followed.

## BASIC POLICIES

**3.** Individual self-development is the main goal in life. Intelligence, individuality, and aesthetic perceptiveness are values of high order. Personal factors should have priority over scientific and institutional matters.

**4.** Honesty is a quality of high order and should be adhered to regardless of consequences.

Boastful accounts of one's alleged abilities or experiences are not considered lying. Such boasts by others are not to be questioned.

Frankness in an authority figure should be rewarded by cooperation and affection.

**5.** Competition is to be discouraged because it distracts from values of higher order, such as human affection. Competition is particularly harmful when women participate.

Competition may be permitted for entertainment purposes, for example, in a poker game.

**6.** No situation is so bad or hopeless that it cannot be turned to advantage. A person's status depends on his ability to see the advantageous aspects of a dilemma and to communicate his insight effectively to others in similar distress.

This rule does not justify dishonesty. It recognizes intellectual achievement that is beneficial to the group.

**7.** Women, if present, are to be treated with chivalry. Derogatory or obscene remarks can be made about them if they are absent. Obscene language is excusable if used as some form of relief in a stressful situation.

**8.** Nobody is supposed to discuss controversial political topics unless this is done in a superficial fashion. (This rule was discarded after I articulated it in a discussion with the penthouse inhabitants; heated political arguments took place thereafter.)

## DEMOCRATIC GOVERNMENT

**9.** All persons are born equal. If discrimination because of race or religion occurs, the fact of discrimination is to be denied. All members of the group are viewed as equal as a matter of principle. A person may be treated differently from others on the basis of his merits or demerits.

**10.** In matters considered crucial, each member of the group has an absolute veto. However, a lone dissenter or a dissenting minority may be harassed to reach a desired unanimity.

In matters relating to minor issues of daily life, a majority vote may be taken. Anyone present is qualified to vote, even if not personally interested in the matter.

**11.** All obligation is based on a notion of consent or voluntary submission. This requires full disclosure of all facets of the obligation, unless they are self-evident. The burden of establishing self-evidence is on the person claiming it.

**12.** Any institutional setting, for instance a scientific experiment involving people, should be democratic and should allow the participants a voice in operation and execution. If the authorities disregard this basic rule, the participants may withhold or delay performance.

If authorities discuss a minor matter with the subjects, it means that implicitly the issue is submitted to their determination. In major matters of concern to both authorities and subjects, a consensus has to be reached.

## EXTERNAL LAW

**13.** Group members should not commit themselves firmly toward outsiders. Any commitment is to be viewed as a working arrangement, to be adjusted to the individual issue by way of renegotiation and consensus.

If inadvertently or under the pressure of circumstances a seemingly firm commitment (personal, financial, or otherwise) has been made, one should deny its existence or reinterpret it in the direction of minimum compliance. This is not considered to be in violation of the demand for honesty since any firm stand on future issues involves an unconscionable limitation of one's basic freedoms.

**14.** Rules originating from outside, regardless of their level of articulation, are less stringent than self-given rules. Such rules may be minimized in their effect, but they should not be altogether abandoned or boycotted. Some measure of compliance is to be observed.

Changes in external law may be introduced by way of gradual interpretation, rather than open confrontation. If there is a difference of opinion about the meaning of a particular rule, the more lenient view shall prevail.

**15.** It is a basic function and responsibility of the group to cooperate in the modification of external law by defining and interpreting law that exists.

**16.** Extraordinary obligations toward the outside should result in extraordinary privileges. A privilege granted to one person has to be granted to everyone else in similar instances.

Any concession in a specific instance implies a concession in any similar instance. A rule is only binding if generally enforced in a uniform fashion.

**17.** General announcements and posted schedules are to be viewed as being directory, not mandatory. Performance may be withheld until a specific demand is made.

If a group is set up for specific purposes, any demand made upon the group or its members has to stay within the scope of such purposes. Matters of doubt are to be resolved in favor of individual group members. The purposes have to be explained in

advance and acquiesced to.

**18.** Irresistible impulse is a defense to the charge of rulebreaking, especially if external law is involved.

## INTERNAL LAW

**19.** While all persons are equal as a matter of principle, every person has his place in life as it evolves naturally over time. One should recognize one's functions and act accordingly.

Functions within the group, such as spokesman toward the outside, counselor in personal problems of members, and watchman in regard to potential internal difficulties or danger from the outside, are to be assumed by natural preferences of the individual. The group should recognize such self-assumed positions if at all possible because it is likely that a person is good at what he really wants to do. In case of serious conflict, the group may take sides by showing greater deference to the more qualified contender.

The functions, once assumed, are to be performed as a matter of fact, but not insisted upon as a matter of privilege.

The internal dynamics in regard to choice of function and recognition are not to be articulated.

**20.** The group is expected to help an individual who is in distress, especially if such distress originates from the outside. Personal distress, depressions, and the like should be regarded with sympathy and respected; they should be acted upon only if a demand is made or if others in the group are affected.

**21.** Serious incidents within the group, whether accidental or not, ought to be concealed from the outside world. Internal frictions and hostilities are to be concealed as horseplay, joking, or in similar fashion. A concerted effort should be made to persuade all members of the group, particularly the participants of the incident, that the matter was actually harmless.

If a member of the group insults another, he is expected to apologize without demand from the offended person or pressure from others. Such apology is to be accepted.

**22.** Benefits obtained by individual members of the group are to be equally divided. This rule does not preclude games of chance for entertainment purposes.

## MATTERS OF PRIVACY

**23.** Everybody is left to his own devices and may do as he pleases as long as the level of utmost toleration is not exceeded. Excessive noise and physical contact are to be avoided.

A desire for privacy has a higher priority than a desire to socialize. If a member of the group makes a nuisance of himself, others are to leave the room rather than remonstrate. Habitual abuse of privileges may result in loss of group status.

**24.** Loyalties are determined by the closeness of the underlying relationship. Loyalty to a friend prevails over group loyalty. Group loyalty prevails over loyalty to larger units. The ultimate responsibility is to the self, to one's conscience.

Loyalties are characterized by their spiritual essence, ideally an inner glow of affection. They may manifest themselves in various ways and actions; yet manual services to others, unless dictated by necessity, are viewed as degrading and should not be expected.

**25.** Any inquiry into personal matters should permit equivocation in response. An inquiry not meeting this standard can be countered by withholding information.

This rule applies equally to all forms of inquiry, such as oral interviews and questionnaires. Tape recordings are suspect as an intrusion on privacy.

**26.** One's proper name, modes of dress, grooming, and hair style are part of one's individuality and should not be interfered with.

Matters relating to intimate bodily functions belong to an inalienable private sphere. The same is true of one's dreams, secret hopes, and aspirations.

## SANCTIONS

**27.** Occasional violations of self-given rules, including basic policies, can be viewed as foreseeable consequences of human frailty and should ordinarily be overlooked.

In case of continued violations, each member of the group is authorized to issue oral reprimands. If this is of no avail, concerted action may be taken in the form of harassment or demonstrative indifference. A concerted show of indifference is to be preferred to more active sanctions, because it leaves the violator alone with his conscience. Permanent loss of status within the group is the ultimate sanction against rulebreakers. The application of sanctions is to be decided upon by loose consensus, for example by joining in the oral reprimand issued by one of the group members.

The same procedure applies if a reprimand is unreasonable. The alleged violator may orally remonstrate, and other group members may join in the remonstration. If a person insists on his unreasonable reprimands, in the face of successful group remonstration he may be harassed and ultimately lose his group status.

Whether a reprimand is reasonable or unreasonable depends upon the circumstances as judged by each member of the group in an essentially intuitive process.

**28.** The group shall not apply sanctions against members for violating external law unless such violation infringes upon other members of the group. External compulsion against some group members should be met by the others with passive resistance, withholding cooperation, quietness, and so forth.

Laws of higher order, such as demands of conscience based on common understandings of humanity, are not to be viewed as external law. They may be considered law of the group and therefore be enforced as such, provided that the matter transcends the private sphere and becomes of group concern.

# CHAPTER 5

# The Moral or Educative Influence of Criminal Law

## —JOHANNES ANDENAES

The threat of punishment contained in criminal law works not only through fear but may also have moral or educative effects. This chapter analyzes these effects and assesses the scanty evidence regarding their importance; it also includes a discussion of the relevance of psychological theory and research for an evaluation of the deterrent effects of criminal law. Although psychological theory and experiment may give suggestions, concepts, and research methods of interest to the lawyer, there is little that can be of direct application. The questions confronting the lawyer are so specific that they ask for specific research.

Punishment is a traditional means of influencing behavior, from a rebuke or slap on the hand of a small child to heavy sentences by courts for serious crime. In criminal law theory a distinction is made between the effects of a threat of punishment and the effects of actual punishment on the punished.

The threat of punishment is directed to all members of society. It is pronounced in the criminal law and is made real by the activities of the police, prosecution, courts, and prisons. The law must always be seen in connection with the machinery of justice that makes it operate. Insofar as this threat of punishment restrains criminal conduct, we speak of *general deterrence.*

When people are punished, they are, in their future conduct, still under the threat of the law, but their motivation is more complex than before. Being prosecuted and punished may influence them in various ways. The threat of the law alone had not been sufficient to make them conform. If they are now deterred by actual punishment, we speak of *special deterrence.*

## LIMITATIONS OF GENERAL DETERRENCE

In this chapter I am concerned only with general deterrence: the effect of the threat of punishment. Two extreme positions often emerge from the literature. One is that of Bentham, who considered people to be rational beings choosing between modes of action based on calculation of risks of pain and pleasure. The consequence of this model is clear enough: If we make the risk of punishment sufficient to outweigh the prospect of gain, the potential lawbreaker will, as a rational being, choose to stay within the limits of the law.

The other extreme, often represented by psychiatrists, discards this model as unrealistic. When people remain law abiding, they maintain, it is not because of fear of the criminal law, but because of moral inhibitions, internalized norms. If an internal restraint is lacking, the threat of punishment does not make much difference since criminals do not make rational choices, calculating gain against the risk of punishment;

they act out of emotional instability, lack of self-control, or because they have acquired the values of a criminal subculture. For convenience I call this the psychiatric model. The extreme representatives of this way of thinking tend to see lawyers as using general deterrence to defend their outmoded system of criminal law or to conceal and rationalize their retributive feelings. In my view each extreme represents only a part of the truth.

## The Danger of Generalization

Offenses are so variously motivated that the role of the criminal law in upholding norms of conduct must be different for every offense. Any realistic discussion of general deterrence must be based on distinctions between various types of norms and analysis of the particular circumstances motivating transgression (Andenaes, 1952). In general it can only be said that general deterrence works well sometimes and works poorly or not at all at other times.

The threat of punishment affects each of us differently. For each kind of criminal conduct, the population can be divided into three groups: (1) law-abiding persons, who do not need the threat of law to remain on the right path; (2) potential criminals, who would have broken the law if it had not been for the threat of punishment; and (3) criminals, who may well fear the law but not enough to keep from breaking it. It is in the intermediate group—potential criminals—that the deterrent effect of punishment is at work. But none of these groups are static. They vary by offense, by geographical area, and with changing conditions (e.g., war or other serious crises). Therefore, there is no easy means of identifying the citizens who belong to each or the proportions of persons in the categories.

## The Moral or Educative Effect
## of the Criminal Law

Both the Bentham and the psychiatric models are concerned with direct deterrent effects. Punishment is not only the artificial creation of a risk of unpleasant consequences. It is also a means of expressing social disapproval that may influence attitudes quite apart from fear of sanctions. The term "general deterrence" is in fact too narrow, insofar as it excludes this moral or educative influence. I prefer to speak of *general preventive effects* of punishment. From the legislator's perspective, creating moral inhibitions is of greater value than mere deterrence, because the former may work even when a person need not fear detection and punishment (Andenaes, 1952, 1966). Moreover, a successful inculcation of moral standards may result in social pressure toward acceptable behavior even for persons who have not personally been influenced by the moral message of the law.

When I speak of moral or educative influence, no value judgment is implied. The expression is used only to designate an influence on attitudes and behavior emanating from the law but not based on fear. Hawkins (1969) has criticized the use of the term "moral" in this wide sense. He prefers to speak about the socializing effects, to me raising a terminological issue of no great significance. The most neutral terminology perhaps is to speak about the attitude-shaping influence of criminal law.

It may seem somewhat artificial to single out for study the influences on human behavior emanating from the system of criminal justice, since these influences at most represent just one thread in a complicated web. The necessity for research into the subject stems from the practical tasks of the legal profession. We are constantly confronted with the problem: What can be achieved by means of criminal law—and at what cost? Traditional legal methods do not provide an answer beyond crude guesswork based on common sense.

## GENERAL PREVENTIVE EFFECTS:
## DIRECT MORAL INFLUENCES

It would not be quite fair to state that the spokesmen of classical deterrence theory totally overlooked the moral influence of criminal law. Thus, in 1770 Beccaria in his discussion of punishment for different categories of crimes said:

If the same punishment be decreed for killing a pheasant as for killing a man, or for forgery, all difference between those crimes will shortly vanish. It is thus that moral sentiments are destroyed in the heart of man ... [Beccaria, 1880, p. 139].

This view in fact expresses a strong belief in the potentialities of criminal law to influence moral attitudes. Even Bentham (1879, p. 184) mentions the power of punishment to act as a "moral lesson." English authors like Stephen (1883) and Kenny (1936) express similar perspectives. But, above all, the doctrine has been developed by German and Scandinavian authors. The idea of moral or educative effects of criminal law is implied when "reinforcement of social values" is mentioned among the goals of criminal law. Sometimes this moral influence is considered more important than the direct deterrent influence. The German criminologist Mayer thus asserts that "the basic general preventive effect of criminal law does not at all stem from its deterrent but from its morality-shaping force. . . . Nothing is so convincing to man as power, provided it appears as expression of a moral order [1936, pp. 26–32]." In Swedish literature Lundstedt (1920, p. 30; 1921, p. 105) was an extreme and eloquent spokesman of the same view. The purely deterrent effects of criminal law, he held, were "hardly worth mentioning" as compared to the moral influence.

Likewise, the Canadian Morton professes that "the most important function of the criminal law is that of education or conditioning [1962, p. 43]." It is often asserted that this effect takes place only when punishment has the character of just retribution. Just punishment "attaches to the criminal a taboo-conception and has the effect that in most cases the possibility of committing the prohibited act is not at all considered

[Mayer, 1953, p. 23]."

These statements are made with great confidence but without much research or practical experience to substantiate them. On closer analysis, it seems that there may be various aspects to the moral or educative influence of criminal law. The following is an attempt to explicate these different aspects.

## Respect for the Formal Law

It is generally believed that legal commands or prohibitions ought to be observed even by those critical of the law in question. This feeling of obligation depends on a respect for legitimate authority. If the conduct in itself is considered reprehensible, the stamp of the law reinforces this feeling. If the act is morally neutral, respect for the law operates alone.

Plato tells that out of respect for the law Socrates emptied the cup of poison instead of following the offer of his friends to bribe his custodians so that he could escape. But Socrates was no ordinary man. In many people this respect for formal law is probably relatively weak, in some it is totally lacking, and in others it may even be negative. Dollard, Doob, Miller, Mowrer, and Sears (1939) contend: "Within any given state internal hostility to the symbols of authority is a common feature of social life. It is manifested alike by labor leaders and capitalists as well as by groups which hope for revolutionary change [p. 85]." A U.S. textbook for police recruits (Germann, Day, & Gallati, 1962) maintains that in almost every community some citizens "resent authority in any form, delight in community disturbances and do all they can to obstruct the conduct of police business [p. 23]." The distribution of such attitudes could be explored by survey research (see Walker & Argyle, 1964).

Attitudes to law compliance vary from one society to another and change over time. European observers of the United States have often remarked that respect for legislation is less in the United States than in most European countries. "The legislative mill grinds as it does in European countries, but the average American cares little what comes out of it [Kinberg, 1935, pp. 68–69]." Similar statements are found in works of many U.S. scholars. Taft (1942) said "American culture does not demand or approve obedience to all laws. . . . The slogan 'obey the laws' is never meant to be taken without qualification. It is but a slight exaggeration to say that people should obey *most* of the *most important* laws *most* of the time [p. 234]." This view may be related both to the highly pluralistic character of U.S. society and to the way the political machinery works. Legislation is looked on, perhaps quite realistically, not as a solemn and authoritative statement of the "will of the state" but as the outcome of a very mundane power structure.

Some respect for the formal law is probably essential for the smooth functioning of society. Without it, law enforcement agencies are like an occupying army in foreign territory, a comparison often made regarding law enforcement in the ghettos of some U.S. cities. For the young, underprivileged black in the ghetto, "law" seems not to be the object of much positive feeling. The National Advisory Commission on Civil Disorders in its 1968 report cited a deep hostility between police and ghetto communities as a primary cause of the riots of 1967. But an absolute respect for formal law may also represent a danger. Blind deference to authority is not considered a virtue in democratic countries. Such obedience lay behind many German war crimes and has often been cited in criticisms of the German people during the Nazi period. In his experiments on obedience, Milgram (1965) called his findings disturbing, since submission to authority led normal people to perform harsh acts.

### Criminal Law as a Moral Eye-Opener

Labeling a certain conduct criminal may make citizens more aware of its socially harmful character. Thus, the Swedish author Thyrén (1970) says that in some cases the effect of the threat of punishment is "not so much that it deters the individuals through fear, but that it opens their eyes to the socially dangerous character of the act and makes their conscience more sensitive on this point [p. 72]." Cameron (1964) reports that when a shoplifter is apprehended, he or she realizes more clearly that a criminal and shameful act has been committed. Before the arrest, the shoplifter had not thought in these terms.

A similar although weaker effect may result from knowing that an act is declared criminal. Such effects could be expected from penal legislation against driving when intoxicated or with negligent homicide. The law may cause drivers to reflect on the dangerous and irresponsible character of driving under the influence of alcohol. For now, opinions on this matter have to remain rather speculative. A British survey (Sheppard, 1968) of drivers before and after a new law on drunken driving offers some relevant data. The law introduced in October 1967 was accompanied by an extensive publicity campaign and led to a substantial decrease in the accident rate. It may be asked whether this was due solely to the deterrent effect of the new law or whether a change in moral attitudes toward drunken driving had occurred. Drivers were questioned about their opinions on the effect of drinking on driving ability and about their attitudes toward drinking and driving. Answers showed little change from the first to the second survey. It seems likely then that behavior change was brought about by the deterrent effect of the new law, not by the publicity campaign and moral eye-opener effects.

### Punishment as Authoritative Statements about Badness

Our attitudes about different behaviors are to a high degree the result of suggestive influences from society. Legislation and the machinery of justice send out messages to the public. Punishment expresses social disapproval, and it does this in a discriminatory way: The heavier the punishment, the stronger the disapproval. If individuals are disposed to accept the evaluations of the authorities, they will be influenced by way of suggestion. Walker (1964), for example, speaks of the "declaratory function" of the criminal law, Feinberg (1965) of the "expressive function" of punishment.

Given our knowledge of how attitudes are formed and sustained, it seems unlikely that legal norms are as influential as are the various primary groups to which an individual belongs. But since primary groups transmit legal norms, there may be a cumulative effect. If the law succeeds in influencing some individuals, the effects may spread as a result of social interaction.

Schwartz and Orleans (1967) conducted a field experiment to test how a sanction threat and a moral appeal influence normative orientation with regard to the payment of federal income taxes. One group of taxpayers was asked questions designed to remind them of the penalties they might risk by tax evasion. Another group was asked questions designed to accentuate moral reasons for compliance. Two control groups had either a neutral interview or none at all. The findings based on analysis of interviews and taxpaying behavior suggest that the punishment threat has some effect on normative orientation, at least in some social groups, but that the conscience appeal in most groups was more forceful. Walker and Argyle (1964) also tested the hypothesis that criminal law has moral effects. Answers to a survey on the morality of attempted suicide showed that knowing that the penal provision against attempted suicide had been replaced did not result in a less strict view; indeed, there was a slight but statistically nonsignificant tendency in the opposite direction. Other questions regarding the normal significance of acts like littering, public drunkenness, prostitution, and use of obscene language yielded parallel findings.

These studies were only concerned with short-term effects. Most believers in the moral effects of punishment have relied on long-term effects. Further, the investigators excluded from their sample that small, but by no means negligible, minority that held that the law automatically governs the morality of conduct. Finally, Walker and Argyle's research dealt only with acts on the borderline of criminal law, not with acts commonly rejected as immoral and deserving of punishment. Arguably, punishment has greater power to support and reinforce commonly held moral judgments than to create a previously nonexistent moral condemnation. While the evidential value of the findings is limited, they do arouse some skepticism about the moral potentialities of criminal law.

Historical data point in the same direction. If the criminal law continues to express moral attitudes, for example, about sexual behavior that represent the views of former generations, often the penal provisions become less enforced and eventually are repealed. Many such provisions stay on the books only as long as they are not enforced. Experience also shows that moral indignation can flow freely without support of the criminal law. In England, incest was not an offense until a statute of 1908, but no one would imagine that the moral indignation toward incest was less intense in the England of Queen Victoria than it is today.

A further question is whether sentencing policy can influence the public's evaluation of a certain type of offense. Imprisonment is normally imposed only for somewhat more serious conduct and expresses a high degree of social disapproval. Is it possible through use of prison sentences to make certain offenses more reprehensible in the eyes of the public? Experience does not give a general answer. On the one hand, Clinard (1952) in studying black market violations during World War II found that imprisonment was more effective than fines. Potential offenders dreaded not only the inconvenience of being incarcerated but also the moral stigma attached to a prison sentence. Further, in the districts where the Office of Price Administration regulations were strictly enforced, compliance was more prevalent.

On the other hand, the public seems to discriminate in its attitudes toward the prison sentence. If the motivation of the offender is considered unselfish or honorable, sentencing does not influence social judgment of the offense or offender, though the sentence may be accepted as justified. The Scandinavian countries have had extensive experience with short sentences for drunk driving. In Norway, more people go to prison for this misdemeanor than for all felonies combined. The sentence carries with it some stigma, but not that much. Klette's study (1964) of 50 drivers with no previous criminal records, sentenced to from one to two months' imprisonment for drunk driving, showed that no offenders had to change employment because of the prison sentence, although the employers in all cases but one knew of the offender's stay in prison. Also the convicted drivers did not consider themselves "criminals" and kept to themselves in prison. In some cases the spouse of the offender reacted strongly, but generally the effects of the prison sentence on social and personal relations seemed to be insignificant.

### Limits on Direct Effects

The effects described above are closely related. In practice it may be difficult to distinguish among them; they all seem to revolve around the concept of *legitimate authority*. However, I have noted above that individuals do not change their views on the morality of the act per se as a result of the formal law; if they now consider the act wrong or immoral, it is only because they generally consider it wrong to act in violation of the law. I have also described situations where the law *has* changed the moral attitude of the indi-

vidual toward the act. The difference between "Criminal Law as a Moral Eye-Opener" and "Punishment as Authoritative Statements about Badness" is that the effect described in the former occurs as a result of the individual's personal thinking and evaluation, whereas the effect described in the latter is due merely to suggestive influence.

A tentative conclusion would be that only within narrow limits can criminal law directly influence moral attitudes, at least from a short-term perspective. This statement refers to the situation in a democratic, pluralistic society with wide freedom of discussion. The situation may be different in an authoritarian setting, where the state has power over the schools, social organizations, press, and other mass media and where all these instruments for indoctrination can support the legal system. For example, Berman (1963; Chap. 8) speaks about the educative role of Soviet law and courts. This idea of educating citizens has found expression in Article 3 of the Russian Code on Court Organization:

By all its activity a court shall educate citizens in the spirit of loyalty to the Motherland and to the cause of communism, and in the spirit of undeviating execution of Soviet laws, of a protective attitude toward socialist property, of observance of labor discipline, of an honorable attitude toward state and social duty, and of respect for the rights, honor, and dignity of citizens and for rules of socialist communal life [Berman & Spindler, 1966, p. 429].

### GENERAL PREVENTIVE EFFECTS: INDIRECT MORAL INFLUENCES

So far I have described the direct moral influences of punishment. The indirect moral influences are probably considerably stronger.

### Punishment as Reducing and Neutralizing the Bad Example

There is much experience to show that a bad example left unpunished can be infectious (Andenaes, 1952). With such trivial offenses as illegal parking, lack of enforcement may easily lead to total breakdown of compliance. But the mechanism of the bad example has a much wider field of application. For example, repeatedly cases are reported of large-scale theft by employees. The more violations, the fewer qualms the individual feels. In the same way, a branch of government can be penetrated by corruption. The unthinkable becomes thinkable when comrades are doing it. Why should one be honest when others are not? The risks seem less real; moral inhibitions are broken down. This danger is probably greatest when an individual learns about offenses committed by others who are in similar situations.

The machinery of criminal law works in two ways to counteract this effect. First, it reduces—through deterrence and in other ways—the number of bad examples. Second, it makes the bad example less attractive. Seeing the criminal law process in action works as a vaccination against the temptation to follow the example. There may be different theories (e.g., Toby, 1964) about the psychological mechanisms, but about the fact itself there can hardly be any doubt.

To understand the importance of this effect, one might visualize the situation if the criminal law or its enforcement were permanently dismantled. To begin with, deviant individuals would commit crimes to a greater extent and more openly than before. The example would be followed by others on the moral borderline who had been kept in check by fear of the law. By a kind of chain reaction more people would gradually be involved in criminal activities, especially of the acquisitive kind. It may be correct that moral inhibitions are sufficient to keep most people from committing serious crimes, but whether this would continue without a machinery of criminal justice is a more doubtful proposition. The experiences during police strikes in urban communities are not encouraging (Andenaes,

1966, pp. 961–962). Perhaps there is much truth in the words of the Swedish author Ekelöf (1942):

If the moral standard of the people is to be maintained, it is in my opinion not sufficient that people get their standards of conduct inculcated in their childhood; they need throughout life to see them applied by their surroundings and conceive of them as an integral part of the prevailing social mores. Man must from the cradle to the grave be exposed to constant moral propaganda. And in this propaganda the activity of the machinery of criminal justice plays an important role [p. 54].

### Criminal Law Shapes the Framework for Moral Education

While punishment can prevent the breakdown of established moral norms by serving a continuing reinforcement function throughout the life cycle, the criminal law system may also have indirect effects on a person's moral education during the crucial early years. This education takes place primarily in the family, in school, and in other small groups, but it is not independent of other conditions in society. The existence and working of the criminal law provide a general framework that must necessarily have deep-rooted consequences for the moral climate of society and the moral education to which children are exposed. It would be difficult to teach honesty, nonviolence, and similar positive values where these rules were openly and commonly broken without punishment. Moreover, the existence of criminal law and the machinery of justice may motivate parents and others in similar authority roles to press those moral rules more strongly. Parents will teach the child not to steal not only because they consider theft immoral but also because the consequences may be serious. Many parents probably use references to police and prison as means of communicating to children the absolute necessity of "going straight."

The Norwegian educator Nordland

(1966) pointed out the parallel functions of discipline in an educational setting and of criminal law in the greater society. In an analogy to the concept of general prevention, she speaks about a general or group-oriented discipline maintained by fixing a set of rules and applying sanctions against violation. The children learn thereby the limits of acceptable behavior and they learn to respond to symbols of what represents forbidden conduct. For the sake of group discipline it may be necessary to apply the prescribed sanction even in cases where it is not considered necessary to prevent repetition by the violator. On the other hand, some children do not react adequately to the normal system of discipline and therefore must be given individual treatment. In practice there may be a tension between those two principles, as there is in criminal law between considerations of general prevention and considerations of individual treatment.

Criminologists, on the whole, have not taken a great interest in the general effects that the criminal law has on human behavior. They have been much more interested in the specific offender and his or her personality and environment. My own perspective is very different. I consider law, especially criminal law, as a fundamental socializing influence. A modern, highly industrialized and urbanized society of the Western type could hardly function without criminal law, police, and a reasonably effective criminal justice system. This system works not only through fear but also through more subtle influences on human thought and behavior. These influences permeate society in so many ways that they are difficult to isolate and measure. In this respect, punishment is as complex as other fundamental institutions of society.

## PSYCHOLOGICAL RESEARCH: CRITIQUE AND CHALLENGE

A contribution to a book on law and psychology would seem incomplete if it did not touch upon the relevance of psychological theory and research. As a layman in psychology, I approach the subject with great diffidence. But a willingness to expose one's ignorance and prejudices may be a necessary step in promoting a fruitful dialogue. The following discussion will be concerned with all general preventive effects of criminal law, the deterrent as well as the moral or educative effects.

It is a commonplace that the general insights into the human being's emotional life and into the processes of social interaction provided by the progress of psychology are indispensable to a realistic understanding of the possibilities of criminal law as a means of influencing attitudes and behavior. These insights exclude any simplistic and generalized conceptualization. It seems, however, to be difficult to find research of direct relevance to the question of the general preventive effects of a threat of legal punishment. Psychologists have been more concerned with the effect of actual punishment than with the effect of threats of punishment.

### Unique Features of Legal Punishment

The threat of legal punishment has four special features that set it apart from most other life situations:

1. The threat is abstract and impersonal. A person tempted to break the law is normally in a very different position from one faced with a command of another person. For this reason Milgram's (1963, 1965) experiments in obedience are of limited relevance to the problem of general preventive effects of criminal law.
2. The threat of punishment is normally directed against forbidden activity. In psychological terms, we have an "approach–avoidance conflict." Sometimes an omission is threatened with punishment, but provisions of this kind do not play an important role in criminal law.

The psychological situation is different for a person who by threat of punishment is forced to do something as compared to a person who has to refrain from a certain activity. Lewin (1935) described the difference as observed in children.

3. The character of legal penalties differs vastly from the negative sanctions applied in punishment experiments or commonly used in education or child-rearing. It is not a question of a succession of short, minor shocks or stimuli. In the case of more serious crime it is a complex, painful, long-lasting experience to be exposed to criminal justice. This is so even if the outcome is only a suspended sentence or probation, and a severe sentence for a serious crime can ruin a life. The other extreme is represented by the traffic ticket, which is more like the punishments ordinarily used in laboratory experiments or for educational purposes. The drastic character of the criminal process and the criminal sanction changes both the empirical and the ethical problems involved.

4. The threat of punishment is only one factor in a complicated motivational process, where personality factors, life situation, and nonlegal pressures combine in a highly varied way.

Criminologists, eager to apply psychological findings to the problems of criminal law, have sometimes overlooked these characteristics of the penal law. Criminological journals have published papers that try to elucidate the problems of deterrence by reference to laboratory animal research. Thus, Jeffery (1965) found that experimental evidence supports the classical school of criminology in its statement that the certainty of punishment—not the severity—deters people from criminal acts; moreover, that a consequence must be applied immediately if it is to be effective. Appel and Peterson (1965) concluded that punishment is essentially ineffective in controlling or eliminating behavior, since its effects usually depend on continuous, repeated applications.

## Threat versus Actual Punishment

These statements about the effects of punishment may or may not be correct. Certainly they cannot be deduced from animal experiments. In the first place the deductions overlook the basic distinction between the threat of punishment and actual punishment. Research into animal psychology has been primarily concerned with the effects of actual punishment; the general preventive effects of criminal law, on the other hand, are achieved through the threat of punishment. The motivational situation is complex; without a certain ability to think in symbols and adjust to future events, threat cannot work. The situation of a person facing the threat of a punishment has nothing in common with the effect of electric shocks or other punishments administered to rats or pigeons following a certain behavior, for example a peck on a disk. It can be confidently stated that animal research cannot make any significant contribution to the problems of the general preventive effects of criminal law.

So, too, with regard to the effects of actual punishment. The application of legal punishment results from the violation of a general norm that prescribes punishment and that the offender normally will know in advance. The whole experience derives its meaning from this relation between the general norm and the specific application of punishment. The situation is very different from that of the confused rat or pigeon desperately trying to adapt its behavior to the incomprehensible manipulations of the psychologist. Azrin (1960) described as punishment any aversive stimulus, such as electric shock or noise, that is explicitly arranged to follow a response. It is doubtful whether there is any similarity at all, apart from the word "punishment," to the situation of a human undergoing punishment because he has committed an offense.

The psychological concept that seems to come closest to the way the problem of general prevention presents itself in criminal law is that of "anticipated punishment." In

Dollard and associates' classic work on "frustration and aggression," this is a key concept: "[T]hose actions cease to occur which, in the past, have been followed by punishment [199, p. 33]." Punishment is here, of course, taken in a wide sense as including all kinds of painful responses from the social environment. The authors did not deal with the pure threat of punishment without actual experience of punishment. They stated as a law of behavior that "*the strength of inhibition of any act of aggression varies positively with the amount of punishment anticipated to be a consequence of that act* [Dollard et al., 1939, p. 33]." (Italics in original.) This postulate fits nicely with classical theories of deterrence and with commonsense notions about the importance of the severity of a threat. But neither the enunciated principle nor the research presented to substantiate it seems to be of much help in the difficult task of assessing what deterrent effects can be expected as a result of a contemplated change of policy.

### Need for Specific Research

In educational research, interest has been concentrated on the problem of whether punishment or reward is more effective as an incentive to moral and intellectual learning. In some fields of life, a similar choice will be open to the legislator. Economic activities may be more conveniently regulated by creating a system of incentives than by legal commands and prohibitions. But in the traditional spheres of criminal law, it is impossible to institute a system of rewards for lawful conduct as an alternative to punishment. The legislator can attach only penalties to theft, tax evasion, or speeding. The preacher can promise heaven to the obedient and hell to the disobedient. The Justice Department has only the last possibility at its disposal.

The conclusion of this raid into foreign territory seems to be the following: Psychological theory and experiments may give suggestions, concepts, and research methods of interest to the lawyer who tries to assess the effects of criminal law or of a change in criminal law policy. I have no doubt that there would be important results if psychologists devoted their interest to these issues. But the questions are so specific that they ask for specific research. Analogies from experimental research may lead us astray if they are drawn without a clear conception of the differences between the life situation and the experimental setting.

# CHAPTER 6

# The Legal Threat as an Instrument of Social Change

## —FRANKLIN ZIMRING and GORDON HAWKINS

Noting that it is important to distinguish threats aimed at shoring up existing norms from those that seek to change customary patterns of behavior, the chapter discusses a number of conditions influencing the outcome of threats that attempt to produce social change. Among the factors considered are variations in the type of custom, the rationale for change, the social characteristics of the threatened audience, and the extent of law enforcement. The implications of these factors for socializing change are presented.

## LAW AND BEHAVIOR

There exist two contrasting views on the relationship between legal precepts and public attitudes and behaviour. According to the one, law is determined by the sense of justice and moral sentiments of the population, and legislation can only achieve results by staying relatively close to prevailing social norms. According to the other view law and especially legislation is a vehicle through which programmed social evolution can be brought about [Aubert, 1969, p. 69].

At one extreme then is the view expressed in Dicey's lectures (1905) at Harvard Law School in 1896 and a few years later in Sumner's celebrated pioneer study (1906): Law is a dependent variable determined and shaped by current mores and the opinion of society. At the other extreme, the view is exemplified by Soviet jurists like Kechekyan (1956) who see the law as an instrument for social engineering. Although some sociologists "try, in a limited way, to confront the two views and determine the conditions under which the law may change social relationships [Aubert,

1969, p. 69]," none appear to have made any systematic attempt to consider the factors that militate for and against the success of law to change customary behavior. This is not to say that no attempt has been made to take account of the variables that determine the effectiveness of law as a means to socialize change. Rather such attention has been limited to the significance of particular variables in specific situations. Thus, Aubert (1966) in his study of the Norwegian Housemaid Law of 1948 emphasized the importance of the level of information and the process of communicating norms. Gorecki (1966) drew attention to the way in which such conditions as the socioeconomic structure of Polish rural areas and social pressures of a customary and religious nature prevented the realization of the legislative aim of the Polish divorce rules. Dror (1959) commented on the failure of law to change family life and marriage habits in Turkey and Israel and formulated a "basic hypothesis" to the effect that "changes in law have more effect on emotionally neutral and instrumental areas of activity than on expressive and evaluative areas of activity [p. 801]." While it is conceivable that such an hypothesis has some validity, it does little more than focus attention on one aspect of an extremely complex problem.

The limited knowledge available on these issues may be due to an ambivalence about discussing the efficacy of legal attempts to control behavior. In casual conversations we have noted a reluctance to formulate objective principles about the extent to which legal threat can change customary behavior. In particular, there seems to be a failure to recognize a distinction between issues relating to the *morality* or *expediency* of prohibiting particular types of behavior and issues relating to the *efficacy* of such prohibitions. There is a tendency for views to vary with the subject from alcohol to firearms to racial discrimination, and to vary according to the speaker's view of the rightness of prohibiting the particular behavior. The conclusion to such discussions is often the comforting one that the law can succeed in doing right but will inevitably fail when authorities attempt to prohibit what should not be prohibited. Unfortunately, since there is a wide variation in moral views among our acquaintances, this general principle leads to contradictory conclusions about the efficacy of particular attempts to control behavior. We attempt here to discuss in objective terms the use of the legal threat of punishment to induce social change. Our emphasis is more on the narrow issue of the deterrent effect of threat of punishment than on the great variety of mechanisms associated with compliance to legal commands. Yet, we feel a discussion of the narrow topic will inform the general topic of law as an agent of social change.

## THREAT AS A SOCIALIZING MECHANISM

By definition, the threat of sanctions cannot achieve a deterrent effect unless that threat results in some individuals acting differently from the way they would in the absence of the legal threat. In this sense at least all legal threat is an attempt to change behavior. Yet, it is important to distinguish between cases where the main thrust of the threat of punishment is aimed at preserving the status quo from those in which the legal threat attempts to change social customs.[1] When the threat of punishment is aimed at preserving the status quo, the formal legal command is usually only one of many forces pushing potential offenders toward conformity. Other social norms will usually complement threat of the law. Thus, knowledge of the law prohibiting burglary is preceded in the socialization process by messages about the wrongness of stealing and home invasion. By the time a citizen reaches adulthood, he or she has heard a consistent stream of messages about burglary—messages that, with the specific legal threat, form a network of restraining influences. And usually when the legal threat is directed at reinforcing a long-standing and important social norm, a demand for compliance does not require learning new behavior patterns. In most cases the traditional habit of imagining that threats are directed by the legal system at specific individuals also seems justified.

When the law is used as an instrument of social change, the achievement of acceptable rates of compliance is likely to require reorientation of the values and behaviors of those who have previously followed the outlawed custom. In all probability the behavior that such threats seek to restrain will have acquired positive social meaning for

---

[1] See Stjernquist (1963), at p. 158: "The above division into behaviour-changing and behaviour-stabilizing norms has proved to be practical in different social sciences. Means . . . uses the terms 'administrative rules' and 'canalizing rules' respectively. . . . Homans . . . applies a similar division of norms but has a special terminology: 'norms apply to the maintenance of established behaviour, orders to future changes in behaviour.' Homans also points out that 'orders are always changing into law and custom.' "

members of a threatened audience far more often than in the case of traditional crimes. Further, there is reason to suppose that, when the law seeks to restrain customary behavior, those whose responses are most important in predicting compliance will be not individuals but groups among whom the forbidden behavior has been customary (Massell, 1968; Stjernquist, 1963).

If these assertions are correct, it is important to know, in understanding the operation of legal threats, whether the aim is change or stability. There are differences in threat effectiveness. But before elaborating on the use of threats to achieve social change, a few qualifications are in order.

*Some of the conditions associated with the use of legal threats to promote social change occur in other situations where law and custom are not synchronized.* In particular, the same kind of circumstances can obtain when the law has not changed but the social values and customs supporting a law have. A change in social conditions without change in legal rules creates much the same kind of disequilibrium between custom and rule that is created by altering the law, and it is this disequilibrium that makes it necessary to consider separately legal threats aimed at social change. In fact, in the contest between an old rule and a new custom, the attempt to return social relations to a prior state can be seen as a subcategory of law as an instrument of social change, albeit a special subcategory, because the old rule will have the support of lip service in the community. For this reason there is a basis for viewing experiences in the U.S. with alcohol in the 1920s and marijuana in the 1960s as similar attempts to legislate social change. However, it is important to distinguish the cases because, among other reasons, we ordinarily expect the new-law versus old-custom contest to provoke more widespread resistance than the old-law versus new-custom; the tradition of lip service is an inertial force of some consequence.

*There are important similarities as well as differences between deterrent threats used to reinforce existing social conventions and those aimed at social change.* It would be naive to suppose that the lessons learned about the operation of threats in other settings can have no relevance to the analysis of threats directed at changing customary behavior. The motive force of deterrence in each case is the fear of unpleasant consequences, and therefore many of the same factors important in predicting the outcome of one will bear significantly on understanding the other. The vocabulary of deterrence —stressing threat credibility, the severity of sanctions, and modes of communication— will thus be a necessary, if inadequate, tool for analyzing this special class of laws.

*There are important differences among threats aimed at social change, and these differences can lead to substantial variations in threat effectiveness.* If this is the case, it is a mistake to base general conclusions about the effectiveness of threats as instruments of change on single observations. To deny, for instance, that stateways can change folkways on the basis of "our experience with Prohibition" is to operate from an insufficient inductive basis. We hope to suggest some of the variations in situations that might explain why some attempts to change customary behavior through legal sanctions succeed while others fail dismally. Among the factors that appear to be most important are variations in the nature of the custom, in the social characteristics of the individuals and groups that have adhered to the custom, and in the way the threat of punishment is carried out.

## VARIATIONS IN THE NATURE OF THE CUSTOM

Differences in the nature of the custom that appear to influence the probability that a custom will be successfully suppressed include: its utilitarian and moral significance to adherents; the extent to which it enjoys popular support; the degree to which its practice is visible to enforcement agencies;

the extent to which its nature is such that a general change may extinguish individual conformity drives; and the degree to which its change meets current community needs.

## The Significance of Customs

Of obvious importance in predicting the effect of threatening customary behavior is the degree of commitment to a particular custom. Public religious observance and burning high-sulphur coal for home heating are both popular social customs in the United States, but the two are poles apart if the first is a central expression of deeply held religious convictions, while the second persists by reason of casual tradition and convenience. Behavior that satisfies important drives is more difficult to extinguish than behavior that satisfies less compelling drives; this axiom provides one basis for ranking the differential significance of customary behavior. A second index for ranking the importance of customs is the extent to which adherents perceive that legitimate alternatives exist to fulfill the drives associated with the customary behavior. Thus, while high-sulphur coal is associated with the admittedly important aim of keeping warm during winter, the availability of other heat sources makes this custom less important. Clearly, some forms of customary behavior are more amenable to substitution than others. It would seem difficult, for instance, to persuade a group associated with a suppressed religion that belief in a nonforbidden dogma would yield the satisfaction they associate with their present faith.

It is also possible that the law might seek to prohibit behavior that has acquired a *moral* significance for many of its adherents (e.g., Mormons who practiced polygamy in the nineteenth century). The possibility of normative support for a custom introduces a problem that traditional criminal law prohibitions do not often encounter. The moral dimension is important when trying to predict the effect that threats might have, because the prohibition of conduct considered morally right or even morally imperative may elicit entirely different reactions from a threatened audience.

Variations in the importance of a custom play a significant role in the simple utilitarian calculus long accepted as a major explanation of the deterrent effect of threats. The more important a custom, the more severe and more certain must be the punishment threatened, if the legal policy is to prove effective as a means of social change. Yet, while this simple formulation might accurately state the relation between variations in the purely utilitarian value of customary behavior and the effect of legal prohibitions, the situation is somewhat more complex when we consider how variations in moral significance affect the prospects for prohibition. To be sure, the greater the moral importance of a custom, the greater the unpleasantness of the penalty that must be attached to that custom to change behavior. But moral support for a prohibited custom can render ineffective two usually powerful reasons for complying with legal threats—respect for law and law-abidingness, and the negative social connotations normally conveyed by punishment. Although most groups in society believe in the law as a system of social control, the belief that violation of any law is wrong may be overwhelmed by a specific moral sense when individuals feel that a customary behavior is of greater importance. Thus, people who find it difficult to commit a petty crime, such as illegal parking, because of their feelings about violations of the law might feel differently when their motives for law violation are altruistic. Those who continue to place a higher moral value on prohibited behavior may feel more like a doctor exceeding the speed limit to visit a patient than like a petty law violator, and even if they continue to express respect for law in general terms, this respect will not be seen as a barrier to violation of the prohibition of the valued custom.

At the same time, the moral significance of a prohibited custom may make the consequences of conviction and punishment less worthy of avoidance. For most people the most degrading aspect of punishment is the social message it conveys. Conviction and punishment for serious offenses carry social stigma, and the fear of stigma is a significant aspect of the unpleasantness. The moral value of customary behavior may result in the would-be offender rejecting the negative significance of punishment received in a worthy cause. Indeed, he or she may invert the moral value of the ordinary symbols of degradation by viewing the discomfort and disrepute suffered as signs of personal dedication. Moreover, if most of the offender's peers share these moral views about a particular type of law violation, severe punishment may result in positive status.

### Extent of Popular Support for the Custom

The popularity of a prohibited custom is an important element in predicting the effects of its abolition. Information about the number of people who have supported a now-prohibited custom should help define the sheer size of the social-control task that faces those attempting to enforce the new law. In addition, such information can also provide clues as to the types of person the legal threat must reach. The smaller the number of adherents, the more the legal system is on notice that potential violators may differ from the general population in ways that might make predicting their responses to threat a special problem. The more widespread the adherence to a custom, the more the legal threat is aimed at normally socialized individuals. Thus, there is greater probability that judges, juries, and other administrative personnel will identify with the custom itself or the type of people who adhere to it; this can undermine law enforcement against all offenders or against a class of offenders with which the rest of the community identifies.

One might question whether in democratic societies customs are often outlawed when there is sufficient public acceptance to

inhibit enforcement. While it is certainly the case that authoritarian and "occupation" regimes more commonly institute laws against popular customs, the democratic process can produce such attempts when groups or even regions are in sharp disagreement over the moral propriety of a particular customary behavior. Any time that the power to declare law is more centralized than, or otherwise removed from, the responsibility of enforcing it, the law itself may not compel the sympathy of the enforcement agencies. Moreover, as long as the group adhering to a particular custom is not considered unambiguously deviant, the attempt to maintain customary behavior may attract members of the community who do not identify with the custom but have no scruples against it.

That it is difficult to prohibit customary behavior should not be interpreted as indicating that success is unattainable. The point is limited to the prediction that suppression of popular custom will require substantial enforcement activity that may be difficult to generate.

### Visibility of the Custom

Since enforcement of law is a significant part of the basis for predicting whether a legal threat will achieve high rates of compliance, the extent to which customary behavior is visible and therefore more easily enforced can play a crucial role in successfully changing custom through law. Some customs may be visible because the public nature of the behavior is part of its defining characteristic. Such is the case with demonstrations, refusals to pledge allegiance to the flag, and so forth. The customary behavior may also achieve high visibility, without involving large numbers of people, if the practice often comes to the attention of a person opposed to the custom. For example, this type of visibility will often occur when a behavior has a victim, as in the case of face-to-face racial discrimination. The fact that a custom is highly visible, however, is no guarantee that a prohibition will be effectively enforced. And substantial enforcement efforts are, of course, no guarantee that punishment on a mass scale will achieve social change. But it is certainly the case that visibility makes enforcement easier if the will and ability to enforce the law exist, and it is clearly more probable that a law against social custom will succeed under conditions of widespread enforcement than under limited or nonexistent enforcement.

## Will General Change Make the Custom Obsolete?

Sometimes the law can succeed in changing patterns of behavior because the change in law, if it reduces the gross rate of a custom or behavior, removes some of the reasons previously supporting the custom. To a certain extent individuals follow a custom usually because most people they know follow that custom and expect them to do so. Any law that changes expectations of other people's behavior and notions of what others expect will go part way toward restructuring the conditions that led to initial compliance. In addition, there are a number of other ways in which the abolition of a general expectation may undercut the incentive for an individual's adhering to a custom. Many people keep firearms at home not because they think other people expect them to but out of fear of guns in the hands of others. For such individuals a change in law might provide a credible promise that others would not be armed. Or the owner of a lunch counter in the South might be unwilling to desegregate if it meant that white customers would attribute the responsibility for this change to him, and if he faced the probability of losing white clientele to other lunch counters. Prohibition of the custom would, however, put him in the position where he could not be personally blamed for the change in policy, and his white patronage would be protected from raids by competitors because of the generality of the change in practice. Thus, prohibiting the

custom of discrimination might be an economic advantage to the individual entrepreneur by increasing the demand for his service, while a unilateral change in conduct might be to his economic disadvantage. Given this type of condition, change in custom can be more easily achieved if preceded by change in law.

## Custom and Current Needs

It is more likely that the prohibition of customary behavior will attract enthusiastic enforcement and secure widespread compliance if a clear need provides a socially acceptable reason. The best reasons yet devised for justifying change in legal relationships are external threat and internal emergency. It is thus much easier during war to explain why previously allowed behavior is being outlawed (featherbedding in the labor market or freedom to determine prices). The drama of changing circumstance and needs can provide a basis for enthusiastic support among the general population and give what is at least a powerful excuse for compliance to those who were following the old custom.

Because the reason for change is of importance, certain types of social change adopted into law during periods of crisis might not be as successfully replicated in the absence of a similar crisis. This does not mean that changing custom through the law may not often survive the crisis that gave rise to it. Though to some extent the end of a war or depression marks the end of a need, it does not automatically herald a return to the status quo. Intervening experience with the new way of doing things and the advantages of the change to some groups (perhaps at the expense of others) provide reasons for continuing the change.

## SOCIAL CHARACTERISTICS OF THE THREATENED AUDIENCE

Different types of groups used to adhering to customary behavior may come in conflict with a new law. Some groups are more cohesive than others, and cohesive group structure can militate for or against change in custom, depending on whether group leadership urges compliance with or defiance of the new law. Perhaps the most important characteristic of groups adhering to custom, from the standpoint of predicting the response to prohibition, is the degree to which group members are integrated participants in the larger social system. The greater the degree of agreement among group members with the values of the larger society, the greater will be the pressure on group members to comply with the command of the law. Similarly, incentive to comply with the new law will increase in proportion to the success that group members have experienced in the larger society. Wealth and status are powerful motives for societal support. Poverty and discrimination, particularly if born of differentiations directly related to group membership, provide fertile ground for rebellion against the prohibition of custom, as well as a basis for generalizing that rebellion into a rejection of the entire value matrix of the legal system.

One complication in the relationship between group identification with the larger society and susceptibility to threat is that high status provides an incentive for compliance only if the threat of punishment is credible. Even those values in accord with the larger society's values will usually require some assurance that the new law will be enforced. And it is precisely the high-status and well-integrated groups in society against whom laws prohibiting customs are most difficult to enforce. But if the will to enforce is sufficient, the incentives enforcement gives a successful group to comply with the prohibition of custom will be large.

## VARIATIONS IN LAW ENFORCEMENT

Any discussion of the variables that explain why some attempts to legislate social change succeed while others fail must deal with law enforcement as both a dependent and independent variable. It must be seen as a dependent variable because such factors as the popularity of a custom and the characteristics of groups who adhere to it may influence the kind of enforcement that legislating change will produce. Yet, the kind and degree of enforcement will itself have a significant impact on the prospects for successful social change. And since many variations in law enforcement are not inevitably determined by situational factors of the type discussed above, the character of law enforcement deserves independent attention. The degree to which enforcement activities entail likelihood of detection, the extent of enforcement across class and group lines, and the severity of punishments meted out for offense—all are included among the significant variations in law enforcement that may condition rates of compliance.

### Likelihood of Apprehension

The simplest statement one can make about the extent of enforcement is that the likelihood of achieving the aim of the law will increase as the perceived likelihood of apprehension for law violation increases. This axiom might deserve some qualification in the situation where a custom is viewed as morally imperative and conscientious objection occurs with a frequency that does not seem to be conditioned by the rate of apprehension or punishment. However, even in the case of a law that generates conscientious objection, increased probability of apprehension and punishment may still reduce the rate of deviation, if only because potential offenders with fewer scruples will respond to such increases.

### Selective Enforcement

A second qualification of the general relation between success in suppressing a custom and perceived likelihood of apprehension is that broader law enforcement means arresting more high-status people for violation. This increases the pressure on enforcement agencies to reduce and re-channel enforcement efforts and confronts the community with the full implications of what it means to punish deviation. Under some circumstances, then, broad law enforcement can lead to an earlier crisis test of the law and perhaps ultimately to its demise. But if broad and nonselective enforcement is somewhat unpredictable in consequence, this in no way implies that the prospects for effective change in custom are any brighter when there is selective enforcement focusing on low-status groups. Aside from its manifest injustice, the principal danger of highly selective enforcement is that groups who are spared will disobey the law because no real risks exist, while target groups will perceive the enforcement as being directed against them rather than against the behavior. If such conditions persist, neither high- nor low-status groups are apt to respect the specific law, and rates of noncompliance in the groups without the threat of enforcement will probably continue to be substantial.

If it is not exclusively based on caste or class factors, selective enforcement can have a profound deterrent effect on those with relatively little chance of being caught, since it is these high-status groups in society that "scare easier" when confronted with the threat of social disapproval. Thus, while a small business owner will doubtless be more impressed if he or she hears of an owner of a like business being jailed for not reporting income, even the incomplete analogy of a racketeer being jailed for such an offense can teach small business owners that people can and do get caught. Unless he or she can be persuaded that enforcement is based exclusively on class factors, this knowledge can produce the kind of anxiety associated with extensive general deterrence.

No doubt enforcement plays a key role in determining whether an attempt to abolish a custom succeeds. We could go further and suggest that, with respect to customary behaviors that are not very important to a

threatened audience, the risk of apprehension and punishment is the most important criterion. The policy value of knowledge about enforcement is less than it might seem, however, for two reasons previously mentioned. First, so many factors relating to the custom and the type of people against whom the law must be enforced have an effect on the enforcement rate that it might be wise to think of the risk of apprehension as shorthand for a complex of variables. Second, because so many factors affect the rate of detection and punishment, it is difficult to estimate the parameters of practical variability in the enforcement of a particular law. Thus, if unalterable conditions make $y$ the maximum achievable level of enforcement, it will be of little comfort to law enforcers to tell them that a rate of detection of twice $y$ rather than $y$ will reduce the rate of crime by half. So the practical importance of enforcement may be far less than its predictive value.

## Rate of Detection

Also important is the degree of detection and punishment needed to suppress customary behavior. If a custom is popular, the punishment for law violation must be severe enough to outweigh, for potential offenders, the advantages of continuing the custom even after the punishment is discounted by the chance of escaping detection. But the risks associated with escalating punishment too far are substantial, because severe penalties may increase pressure on sympathetic jurors, judges, prosecutors, and police, thereby contributing to a breakdown in law enforcement and, ultimately, nullification of the law.

As to what rate of detection will suffice to suppress customary behavior, we would make one comment. The minimum level of apprehension sufficient to abolish customs may be lower than one would expect. While some early authors speak of "certainty" of punishment, rather than some less absolute term, as the key to deterrence, it is not inconceivable that for some customs a detection rate of one per several hundred offenses could lead to the general abandonment of a custom, or at least to substantial repudiation. It must also be added that such a detection rate would be a tribute to efficient enforcement in light of the present rates of one in many thousands that obtain for many victimless crimes in the United States.

## UNFINISHED BUSINESS

We conclude this discussion with the list of significant variables hopelessly incomplete. It may be well therefore to indicate briefly some of the more important lacunae.

We have not speculated on what differences between cultures make it easier for some legal systems to engineer change than others. The possibilities are manifold, but we leave them for another time.

We have also failed to mention variations in the conditions of government that would influence the prospects of social change. Rather, we have assumed a legitimate government; occupation forces and other nonlegitimate governing bodies will operate under a set of further handicaps—and possibly also with some advantages—that we have not discussed.

A third gap is the absence of sustained speculation about how variations in social-change situations might affect the extent to which the law can succeed in prohibiting

custom through its moral and educative effects. We have suggested that this is more difficult to achieve when the custom has acquired positive moral value among its constituency, and we have hazarded a guess that selective enforcement based on caste or class and the lack of an adequate rationale for change might impede the moralizing potential of criminal law. But there are other, more basic, questions. Does the criminal law have the same moralizing and habit-building potential when it acts against the grain of custom? Under what circumstances will the prohibition of custom act as a negative socialization force by turning parts of a threatened audience against the legal system in general? Our failure to treat these issues in detail is no indication that they lack importance but rather a tribute to their richness and complexity.

We have not discussed the many costs associated with regimes of threat and punishment. Thus, it does not follow from the fact that abolition of custom is possible that legal prohibitions will be worth their cost. At what point, for example, will citizen loyalty snap under the pressure of coerced social change? Again, such questions remain.

Finally, we have failed to examine, in detail, a single episode of attempted social change through legal threat in order to demonstrate the importance of some of the variables we have considered. We look forward to pursuing this path at some later date.

# CHAPTER 7

# The Idea of Right as a Social and Legal Concept

*—LAWRENCE M. FRIEDMAN*

The legal system consists of authorizations and rights as well as commands. Some claims of right are demands for major changes in society. These claims may act as an important alternative to violence; on the other hand, denial of such claims may lead to serious frustration. This is particularly so because although the essence of a right is that it is theoretically without limits as to supply, in actual practice no right can be absolute, and rights are in constant conflict. The use of claims of right to bring about social change seems to be rapidly increasing in the United States, and the socialization process that leads to a consciousness of right should be further explored.

Socialization has been defined as the "developmental process through which persons acquire societal orientations and behavior patterns [Tapp, 1970b, p. 1]." Socialization is a vital, elemental social process. It is important to know how children learn the legal culture; how they learn about law and authority, about rules, punishments, and norms. The research reported in this volume sheds light on that process. I intend to focus on one aspect: the socialization of the concept of right. In other words, I am concerned about the acquisition of a claims-consciousness or consciousness of rights. This is basic to understanding orientations to the legal system within a culture.

As several of the chapters in this book remind us, there is a literature that looks at the internalization of the moral—and legal—code (Aronfreed, 1968; Berkowitz, 1964; Kohlberg, 1969; Maccoby, 1968). The vast bulk of the population is generally law abiding even when there is not the slightest chance that real punishment will pursue the deviant. The explanation for this phenom-enon is not complex. People tend to do what they think is morally right. They follow the dictates of conscience, the product of their socialization (Freedman, Wallington, & Bless, 1967).

Socialization, however, does not *necessarily* produce obedience to law. Many who do what they think is correct do not equate morality and obedience. For other reasons as well, not every person is as compliant as authorities would like. A great deal of effort has gone into studying deviant behavior, what it is and where it comes from (Becker, 1963; Cloward & Ohlin, 1960; Cressey & Ward, 1969; Hirschi, 1969; Matza, 1964). The problem is more than one of theory. It covers a wide range of behavioral orientations, sometimes moral, sometimes immoral, from civil disobedience to murder, robbery, and riot—all of considerable social importance.

Deviance and obedience are so important that they tend to obscure the full range of orientations toward law. A general inquiry cannot look only at commands and prohibitions. It should include more than analyses of the conditions for obeying the penal code, rules, and regulations laid down from above. A full theory of legal socialization must take into account all legal phenomena. Law contains more than a set of commands. There are, in addition, rules that authorize action but do not require it—rules that facilitate the exercise of individual initiative.[1] These too are important.

## INDIVIDUAL RIGHTS AND THE LEGAL SYSTEM

Particularly on the civil side, the legal system is a kind of department store of goods and services, at which people are invited to shop and buy. Take, for example, the law of contract and rules about the possible consequences of a breach. These rules imply that if A, who agreed to sell a carload of lumber to B, does not perform as promised, then, under certain circumstances, the buyer can go to court, sue A, and collect the damages. What to do is left entirely up to B. Certainly there is no moral stigma if B lets the matter go. There are all sorts of reasons why B might or might not sue. Indeed, most of the time, B would choose not to go to law (Macaulay, 1963), but might adjust the matter out of court or simply forget it. The aggrieved party decides whether to press the claim. Whether B does or not is (theoretically) a matter of indifference to the judges, Congress, the police, and all authority. The legal system only makes an opportunity available and defines what the opportunity is.

Of course, in a sense it does much more than that. The system socializes individuals to believe they can or cannot avail themselves of various modes of recourse, and that they should or should not do so. It makes it

cheap or expensive to sue, and it manipulates its rules so as to raise or lower the likelihood that many people will take advantage of the rules (Friedman, 1967). Nonetheless, when a person decides to bring a lawsuit, this is not a case of compliance, nor is it deviant not to sue. The person who breaches a contract is not a deviant. The most we can say is that he or she acts in such a way as to be exposed to a lawsuit. Deviance depends on very different considerations. Although societal norms teach and reinforce a consciousness of *rights,* whether people do go to law, in the final analysis, is a matter for them to decide. In particular, they must consider if they are likely to be better or worse off for bringing the case— win or lose. Plaintiffs are also affected by norms, ethics, and ideas of right or wrong, which may be weak or strong depending on the case.

Put another way, criminal law, and regulatory law in general, is the domain of duties and obligations. Civil suits fall in the domain of rights as well. An aggrieved wife has a "right" to a divorce, a buyer has a "right" to sue for breach of contract, and so on. On the civil side, the impulse to use law can be said to be a propensity to avail oneself of one's rights.

The consciousness of right is important, too, in another area that cannot be quantitatively compared to regulatory and criminal law or to ordinary civil law. There are legal actions occasionally pursued in which the assertion of a right would not restore a disturbed equilibrium, but rather would effect some major social change. Many civil liberties cases are of this order. In school desegregation, reapportionment, and right-to-counsel cases, plaintiffs asserted claims of right that called for profound changes in power or wealth or social position, while demanding at the same time major changes in the law.

Law, of course, is made (that is, changed) all the time. Appellate judges make law, at least in small nibbles and bites, in the ordinary course of deciding cases. Legislatures

---

[1] The literature, of course, does concern itself with ideas of fairness, equality, and justice, and hence does shed some light on the growth of the idea of right (see, e.g., Piaget, 1932, pp. 283–285).

make law when they pass statutes. Administrative rulings are new law. The kind of claim we are discussing, however, occupies a curious place between judicial and legislative lawmaking. It speaks of *rights* as somehow already guaranteed. Even when these claims do result in changing the law, in redistributing social goods, they wear this special clothing. When blacks argued in court their rights to nonsegregated schools, they were saying that their claim was different from claims in the ordinary sense. It was not an interest but a right. They were demanding social change, not by invoking their power as voters or buyers; they were demanding a right through law. As a right, of course, their claim had a normative basis. But it was not a norm of mere compliance; it was a norm that led to demands for significant change.

## THE SOCIALIZATION OF RIGHTS

The claim of right is a crucial phenomenon in that it sometimes calls for drastic societal change. Since this sort of claim seems to be common, the socialization process that leads to it must be understood. Research and speculation about socialization tend to stress how society sees to it that children grow up in the image of adults. As Maccoby (1968) has recognized, theories of socialization do not adequately handle the dynamics of social change. In part this may be because such theories have not taken into account the growth of the consciousness of right. The present age is anything but static. In addition to violent change through riots, wars, and revolutions and change in the classic political way through elections and the push and pull of interest groups, there is change that occurs through claims of right, usually presented to a court.

### Socialized Values: The Concept Defined

To understand the socialization of rights, one must define certain terms. What, after all, is a right? The term, as used in ordinary speech, has a number of important characteristics.

First, a right is a claim asserted against or through public authorities. It is essentially a claim against the state. Now it is certainly possible to analyze the concept differently. Many claims of right are or seem to be asserted not against the state but against some other person or persons. This is true of most ordinary civil claims: a landlord's rights against a tenant, a child's rights against a parent, a person's right against a creditor, and vice versa. Some legal scholars have argued that the concept of a right *always* implies two parties. So, to say that one "owns" a piece of property means that one has the right to exclude A, B, C, D . . . *n,* that is, everybody in the world—an infinite number of dyadic partners—from possessing and enjoying it.[2]

Admittedly, all rights can be reduced analytically to two-person legal relationships. But it is equally true that all rights can be looked on as claims against the collectivity, that is, against the state. A right against a particular person is a ticket, allowing the holder to invoke the protection or participation of the state in some particular way. A woman's right to a divorce "against her husband" can be analyzed as a right to make the state give the divorce. A landlord's right to evict a tenant can be analyzed as a right to make the state throw the tenant out.

Neither mode of analysis is wrong or right in itself; each can be used for different purposes. Clearly, rights have a public aspect; they depend on public institutions for vindication or enforcement. This means that the frame of mind that leads a person to assert a right is one of willingness to make demands on the state. There is no reason to think this frame of mind is culture-free. In certain societies, socialization may work against claims-consciousness, and individuals may be discouraged from pressing such

---

[2] This view was expounded by Wesley Hohfeld (see Julius Stone, 1964, pp. 150–152).

claims. Other societies may foster it, willingly or not.

The first aspect, then, of a right is that it is a claim against or through authority. Second, it is a claim that (if it is truly a right) *has* to be granted. Individuals are taught that authorities have no right to withhold a right. If a matter is in the discretion of authority, then the claim is not a right.

Since this is so, a right is a claim to a "free good" that, theoretically at least, is in unlimited supply. This is what we mean when we say that adult citizens have the right to vote, provided they register. If more people register, more people vote. There is no limit on the number of "tickets" to vote that the government can and must issue. The right of free speech and all the other basic rights are of precisely the same quality. They are rights because there is no limit on supply.

## Social Realities:
## The Concept in Operation

A claim of right, then, denies that it has anything to do with the zero-sum games of the world. That, we believe, is part of its subjective nature. In practice, however, this second aspect of the concept is objectively false. All things of value are in limited supply. What government can grant or allow is never absolute. This is even true of basic rights, like the right of free speech. Theoretically, everyone can say what he or she likes, whenever and wherever he or she likes. In fact, the right depends on certain expectations—probabilities about supply and demand. If five million people decided to sing "The Star Spangled Banner" in Times Square on a Tuesday at noon, it would be physically impossible for them to do so. Nor would the government allow them to try, if only for reasons of traffic and safety. It is not enough to say that this is a case where one right— free speech—conflicts with other rights and that therefore some sort of balancing is required. If *any* right is exercised in a way far

beyond expectation, it will conflict with some other right or some other consideration of law or public policy. Subjectively, the essence of a right is that it is absolute. Objectively, no right can be absolute—not as a matter of theory, but as a matter of fact.

To take another example, the right to use the courts has no theoretical limit. But there are only so many judges and lawyers and courts. How many are provided depends on a number of factors; one of these is the expected demand. Past experience is the usual guide. Courts are crowded, which materially affects the reality of the right. But the litigating public has, over the years, adjusted itself to a certain level of supply of courts, and government has likewise adjusted the supply more or less to the level of tolerable demand. This balance could, obviously, be completely disrupted if the number of people wanting to use the courts suddenly rose. This would be a revolutionary situation, even though nobody demanded anything except the right to a day in court, a right citizens learn to consider as legally guaranteed. Welfare rights can create a similar situation. The government appropriates money not by computing how many people are potentially bearers of rights but on the basis of past experience. If everybody suddenly claimed his or her due, the system would be gravely overloaded. In fact, some militants have tried to mobilize ghetto people to demand their full share of welfare for exactly this reason: to bring the system tumbling down (Friedman, 1969b).

When claims of right, then, are asserted suddenly and in great volume and intensity so that the institutions that normally supply the rights cannot handle the demand, a gap appears between socialized values and social realities. It is fruitful of conflict, since the legitimate expectations of individuals may be frustrated or totally denied. A whole social system has grown up on the hidden assumption that some rights—even those that everyone concedes in theory—will not in practice be claimed. Ironically, to claim them now may have a devastating effect, although the claims themselves are simple, obviously just, and have in theory always been treated as valid.

In an important sense, however, claims of right are nonviolent. They are, indeed, alternatives to violence. In the U.S. there is no more hackneyed preachment than the advice to take grievances to court or to Congress rather than to take them to the streets. People are socialized to use these institutions as legitimate avenues of participation and dissent. A claim of right is a demand that wears a peculiarly ethical, even conservative, dress. In form, it is not revolutionary. Frequently, it asks for what is already and concededly due, or for restitution of what has been unjustly taken away. Claims of right may even ask for restoration of some mythical golden age. The words of the Constitution change very little and very slowly. When blacks demand full equality on the basis of the Fourteenth Amendment, they are not in theory asking whites to *grant* them equality, but to stop their incursions on rights that in some ethical or legal sense inhere in the words or the spirit of the Constitution, though, in fact, they have never had full objective reality. For those who would like to hold out hope for the ethical transformation of society in the U.S., it would be good to argue—or to prove—that claims of right could act as effective instruments of peaceful reform. For this would mean that the social system had developed, through the consciousness of right, a nonviolent mechanism of effective social change.

But for now, it seems, there is no proof. Obviously use of this socialized mechanism has dramatically increased. The growth, in the twentieth century, of the law of civil rights and civil liberties, for example, clearly suggests an escalation in claims of right. Those who feel oppressed fight back on every front, including the courts, and this produces law. But why does this uprising occur? Is it because the nation is more materialistic, hypocritical, blood-thirsty, or op-

pressive than before? And why in this form? Has there been for some people and groups a real change in state of mind? In any case, the escalation of claims of right must reflect some change in the social-psychological mind.

## RESEARCH IMPLICATIONS

Very little has been written by sociologists or psychologists about this important concept of right. The literature touches on related and relevant matters but does not get to the heart of the matter. What is the relationship between claims of right and aggression? In a sense, claims-consciousness is aggressive; perhaps only a certain personality type is strongly claims-conscious. On the other hand, claims of right are certainly an oddly ceremonial and legitimate *form* of aggression, if they can be called aggressive at all (Dollard, Doob, Miller, Mowrer, & Sears, 1939).

Those concerned with socialization and compliance will want to know more about this sense of right. At what age, how, and why do people become aware of the concept of right? Who teaches it and how is it learned? Why are some people more conscious of rights than others? What sets the process so thunderously in motion at a particular time?

This is also a fertile field for cross-cultural research. Societies differ in what Almond and Verba (1963) have called their civic cultures; they also differ in their legal cultures (Friedman, 1969a). In some cultures, people love to go to court and press their claims. In other cultures the same behavior would be considered reprehensible; litigation is avoided if at all possible.

Obviously, structural differences account for some of these features. But is the type of claims-consciousness discussed here particularly a U.S. or Western phenomenon? Clearly, the natural law tradition in the West has left a mark on the concept of right. It would be hard to imagine a rights movement without the written constitution and doctrines of judicial review. There is a particularly ingrained habit in the U.S. of judicializing all sorts of conflicts, turning interest claims thereby into claims of right (Aubert, 1963). In this country, too, the process of vindication of rights has demonstrated that it has a tremendous payoff.

But structural bases should not be overemphasized. Rights movements may crop up where there is no written constitution, and some claims (for improved civic services, higher pensions, better schools) have little or nothing to do with the Constitution. There are many imitations now abroad of the U.S. brand of judicial review.[3] This may suggest something stirring in the soil of world culture that is especially conducive to this growth. No doubt this new cultural phenomenon is deeply rooted in economic and social facts. But like other elements of the culture, it must ultimately be carried out by specific people, as individuals, in their homes, on the streets, in their places of work. There must be some process of teaching it to children. By looking beyond the formal structure, we may shed light on this process in the coming years.

[3] A number of countries since World War II have created constitutional courts, among them Italy (Merryman & Vigoriti, 1967).

# CHAPTER 8

# The Use of Law to Guide People to Virtue

## A Comparison of Soviet and U.S. Perspectives[1]

—*HAROLD J. BERMAN*

Soviet law, in contrast with U.S. law, places heavy emphasis on the conscious use of official law, including court proceedings, to nurture the unofficial law-consciousness of citizens. As in Soviet psychology generally, emphasis is placed on social conditioning of attitudes and beliefs. Shaming the offender and ultimately withdrawal of love, exemplified by expulsion or isolation, are viewed as important techniques for inducing change. This approach bears resemblance to Western "social learning" theories of child development. It is questionable, however, whether official law can best nurture unofficial law-consciousness when it is deliberately used for that purpose.

Law is usually understood (I would say *mis*understood) as primarily a political phenomenon, an instrument of control by political authorities, which operates chiefly by deterring recalcitrant people from undesired conduct by threat of penalties. This view of law is expressly taken by the "positivist" or "analytical" school of legal thought, which defines law as a body of rules imposed by the state in order to effectuate its will. Adherents of competing legal theories often reach the same results by other routes. Thus "natural law" theorists, who find the ultimate sources and the ultimate sanctions of law in morality and reason rather than in power and will, nevertheless—when they discuss what the law actually *is*—often focus on the rules and penalties laid down by agencies of government in order to effectuate their will. Similarly, the "historical" and "sociological" schools of legal theory, which

find the ultimate sources and sanctions of law in the historical development of a society or in its social and economic structure and its cultural values, are also usually concerned chiefly with explaining the same phenomenon: the rules laid down by the state and the adverse consequences attached to their infringement. The view that law is something more, and something other, than a body of rules enacted by lawmakers and enforced by administrators is not often affirmed today, and even when it is affirmed, it is not often taken as a starting point of analysis.

In contrast to the conventional approach, I begin with the view that law is primarily a psychological phenomenon, that it is primarily rooted in the intellectual, emotional, and spiritual life of the people of a community. Here I follow in the footsteps of the great Polish-Russian jurist of the early twentieth century, L. I. Petrazhitskii, who distinguished between the "official" law of the state and the "unofficial" or "intuitive" law

[1] The present chapter in part extends an earlier article (Berman, 1972).

that exists in the consciousness of people (Babb, 1937, 1938; Gorecki, 1975; Petrazhitskii, 1955; Timasheff, 1947).

## LAW-CONSCIOUSNESS AS A PSYCHOLOGICAL PHENOMENON

Each person, according to Petrazhitskii, has his or her own law-consciousness, own conceptions of rights, duties, privileges, powers, and other legal relations. These derive primarily from the unofficial, intuitive pattern of entitlements and obligations that exists within the family, the school, the church, the neighborhood, the factory or business enterprise, the profession, the city or region or nation. Such legal emotions are distinct from moral sentiments in the Kantian sense. In Kant's theory, moral sentiments are intuitions that people in general have about their moral obligations, that is, about their duties to avoid what is wrong and do what is right. Legal sentiments, on the other hand, as Petrazhitskii saw, are intuitions (or emotions, as he called them) that people in general have about their *rights* and about their duties correlative to rights. A sense that it is right to aid (or not to aid) a person in distress is a moral sentiment; a sense that a person in distress has a right (or does not have a right) to be aided is a legal sentiment.

Legal sentiments include an aversion to inconsistency in the treatment of people ("like cases should be decided alike"), a felt need for an impartial hearing before a judgment is passed on another, an abhorrence of illegality, a commitment to legality. If one person, for example, has taken something belonging to another without justification or excuse, we are outraged not only because the owner has suffered a loss and because the other person has behaved immorally but also because there has been a breach of the legal order. Even if the general moral position of the thief is superior to that of the owner, as it may be in some cases, all concerned are apt to view the matter not in general moral terms but in intuitively recognized legal terms of the violation of rights of ownership. Conversely, the violation of a moral duty to give alms to a beggar offends moral but not legal emotions since the beggar, by definition, does not claim the alms as a matter of right.

If the official law of the state varies significantly from the unofficial law of the people, then officials may be driven to impose their will by a body of rules sanctioned by threat of penalties. This is apt to be both more efficient and more humane than the imposition of their will by naked force. At a time when Soviet jurists tended to view all law as an instrument of coercion, N. V. Krylenko, who became a People's Commissar of Justice in the early 1930s, observed, "a club is a primitive weapon, a rifle is a more efficient one, the most efficient is the court [Berman, 1963, p. 36]." Yet there is another alternative: The state may attempt to persuade and educate people to adapt their intuitive legal ideas and feelings to the official law. In so doing, the state may also find it both necessary and desirable to adapt the official law to the unofficial law of the community it is seeking to regulate.

In stable societies, however, the basic values and concepts of the official law will correspond in most respects to the basic values and concepts of the unofficial, intuitive law. From the standpoint of a positivist legal theory, it only remains for the official law to impose its sanctions on violators. Yet even in that case there also remain felt needs—which positivism does not address—to persuade the offender to acknowledge the wrongful character of the offense, to educate him or her not to offend again, and to reassure others of the rightness of their intuitive legal feelings and of the correspondence of such feelings to official legal values.

## NURTURING ROLE OF SOVIET LAW

In what has been said thus far there is little to distinguish Soviet from U.S. perspectives. In both societies the predominant legal theory does not recognize that people's ideas, feelings, and attitudes concerning law constitute something that itself can be called law. Yet Krylenko's concept of law as a mere instrument of coercion has been repudiated in the Soviet Union; there, as in the United States, it is asserted that law should also reflect justice. In both societies, too, there are strong efforts on the part of a wide range of social and political agencies to educate citizens to respect the official law and to internalize official legal values.

In the Soviet Union such efforts are more highly organized than in the United States. A conspicuous place is occupied in Soviet public affairs by what is called, in Russian, *pravovoe vospitanie,* literally, "legal nurturing" or "legal upbringing." Also much attention is given to what is called *pravovaia propaganda,* literally, "legal propaganda," that is, the propagandizing of law or the circulation of information about law. Basic codes and statutes are sometimes published in hundreds of thousands of copies. A monthly magazine about law, entitled *Chelovek i Zakon, "Man and the Law,"* contains articles, short stories, pictures, cartoons, and the like. In 1974 it had a circulation of over three million, and a nationwide television show of the same name and purpose is broadcast each week. On the other hand, the U.S. press gives far more detailed and far more objective coverage of court cases and of legislative debates than is given in the Soviet Union, and U.S. television and press reports of such legal events as the 1973 Senate Watergate hearings and the 1974 House Judiciary Committee debate on impeachment of the President constitute a "legal nurturing" and a "legal propaganda" that have no equal in the Soviet Union.

What sharply distinguishes the Soviet from the U.S. concern for the shaping of popular law-consciousness, however, is the heavy Soviet emphasis on using the official law itself for that purpose. This is called, in Russian, *vospitatel'naia rol' sovetskogo prava,* "the nurturing role of Soviet law." The law itself, through its procedures and substantive provisions, is intended, above all, to educate,

guide, and train Soviet citizens in official legal values as well as in Soviet moral and social values generally. The ideas and feelings of Soviet citizens concerning the law are supposed to be fostered not only by the family, the school, the press, the trade unions, and other social and state agencies but also by the courts in the conduct of cases and by legislators and administrators in the performance of their official duties. The purpose of Soviet law itself is not only to make people behave, by threat of sanctions or promise of rewards, according to the official rules. It is also, and more fundamentally, to educate offenders to change their attitudes and to reinforce among nonoffenders their belief in the basic goals of Soviet society. Thus law is intended to help create the "new Soviet person" needed for the building of Communism.

## CHRISTIAN AND COMMUNIST PARALLELS

Perhaps the closest historical parallel to these Soviet concepts is found in sixteenth-century Protestant writings on the use of the law. In both Lutheran and Calvinist thought, law, including both the moral law of scripture and the secular law of the state, had a threefold purpose: first, to deter recalcitrant people from misconduct by threat of penalties; second, to make people repentant of their sins and conscious of their obligations; and third, to guide faithful people in the paths of virtuous living. Of the last purpose, John Calvin wrote:

The third use of the law, which is the principal one, and which is more nearly connected with the proper end of it, relates to the faithful, in whose hearts the Spirit of God already lives and reigns. For although the law is inscribed and engraven on their hearts by the finger of God—that is, although they are so excited and animated by the direction of the Spirit, that they desire to obey God—yet they derive a twofold advantage from the law. For they find it an excellent instrument to give them, from day to day, a better and more certain understanding of the Divine will to which they aspire and to confirm them in the knowledge of it. As, though a servant be already influenced by the strongest desire of gaining the approbation of his master, yet it is necessary for him carefully to inquire and observe the orders of his master, in order to conform to them. Nor let anyone of us exempt himself from this necessity; for no man has already acquired so much wisdom, that he could not by the daily instruction of the law make new advances into a purer knowledge of the Divine will. In the next place, as we need not only instruction, but also exhortation, the servant of God will derive this further advantage from the law; by frequent meditation on it he will be excited to obedience, he will be confirmed in it, and restrained from the slippery path of transgression [Berman, 1974, pp. 94, 166–167; Calvin, 1816, pp. 176–177].

If the language of Christianity in Calvin's statement is replaced by the language of Leninism—if "Spirt of God" and "finger of God" are replaced by "vision of communism," "obey God" is replaced by "serve the Party," and "Divine will" by "will of the Party"—the above passage could be found duplicated throughout Soviet legal writings today.

In contrast, the prevailing theory of law in the United States not only does not acknowledge a law "inscribed and engraven on the hearts of the faithful" but also does not acknowledge that it is a principal purpose of law to bring people to repentance or guide them to virtue. It is widely recognized that law does, in fact, influence moral and legal conceptions. However, it is generally presupposed that this is only a by-product of law, a latent social function of legal rules and procedures, and not part of their express purpose, not part of the law itself. The purposes of law, it is said, are to keep the peace, to delimit interests, to prevent interference by one person in the domain of another, to enforce rights and obligations established by government or by the voluntary agreement of individuals, and generally

to promote order and justice. Traditionally, at least, reinforcing or changing people's ideas and attitudes, including their ideas and attitudes concerning law, is thought to be the task of the family, the school, the church, the local community, the various informal associations in which we live and, increasingly, the political system, but not of the law as such, and especially not of the courts.

## THE NATURE OF LEGAL MAN

These contrasting U.S. and Soviet views of the role of the official legal system with respect to popular legal ideas and attitudes reflect contrasting assumptions concerning the nature of the person who is the "subject" of legal rights and duties, that is, of the person to whom law is addressed and who participates in legal processes as a litigant or potential litigant or as a voter or in other ways. The assumption implicit in the U.S. view is that *legal man* is an independent adult who knows his (or her) interests and is capable of asserting them. His sense of law-consciousness has already been formed. He is a rugged individualist, a "reasonable, prudent man" who stands or falls by his own claims and defenses and is presumed to have intended the natural and probable consequences of his acts. The Soviets, on the other hand, in emphasizing the "nurturing role" of law, assume that legal man is a person in need of nurturing and capable of being nurtured. In effect he is a youth, a dependent member of the collective, whom the law must guide and train and discipline. He is treated as a member of a growing, unfinished society that is moving toward a new and higher phase of development.

Some may object that these contrasts are overdrawn. U.S. law is no longer so "bourgeois" as it was 50 or 100 years ago. Soviet law is no longer so "moralistic" or "ideological" as it was in Stalin's time. In both systems a balance has been struck between the use of law, on the one hand, to shape people's moral and legal attitudes and, on the other, to protect their rights and keep the peace. In both systems people are treated for some purposes as mature, independent, right-and-duty-bearing adults and for other purposes as dependent, collective youth. Is there not at least a tendency toward convergence between the two "models"?

To do full justice to this question would require a detailed analysis of many aspects of both legal systems. In certain areas of Soviet law, a person's rights are treated as virtually absolute and no argument based on communist morality and the educational role of law can prevail against them. Conversely, in certain areas of U.S. law, a person's rights are treated as subordinate to considerations of morality and public policy. In fact, a long list of important similarities could be drawn up between Soviet and U.S. law. Yet despite all the particular similarities the ensemble of each legal system is strikingly different from the other. These differences are usually expressed by Western observers in terms of *Rechtssicherheit* and the rule of law; they are usually expressed by Soviet writers in terms of state ownership of the means of production and Marxist-Leninist ideology (Tumanov, 1965).

Even more fundamental, in my view, are the differences in concepts of the relationship of the law to the people who are addressed, so to speak, by it. These differences are manifested in the Soviet emphasis on the educational or "nurturing" role of law. Another way of expressing them is by the phrase "parental law," which refers to the role of Soviet law as parent or teacher and to Soviet legal man as a youth to be guided and trained—a phrase that I have used elsewhere and which has incurred the wrath of a Soviet reviewer (Berman, 1965; Tumanov, 1965). A similar concept is expressed by the phrase "legal socialization," or, as Petrazhitskii (1955, pp. 310–312, 328) put it, the use of law for "the socialization of the psyche." Such socialization, above all, is the *raison d'être* of Soviet legal institutions.

## SOVIET TECHNIQUES OF SOCIALIZATION THROUGH LAW

Soviet legislation furnishes abundant examples of the conscious use of law for the "socialization of the psyche." Thus, Article 3 of the Fundamental Principles of Court Organization of the U.S.S.R. provides:

By all its activity a court shall educate citizens of the U.S.S.R. in the spirit of devotion to the Motherland and the cause of communism, in the spirit of strict and undeviating execution of Soviet laws, care for socialist property, observance of labor discipline, an honorable attitude toward public and social duty, [and] respect for the rights, honor, and dignity of citizens [and] for rules of socialist community life [Berman, 1972, p. 83].

This provision is the foundation stone of Soviet judicial procedure. In implementing it, the Soviet republican codes of criminal procedure require the court not only to determine the guilt or innocence of the accused and to pass sentence but also to "expose the causes and conditions facilitating the commission of the crime and to take measures to eliminate them [Berman & Spindler, 1972, p. 259]." A similar provision exists for civil disputes. In order to bring such causes and conditions to light, wide use must be made of the help of the public. Representatives of so-called social organizations—the trade union, the collective of the apartment house, the collective of the institute, and so on—are encouraged to appear in court on one side or the other (e.g., see 1960 RSFSR Code of Criminal Procedure, Arts. 128, 228, 236, 250, 276, 288, 291, 293–298, & 302 in Berman & Spindler, 1972; 1964 RSFSR Code of Civil Procedure, Arts. 141(6), 147, & 225 in Kiralfy, 1966). In both civil and criminal cases trials are often held in the clubroom of a factory or apartment house or other place where the parties or the accused live or work or study (Berman, 1972, pp. 84–87).

In trying a case, the judges—a professional judge and two lay assessors—are supposed to pay special attention to the educational effect of the proceedings not only on the accused or the litigants but also on the courtroom spectators and on the broader public. As stated in Article 243 of the RSFSR Codes of Criminal Procedure (Berman & Spindler, 1972, p. 351), the presiding judge of the court in directing the judicial session "shall [secure] the educational influence of the trial." Indeed, a Soviet book on the legal profession states that the court "is one of the places where . . . people are educated in the spirit of respect for law and for the norms of socialist morality [Zaitsev & Poltorak, 1959, p. 120]." Therefore, the authors conclude, not only the judges but also counsel for the parties must analyze the social and political aspects of the case and in so doing must attempt to persuade both the court and the spectators (see also Feifer, 1964, pp. 104–105).

The Soviet use of law to guide people to virtue is nowhere more evident than in the institution of Comrades' Courts. These are popular laymen's tribunals in factories, apartment houses, educational institutions, and elsewhere, which hear cases of minor offenses and are empowered to issue warnings and reprimands and to impose small fines. In extreme cases they may recommend discharge from jobs or eviction from apartments. Comrades' Courts' sanctions are termed "measures of social pressure" (Berman, 1963, pp. 288–291). Hundreds of Soviet citizens serve on these "courts" and millions attend their sessions (Berman & Spindler, 1963; Feifer, 1964, pp. 115–120).

Another striking example is the People's Guard, a mass organization of volunteer auxiliary police, which patrols streets, directs traffic, and generally assists in law enforcement. As stated in the 1960 RSFSR Statute on Voluntary People's Patrols, its purpose is "[t]o participate in educational work among the population concerning the observance of the rules of socialist community life and the prevention of anti-social offenses

[Berman, 1963, p. 287]." Some six million young men serve in the People's Guard.

Soviet substantive law also is permeated with provisions intended to induce belief in and conformity to the ideals of civic virtue. The criminal code not only makes punishable—as do non-Soviet criminal codes—immoral acts considered to be socially dangerous but also proscribes the malicious refusal to take an assigned job by a person who "is leading an antisocial way of life" and conducting a "parasitic existence" (see 1960 RSFSR Criminal Code, Art. 209 & 210 in Berman & Spindler, 1972). The civil code expressly declares that private ownership ("personal ownership") is derivative from socialist ownership and that rights granted by the code are protected only to the extent that they are exercised in conformity with the social-economic purpose for which they are granted (see 1964 RSFSR Civil Code, Preamble & Art. 5 in Gray & Stults, 1965).

Soviet limitations on rights of private property and private contract have often been viewed both in the West and in the East simply as manifestations of a state that has greatly extended the range of its interests and activities at the expense of individual economic autonomy. However, something more fundamental is also involved, namely, the subordination of *all* individual property and contract rights—however extensive they may be (and they are much more extensive in the Soviet Union than is often supposed)—to the interests of the society as a whole. The same is even more true of rights of speech. What the law intends is to manifest and to instill a sense that individual rights are conferred in trust, so to speak, for the future communist society. A good example is provided by Article 125 of the Soviet Constitution, which provides for freedom of speech, press, and assembly, but only to the extent that it is exercised in "conformity with the interests of the working people and in order to strengthen the socialist system [Berman & Quigley, 1969, p. 24]."

## POSITIVE LAW AND POPULAR LAW-CONSCIOUSNESS

Is it possible to change people's beliefs and feelings by law? The eighteenth-century Enlightenment view, which still prevails to a considerable extent in the United States, is that it is not possible and that even if it were possible it would be wrong to try. The law, it is said, should concern itself with people's conduct and their expectations of its consequences, not with their beliefs and feelings. This view of law is built into our legal system, where it survives long after the virtual disappearance of the Enlightenment presuppositions on which it is based.

At least so far as the judicial process is concerned, it would be considered improper, in most cases, for a U.S. court to undertake the kind of broad-ranging inquiry into surrounding circumstances that is required by the Soviet procedural codes. Also it generally would be considered improper for the court to shame litigants or the accused into revealing, and repenting, the sources of their waywardness. The systematic use of representatives of extrajudicial bodies—"the collective" of the factory or neighborhood or institute—as aids to the court in determining the outcome of cases would likewise not be tolerated by legal thought in the United States.

There are, to be sure, some U.S. parallels to the Soviet Comrades' Courts; for example, tenants' councils in low-cost housing projects authorized under guidelines of the Department of Housing and Urban Development (see also Levine & Tapp, Chap. 15). But these are scattered instances and are not integral in the legal system. Similarly, U.S. parallels to the Soviet People's Guards may be found in various volunteer neighborhood law enforcement organizations, especially in big cities; but these, too, are only somewhat comparable to the nationwide mass organization found in the Soviet Union.

Connected with the question of the propriety of attempting to influence beliefs by law is the question of the effectiveness of such an attempt. Here, however, we face insuperable difficulties of proof. On the one hand, a very considerable amount of vice persists in the Soviet Union, including crime, corruption, drunkenness, sloth, and various other kinds of sins; since the Soviets do not publish statistics on these matters, the suspicion is aroused that the rate of vice has in fact increased, rather than decreased, over the years. On the other hand, even assuming that virtue is declining despite all efforts to promote it, it does not necessarily follow that those efforts are in vain, for the rate of decline might possibly have been much greater if such efforts had not been made.

It should also be stressed that not only the law but all social institutions and all forms of social control in the Soviet Union, including the Communist Party, economic organizations, trade unions, the press, the school, the arts, and a host of others, are used to guide people to virtue. If the educational or "parental" role of law were to be abandoned or substantially reduced, the law would become strikingly different from every other official activity of the Soviet social, economic, and political system. Thus, it is impossible to isolate the consequences of moral education through law from those of moral education through social, economic, and political institutions in general.

The experience of the United States seems to be equally inconclusive as to whether law can in fact change people's attitudes and values. Prohibition is often cited to show the ineffectiveness of legal control over morals. Apparent changes in attitudes toward racial equality following court decisions and legislation denouncing racial discrimination are often cited for the contrary position. Again, the multiplicity of factors involved and the "iffiness" of the question make it difficult to test the specific influence of law on beliefs. It is doubtful whether under any circumstances the efficacy of law as an educational instrument

—or its inefficacy—can ever be tested by objective criteria.

## THE RELATIONSHIP OF LEGAL THEORY TO PSYCHOLOGICAL THEORY

Soviet concepts of the educational role of law reflect Soviet concepts of psychology generally and of educational psychology in particular. As is well known, Soviet psychological theory, in comparison with theories such as those of Piaget (e.g., 1928, 1929, 1932), which are widely held in Western countries, emphasizes the plasticity of the human psyche and the possibility of influencing attitudes by social conditioning (see Cole & Maltzman, 1969; Rahmani, 1973). In part, this Soviet emphasis rests on behaviorist premises that derive historically from the work of the great prerevolutionary Russian psychologists I. P. Pavlov and V. M. Bekhterev on conditioned reflexes (Bauer, 1952; Langer, 1969; Pavlov, 1957). However, Soviet psychologists have gone far beyond behaviorism in their recognition of the autonomous role of consciousness and their belief that conscious social effort can overcome both hereditary and environmental obstacles to the development of socially desirable beliefs and attitudes (Leontiev, Luria, & Smirnov, 1966). They state that the internalization of social norms is effectuated primarily by communication (especially persuasion and suggestion) and by example within the context of the social group (Kovalev, 1964, 1965). Thus, Soviet psychology matches Soviet philosophical theories of the perfectibility of human nature and Soviet sociological theories of the ultimate dependence of personal values on social conditions, as well as Soviet legal theories of the educational role of legal institutions.

In conformity with these theories, Soviet educators place great stress, from the earliest years of children's schooling, on collective living, cooperative play and work, and the express goals of Communist morality (Barghoorn, 1972). Competition among pupils (like competition among state economic enterprises) is "socialist competition"; that is, it is not primarily competition between individuals but rather competition between collectives. In elementary schools, it is competition between rows, between classes, between schools, and so on. According to Urie Bronfenbrenner, in Soviet schools peer evaluation occurs weekly and the "tattletale," as he or she is viewed in other countries, is valued positively as a person who contributes to group achievement. At the same time, Soviet children are taught to be even more sensitive to adult evaluation than to peer evaluation. The most important adult sanction is withdrawal of love, and the ultimate adult sanction is expulsion from the class, from the school, and so forth (Bronfenbrenner, 1970).

All these characteristics of Soviet educational psychology have important parallels in Soviet legal psychology. The substantive law, as we have already noted, imposes heavy duties of cooperation. The Constitution itself imposes social duties on Soviet citizens, such as the duty, under Article 130, "to respect the rules of socialist community life [Berman & Quigley, 1969, p. 25]." Trial procedure, in both criminal and civil cases, is supposed to expose the shame of the offender and to induce him or her to repent (Feifer, 1964, pp. 38–44, 147–148). Withdrawal of love is manifested in expulsion to a correctional labor colony, exile to remote regions, or banishment from particular cities or regions.

The psychological presuppositions of both Soviet law and Soviet education bear a considerable resemblance to the social learning theory of child development expounded in the United States by Miller and Dollard, Whiting, Sears, and others (Langer, 1969). Briefly stated, the social learning theory emphasizes the child's imitation of, and identification with, adults. The child internalizes the norms of behavior due to a desire for approval, which, in turn, reinforces self-confidence. For Western social learning theory, as for Soviet educational and legal theory, the most important negative stimulus to moral development is the withdrawal of love.

What Soviet psychologists add to the social learning theory of Western (and especially U.S.) psychologists is an emphasis on the child's membership in the group. Western psychologists tend to start their analysis by making a division between the consciousness of the individual child and the surrounding environment; the family, the school, the neighborhood, and so on are treated as external factors with which the child interacts. Soviet writers, on the other hand, do not consider the psyche in exclusively individual terms. The child who is influenced by the peer group is not, after all, outside that group: As part of it, his or her interaction with it is also an interaction within the self. Similarly the parent, the teacher, the group, the society are both inside and outside the child and at the same time are both inside and outside the child's environment. This, I believe, is what Soviet writers mean when they speak of "training" as something additional to both heredity and environment (Bauer, 1952). A closely related insight is that of the famous Soviet psychologist L. S. Vygotsky that language forms an important link between the social context and the individual consciousness (1962, 1966).

In light of the close connection drawn by Soviet scholars between individual psychology and group psychology, and in light of the emphasis they place upon group persuasion and example as means of influencing individual attitudes, it is not surprising that in the past decade there has developed a special branch of psychology called "judicial psychology." Indeed, a decree of the Central Committee of the Communist Party (1964) called for the development of judicial psychology as a separate branch of science. In accordance with this decree, articles have appeared and a textbook has been published dealing with psychological aspects of crime, psychological factors in investigative and judicial proceedings, psychological aspects

of the re-education of convicted persons, and, more broadly, psychological effects of legal proceedings on the attitudes of people who participate in them, witness them, or are affected by them.[2]

Yet, despite these brave words, an examination of this new literature shows that Soviet judicial psychology is in a very primitive state as both a scholarly discipline and a practical art. An evaluation of its deficiencies would require analysis of Soviet theory and practice with respect to the two primary means of social learning: communication and example. It would also require an analysis of the underlying premise that the official law can best nurture unofficial law-consciousness when it is deliberately used for that purpose.

## CONCLUSION

There is a very great difference between a sociological or psychological generalization concerning the nature and functions of law and an incorporation of that generalization into the legal system. For example, the sociological generalization that in every society law serves the interests of the state may be quite innocent, but a legal principle that law in the given society *must* serve the interests of the state may be quite harmful. It is not accidental that all legal *systems*—as contrasted with legal *philosophies*—put themselves forward as embodiments of universal justice.

---

[2] Dulov (1970) wrote this textbook for higher educational institutions. A bibliography on p. 382 lists 17 items published between 1964 and 1969, chiefly dealing with methods of conducting investigations, methods of examining witnesses, and the like. Several of the articles listed sketch general programs of study of legal psychology. Compare, for example, O. A. Gavrilov's "O problemakh sovetskoi sudebnoi psikhologii"—"On problems of Soviet judicial psychology" (1965). However, Dulov's book is the first textbook in the subject.

What the Soviets have added to the legal concept of law as an embodiment of universal justice, and what the United States and other non-Communist societies are coming more and more to add, is the legal concept of law as a *teacher*. The question is what kind of teacher. The Soviet concept implies that the bearer of rights and duties —"legal man"—is a youth to be guided and trained. The socialization of popular law-consciousness is conceived as a process by which the society's unofficial sense of law is raised to the level proclaimed by the official lawmaking authorities. There are obvious dangers in the implicit belief that the movement between official law, with its technical language and professional practitioners, and unofficial law, with its diffuse relationship to custom and morality, may go in only one direction.

# PART III

# The Pattern of Legal Development

## INTERSTITIAL BRIEF

*JUNE LOUIN TAPP*
*FELICE J. LEVINE*

Legal socialization has been an area of inquiry since the late 1960s and is a core construct of the 1970s. Regardless of nomenclature (e.g., compliance to laws, respect for authority, conformity to rules, moral internalization, and/or conscience formation), psychologists have attended to the phenomenon of conforming behavior as an aspect of socialization that is crucial to the stability of a society. Succinctly put, socialization entails incorporation of cultural standards as well as the development of independent relations within normative prescriptions. It is the process whereby members of a culture articulate norms and evolve values and behavior patterns. Optimally, this process implies the emergence of mutually acceptable social roles and expectations, not merely uncritical adherence to stipulated norms. Socialization so defined denotes the complementary not necessarily equivalent bases of social control and social order.

The term "legal socialization" delineates that aspect of the socialization process dealing with the expression of legal beliefs and behaviors, the internalization of "rule" norms, the conditions obtaining legal compliance, and the learning of deviant and compliant modes. It focuses on the development of individual standards for making sociolegal judgments *and* for using the legal network for resolving conflicts, pressing claims, and settling disputes. Covering the "positive" and "negative" sides of learning, specifically for the institution of law and generally for all human rule systems with authoritative validity, legal socialization considers both the processes and products of reasoning about "legal" norms. Whether "law," "norm," or "rule" is used, each conveys some obligation and expectation of compliance; but none precludes the possibility of disobedience. Compliance and independence are inseparable aspects of a democratic, humanistic social order. While rules and laws are structures for guiding choice, a crucial goal of legal socialization is to encourage the assessment of the underlying purpose of normative standards that only committed but autonomous participants can perform.

To some degree, work in legal socialization—emerging from political socialization and moral development research—overlaps both traditions. However, it is useful to demarcate legal socialization from political and moral socialization. There are important differences among these three realms of ideological socialization with regard to contexts of expression (jury vs. precinct caucus), indicators of authority (judge vs. president), and topics of research (justice vs. party loyalty). Further, though all three focus on the growth of ideas especially in youth and increasingly into adulthood, the moral development research in the traditions of moral psychology and moral philosophy emphasizes general "valuation" processes, and the political development literature primarily provides descriptive information on attitudes and opinions relevant to political-legal settings. Given these points of attention, some of the chapters in Part III might have been included in a handbook of political socialization, political psychology, or moral development. Yet, these original contributions taken together demonstrate that legal development and orientations toward law are identifiable phenomena.

The following four chapters—all by psychologists—report studies surveying aspects of individual legal development. The first by Tapp and Kohlberg describes cross-cultural and developmental data from the authors' respective studies in an exercise crossing methods and materials. The purpose of this chapter is to corroborate a universal progression in legal values parallel to moral judgments. In analyzing cross-cultural preadolescent and U.S., white, kindergarten-to-college interview data, a legal levels construct is explicated that uses Kohlberg's terminology of preconventional, conventional, and postconventional modes of thought. While the data disclosed a conceptual shift in orientation from preconventional law-obeying, to conventional law-maintaining, to postconventional law-creating, overall the conventional law-and-order perspective was modal in the U.S. and cross-culturally. By late preadolescence and particularly by college age, sizable minorities exhibited postconventional principles, but this form of reasoning did not dominate in any of the groups. Since one goal of legal socialization is to achieve a balance of compliance tempered by critical independence, the authors initiate discussion on the ethical and pragmatic value of developing the capacity to reason judgments of more than a system-maintenance sort. In this chapter and a subsequent one by Levine and Tapp (Chap. 15), socialization procedures such as role participation and conflict confrontation are proposed that could accomplish the principled legal development of the individual. In a very real sense such stratagems should also result in socializing social institutions to the same justice level—that of a postconventional ethical legality.

Gallatin and Adelson's study, also presenting cross-cultural developmental data, focuses on the relation between individual rights and the legal system. Youth's responses to a series of open-ended hypothetical dilemmas highlight two key issues at the nexus of political and legal decision making: legal infringements on liberty and legal guarantees of individual freedom. Gallatin and Adelson discuss specific cross-cultural differences (e.g., concern about individual freedom is highest in the U.S.), but here too the primacy of developmental trends is the most impressive finding. Changes occurring from ages 12 to 16 underscore that this period is a "watershed" for thought on matters of government and law. Neither sex nor social class accounts for substantial differences in youth's ideas. For example, while younger children tended to comply with any state law, older subjects increasingly emphasized that individual liberties weighed against accepting certain laws. Adolescents in comparison to younger children were able to recognize the potential for intrusions on the privacy of the individual, the importance of safeguarding certain individual freedoms with formal legislation, and the necessity of balancing societal needs and the costs to individual rights. Gallatin and Adelson attribute these changes to cognitive ability as well as to an opportunity to understand oneself and others through participation. However, one caution should be invoked in assessing the apparent level of growth in individuals across cultures: As in the preceding chapter by Tapp and Kohlberg, the age-related attention to principles is typically not the modal response.

This caution appears well founded. Zellman and Sears report that, although tolerance of the right to dissent is accepted in principle, there is little generalization to concrete situations. Among children in grades 5 through 9, the right of free speech was endorsed primarily as an abstract slogan; this pattern held comparatively with adults. While 12- to 14-year-olds were generally more tolerant of free speech than 9- to 11-year-olds, even by age 11 most children acknowledged the existence of such a right, with tolerance not increasing substantially thereafter. These findings again mark preadolescence as a crucial period. Furthermore, the single most important determinant of tolerance and endorsement of free speech was self-esteem. Confident individuals are less likely to be threatened by the divergent ideas of others—suggesting that socialization experiences that encourage tolerance for and incorporate tolerance from others should bring greater acceptance of rights in real-life contexts. Zellman and Sears suggest that civil libertarian principles be taught as part of a larger schema for handling conflict and dissent from norms—whether in the setting of home, school, or law. This counsel is consistent with programmatic changes suggested in later chapters as well (see Chaps. 13, 15, 16, 17).

Torney also emphasizes the role of multiple legal contexts in socializing orientations to law. Her perspective is consistent with assumptions of continuity among authority rule systems. Using data on children in grades 2 through 8, Torney posits four models of socialization—accumulation, identification, role transfer, and cognitive development—to explain changes and differences in legal development. To test the models' viability, she considers attitudes on a variety of issues ranging from the police and the Supreme Court to the function and fairness of rules and laws. Generally, Torney finds differences in legal orientation affected more by age and sex than by social class or intelligence. She explains these variations primarily in terms of the cognitive developmental and role transfer processes. For example, with age children differentiated among the role functions of police. While younger children tended to view all authorities as legitimate per se, the older groups separated "power attributes" from "personal goodness." However, girls were significantly more likely to rate police positively. Since parents typically rear girls to be more accepting of authority, transfer of expectation within the legal institution might be expected. Likewise, role transfer from authority figures in the home to other rule systems may explain the lower-middle class overglorification of police. Such social class and other contextual differences in attitudes toward police suggest that the law is not uniform in its effect or administration—which could have crucial implications for the maintenance of a legal system.

In sum, the chapters in this section focus on aspects of the how, why, and what of children's and youth's emergent orientations in the legal network. Investigators draw on cross-cultural, developmental, and/or age-cohort groups to explore the patterns of legal development. In these empirical examinations some socializing effects of adults in different settings are also unveiled. In considering the issues addressed in these chapters, the following queries on patterns of legal development might serve as a guide:

**1.** Although the frequency of children and youth offering principled reasons varies, what might explain the recurrent evidence of substantially more principled responses to abstract questions than to realistic, pragmatic probes?

**2.** Self-esteem is one explanation for the ability to tolerate dissent. Are there others that might be used to connect the constructs of personality and legality? Put another way, what is the effect of personality on legal socialization?

**3.** To some, a "universal" explanation is a trap that seemingly obviates the effect of cultural values (e.g., individuality) and of cultural conditions (e.g., poverty) on socialization. In the case of individual freedom, for example, what are the arguments for its being a universal category rather than a cultural value? What are the arguments for the primacy of age over education?

**4.** Findings from the various chapters raise questions about the meaning of culpability and the relation between attitude and action. If children and adults are held responsible in the "eyes" of the law, should the law take a more active and/or conscious role in legal socialization? From another perspective, should a person's legal knowledge and legal reasoning capacity be considered in assessing responsibility? By whom, the police, the prosecutor, or the court?

# CHAPTER 9

# Developing Senses of Law and Legal Justice[1]

## —JUNE LOUIN TAPP and LAWRENCE KOHLBERG

A theory of legal development, derived from cognitive developmental theory, is set forth using U.S. kindergarten to college and cross-national preadolescent data. Paralleling evidence on universal moral levels, the development of individual orientations vis-à-vis legal or rule systems shows consistent movement from a preconventional law-obeying, to a conventional law-maintaining, to a postconventional law-making perspective. In both the U.S. and cross-national samples, "law and order" conventional reasoning is modal, reflecting that socialization experiences can accelerate, retard, or crystallize the growth of legal values and roles. Implications of the theory and findings are discussed for legal socialization.

Rules and laws are the mechanism for achieving a just or moral social order. Wherever both operate, they are intended to facilitate human interaction insofar as they include views of obligation, authority, and justice (Fuller, 1969b; Selznick, 1969). These concepts, so closely related to the institution of law and legal process, are also central in moral thought, suggesting a consistency in moral and legal development. The law is the most venerable and specialized institutionalized expression of rule- or norm-guided behavior to which basic moral categories may apply. We may ask: What is an individual's legal right? Why should he or she obey? What is the relation of law to justice? Thus, understanding a person's orientation to rule and law should be enhanced by understanding one's orientation to fundamental moral principles. In this chapter we present and extend evidence on universal moral stages to concepts of law and rule and their development.

Despite great diversity in detailed definition, in all cultures there are universal institutional structures—law, family, education —and universal concepts—justice, rule, responsibility—that are basic to human development. Moral development and by extrapolation legal development result from interaction between universal structures of the social environment and the natural structuring tendencies of organisms (Allport, 1961; Asch, 1952; Dewey, 1910, 1930; Dewey & Tufts, 1932; Kohlberg, 1969; Mead, 1934). But many concerned with individual legal development have failed to appreciate the universality and the dynamic of either moral or legal reasoning. Instead, they have transmitted fixed clichés about moral and legal dilemmas rather than a

---

[1] This chapter was written with the invaluable assistance of Felice J. Levine to whom the authors express gratitude. We also wish to thank Brenda Smith and Roberta Tabor for their services in the preparation of this manuscript.

conflict-solving approach. If societies' agents are not merely to institutionalize blind obedience, but are to stimulate principled perspectives, they must understand more entirely the process of developing and crystallizing legal values.

The purpose of this chapter, then, is threefold: (1) to present data on the cultural universality of moral development; (2) to investigate the universal applicability and utility of Kohlberg's moral development theory to concepts of law and legal justice; and (3) to explore the implications of these findings for legal socialization and education. To accomplish this exercise in crossing theories and methods, we first review some assumptions and findings from Kohlberg's research on morality. Next, we present Tapp's findings, derived in part from a cross-national study (Hess & Tapp, 1969; Minturn & Tapp, 1970; Tapp, 1970a). Finally, we consider some implications for legal socialization of conceptualizing legal development as part of a more general process of sociomoral development.

## MORAL DEVELOPMENT

### Theoretical Antecedents

Research by Kohlberg and associates has elaborated a cognitive approach to moral development (Blatt & Kohlberg, 1969; Kohlberg, 1963a, 1964, 1969; Kohlberg & Kramer, 1969; Kohlberg & Lockwood, 1970; Kohlberg & Turiel, 1971; Turiel, 1966). Its major thrust is that the development of moral thought follows a universal sequence of distinct stages. The theoretical bases for this model are primarily inspired by Dewey's genetic, experiential, and purposive reasoning (1910, 1916, 1930); Piaget's structural approach to moral development and cognitive thought (1928, 1929, 1932); and Kant's ethical analysis (1949).

These traditions posit continuity in sociomoral development. Dewey assumes that behavior is determined by valuation of current situations, prior activity influencing the choice of the sequence of development. Piaget's work on morality also issues from a general theory about the developing child's cognitive conception of the world. Using such basic categories as logic, causality, and space in a structural analysis of cognition, he defines relationships for construing any physical experience (e.g., it must be located temporally). Piaget's cognitive categories, in turn, derive from Kant's analysis of the categories of pure reason. Both Piaget's moral dimensions (e.g., intentionality, reciprocity) and most of Kohlberg's categories (e.g., justice, rule obedience, rights) correspond to aspects of moral judgment used in systematic moral philosophies (e.g., Dewey, 1909; Dewey & Tufts, 1932; Hare, 1952; Kant, 1949).

### Stage Theory

Stage and structure are core concepts of the moral development position. Each stage represents a qualitatively different organization of thought, not a set of specific beliefs. Cognitive structures are the rules for processing information, i.e., connecting experiences. Stages, basically ideal-typological constructs, represent different psychological organizations of thought. The order of the stages is always the same. Culture may accelerate or retard movement through the stages but not change the quality or order. While movement through all the developmental stages is not inevitable, each stage is characterized by increasing differentiation and integration, extending the individual's ability to resolve conflicts. In sum, this cognitive stage model is characterized by a distinctive response form in modes of thinking; situational generality; stage consistency across core aspects or categories; differentiative and integrative hierarchical functioning; invariant sequence; and a sequential rate only affected by environmental conditions (Kohlberg, 1963a, 1968a, 1968b, 1969).

## Method

The modes of thinking that characterize moral development were first derived from 72 U.S. boys, ages 10, 13, and 16, half from upper-middle class and half from lower- to lower-middle class homes (Kohlberg, 1958). Longitudinal retests were done on this sample at three-year intervals so that the data extend from ages 10 to 28. Also other cross-cultural studies were conducted using the same measures.

The stages and categories were derived from free interview responses to 10 hypothetical moral dilemmas. The dilemmas put customary moral rules in conflict with specific situational demands. Philosophical value judgments are elicited during an inquiry period. The dilemmas permit defensible but mutually exclusive solutions. Since the issues are structural, dilemmas can be modified for cross-cultural use. For example, the dilemma, used extensively with U.S. groups, about the city man stealing a drug for his dying wife was adapted for village life:

A man and his wife had just migrated from the high mountains. They started to farm but there was no rain and no crops grew. No one had enough food. The wife got sick and finally she was close to dying from having no food. There was only one grocery store in the village, and the storekeeper charged a very high price for the food. The husband asked the storekeeper for some food for his wife, and said he would pay for it later. The storekeeper said, "No, I won't give you any food unless you pay first." The husband went to all the people in the village to ask for food but no one had food to spare. So he got desperate and broke into the store to steal food for his wife.

While an ethnographer is indispensable for content interpretation, the assessment of stage differences in forms of thought is definable independent of a particular culture. (A complete treatment of the dilemmas and their scoring is in Kohlberg & Turiel, in prep.)

## Moral Levels

Kohlberg identifies three general levels of moral judgment: preconventional, conventional, and postconventional. Each level has two distinct stages.

At the *preconventional level (I)*, the cultural labels of "good" and "bad" are interpreted in terms of physical consequences (e.g., punishment, reward, exchange of favors) or in terms of the physical power of those who enunciate the rules and labels. The Physical Power stage (1) characteristically orients toward punishment, unquestioning deference to superior power and prestige, and avoidance of "bad" acts. Regardless of value, physical consequences determine goodness or badness. The Instrumental Relativism stage (2) is basically hedonistic. Right action consists of that which instrumentally satisfies one's own needs and occasionally the needs of others. Elements of fairness, equality, and reciprocity are present, but interpreted pragmatically, not as a matter of loyalty, gratitude, or justice.

The *conventional level (II)* is characterized by active support of the fixed rules or authority in a society. Maintaining the expectations and rules of the family, group, or nation is valued in its own right. The Interpersonal Concordance or good-boy/good-girl stage (3) orients toward pleasing others and gaining approval. There is conformity to stereotypical images of majority behavior. Also behavior is frequently judged by intention: "He means well" becomes important for the first time. The Law-and-Order stage (4) is typified by doing one's duty (obeying fixed rules), showing respect for authority, and maintaining the given social order. Respect is earned by performing dutifully.

The *postconventional level (III)* is characterized by a clear effort toward autonomous moral principles with validity apart from the authority of the groups or persons who hold them and apart from individual identifications. The Social Contract stage (5) has legalistic and utilitarian overtones; strong constitutionalism pervades. Right action is defined in terms of individual rights, critically agreed upon by the whole society.

Awareness of the relativism of personal values is attended by an emphasis upon procedural rules for reaching consensus. The stress is on the legal point of view, but with the possibility of changing law in terms of rational, social utility rather than freezing it in terms of law and order. The Universal Ethic stage (6) moves toward conscientious decisions of right based on principles that appeal to logical comprehensiveness, universality, and consistency. These principles are abstract and ethical; they include justice, the reciprocity and equality of human rights, and respect for individuals.

For this chapter the relevant institution is "law," the norm "rule," and the principle "justice." As might be expected, at the preconventional level (I), a *rule-obeying* perspective guides legal judgments; at the conventional level (II), a *rule-maintaining* perspective prevails, and the main concern is law and order; and at the postconventional level (III), the *legislative* or *rule-making* perspective is dominant. These perspectives are based on global ratings of law orientations from international cross-sectional and longitudinal small samples (Turiel, Kohlberg, & Edwards, in prep.) and thus are less explicitly formulated than the legal development stages presented in the next section. In short, preconventional and conventional persons respond primarily to the fixed rules and values of society, but their reasoning varies systematically. In contrast, those with a postconventional perspective want rationally created laws *ex nihilo*. The distinction between rule-maintaining and rule-making perspectives is typified by the difference between justifying an action falling under a practice and justifying the practice (Rawls, 1955). The rule-making perspective recognizes the possibility of conflict between what is rationally right for the individual and what is legally or rationally right for society. As the criteria for moral choices (e.g., universality, impartiality) extend beyond the sphere of law, a universalistic moral orientation is possible. Such cognitive

development permits judgments of a moral-legal genre.

The conventional level (II) is modal for most cultures; the dominant moral stage is the law-and-order one (50 to 60%). The rest of the moral judgments distribute around this mode in decreasing fashion with successive movement up the ordinal scale. As children develop, they are partly in their major stage (about 50% of their ideas), partly in their previous stage, and partly in the stage being entered. While no one is totally at one stage, a person with, for example, a postconventional orientation to drug stealing is likely to be at the same level on a civil disobedience dilemma.

**Previous Research**

*Early childhood.* Exploratory work on young children's concepts of rule and law supports the relation between moral and legal development. Epstein (1965), studying upper-middle class children at ages 4, 5, and 7, finds similar six-attribute Guttman scales in concepts of game rules, classroom rules, and law. With maturity, children show increasing comprehension of rules culminating in a Piagetian autonomous stage with rules representing shared consent. Further, age trends on changing rules parallel those on conceptions of rules. Verbal concepts of breaking or changing rules are meaningless to 4-year-olds, but by age 7 most accept change for all three types of rules.

*Cross-cultural.* Substantial evidence on the cultural universality in the sequence of stages comes from studies done in Mexico, Taiwan, Turkey, and the United States. In addition to middle- and lower-class urban boys, the studies include illiterate villagers in Turkey, Mexico, and Taiwan (Kohlberg, 1968a, 1968b, 1969; Kohlberg & Turiel, 1971). For middle-class urban boys in the U.S., Taiwan, and Mexico, moral level at age 10 reflects a lack of cognitive sophistication: Stage 1 preconventional thinking is used the most; stage 6 postconventional, the least. By age 16, U.S. boys reverse the use of the stages from the highest to the lowest (except for stage 6); at age 13, the good-boy stage 3—a conventional mode—is most used. In Mexico and Taiwan parallel findings emerge, but the rate of development is slower. Whereas in the U.S. postconventional thinking is prevalent at 16, in Taiwan and Mexico conventional morality prevails. The presence of postconventional thinking in other countries demonstrates it is not purely a Western democratic construct. Also, developmental patterns from two isolated villages in Yucatan and Turkey are strikingly similar. Conventional moral thought increases steadily from ages 10 to 16, but does not clearly ascend over the preconventional level. Postconventional level responses are only minimal in these villages.

*Longitudinal.*    High correlations (i.e., from .78 to .92) between moral maturity scores at ages 13 and 16 and at the mid-twenties suggest that moral development is an excellent predictor from preadolescence to adulthood (La Crosse & Kohlberg, 1969). Also, Kohlberg and Kramer (1969) report that the correlation between ages 16 and 25 is .89 (Kramer, 1968). Basically, postconventional conceptions (level III), especially social contract ideas (stage 5), substantially develop by the end of high school; universal ethical principles (stage 6) crystallize in the mid-twenties. Adult maturity seems more a matter of increasing consistency and integration than further development.

## LEGAL DEVELOPMENT

To assess the applicability of Kohlberg's typology of moral development to concepts of law and legal justice, two of Tapp's studies will be described: a developmental study of U.S. white youths from kindergarten to college, and a six-country, seven-culture study of middle-school preadolescents. These studies preceded and formed

the basis of a cognitive model of legal development (Tapp & Levine, 1971, 1974).

## Method

*Sample.*    The U.S. developmental study had 115 white subjects of high socioeconomic status (from professional or semiprofessional homes). Each group had about equal numbers of females and males. The primary group, spanning kindergarten through grade 2, had 20 subjects; the middle school, covering grades 4, 6, and 8, had 30 subjects; and the college group had 65 first- and second-year students. The cross-national sample was 406 children, selected randomly from a 1965 research project of almost 5000 children from Denmark, Greece, India, Italy, Japan, and the U.S. (black and white). There were about 60 preadolescents per country, 30 per sex, 30 per social class (professional and working), and 20 per grade (4, 6, 8).[2]

---

[2] The cross-cultural data were gathered pursuant to a contract with the United States Department of Health, Education and Welfare, Office of Education, Project 2947 under Contract OE 5-10-219, entitled "Authority, Rules, and Aggression: A Cross-national Study of Socialization into Compliance Systems." The cross-national investigators in the study were Robert D. Hess, Leigh Minturn, and the first author of the present chapter. The middle-school (preadolescent), high-status data were collected in 1965 as part of that investigation. The primary-school material was gathered in 1967 as part of a graduate research project (Kleiman, 1967) under our supervision; however, the coding categories and analysis presented here are markedly different from those in the original trial research. The college information was obtained in 1970 as part of an assessment of the impact of an undergraduate law and behavioral science course taught by the first author. Subsequent analyses of the cross-national data and the developmental data were completed with the support of the American Bar Foundation. Cross-cultural data tables are available from Tapp; patterns are here summarized.

*Interview.* The open-ended interview administered in the cross-national study had 79 questions on law, justice, compliance, punishment, and authority (Hess & Tapp, 1969; Minturn & Tapp, 1970). The interview was adapted for the primary and college groups. This chapter focuses on seven questions in three substantive areas: the value and function of rules and laws; the dynamics of legal compliance; and the changeability and breakability of rules.

Coding categories were initially developed using responses from 42 cross-cultural interviews translated into English; additional categories for the U.S. were also empirically derived. The cross-national overall scoring reliability was 77 percent; the overall reliability for the three U.S. groups averaged 83 percent.

*Data analysis.* In the U.S. developmental study, differences between category response percentages for the age levels were tested using *t* tests. Significant differences at the *p* ≤ .05 level are discussed comparatively as developmental changes; at the *p* ≤ .10 level, as developmental trends. In the cross-national study, response percentages were compared for total country and age trends. A pattern was universal if it held across all seven cultures; a cross-cultural one held across at least five cultures.

In addition to presenting developmental and cross-national results, the findings are analyzed in terms of a hypothetical model developed by Tapp and Levine (1971, 1974) that relates empirically derived interview categories to Kohlberg's three moral levels (see Table 1). Since these legal concepts and the moral levels were derived from studies based on very different methodologies, the classification schemas are not isomorphic. Therefore, in several instances certain categories have transitional qualities of two levels. We have noted when this is the case. Further, we do not intend that a concept at one level necessarily replaces another, only that it is no longer the preeminent or characteristic quality (see also

Tapp & Levine, 1971, 1974). As Kohlberg has previously indicated (1969), whether a replacement or additive scale emerges is determined to a large extent by the methodology employed. However, despite differences in reconciling these two approaches, we are struck by the astonishing similarities in the findings.

## Results: The Value of Rules and Laws

*U.S. developmental study.* Youth's developing notions about the need for laws and rules in society were examined by asking, "What would happen if there were no rules?" The youngest children, primary- and middle-schoolers, thought rules prevent *violence and crime* (level I, see Table 2). As a second-grade girl cautioned, "Then people would go around killing other people, and they'd be stealing things, and they'd be kidnapping people. . . ." Also an infrequent, but developmentally stable, *personal desire over principle* response (level II) indicated some apprehension about impulse control, for example, about greed, weakness, or indolence. *Anarchy-disorder-chaos* (level II), a major prediction by middle-school and college subjects, revealed that laws are valued primarily for maintaining the social order. The words of a grade 4 boy, "Well, it would be a lot of disorganizing in the world," were mirrored by a college male's reply, "There would be utter chaos and confusion."

Between primary and middle school the chaos response (level II) increased significantly. Further, while equal numbers (57%) of middle-school children predicted violence-crime (level I) and anarchy-disorder-chaos (level II), only 6 percent of the college students continued to focus on the former consequences. Instead, 32 percent of them, viewing a rule system as essential, found it *impossible to imagine a world without rules* (level II). Several also, seeing *human beings as self-regulatory* (level III), reasoned that ominous events are not necessarily inevitable. In the words of a college female, "If people were capable of acting responsibly and morally, nothing would happen."

To summarize developmental trends, primary-school children favored a preconventional over a conventional orientation; in contrast, the majority of preadolescent and college students were at the conventional level. While by college few shared the notion that rules prevent violence or crimes, most students in both older groups saw rules in conventional terms. Only college students presented the postconventional position that autonomous persons can guide behavior using universal principles.

*Cross-cultural study.* Cross-culturally the preadolescent perspective was remarkably consistent with the pattern revealed in the U.S. high-status, developmental study. Violence-crime and personal desire were important, but prevention of chaos was the universal concern. Further, older middle-school children were more likely to express a conventional position.

## Results: The Function of Rules and Laws

*U.S. developmental study.* The responses of the primary-school, middle-school, and college groups to "What is a rule?" and "What is a law?" further clarified their concepts of rules and laws (see Table 2). Basically children saw no distinction between the two formulations, defining both primarily in functional terms: *prohibitive* (level I), a restrictive guideline forbidding a class of behavior; *prescriptive* (level II), a general, neutral regulatory guideline; and *beneficial-rational* (level III), a personally or societally purposive reasonable guideline. (Since beneficial-rational responses may contain components of level II reasoning, we considered this category transitional.) A primary-school boy gave this prohibitive response: "A rule is not to run around, not to hit anybody, not to break anything"; an eighth-grade girl described the prescriptive quality: "It's a guideline to follow. Well, you just follow it." A college male demarcated

the beneficial aspect: "A judgment or standard arrived at morally or pragmatically, affecting, directing, and/or compelling behavior."

On "What is a rule?" there was significant movement between primary school and college from prohibitive statements, often confusing the rule and the act, to more general prescriptive views of rules as guiding modes of interaction (level II). While the beneficial-rational aspect (level III) increased only slightly, by college—with the sharp decrease in prohibitive (14%)—beneficial-rational concerns (26%) became salient.

On "What is a law?" again there was developmental movement toward the prescriptive and away from the prohibitive. Beneficial-rational considerations also increased significantly with college students defining laws more in these terms (29%) than in prohibitive ones (11%). The dramatic decline in defining rules and laws prohibitively contrasted to the relative importance of rational benefit showed a more complex appreciation of the purpose behind "legal" guidelines.

While the functional assessment of rules and laws was basically the same, there was some difference across the age groups in ideas about *enforcement* (level II). For rules, few middle-schoolers cited this element, which reduced further by college. For laws, enforcement appeared initially at the primary grades (10%) and increased noticeably from middle school (23%) to college (37%). Apparently transgression against *the law* was deemed more likely to incur severe sanctions.

On both the rule and law questions expected changes occurred. Most primary-schoolers were preconventional, seeing only negative functions. By middle school and college, most students expressed a conventional orientation toward rules as maintaining and facilitating striving to be good or getting along with others. This level also included a shift from proscriptive definitions confusing punishment to definitions differentiating the enforcement quality from the

**TABLE 1 Classification of Interview Categories by Moral Levels***

| Subject/Question | Level I Preconventional Categories | Level II Conventional Categories | Level III Postconventional Categories |
|---|---|---|---|
| 1. *Value of Rules and Laws* What if there were no rules? | *Violence-crime:* Laws prevent concrete physical harm, i.e., specific bad acts or crimes and secure physical necessities. | *Personal desires not principles:* Laws restrain bad, guide weak, e.g., insure personal control over greed. | *Human beings as self-regulatory:* human beings guiding behavior via principles; distinguishes law from moral principles. |
| | | *Anarchy-disorder-chaos:* Laws maintain social order. *Impossible to imagine:* Society cannot exist without rules; accepts abstract regulation as requisite for society. | |
| *Function of Rules and Laws* What is a rule? What is a law? | *Prohibitive:* Functions as proscription or fiat command restraining actions; serves no positive social good. | *Prescriptive:* Functions as shared guide interpreted by normal actor; generality to whole system of rules as facilitating, e.g., "maintaining society" or "preventing antisocial behavior." *Enforcement:* Distinguishes between badness of act and consequent punishment. | *Beneficial-rational:* Functions to achieve rational purpose behind law, usually for maximizing personal and social welfare consequences; cognizant of the utility of agreed-upon standards. |
| 2. *Dynamics of Legal Compliance* Why should people follow rules? Why do you follow rules? | *Avoid negative consequences:* Punishment reason for conformity or reason why act is bad; simple compliance, not respect, for rules. *Authority:* Obedience to power figures as ultimate guides; rules derived from them; badness of proscribed activity confused with badness of disobeying authority's rule. | *Personal conformity:* Confuses obedience with stereotypes of socially desirable in order to be good and maintain what lawmakers think is good individual behavior. *Social conformity:* Role requires compliance to be fair to other obeyers and to avoid chaos; law-and-order–maintaining perspective. | *Rational-beneficial-utilitarian:* Obedience to maintain individual and social welfare based on rational, mutual, decision-making and utilitarian considerations; no fixed obligation; obedience from weighing consequences. *Principled:* Obedience guided by principles, e.g., sense of justice independent of society; conform only with principled rules. |

| 3. Changeability of Rules and Laws<br>Can rules be changed? | *No:* Laws fixed; permanent, or quasi-physical things. | *Yes:* Laws not for "good of all" because they permit unkindness or are made by uncharitable persons. | *Yes:* For reasons of social utility, rational purposes; law-making perspective; can change unprincipled laws. |
|---|---|---|---|
| Breakability of Rules and Laws<br>Are there times when it might be right to break a rule? | *No:* No differentiation between legal and moral; badness of breaking equated with badness as such.<br>*Yes:* Simple "yes" but does not differentiate moral norm from prudential directives. | *Morality of circumstance:* Extreme circumstances justify breaking, recognize sociomoral function of rules (e.g., preservation of life) to which law obedience is instrumental; conformity with personal judgment. | *Morality of rule:* Justify breaking when law immoral or unjust, when law violates moral principles (e.g., fundamental individual rights). |

Note.—Because of our differing methodologies, the beneficial-rational category on "What is a law?" and the rational-beneficial-utilitarian category on "Why should people follow rules?" and "Why do you follow rules?" seemed to have transitional qualities between levels II and III. However, the empirical criteria for coding these categories suggested they were predominantly, though not exclusively, level III.

*The classification schema is part of the more extensive conceptualization of legal development in Tapp and Levine (1971, 1974).

**TABLE 2  Response Percentages on Legal Development Questions by Age:
U.S. Developmental Study**

| | EDUCATIONAL GROUP | | | COMPARISONS (by *t* test) | |
| LEVELS: CATEGORIES | Primary (1) | Middle School (2) | College (3) | (1) × (2) | (2) × (3) |
|---|---|---|---|---|---|
| | *What would happen if there were no rules?* | | | | |
| I:  Violence-crime | 50 | 57 | 6 | | *** |
| II:  Personal desires not principles | 15 | 20 | 15 | | |
| II:  Anarchy-disorder-chaos | 25 | 57 | 46 | ** | |
| II:  Impossible to imagine | — | 7 | 32 | | *** |
| III:  Human being as self-regulatory (nothing would happen) | — | — | 8 | | * |
| | *What is a rule?* | | | | |
| I:  Prohibitive | 60 | 30 | 14 | ** | ** |
| II:  Prescriptive | 20 | 40 | 58 | * | * |
| II:  Enforcement | — | 10 | 5 | * | |
| III:  Beneficial-rational | 15 | 27 | 26 | | |
| | *What is a law?* | | | | |
| I:  Prohibitive | 60 | 43 | 11 | | *** |
| II:  Prescriptive | 20 | 43 | 34 | ** | |
| II:  Enforcement | 10 | 23 | 37 | | * |
| III:  Beneficial-rational | — | 13 | 29 | ** | ** |
| | *Why should people follow rules?* | | | | |
| I:  Avoid negative consequences | 50 | 13 | 3 | *** | ** |
| I:  Authority | 5 | — | — | | |
| II:  Personal conformity | 35 | 13 | 9 | ** | |
| II:  Social conformity | 10 | 53 | 25 | *** | *** |
| III:  Rational-beneficial-utilitarian | 5 | 27 | 51 | ** | ** |
| III:  Principled | — | — | 5 | | |
| | *Why do you follow rules?* | | | | |
| I:  Avoid negative consequences | 60 | 47 | 25 | | ** |
| I:  Authority | 10 | 10 | 3 | | * |
| II:  Personal conformity | 20 | 40 | 34 | * | |
| II:  Social conformity | — | 40 | 12 | *** | *** |
| III:  Rational-beneficial-utilitarian | — | 7 | 22 | | ** |
| III:  Principled | — | — | 11 | | ** |
| | *Can rules be changed?* | | | | |
| I:  No | 20 | — | — | *** | |
| II & III:  Yes | 70 | 100 | 95 | *** | |

**TABLE 2    Response Percentages on Legal Development Questions by Age:
U.S. Developmental Study—Continued**

| | EDUCATIONAL GROUP | | | COMPARISONS (by $t$ test) | |
|---|---|---|---|---|---|
| LEVELS: CATEGORIES | Primary (1) | Middle School (2) | College (3) | (1) × (2) | (2) × (3) |
| | *Are there times when it might be right to break a rule?* | | | | |
| I: No, unqualified | 55 | 7 | 3 | *** | |
| I: Yes, unspecified | 25 | — | 5 | *** | |
| II: Morality of circumstance | 20 | 73 | 35 | *** | *** |
| III: Morality of rule | — | 17 | 54 | ** | *** |

*Note.—All questions except "Can rules be changed?" and "Are there times when it might be right to break a rule?" are multiple coded; therefore, percentages may total over 100%. Where answers were idiosyncratic or uncodeable, the categories were omitted from the table. Level I: Preconventional; Level II: Conventional; Level III: Postconventional.*

*p < .10
**p < .05
***p < .01

guideline. Further, a minority in the older groups expressed postconventional ideas about the rational purpose behind rules and laws and the utility of agreed-on standards for gaining personal and social welfare consequences.

*Cross-cultural study.* Similarly, the cross-national middle-school subjects saw no substantial distinction between rules and laws. In five of the seven cultures, preadolescents thought rules and laws were functionally equivalent although there was variation in emphasizing prohibitive, prescriptive, or beneficial-rational. Cross-culturally for both rules and laws many subjects focused on the prohibitive quality (preconventional level). In all seven cultures the prescriptive dimension was the most pervasively recognized, underscoring the modality of a conventional orientation. This conventional mode increased between grades 4 and 8: Older preadolescents in six cultures more often stressed the prescriptive nature of law, but few postconventional answers emerged.

**Results: Dynamics of Legal Compliance**

*U.S. developmental study.* Given the growth of children's ideas about the value and function of rules and laws, we could expect parallel changes in perceiving the individual's relationship to rule systems. Two questions, "Why should people follow rules?" and "Why do you follow rules?" probed the dynamics of legal compliance (see Table 2).

In telling why people ought to obey, half the primary-school children emphasized to *avoid negative consequences* (level I). A second-grade girl reasoned, "Because people would be doing anything and the police would try to catch them and it would be bad." By middle school and college this rationale significantly decreased. Also a substantial minority of primary-schoolers equated following rules with *personal conformity* (level II). A second-grade boy's comment, "Not to be bad; not doing things they are not supposed to do," exemplified the good-boy/good-girl view that rules should be obeyed because they maintain authority's expectations and represent what people think is good behavior. Unlike the level I orientation, "being good" responses reveal an interpersonal sense of respect for rules, generally characteristic of level II.

By middle school, personal conformity motives significantly decreased. However, a majority, still at level II, offered a broader *social conformity* explanation. This perspective held that compliance with law prevents societal chaos and so is the best way to behave (level II). A social conformity orientation was typically adolescent, up significantly at middle school (53%) and down by college (25%). In the words of an eighth-grade boy, "Well, sometimes it's for their own good. Or they should follow rules because like you go back to where you had confusion again if you didn't have any rules."

Unlike primary-graders, 27 percent at middle school also gave *rational-beneficial-utilitarian* reasons (level III). An eighth-grade girl observed that people ought to obey "for the benefit of everyone, and it makes everything easier actually and easier to live with." This perspective generally implied a legal compliance based on rational decision making and utilitarian considerations of individual and social welfare. In contrast to conformity responses, such explanations support a weighing of conflicting values and consequences, not a fixed obligation to obey. By college, slightly over half the students answered thus. A few also took a *principled* position (level III) that internal commitment, not conformity per se to concrete rules, should dictate obedience. "People should only follow those they think are fair and just," said a college female.

While youth's reasons for their own obedient behavior showed the same cognitive developmental progression, their responses also differentiated between what ideally should motivate them to obey and what often does. For example, under ideal conditions few middle-school and college students reported negative consequences (level I) as a compelling reason for legal compliance. But in the real situation, punishment consequences were an acknowledged force through adolescence, only significantly declining between middle school and college. Similarly, another level I response, *authority,* though minimal for both questions, was slightly more frequent in the realistic situation. Obedience to powerful authorities resonated in this sixth-grade girl's statement, " 'Cause my parents want me to and school wants me to and the city wants me to."

Consistent with the slower decline of level I answers, there was less movement to level II and III positions on the real than on the ideal question. At college, even with a significant increase in the postconventional position, more students expressed a conventional than a postconventional orientation: In the ideal situation 51 percent expressed transitional, rational-beneficial-utilitarian-reasoning; in the real only 22 percent did.

Evidently the rate of development varied on the ideal "should people" and the real "do you" questions. On the ideal, primary-school children took a preconventional rule- and authority-obeying stance, with punishment a major concern; however, a substantial minority progressed to a conventional position. By middle school, while a large majority expressed a conventional law-and-order-maintaining perspective, some moved to a postconventional orientation. And at college the primary focus was postconventional. On the real "do you" question, primary-schoolers were basically preconventional; middle-schoolers, preconventional and conventional; and college students, generally conventional with only a modest inclination toward a postconventional posture. By their own self-assessment, these youth recognized that their daily behaviors were guided predominantly by a conventional frame, although they realized that ideally principles should determine compliance.

*Cross-cultural study.* Universally, on both the ideal and the real question, most children took a conventional posture. Supportive cross-cultural age trends also emerged. Younger children were more inclined toward preconventional responses. The few children with a postconventional orientation were primarily at grade 8. These two cross-national age trends over grades 4 to 8 again supported the contention of a universal development in concepts of law and legal justice.

## Results: The Changeability of Rules

*U.S. developmental study.* Children's ideas about flexibility of rules and laws further illuminated the stages of legal development. With cognitive maturity children should see rules as less authoritative and immutable; such a developmental pattern emerged in response to "Can rules be changed?" Most primary-schoolers said *yes* (levels II–III); by middle school this pattern increased significantly (see Table 2). Typical preadolescent responses were: "Yes, if it's more harmful than good or not enough good," and "Some rules, they can be voted unconstitutional or something." But while 20 percent of the youngest group felt rules could not be changed (level I), *no* middle-school or college youth responded negatively—also developmentally significant.

That only a minority of the primary-schoolers were still preconventional attests to social and cultural experiences accelerating development. Most kindergarten to college students acknowledged flexibility in rule systems. While specifications varied—from conventional explanations that laws made by "mean" persons should be changed to postconventional statements for change based on social utility and mutual agreement—there was little doubt that rules and laws are mutable.

*Cross-cultural study.* Cross-cultural data on middle-school children corroborated the U.S. developmental pattern. Preadolescents overwhelmingly responded that rules can be changed. In the U.S. *all* grade 4, 6, and 8

children said yes; in the other five countries, consistent developmental results were evident. Regardless of cultural background, preadolescents increasingly recognized the changeability of rules.

## Results: The Breakability of Rules

*U.S. developmental study.* The legitimacy of rule violation was probed by asking, "Are there times when it might be right to break a rule?" While only 20 percent of the primary-schoolers maintained that rules cannot be changed, 55 percent were against rule breaking (level I) (see Table 2). There was again marked developmental progression toward greater flexibility. By the middle grades, only 7 percent adopted an absolutist position. Furthermore, 25 percent of the primary-schoolers indicated only a general awareness of reasons that might cause them to act deviantly (level I), but by preadolescence, significantly more children conceptualized the kinds of conditions precluding compliance.

One condition was the *morality of the circumstance* (level II): Rule modification is permissible if the rule is less important than the reason for breaking it; transgressions are legitimate *in extremis*, especially where potential harm to another may be involved. While a minority of primary-school children (20%) used such logic, it was typically a middle-school (73%) approach, significantly decreasing by college (35%). As a grade 8 preadolescent said: "Well, it depends on what's going on. If it's a matter of life and death or you know something pretty important, then it's all right. But it should be followed as much as possible."

By college this rationale was superseded by concern about the *morality of the rule* (level III). Although significantly more preadolescents than primary-schoolers felt that an immoral rule provides a justifiable reason for violation, by college this motive increased significantly (54%). These students argued that expected compliance must be weighed against the inherent rightness or morality of the rule, independent of circumstances. Rather than hardship justifying deviation, the justice of the rule was *the* primary condition for disobedience. A college female's comment was typical: "When the rule is immoral or unjust because I believe that people are morally accountable for their actions, and this is above the law or rules."

Again, then, the interview data revealed a sequential progression. Predominantly preconventional, primary-schoolers did not distinguish between legality and morality. By middle school, most children had internalized a conventional orientation where extenuating circumstances provide moral justification. At college, while a minority were conventional, slightly over half expressed a postconventional ethic where universal moral principles—above *the law*—should dictate relations.

*Cross-cultural study.* Congruent cross-cultural results further validated the legal development model. In five of the seven cultures children readily accepted the possibility of rule breaking; only in two cultures was the preconventional "no rule is breakable" the modal response. In five out of seven cultures there was strong support for the conventional notion that rules can be broken under certain circumstances; also, older preadolescents more willingly maintained that rules or laws are breakable. They increasingly adopted a conventional posture. The postconventional focus on the morality of the rule, which strongly emerged by college in the developmental study, was not a dominant cross-cultural justification for rule violation.

## Discussion

*Applicability of moral development theory.* The foregoing analysis of Tapp's research shows the utility of a cognitive theory for studying legal development. The U.S. kindergarten to college data revealed a shift in conceptualizations from preconventional to postconventional orientations. In addition, the cross-cultural adolescent data corroborated the universality of a progression in legal values. Lastly, both sets of data confirmed that a conventional mode was the typical societal level, that is, most individuals move beyond level I, but generally only small minorities move beyond II to III.

In the U.S. study, preconventional thinking decreased dramatically from kindergarten to college on *all* questions. A conventional approach was generally modal at middle school and college. Postconventional reasoning, virtually nonexistent in the primary grades, increased steadily to college. Cross-nationally, children from grades 4 to 8 generally exhibited a marked decline in preconventional notions. Conversely, conventional responses were generally modal at grades 6 and 8, often peaking at grade 6. By grade 8, a growing number used a postconventional frame. Although the cross-national study only spanned grades 4 to 8, the data provided supportive evidence that changes in legal development occur in consistently ordered stages.

*A cognitive theory of legal development.* Valid determinations about legal socialization require an understanding of legal development. In answer to interview questions, children at the preconventional level expressed an "obedience and punishment orientation." Their sense of law and justice was based on punishment avoidance and unquestioning deference to power. They neither conceptualized a generalized legal system or underlying moral order, nor recognized a difference between legality and morality. They accepted rules or laws as fixed and immutable acts made and enforced by authority to restrain "bad" behaviors and prevent physical harm.

By the conventional level, children's responses shifted from a law-obeying perspective to the modal law-maintaining one. They either embedded justice in concern for another's approval or equated justice with the maintenance of the basic rules and structure of society. Conventional children respected rules or laws as guiding social or "good" behavior and preventing disorder; they posited that rules and laws do not prohibit behavior but function as general prescriptions. While rules and laws may be changed or even broken in extreme circumstances, conventional youth considered obeying law —and thus fulfilling one's obligation to society—instrumental in sustaining sociomoral values.

While both preconventional "obedience and punishment avoidance" and conventional "law and order" were heavily oriented to fixed law in defining right and wrong, there were marked differences. The former was rigidly oriented without any conception of social welfare or social order; the latter was rigidly oriented to systems of law as identified with and at the core of social order and social welfare.

Those who reached the postconventional level described a far more flexible perception of relations to the legal or rule system, one oriented to principles of morality and justice directing compliance. Thus, postconventional youth viewed rules and laws as norms mutually agreed on by individuals for maximizing personal and social welfare. They judged that laws should be obeyed for rational considerations or because they are coincident with universal principles of justice. This perspective offered a coherent, responsive guide to social change and the creation of new norms: Those that served no purpose or were unjust should be changed; those that violated fundamental individual rights and universal moral principles could be legitimately broken. While conventional morality also permitted rule breaking in extreme circumstances, it did not relate law to ideal principles of justice in defining the limits of obedience. Effective and impartial maintenance of the legal system was equated with justice.

## IMPLICATIONS FOR LEGAL SOCIALIZATION

The joint concern of social scientists and law operatives alike remains: What procedures seem key or instrumental in moving individuals toward principled legal development?

### Conflict, Participation, and Match as Socializing Procedures

The ease and strength of fit of the Kohlberg moral development model to the Tapp U.S. developmental and cross-cultural preadolescent data and model signify an approach to legal socialization procedures. The interactional models of legal development (Tapp & Levine, 1971, 1974) and moral development (Kohlberg, 1969) view participation and conflict resolution as key concepts to evolving mature, principled thought. Since legal development is fundamentally a process of restructuring perceptions of self vis-à-vis legal or rule systems, role-taking opportunities in family, peer group, and secondary institutions should provide necessary inputs (Baldwin, 1906; Mead, 1934; Piaget, 1932). Research results suggest that these role-taking experiences operate by stimulating cognitive development rather than producing a particular value system. For example, peer group "stars" who are more active than "isolates" display both more rapid development and a more mature moral ideology (Kohlberg, 1968b). It is the structural conflict between these value-role inputs and the child's developmental level that stimulates transition from one stage of development to the next (see, e.g., Haan, Smith, & Block, 1968).

Socialization procedures that ignore the learning modes of conflict and participation —and the basic psychological processes of cognition, interaction, and valuation—cheat the child. Traditional social education has typically urged compliance with the predominant adult rules and attitudes of the particular social system. This transmission of clichés or slogans (Zellman & Sears, Chap. 11) by conventional adults is documented by the push toward an unexamined, narrowly defined law-and-order orientation, society's modal legality. It is accompanied by a proliferation of materials usually unmatched to levels and experiences of development.

It is not that in the short-term preachment, pronouncement, and punishment may not control behavior. Rather, we emphasize that we are concerned with approaches that have a long-term, persistent effect in developing the capacity to reason judgments. We would argue that experience-based activity involving conflict resolution, problem solving, participation in decision making, and role taking beget compliance and independence of more than an uncritical law-and-order sort. Such educational experiences extend the human's capacity to differentiate and integrate and to contemplate different points of view, in other words, to develop principles for evaluating "right" and "wrong" and perfecting a sense of responsibility, obligation, law, and justice (Asch, 1952; Dewey, 1910, 1930; Dewey & Tufts, 1932).

The match problem for affecting change in legal development is one of presenting stimuli sufficiently incongruous to stimulate conflict in a person's existing cognitive schema and sufficiently congruous to be assimilated with some accommodative effort. Techniques and materials used in socializing encounters should match the level of comprehension of the subject—child or adult. For the most successful match, the socializer should be one level above the learner (Blatt, 1969; Blatt & Kohlberg, 1969; Turiel, 1964). As Turiel's study (1964) reveals, children are almost as likely to reject moral reasoning and behavior beneath their level as to fail to assimilate reasoning and action too far above it. Socializing agents, in addition to knowing the subject's level of development, must know

their own. Working knowledgeably with these bits of information should enable the socializers (teachers, parents, or law operatives) to develop meaningful and provocative programs. Fitting experiences, guidance, and/or explanations by elders can accelerate the growth of moral outlooks and ethical legal perspectives.. This is the hidden curriculum of socialization—be it political, moral, or legal.

## Contexts for Legal Socialization Procedures

Since an individual's legal reasoning guides interaction in a variety of systems of law, multiple settings beyond government (state law) likewise provide the opportunity for developing senses of legality and justice (Tapp & Levine, 1971, 1974). Such a perspective is consistent with Fuller's jurisprudential definition of law as "the enterprise of subjecting human conduct to the governance of rules . . . in clubs, churches, school, labor unions . . . and a hundred and one other forms of human association [1969b, pp. 106–125]." Also, Barton and Mendlovitz (1960) report that legal development occurs in traditionally legal and nonlegal settings. For example, of 114 incidents of injustice reported by 21 law students, only 13 percent involved the formal legal system, 19 percent were experienced in school settings, 10 percent in parent–child relations, and 32 percent in bureaucratic organizations. For these reasons, we direct our attention to the family, school, and legal system.

*Family.* The family is not unique or indispensable for moral (Kohlberg, 1969) or political education (Torney, Chap. 12; Zellman & Sears, Chap. 11). Too many developmental and cultural forces tend to produce normal morality and legality to make these values contingent primarily on the kinship relationship. Nevertheless, in the cycle a "good parent" may be critical. While many findings (McCord, McCord, & Thurber, 1962; Terman & Miles, 1936) contradict claims that good parent relations are necessary for normal social development, some findings suggest that bad parent relations retard or disrupt such development (Hetherington & Frankie, 1967; McCord et al., 1962).

*School and legal systems.* The two most important institutions for stimulating legal development are the public school and the legal system. The school particularly provides an accessible forum for participation and conflict resolution. For example, rather than attempting to teach students by chronicling statutes or situations in which laws are mechanically applied, a persuasive way to accelerate legal reasoning is to engage students, both within and without the school context, in contemporary legal issues (e.g., student rights, tenant unions, drug addiction). Further, legal education is taught not only formally through curriculum materials but also informally through the process of instruction, the organization and administration of the school, and the relations of the school to the community (Westin, 1970).

The experiences of children, as well as adults, in such institutions of law and government as courts, legislatures, prisons, public housing, and city councils affect their perceptions of these institutions and, more generally, the development of their senses of law and legal justice. The law and the government are perceived quite differently by those who have participated in the social order. Further, participation leads to comprehending another's condition—for example, children's understanding of the dilemmas and stresses of the policeman's role. Thus, participation and equality are requisite characteristics of both teaching and achieving justice.

Interaction with just socializing agents in school and legal systems—the teacher and the police, or the principal and the judge—is crucial to legal development (Tapp & Levine, 1970, 1974). The possibility of developing mature ethical-legal judgments is affected substantially by whether the environment affords the opportunity for dialogue, sharing responsibility, and taking part in decision making. If such opportunities are negligible, some individuals may be fixated at low levels of development while others ultimately may seek conflict resolution across the barricades (rioters) and/or across the bars (delinquents).

## Legal Socialization Goals

Whatever the social context, legal socialization procedures that do not incorporate knowledge about (1) the relation between ethical and legal judgments, (2) the natural sequencing of sociomoral development, (3) the utility of role taking and conflict resolution, and (4) the value of presenting modes of thought beyond the conventional, not only ignore major psychological findings but also reveal a view of humanity as potentially less than rational, purposive, and principled. A more complete, parsimonious theory of legal socialization must draw on the natural tendencies of the individual interacting with the environment. Further, it must envision participation and conflict, cooperation and rationality as congruent with the requirements of a just legal order. Such an approach tends to view the law as a construction of values to promote individual rights. It tends to produce individuals who view the law as a resource for facilitating needed change, not a mechanism for sanctifying tradition. More than that, it would encourage citizens to look beyond "law and order" narrowly conceived to more responsive and inclusive concepts of legality. The legal order has vicissitudes that stem from the inherent dilemmas of law making and law enforcing. But the process of developing rule systems and comprehending the meaning of law and legal justice calls on our ability to design procedures for establishing justice and, therefore, provides an experience essential to achieving the ideal of a just person in a just society.

# CHAPTER 10

# Legal Guarantees of Individual Freedom

## A Cross-National Study of the Development of Political Thought

—*JUDITH GALLATIN and JOSEPH ADELSON*

U.S., British, and German adolescents between the ages of 11 and 18 were asked to weigh the merits of two potentially intrusive laws and to state whether or not individual freedoms ought to enjoy certain legal safeguards. Older subjects were both more aware that the proposed laws might constitute an invasion of privacy and more interested in obtaining legal guarantees of individual liberties, even in the event of an emergency. While the developmental results were more striking than the cross-national ones, the concern for preserving individual liberties was especially marked among U.S. adolescents. These findings are taken as evidence for the development of an "ideology" or "feeling for ideals" during adolescence.

As student activism became increasingly visible in the 1960s, even spreading to the nation's high schools, the common view of youth underwent a rather startling transformation. During this period, adolescents became more socially aware, more politically concerned, more sensitive to limitations of their personal freedom than did their supposedly apathetic predecessors of the late 1950s. It has been argued (Adelson, 1964, 1970) that this discrepancy—between the complacent youth of the 1950s and the activists of the 1960s—is largely illusory, more a myth unwittingly promoted by the media than a social reality. Illusion or not, the contrast points up a very real gap in our research on adolescents. We know very little about how political ideals and activities are acquired, how the cognitive map that presumably underlies such activities develops.

The pioneering studies of political socialization (Greenstein, 1965; Hess & Torney,

1967) have, for the most part, concentrated on grade-school children, or alternatively have traced the impact of specific factors such as civics courses and parental affiliations on a single age group—for example, high-school seniors (Jennings & Niemi, 1968b; Langton & Jennings, 1968). They also have focused on the acquisition of political attitudes rather than on the development of political cognition. Hence, although these studies may tell us when attachment to country begins to develop, we know much less about how political principles mature. At what age, for instance, does an awareness of individual freedoms begin to emerge? At what point does the child become able to distinguish between rules that make a legitimate demand and those that infringe on liberty? Further, how closely does the developmental pattern of U.S. youth resemble the pattern of youth in other countries?

Earlier research indicates that the answers

to such questions should be sought among adolescents rather than children. Both Greenstein (1965) and Hess and Torney (1967) have concluded that early in life children acquire feelings about government without being able to comprehend how it actually functions. Indeed, studies by the present authors and associates (Adelson, Green, & O'Neil, 1969; Adelson & O'Neil, 1966; Gallatin & Adelson, 1970) confirm that preadolescents are in many respects unable to grasp political principles. Abstractions such as "law" and "government" that encompass a realm outside the face-to-face encounters of family, schoolroom, and street are usually beyond them. Apparently only in midadolescence, at the age of 15 or so, is one's intellectual capacity sufficient to understand the basic tenets of the social contract and to envision the self as part of a larger political-legal community.

In this chapter we will examine various aspects of a principle fundamental to just democracy: the concept of individual freedom. This concept is often defined negatively—as *freedom from* coercion by other individuals or the state. As the political philosopher Barry (1965) observed, individual freedom is "contrasted with interference, censorship, control, regulation. . . . Examples are freedom of speech, freedom of worship . . . freedom to paint one's house any colour one chooses [p. 141]." It is our intention to trace the growth of ideas concerning this principle during adolescence. Using a research strategy that is both developmental and cross-national, we will ascertain how the conceptualization of individual freedom changes between the ages of 11 and 18 in three Western countries—the United States, Great Britain, and West Germany.

## METHOD

### The Interview

The data were obtained by an interview schedule that proposed the following hypothetical situation: A thousand people, dissatisfied with their government, have moved to a Pacific island to form a new society; once there, they are confronted by the task of establishing a political order. The schedule then posed wide-ranging questions on the nature of law and government, political forms and functions, the sources of crime and the strategy of punishment, utopianism, and so on. The questions were primarily open-ended and semiprojective. In complexity they ranged from the simple type (e.g., on the purpose of government or law) to complex sequences that considered in some detail specific dilemmas the society faced (e.g., control of cigarette smoking).

The interviews, 60- to 90-minutes long, were conducted in school, tape-recorded, and transcribed verbatim. Interviewers were graduate students with previous experience in clinical interviewing.

### The Sample

In all, 330 boys and girls between the ages of 11 and 18 were interviewed. Fifth, seventh, ninth, and twelfth grades were sampled with average ages of 11, 13, 15, and 18, respectively. There were 120 U.S. subjects drawn from a midwestern suburb, 120 British subjects from the London suburbs, and 90 German subjects from Hamburg and environs. For each age level, 15 boys and 15 girls were chosen; two-thirds of average intelligence (IQ 95–110) and one-third superior intelligence (IQ 125 plus). Due to fund limitations, German fifth-graders were not interviewed; therefore, cross-national comparisons to be reported here do not include that grade for any of the national samples.

With respect to social status, the U.S. and German samples are roughly comparable—largely middle class, with the U.S. sample having a somewhat higher number of upper-middle class cases. The British sample is somewhat lower overall in social status, containing a larger number of subjects from working and lower-middle class backgrounds.

The data reported here were analyzed by social class, sex, and IQ without significant differences. Consequently, this chapter focuses on differences related to age and national origin.

### Reliability

Of the total interview sample, 10 percent were selected randomly to test reliability. Intercoder agreement ranged from 80 to 90 percent.

### RESULTS

### The Infringement of Liberty

Implicit in the concept of freedom is the notion of privacy. The state may regulate the lives of people in some respects (requiring them to obtain a minimum education, for example) but not in others without infringing their liberties. To get at this aspect of the concept of freedom, we asked the following:

*Question 26*: Let us return to some of the laws that were proposed. One was a suggestion that men over 45 be required to have a yearly medical check-up. What do you think of that suggestion?

*Question 27*: Some people of the island proposed the following law: that people paint their houses at least once every five years. (a) What would be the argument for such a law? (b) What would be the argument against such a law?

*Developmental differences.* Perhaps most striking is the greater recognition with increased maturity that the proposed laws involve an infringement of personal freedom (Tables 1 and 3, category 4). Younger adolescents are more likely to respond to the evident "good" that might be obtained and more willing to grant legitimacy to any claim the state may make. The ideal of privacy is too tenuously held, or perhaps too abstract to prevail in the face of such concrete virtues as good health and brightly painted homes (Table 2). But by the end of

**TABLE 1  Percent Offering Various Arguments For or Against Law Requiring Men Over Forty-five to Have Annual Medical Exams (Question 26)**

|  | AGE | | | | NATIONALITY | | |
|---|---|---|---|---|---|---|---|
|  | 11 | 13 | 15 | 18 | U.S. | British | German |
| 1. Uncritical compliance; security orientation: Government should protect older people | 83 | 64 | 56 | 41 | 51 | 48 | 61 |
| 2. Community welfare: Society is enhanced by having healthy citizenry and work force | 8 | 16 | 17 | 23 | 24 | 14 | 18 |
| 3. Lack of utility: Cost of exam would outweigh benefit to community | 5 | 11 | 8 | 6 | 5 | 18 | 3 |
| 4. Individual freedom: Exam would infringe individual liberties | 4 | 9 | 19 | 30 | 20 | 20 | 18 |
| (N) | (59) | (88) | (88) | (86) | (88) | (85) | (89) |

*Note.—Overall chi-squares significant for age at $p < .001$, for nationality at $p < .01$.*

**TABLE 2     Percent Offering Various Arguments For Law Requiring
House-Painting Every Five Years (Question 27a)**

|  | AGE | | | | NATIONALITY | | |
|---|---|---|---|---|---|---|---|
|  | 11 | 13 | 15 | 18 | U.S. | British | German |
| 1.  Immediate effect:  Houses would look nice | 44 | 24 | 38 | 19 | 24 | 33 | 26 |
| 2.  Maintain order and  cleanliness | 13 | 22 | 15 | 29 | 14 | 28 | 24 |
| 3.  Appearance of community; maintain  morale | 33 | 32 | 29 | 40 | 55 | 23 | 23 |
| 4.  Enhance tourist trade | 10 | 22 | 17 | 12 | 7 | 16 | 27 |
| (N) | (46) | (74) | (78) | (75) | (76) | (69) | (82) |

Note.—Overall chi-squares significant for age at $p < .05$, for nationality at $p < .001$.

**TABLE 3     Percent Offering Various Arguments Against House-Painting Law
(Question 27b)**

|  | AGE | | | | NATIONALITY | | |
|---|---|---|---|---|---|---|---|
|  | 11 | 13 | 15 | 18 | U.S. | British | German |
| 1.  Economic hardship:  Some people could not  afford cost | 9 | 12 | 5 | 13 | 8 | 7 | 18 |
| 2.  Lack of utility: Houses  would not need painting as often as required by law | 52 | 50 | 61 | 29 | 44 | 53 | 39 |
| 3.  Individual discretion:  Painting should be up  to owner | 13 | 16 | 11 | 17 | 8 | 18 | 19 |
| 4.  Individual freedom:  Law would infringe  rights | 27 | 22 | 23 | 41 | 40 | 22 | 24 |
| (N) | (46) | (64) | (74) | (83) | (80) | (74) | (67) |

Note.—Overall chi-squares significant for age and for nationality at $p < .05$.

adolescence, substantial numbers not only recognize the intrusiveness of such laws but also can adduce a counterprinciple—individual freedom—to weigh against their apparent merits.

*National differences.* Though the national results are somewhat less vivid, there are a number of interesting trends. Among the U.S. sample, a dual theme emerges. They are more likely than either Germans or the British to justify the potentially repressive laws in terms of their benefit to the community as a whole (Table 1, category 2 and Table 2, category 3)—although their justification for the house-painting law may be rather half-hearted. Also they are apparently more sensitive to the infringement of personal liberties implicit in the house-painting law (Table 3, category 4), but not in the law about medical check-ups. Since they are no more likely to say that keeping up one's house should be "left to the individual" (indeed, if categories 3 and 4 in Table 3 were combined, there would be no visible difference between the national groups), they may merely be more inclined to label the proposed law an outright invasion of privacy.

By contrast, the British reveal, in opposing both laws, an orientation that seems more "utilitarian" than that of either the German or U.S. respondents. They are more likely to dismiss annual medical examinations and house-painting at regular intervals with the argument that "they would cost too much" (Table 1, category 3 and Table 3, category 2). Utility rather than public welfare or infringement appears to be the overriding concern.

If any trend is visible among the Germans, it might be described as a desire for security or protection. They are more likely than either the U.S. or British respondents to approve the law requiring annual medical examinations with a statement like, "Older people need to be cared for" (Table 1, category 1). Interestingly enough, they oppose the more intrusive house-painting law on similar grounds—that is, that it would work an economic hardship on some individuals (Table 3, category 1).

## Legal Guarantees of Individual Freedom

There is an awareness in most Western democracies not only that the state may sometimes pose a threat to an individual's autonomy but also that it should formally guarantee liberties to a certain extent. Citizens refer to such formal sanctions as "Constitutional" or "inalienable" rights, meaning that they have been incorporated into the legal structure and can be altered only by amending that structure or by specifying a special set of conditions (e.g., a national emergency). To study these particular facets of the concept of individual freedom, we followed up the infringement questions with the following series:

*Question 29:* After a great deal of discussion the people of the island developed a fairly complete system of principles and laws. At this point, another issue arose. There were some who felt that certain laws, such as those guaranteeing freedom of speech, were so important they should never be changed, and that it should be agreed that no future government would ever be able to change those laws. On the other hand, there were those who felt that as times change then laws must change and that there ought to be no laws which future governments could not change if they wanted to. What do you think of these arguments?

*Question 30:* Could you give me some examples of the kinds of laws that should be permanent and unchangeable?

*Question 31:* There were some people who felt that permanent laws might be a good idea except in times of war or emergency. They said that when there is a really serious crisis, the government should have the right to suspend all those laws until the emergency was over. What do you think of that?

*Developmental differences.* The responses to this set of questions demonstrate that the ability to recognize concrete instances of infringement is accompanied by an increased commitment to the principle of individual freedom. Indeed, the most dramatic evidence of this particular trend appears in Table 5: Fully 65 percent of the 18-year-olds but only 12 percent of the 11-year-olds believe that certain individual freedoms should be permanently guaranteed by law (category 3). A similar developmental trend is evident in response to Question 29 (Table 4). Not only are older subjects more likely to declare that there should be no tampering with legal guarantees of free speech (category 2), they also are more likely to insist on such safeguards even

**TABLE 4   Percent Offering Various Opinions as to Whether Laws Should Ever Be Amended (Question 29)**

| | AGE | | | |
|---|---|---|---|---|
| | 11 | 13 | 15 | 18 |
| 1. Unelaborated response: Opinion that laws should either change or be permanent; no reference to amendment | 50 | 36 | 10 | 8 |
| 2. Individual freedom: Laws insuring civil liberties should be retained; no reference to amendment | 10 | 11 | 11 | 26 |
| 3. Amendment concept: Legal system should be stable but not inflexible | 36 | 38 | 53 | 36 |
| 4. Amendment with guarantee of permanent freedom laws | 4 | 15 | 26 | 30 |
| (N) | (58) | (82) | (88) | (88) |

*Note.—Overall chi-square significant for age at* p < *.001.*

**TABLE 5   Percent Naming Various Laws Which Should Be Permanent (Question 30)**

| | AGE | | | | NATIONALITY | | |
|---|---|---|---|---|---|---|---|
| | 11 | 13 | 15 | 18 | U.S. | British | German |
| 1. Misdemeanor: Traffic laws, disturbance of peace | 41 | 26 | 14 | 18 | 14 | 22 | 22 |
| 2. Criminal: Murder, robbery | 47 | 45 | 26 | 17 | 15 | 44 | 28 |
| 3. Individual freedom: Freedom of speech, religion | 12 | 29 | 60 | 65 | 71 | 34 | 50 |
| (N) | (51) | (78) | (78) | (77) | (78) | (77) | (78) |

*Note.—Overall chi-squares significant for age and for nationality at* p < *.001.*

while recognizing the necessity for changing other laws (category 4). In addition, they are slightly more likely to uphold the principle of free speech even during a national emergency.

Some accompanying trends, though less obvious, are perhaps equally important. Although our questions were designed primarily to study a particular political ideal, they inevitably raised other issues as well. During adolescence, in addition to an increased regard for certain fundamental principles of democracy, such as individual freedom, there is also a greater understanding of the complex governmental machinery that insures these principles. The younger respondents display a marked tendency to be one-sided and arbitrary in their judgments in

**TABLE 6    Percent Offering Various Opinions as to Whether Laws Should Be Suspended during Emergency (Question 31)**

|  | AGE | | | | NATIONALITY | | |
|---|---|---|---|---|---|---|---|
|  | 11 | 13 | 15 | 18 | U.S. | British | German |
| 1. Compliance: Laws should be suspended | 35 | 24 | 18 | 12 | 11 | 19 | 24 |
| 2. Security orientation: Government should protect citizens, ease laws | 41 | 42 | 31 | 11 | 16 | 34 | 35 |
| 3. National security: Laws should be suspended to further war effort | 6 | 11 | 12 | 20 | 22 | 16 | 6 |
| 4. No suspension of freedom laws | 18 | 9 | 23 | 24 | 31 | 12 | 11 |
| 5. Conditional: Should be decided by government at time of emergency; depends on situation | 0 | 14 | 16 | 33 | 20 | 19 | 24 |
| (N) | (46) | (80) | (84) | (83) | (84) | (83) | (80) |

*Note.—Overall chi-squares significant for age and for nationality at* $p < .001$.

addition to being unthinkingly compliant on occasion. Not only are they less explicit about their regard for personal freedom than the older subjects, but also they demonstrate less comprehension of the concept of amendment (Table 4, categories 3 and 4); are more likely to include misdemeanors among laws that should be made permanent (Table 5, category 1); and are more willing to yield their liberties for some vaguely defined "protection" (Table 6, category 2).

The increased capacity to appreciate various facets of a political-legal issue is perhaps best shown by the responses to Question 31 (Table 6). We have already noted that older subjects are only slightly more likely than younger ones to insist on retaining free speech laws (category 4). However, older adolescents who do recommend suspension seem more inclined to offer some reasoned justification—for example, the need to abridge individual rights to "support the war effort" or "unify the country" (cate-

gory 3). Rather than decide the matter by fiat, they allow one principle to override another. Even more striking is the tendency to take a conditional stance on the issue. None of the 11-year-olds but fully a third of the 18-year-olds declare that the procedures to apply during emergencies cannot always be decided in advance and "depend on the circumstances" (category 5). This type of response in particular underscores the development of a sense of perspective during adolescence, an increased ability to anticipate future events and deal with them flexibly.

The responses to Question 30 (Table 5) may partially explain this increased flexibility and detachment. Generally unconcerned about preserving free speech, younger respondents exhibit a rather marked interest in retaining legal penalties against murder and robbery (category 2). Perhaps this concern about violence in early adolescence reflects a deeper preoccupation with problems of impulse control (Freud, 1936). Possibly the older adolescents, having a greater degree of internal control, can better afford to insist on guarantees of individual freedom.

*National differences.* As with the previous set of items, the developmental differences on Questions 29, 30, and 31 are more pronounced than the national differences. (Indeed, the national groups did not differ significantly in responding to Question 29; thus we have not presented the separate response patterns for this question.) Nonetheless, some trends observed earlier are repeated, accompanied by some interesting new trends. Most noteworthy is the U.S. preoccupation with individual freedom, implied previously in objections to the house-painting law (Table 3) and now underscored far more emphatically in response to Questions 30 and 31. When asked which laws should be permanent, an overwhelming percentage of the U.S. subjects, 71 percent, refers to one or more of the civil liberties guaranteed by the Bill of Rights (Table 5, category 3). Confronted even by a national emergency, they are considerably more likely to oppose the suspension of free-speech laws than either British or German adolescents (Table 6, category 4). But note that the dual theme that emerged in response to the law proposing annual medical check-ups (Table 1) also figures in the responses to Question 31. Although a substantial percentage of U.S. citizens may argue against abridging free-speech laws even in a crisis, a smaller but still notable number favors suspending them "in the interest of national security."

The British perception of the relation between the individual and the state appears to be quite different. They seem to want the state to assure its citizens safeguards from *each other* and to relax demands on them in times of crisis, rather than to offer an open forum for their opinions. They are, for instance, much more likely than either U.S. or German respondents to suggest putting criminal laws above the process of amendment (Table 5, category 2). They are

also more likely than the U.S. sample to respond to the threat of a national emergency with what sounds like a plea for protection rather than an insistence on the right of free speech. One gathers that for most of the British, the issue of free speech simply does not enter the picture. Many apparently interpreted the phrase "permanent laws" in Question 31 to mean laws restricting freedom rather than insuring it. Thus, they replied that in times of crisis a government should not expect its citizens to toe the mark, that it should defend them and ease up on the more demanding regulations (Table 6, category 2).

The Germans appear to steer a middle course. They are more likely than the British but less likely than the U.S. sample to advocate a permanent guarantee of free-speech laws. However, confronted with a crisis, they appear to retreat somewhat from this civil libertarian position to one of acquiescence. As many German as British subjects declare that government should require less of its citizens in an emergency (Table 6, category 2) rather than addressing whether citizens can insist on free speech in such circumstances. In addition, a smaller but still considerable percentage of the Germans categorically advocate suspending all "permanent laws" during a crisis (Table 6, category 1). Note, however, in this connection that the absolute number of German adolescents who favor suspension is actually smaller than the absolute number of U.S. adolescents favoring it (if categories 1 and 3 in Table 6 are combined, 33 percent of the U.S. and 30 percent of the German respondents advocate this move). The Germans seem less inclined to offer much justification for their position.

## DISCUSSION

### Developmental Differences

Our developmental data are quite clear-cut. The adolescent's grasp of the concept of individual freedom increases with age.

Not only is the 18-year-old more capable than the 11-year-old of recognizing intrusions into the privacy of the individual, but also much more committed to liberty as an abstract principle, recognizing the need of safeguarding certain freedoms with formal legislation. Concomitant with this increased regard for the individual is a heightened comprehension of governmental functions. The 18-year-old is not so irrevocably committed to any single principle that he or she cannot envision waiving it under any circumstances. The stance is prima facie rather than absolutist, ready to invoke a particular rule where it seems fitting, prepared to yield it where there are overriding concerns.

What our findings point to is an integral and highly significant part of a larger development, what Erikson (1959, 1963) has termed the formulation of an ideology: "The adolescent learns to grasp the flux of time, to anticipate the future in a coherent way, to perceive ideas and to assent to ideals, to take . . . an ideological position for which the younger child is unprepared [1963, p. 417]." The question is why such development takes place only in adolescence—relatively late in adolescence at that. Until recently, there has been a tendency to attribute the growth of conceptual thinking during the teenage years to "cognitive maturation," the implication being that this was principally a neurological phenomenon and hence inaccessible to further study. But researchers are beginning to recognize that cognitive abilities do not mature in vacuo, that there is an interaction between what might be termed "cultural expectations" and intellectual capacities. Elkind (1968) exemplifies this new orientation when he observes, "The awareness of the discrepancy between the actual and the possible . . . helps to make the adolescent a rebel. He is always comparing the possible with the actual and discovering that the actual is flagrantly wanting [p. 152]."

Conversely, we suspect that the adolescent's growing concern and respect for in-dividual freedom are due also to a multitude of pressures and opportunities that encourage him or her to formulate an increasingly differentiated sense of self. Indeed, this burgeoning awareness of one's own identity, an identity apart from and yet somehow dependent on other people, is probably the most significant development of the adolescent period. Despite the large-scale publicity given to "youth" and "identity crises," it is a phenomenon at present only dimly understood.

Yet, it seems reasonable to assume that in day-to-day existence the adolescent undergoes a vast range of experiences that make the principle of individual freedom increasingly relevant and comprehensible. As Sullivan (1953) observes, close friendships provide the adolescent with the opportunity to view the self through the eyes of others, thus promoting a heightened sense of his or her own uniqueness. One is expected to take greater responsibility for one's own actions; and at the same time more decisions are left to the adolescent's discretion. Needless to say, he or she also becomes increasingly aware of civic responsibility and at the same time begins to look forward to exercising the right of franchise. To lend coherence to the anticipated adult life and some order to decisions, the adolescent needs to develop what Erikson (1959) has loosely termed an "ideology" or "religion," or what Inhelder and Piaget (1958) call "a feeling for ideals." Simultaneously he or she becomes increasingly capable of comprehending the ideological principles that make up the particular creed of the mother nation. In Western democracies, the concept of individual freedom is one of the most sacrosanct, and it is also one of considerable relevance to the late adolescent.

## National Differences

While generally less pronounced than our developmental findings, the national differences suggest that even countries sharing a more-or-less common cultural tradition may foster somewhat different political orientations among their adolescents. Certainly, our U.S. respondents demonstrate more concern with individual freedom than either German or British respondents. But this is the least problematic of the cross-national results. Individual autonomy is a U.S. preoccupation. School children are taught about the Bill of Rights long before they can comprehend its significance.

More intriguing is the less visible tendency to justify measures that might infringe on individual autonomy by citing the national interest. This tendency emerged much more clearly in a previous study designed to evoke it (Gallatin & Adelson, 1970), but its appearance here serves to underscore once more the peculiarly U.S.-form of phrasing of the social contract. The U.S. adolescent finds considerations of personal freedom particularly compelling, but considerations of "public welfare" may prove even more so. While emphasizing the speculative nature of any interpretation of our findings, we point out that this dual commitment is a great potential source of tension in the politics of the U.S. As long as there is consensus about which matters are to be left to individual discretion and which require a national commitment, these principles do not conflict. When consensus breaks down, the basic tension is exposed.

Even more intriguing, and somewhat surprising, is the relative absence of these two themes in our British sample. The British have a tradition of tolerance for free speech that is, if anything, more impressive than that of the U.S. England is also a "welfare state," so we might expect references to the common good to be more prominent. But, if any consistent impression emerges from the data, it is the British tendency to characterize this relation as pretty much a "business arrangement."

One suspects that this rather laissez-faire attitude may stem from taking for granted in Britain what is still a matter of issue in the United States. The British do not seem to share U.S. qualms about strong central government. It is simply the government's job to provide services and to protect its citizens. Objections to government policy are voiced more in the tone of a stockholder than of a civil libertarian or a participant. The cost outweighs the gain, and the whole matter becomes a "bloody nuisance." Or, as one subject put it in referring to the house-painting law, "That's something thought up by a bureaucrat sitting off in an office somewhere." These kinds of differences have been pointed to also by Banfield (1960) and Almond and Verba (1963).

The Germans, with their slightly greater willingness to acquiesce to potentially restrictive laws and their concern with being protected, reveal a somewhat childlike approach to government, an orientation that has been characterized as "authoritarian submissive" (Gallatin & Adelson, 1970; Pinson, 1954; Rodnick, 1948). Certainly, the German group seemed more inclined than the U.S. youth to trade individual freedoms for collective security. But how are we then to explain why fully half of the Germans advocated making freedom of speech laws permanent?

These apparently contradictory findings suggest a rather sharp cleavage within the German sample. Our data indicate that a great many of these youth—somewhat more than a majority in most instances—are democratic in outlook. But a substantial minority—we estimate as many as one-third—display a degree of submissiveness to the state that strikes U.S. citizens as extraordinary. They feel that the citizen exists to serve the state; they fear independence of judgment, arguing that it leads only to confusion and anarchy; they doubt that the citizen is competent to make his or her own political judgments and suggest that it is better to pay heed to the wisdom of leaders. It is the presence of this large minority that makes the German sample as a whole turn out to be so authoritarian in sentiment. The conflict between democratic and authoritarian principles is not so much within the German mind as within the German polity.

As fascinating as the national differences are, we would nonetheless like to emphasize once more that the developmental differences seem on the whole more impressive. Though the degree of commitment to individual freedom may vary from country to country, the overall developmental pattern is similar. As adolescents in the United States, West Germany, and Great Britain mature, they appear to develop a more differentiated view of the political-legal world and to become increasingly concerned with guaranteeing certain individual rights.

# CHAPTER 11

# Childhood Origins of Tolerance for Dissent[1]

## —GAIL L. ZELLMAN and DAVID O. SEARS

The origins of children's attitudes toward freedom of dissent were investigated using questionnaire data from 1384 children in grades 5–9. Political socialization of attitudes toward free speech apparently does occur during late childhood and early adolescence. Most children acquire support for the abstract principle of free speech in slogan form, without learning its concrete implications. Support for free speech in concrete instances is dictated largely by the child's attitude toward the dissenting out-group in question and only rarely by the general principle of free expression. There are indications that the child's confidence in his or her ability to think divergently contributes to tolerance, presumably by reducing the personal threat posed by deviant out-groups.

When asked what is most desirable about the U.S. political system, most U.S. respondents generally cite such abstractions as "freedom," "democracy," "equality," "majority rule," or tolerance for diversity (see, e.g., Dahl, 1961; Lane, 1962). Surely a unique aspect of the U.S. system is the constitutional guarantee of certain individual rights, particularly the right to free and open dissent from conventional social norms or from official government policy. But over two decades of research have shown that the U.S. public is often uninformed at best, and hostile at worst, toward extending such rights to political and social dissenters (see, e.g., Erskine, 1963; Key, 1961; McClosky, 1964; Prothro & Grigg, 1960; Stouffer, 1955). In fact, the most striking feature of adult attitudes toward free speech is their acceptance of the principle coupled with their unwillingness to apply it to concrete contexts.

Because basic civil liberties are fundamental to U.S. democratic process, this gap between attitudes and ideology is of substantial importance. Why the intolerance for free dissent in concrete situations? What explains the inconsistency between tolerance in the abstract and intolerance in the concrete?

There are, of course, variations among demographic groups. The college-educated and the young are far more likely to support concrete extensions of civil liberties than are less educated or older individuals (D. O. Sears, 1969; Stouffer, 1955). It is

[1] The research was supported by grants from the Ford Foundation to the UCLA Committee on Civic Education, from the U.S. Office of Education to the second author, and by a USPHS predoctoral fellowship to the first author. The authors wish to express thanks to Joan E. Laurence, who supervised the data collection, and to Charles N. Quigley, Richard P. Longaker, June L. Tapp, Richard Whinnery, and the students and staff of the Sacramento City Unified School District, whose cooperation made the research possible.

**117**

possible that a college education directly teaches tolerance. But this does not systematically seem to be the case (Jacob, 1957; and Selvin & Hagstrom, 1960, for a possible counterexample). Also, Langton and Jennings (1968) reported greater tolerance for civil liberties among high-school seniors bound for college than among those not college bound. Thus correlations between tolerance and educational level among adults must be due in part to differential socialization prior to college.

Research indicates socialization of major political dispositions in childhood and adolescence. Most notably, support for authority (and for the political system more generally) is evident among preadolescents (Easton & Dennis, 1969; Hess & Torney, 1967). Also, there is early socialization of group-related attitudes such as party identification and racial prejudice (Greenstein, 1965; Harding, Proshansky, Kutner, & Chein, 1969; Hyman, 1959; Jennings & Niemi, 1968b; D. O. Sears, 1969).

The fact that significant socialization occurs in childhood and/or adolescence does not clarify how it occurs. Elementary and secondary schools attempt little teaching of concrete extensions of liberties (Hess, 1968); high-school civics courses are ineffective in increasing tolerance (Langton, 1969; Langton & Jennings, 1968). Also the home does not seem to be vital in socializing tolerance; Jennings and Niemi (1968b) reported almost no relationship between the civil liberties attitudes of high-school seniors and their parents.

## PURPOSE

The primary purpose of this study is to determine why in the U.S. political socialization fails to provide broad public support for basic civil liberties. The secondary purpose is to determine under what conditions children *do* acquire supportive attitudes. These purposes raise three specific questions.

First, what are children's attitudes toward free speech? Remmers and Franklin (1970) showed that high-school students, like adults, are unenthusiastic about civil liberties. Does the same hold for younger children? Are their attitudes stable and internally consistent, or are they semi-random, ephemeral "nonattitudes" of only passing interest (Converse, 1970)?

Second, what cognitive process do children use to decide in a concrete case of freedom of dissent? What attitudes do children bring to bear? The answer might seem simple. Almost everyone expresses antagonism toward ideas or behavior widely discrepant from one's own. An individual generally dislikes those with dissimilar values and beliefs (Byrne, 1961; McGuire, 1969; Newcomb, 1961; Rokeach & Mezei, 1966; Stein, Hardyck, & Smith, 1965) and derogates their positions (see, e.g., Hovland, Harvey, & Sherif, 1957). Presumably a person would block free expression of dissenting, deviating political groups both because he or she dislikes them and thinks their ideas foolish and possibly dangerous. If this holds, the best predictor of free-speech attitudes would be the child's degree of sympathy or antagonism toward the out-group in question.

Yet the general purpose of political socialization is to train the individual to redirect those natural impulses that conflict with the goals and needs of the political system. For example, much effort is devoted to giving the child a strong internalized motive to obey the law and identify with his or her national group. (The schools are particularly active in this endeavor; see, e.g., Easton & Dennis, 1969; Hess & Torney, 1967; Litt, 1963). For civil liberties, the main formal mechanism is presumably teaching abstract principles of justice, fair play, and free expression. The young person is supposed to generalize from these abstract principles to concrete cases. If this is effective, the best predictor of attitudes toward free speech in concrete situations would be the child's support for the abstract principle. Therefore, the second part of our investigation analyzes how the child weights antagonism toward dissenting groups against application of the free-speech principle in deciding concrete situations.

The third area of investigation deals with the antecedent variables determining these mediating attitudes and the main dependent variable, tolerance for free dissent in concrete situations. A variety of questions can be distinguished: (1) In terms of direct political socialization in the home, is there evidence for intergenerational transmission of tolerance? (2) Do nonpolitical socialization processes in the home indirectly account for political socialization? Research from the 1950s suggests that the psychologically "healthy" individual is more tolerant (see Adorno, Frenkel-Brunswik, Levinson, & Sanford, 1950; Lane, 1959, 1962; Mc-Closky, 1958). In particular, are children who are confident in their divergent thinking —their intellectual ability to think up imaginative ideas—not so threatened by variant ideas and therefore more tolerant of such expression in others? (3) What are the effects of peer-group influence; is there evidence of the early emergence of a college-bound reference group with tolerant norms? (4) Does socialization in the schools facilitate the development of tolerance?

## METHOD

### Sample

The sample consisted of 1384 children in grades 5 through 9 in Sacramento, California schools. The children, equally divided by sex, were ranged in age from 9 to 14 (with 10 exceptions). The racial distribution came to 67 percent white, 14 percent black, and 11 percent Mexican-American. Protestants constituted 50 percent of the sample, Catholics 30 percent, Jews 2 percent, and the rest were either from religiously mixed families or had no religious preference.

In April 1968 a self-administered questionnaire designed to assess political attitudes was completed during regular class time. About half of the children were in an experimental treatment group with a specially designed civics curriculum stressing the importance and legitimacy of group interests and political conflict instead of emphasizing only the consensual aspects of our political system. Controls were taught according to the standard curriculum. In June 1968 both groups completed a second questionnaire. Unless otherwise noted, the data are drawn from the first questionnaire.

### Attitudes toward Free Speech

The main dependent variables were four measures of attitudes toward free speech. One measured support of the abstract principle of free speech: "I believe in free speech for all, no matter what their views might be." The other three measured support for extending free speech to dissenting or nonconforming political groups in concrete situations: the right of a Vietcong sympathizer to buy TV time, the right of a Communist to make a public speech, and the right of the head of the American Nazi Party to have a meeting on a street corner.

### Attitudinal Mediators

Ethnocentrism, chauvinism, and attitude about communism were treated as possible mediators of the effects of our main independent variables on free-speech attitudes. The ethnocentrism scale measured whether children liked or disliked five peoples— Mexicans, Russians, Negroes, Chinese, and Africans (Lambert & Klineberg, 1967). Based on a median split, lows liked at least three groups of the five; highs liked two or less. High and low degrees of chauvinism were determined by agreeing or disagreeing with two items: "Our government is the best in the world" and "Other countries should try to make their governments exactly like our government." Finally, attitude about communism was assessed on the basis of a single item.

## Independent Variables

The independent variables were age, IQ, college motivation, self-esteem, and politicization. Based on a median split, the young group was 11 and under; the old group, 12 and above. For IQ, children again were divided at the median—110. College- and noncollege-bound groups were constructed on the basis of answers to, "Do you think you'll go to college?"

Self-esteem was measured by three scales —divergent thinking self-esteem, convergent thinking self-esteem, and schoolwork self-esteem—developed by P. S. Sears (1963). For each, high and low groups were determined by a median split. Divergent thinking self-esteem was measured by these items: "Compared with other boys and girls my age, how do I rate now? (1) interested in new things and excited about all there is to know; (2) having new original ideas; (3) letting my imagination go when I want to; (4) studying about things on my own; (5) seeing new ways of thinking about things and putting ideas together." Convergent thinking self-esteem was assessed through items like: "Compared with other boys and girls my age, how do I rate now? Knowing what to do to get the right answer to a problem." Schoolwork self-esteem was assessed through such items as "I sometimes feel that I just can't learn." We also included items on acquiescence response set (Couch & Keniston, 1960) and internal–external control (Coleman, Campbell, & Hobson, 1966), but the scales they comprised were insufficiently reliable.

Politicization was determined by scores on three scales: political knowledge, media exposure, and political involvement. The political knowledge scale assessed factual political information through multiple-choice questions such as, "The President of the United States is elected for how many years?" Media exposure was determined by such questions as, "Do you watch news programs on television?" Political involvement was measured by asking how many of a list of nine forms of political participation (e.g., "talked with my parents about our country's problems") the child had done. For each scale, children were classified as high or low based on a median split. We used political knowledge most often as the politicization variable because it was least dependent on the child's age or developmental level.

## Parents' Questionnaire

We also had data from parents of 23 percent of the children. Parent questionnaires were taken home by all responding children and returned by mail. They were completed anonymously but were coded to match their children's (also anonymous). Among the parents, 49 percent had some college exposure; 57 percent reported an annual income of over $9000 for head of household; 67 percent considered themselves Democrats, 21 percent Republicans, and 11 percent Independents. No items on free speech were included in this questionnaire, unfortunately.

## Comparisons with Adults

One goal of this chapter is to establish that socialization of attitudes toward free dissent does occur before adolescence. To show that preadolescents' attitudes already resemble those of mature adults, we intend to show that subjects' attitudes: (1) had about the same marginal distributions as those normally obtained from adult U.S. respondents, and (2) differed from those held by children of unusually high socioeconomic status in the same way that ordinary citizens' attitudes typically differ from those of adults in high-status, leadership, and/or decision-making positions. Although the methodology of our work differs from that of previous studies, the same free-speech items were used. Comparisons draw upon the following earlier studies:

*Adult mass samples.* McClosky's (1964) data are based on a 1957–1958 national sample of 1484 adults, each of whom mailed in a questionnaire left at his or her house. With a mail-back rate of about 50 percent, the sample overrepresented persons at higher educational levels. Stouffer (1955) reported the results of interviews in 1954 of a national cross-section sample of 4933 respondents. Prothro and Grigg (1960) interviewed 243 registered voters in two university communities in the late 1950s; the data of interest are from the 106 of their respondents with no college education.

*Adult elite samples.* Stouffer's (1955) elite sample consisted of 1500 community leaders selected by position (mayor, chairman of Democratic organization, American Legion post commander, etc.) from medium-sized cities. McClosky's (1964) elite consisted of 3020 delegates and alternates to the 1956 Democratic and Republican national conventions. From Prothro and Grigg's (1960) study, we have classified as "elite" their 137 college-educated respondents.

*Child elite sample.* Laurence and Scoble (1969) conducted a questionnaire study in 1965 with 48 children aged 9 to 12 attending University Elementary School at UCLA. These children are "elite" because 79 percent of their fathers had college degrees, 54 percent had some post-graduate professional work, and 65 percent were professionals or business executives.

**Data Analysis**

Analyses are based on chi square and a test of the significance of the difference between two sample proportions (yielding a z-score). Nonsignificant differences failed to attain the $p < .05$ level, using two-tailed tests of significance.

## CHILDHOOD ATTITUDES TOWARD FREEDOM OF DISSENT

Children's attitudes toward free speech are presented in Table 1. Most children,

even the youngest, have acquired attitudes on these matters; the largest proportion of "don't knows" was 34 percent. Also tolerance was expressed much more freely as an abstract principle than as a concrete policy. In the abstract, tolerance was more common than intolerance by a 4 to 1 margin; in concrete situations, margins ranged from 2 to 1 and up. In the section below, we present evidence for these two observations: (1) basic attitudes toward free speech are normally acquired in childhood, and (2) few children learn how to apply the abstract principle to cases involving dissenting political groups.

**Early Socialization**

Most children even by age 11 have some attitude about free speech both in the abstract and in the concrete, but attitude acquisition is still occurring. In our sample, the proportion of children with any attitudes at all on free speech tends to increase with age (Table 1). The difference is significant on two items and nonsignificant on the other two, suggesting that substantial acquisition of free-speech attitudes occurs before and during this period of late childhood.

Moreover, these early attitudes resemble those typically held by adult U.S. respondents, at least in gross respects. Table 2 compares tolerance in our sample with that obtained from earlier samples of adults and elite children (these comparisons across diverse studies cannot be precise but can yield useful approximations). Three parallels between adults and preadolescents clearly emerge. The distributions of opinion on free-speech items in our sample are strikingly similar to those obtained previously for adults (compare cols. 1 and 2). Also, among children, as among adults, the overwhelming majority of those with opinions endorse the abstract principle but refuse to grant free expression to dissenting political groups in concrete situations (compare, for mass samples, the top two rows with the bottom two rows). And finally, children

**TABLE 1   Tolerant Responses to Free-Speech Items by Age (Percentages)**

| | % TOLERANCE | | | % DON'T KNOW | | | % INTOLERANCE | | |
|---|---|---|---|---|---|---|---|---|---|
| | Young | Old | Total | Young | Old | Total | Young | Old | Total |
| *In the abstract* "I believe in free speech for all, no matter what their views might be."[a] | 55 | 65 | 60 | 30 | 20 | 25 | 15 | 14 | 15 |
| *In concrete situations* "Should a Communist be allowed to make a speech in this city saying that Communism is good?"[a] | 17 | 25 | 21 | 34 | 24 | 29 | 49 | 52 | 50 |
| "Should this man who wants to help the Vietcong be able to buy time on television to make a speech?" | 27 | 29 | 28 | 19 | 16 | 18 | 53 | 55 | 54 |
| "Should the police give the head of the American Nazi Party permission to have a meeting on a street corner?" | 12 | 14 | 13 | 23 | 21 | 22 | 65 | 65 | 65 |

Note.—*The "young" children were almost all aged 9 to 11, and the "old" 12 to 14; the smallest N on which the percentages are based is 563 for a within-age entry, 1226 for a total.*

[a]*Significant age differences in percent tolerant and in percent "don't know," p < .01.*

from elite groups, like adults from high SES or leadership groups, are considerably more favorable than nonelites to concrete extensions of free speech (compare the mass and elite samples in the bottom two rows).

The combination of widespread support for the principle of free speech with opposition to its extension to concrete situations is crucial in both children's and adults' opinions. Our data indicate further that it holds as a dominant pattern at the individual level of analysis. Table 3 shows that the most common pattern for the individual child in our study (excluding those without any attitude) was tolerance in the abstract and intolerance for concrete extensions. For example, 30 percent endorsed free speech in the abstract but would at the same time refuse to allow a Communist to make a speech favoring Communism. This exceeded the *combined* total of those consistently tolerant (15%) or consistently intolerant (9%) across both the abstract and concrete levels. Thus, this combination of tolerance and intolerance not only is most typical for large samples of children or adults but also is most commonly found for each individual child.

**The Slogan Nature of "Free Speech for All"**

The data suggest that belief in free expression is taught only as a slogan and that children therefore do not learn to apply it to concrete situations. Thus, when asked about the desirability of free speech for dis-

**TABLE 2    Typical Findings from Studies of Children's and Adults' Tolerance for Freedom of Speech**

|  | MASS SAMPLES | | ELITE SAMPLES | |
|---|---|---|---|---|
|  | Children | Adults | Children | Adults |
| *In the abstract* | | | | |
| "I believe in free speech for all no matter what their views might be." | 60[a] | 89[b] | 98[c] | 89[b] |
| "People who hate our way of life should still have a chance to talk and be heard." | 71[a] | 82[b] | 98[c] | 87[b] |
| *In concrete situations* | | | | |
| Allow Communist party member to make a speech in this city. | 21[b] | 27[d] | 88[c] | 51[d] |
| If a Communist were legally elected mayor of this city, the people should not allow him to take office. (*Disagree*) | 26[a] | 34[e] | 75[c] | 56[e] |

*Note.—In each case, entry is percent tolerant responses out of total sample tested.*
[a]*Zellman and Sears, described in text.*
[b]*McClosky (1964).*
[c]*Laurence and Scoble (1969).*
[d]*Stouffer (1955).*
[e]*Prothro and Grigg (1960).*


**TABLE 3    Consistency between Abstract Principle of Free Speech and Application in Concrete Situations as a Function of Age**

| | TOTAL SAMPLE | | | CHANGE WITH AGE | | |
|---|---|---|---|---|---|---|
| CONCRETE SITUATION | Commu-nist Speech | Viet-cong TV | Nazi Street Corner | Commu-nist Speech | Viet-cong TV | Nazi Street Corner |
| Consistent tolerance | 15 | 18 | 9 | + 7* | +3 | +2 |
| Abstract tolerance + Concrete intolerance | 30 | 33 | 40 | + 4 | +4 | +5 |
| Consistent intolerance | 9 | 10 | 10 | + 1 | +1 | −1 |
| Don't know | 44 | 36 | 39 | −12* | −7* | −6* |
| Other | 2 | 3 | 2 | 0 | −1 | 0 |

*Note.—The entry is the percent holding the specified combination of attitudes toward free speech in the abstract and concrete situations. For example, 18 percent both agreed with free speech in the abstract and felt it should be extended to the Vietcong, while 33 percent agreed with it in the abstract but refused to extend it to the Vietcong; 36 percent replied "don't know" to at least one of these two items. These percentages were 3 percent and 4 percent higher, and 7 percent lower, respectively, in the older than in the younger age group.*

*\*Age changes significant beyond the .01 level.*

senting political groups, they respond primarily in terms of their attitudes toward the group, rather than generalizing from the principle. There are several kinds of evidence for this assertion.

*"Free speech for all" as mainstream norm.* First, children more likely to be in contact with the mainstream of adult political norms are considerably *more* likely to adopt the abstract slogan of "free speech for everyone," but *not* to be substantially more tolerant in concrete situations. Older, more intelligent, and more politicized children all should be more informed about the dominant political norms, and thus can be considered closer to the political mainstream of society. As expected, (1) older, significantly more than younger, children agreed with the slogan, as shown in Table 1; (2) a greater proportion of high- (66%) than of low- (56%) IQ children likewise agreed with the slogan ($p < .05$); and (3) on all three indices, more politicized children were more likely to accept it. Children high in political knowledge were 9 percent more likely than those low ($p < .01$); the difference was 9 percent for media exposure ($p < .01$) and 14 percent for political involvement ($p < .01$). However, mainstream children were not consistently more likely to support free speech in concrete situations. Of fifteen possible relationships—three free speech items by age, IQ, and three politicization variables—only three were significantly positive.

In short, mainstream children, though more attuned to the rhetoric of free speech, are no more cognizant of its practical implications. These data support the conclusion that civil liberties are taught as slogans and concrete applications are taught not at all.

*No deductive generalization.* If children derive their opinions about concrete situations from applying abstract principle, one should expect consistency of two kinds. First, attitudes on abstract and concrete items should be consistent. But as shown in Table 3, fewer than a third of the children manifest consistency in this sense.

Second, application of general principle should lead to consistency across groupings of concrete situations (Table 4). Here the picture is even more dismal. Across groupings, at most only 7 percent consistently allowed free expression. In contrast, from 30 percent to 53 percent consistently *denied* free speech to deviant political groups. Thus, very few children, fewer than 10 percent in every case, could possibly be applying any common abstract principle to concrete situations.

*No broader context.* Children do not see freedom of speech as part of a larger scheme for managing interpersonal, social, and/or political conflict. We included questions on conflict at the personal level, for example, feelings about arguments between parents and children; and at the political level, for example, whether it would be better if people in government did not argue with each other. Over many comparisons between these items and those on free speech, the relationships vary in direction and are generally nonsignificant. If civil liberties are not taught in broader terms, one can readily understand why children oppose extending free speech to possibly dangerous political deviants.

*Antagonism toward dissenters.* Attitude toward dissenting political groups emerges as a major determinant of support for civil liberties in concrete situations. For example, antagonism toward communism was closely related to rejection of free speech for Communists (Table 5). Of those who said, "I don't agree with Communism but some of its ideas are good," 39 percent were willing to permit a Communist speech, but of those who felt Communism is "completely wrong," only 13 percent were willing to permit this. In fact, attitudes toward dissenting groups accounted better than chauvinism or nationalism for intolerance about free speech.

**TABLE 4    Consistency of Tolerance or Intolerance across Concrete Free-Speech Situations (Percentages)**

|  | Consistent Tolerance | Consistent Intolerance | Mixed | Don't Know |
|---|---|---|---|---|
| *Consistency across situations* |  |  |  |  |
| Nazis: Street-corner meeting, auditorium, speech attacking Jews, newspaper ad attacking President | 2 | 45 | 14 | 39 |
| Vietcong: TV speech, auditorium speech to raise money, street corner for meeting | 7 | 40 | 21 | 32 |
| *Consistency across groups* |  |  |  |  |
| Auditorium: Vietcong speech to raise money and Nazi for speech attacking Jews | 5 | 53 | 12 | 30 |
| Street corner: Vietcong meeting, Nazi meeting, and Communist speech | 4 | 30 | 21 | 45 |
| Media: Vietcong TV speech and Nazi paper ad attacking President | 7 | 41 | 19 | 34 |

*Note.—The "don't know" column includes all subjects giving "don't know" on one or more items. Additional concrete items not directly dealt with in the text are included in this table for purposes of explication.*

**TABLE 5    Tolerance for Free Speech as a Function of Attitudes toward Communism**

|  | ATTITUDE ABOUT COMMUNISM | | | | | |
|---|---|---|---|---|---|---|
|  | "I think Communism is completely wrong" | "I think Communism is wrong but I can understand why some people like it" | "I don't know what I think about Communism" | "I don't agree with Communism but some of its ideas are good" | "I agree with Communism" | *p* |
| *In the abstract* |  |  |  |  |  |  |
| Free speech for all | 64 | 66 | 51 | 69 | 39 | n.s. |
| *In concrete situations* |  |  |  |  |  |  |
| Communist speech | 13 | 24 | 21 | 39 | 38 | <.001 |
| Vietcong on TV | 22 | 31 | 30 | 39 | 47 | <.001 |
| Nazi on street corner | 11 | 17 | 12 | 19 | 26 | <.001 |
| *N* | 482 | 324 | 411 | 200 | 51 |  |

*Note.—Entry is percent giving a tolerant response on the free speech item among those holding the attitude toward Communism specified. P values index significance of variation due to linear regression.*

Also, antagonism toward dissenting or deviant groups generalizes to other groups and thus contributes to rejection of free speech more generally. Table 5 indicates that antagonism toward Communism was related significantly to rejection of free speech for the Vietcong and the Nazis. Most important, though, rejection of free speech in concrete situations is better predicted by antagonism toward the dissenting group than by support for the abstract principle. This too may be illustrated with attitudes toward Communism, which are more strongly related to decisions in free-speech cases involving Communists than are feelings about free speech as a principle (Table 6). A child will grant free speech to Communists only if Communists have some good ideas; apparently believing that "*anybody* should be given free speech" is not sufficient for extending this basic right.

## Summary

Attitudes about free speech for dissenting or nonconforming political groups are acquired by a socialization process different from that involved in acquiring the abstract

TABLE 6   Tolerance for Free Speech in Concrete Situations as a Joint Function of Attitudes about Communism and Free Speech in the Abstract

| TYPE OF CONCRETE SITUATION | ATTITUDE ON FREE SPEECH PRINCIPLE | ATTITUDE ABOUT COMMUNISM | | | | |
|---|---|---|---|---|---|---|
| | | "I think Communism is completely wrong" | "I think Communism is wrong but I can understand why some people like it" | "I don't know what I think about Communism" | "I don't agree with Communism but some of its ideas are good" or "I agree with Communism" | p |
| "Should a Communist be allowed to make a speech saying that Communism is good?" | Supports | 16 | 29 | 27 | 47 | <.001 |
| | Opposes | 4 | 21 | 16 | 28 | <.001 |
| "Should a Communist be allowed to teach in this school?" | Supports | 12 | 21 | 17 | 26 | <.001 |
| | Opposes | 4 | 18 | 20 | 28 | <.01 |

*Note.—Entry is the percent tolerant in concrete situation cited, among those with specified attitudes toward abstract free-speech principle and communism. For example, of those thinking Communism is "completely wrong" and supporting free speech in the abstract, 16 percent were willing to allow a Communist to make a speech (the remaining 84 percent either would not allow it or gave no opinion). Significances are based on a test for trends in the chi-square contingency table (Maxwell, 1961).*

principle of free speech. The abstract belief in "free speech for all" is learned as a slogan bearing no concrete implications. In contrast, most children's attitudes toward rights of free expression for specific dissenting political groups depend more on their attitudes toward the groups. Children do not deduce from an abstract principle to concrete situations, and there is no evidence that free speech in concrete situations is taught as a dominant norm of the adult political world.

Specifically, (1) mainstream children (older, more intelligent, more politicized) were not more tolerant than nonmainstream children about free speech in concrete situations; (2) attitudes toward the abstract slogan were not related to support for free speech in concrete situations; (3) few children showed consistent tolerance across concrete situations as might be expected if they were applying a general abstract principle; (4) tolerance was unrelated to general acceptance of political, social, and interpersonal conflicts; (5) tolerance for free expression in concrete situations *was,* however, closely related to the degree of sympathy or antagonism children had for a dissenting political group and, to a lesser degree, to their attitudes toward other such groups; and (6) chauvinism or nationalism did not itself represent a force toward intolerance of deviant political groups. Rather, intolerance and repression seemed to be evoked mainly by negative reactions to symbols of political nonconformity.

In February 1971 a replication study was conducted on sixth- and eighth-graders ($N = 946$) in Fresno, California. For the most part, the similarities in the findings are striking. We again observed that support for the abstract principle far outstripped tolerance in concrete situations. The "mainstream" children again were the strongest boosters of the slogan of free speech, but not of civil liberties in concrete situations. Attitudes toward conflict, indexed by five new scales, were related only haphazardly to either abstract or concrete versions of free speech. Attitudes toward Communism

again related extremely strongly to tolerance for Communists' civil liberties ($p < .001$), but not to the slogan. And attitudes toward Communism accounted for tolerance in concrete situations much better than did the slogan, and even more so than they did in Table 6 above.

One point does represent some departure. A scale measuring political chauvinism was significantly ($p < .05$) related to intolerance for concrete extensions of civil liberties. So also were several items on U.S. war policy not used before: Children who were more open to criticizing U.S. policy were much more likely to support concrete extensions of civil liberties. By 1971, conflicts over the Indochina war may thus have had the unfortunate side effect of associating loyalty to the nation with intolerance for dissent. This had not been true of children in 1968.

## ORIGINS OF TOLERANCE

Although most children did not show consistent tolerance for dissenters across concrete situations, some did consistently grant free speech. This tolerance could be acquired in a number of ways: in the home directly by indoctrination or modeling or indirectly through the socialization of nonpolitical personality dispositions; as part of peer-group norms; or even in school. In this section we consider the relative contributions of these socializing agents.

### Political Socialization in the Home

Much literature on political socialization has emphasized the role of the family in socializing basic political predispositions (see particularly Hyman, 1959). A family might influence the child's political orientations in a number of ways (e.g., Dawson & Prewitt, 1969). Most obviously, parents could teach directly by selective reinforcement and punishment or by serving as models for attitudes by open communication but not overt teaching. Additionally, nonpolitical dispositions such as personality characteristics might ultimately lead a child to adopt parental attitudes. In such cases, the child need not be exposed to the parent's political attitudes; personality predispositions would inevitably lead the child to replicate the political and social attitudes held by the parents.

Our inquiry about the possibility of direct transmission of political attitudes from parents to offspring begins with an assessment of the political climate in the home. Unfortunately, except for party identification, we have no direct measures of parents' political attitudes. But unlike most studies, we do have reliable demographic information on a subsample of parents. As mentioned above, adults' demographic variables (especially educational level) are closely associated with tolerance for free speech. Thus they provide a measure—even if somewhat indirect—of variation between families in tolerance for civil liberties.

*Education.* While college attendance is an excellent indicator of adult support for civil liberties (Key, 1961; Prothro & Grigg, 1960; Stouffer, 1955), in our data parental education bore virtually no relation to children's attitudes about free speech. This finding is consistent with Pock's report (1967) that parental education was unrelated to civil liberties attitudes among high-school students.

*Income.* Paralleling previous research (Prothro & Grigg, 1960), family income was rather strongly associated with tolerance for free speech. On both the abstract principle and the three concrete situations, higher income was associated with greater tolerance. Differences between high- and low-income groups are significant for the Communist speech item (25% versus 14% tolerance) and the Nazi street-corner item (19% and 9%).

A more complex hypothesis is that discrepancies among the various dimensions of one's status (such as education and income) are associated with ultraconservatism, intolerance, racism, and so on (see Rush, 1967). D. O. Sears' review (1969) of the relevant adult data found relatively little support for this hypothesis; in our data, if anything, the exact opposite occurs. Tolerance in concrete free-speech situations occurred among children whose parents' income and education were inconsistent with each other. However, the effect is statistically significant on only one item.

*Religion.* Children from Protestant and Catholic families differed little in tolerance of political nonconformists. They did not even differ in degree of anti-Communism, despite the Catholic Church's longstanding hostility toward Communism. If anything, Catholic children were somewhat more tolerant.

*Party identification.* Children with Democratic parents were somewhat more tolerant in general, though significantly so only on one item. With parental education controlled, party identification was not significantly related to the free-speech items.

In sum, such parental demographic characteristics as education, party preference, and religion did not relate significantly to tolerance (nor did race; see Laurence, 1970, for a complete analysis). But higher-income families had more tolerant children than did lower-income families. These data correspond to Jennings and Niemi's findings (1968b) that parents and children agree relatively little on civil liberties issues. Basically the political environment of the home seems not to have an important effect.

## Nonpolitical Socialization in the Home

The family may, however, have a crucial impact on the child's level of tolerance in less direct ways. The child's general values and personality development may influence interpretations of the political world, including political tolerance.

*Self-esteem.* The main personality variables we considered were *divergent thinking self-*

*esteem, convergent thinking self-esteem,* and *schoolwork self-esteem.* In every case but one, tolerance for free speech was greater among high self-esteem children (Table 7). Although all three scales generated statistically significant differences, *divergent thinking self-esteem* was the strongest predictor of tolerance for political nonconformity.

Similarly, *divergent thinking self-esteem* was closely related to tolerance for Communists. Favorable attitudes toward Communism were significantly more common among the high *divergent thinking self-esteem* children than the low ($p < .01$), whereas the feeling that Communism is "completely wrong" was equally common at each level of self-esteem. No such relation held between *divergent thinking self-esteem* and ethnocentrism: Liking for various foreign nationalities was not related to confidence in divergent thinking.

That low self-esteem was related to anti-Communism but not ethnocentrism suggests that threat mediates the relation between self-esteem and tolerance. Whereas there is a distinct threat posed by Communists, Vietcong, and Nazis, no threat is posed by most of the various foreign nationalities in the ethnocentrism index. That *divergent thinking self-esteem* acts primarily by reducing the threat posed by deviance is also suggested by its relation with racial tolerance. Across a variety of racial items, high self-esteem white children tended to be more tolerant. So anti-Communism provokes intolerance for concrete extensions of civil liberties partly because it threatens the child's confidence in his or her own ability for entertaining divergent thoughts.

However, personal threat is not the sole explanation for the effect of anti-Communism on intolerance for free speech. Anti-Communism is related to intolerance quite independent of variations in *divergent thinking self-esteem* (Table 8). On the most relevant item, measuring tolerance for a Communist's making a pro-Communist speech, both high self-esteem and sympathy with Communism significantly contributed to free-speech tolerance with the other dimension controlled. We suspect, therefore, that

**TABLE 7   Tolerance for Free Speech as a Function of Self-Esteem**

| | | | TYPE OF SELF-ESTEEM | | | | |
|---|---|---|---|---|---|---|---|
| | | Divergent Thinking | | Convergent Thinking | | Schoolwork | |
| *In the abstract* | | | | | | | |
| I believe in free speech for all . . . | | high | 64* | high | 64** | high | 65* |
| | | low | 57 | low | 56 | low | 58 |
| *In concrete situations* | | | | | | | |
| Communist speech | | high | 25** | high | 23* | high | 22 |
| | | low | 15 | low | 18 | low | 20 |
| Vietcong on TV | | high | 31** | high | 29 | high | 26 |
| | | low | 24 | low | 27 | low | 30 |
| Nazi on street corner | | high | 15* | high | 16** | high | 16* |
| | | low | 11 | low | 10 | low | 11 |

*Note.—Entry is percent giving a tolerant response on the free-speech item among high and low self-esteem children. Starred entries indicate significant difference between self-esteem levels.*

   *$p < .05$.

   **$p < .01$.

**TABLE 8** **Percent Tolerant on Free Speech as a Joint Function of Divergent Thinking Self-Esteem and Attitude toward Communism**

| | DIVERGENT SELF-ESTEEM | ATTITUDE TOWARD COMMUNISM | | |
| --- | --- | --- | --- | --- |
| | | I think it is completely wrong | Tolerance or acceptance of Communism | Difference |
| *In the abstract* | | | | |
| I believe in | High | 67 | 69 | + 2 |
| free speech | Low | 63 | 59 | − 4 |
| for all . . . | Difference | + 4 | +10 | |
| *In concrete situations* | | | | |
| Communist speech | High | 16 | 35 | +19** |
| | Low | 9 | 19 | +10** |
| | Difference | + 7* | +16** | |
| Vietcong on TV | High | 24 | 38 | +14** |
| | Low | 18 | 28 | +10* |
| | Difference | + 6 | +10 | |
| Nazi on street corner | High | 11 | 19 | + 8* |
| | Low | 9 | 17 | + 8* |
| | Difference | + 2 | + 2 | |

Note.—*Entry is percent giving a tolerant response on the free-speech item. For example, of those high in self-esteem and thinking Communism completely wrong, 67 percent believed in free speech for all; the remaining 33 percent either did not or had no opinion.*
*p < .05.*
**p < .01.*

children's intolerance for political nonconformity is due *both* to insecurities about their own thinking and to direct socialization of antagonism toward dissenting political groups.

*Intelligence.*   On none of the three concrete free-speech items was intelligence significantly associated with tolerance. It was significantly associated with acceptance of the general principle of free speech. With IQ controlled, *divergent thinking self-esteem* remained positively related to tolerance in all three concrete situations, both among high- and low-IQ children (though not significantly so in five of the six comparisons because of the reduced number of subjects). Evidently intelligence does not explain away the effects of self-esteem.

In short, the direct socialization of political attitudes inimical to nonconformist groups lessens the child's tolerance for extensions of free speech. In addition, the child apparently develops attitudes toward such groups less directly based on confidence in his or her own capacity for divergent thinking. When there is little confidence, the child tends to be harsh and unwilling to extend the privileges of free speech. With greater self-confidence, he or she is more likely to see some good in such groups and extend this right. These self-esteem effects hold, controlling for any of our other variables: They hold within almost any demographic group, controlling for intelligence and age; indeed, they generally are strengthened with controls.

This consistent relationship between self-esteem and tolerance was not found in the 1971 data. Instead, the relationships with convergent and divergent thinking self-esteem were mixed and nonsignificant. High self-esteem was actually negatively (though not significantly) related to tolerance for civil liberties among black children. Blacks were generally somewhat more tolerant than whites. We attempted to relate this finding to the Angela Davis case, the black self-professed Communist who had been fired from UCLA. However, black children's highly favorable attitudes toward Angela Davis were totally unrelated to their considerable support for concrete civil liberties. They seem to have responded to her mainly as a black; their attitudes toward her were unrelated to their attitudes toward Communism or civil liberties. On the other hand, white children's antagonism toward Angela Davis was closely related to intolerance for concrete civil liberties, even with attitude toward Communism controlled. They appeared to respond to Angela Davis as a Communist; thus their attitude toward Communism determined their support for her, just as it had determined their tolerance for concrete civil liberties.

## Peer-Group Influence and Intent to Go to College

Previous research has found that college-bound high-school students are more tolerant than those not college-bound (Langton & Jennings, 1968). Our data replicate this basic finding, even in the preadolescent years. The differences are significant in two of the three concrete situations. Such findings have puzzled researchers. Family influence does not seem to account for this greater tolerance, since parental and offspring attitudes were essentially uncorrelated (Jennings & Neimi, 1968b). Nor could it be due to direct effects of college, since the students were still in high school.

One possible interpretation is that the college-bound have high *divergent thinking self-esteem*, which both points them toward college and makes them more tolerant. The second is that a reference group of chil-

dren bound for college forms in high school, resulting in a set of common political and social norms. One norm might well be tolerance for dissenters. Our data test for the possibility of such a reference group emerging even prior to high school.

As implied by the first interpretation, the college-bound are considerably higher in *divergent thinking self-esteem*. Of the high self-esteem children, 74 percent think they would go to college, as compared with only 61 percent of those low in self-esteem ($p < .01$). Not surprisingly, confident children are more likely to make college plans.

But the differences in self-esteem do not entirely account for this greater tolerance. Intent to go to college was associated with somewhat greater tolerance even with self-esteem controlled (though the strength of the relation is diminished). Also this relationship was somewhat stronger among older children in all three concrete free-speech situations, suggesting the formation with age of a cadre of children bound for college with attitudes typical of college-educated adults. The evidence of a reference group is admittedly indirect. Additional evidence is provided by the finding that college-bound white students were considerably more tolerant of racial matters than those not college-bound.

*Personal threat versus social influence.* Two processes of political socialization seem operative in the independent contributions of self-esteem and college-boundness. The effects of *divergent thinking self-esteem* are most powerful when threat is involved. As indicated earlier, self-esteem was closely related to tolerance for the gravest threat of all, Communism, but not at all related to ethnocentrism, which refers mostly to non-threatening foreign peoples. Apparently self-esteem affects tolerance only when threatening out-groups are involved.

On the other hand, the emerging reference group indexed by college motivation evidently inspires tolerance for nonthreatening out-groups. College motivation was significantly related to absence of ethnocentrism ($p < .01$), but only to having an opinion regarding Communism ($p < .01$), not to antagonism toward it. The presence or absence of political threat may, then, serve as one index regarding the probable contributions of college motivation and self-esteem to tolerance for political diversity.

*Politicization and budding elites.* Political elites are more favorable than the public at large to civil liberties in concrete situations, and there is some evidence as well that elite preadolescent children are also distinctive (see Table 2). The final question is whether we can discern a group of children that might be described as a budding elite, that is, highly politicized, unusually tolerant, and so on.

As indicated earlier, politicization alone does not seem to be related to tolerance at this early age: It is closely related to acceptance of the slogan, but generally not to understanding its concrete applications. Is there though some cadre of highly politicized children who begin to apply the slogan to concrete situations? The evidence is ambiguous. There is some increase in consistent tolerance with age but the difference is small (Table 3). Age and politicization do interact to produce increases in consistency between the abstract principle and concrete situations. On the other hand, age and politicization do not together increase consistent tolerance *across* concrete situations. Thus, it is unclear whether any group of children normally exists at this age that both has the impulse of tolerance and understanding for nonconforming groups *and* thoughtfully applies the basic principle of free speech to concrete situations involving such groups. Perhaps the socialization of future elites requires more advanced age or special situations.

## DISCUSSION

We have presented evidence for the socialization during late childhood and early adolescence of free-speech slogans, attitudes toward deviant political groups, and tolerance of free speech for political dissenters. The strongest data indicated that support for concrete civil liberties is dictated largely by the strength of the child's antagonism toward the dissenting out-group; rarely does it stem from applying a general principle of free expression or broader views about conflict management. Somewhat weaker data indicated that children's confidence in their ability to think divergently contributed to tolerance, presumably by reducing the personal threat posed by nonconformist or deviant groups.

To what extent does this pattern persist throughout adulthood? It is likely that attitudes toward out-groups are formed in childhood, and, when later reinforced, persist in similar (though perhaps cognitively more complex) forms throughout life. The same is also true for such slogans of U.S. democracy as "I believe in free speech for all" and other symbolic representations of fealty to the U.S. system (Easton & Dennis, 1969; Hess & Torney, 1967; Lane, 1962).

Concrete extensions of civil liberties, however, are more likely another matter. We have little evidence that children are taught this directly either in the schools or in the home. Rather, they seem to deduce their positions from their attitudes toward the dissenting group in question. Therefore, we would not expect this early socialization to produce consistent tolerance (or even intolerance) across groups. Greater consistency and greater tolerance alike could be expected if the child were taught how to apply the principle of free speech to concrete instances. But such teaching is not common, and thus the child is left to apply rather narrowly any prejudices or sympathies felt toward the group or individual in question.

Finally, to what extent do the schools contribute to tolerance for dissent—and what potential do they have? The data do not indicate that much positive teaching of concrete civil liberties occurs in most elementary and junior high schools. And children do not markedly increase in tolerance with age (Table 1). Attitudes toward concrete liberties do not suggest that they are the product of careful school training. It would appear that the best that schools accomplish is to allow a self-confident child to respond self-confidently to symbolic political threats, that is, to respond empathically to nonconformist groups and in a way that does not deprive them of their rights. This behavior, so obviously consistent with democratic ideology, unfortunately characterizes only a minority of these preadolescents.

It may be idealistic to hope that tolerance for basic civil liberties could be related to a larger view of conflict management. But there is evidence that providing such a larger context does increase preadolescents' understanding and thus their tolerance. Our data were collected as part of an experiment in teaching a more sophisticated view of political conflict to fifth- through ninth-graders. The experimental program produced consistent increases in children's acceptance of political conflict; more important, tolerance for civil liberties also increased somewhat more in the experimental than in the control group (e.g., on the Communist speech item, experimentals became 5% more tolerant, while controls became 3% less toler-

ant). These findings indicate that teaching a more sophisticated view of conflict can produce both more accepting attitudes toward conflict and greater tolerance for civil liberties.

Nevertheless, our data show that the main "message" that young children normally get about nonconforming minorities is that they should be repressed. If Communism is bad, then Communists should not be allowed to speak freely. They are taught free speech only in slogan form, not how to apply it to concrete situations; and clearly they are not taught any larger view of society that would convey why such extensions *must* be made. Early political socialization in this area does little or nothing to keep the child from exercising a natural human proclivity to derogate and repress those with differing or rejected values and ideas.

In this sense, early political socialization fails to teach the meaning of U.S. democracy. It succeeds in teaching the child affection for the U.S. system and distaste for its ostensible enemies. It succeeds in teaching the conventional slogans of the U.S. system. However, it fails utterly to convey the unique and desirable feature of the U.S. system—its tolerance for diversity and individual liberties.

# CHAPTER 12

# Socialization of Attitudes toward the Legal System[1]

## —JUDITH V. TORNEY

Socialization to the legal system was explored with data on attitudes toward police, the Supreme Court, and the fairness of laws obtained from about 9000 elementary-school children tested in 1961–1962. Analysis of variance was used to examine differences by school grade, sex, social class, and intelligence. Four models of the socialization process were discussed. Lower-middle class children tended to give higher ratings to the police than either upper-middle or lower-class children. There was also a significant increase with age in the amount of difference between the attitudes of boys and girls.

The socialization of children into the legal system includes diverse objectives; children must come to recognize laws, perceive their functions, accurately view their sources, develop relevant attitudes toward those who enforce them, and guide their own behavior to conform to morality and legality. The ways a society encourages the development of these capacities are also diverse. No one agent can claim full responsibility for success or failure of socialization. No single process is adequate to explain how the objectives are attained.

[1] The questionnaire data analyzed in this chapter were gathered with support from the U.S. Office of Education, Cooperative Research Project 1078 (Robert Hess and David Easton, Senior Co-Directors). Support for the phase of analysis presented herein comes from a Grant-in-Aid from the Society for the Psychological Study of Social Issues and from the Urban Education Research Program, University of Illinois at Chicago Circle. The author is grateful to Anne Vollmar and Tony Kay, and to students in an Education 210 Class, University of Illinois, Chicago Circle, Winter 1970.

The kind of socialization that results in children's viewing themselves as part of the political and legal process has been studied extensively (Adelson & O'Neil, 1966; Easton & Dennis, 1969; Hess & Tapp, 1969; Hess & Torney, 1967; Langton, 1969). The contents of political socialization have been mapped by these and other studies (Adler & Harrington, 1970). Many authors have given tentative answers to where and in what context socialization occurs. But, for the most part, they have not dealt with the more critical question of how socialization takes place. The questions of locus and process are not the same. For example, the home may exert an influence as children model the ideas of their parents without parents' dispensing any reinforcement for the modeling. Or parents may reward their children for behaving toward the legal system in ways they consider appropriate.

The socialization process has been treated in so limited a way chiefly because process, a dynamic concept, is more difficult to conceptualize and deal with than locus or structure. So strong is our awareness of the influences of home and school on children's attitudes that we easily take a simplified, stereotyped view of the process: The parents state the rules, the teacher provides factual information about laws, both punish deviance, and the child absorbs and accumulates attitudes and modes of behavior (see, e.g., Truman, 1963).

## PSYCHOLOGICAL MODELS FOR SOCIALIZATION TO THE LEGAL SYSTEM

Four models of the socialization process are useful for understanding the sources of attitude development and change (Hess & Torney, 1967).

### Accumulation Model

The child gathers much raw material about laws and legality in single, often unrelated units. The child learns what behaviors are prohibited by laws and is taught rather directly that Congress makes laws, police can arrest the lawbreakers, and so forth. The *accumulation model* assumes the teacher or parent controls the information flow and the child is a passive recipient. The model does not assume a consistent relation among elements of the child's information and makes few assumptions about his or her attitudes or needs. That the child vastly overrates an officer's range of authority, for example, cannot be explained by this model. Because reactions to rules and authorities are complex responses largely affected by the child's needs, the accumulation model alone is inadequate for understanding legal socialization.

### Identification Model

The *identification model* focuses most directly on the child's imitation of adults. While the parent may wish to see the child imitate law-obeying behavior, he or she does not want imitation carried to the point of the child's trying to make rules for others.

Thus, while identification is important to the socialization process, this model cannot account for most legal socialization.

### Role Transfer Model

The *role transfer model* is in some respects the reciprocal of the identification model. Instead of copying the behavior of an authority, the child takes the role as a subordinate (as a child in the home, as a pupil in school) and transfers or generalizes role-appropriate behavior to the political system without any direct reinforcement from socializing agents. Children structure and sometimes distort information in accord with these transferred role expectations. They may make assumptions based on vague information. But similarities among many levels of social authority (family, school, nation) make the role transfer model particularly important.

### Cognitive Developmental Model

A fourth model is the *cognitive developmental model*. Development is defined by cognitive developmental psychologists like Piaget (1932), Kohlberg (1969), and Zigler (1963) as sequential change in the organization of knowledge and the basis of judgment. The thought processes of the 7-year-old differ radically from those of the child of 14 in using, transforming, and synthesizing information. The older child has more ability to deal with complex, abstract aspects of the social world and take the perspective of others. The tendency to process information in a personalized, egocentric fashion declines with age, while the ability to reverse a situation increases. Like the role transfer model, the cognitive developmental model stresses that a child develops attitudes in somewhat the same way he or she acquires a native language—by evolving and then applying expectations in new situations, by forming specific concepts through generalization from scattered experience, and by detecting various kinds of deviance from already established expectations.

A number of cognitive developmental processes originally detailed by Piaget are important for understanding this model (see Flavell, 1963; Flavell, Botkin, & Fry, 1968; Piaget, 1932). Data from political socialization studies generally do not allow delineation of age-bound stages. The cognitive developmental model is best studied through interview data, where it is possible to explore the thinking behind attitudes, their sources, and links with other beliefs (see Adelson & O'Neil, 1966).

Consideration of the four models suggests that simple models do not adequately account for attitude acquisition. Sensitivity to several processes by which such attitudes are formed seems to be most useful. Therefore this chapter adopts a broad perspective. Drawing on all four models, it presents an analysis of children's attitudes toward the legal system, taking into account age, IQ, social class, and sex differences.

## SOURCES OF DATA

Data were gathered primarily from a questionnaire and an interview. Questionnaire ratings of agreement with attitude statements come from a comprehensive political socialization study begun at the University of Chicago in 1961–1962. About 12,000 white children in elementary school (grades 2 through 8) were selected from one large city and one small city of each major region of the United States (about 1500 from each city). Details of this study are presented in Hess and Torney (1967). In addition to the questionnaire material, information about IQ was collected from school records (different tests converted to a common scale); father's occupation was also recorded. Besides describing their current curriculum, teachers answered a questionnaire similar to that administered to the children.

The interview, a relatively structured pro-

**TABLE 1    Content of Questionnaire Items**

| ITEM | SCALE | | |
|---|---|---|---|
| 1. How much do policemen help decide which laws are made for our country: | 1<br>very much | . . . | 4<br>not at all |
| 2. The policeman: | 1<br>I like him more than anyone | . . . | 6<br>less than almost anyone |
| 3. The policeman: | 1<br>would always want to help me if I needed it | . . . | 6<br>would not usually want to help me if I needed it |
| 4. The policeman: | 1<br>makes important decisions all the time | . . . | 6<br>never makes important decisions |
| 5. The policeman: | 1<br>can punish anyone | . . . | 6<br>can punish no one |
| 6. The policeman: | 1<br>can make anyone do what he wants | . . . | 6<br>can make almost no one do what he wants |
| 7. The Supreme Court: | 1<br>can punish anyone | . . . | 6<br>can punish no one |
| 8. All laws are fair: | 1      2<br>YES    yes | | 3      4<br>no      NO |

tocol, was administered by students at the University of Illinois, Chicago Circle, in 1970 as part of a class project. Forty children were studied from grades 3 through 8. No information about IQ was available for these subjects.

## RATIONALE OF THE ANALYSIS

Data on children's attitudes toward the legal system, law, and legality were analyzed for socialization effects. (See Tables 1 and 2.) Analyses of variance performed on questionnaire responses tested for age, IQ, social class, and sex differences.[2] The interviews provided qualitative insights particularly on developmental differences in children's perspectives.

On one level, differences in attitudes by age (indexed by grade in school) are the basis of normative descriptions of attitude endorsement. On a second level, age changes in attitudes, as supplemented by interviews, measure the impact of cognitive development. Differences in attitudes expressed by children of different intelligence levels also are consistent with cognitive development factors. But note that IQ as measured by standardized tests is not identical with cognitive ability as defined by psychologists like Sigel (1963) and Kohlberg (1969).

Three social class groups were compared: children whose fathers were unskilled workers (lower class), skilled sales or clerical workers (lower-middle class), and executives or professionals (upper-middle class).[3] Social class is important as an index—some-

---

[2] In previous reports of these data (Hess & Torney, 1967), a special graphing technique was used to suggest which differences were likely to be statistically significant. In this chapter, the differences previously observed are examined statistically.

[3] These class labels vary somewhat from the status labels used earlier in Hess & Torney (1967). As indicated by the occupations listed, for this more careful analysis the present terms seem more descriptive of the actual levels.

times a rough one—of a child's experiences with authority, particularly in the family. This experience may affect the need structure brought to the wider political and legal world. Strong social class differences in roles and expectations suggest the importance of the role transfer model for understanding attitude development.

Children's social class and intelligence have been found to be positively correlated. Some investigators infer the influence of intelligence from observed differences between social classes (Greenstein, 1965). However, it is important to determine the effects of intelligence within a particular social class. Also, with children of a given intelligence level, how do those from the lower class differ from those of the upper-middle class? Are there striking interactions between social class and intelligence? Does low IQ have a different impact on children of low social status than on those higher in position? Or is the effect of IQ the same regardless of class? Significant interaction terms in analyses of variance would indicate differential impact.

Sex differences have an emerging place in socialization research. The accumulation model may explain sex differences—for example, the girl who is reinforced for expressing certain feelings about law and politics because agents of socialization feel they are appropriate for females. The identification model would focus on the female child's identification with political and legal attitudes expressed by her mother. But these explanations seem less useful than the view that the child's relations with authority at home and in school are transferred to the political and legal systems.

In sum, information about laws gained from adults through accumulation and identification provides important raw material. However, the child's own framework as it is imposed on that material—the connections (sometimes false), the differentiations (sometimes unusual), and the generalizations (sometimes unduly wide)—are vitally important. These are the processes deline-

**TABLE 2   Summary of Analysis of Variance Findings (Questionnaire Data)**

| ITEM AND DIRECTION | MAIN EFFECT | | | | SIGNIFICANT INTERACTIONS |
| --- | --- | --- | --- | --- | --- |
| | Age (Grade) | IQ | Social Class | Sex | |
| 1. Policeman has more influence over lawmaking as seen by | Younger | Less bright | Lower | —[a] | None |
| 2. Policeman liked more by | Younger | (n.s.)[b] | Lower-middle | Girls | Sex difference more pronounced for older |
| 3. Policeman seen more willing to help by | Younger | Brighter | Lower-middle | Girls | Sex difference more pronounced for older |
| 4. Policeman seen making more important decisions by | Younger | (n.s.) | Lower-middle | Girls | Sex difference more pronounced for older |
| 5. Policeman seen as more capable of punishing by | (n.s.) | (n.s.) | Lower-middle and Upper-middle | Girls | None |
| 6. Policeman seen as able to make people do what he wants by | (n.s.) | (n.s.) | (n.s.) | Girls | IQ differences are of different pattern in the SES groups |
| 7. The Supreme Court seen as more capable of punishing by | Older | Brighter | (n.s.) | Boys | Sex difference more pronounced for older |
| 8. More laws seen as fair by | Younger | Less bright | Lower and Lower-middle | Girls | Sex difference more pronounced for older. IQ differences more pronounced for older |

[a]Factor not included in this analysis.

[b]Not significant at $p < .01$.

ated by the role transfer and cognitive development models of attitude acquisition.

## RESULTS AND DISCUSSION

### Police and the Supreme Court

The legal system has a major impact on children through its personal representatives. Thus, the origin of many attitudes toward the legal system may be found in attitudes toward authorities. Taking the policeman as an example, there is a link in the child's mind between power to enforce laws and possession of influence on lawmaking. An analysis of variance of the effects of grade, social class, and IQ (sex was not entered in this analysis) on children's responses to a question about the policeman's influence on what laws are made for our country indicated that grade in school has the most striking and highly significant effect ($p <$ .001). For younger children the policeman has much more influence; they see lawmaking and law enforcement joined syncretically. This may be because children transfer expectations to the legal system from situations they know (home and school) where the same authority (parent or teacher) makes and enforces rules.

Social class and IQ also show strong effects ($p <$ .001); children of lower IQ and lower SES see the policeman as more involved in lawmaking. There were no stable interactions among the three variables. The tendency for lower SES children to view the policeman as more influential may be due to their inclination to transfer expectations from the more authoritarian atmosphere they experience at home. The IQ differences that were apparent may reflect the higher level of cognitive development that is required before a child can separate functions seen occurring together in the social realm. Both IQ and grade effects support the importance of cognitive factors but, of course, do not rule out the importance of the child's learning in school about the functions of the legislatures.

The importance of the models for understanding legal socialization is further clarified by examining the relation of five additional scale judgments about the policeman. Two judgments concerned his personal attributes, one his decision-making influence, and two his power to control. An analysis of variance testing for grade, IQ, social class, and sex effects (plus interactions) was performed for each scale.

Significant differences were attributable to grade in three of five ratings. Older children liked the policeman less ($p <$ .001) and thought less of his helpfulness ($p <$ .001) and his decision making ($p <$ .001) than did younger ones. On the two items most clearly part of the policeman's role—power to punish and power to make people do what he wants—there were no significant age differences. These latter functions are major components of police job-related activity rather than characteristics merely associated with law enforcement.

Only one "policeman" rating was related to IQ; the policeman was perceived as more helpful by the brighter children ($p <$ .001). Regardless of IQ, there seems to be strong agreement at all age levels about the power of the policeman.

Younger children seem to link, in a syncretic fashion, the power to punish and control with other positive qualities they see in the policeman. When they mature, their cognitive development enables them to separate power attributes from other facets of the policeman's activity just as they have separated lawmaking and law enforcement. This tie between power and positive feeling is important for understanding children's more general reactions to authority systems. For most young children, might is right. Power is admired and its possession implies personal goodness. In the early political socialization literature this was commented on in explaining the child's changing image of the President (Torney, Hess, & Easton, 1962).

On the three nonpower police items, there were significant social class differences—all in the direction of more positive ratings by children in lower-middle class families. These children thought more of the policeman's decision making ($p < .001$), helpfulness ($p < .01$), and personal likeability ($p < .01$) than did either lower- or upper-middle class children. These data, collected in 1961–1962, were an interesting precursor of the law-and-order attitudes later found among lower-middle class adults. In that social group, positive attitudes toward the authoritarian function of legal systems were visible in young people. Lower-class children differed in a linear fashion from the middle-class groups on only one policeman rating— they saw the policeman as having less power to punish ($p < .01$). No significant social class effect was associated with the "power to control."

In summary, a statistically significant tendency for lower-middle class children to glorify authority as represented by the policeman was found. This pattern contrasts with general findings about other parts of the political system (political parties, other governmental institutions), reported in Hess and Torney (1967). In those analyses, when there were significant social class variations, the lower-middle and upper-middle classes were similar while the lower class gave different responses. On the items analyzed here on perceptions of laws and the policeman, there was a "lower-middle class effect"; that is, the lower-class and upper-middle class children are generally similar while the lower-middle class children stand out in their positive attitudes.

The source of these observed differences can be surmised. The lower-class child is more likely to interact with the police in situations with substantial negative emotion; he or she may also model negative attitudes seen expressed by parents and peers. The source of the more negative feeling on the part of the upper-middle class child, on the other hand, may result from viewing the police as social inferiors and from hearing parents express negative attitudes, but seldom through direct interaction. The lower-middle class child, in contrast, does not have extensive negative personal contacts with police or see them as social inferiors, but instead perhaps considers them occupational models and hears parents glorify authorities and authority roles. We cannot determine from the available data which of these factors is most important.

Finally, sex was a crucial factor. On all five dimensions, girls rated the policeman more positively than did boys ($p < .001$ in each instance). In the three ratings where the main effect for grade was significant (liking, helpfulness, and decision making), there was also a significant interaction between sex and grade due to an increase with age in the sex differences in attitudes toward this legal authority figure. While boys showed a striking decline with age in these ratings of the policeman, the decline with age for the girls was less pronounced.

The role transfer model helps interpret these sex differences. In home and school girls learn to be submissive and respect authority; they transfer these orientations and role expectations to relations with other authorities. These differences are congruent with Lynn's (1969) theory of sex-role development. According to Lynn, the process of acquiring sex role determines the characteristics of that role. The girl, learning the female role directly from a personal relation with her mother, interprets personal cues and is sensitive to affiliative ties. In contrast, the boy, generally abstracting masculine qualities from a number of models, develops this ability to abstract and is less likely to focus on personal relations.

While girls' attitudes toward the policeman are clearly more positive, boys rate the Supreme Court higher ($p < .001$), perhaps because it is an institution requiring greater abstraction to comprehend its process. Boys see the Supreme Court as able to punish more people than do girls; girls see the policeman as able to punish more people than do boys. These findings are consistent with other rating scales of both policemen and the Supreme Court given in Hess and

Torney (1967). The rating of the Supreme Court confirms the importance of cognitive factors in the child's differentiation of the political-legal world. Older children view legal authority in a more abstract and less personalized fashion ($p < .001$); boys and children of high IQ ($p < .001$) also take a more abstract view. There were no social class differences in this more abstract attitude toward the Supreme Court.

## Functions of Laws

Moving from lawmaking and enforcement (and from questionnaire to interview), we examine the source of children's ideas about the functions of laws. Many of the attitudes seem to have transferred from attitudes toward school rules. First, a third-grader:

INTERVIEWER: What do you think would happen if we didn't have any more rules in school?

THIRD-GRADER: Someone could get hurt or fall. . . .[4]

INTERVIEWER: What do you think would happen if there weren't any more laws?

THIRD-GRADER: Lots of people would be hurt and there'd be accidents. That's all.

While younger children see laws more as preventing individual misfortune rather than regulating group functions, all children describe the same consequences of suspending rules or laws. First, a third-grader and next an eighth-grader:

INTERVIEWER: Why does the school need to have rules?

THIRD-GRADER: If you don't have rules, you could do anything you want and the teachers couldn't teach. . . .

INTERVIEWER: What would happen if there were no laws?

---

[4] Ellipsis indicates that a number of other questions were asked between the questions about functions of rules and functions of laws.

THIRD-GRADER: Then there wouldn't be traffic signs. Criminals would be loose and people would do anything that they want.

INTERVIEWER: Why do you imagine it is necessary to have rules in school?

EIGHTH-GRADER: Well, because it would cause a lot of disorder. There are 1600 children in our school, and if they could do anything they want, there would be no learning really. They'd do just what they want and they wouldn't learn. . . .

INTERVIEWER: Do you have any idea as to what might happen if all laws were abolished?

EIGHTH-GRADER: Complete disorder, and people would do what they wanted, and there would be absolute, complete disorder. There would be no control at all over people. Life would not be safe.

There is considerable transfer of beliefs about laws from beliefs about school rules. Children even use the same words. Also older children perceive laws as serving social functions, not just preventing personal accidents. They predict the existence of chaos under conditions either of no rules or no laws. Children by 12 or 13 believe that the innately evil nature of humankind is controlled by rules and laws; social order would collapse without them (Adelson & O'Neil, 1966; Tapp, 1970a; Tapp & Levine, 1970). No students said that abolishing rules or laws would make no difference because people would behave well anyway. Social scientists may see development of conscience or moral scruples as a bulwark against immoral behavior even in the absence of enforceable laws. But children, whose sense of moral judgment is less developed, do not view conscience as a deterrent to wrongdoing. A recent cross-national survey of civic attitudes found that the functions of laws and of the police were perceived more clearly by preadolescents than were the functions of eight other social institutions (Torney, Oppenheim, & Farnen, 1975).

### Fairness of Laws

Children believe all laws should be fair. Although some show changes at a relatively early age toward what fairness entails, other young children, in judging what makes laws fair, show much the same general pattern as that of young children in dealing with problems of personal moral action (Kohlberg, 1969). What is important in judging the "right thing to do" is often whether they personally will be hurt or punished. As this third-grader cites:

INTERVIEWER: What makes a law fair?
THIRD-GRADER: If you don't do what's right, you'll get hurt.
INTERVIEWER: What is the most fair law you can think of?
THIRD-GRADER: One-way streets—that you go one way. If you don't obey, you will get hurt.

Likewise, to a fifth-grader unfair rules and laws are those that prevent people from gratifying their wishes:

INTERVIEWER: What is the most unfair rule in your school?
FIFTH-GRADER: When you eat candy or chew gum you got to spit it out or else you get in trouble.
INTERVIEWER: Why is this rule unfair?
FIFTH-GRADER: Because kids love to chew gum and candy. . . .
INTERVIEWER: What is an unfair law you know that they have made?
FIFTH-GRADER: They have a curfew law for young children and you can be arrested. That's unfair. Us kids would like to get out, too . . . go to parties, movies.

Younger children tend to link fairness with adjectives that describe general goodness as in this interchange with a third-grader:

INTERVIEWER: What is the most fair rule in your school?
THIRD-GRADER: You should stand up when someone comes in our room and listen to him.
INTERVIEWER: What makes that a fair rule?
THIRD-GRADER: Because it's polite.

Universal compliance defines the fairness of rules and laws for this fourth-grader:

INTERVIEWER: What is the most fair rule in your school?
FOURTH-GRADER: All of them are fair.
INTERVIEWER: What makes them fair rules?
FOURTH-GRADER: People follow them. . . .
INTERVIEWER: What makes a fair law?
FOURTH-GRADER: I don't know . . . when everybody follows it, I guess.
INTERVIEWER: What is the most unfair law that you can think of?
FOURTH-GRADER: I don't think there's any. All laws are fair.

Again, the similar wording of fair school rules and fair laws is striking, though several questions intervened.

Some third-, fourth-, and fifth-graders have advanced beyond hedonism, universal compliance, and general goodness. For instance, this third-grader perceives equality as the criterion of fairness for both rules and laws:

INTERVIEWER: Can you think of a rule at your school that's fair?
THIRD-GRADER: You're not supposed to play ball.
INTERVIEWER: Why do you think that's fair?
THIRD-GRADER: Because they don't let anyone. They don't let any one person.
INTERVIEWER: What do you think is an unfair rule at your school?
THIRD-GRADER: Running. Some people get hollered at but some people don't. . . .
INTERVIEWER: What do you think makes a law fair?
THIRD-GRADER: That just no one person has to obey it. The whole country, like all the people have to obey it.
INTERVIEWER: Can you think of a law that's fair?
THIRD-GRADER: That you're not supposed to steal stuff.

INTERVIEWER: Why do you think that's fair?

THIRD-GRADER: Because people don't get away with it. Like when they steal something they always get caught. . . .

INTERVIEWER: What do you think makes a law unfair?

THIRD-GRADER: That they catch some people but like other people don't get caught.

Although certain enforcement is intimately involved with laws for this student, there is a feeling for equality in defining fairness that is absent from the earlier interviews.

Furthermore, the questionnaire data indicate a very marked decline with age ($p <$ .001) in the belief that all laws are fair. Although it is a less striking difference, children of low IQ ($p < .001$) are also more likely to view laws as universally fair. The IQ difference increases with age. These two relations suggest the importance of cognitive developmental factors to judgments of fairness. Social class differences ($p < .001$) are less pronounced than IQ differences, but—quite consistently—lower- and lower-middle class children are more inclined to rate law as fair. Girls as well are more positive in their evaluations of law ($p < .01$). Although significant and increasing with age, the sex difference is not nearly as great as those differences reported in attitudes toward authority figures. The developmental changes in belief that laws are fair cannot be accounted for solely by the accumulation of taught values. Few schools even at grade 8 point out unfair laws to children. It seems rather that older and brighter children embrace the ideal of fairness and yet recognize that the administration of laws may not always be fair. Injustice occurs "if the law is not carried out right," as an eighth-grader put it. Likewise, the concept of what makes a law fair differs in different children, as indicated in the analysis of interviews. The younger child sees all laws as good, preventing bad occurrences. The older child may still believe that laws serve positive functions but fairness now includes the equal distribution of justice.

## SUMMARY AND CONCLUSIONS

The analysis was based on two types of data concerning legal socialization. The first was questionnaire ratings related to age, in most cases showing pronounced changes leading to less syncretic, more differentiated perspectives toward legal functions and authority figures, greater abstraction, and less idealistic views of the operation of the legal system. Likewise, the sex differences were pronounced, particularly at the older age levels. Girls viewed the system in a more personalized way and in most cases retained these attitudes, which were characteristic of young children, longer than did boys. Although this analysis also probed the influence of social class and IQ on legal socialization, these dimensions accounted for less variation than did grade and sex. Some data could be interpreted as indicating a glorification of police authority by lower-middle class children (tested in 1962). Such evidence allows us to see linkages between attitudes prevalent in youth in one period and a rise in similar attitudes in adults at a later period and further verifies the importance of studies of socialization as predictors of future adult political attitudes. Contrary to expectation, there was also a general absence of significant interactions between IQ and social class. The second data source, an interview, was suggestive particularly of the age differences in how problems of legal justification and fairness are conceptualized and handled.

The questionnaire and interview data are fascinating descriptions of major group differences in legal attitudes. They also have implications for understanding the socialization process. For example, age and IQ differences in attitudes toward the legal system (questionnaire) and age-linked changes in judgments regarding school rules and laws (interview) illuminate the role of the cognitive developmental model in understanding the socialization process. Sex differences in attitudes (questionnaire) and similarities in children's judgments of school rules and laws (interview) suggest the importance of the role transfer model.

The next step in understanding socialization process must include studies that *a priori* have tests for alternative processes or models. Questionnaire data or small numbers of interviews enable a researcher to do no more than hint at the model of process involved. Cognitive abilities—particularly ability to reason abstractly and use moral principles in nonlegal situations—would be important components of such a study. Experimental work comparing the efficiency of different methods based on the four models of socialization process would be another useful step. Such research could well have an impact on fields as divergent as school organization, school–community power relations, social studies curriculum, and cognitive training programs.

Although some social forces are not predictable, understanding the way in which current ideas and attitudes have come about is crucial for predicting the course of future events. It would be shortsighted to assess, understand, or attempt to change only the attitudes of adults. Early socialization is a crucial precursor to any kind of long-standing change in overall social forces. Political scientists discovered this 15 years ago; those interested in law are discovering it now (in this regard, see Buergenthal & Torney, 1976). Concurrent interest in process and in attitude content as expressed by growing children is crucial to progress in this research area and in society at large.

# Socialization into Legal Systems

## INTERSTITIAL BRIEF

*JUNE LOUIN TAPP*
*FELICE J. LEVINE*

The impact of social variables on the legal socialization and resocialization of individuals is specifically considered in Part IV. In these chapters, psychologists and lawyers seek to clarify the potential effects of situational and institutional contexts on legal behavior not by examining formal structure but by evaluating the network of opportunities, goals, pressures, and constraints. These contributions in no way purport to describe all the environmental influences that might affect people's perceptions of themselves, the law, and their roles in relation to rule systems. As a unit, however, they should reveal how the treatment and training that people receive, the nature of their interactions in diverse climes, and the consequent definitions they experience about rules, rights, and roles are vital to the development of the individual and society.

The first chapter by Rokeach, Miller, and Snyder assesses situational determinants of behavior and presents the results of an empirical study of police value patterns. They found that typically policemen were more concerned than were a representative national sample with personal values and less with social values. Policemen ranked equality as less important than did white and especially black U.S. respondents. The obvious question, of course, is the extent to which occupational exposure contributes to this discrepancy. The answer is very little. Rokeach, Miller, and Snyder report that police value patterns were not attributable to occupational socialization. Matching policemen to a sample of working-class whites revealed homogeneity of values with those of similar background. While matching did not account for all discrepancy, personality factors—and not age or years of service as a police officer—would seem to account for the rest.

These data should not be interpreted as support for the view that situational contexts do not or cannot have an impact. The high visibility of the police organization in a community may contribute to a strong self-selection process among individuals with compatible personalities and belief structures. To alter this situation, Rokeach, Miller, and Snyder propose broadening the recruitment base and intensive professional resocialization programs including such techniques as feedback to the police about conflict between their values and those of others. Introducing such socialization procedures might ultimately modify not only police values but also the environment of the police organization itself.

The Rokeach, Miller, and Snyder chapter underscores the significance of initial socialization and yet the potential of socializing strategies to effectuate change. Both of these themes are addressed directly in the chapters by Freund and by Levine and Tapp. Freund argues that the school should be a more active agent of legal socialization by exposing children early to both the substantive content of the law and the principles of legal reasoning. Taking the view that law is a dynamic process that facilitates "everyday events and transactions," Freund emphasizes the need for educational programs that, besides imparting information, encourage alternative views, convey the ambiguity of the decision-making enterprise, develop a sensitivity to ethical dimensions, and explicate the multiple purposes for sanctions. To Freund, these skills are an essential for "ethically sensitive and socially resourceful individuals." Further, they can best be cultivated in the school setting by the use of relevant age-related materials and the introduction of participatory and role-playing opportunities.

Integrating psychological and jurisprudential assumptions, Levine and Tapp further elaborate the strategies and contexts for effective legal socialization. From the framework of a biosocial interactive model, these investigators seek to provide a set of working hypotheses on the "legal worlds" of individuals and institutions. To evaluate the "match" (or "mismatch") between social inputs and the individual's natural capacity, Levine and Tapp assess the legal reasoning of adults (graduating law students, elementary and high-school teachers, and prisoners) who are both products and potential agents of socialization. Basically, adult groups (like the college sample presented in greater detail in Chap. 9) exhibited a system-maintenance, law-and-order orientation to rule systems. Further, the commonalities between the adult and child data suggest that stabilization occurs during the adolescent years and that substantial consistency is demonstrated during adulthood. Given these data, Levine and Tapp discuss the social conditions that should stimulate legal development regardless of age or circumstance. Abstracting variables previously tested only in a limited way and/or in experimental settings, the authors posit four strategies for effective socialization—acquisition of legal knowledge, mismatch and conflict, participation, and continuity among rule systems—and analyze how these approaches could be implemented in the legal systems of community and school.

Compatible with the perspective on law and legal socialization elaborated by Levine and Tapp, Parke in his chapter on child abuse similarly locates the family "within a structure of multiple, interactive, and overlapping rule systems." Rejecting the blame/responsibility or health/disease emphasis of the psychiatric model, Parke analyzes the ways in which cultural, community, and familial factors affect the development of abusive patterns and conversely how they could be employed to achieve rehabilitative goals. This interactional perspective shifts the focus from the individual parent to the environment—both within the family and between the family and other rule systems. Through an integrative review of research on child-abuse patterns, Parke highlights the dysfunctional effects of such conditions as "abuse" labeling and punitive punishment techniques. Taking the view that learned behavior can be modified, the author elaborates resocialization alternatives that involve the police, courts, and social services agencies undertaking constructive measures (e.g., accessibility, support, participation) in addition to social control functions.

Like Parke, Haney and Zimbardo also consider the situational versus personal determinants of legal behavior. To illuminate the effects of interpersonal dynamics and situational control across criminal justice settings, these investigators report on their simulated prison experiment and present scenarios of prisoners and guards based both on real prisons and on the prison simulation. In their experiment they found that individuals randomly assigned to role-playing conditions *unknowingly* were socialized into criminality, whether they were prisoners or guards. Within six days, the behavior of stable, representative, middle-class Caucasian males became pathological and antisocial. Haney and Zimbardo assess the emergence of these patterns not as the product of deviant personalities *but* as the result of pathological situations that rechannel and distort the behavior of normal individuals. Beyond dramatizing the impact of social situational variables within the context of total institutions, Haney and Zimbardo more generally convey the potential power of situations to socialize individuals into dehumanizing—or likewise humanizing—roles.

Parke's as well as Haney and Zimbardo's chapters emphasize that locating the causes for individual pathology and "criminality" in the individual has led to insufficient attention to interactive variables. The authors persuasively demonstrate that the definitions, roles, and labels constructed in situational contexts can significantly affect the way people come to view themselves and the way they are viewed by others. These contributions well illustrate how traditional rehabilitative and therapeutic approaches neglect social factors and are biased against evaluating—and potentially reordering—the network of legal arrangements. It is these very issues, addressed in systemic terms, that Levine and Shuman, respectively, consider in their chapters.

Levine's chapter deals with the conceptual confusion in labeling and handling criminality, mental illness, and political behavior. Levine points out how, with each of these terms, there is great diversity in definition and use from place to place and from time to time. Further, he emphasizes that the problem is compounded by the fact that there is considerable overlap in applying these labels to the same or similar manifestations of social deviance. This problem he views to be symptomatic of a more basic ambiguity about the appropriate goals for systems of social control—whether criminal justice or mental health. In light of the potential for social injustice, Levine calls for a careful scrutiny of the premises on which regulatory systems operate. Throughout his review and presentation of empirical data, he is mindful of the need to evolve rules compatible with human dignity and due process, however well-meaning the effort to reduce deviance or disease.

Shuman also presses for a critical look at the objectives and assumptions underlying the criminal law. In his view, insufficient knowledge and specificity have been brought to bear at each stage of the criminal justice process—from labeling deviance to articulating solutions for its control. Within this framework, Shuman primarily focuses on the rehabilitative and punishment objectives of the criminal law. Not persuaded by the Skinnerian view that the more humane way to deal with individuals is to absolve them of the responsibility of being free, Shuman rejects the notion that criminal deviance is sufficient basis for involuntary or indeterminant therapy in the name of rehabilitation: After analyzing several solutions to deviance—institutionalization, conditioning, and biological reconstruction—he suggests that the criminal law system may not be worth the cost of its maintenance. As an alternative he proposes that we speculate what life would be like if only tort remedies were available for deviant conduct.

Though diverse in scope, the selections in Part IV raise important questions regarding the socialization impact of various modes of governance whether in the microsystems of family, school, professional group, and prison or the macrosystems of community, criminal justice, and mental health. In each case, one might ask, what are the styles of legality that individuals bring to these settings and what are the distinctive and common characteristics across these climes? What effects, both functional and dysfunctional, evolve in the course of an individual's interactions in legal systems? Part of understanding the nature of law requires describing the realities as well as contemplating the institutional potentialities. Therefore, as the reader embarks upon this group of chapters, the following queries might serve as a guide: Given the observations in Parts II and III on "The Role of Law as Socializer" and "Patterns of Legal Development," what are the possibilities of creating a legal clime where reciprocity, cooperation, and shared expectations may prevail? Further, what procedural and substantive values are compatible with such ends?

# CHAPTER 13

# The Value Gap between Police and Policed[1]

—MILTON ROKEACH, MARTIN G. MILLER, and
JOHN A. SNYDER

This chapter describes a study on the value patterns of a midwestern municipal police force, and compares police values with those of representative samples of black and white U.S. respondents. The data on police values support the hypotheses that personality factors and social backgrounds are more important than occupational socialization in understanding police value systems. The police values are not necessarily representative of U.S. value patterns, either black or white, suggesting that either more differential recruitment and/or more direct resocialization procedures are needed for improving police–citizen relations in this country.

Descriptive data on values in U.S. society have been reported for representative samples of blacks and whites varying in income (Rokeach & Parker, 1970), religious devotion (Rokeach, 1969a, 1969b), and voting preferences in the 1968 presidential campaign (Rokeach, 1971). From these we have arrived at some understanding of what U.S. value patterns are and how experience and environment affect socialization. Our purpose here is (1) to extend these descriptions to include data on the value patterns of police, (2) to determine the extent to which police values coincide with those found for U.S. blacks and whites, (3) to evaluate whether the values police express result more from early preoccupational socialization or from socialization in this particular occupational group, and (4) to consider some policy implications.

There are theoretical and empirical grounds for anticipating identifiable value patterns among police. The role that police officers are asked to play in their community includes control, service, and order-maintaining functions (Wilson, 1968). We may thus expect that values stressing the desirability of preserving the status quo, concerning obedience and conformity to the laws and norms of society, would be emphasized. Police personnel are expected to be recruited, or recruit themselves, to law enforcement from politically conservative strata of society and from among those whose personalities predispose them to gain special satisfaction from police work. After recruitment, we would expect to find, as with any other occupation, increasing socialization into prevailing police value patterns.

Available evidence suggests that police attitudes and also personality characteristics are indeed distinctively different. Westley (1951), Guthrie (1963), Watson

---

[1] The research reported herein and preparation of this chapter were supported by a grant from the National Science Foundation.

(1967), and Bayley and Mendelsohn (1969) reported the police to be generally homogeneous in their attitudes and beliefs on such topics as law enforcement as a worthwhile occupation, the courts and the law, youth and minorities, and the public. Bayley and Mendelsohn (1969) found, for example, that 89 percent of police officers feel that police work is more important than other jobs. The state police officers of Preiss and Ehrlich's study (1966) showed attitudes stressing departmental loyalty, self-sacrifice, and unquestioning acceptance of orders. The officers in Goldman's study (1963) viewed the juvenile court as unfair to the police and too lenient with offenders. Reiss (1967) found that most police officers studied in Boston, Chicago, and Washington perceived jurists as unfair, judges as too lenient, and probation officers as not doing a good job. Similarly, negative attitudes by police toward correctional agencies, probation officers, and juvenile court judges were reported by Piliavin and Briar (1964) and by Cicourel (n.d.). Generally negative attitudes of police toward youth were reported by Reiss (1967), Wilson (1968), and Bayley and Mendelsohn (1969) due to youth's defiance, rebelliousness, and disrespect for the law. Goldman (1963) and Reiss (1967) found police to be generally critical of the public because of their lack of cooperation or interest in effective law enforcement.

Studies have focused on the "police personality." Police personnel were reported to be suspicious (Dodd, 1967; Skolnick, 1966), cynical (Toch, 1965; Westley, 1951), isolated from personal friends and the public (Clark & Gibbs, 1965; Dempsey, 1967), and suffering from feelings of powerlessness and self-hate (Chwast, 1965). Several studies found that police generally suffer from feelings of low self-esteem and are preoccupied with the importance of obtaining "respect for the law" (Becker, 1963; Pfiffner, 1967; Reiss, 1967; Westley, 1951; Wilson, 1963). But contrary to popular belief, police scores on authoritarianism and dogmatism are sim-

ilar to those obtained by groups of comparable education (Bayley & Mendelsohn, 1969; Niederhoffer, 1967; Smith, Locke, & Walker, 1967). Niederhoffer (1967) found a mean $F$-scale score of 4.15 for 166 police recruits —close to the mean of 4.19 for the working-class sample reported in *The Authoritarian Personality* (Adorno, Frenkel-Brunswik, Levinson, & Sanford, 1950). Moreover, police score relatively low in anomie (Bayley & Mendelsohn, 1969; Nierderhoffer, 1967), and contradictory findings were reported for punitiveness (Marshall, 1966; McNamara, 1967).

The literature has consistently pointed to the conservative political orientation of police officers. Guthrie (1963) saw police as typically approaching problem solving in an either–or, black–white manner. Wilson (1967) observed that Chicago police officers are unreceptive to social change. Skolnick (1966) concluded about the California police in his study that "a Goldwater-type of conservatism was the dominant political and emotional persuasion [p. 61]." Watson (1967) found that patrolmen and detectives are more conservative than command personnel. Bayley and Mendelsohn (1969) reported that Denver police are more conservative and more Republican than the community as a whole. They also found that age is not related to political orientation, concluding that selection rather than socialization after recruitment explains police conservatism. Lipset (1969) summarized the findings on police personality:

On the whole, the less education people have, the more likely they are to be intolerant of those who differ from themselves, whether in opinions, modes of culturally and morally relevant behavior, religion, ethnic background, or race. The police, who are recruited from the conservative, less-educated groups, reflect the background from which they came . . . [p. 78].

Several general hypotheses can be formulated: (1) Police value systems differ distinctively from those of other groups in U.S. society; more specifically, the greater conflict between police and blacks leads us to expect a greater value gap between them than between police and whites. (2) Police value systems should be highly similar to the value systems of those from comparable social backgrounds; that is, police values are a function, at least in part, of selective recruitment from among certain strata of society whose members had been similarly socialized. (3) Police values are also a function of personality predisposition; that is, police are selectively recruited from among those whose value systems predispose them toward a career in law enforcement. (4) Police values are a function of occupational socialization; that is, distinctive police value patterns should become increasingly evident as a function of length of exposure, training, or identification with the value patterns of law enforcement institutions.

## METHOD

### Value Instrument

The concept of value has previously been defined as a preferred end-state of existence (terminal value) or a preferred mode of behavior (instrumental value): "To say that a person 'has a value' is to say that he has an enduring belief that a specific mode of conduct or end-state of existence is personally and socially preferable to alternative modes of conduct or end-states of existence [Rokeach, 1968a, pp. 159–160]." A *value system* is a rank-ordering of values along a continuum of importance. Operational measures of value are obtained by the Rokeach Value Survey, which provides separate, rank-ordered data for 18 terminal and 18 instrumental values. The two sets of values are presented in alphabetical order to the respondent with the instruction to rank them "as guiding principles in your daily life." Each value, along with a defining phrase, is printed on a label. The respondent merely

rearranges each set of 18 values by ranking them in order of importance into boxes 1 to 18. Median test–retest reliability of the value systems (with time intervals ranging from three to seven weeks) ranges between .78 and .80 for terminal values and between .70 and .72 for instrumental values (Penner, Homant, & Rokeach, 1968; Rokeach, 1970a). For comparable time intervals, test–retest reliabilities of individual values range from .51 to .88 for the 18 terminal values, and from .45 to .70 for the 18 instrumental values.

### Subjects and Procedure

The Rokeach Value Survey was completed by 153 white, male police officers of a middle-size, Midwest police department in April 1968. At the time of the survey, the department had a sworn force of 188 white members—181 men officers and 7 policewomen. The women were excluded from the study. Of the 181 men, 28 did not complete the survey mainly because of sickness or vacations.

The survey was administered to command officers (sergeant and above) at two sessions of a command officers' in-service training school held at a nearby police headquarters. To lower-ranked personnel the value survey was administered at police headquarters in 16 small groups of from 4 to 30 police officers. All officers had been directed to attend these sessions by the chief of police. Sessions were scheduled throughout the day and evening for 7 days so that all personnel could take part in the study. (For a report of additional data, see Miller, 1971.)

The same survey was also administered by the National Opinion Research Center in April 1968 to an area probability sample of U.S. residents over age 21. Some of these data are reported elsewhere (Rokeach, 1969a, 1969b, 1970, 1971; Rokeach & Parker, 1970). Of major interest here are the value similarities and differences found between police personnel and representative national samples of 561 male whites and 93 blacks. A national rather than local police sample would have permitted a more robust comparison with national samples of blacks and whites. Practical considerations, however, dictated the selection of this more readily available group.

## RESULTS

Tables 1 and 2 show the data on both terminal and instrumental values. For all values we show median rankings and the rank ordering of these medians from 1 to 18 (composite rank order). Tests of significance were obtained by the Median Test (Siegel, 1956)—between police and male whites and between police and male blacks.[2]

_____

[2] For analysis of similarities and differences between black and white values see Rokeach and Parker (1970).

## Similarities Between Police and National Sample

Note, first, that the value systems of the three groups are in important respects similar—reflections, no doubt, of general values in the U.S. All three samples placed a relatively high value on such end-goals as *a world at peace, family security,* and *freedom* and low value on *an exciting life, pleasure,* and *a world of beauty.* Also, police did not differ significantly from whites or blacks on 9 of the 18 terminal values—*a comfortable life, freedom, happiness, inner harmony, pleasure, salvation, self-respect, true friendship,* and *wisdom.* On instrumental values, all three groups placed a relatively high value on being *honest, responsible,* and *ambitious* and a low value on being *obedient* and *imaginative.* Police did not differ significantly from whites or blacks on 6 of the 18 instrumental values—*ambitious, clean, courageous, imaginative, loving,* and *polite.*

**TABLE 1   Terminal Value Medians and Composite Rank Orders for Police Sample and for National Samples of Male Whites and Blacks**

|  | Police N=153 | | NORC Whites N=561 | | NORC Blacks N=93 | |
|---|---|---|---|---|---|---|
|  | Md. | Rank | Md. | Rank | Md. | Rank |
| A comfortable life | 8.0 | (8) | 8.1 | (6) | 6.6 | (5) |
| An exciting life | 12.9 | (15) | 14.5* | (18) | 15.1** | (18) |
| A sense of accomplishment | 7.3 | (5) | 8.1 | (5) | 10.6** | (11) |
| A world at peace | 5.3 | (2) | 3.6** | (1) | 4.1 | (1) |
| A world of beauty | 16.0 | (18) | 13.4** | (15) | 14.6** | (17) |
| Equality | 11.7 | (14) | 10.1* | (12) | 4.3** | (3) |
| Family security | 2.9 | (1) | 3.7 | (2) | 4.7* | (4) |
| Freedom | 5.3 | (3) | 5.0 | (3) | 4.2 | (2) |
| Happiness | 7.7 | (6) | 8.0 | (4) | 7.4 | (7) |
| Inner harmony | 11.3 | (13) | 11.1 | (13) | 10.7 | (12) |
| Mature love | 10.2 | (10) | 12.3** | (14) | 13.4** | (15) |
| National security | 11.1 | (12) | 8.8** | (9) | 10.9 | (13) |
| Pleasure | 13.7 | (16) | 14.2 | (17) | 13.6 | (16) |
| Salvation | 10.5 | (11) | 9.8 | (11) | 10.4 | (10) |
| Self-respect | 7.0 | (4) | 8.4 | (7) | 6.9 | (6) |
| Social recognition | 14.4 | (17) | 13.9 | (16) | 12.9* | (14) |
| True friendship | 9.1 | (9) | 9.5 | (10) | 10.3 | (9) |
| Wisdom | 8.0 | (7) | 8.4 | (8) | 9.0 | (8) |

*Differ from police at .05 level by median ($x^2$) test.
**Differ from police at .01 level by median ($x^2$) test.

**TABLE 2    Instrumental Value Medians and Composite Rank Orders for Police Sample and for National Samples of Male Whites and Blacks**

| | Police N=153 | | NORC Whites N=561 | | NORC Blacks N=93 | |
|---|---|---|---|---|---|---|
| | Md. | Rank | Md. | Rank | Md. | Rank |
| Ambitious | 6.1 | (3) | 5.5 | (2) | 5.8 | (2) |
| Broadminded | 8.8 | (7) | 7.0* | (4) | 7.4 | (6) |
| Capable | 7.7 | (5) | 8.6* | (8) | 10.1** | (11) |
| Cheerful | 12.6 | (17) | 10.3** | (11) | 10.6 | (13) |
| Clean | 8.2 | (6) | 9.9 | (10) | 6.6 | (3) |
| Courageous | 8.9 | (8) | 7.6 | (5) | 6.9 | (5) |
| Forgiving | 10.3 | (10) | 8.2** | (6) | 8.3 | (8) |
| Helpful | 11.6 | (13) | 8.4** | (7) | 8.2** | (7) |
| Honest | 2.6 | (1) | 3.3 | (1) | 4.2* | (1) |
| Imaginative | 14.5 | (18) | 14.3 | (18) | 15.4 | (18) |
| Independent | 11.8 | (14) | 10.4* | (12) | 9.6 | (9) |
| Intellectual | 11.0 | (11) | 12.9* | (15) | 12.2 | (15) |
| Logical | 10.2 | (9) | 13.3** | (16) | 14.5** | (17) |
| Loving | 11.9 | (16) | 10.8 | (13) | 11.6 | (14) |
| Obedient | 11.9 | (15) | 13.7** | (17) | 12.4 | (16) |
| Polite | 11.4 | (12) | 10.9 | (14) | 10.3 | (12) |
| Responsible | 5.0 | (2) | 6.6* | (3) | 6.8 | (4) |
| Self-controlled | 6.3 | (4) | 9.7** | (9) | 9.9** | (10) |

*Differ from police at .05 level by median ($x^2$) test.
**Differ from police at .01 level by median ($x^2$) test.

## Differences in Terminal Values

Tables 1 and 2 also show that police differ consistently from whites and blacks (with one or both of the differences being statistically significant) on many terminal and instrumental values. Police regard 4 terminal values as more important than black and white samples—*an exciting life, a sense of accomplishment, family security*, and *mature love* —and 5 terminal values as less important— *a world at peace, a world of beauty, equality, national security*, and *social recognition*.

## Personal and Social Values

These findings suggest that police generally place a higher emphasis on personal than social values. Not surprising, they place a greater value on *family security* than do the national sample of blacks and whites. Somewhat surprising, in view of contempo-

rary stereotypes, is that police place a higher value on *a sense of accomplishment*. Does this mean that police are more upwardly mobile or more motivated by a desire for self-fulfillment in work? We will return to this question in discussing instrumental values.

## Valuation of Equality

The difference between police and the other two samples on *equality* is especially noteworthy because of its social implications. Police rank it fourteenth, whites twelfth, and blacks third in importance. The equality difference between police and blacks is highly significant. Data from research by Rokeach (1971) and Bishop (1969) suggest that the ranking on *equality* is the best single predictor of political conservatism. Those who rank *equality* high when compared with those who rank it low have been found to be significantly more favorable toward equal rights for blacks and the poor, more sympathetic with student protest movements, and more sympathetic with the Church's participation in the daily affairs of society. Ranking on *equality,* moreover, has been found to be the best single predictor of political identification (Bishop, 1969; Rokeach, 1971). Those who ranked *equality* high were more likely to favor Kennedy, McCarthy, and Johnson in the 1968 campaign; those ranking *equality* somewhere in the middle were more likely to favor Rockefeller, Nixon, and Reagan; and those ranking *equality* toward the low end of the scale were more likely to support Wallace. Average police rankings on *equality* are closest to those we earlier obtained for Wallace supporters.

### Differences in Instrumental Values

Among the instrumental values (Table 2), police consistently placed higher value than blacks and whites on being *capable, honest, intellectual, logical, obedient, responsible,* and *self-controlled.* But they consistently placed lower value on being *broadminded, cheerful, forgiving, helpful,* and *independent.* That police care more than the other two groups about being *capable, intellectual,* and *logical* is consistent with the differences on a *sense of accomplishment.* Together these differences suggest that the policeman sees himself functioning in a professionally competent and responsible manner. But this professional orientation has a special quality that distinguishes it from role conceptions prevailing in other professions.[3] The data suggest that police place a relatively higher value on professional fulfillment within an authority-dominated and rule-oriented social organization, which provides a framework for dealing with people impersonally and according to bureaucratic rules. Police role conceptions seem to place less emphasis on individual spontaneity or

---

[3] Unpublished data.

being cheerful, lenient, or tolerant, while placing greater emphasis on obedience and self-control. Thus, the first hypothesis, that police have value systems that are distinctively different from those of other U.S. residents, is supported.

### Differential Recruitment or Socialization?

What can be said about the personal or social "etiology" of police values? Do such patterns originate with personality factors that predispose certain persons to go into law enforcement? Do they reflect the fact that police are recruited, as Lipset (1969) suggests, from a working-class milieu that shares generally similar values? Or do they perhaps reflect an occupational socialization process that takes place after recruitment?

First, to find out to what extent personality and working-class background account for police value patterns, we matched 153 male whites of the national sample with the 153 policemen on education and age. (On education, 6 policemen reported that they had some high school, 77 were high-school graduates, 61 had some college, and 8 were college graduates; on age, 61 were under 30, 51 were between 30 and 39, and 40 were over 40.) Table 3 shows the *significant* value differences that were found between the police and the matched white sample.[4]

In this analysis we find only 8 of 36 statistically stable value differences, suggesting that police value patterns are indeed more like those held by matched white males. This supports Lipset's idea that police "reflect the background from which they came [1969, p. 78]," but it is evidently not the whole story. Police still differ in important respects from other whites of comparable age and status, suggesting that personality and social factors are at work. Within the less educated groups from which police

---

[4] We include *equality* even though the difference does not quite reach statistical significance ($p = .06$).

**TABLE 3    Terminal and Instrumental Values Differentiating Police Sample and National White Male Sample Matched for Age and Education**

| | Police (N=153) | | NORC Whites (N=153) | | Median Test | |
|---|---|---|---|---|---|---|
| | Md. | Rank | Md. | Rank | $\chi^2$ | p= |
| *Terminal values* | | | | | | |
| A comfortable life | 8.0 | (8) | 10.3 | (12) | 4.61 | .03 |
| A world of beauty | 16.0 | (18) | 14.2 | (16) | 10.08 | .01 |
| Equality | 11.7 | (14) | 10.2 | (11) | 3.54 | .06 |
| Freedom | 5.3 | (3) | 4.2 | (2) | 4.93 | .03 |
| Pleasure | 13.7 | (16) | 15.1 | (18) | 6.81 | .01 |
| *Instrumental values* | | | | | | |
| Independent | 11.8 | (14) | 8.0 | (5) | 5.86 | .02 |
| Obedient | 11.9 | (15) | 14.6 | (18) | 13.16 | .01 |
| Self-controlled | 6.3 | (4) | 9.5 | (8) | 12.93 | .01 |

are traditionally drawn, our data suggest recruitment is more likely to take place from among those who place a relatively lower value on *freedom, equality, independence,* and *a world of beauty* and a relatively higher value on *obedience, self-control, a comfortable life,* and *pleasure.* Thus it seems that hypotheses (2) and (3) are empirically supported. Both social background and personality seem to be selective determinants of police recruitment.

What role does socialization play after recruitment? If occupational socialization is also a determinant of police values, we would expect to find that the value patterns are more characteristic of older than of younger policemen, and are more charac-

teristic of policemen with more years on the force. When we compared the value patterns of police under the age of 30, between 30 and 39, and over 40, there was not a single significant difference. Young police officers seem to have essentially the same value systems as older police officers. Evidently the police force is not the primary or even a secondary socializer of the police. When police officers of varying experience were compared, we found only a few values —4 out of 36—that differentiated significantly among them (Table 4). Among those with over 20 years' experience, there is a large increase in the value placed on *equality, inner harmony, mature love,* and *being polite.*

**TABLE 4    Terminal and Instrumental Values Differentiating among Police Sample Varying in Years of Experience**

| | Under 3 years N=41 | | 4–10 N=46 | | 11–20 N=44 | | Over 20 N=18 | | Median Test | |
|---|---|---|---|---|---|---|---|---|---|---|
| | Md. | Rank | Md. | Rank | Md. | Rank | Md. | Rank | $\chi^2$ | p= |
| *Terminal values* | | | | | | | | | | |
| Equality | 12.3 | (14) | 12.0 | (13) | 14.0 | (16) | 6.5 | (4) | 9.37 | .03 |
| Inner harmony | 11.2 | (12) | 12.7 | (15) | 10.8 | (12) | 9.5 | (11) | 7.99 | .05 |
| Mature love | 10.8 | (11) | 9.3 | (10) | 8.8 | (10) | 13.0 | (14) | 7.78 | .05 |
| *Instrumental values* | | | | | | | | | | |
| Polite | 10.1 | (10) | 10.1 | (8) | 12.7 | (16) | 12.8 | (15) | 7.73 | .05 |

It is difficult to say how seriously we should take these findings, since so few differences could have arisen by chance. But even if these are indeed reliable differences, they provide little support for postoccupational socialization. The distinctive patterns of police values shown in Tables 1, 2, and 3 are, if anything, somewhat less evident among more experienced police officers. These data, in conjunction with the data showing no value differences among younger and older police officers, therefore suggest that police value patterns are probably not a function of occupational socialization (hypothesis 4), but of recruitment from certain social strata and of personality factors operating within these strata.

## DISCUSSION

We find a somewhat larger value gap between police and blacks than between police and whites matched on age and education, but the value gap is considerable in both cases.[5] Of the 36 values 21 show consistent differences (with one or both being statistically significant) between police and the national samples of blacks and whites; 13 of these show larger differences between police and blacks, and 8 show larger differences between police and whites. Police differ from both groups in their priorities for both idealized means and idealized ends.

In general, police are relatively more concerned than are the two national samples with certain personal values and less concerned with social values. Some of these personal values involve self-actualization and competence needs; contrary to popular conception, police give these values higher priority. Recall that police rank *a sense of accomplishment, capable, intellectual,* and

*logical* higher than do the national samples. But, paradoxically, such value strivings by police exist side by side with a relatively higher value for obedience to authority, a devaluing of autonomy, and a punitive and unsympathetic orientation toward people in general. Recall especially that police devalue such modes of behavior as being *broadminded, forgiving, helpful,* and *cheerful.*

We see that the value gap involves not only a discrepancy in value patterns but also a discrepancy that implies value conflict between police and policed. These data were collected during a period of mass protest about such social values as *a world of peace* and *equality,* the war in Vietnam, and equal rights for blacks. The protest behavior reflects the existence of value patterns that were highly incongruent with police value patterns. It is thus hardly likely that police view such behavior with sympathy or even tolerance.

The significant differences found for *equality* are disturbing. Police rank *equality* significantly lower than whites, lower than whites matched for age and education ($p < .06$), and far lower than blacks.[6] As already stated, ranking for *equality* is the best single indicator of conservatism in the U.S. This finding not only supports Lipset's observation (1969) that many police were attracted to Wallace's campaign in 1968 but also identifies the value that best accounts for the attraction. This discrepancy in value for *equality* we regard as the most significant component of the value gap between police and policed. Given that the discrepancy was especially apparent between police and blacks, it is hardly surprising that black ghetto residents view the police as enemies

---

[5] That more significant value differences were found between police and the total sample of whites than between police and blacks is probably due to differences in sample size between NORC samples of white ($N = 561$) and blacks ($N = 93$).

[6] An earlier analysis of police values ($N = 50$) using a 12- rather than 18-value scale showed that police ranked *freedom* first and *equality* last, supporting the findings reported here. On 12 instrumental values, police ranked *forgiving* and *tender* as significantly less important than did students; retail store owners, managers, and salesclerks; and executives in the federal government.

who preserve "law and order," that is, preserve the conservative value pattern of a white power structure.

Considering the similarity of police and matched white value patterns, our findings support Lipset's contentions that police derive their conservatism from prior socialization. Further, our data indicate that police work appeals primarily to those members of the working class whose personalities are such that they value subservience to authority. It seems that their value preferences represent predispositions that lead to police work rather than to other occupational careers.

Theoretical considerations suggest that police values would be further shaped after recruitment by reinforcement or socialization to institutionalized police values. Our data provide very little support for such a hypothesis, supporting similar conclusions reached by Bayley and Mendelsohn (1969).

## Policy Implication

While police hold certain values in common with U.S. residents in general, police value patterns as a whole do not seem to represent U.S. value patterns. Law enforcement agencies that seek a police force with values more representative of the public might well ask what changes in recruitment or training, what resocialization program, can lead to greater congruence between the value patterns of police and policed. One solution, already being tried in many police departments, is to recruit officers from other social backgrounds and other racial and ethnic groups. But such a policy has met with limited success because of low pay scales and strong minority group biases against police careers. Ways must be found to overcome both obstacles. Or perhaps applicants exhibiting clearly undesirable value patterns should be weeded out. We can, for example, ill afford to accept recruits who rank too high on such values as *obedience* and too low on such values as *equality* and *forgiving*.

Specific techniques might also be used to resocialize police values to coincide more with those of other citizens. Police training could include feedback about what is known concerning police value patterns and associated attitudes, how they resemble and differ from those of other significant groups in our society, and how they are related to behavior. Research has shown that such feedback effectively induces enduring value change and change in associated social attitudes (Rokeach, 1968a, 1968b). More recent work (Rokeach, 1973) extends the chain to related changes in behavior. It is anticipated that such training, specifically designed to raise certain values and to lower others in the value hierarchy, will contribute to the increasing professionalization of law enforcement personnel.

Consistent with the data reported here, a study by Black and Reiss (1967) has characterized police interactions with the policed as routine, impersonal, businesslike, civil, rational, and bureaucratic. Police training needs to discourage such presentations of the police to the policed. A greater emphasis on training in human relations might lead to a resocialization or reorganization of value priorities, thus bringing the police into more harmonious daily interactions with the policed than is now the case.

# CHAPTER 14

# Law in the Schools

## —PAUL A. FREUND

Since the law is a dynamic process that structures "our" common life, understanding the rules and processes of law as well as developing critical modes of reasoning are neither esoteric nor theoretical concerns. This chapter focuses on the objectives of law teaching as a component of elementary and high-school education. Not only should legal education teach the content of law, it should also emphasize an ability to reason dialectically, cope with uncertainty, appreciate the ethical dimensions of problems, and weigh the consequences of diverse action. The complexities of achieving these goals are discussed.

For most individuals, adults and youngsters alike, law remains the "mysterious science" that Blackstone undertook to explain.[1] It is either a conglomeration of technical rules or the manipulation of symbols by practitioners licensed to carry on the black art. Even worse, law may seem to be both these things at once. The idea of law as a system of principles and processes for reaching just results, and thus a rich quarry of ethical problems and moral reasoning, shaped by thought and experience over the generations, is largely unapprehended.

We neglect the quarry of law at our peril. Ours is a time of intense interest in law. No one who reads the newspapers or watches television can be unaware of the degree to which law does indeed structure our common life. This is made plain, often painfully so, by the ceaseless flow of reports of trials, investigations, legislation, enforcement measures, and all the fascinating paraphernalia

of coercive law. What is not so plain are the rules and processes of which these happenings are only instances, or the mode of thinking that governs the method of law. Not so plain, either, is the noncoercive role of law, the function of facilitating certain kinds of transactions and encouraging certain kinds of behavior through pervasive sheltering institutions such as contract, property, and inheritance.

Law teaching in the schools may reflect a similar balance or imbalance in communicating the essence of law. Any consideration of law as a component of elementary and high-school education must focus on the goals of the program and the problems it presents. To be more concrete the following discussion aims to set forth the kinds of objectives law programs might well include.

### OBJECTIVES

#### Learning the Content of Laws

This objective is put first not because it is the most significant (on the contrary, it is one of the lesser ones) but because it is the most obvious. A good deal of important law

---

[1] See Boorstin (1941) on Blackstone's *Commentaries*. The *Commentaries,* highly influential in the United States in the late eighteenth century, derived from Sir William Blackstone's Law lectures at Oxford (1753), designed for the general education of gentlemen.

should be accessible to pupils, in the sense of being worth knowing and within the competence of young people to grasp. Everyday events and transactions, within the experience or observation of students, raise questions that are addressed by law: the rights of landlord and tenant, of the purchaser and seller of a product that proves unsatisfactory, of the householder faced with a police officer at the door, of a writer or speaker defaming a public figure, of a journalist publishing information about a criminal suspect. But, as I have suggested, there is a danger that learning rules of law may so engage the interest of pupils that the processes whereby rules are arrived at, tested, criticized, and revised are neglected.

### Reasoning Dialectically

Rules of law are often accommodations between right and right rather than condemnations of obvious wrong. Legal thinking strives to resolve in an acceptably fair way, and in specific contexts, the great antinomies of freedom and constraint, privacy and the right to know, free press and fair trial, security of acquisitions and freedom of transactions, national citizenship and local autonomy, blameworthiness and compensation for harm. For example, the last-mentioned antinomy is inherent in the problem of compensating highway accident victims: Should the outcome turn on the fault of those involved, or should it be resolved irrespective of fault, as in the case of fire or casualty insurance? Is there a way of incorporating elements of fault in the solution without sacrificing the end of compensation to the victim? These are hard questions of justice that challenge the powers of creativity. It is precisely with such issues that the study of law differs crucially from the art of debating. While both call for the confrontation of claims with counterclaims, legal thinking requires a resolution in the individual mind and encourages the finding of solutions that transcend, as by a synthesis, the polar opposites of a debate.

This process is not easy, but on its cultivation may depend the pursuit of justice in society (Freund, 1968, pp. 61–115). Our neural systems seem better adapted to the binary program of yes–no responses than to the responses yes/but or no/but. The educated person must be able to make the qualified response without paralysis of judgment or the will to act, and be able to believe without being a true believer. This capacity is critical: The process of conflict resolution calls for delicate accommodations. Learning the law is not merely learning principles. In fact, we do not really "know" a principle until we know its opposing principles and reshape them all in the process.

### Coping with Uncertainty

Not unrelated to the dialectical mode of thinking is the need to come to terms with uncertainties. These may be the uncertainties of predicting the future. Here the insurance principle, or pooling of risks, and attendant ethical issues come into play: Should participation in the system of insurance be made compulsory, so that the stronger or braver spirits are deprived of an option to take risks, or is social interdependence the dominant consideration? Uncertainties may relate as well to the truth about past events, as in a trial. Here the devices of the adversary system and cross-examination emerge. If these fail to yield a confident conclusion, legal presumptions and burden of proof may resolve the issue in accord with a chosen public policy—the presumption of innocence, for example. Or the uncertainty may relate to more general facts of a physical or scientific nature. If there is no assured finding regarding the harmfulness of marijuana or obscenity, on what side of the scales should the finger of the law be pressed? Shall abundance of caution or free self-determination (or family determination) be the controlling principle? It is perhaps less important that such questions be answered than that they be asked, because the process of question asking conveys a view of law as a dynamic, fluid process, not as a set of rules that must only be "learned" to be "known."

## Perceiving the Ethical Dimensions of Justice

It is difficult enough to decide where justice lies in disputes between A and B, where the ethical issue is problematic because of its dialectical nature or where the facts are uncertain. Even where the facts are clear, their significance for legal liability may not be so, for they must be fitted into a legal rule or principle that contains a term apparently of an empirical character but actually dependent for its meaning on an ethical judgment. Consider the term "cause." What "caused" the Civil War? The question might be answered differently by a sociologist, a political historian, and a modern statesman concerned to avoid a similar catastrophe. The first answer, with all respect, should be: "Why do you want to know?" Suppose a law provides that whoever, without good reason, causes physical injury to another shall be liable to that other for damages; suppose further that A playfully taps the head of B, unaware that B's skull is abnormally thin: B thereby suffers serious injury. Was the injury "caused" by the tap or by the dangerously vulnerable condition of the skull? The question might be answered differently by a moralist, a physician, and an onlooker. Purposes vary in law itself. The aim may be to affix blame, or to provide compensation in a just way, or to deter future misadventures. That the same term may have different meanings in different contexts, and that the differences are purposive, indeed ethical, in nature is surely an insight that can, and deserves to, be cultivated as part of the education of youth.

Our illustrations have concerned simple cases of A and B. When a third party, C, enters the equation the difficulties of framing rules of justice are likely to mount. If B steals A's bicycle and then sells it to C, who is unaware of the theft, two innocent parties are in conflict. As between A, who wants the bicycle returned, and C, who wants to keep it, the law can be expected to prefer A's claim. B, it may be said, had no rightful title to the property and (therefore?) could pass none to C. Now suppose that B steals A's ten-dollar bill, pays it to C for a book, and then disappears. As between A and C, again two innocent parties, in a contest for the ten dollars, should A again prevail? If not, why not? Would it make a difference if C received the money from B as a gift? Obviously the dimensions of justice should encompass not merely A and C but the social presuppositions and requirements of the market. What are needed are middle axioms of justice between large generalizations like "No one can transfer a greater title than he or she possesses" and the atomism of situational ethics. This is the familiar task of law. Pursuing such issues is neither esoteric nor theoretical. The meaning of just expectations, on which the social order ultimately rests, can be explored in considerable depth within the parameters of the student's personal fields of reference and experience.

## Choosing Sanctions

Problems of ethical choice can sometimes be resolved, or compromised, by a judgment that draws on sanctions in the law's procedural arsenal. Two major sanctions are the imposition of a judgment for money damages, payable to the injured party, and a direct order addressed to the offender, enforceable by fine or imprisonment for noncompliance, to cease and desist from the offensive conduct. As ethical sensibilities become more refined, conduct that was once deemed tolerable may be regarded as reprehensible; invasions of privacy may be an example. Yet a court may hesitate to frame a new rule if it would force individuals to pay damages for actions that were not condemned by law when they were taken. In this impasse, the choice of an injunctive remedy—to desist henceforth—may provide the fairest solution.

The choice of sanctions may work the other way around—in favor of money damages rather than injunctive order. An actual case, several generations ago, illustrates the point. The International News Service, unable to operate in certain countries abroad, pirated from Associated Press bulletin boards news items that were then wired to International's newspaper clients. Associated Press sued to enjoin this misappropriation, and an injunction was approved by the Supreme Court (*International News Service* v. *Associated Press*, 1918). In a dissenting opinion, however, Justice Brandeis argued that, although a private wrong had been committed, nevertheless the public interest in the widest dissemination of news, together with AP's then restrictive membership policy, weighed against that form of remedy. One alternative might be the denial of an injunction but the imposition of money damages against INS as a condition of its continuing use of the bulletins, thus compensating the injured party without curtailing the flow of news. The dimensions of justice would be perceived to extend beyond A and B, and an appropriate ethical solution would be found in the flexible procedures of the law.

## PITFALLS AND WINDFALLS

Enough has been said to indicate the relevance and the cognitive challenge of legal materials and to suggest that the distinctive mode of thinking in law has its place in the education of ethically sensitive and socially resourceful individuals. A number of difficulties are, of course, presented and need to be discussed.

The most obvious difficulty is the unpreparedness of teachers to give instruction in "law," a difficulty easily exaggerated. It would be critical if professional training were the goal, but it is not an excessive

burden to become familiar with fundamental legal concepts and their relevance to commonplace situations. Indeed, a background in moral philosophy would go a long way to prepare a teacher to guide discussions of the kind envisaged here. The stuff of law can be related to such normal experiences as association in clubs, disciplinary proceedings, simple commercial transactions at neighborhood shops, and reading facts, opinions, gossip, and untruths in newspapers. There is, to be sure, a need for teacher training programs in this field, and there is an upsurge in these offerings and in support for them. Likewise, there is a need for graded materials, and these too are increasingly available.[2] This assistance can be invaluable, provided the objectives are not distorted to become the purveying of information about "the law" or the glorifying of our system in contrast to others (see also Levine & Tapp, Chap. 15).

A more troublesome difficulty is the risk of cynicism as the law perceived on the streets is held up against the law presented in school. The strain may be accentuated when pupils who are expected to participate in formulating, criticizing, and revising rules as a classroom exercise feel themselves to be remote from actual lawmaking. The emotional gulf between "we" and "they" may be widened. But alienation need not be the outcome. On the contrary, a greater appreciation of the tasks of law, the complexities and genuine problems for accommodation, and the demonstrated capacity of law for adaptation can produce a more balanced critique of the system and a greater respect for the legal order. Participation in school may give motivation for participation in the larger arena. Better to put the program to

---

[2] See the *Directory of Law-Related Educational Activities* prepared by the American Bar Association's Special Committee on Youth Education for Citizenship (1974). See also the second edition of the Special Committee's comprehensive bibliography of law-related educational materials (1976).

a test than to indulge in evasion, which itself breeds not only cynicism but invincible ignorance.

What has just been said is bound up with questions of the stages of child development at which various materials and approaches should be employed. Those who prepare materials will need the counsel of teachers and psychologists. Impressionistic experiences with the teaching of law in the schools suggest that pupils are readier than might be supposed to discuss ethical issues in more advanced terms than simple rule obedience, given challenging and interesting problems with which to wrestle.[3] Those who have experimented along these lines have reported a number of rewarding by-products of the enterprise. Pupils generally apathetic or hostile in class have entered enthusiastically

---

[3] These impressions are based on personal communications to the author by teachers from the Boston-area schools.

into the role of legislator or judge. Unexpectedly acute powers of comparison and differentiation of cases have been displayed. And beyond the classroom, communication between parent and child has improved as the cases of the day are carried home and discussed. Issues of right and wrong conduct, or right against right, and of just sanctions can be discussed on equal terms with forceful concern, yet free from the emotionally disturbing element of personal involvement.

Evaluation research will inevitably evolve to assess more scientifically the results of school programs of instruction in law. Testing and measurement will not be easy, since what is at stake is least of all the absorption of information. Most superficially the results should be observable in the classroom atmosphere. Most profoundly they may call for the wisdom of the ancient judges of the Areopagus, who when faced with an especially subtle case asked the litigants to come back in a hundred years.

# CHAPTER 15

# The Dialectic of Legal Socialization in Community and School[1]

—FELICE J. LEVINE and JUNE LOUIN TAPP

The goal of legal socialization is to stimulate legal reasoning skills that reflect a reciprocal rights-consciousness and legal competence. Premised on an interactive view of the individual's relations to rule systems, this chapter examines the impact of social variables on legal development. First, a social-psychological stage model of legal reasoning and empirical data on the reasoning of adults are presented. Then the chapter describes possible socializing strategies compatible with legal growth and demonstrates how these strategies may be applied to two naturalistic settings—the community and the school.

---

[1] "Dialectic" is defined in the Oxford English Dictionary (1971) as "[t]he art of critical examination into the truth of an opinion; the investigation of truth by discussion . . . the art of reasoning or disputation by question and answer. . . ." According to Hegel, "the term is applied (a.) to the process of thought by which . . . contradictions are seen to merge themselves in a higher truth that comprehends them; and (b.) to the world-process, which being . . . but the thought-process on its objective side, develops similarly by a continuous unification of opposites." Our application of the term "dialectic" in this chapter is consistent with these definitions: Legal socialization is viewed as a dialectical process that optimally encourages in individuals and institutions the facility to accommodate both insights and inconsistencies.

We gratefully acknowledge the support of the American Bar Foundation in sponsoring F. J. Levine's research on "How the Public Relates to Law" and a University of Minnesota Graduate School Grant-in-Aid on Ethnicity and Legality to J. L. Tapp. We wish to thank Glenda Hargrove of the Foundation for her competent and concerned secretarial assistance in this manuscript. Parts of this chapter appeared previously in somewhat different form in Tapp and Levine (1973, 1974).

The burgeoning trend toward legal activity, revealed in a greater use of legal resources and solutions, underscores the increased significance of individuals' ability to mobilize the law. Theoretical and empirical work on the relation of the individual to legal systems has employed a concept of "legal competence" to denote effective utilization of law (e.g., Carlin, Howard, & Messinger, 1967; Levine & Preston, 1970; Nonet, 1969; Selznick, 1969). Simultaneous to these efforts, other studies have contributed to identifying the development of orientations toward law (e.g., Adelson, Green, & O'Neil, 1969; Rodgers & Taylor, 1970; Tapp & Levine, 1970, 1972). The underlying theme in much of this research suggests that individuals acquire their notions of rules, laws, and compliance and develop strategies for using legal institutions through interaction between natural cognitive structures and a host of "legal" environments such as the home, school, friendship circle, or court. In this chapter we seek to address the second half of this interaction: the impact of social conditions on the development or the expression of standards for guiding behavior, pressing claims, and settling disputes.

To this end, we first review our model of legal reasoning, emphasizing its congruence with other psychological and jurisprudential frameworks. Second, we present data on the legal reasoning potential of adults who are both agents and products of socialization. Next, we assess the socializing strategies compatible with legal growth, whatever the age, situation, or circumstance. In the final section, we apply these stratagems to two naturalistic settings—the community and the school—to sketch the components of a constructive social context and a viable educative experience. Throughout, the purpose is to characterize situational conditions that can enhance the capacity to make competent, ethical judgments about law and that are thereby compatible with the administration of justice.

## AN INTERACTIONAL COGNITIVE MODEL OF LEGAL REASONING

Our approach to understanding human reasoning about law and legal institutions considers the legal socialization process in its totality—an infinite set of continuous interactions between social variables and natural potentialities. We posit three distinct levels of legal reasoning: the preconventional, a sanction-oriented, deference stance; the conventional, a law-and-order, conformity posture; and the postconventional, a law-creating, principled perspective. While this model is presented from the vantage of cognitive stage theory, that perspective was adopted largely for heuristic purposes. Our approach also reflects the impact of social-psychological and jurisprudential thought. Ultimately the purpose in clarifying modes of legal reasoning is to understand more fully the relation between persons' role conceptions and their legal attitudes and actions. In this quest, we have sought to integrate multiple sources of data and theory (e.g., the research presented in DePalma & Foley, 1975; Knutson, 1973; Lickona, 1976)

that are coterminous with our focus on individuals' interactions with systems of law.[2]

## Theoretical Congruency

*Social psychology.* Social psychology has long employed an interactive levels approach for interpreting individual, social, or cultural phenomena. Our work is consistent with the tradition of such pioneers as Dewey (1909, 1910, 1930), McDougall (1908), Mead (1934), and Heider (1958). In 1895 Dewey presented an interactional developmental conception of moral stages "to insure the full meaning and free, yet orderly or law-abiding, exercise of the psychological powers [1964, p. 207]." A few years later, McDougall delineated a stage theory culminating in a principled position, noting, "while the lower forms of social conduct are the direct issue of the prompting of instinct . . . the higher forms of social conduct, which alone are usually regarded as moral, involve the voluntary control and regulation of the instinctive impulses [1908, p. 150]." With a focus more on the potency of participation and interpersonal exchange, Mead postulated that moral development reflected a transition from the centrality of "significant others" to the primacy of the "generalized other [1934, p. 154]." Likewise, Heider considered judgments of causality, blame, responsibility, and the like to be a function of stage-related cognitive processes (see also Ross & DiTecco, 1975; Rubin & Peplau, 1975). For example, in his

---

[2] In a recent paper, Hogan (1976) proposes a three-level model of development: attunement to rules, sensitivity to social expectations and concern for the well-being of others, and ideological maturity. Although Hogan perceives differences in basic assumptions between his model and the Tapp-Levine framework, we are struck by the commonalities. Our theoretical antecedents in social psychology, cognitive developmental psychology, and jurisprudence indicate our integrative orientation.

analysis of interpersonal relations, Heider outlined five Piagetian stages in the attribution of responsibility "in which attribution to the person decreases and attribution to the environment increases [1958, p. 113]."

Other social psychologists have pursued work congruent with a levels framework. Key among them is Kelman, who developed models of attitude change (1958) and personal involvement in the national political system (1969). While Kelman considers modes of conformity largely in terms of situational conditions and consequences, the similarities between his analysis and our levels of legal thought suggest the validity of a developmental interactional perspective.

Kelman, too, attends to the interaction between a person's value orientation and patterns of relating to authorities and authoritative institutions. In general terms, his characterizations of compliance, identification, and internalization processes as responses to social influence are analogous to the three levels of legal thought. To Kelman, simple compliance occurs when situational rewards or punishments dominate (preconventional); identification occurs in the service of the maintenance of role relationships (conventional); and internalization—the most stable form of attitude change—occurs when a social influence is intrinsically rewarding, that is, compatible with one's value system (postconventional). Kelman postulates further that (1) normative integration is based on unquestioning adherence to the rules (preconventional); (2) role participant integration reflects a commitment to and identification with social roles within the system (conventional); and (3) ideological integration is rooted in an endorsement of the underlying values of the system (postconventional).

*Cognitive developmental psychology.* The cognitive-structural-stage theories of moral development and thought advanced by Piaget (e.g., 1928, 1932, 1947) and elaborated by Kohlberg (e.g., 1963b, 1969,

1971) also significantly influenced our levels model of legal reasoning. In Chapter 9, Tapp along with Kohlberg viewed the continuities between a cognitive theory of legal development and Piaget's and Kohlberg's moral development theories. In his explorations of children's morality, Piaget stressed the interaction of "natural" and "social" influences on emergent concepts of rules and justice. Recognizing a premoral stage wherein the individual is incapable of causal thought, he primarily emphasized two levels of morality —heteronomous and autonomous. At the heteronomous stage the individual sees authorities as warranting unilateral respect and their rules as obligatory, sacred, and immutable (Piaget & Inhelder, 1969, p. 125). By the autonomous stage, obligations are defined in terms of mutual respect, reciprocity, and responsibility, and "an essential product . . . is the sense of justice . . . [wherein] justice prevails over obedience itself [p. 127]."

Extending the Piagetian model, Kohlberg postulated six stages (three levels) of moral development and tested cognitive developmental theory both longitudinally and cross-culturally (see, e.g., 1963b, 1968a, 1969). Since the relation between the Tapp-Levine legal levels model and Kohlberg's moral stage typology is considered in Chapter 9, Kohlberg's assumptions are not reiterated here. We do note, however, that Kohlberg's theoretical orientation, despite critiques (e.g., Kurtines & Grief, 1974), is valuable for analyzing a number of areas of social development. For example, other investigators have used his framework for studying political ideological thought (e.g., Fishkin, Keniston, & MacKinnon, 1973; Haan, Smith, & Block, 1968; Merelman, 1969, 1971). While we adopt and extend Kohlberg's descriptive labels to characterize modes of legal reasoning and describe "ideal" types, our theoretical and empirical roots reside as much with Piaget, who attends to the impact of cultural and social determinants on cognitive capacities (Piaget, 1970;

Piaget & Inhelder, 1969; see also Berg & Mussen, 1975).

A major thrust of Kohlberg and associates' research to date has aimed at verifying an invariant sequence of moral stages (see, e.g., Blatt & Kohlberg, 1969; Kohlberg, 1969; Rest, Turiel, & Kohlberg, 1969; Turiel, 1966). We depart from a strict stage model that sees change as a function of an ordered, mutually exclusive progression. We share the conviction that the maturing individual has the capacity to advance through a series of reasoning stages from simple to complex, from concrete to abstract. We emphasize, however, that the dialectic of reasoning simultaneously at diverse stages can stimulate stable, integrated cognitive growth in the individual.

This view is compatible with the position enunciated by Flavell (1972). To clarify further the process of cognitive development, Flavell elaborates a concept of bidirectionality for stage learning, where increments appear in a cyclic or "spiral sort of pattern." He commends this "mixed sequential–asequential view" to explain subject inconsistency as well as variability in stage or level: "As in the history of science, there is . . . a good deal of recycling, of doubling back to reanalyze and reinterpret earlier-received elements in the light of currently-processed ones [1972, pp. 340–342]." Since much of the research, including ours, indicates that no individual reasons totally at any one stage (e.g., Kohlberg, 1969; Rest, 1976; Turiel, 1973), a dialectical model of learning extends the promise of cognitive developmental theory for illuminating patterns of cognitive competence—whether legal, moral, or political.

*Jurisprudence.* The commonalities between our legal levels theory and jurisprudential frameworks provide a measure of concurrent validity (see also Tapp, 1974). Foremost among those who have enhanced our perspective on legal socialization are Fuller, a proponent of legal naturalism (e.g., 1969a,

1969b, 1969c), and Rawls, a moral philosopher (e.g., 1969, 1971). Both appreciate the interdependence of the moral, legal, and psychological. Their analytic constructs take account of the interactive components of both individual and institutional development.

Many of Fuller's ideas informed our general theory (e.g., communication, shared activity), but his discussion of the relation between the morality of duty and the morality of aspiration is especially germane to a legal levels typology. Fuller's perspective implies a development progression, most clearly evident in his "invisible pointer that marks the dividing line where the pressure of duty leaves off and the challenge of excellence begins [1969b, pp. 9–10]." In moving from duty to aspiration, Fuller's analysis resembles Piaget's shift from an amoral to a juridical position. Such a shift is reflected in the understanding that "[a] mere respect for constituted authority must not be confused with fidelity to law [p. 41]." Philosophically and psychologically, there is an advance from a dependent, hedonistic, and uncritical state to an independent, altruistic, and rational manner. As with Piaget, Fuller reveals a basic commitment to seeing humans as increasingly interactive and intellective, capable of rationality and, therefore, of an ethical legality.

Rawls's philosophic, analytic constuct also helped to clarify our ideas about law, justice, and compliance as well as corroborate our model. To Rawls, "moral feelings are a normal feature of human life [1971, p. 487]." Although postulating that a "sense of justice may be viewed as the result of a certain natural development [pp. 281–282]," he emphasizes that this development is enhanced through the social interaction and communication found in a stable, well-ordered society (see also pp. 453–462). Drawing on Piaget's model, Rawls details three "natural" stages of justice based on authority, association, and principle. Progression to a principled position, however, is triggered by the "social" nourishment of love and trust, participation and mutuality, shared activity and reciprocity.

## Theoretical Assumptions

*Nature of construct.* The adoption of a legal levels typology stems from the assumption that there are detectable regularities in modes of reasoning about legal values and interacting with legal systems. This focus on forms of thought offers a "universal" framework for organizing and structuring legal cognitions that simultaneously incorporate diversity. Although a specific legal attitude or action may vary by culture, group, or even person, an individual's level of reasoning is expected to explain variations in the content of expressions or orientations toward law. While no one is totally stage-consistent in reasoning across issues (see, e.g., Turiel, 1975), on balance one's cognitive structure should determine how he or she reasons about accepting or rejecting a substantive law and attempting to reform or maintain it (see Rawls, 1971, p. 494).

We recognize, in addition, the impact of affective states. Although concerned with stable, distinguishable, and cumulative reasoning competencies, we view cognitive structure "as the framework by which affective experiences are interpreted, and by which the strong emotional experiences of today are translated into the commitments of tomorrow [Rest, 1974, p. 242]." Thus, while we realize that to some degree ideal-type models represent a distortion of reality, we see a legal levels theory as providing a set of working hypotheses useful in attempting to clarify and map the legal worlds of individuals and institutions.

*Progression of reasoning.* Since the various levels of legal reasoning are depicted as successive restructurings in modes of thought, the meaning of "higher" or "highest" levels of development often troubles the cognitively oriented psychologist in the creation of paradigms or the interpretation of results. We are persuaded by the Piagetian notion that higher implies better at problem solving, integrating differences, and incorporating logical and psychological concepts. The view that the sequence of stages represents a progressive development has also guided Rawls: At the last stage "all the subordinate ideals are finally understood and organized into a coherent system by suitably general principles. The virtues of the other moralities receive their explanation within . . . the more comprehensive conception . . . [which is] continuous with these principles but extending beyond what they enjoin [1971, pp. 478-479]."

From an empirical perspective, the Tapp-Levine legal levels typology (Tapp, 1973, 1974; Tapp & Kohlberg, Chap. 9; Tapp & Levine, 1971, 1974) derives from an interpretation of cross-cultural and developmental responses to open-ended, classic jurisprudential questions. We noted earlier that the configuration of legal reasoning is best characterized by three major progressions: the preconventional (I), the conventional (II), and the postconventional (III). Of these the second, or conventional system-maintenance level, is modal in most cultures and groups (see, e.g., Kohlberg, 1968a; Tapp, 1970a, 1973; Tapp & Levine, 1970). In addition, ample research supports the hypothesis of a universal age-related sequence in the growth of ideas concerning law, justice, and morality (see, e.g., studies cited in Adelson, 1971; Berg & Mussen, 1975; DePalma & Foley, 1975; Tapp & Levine, 1974).

In this chapter, we neither review evidence on the patterns of legal development nor test the validity of a levels typology. The reader is referred to Chapter 9 and Part III for exemplary cross-cultural and developmental data. The focus here is on the socializing conditions that would seem to increase the number of ethical and critical persons who can act on a principled basis in developing and evaluating rule norms.

## EMPIRICAL ASSESSMENT
## OF SOCIALIZING AGENTS

We first evaluate the legal reasoning of adults—who both socialize and are themselves the products of socialization. We are guided by the observation that adults constitute a critical and continuing component of the social environment for developing individuals. If children, youth, and adults almost exclusively confront persons, situations, and institutions that are guided by homogenous frames of reference and low-level modes of thought, they are less likely to engage in or move toward the intellectual exploration and integration compatible with cognitive legal growth. The question, then, is whether adult socializing agents are simply passing on conventional slogans and clichés or whether they can create an environment that encourages the development of a principled perspective.

To address this issue, we use data from preliminary studies on the legal reasoning of graduating law students (law professionals), elementary and high-school teachers (law educators), and federal penitentiary inmates (law deviants). These adult samples, totaling 120 subjects, completed an open-ended questionnaire during 1970–71.[3] The instrument was group-administered to law students and teachers who consented to participate on a voluntary basis. The prison inmates were asked individually to complete the questionnaire and also did so voluntarily. All data were confidential and recorded anonymously.

_____
[3] The data on the graduating law students ($N = 24$) were gathered in 1971 by Deborah Seabury and Judith Rumreich as part of a research project in J. L. Tapp's course on law and psychology. The interviews were administered to the prison inmates ($N = 25$) by a graduate student, David Clarke, as a part of an independent study project in 1970. The data on elementary and high-school teachers ($N = 71$) were collected by J. L. Tapp and F. J. Levine in 1971 as part of a teacher-training institute sponsored by the American Bar Association.

The questionnaire instrument was derived and modified from an interview schedule developed in 1965 as part of a six-country, seven-culture study of socialization into compliance systems.[4] Aspects of that cross-cultural study and our subsequent developmental work are described in Chapter 9. In coding and analyzing the adult data, parallel procedures were followed to those reported in that chapter: Responses to the open-ended questions from all research samples were coded in terms of categories empirically derived from the cross-cultural and developmental data. Prior to data analysis, each category was distributed according to the preconventional, conventional, postconventional levels schema. In "leveling" an empirical category, we sought to characterize its dominant structure of legal thought. Therefore, assignments were agreed on _a priori_ by Tapp and Levine on the basis of conceptual issues, not on the basis of response distributions between or within groups.

As with the developmental and cross-national samples presented in Chapter 9, aggregate data were inspected and the legal level of adults was assessed by analyzing group response distributions on selected interview questions. Group differences in category response percentages were tested using $t$ tests, with a $p \leq .05$ minimal criterion of significance. We also focused on within-group patterns. Rank order and trend analyses are highly important in understanding the orientation of greatly disparate groups because significant differences may represent only variations in response set and thus may not be as revealing as comparative analyses of general patterns (Bakan,

_____
[4] Robert D. Hess, Leigh Minturn, and June Louin Tapp conducted this cooperative, cross-cultural study along with European and Asian field teams under the direction of Svend Skyum-Nielsen (Denmark), Vasso Vassilou (Greece), B. Kuppuswamy (India), Marcello Cesa-Bianchi (Italy), and Akira Hoshino (Japan). (See Chap. 9, Footnote 2 and accompanying text, by Tapp and Kohlberg.)

1967; Minturn & Lambert, 1964; Pick, 1974). Although in different areas of legal thought individuals may be more apt to express higher-stage reasoning (see Turiel, 1975), over a series of questions stable patterns can be identified among groups of adults and between adults and children. For comparative purposes, discussion of the developmental kindergarten to college data is also included (see Table 1 and Chap. 9).

## What Would Happen If There Were No Rules?

In response to "What would happen if there were no rules?" the adult groups generally considered legal norms in system-maintenance terms: A small number of adults expressed conventional concerns about impulse control—personal desires would prevail. Further, 88 percent of the graduating law students, 90 percent of the teachers, and 56 percent of the prisoners could not imagine a ruleless order or reasoned that anarchy and chaos would engulf society. These combined percentages capture the modal reasoning for all three adult groups. The lower response of 56 percent by prison inmates may partly be explained by the fact that a somewhat greater number of prisoners expressed a postconventional perspective on the value of rules (16%) and/ or by the higher rate of noncodable (12%) answers by them to this question.

Strikingly parallel to youth's observations, a 25-year-old lawyer-student predicted "disorder, chaos, and stifling of the advancement of society." A 50-year-old teacher similarly concluded, "Anarchy, we would all be savages; there would be no technological advances. . . ." And a 36-year-old who had been in prison a total of thirteen years felt that "everyone would create his own [rules] and nobody would know what to do to maintain harmony." As these statements illustrate, most adults emphasized conformity to the social order. While few expressed a preconventional view of rules as preventing

violence and crime, there was likewise little postconventional differentiation between the social system and the basic principles it promotes.

In considering the lawyer's role as socializer, it is noteworthy that third-year law students were just as conventional in their perspectives as teachers and college students. Professional legal education seemed to exert little influence in changing views of the purpose of law. The focus of these graduating lawyers was on rules serving to prevent chaos, not on their establishing consistency, clarity, and due process or guaranteeing personal liberties and human rights. Although a few fledgling lawyers (8%) and slightly more prison inmates (16%) demonstrated an appreciation of postconventional principles, the modal orientation of system maintenance was dominant for all adult groups.[5]

The adult data were strikingly consistent with developmental patterns. Most youth by preadolescence emphasized a conventional, system-maintenance view of rule guidelines that matched adult modes of thought. Across these samples, no one regardless of age or situation inferred that rules are needed to protect rights, establish legitimate claims, or guarantee freedoms—reasoning that would have demonstrated aspects of an ethical legality.

---

[5] These data are consistent with Simpson's study (1973) of 784 teachers, 65 of whom were interviewed on questions replicated from the Tapp-Levine Rule-Law Interview. Paralleling our finding that 83 percent of the teachers had conventional apprehension about anarchy, disorder, and chaos with none saying that humans are self-regulatory, Simpson also reported that 83 percent of her sample "responded conventionally to the idea of a world without laws, with no indication of belief that human beings are capable of social restraint, self-imposed [p. 15]." On other questions, Simpson also found instances of preconventional and postconventional thought but conventional reasoning strongly predominated.

**TABLE 1   Response Percentages on Legal Reasoning Questions for U.S. Youth and Adult Samples**

| LEVELS: CATEGORIES | SAMPLE GROUP | | | | | | COMPARISON (by t-test) | | | | |
|---|---|---|---|---|---|---|---|---|---|---|---|
| | Primary (1) | Middle School (2) | College (3) | Law Students (4) | Teachers (5) | Criminals (6) | (1)×(2) | (2)×(3) | (3)×(4) | (3)×(5) | (3)×(6) |
| *What would happen if there were no rules?* | | | | | | | | | | | |
| *I: Preconventional* | | | | | | | | | | | |
| Violence-crime | 50 | 57 | 06 | — | 03 | 08 | | ** | | | |
| *II: Conventional* | | | | | | | | | | | |
| Personal desires not principles | 15 | 20 | 15 | 04 | 10 | 08 | | | | | |
| Anarchy-disorder-chaos | 25 | 57 | 46 | 38 | 83 | 44 | * | | | ** | |
| Impossible to imagine | — | 07 | 32 | 50 | 07 | 12 | | ** | | ** | * |
| *III: Postconventional* | | | | | | | | | | | |
| Human being as self-regulatory (nothing would happen) | — | — | 08 | 08 | — | 16 | | | | ** | |
| *Are there times when it might be right to break a rule?* | | | | | | | | | | | |
| *I: Preconventional* | | | | | | | | | | | |
| No, unqualified | 55 | 07 | 03 | — | — | 04 | ** | | | | |
| Yes, unspecified | 25 | — | 05 | — | 13 | 16 | ** | | | | |
| *II: Conventional* | | | | | | | | | | | |
| Morality of circumstance | 20 | 73 | 35 | 67 | 54 | 36 | ** | ** | ** | * | |
| *III: Postconventional* | | | | | | | | | | | |
| Morality of rule | — | 17 | 54 | 46 | 34 | 40 | * | ** | | ** | |

*Why should people follow rules?*

| | | | | | | | | | |
|---|---|---|---|---|---|---|---|---|---|
| **I: Preconventional** | | | | | | | | | |
| Avoid negative consequences | 50 | 13 | 03 | 13 | 03 | — | ** | * | * |
| Authority | 05 | — | — | — | — | — | | | |
| **II: Conventional** | | | | | | | | | |
| Personal conformity | 35 | 13 | 09 | 04 | 04 | 08 | * | ** | * |
| Social conformity | 10 | 53 | 25 | 54 | 28 | 36 | ** | ** | ** |
| **III: Postconventional** | | | | | | | | | |
| Rational-beneficial-utilitarian | 05 | 27 | 51 | 38 | 62 | 48 | * | * | * |
| Principled | — | — | 05 | — | 04 | — | | | |

*Why do you follow rules?*

| | | | | | | | | | |
|---|---|---|---|---|---|---|---|---|---|
| **I: Preconventional** | | | | | | | | | |
| Avoid negative consequences | 60 | 47 | 25 | 29 | 17 | 04 | | | * |
| Authority | 10 | 10 | 03 | — | 01 | 04 | | | |
| **II: Conventional** | | | | | | | | | |
| Personal conformity | 20 | 40 | 34 | 29 | 18 | 32 | | * | * |
| Social conformity | — | 40 | 12 | 21 | 46 | 28 | ** | ** | ** |
| **III: Postconventional** | | | | | | | | | |
| Rational-beneficial-utilitarian | — | 07 | 22 | 25 | 42 | 20 | * | * | ** |
| Principled | — | — | 11 | — | — | 16 | * | ** | ** |

*Note.—All questions except "Are there times when it might be right to break a rule?" are multiple coded; therefore, percentages may total over 100%.*

*p ≤ .05
**p ≤ .01

## Are There Times When It Might Be Right To Break a Rule?

Adults' conceptions were also probed on the legitimacy of rule violation. How does the legal ideology of adult socializers compare to that of developing youth? Does their legal reasoning coincide with that of most middle-school preadolescents (73%), or does it more closely match that of college youth who showed a preference for a post-conventional (54%) above a conventional (35%) legality? The majority response for adults again fell short of a principled perspective: Of the graduating law professionals, 67 percent reflected a conventional orientation; of the teachers, 54 percent exhibited conventional reasoning with 13 percent at the preconventional level; and of the prison inmates, 36 percent showed conventional and 20 percent, preconventional models of thought. A 28-year-old serving a life sentence typified the conventional, circumstantial approach: Rule violation was legitimate "when a life is in danger." In short, these conventionally oriented adults conceived legitimate rule violation as an exception—representing what any "good" actor has a role obligation to perform. They typically did not acknowledge the legitimacy of a rule-rejecting posture.

While adults generally gave conventional responses to this question, sizable minorities revealed postconventional thought, ranging from teachers at 34 percent to law students at 46 percent. Evidencing concern about the morality of the rule, a 40-year-old junior-high-school teacher firmly stated "yes, when it violates morality and human dignity." As with the findings on college youth, these data indicate that adult respondents could evaluate rule systems in terms of underlying principles. College students, however, across questions seemed to exhibit a greater ability to *comprehend* or express higher-stage notions.

The somewhat higher proportion of post-conventional reasoning by college students suggests greater stage mixture in decision making, perhaps in response to their situation. College youth, in an environment that encourages dialectical inquiry, may draw upon higher-order reasoning to supplement their predominant legal level. Social contexts due to their social structures and/or socializing agents can accelerate, retard, or fixate—even temporarily—the development of legal reasoning (see Kohlberg, Scharf, & Hickey, 1971). As Turiel (1973, p. 737) pointed out: "[I]f the individual's existing structure is inadequate to deal with events encountered, the resulting state of heightened disequilibrium (manifested in conflict and confusion) could lead to compensatory activity. In such a case the feedback of new information could result in transition to a new stage."

The dominant patterns in the adult data, however, reveal a continuity in legal reasoning between childhood and adulthood. Apparently most of these adults had not fully developed their capacities to be competent rule-creating as well as rule-maintaining agents. Thus as socializers, they are unlikely by example or intention to create social climes that on a sustained basis stimulate an ethical legality.

## Why Should People Follow Rules? Why Do You Follow Rules?

Responses to two questions, "Why should people follow rules?" and "Why do you follow rules?" probed how individuals defined obligations to rule systems. Overall, the adult groups justified legal compliance in terms of conformity to the status quo. Congruent with the developmental data, all three adult samples exhibited a higher level of reasoning about what ideally should motivate obedience than about what prompts their compliance in practice. Further, a comparison of the adult and child data strengthened the conclusions that among these respondents crystallization occurred during the adolescent years and that substantial consistency in legal reasoning was demonstrated during adulthood. While for most adults a system-maintenance orientation obtained, several patterns are worthy of discussion.

Prisoner responses to the ideal "should people" and the real "do you" questions revealed that their reasoning structure did not differ significantly from that of other adult groups, a finding consistent with the data in many of the studies measuring criminal and noncriminal attitudes toward law (see, e.g., Kutchinsky, 1972, 1973). On the ideal questions, answers were about evenly split between conventional (44%) and postconventional (48%) responses; on the real question, a conventional orientation (60% vs. 36%) was dominant. And in neither case did prisoners focus extensively on avoiding negative consequences as a motivation for compliance. In the words of a 40-year-old with a 12-year prison record, people should follow rules "to insure peace and order which previous social preconditioning has failed to instill in those who tend to disrupt peace and order." In sum, these law deviants did not express an idiosyncratic "criminal" orientation to issues of rights, roles, and rules. They were not more postconventional or preconventional than college youth, teachers, or law professionals. This finding supports the view that deviance may be as much a function of the psychopathology of the social milieu as of the individual (see Haney & Zimbardo, Chap. 17).

Particularly on their ideal question, teachers expressed a somewhat greater degree of postconventional reasoning (66%) than other adults (38% and 48%) and even college youth (56%). A 60-year-old high-school teacher said that people should obey "to accomplish the greatest good for all concerned." Since as part of their professional role, teachers function directly in socializing and resocializing activities, their ability to comprehend higher-level reasoning is of paramount importance. To the extent that teachers can at least understand postconventional thought, as professionals and socializers they can move beyond the slogans and clichés of uncritical, maintenance-oriented perspectives.

Juxtaposed with other adults, graduating law professionals were seemingly more entrenched in a conventional pattern of reasoning. A 25-year-old reasoned that people should obey "to achieve the rewards that following the rules brings." On the ideal question, in comparison to college undergraduates (34%), teachers (32%), and criminals (44%), 58 percent of the law students focused on social conformity explanations. Prospective lawyers in comparison to other adults and college youth did not appear to be better equipped for autonomous, principled rule-making activity, even though they have greater technical skill and are trained to expect to assume more powerful and demanding societal functions.

Analyzing the responses to both obedience questions together revealed that both adults and youth primarily saw the conditions of compliance not in terms of a simple punishment model but rather in terms of a respect for and obligation to maintain rule systems. Preconventional limits of legality based on enforcement and sanction concerns were expressed infrequently. Conventional conformity to majority norms was exhibited by preadolescence and basically remained stable in adulthood.

## Summary

Overall the data indicate that developing children and adults express rather similar conceptions vis-à-vis authoritative rule systems. By preadolescence, individuals are basically consumers of the legal process and are oriented to system maintenance. In stabilizing at a law-and-order conforming level, most individuals make no distinction between underlying principles of justice and the legal system itself. These adults from diverse backgrounds seemed to articulate a value structure that mirrored the reasoning of youth during preadolescent to college years. To encourage more advanced modes of legality, socialization agents may need to embrace alternative structures of thought, define new educative goals, appraise old strategies, and consider the impact of legal experiences and settings.

## SOCIALIZATION STRATEGIES: PROCEDURES FOR JUSTICE

The predominance of a conventional legality in youth and adults suggests that the legal environment or culture can indeed limit an individual's natural capacity (see also Tapp, 1974). Therefore, in this section our primary concern is to discover the socializing conditions that engender an ethical use of law in the populace, both within the present adult generation (resocialization) and the next (initial socialization). Since the socializing strategies elaborated below were abstracted from specific variables tested in a limited way and/or in experimental settings (see, e.g., Staub, 1975; Turiel, 1973), we proffer them solely as working hypotheses that need further evaluation and refinement.

### Legal Knowledge

The first of the socializing strategies is the transmission of legal knowledge. By focusing on legal reasoning, we did not intend to obscure the importance of substantive information about law and the legal network. To the contrary, developing substantive competence is critical to the expansion of one's capacity to analyze and make decisions (see also Freund, Chap. 14; Hogan, 1970). Effective socialization should impart and make accessible knowledge about rights, rules, resources, and remedies if individuals are to become creators as well as "informed" consumers of law and if critical competence rather than compliance is the prevailing goal. The goal is not to learn the technical skills and art of the practicing lawyer, or indoctrination or the incorporation of legal facts—or fictions—into one's repertoire. Yet, the law should not be re-

garded merely "as a system of rules to be mastered by those self-doomed to work with them. . . [Freund, 1968, p. 108]."

In our view, acquiring knowledge about law (whether one endorses the law or not) *is* essential because it expands the ability to understand problems, define expectations, relate to events, press claims, and structure choices. Without a basic comprehension of substantive law and legal process, individuals cannot effectively use a service, invoke a right, or redress a grievance. We do not contend that knowledge about law determines either attitudes or behaviors (see also Andenaes, Chap. 5; Berkowitz & Walker, 1967; Walker & Argyle, 1964). Recall, for example, the conventional legality revealed by the graduating law students: They were no more principled than adults *not* exposed to substantive legal training. The point is simple: While the development of legal competence requires substantive information, the acquisition of knowledge alone is insufficient for stimulating integrative, accommodative, and critical thought.

### Mismatch and Conflict

"Successful match as mismatch" succinctly describes the staging of value conflicts as a socializing condition for achieving legal competence. A mismatch in value orientations should stimulate one's intellective, differentiating capacities and thereby more complex forms of thought. The role of "mismatch" or constructive conflict is revealed in Turiel's discussion (1973, 1974) of the Piagetian principle of equilibration: "The ideal equilibrium is not passive adjustment or conformity to external demands. . . . [I]ncreases in disequilibrium are viewed as the conditions for development [1973, p. 737]."

Conflict has increasingly and persuasively been used as a strategy in value education. Research in moral development described in Chapter 9 indicates that it is advantageous for the socializer to be one stage ahead of the socializee or at least cognizant and appreciative of alternative arguments and modes of reasoning (see also Kohlberg & Turiel, 1971; Rest *et al.,* 1969; Tracy & Cross, 1973; Turiel, 1966). Social learning paradigms too are drawn to the role of conflict, though they rely more on modeling and experience than on maturation and movement (Bandura & McDonald, 1963; Hoffman & Saltzstein, 1967; Sears, 1974). Social learning theories stress the conflict of content and experience, rather than the conflict of reasoning structures, as very crucial in elaborating an ideological perspective. In terms of socialization practice, conflict in content and structure are neither incompatible nor mutually exclusive; probably both conditions are at work in the interactive process necessary to ideological development.

The introduction of conflict should provide the individual with practice in managing and integrating diversity. The research cited above indicates that reasoning can be advanced by experiences that question one's problem-solving modes; our data suggest that the orientation of adults is not sufficiently disparate from that of youth to create a dialectical exchange. Legal socializers need not endorse higher-stage thinking, but they must recognize and comprehend such reasoning to encourage the learner to generate his or her own conceptualization. As Haan, Smith, and Block emphasized, "conflictless experiences are probably incompatible with both moral and cognitive growth [1968, p. 200]."

## Participation

Participation is crucial for stimulating legal development. It offers varied opportunities for role taking and communication, emphasizes reciprocity and cooperation in reaching legal decisions, and encourages evaluation and open inquiry. Through participation one can gain an appreciation of the frameworks of others, the interdependence of rights and responsibilities, the meaning of power and powerlessness, and the need to allocate resources and establish

priorities. Such experiences can put the locus of control internal to the individual, with each person contributing to the ultimate configuration of legal norms and judgments (see Fuller, 1969b, pp. 162, 186; Rawls, 1971, p. 526).

Socializing strategies based on participation should further advance legal development; under such conditions individuals are more likely to evaluate their own acts, compare them to others', and reconsider the adequacy of their reasoning modes. The centrality of cooperation and role taking to cognitive development has been emphasized by Piaget and Kohlberg (see Berg & Mussen, 1975, pp. 189, 193). Selman and Damon (1975) concluded on the basis of their research that perspective taking is "an important component of more mature moral thought and action [p. 72]." Staub (1975) drew a similar conclusion from his experimental studies of helping behavior. He found that assigning responsibility to children for the welfare of others and/or having children teach other children prosocial behavior (both activities are functionally participatory for the subjects) affected later prosocial behavior. To the extent that participatory experiences stimulate empathy, enhance tolerance for diversity and dissent, and foster critical abilities and internal controls, they embody—if not rehearse—the attributes of a postconventional legality. The value of participation for realizing a postconventional orientation is well captured in Nonet's discussion of legal competence (1969, pp. 8–9):

Legal participation is not submission to authority but . . . a way of insisting that authority is problematic, open to criticism, and in need of justification. A new form of authority is envisioned, one that is less preoccupied with stability and acceptance, and that values the unsettling impact of controversy and the participaton of an assertive citizenry. . . . A commitment to [the] law as a mode of governance requires that more thought be given to means of promoting the growth of a competent citizenry, including the possibility that legal institutions might assume more affirmative responsibilities for developing the capacities of their constituencies.

## Legal Continuity

To encourage individuals to fulfill their potential as creative legal forces—in Nader's terms, to exercise their justice motive (1975, p. 169), social institutions and their socializing agents should promote conditions for valuing multiple legal systems and diverse legal cultures. In daily life, rule-creating and -administering processes occur in an infinite variety of contexts—a network of rule systems that are experientially "legal." A broader approach to law than the common but restrictive, unitary focus on government regulation is needed. This expanded perspective is consistent with cross-cultural, developmental data on children's similar conceptions of the attributes of various compliance systems from government and community to family and school (Hess & Tapp, 1969). It also parallels the work of others (e.g., Fuller, 1969a, 1969b; Hogan & Henley, 1970; Pospisil, 1967, 1972; Selznick, 1969; Weyrauch, Chap. 4), who view societies as composed of countless and multiple "social unions" with shared ends and common activities, ranging in size "from families and friendships to much larger associations [Rawls, 1971, p. 527]."

The advantage of socializing strategies that reflect a broad conception of law is substantial. Such a perspective should increase the probability of one's using complementary, yet diverse "legal" alternatives to redress grievances, accommodate interests, or secure rights. For example, an individual can reason whether to press a claim through formal or informal "law" or through adversary or conciliatory techniques. Further, continuity enhances a conception of the individual as instrumental in determining the nature of the network of "legal" activity, as opposed to passively receiving an externally imposed set of regulations. Thus, the individual is more likely to develop an ethical legality,

and the law is more likely to be, or to become, an expresive, participatory institution.

## SOCIALIZATION MODELS: TWO CASES IN POINT

In the preceding section we outlined socialization strategies deemed compatible with stimulating an ethical legality. A basic question is the extent to which legal institutions, as presently constituted, can use such techniques. In earlier work we found little evidence that the legal profession and legal services were prepared to educate the public effectively (Tapp & Levine, 1974; see also Rosenthal, 1974). As additional cases in point, we here examine the possibility of implementing socializing strategies in two other legal contexts—the community and the school. Our goal is to offer guidelines for social situations that could bring individuals regardless of age into the practice of justifying as well as implementing procedure. Encouraging equal access to and participation in the administration of justice are crucial components of a postconventional competence to use the law, whatever the institutional forum or setting.

### Community Legal System

In our view a community with decentralized institutional and procedural supports could be instrumental in developing people's legal reasoning. With regard to legal socialization goals, a community legal system—whether in the city neighborhood, village, or rural locale—is particularly promising because it is an existing framework for involving individuals in public life. At present, except as witness, suspect, plaintiff, defendant, informer, or juror, most people have little or no access to or acquaintance with the institution of law. But a community legal structure could provide essential opportunities for participation in rule- and decision-making activity.

We are aware of the problems involved in establishing a decentralized, complementary legal system. There is substantial risk merely of transferring power from central to local elites. While efforts to enhance local control may reinforce instead of eradicate power and privilege, awareness of the problems should not obscure the promise of expanding legal institutions and developing the public's competence to criticize or challenge authority. As Cahn and Cahn (1966, p. 951) emphasized, "the possibility of advancing the cause of justice through increasing lay involvement in fact finding, adjudication and arbitration should not be sacrificed a priori out of fear of abuse."

Overall, local communities are conducive to implementing a horizontal legal system (Franck, 1972) with open channels of communication (Fuller, 1969b, p. 186). This type of social structure is an apt context both for imparting knowledge (substantive competence) and for encouraging its effective use (psychological competence). In comparison to a hierarchical model based on representative authority and the delegation of power, a horizontal, participatory social structure emphasizes "an authority by equals . . . jointly sharing tasks and responsibilities [Franck, 1972, p. 775]." Whether a child or an adult is concerned, learning is most difficult when theory is divorced from practice. The socializing value of a community legal system lies in providing a means for persons to apply abstract principles to real situations —a key component for effective education (Dewey, 1910, 1930).

In proposing a community legal system, we contemplate building on extant legal foundations, not dismantling presently existing legal institutions. As indicated previously, alternative, multiple rule contexts are continuous, legitimate, and valuable expressions of law. As Danzig observed, "if decentralization is to be successful it will involve the construction of a complementary system, supplementing and in some areas substituting for, but nowhere destroying or totally displacing, the existing apparatus [1973, p. 7]." In this chapter, we view the socializing goals that a complementary system could promote. Other advantages of a decentralized

system are well outlined by Danzig (1973) and by Cahn and Cahn (1966, pp. 948–955). We sketch three operational features (procedural, programmatic, and institutional) of a community legal system to characterize its socializing role.[6]

*Community exchange.* Effective outreach is required to raise the general level of legal consciousness and competence and to enhance the knowledge and efficacy of individual citizens. Relaying information to persons individually, however, is insufficient. As Fuller in Chapter 3 succinctly put it, "[l]ike any joint enterprise, the operation of a legal system is collaborative." Therefore, opportunities for individuals to communicate and cooperate during the process of legal decision making are indispensable.

Both individual citizens and professional groups need to take part together in public forums (town meetings, speakouts, accountability sessions, precinct caucuses, workshops). Practicing lawyers, police, probation officers, legislators, welfare workers, prosecutors, and judges should view participation as part of their role responsibility, the neglect of which constitutes an abrogation of the ethics of their role (see Fuller, 1969c). Such exchange is one way to confront the problems associated with establishing a balance of power between the community and the professional. In proposing short-term, problem-solving groups, Glidewell emphasized that, in contrast to larger social systems, temporary groups "[can] take greater risks, examine more different alternatives, conduct more experiments, and confront more threats [1968, pp. 103–104]."

---

[6] Danzig (1973) presented a comprehensive analysis of the advantages of a decentralized system and described "what a decentralized [criminal justice] system performing [certain] legislative, police, prosecutorial, court, and prison functions could look like [p. 2]." His model calls for a neighborhood attorney (p. 37) and neighborhood court system (p. 41). In the next section of the text, the potential of these two reforms are considered in terms of their socialization impact.

Such face-to-face, open forums can transmit knowledge, reveal mutual goals, develop the ability to question and evaluate responses, and foster an understanding of diverse frames of reference. For example, a precinct caucus could focus on such relevant issues as abortion, police, taxes, drug use, or housing. Besides imparting legal knowledge, such sessions should promote exchange of information about local practices and personal experiences as well as encourage participation in self-government. In short, communicating with people in their idiom (bilingually as needed), in familiar contexts, and with identifiable problems can considerably enhance substantive and psychosocial legal competence.

*Community legal counsels.* Lawyers, if available, or a cadre of trained paraprofessionals can usefully function as "house counsel" for a community legal system (see also Cahn & Cahn, 1966, pp. 954–957; 1970, pp. 1019–1022; Conn & Hippler, 1973). The "house counsel" would serve some functions analogous to the community psychologist in the community mental health field (see, e.g., Glidewell, 1972). Whether a community is urban or rural and whether there are strong customary "laws," the community legal counsel can inform, advise, translate (literally and figuratively), and investigate relevant issues. For the community counsel, the collectivity is the client. As part of the legal community, these workers would come to know the local citizens, try to understand their problems, encourage their participation, function as outreach liaisons, and hopefully develop shared bonds of trust.

Instead of traditional case-by-case practice, community counsels can function as justice facilitators by assuming educative, experimental, and ethical responsibilities (see also Cahn & Cahn, 1966, pp. 939–941; Rosenthal, 1974, pp. 7–28; Silberman, 1970, p. 45; Tapp, 1974, p. 165). These law advisors can protect and enlarge the compass of basic human rights—of "generating conflict, of bringing latent conflict into the legal and political arenas and mobilizing interests

on both sides of an issue [Casper, 1970, p. 173]." It may be unrealistic to expect community counsels to undertake extensive investigations or complex litigations, particularly when resources are scarce, but they could hold local public hearings, aid criminal suspects, witnesses, and victims, and inform community groups (see also Danzig, 1973, p. 37). Such efforts can clarify the limitations and potential of current law as well as of alternative legal forums (e.g., consumer arbitration). In sum, the role of community counsels in raising legal consciousness and competence is limited only by their own creativity and imagination in devising programs for improving community life (see Danzig, 1973, p. 40).

*Community courts.* Perhaps most importantly, the community legal system as a complementary subsystem of the law provides expanded opportunities for institutionalized legal activity. While many contexts (e.g., clubs, unions, work groups) offer "legal" experiences, actual participation in the institution of law (e.g., proceedings before courts, legislative councils) is crucial to individual legal development. Jury participation is now the major institutionalized mechanism for citizen involvement in legal decision making (see, e.g., Black, 1973, p. 149; Kadish & Kadish, Chap. 24; Kalven & Zeisel, 1966). But otherwise individuals in the United States are, for the most part, consumers of law, not participants in the administration of justice. Localizing dispute settlement in the community can significantly increase access to and participation in decision making. Community experience with legal tribunals (e.g., arbitration commissions, courts of reconciliation, popular tribunals) brings laws closer to the people's daily lives.[7]

---

[7] For illustrations of local tribunals across cultures, see Berman (1969), Berman and Spindler (1963), Gibbs (1963), and Nader (1960). Also Berman's analysis in Chapter 8 of the socializing role of the Soviet court system is particularly relevant—and perhaps reveals some of the potential for abuse.

Developing countries have had local tribunals as part of their customary legal systems (e.g., Gibbs, 1963; Nader, 1969; Nader & Yngvesson, 1973; Smith, 1972). The anthropological literature considers many dispute settlement institutions that have well served traditional legal cultures (e.g., Bohannan, 1957; Gluckman, 1955; Gulliver, 1963; Nader & Metzger, 1963; see also Nader, 1975). The more highly developed countries have generally not been committed to preserving multiple legal systems, but they are beginning to acknowledge the value of alternative mechanisms for processing disputes, resolving grievances, and handling claims (see also Felstiner, 1974; Yngvesson & Hennessey, 1975). Establishing community courts with complementary jurisdiction can serve to integrate individuals into their systems of law, both national and local. Economy, accessibility, and shared bonds are only three of the many factors that should encourage the development of legal competence (see Fuller, 1969c). They are almost necessarily characteristic of a community legal system.

Individuals who sit on, appear before, or observe courts of conciliation, mediation, or arbitration witness attempts to reconcile preferences and values in the process of accommodation. Whether a dispute is civil or criminal, the purpose is basically the same: to reestablish cooperation and communication between individuals whether they bring common or divergent goals. Community courts not only reduce the social distance between legal professionals and the citizenry, increase people's comfort and experience in legal settings, and bring cases expeditiously to conclusion; they also offer opportunities for pursuing open inquiry, managing conflict, and appreciating the rights and responsibilities of participating in shaping laws.

## School Legal System

The school setting can have a significant impact on the legal socialization of youth. Our focus on stimulating ethical use of the law during childhood is based on two assumptions—the primacy of the formative years in determining patterns of legal reasoning and the potency of initial socialization over resocialization. While socialization and resocialization continue through life (see, e.g., Brim & Wheeler, 1966; Jennings & Niemi, 1968a, 1974), strong evidence in our adult data and in the studies presented in Part III indicates considerable persistence of early values, reasoning processes, and modes of behavior. In addition, compared to resocialization, initial socialization stimulates a fluid developmental process rather than trying to alter crystallized reasoning structures or reorganize accumulated experiences (Kennedy & Kerber, 1973, pp. 43–47). The community legal system may avoid the pitfalls of resocialization that is sporadic and divorced from people's lives. But the strengths of early development and primary socialization, coupled with the educational system's function of teaching basic cognitive competencies to the young, underscore the potentially crucial impact of a school milieu.

*Importance of school setting.* The school, through its policies and substantive programs, can direct students toward an ethical utilization of law or retard the development of such a legality. The school is particularly appropriate for implementing effective socializing conditions: It is an accessible, salient, and controllable setting. As such, it sets the tone for comprehending both rule making and justice seeking. In addition to formal curricula and instructional pedagogy, legal education occurs indirectly in the classroom and school, as Silberman emphasized:

What educators must realize . . . is that how they teach and how they act may be more important than what they teach. . . . Certainly administrative procedures like automatic promotion, homogeneous grouping, racial segregation, or selective admission to higher education affect "citizenship education" more profoundly than does the social studies curriculum. And children are taught a host of lessons about values, ethics, morality, character, and conduct every day of the week, less by the content of the curriculum than by the way schools are organized, the ways teachers and parents behave, the way they talk to children and to each other [1970, p. 9].

In essence, the school is a functioning legal system for student and teacher alike. Opportunities for dialogue and participation within this system can substantially enhance the legal competence of all.

*Current trends.*   Since 1971 interest in legal education for youth in both elementary and high schools has grown enormously in the U.S. The organized bar, educators, and law enforcement agencies have made major commitments to promoting law-related programs in the school systems from kindergarten to grade 12. The result has been a proliferation of materials, curriculum programs, demonstration projects, and teacher-training institutes. Some programs indeed attempt to stimulate open inquiry, active participation, confrontation, and controversy appropriately "matched" to the cognitive level of the student. Their goal is to develop the individual's capacity to analyze, interpret, and make decisions regarding legal order, indoctrination for obedience, support of the government, and assimilation of legal "facts."

Although we recommend evaluation research, in this section we do not evaluate current programs. We review recent activity because, viewed as an experiment (see Campbell, 1969), it can usefully inform legal education planning. In so doing, we are guided by two questions: What is the nature of legal education in the schools? Is it compatible with stimulating an ethical utilization of law?

There are well over 200 law-related educational projects outside of professional law schools in the United States, according to a survey done in 1973.[8] The programs are predominantly urban or metropolitan based, with almost none in small urban (under 100,000 population) or rural communities. As with social services, it is generally easier to conduct an urban program. Unfortunately, city projects often do not reach effectively into inner-city, rights-deprived areas, and they have no contact at all with the rural periphery. A further problem of program outreach is revealed by the survey data on target audiences. Only about 20 percent of the projects focus on the entire school career from kindergarten through high school. In addition, almost half are oriented exclusively to high-school students; comparatively few reach solely to those in grade school.

Overall, legal education in the schools seems to reflect a conventional, system-maintenance perspective. Few declarations in support of the ritual of compliance are as blunt as "[a]ll we ask is that they behave themselves."[9] But typically programs emphasize responsibilities much more than rights. For example, a common guiding principle or ultimate goal is to "show students the values of the system under which they live [and] . . . to subdue violence and defiance of authority of the majority as expressed through law." There is little focus on the rights of children and youth or on active participation in rule making and in seeking redress through system procedures.

---

The primary data source was a mailed questionnaire ultimately obtained on 145 programs. We wish to thank Vivian Monroe, Executive Director of the Constitutional Rights Foundation (CRF), and Joel Henning, former Staff Director of the ABA Special Committee on Youth Education for Citizenship, who granted us access to the survey materials. We also especially wish to thank H. Dietmar Starke, research assistant at the American Bar Foundation, for undertaking a preliminary analysis of these data.
[9] This statement and those that follow in the text are direct quotes written by project representatives in response to a series of questions about goals and objectives.

---

[8] The survey was jointly sponsored by the Los Angeles-based Constitutional Rights Foundation and the American Bar Association's Special Committee on Youth Education for Citizenship.

Only rarely is the objective of a law-related program to "organize students to protect their rights and involvement in school decision making."

A number of programs do seem to incorporate educational strategies compatible with an ethical utilization of law. One major effort—reaching 93,000 students in 50 school systems of California—is the Law in a Free Society Project,[10] which offers programs from kindergarten through grade 12. By curriculum development, teacher-training workshops, and consultation services, this project caters to the cognitive capacity of the audience, matching innovations to student comprehension. Particularly noteworthy is the project's teacher-training program. Far from imparting legal "truths" to teachers for their dissemination to students, practical, problem-solving courses encourage adults to reason about law and evaluate the potential of diverse alternatives.

Most illuminating from our perspective, however, is that direct student participation in the school context on anything other than an audience level is minimal. There is, for example, very little joint activity in school governance. Of the 145 projects responding to the survey, 15 percent attempted to involve students in "School Decision Making or Disciplinary Measures," 18 percent in "Student Government Activities," and 24 percent in "Outside Voluntary Activities." This profile reflects little progression beyond the 1969 characterization that what students "learn from school practices is often a conscious or unconscious denial of the participation, liberty, equality, and justice theories they heard about in civics class. Students hear about libertarian precepts, but they see

---

[10] This project is listed in the Directory of Law-Related Educational Activities disseminated by the ABA Special Committee on Youth Education for Citizenship (1974). The core materials of this project consist of four books (*Casebook, Lesson Plans, Curriculum, Guide for Teacher Education*) on each of eight topics (authority, diversity, freedom, justice, participation, privacy, property, and responsibility).

and experience authoritarian treatment [Schwilch & Mead, 1970, pp. v–vi]." Evidently while legal competence and principles of justice may be taught in the classroom, these data suggest that they are not sufficiently put into practice in real-life situations.

*Future perspectives.* The present thrust of U.S. legal education programs in the schools is oriented toward high-school students through course curricula. To maximize the socializing potential of the school environment, greater efforts should commence in the primary school. Young children have the capacity to confront legal and ethical issues (see also Cahn & Cahn, 1970, p. 1022; Freund, 1968). Since the development of legal reasoning is a continuous, life-cycle process, it is crucial to consider this cognitive skill at an early age.

Attention should also focus on the school (or classroom) itself as a functioning legal system. We are not saying that direct teaching and learning are unimportant to developing legal competence. Exposure to substantive legal knowledge and pedagogic techniques such as role playing, examining historical and cross-cultural experiences, or conducting simulations should increase the ability to comprehend other points of view, appreciate the continuity of law, and value open inquiry. However, participation and role-taking experiences (appropriately matched for age level) in governing the classroom and/or the school are critical to enhancing legal reasoning and to implementing a just administration.

Any complete program of legal education must confront real problems and encourage initiative and meaningful participation (or freely elected nonparticipation). The credibility of a system is enhanced when there are significant opportunities for dialectic and dialogue. Such early experiences lay the foundations for more complex legal reasoning and activity. As Piaget observed:

[S]ocial life, introduced into the classroom through the agency of effective collaboration among the students and the autonomous discipline of the group, implies the very ideal of the activity we have already described as being characteristic of the new school: it is morality in action, just as "active" work is intelligence as act. And even more than this, cooperation leads to the formation of a number of particular and interrelated values such as those of justice based on equality and those of "organic" interdependence [1970, p. 180].

## CONCLUSION

This chapter has aimed to clarify the relation between the individual's natural reasoning ability and the impact of social variables. Essentially the goal of legal socialization is to stimulate legal reasoning skills that embody a reciprocal rights-consciousness and legal competence. To this end, more is required than increasing legal resources and legal knowledge. Legal education should be part of a broad societal commitment to socialize and resocialize individuals to become more interactive, self-reliant participants in multiple systems of law.

Implicitly this charge acknowledges the necessity of appraising social settings, institutions, and rule systems not only because we are concerned about their impact on human development but also because we are equally concerned about their functional compatibility with basic values. If systems of law and the general public are to gain a postconventional orientation, the dynamic relation between the two must be recognized and both socialized simultaneously. Participation, the support of dissensus and consensus, communication of information, as well as role-taking opportunities, are crucial in such an educative process. These conditions promote a dialectical exchange between individuals and institutions that can only advance the comprehension and administration of justice.

# CHAPTER 16

# Socialization into Child Abuse
## A Social Interactional Perspective[1]

*—ROSS D. PARKE*

A social-psychological theory of child abuse is outlined that stresses how the social environment elicits and maintains abusive behavior. Social environmental influences are examined in the culture, the local community, and the family. Cultural sanctioning of violence and lack of community support systems for families are viewed as supporting the development of abusive patterns. An analysis of family interaction patterns that lead to abusive incidents is offered, with emphasis on the role of both the child-victim and the spouse. Resocialization of abusive families can be achieved by therapeutic modification of family interaction patterns and by improving the availability of social support systems. It is argued that professionals in the legal system can serve as facilitators of effective family functioning rather than merely agents of law enforcement. Finally, children's rights need to be given wider recognition, and arguments limiting the scope of children's rights in terms of sociolegal competence are questioned.

Child abuse has received much recent attention due in part to a reported rise in child abuse and in part to a societal reawakening to the rights and treatment of children. The purpose of this chapter is to advance a social interactional analysis of child abuse as an alternative to the traditional personality–psychiatric approach. The model presented here builds on the view that the family is one rule system within a structure of multiple, interactive, and overlapping rule systems (for this approach, see Fuller, 1969b; Tapp, 1971a; Tapp & Levine, 1974). Abuse,

it will be argued, is an orderly outcome of a network of cultural and community forces that, in turn, affect the development of family interaction patterns leading to abusive incidents. Furthermore, by reducing isolation and enhancing educative experiences, family exposure to and interaction with other rule systems can modify and/or deter abuse. In contrast to an emphasis on blame/responsibility or health/disease, this approach suggests that social problems can be managed more effectively by using the link with other "legal" systems as "complementary, yet diverse . . . alternatives to redress grievances, accommodate interests, or secure rights [Levine & Tapp, Chap. 15]," whether for children or adults.

## DEFINITION OF ABUSE

Definitions shape theory and research; the area of child abuse is no exception. Most definitions have been largely asocial, focus-

[1] The chapter was prepared with the support of the National Science Foundation grant GS-31885X to the author. Parts of this chapter are derived from an earlier review by Parke & Collmer (1975). Thanks to M. Gillian Parke and June Louin Tapp for comments on earlier drafts of this chapter. Finally, a special note of appreciation to Frances Hall and Cathy Prinslow for their able assistance in the preparation of the manuscript.

ing on the parent as the sole agent inflicting injury on a passive child-victim. Kempe and Helfer, medical experts on child abuse, defined the phenomenon as "any child who received nonaccidental physical injury (or injuries) as a result of acts (or omissions) on the part of his parents or guardians [1972, p. 1]." The same perspective is revealed in the nonmedical definition offered in Gil's influential volume *Violence against Children:* "Physical abuse of children is the intentional, nonaccidental use of force, on the part of a parent or other caretaker interacting with a child in his care aimed at hurting, injuring or destroying that child [Gil, 1970, p. 6]."

While these two definitions recognize the need to exclude accidental occurrences of physical harm, serious conceptual problems remain. They imply that child abuse can be clearly identified as a set of behaviors imposed on a child by an adult. Ignoring the obvious inferential difficulties of attributing intentionality accurately (Kelley, 1973), these definitions are too narrow. First, they direct attention to only one side of the parent–child dyad, namely the adult. No recognition is paid to the child's role in eliciting abuse from his caretakers. Second, the sociocultural context of behaviors is not recognized, in part stemming from the assumption that an absolute standard for judging the occurrence of abuse is obtainable. Such a definition is neither empirically possible nor logically valid.

### The Role of Contexts in Definitions

Child abuse is not merely a set of behaviors but is rather a culturally determined label applied to injury patterns as an outcome of a judgment process by an observer. According to a social judgment approach (Bandura & Walters, 1963; Parke & Sawin, 1975a; Walters & Parke, 1964), an observer takes into account various factors in deciding whether a particular injury is an instance of child abuse. Intention is merely one criterion. Other variables include the

antecedents, form, and intensity of the response, the extent of the injury, and the role and status of agent and victim. For example, the same injury labeled abuse in one situation, for one child, or in one social class may not be judged abuse in another situation, for another child, or in another social class. Even a simple definition in terms of injuries must include estimates of severity based on culturally defined standards.

In short, child abuse is a phenomenon that must be viewed in the context of community norms. To date, insufficient attention has been paid to developing an empirically derived set of standards based on community consensus concerning the rights of children and parents. For purposes of this chapter, a modification of the Kempe-Helfer definition of the abused child is used: any child who during the course of parent–child interaction receives nonaccidental physical injury (or injuries) resulting from acts on the part of his or her caretakers that violate the community standards concerning the treatment of children.

### The Implications of Being Labeled Abusive

Labeling a family as abusive has important implications for treatment both informally by friends, neighbors, and relatives and from formal agencies such as social welfare and law-enforcement groups, school authorities, and employers. Once an agency within an interrelated services structure labels a parent as abusive, other agencies tend to accept this label and treat the family accordingly. Consistency across agencies occurs even though initially a second agency may not have labeled the family as abusive by its own criteria. Similarly, informal communication of the label through the family's court appearances or social worker's visits may promote adoption of the abuse tag by friends and relatives in the informal social network.

Once a family has been labeled "abusive," treatment may vary. For example, the adequacy of the home may be assessed; legal machinery may be activated with ensuing public exposure; a child's subsequent bruises may be more readily defined as abuse by school officials. Friends and relatives may avoid the "accused" family from fear of guilt by association or the embarrassment of interacting with a "deviant" individual. The alterations at informal and formal levels can significantly affect a parent's attitudes and behaviors. As Gelles (1975, p. 365) wisely argued, "being labeled an abuser may have produced the personality characteristics— anxiety, depression, etc.—which were later called the causes of the abuse!" Nor should this argument be restricted to personality characteristics. The social isolation characteristics of the abusive family (Elmer, 1967) may also result from community rejection of the labeled family.

This exploration of labeling effects may challenge the oft-made claim that child abuse is a lower-class phenomenon (Gil, 1970). The social network used by middle-class families in crisis importantly differs from that available to lower-class families. Middle-class families are likely to use private agencies, while lower-class families rely on public agencies, clinics, and hospitals. Private physicians and social agencies are less likely to report and publicly label child-abuse incidents. For example, in one national survey hospitals, police, and public social agencies accounted for 80 percent of reported incidents, while private sources contributed only 3 percent of the cases (Gil, 1970). In short, lower-class individuals are probably overrepresented in child-abuse estimates and thus more likely to suffer the consequences of being officially designated as abusive.

The implications of labeling errors merit attention. Although labeling permits institutionalized response in the form of state-sponsored intervention and support, mistaken labeling can have harmful effects for the mislabeled family. Recent suggestions (see Kempe, cited in Light, 1973) for programs to improve detection of abused chil-

dren increase the probability of misidentification. Even with such a low base-rate event, small margins of error can result in high levels of false positive predictions. For example, when an abused child is detected 90 percent of the time and nonabuse is correctly identified 95 percent, only 15.4 percent of the children are actually abused— estimating the abuse incidence rate at .010. Thus, 85 percent of the parents accused of abuse would be mistakenly labeled (Light, 1973, p. 570–571)! Given such an error rate, the justification for massive screening programs is questionable. Further, the public labeling of families as abusive by the legal or welfare systems may interfere with the resocialization process. Recidivism rates of labeled and nonlabeled families would provide an important index of the consequences of labeling.

## SOCIALIZATION INTO CHILD ABUSE

How do families become socialized into abusive patterns of child treatment? The most influential and popular model, derived from psychiatric analyses, focuses on the parent as the principal cause: Abusive parents are assumed to have personality characteristics distinct from other parents. There is also the implicit assumption that abusive parents are abnormal or "sick," therefore requiring extensive psychiatric treatment to overcome their "illness." Recently the utility of this approach has been questioned (e.g., Gelles, 1973; Parke & Collmer, 1975). An alternative model of child abuse shifts the causal focus from an analysis of the individual parent to the social environment.

To understand this socialization process, three levels of social-environmental influence require attention. In contrast to a traditional psychiatric emphasis on abnormality, I assume that normal parents are socialized into abusive child-care patterns through the interaction of cultural, community, and familial influences. Child abuse is viewed not as an isolated social phenomenon but as a manifestation of a general cultural attitude to violence. Accordingly, I first explore the cultural sanctioning of violence and aggression, then examine the familial context in which abuse is executed, and, third, analyze the community rule systems in which the family system operates.

## Cultural Sanction of Violence as a Contributor to Child Abuse

Some commentators have argued that the level of child abuse in U.S. society is partly due to cultural sanctioning of physically violent tactics for resolving social conflict (Gil, 1970; see also Palmer, 1972; Pinkney, 1972). For example, in the United States in 1972 there were nearly 20,000 murders known to the police, a rate of 8.9 per 100,000 inhabitants (Kelley, 1973); yet, the rate was only one-tenth as high in England (Geis & Monahan, 1976). Similarly, the assault and battery rate for Canada in 1968 was 28.6 per 100,000, while the U.S. rate was 141 per 100,000 (Steinmetz, 1974a). Nor are law-enforcement officers exempt from violent tactics. Stark (1972) has estimated that there are three million instances of unnecessary physical abuse by police officers (see also Black & Reiss, 1967).[2]

The level of television violence is also higher in the U.S. than in countries such as Sweden, Israel, or Britain (Liebert, Neale, & Davidson, 1973). Gerbner's careful analysis (1972) of the content of TV programs over five years revealed that over 75 percent contained violence. Stein and Freidrich (1975) summarized these effects: Both behaviors and attitudes are shaped by TV programming. In fact, children and adults are repeatedly and consistently exposed to the moral lesson that violence is an appropriate means for resolving conflict.

---

[2] There are other forms of institutionalized violence commonly executed by corporate and government officials such as failing to enforce pollution standards and permitting dangerous drugs to be profitably marketed (Geis & Monahan, 1976).

Other evidence suggests that levels of violence in a society are reflected in levels of violence within the family. In a comparison of German, Italian, and Danish cities, Bellak and Antell (1974) found that higher suicide and homicide rates corresponded to higher levels of both parental and child aggression. Similarly, Steinmetz (1974a) in a U.S.–Canadian comparison found lower levels of intrafamilial aggression in Canada, where criminal aggressive activity is also lower. In a U.S. study, Steinmetz (1974b) reported that parents who used verbal and physical aggression to resolve husband–wife disputes tended to use similar techniques in disciplining children—with children duplicating these tactics with siblings.

Given these repeated patterns of violence, it is not surprising that physical punishment is a widely used disciplinary and child-rearing technique. Stark and McEvoy (1970) reported that 93 percent of all parents employed physical punishment, although some only rarely and only on young children. In fact, one investigation by Korsch, Christian, Gozzi, and Carlson (1965) revealed that of a sample of 100 Los Angeles mothers, a quarter spanked infants in the first six months of life, and nearly half spanked infants by the end of the first year. However, later studies (Steinmetz, 1974c; Straus, 1971) showed that physical punishment was not restricted to young children. Straus found that 52.3 percent of his adolescent sample experienced actual or threatened physical punishment during their last year of high school. Erlanger's recent study (1974) indicated that physical punishment as a disciplinary technique was used at all social levels—contrary to earlier reports (Bronfenbrenner, 1958). Professional groups also have advocated the use of physical punishment in child-rearing. Viano (1974) found that of the educators, police, and clergy questioned, two-thirds condoned spanking children for disciplinary purposes with belts, straps, and brushes!

Is physical punishment as a child-rearing technique in U.S. society a factor in the level of child abuse? Gil argued:

A key element to understanding child abuse . . . seems to be that the context of child rearing does not exclude the use of physical force. . . . Rather, American culture encourages in subtle and at times not so subtle ways the use of "a certain measure" of physical force in rearing children . . . [1970, p. 134].

Support for this assertion comes from other cultures where physical punishment is not sanctioned. Recent reporters on China (Sidel, 1972; Stevenson, 1974) described only rare use of physical punishment, little aggression among children, and no incidents of child abuse. Data from Taiwan and the U.S. (Niem & Collard, 1971) indicated that physical punishment in any form was used less than half as often by Taiwanese families and spankings were only a quarter as frequent (see also Freedman & Freedman, 1969). Goode (1971) noted a similar situation in Japan, where physical punishment is not a common disciplinary tactic and child abuse is infrequent. Also this pattern is evident in other cultures such as the Arapesh (Mead, 1935) and the Tahitians (Levy, 1969).

These examples suggest that variations in the cultural level of violence are reflected in family violence, particularly in the use of physical punishment in child rearing. Whether these variations are responsible for different levels of child abuse is left unanswered. However, in the next section the processes by which physical punitiveness *can* lead to child abuse are analyzed in detail.

## The Family as the Context of Child Abuse

To understand how abuse develops within a family, a variety of factors must be examined. First, parents' histories define the guidelines for child rearing. Second, the nature of parent–child interaction helps explain the development of abusive tactics. As noted earlier, it is not enough to view child abuse as unidirectional, with the main cause located in the parent; husband, wife, and child-victim each may play a role. Finally, the social and community support available to the family for providing alternative "rule" guidelines or assistance in times of crises must be considered.

*Transmission of cultural attitudes to parents: The impact of punitive child-rearing.* Although child-rearing information, norms, and rules are transmitted in a variety of ways, such as through schools and the news media, the most powerful vehicle within a culture is the family. Steele & Pollock (1968) have documented that abusive parents were themselves abused as children. There is a clear parallel between this finding and the more general relation between exposure to physical punishment during childhood and the high rate of aggression of both children and adults (Erlanger, 1974). Physically punitive tactics are probably learned through imitation of parents. Bandura (1967) summarized how parental modeling may account for the physical discipline-aggression relation:

When a parent punishes his child physically for having aggressed toward peers, for example, the intended outcome of this training is that the child should refrain from hitting others. The child, however, is also learning from parental demonstration how to aggress physically. And the imitative learning may provide the direction for the child's behavior when he is similarly frustrated in subsequent social interactions [p. 43].

In essence, one's history of treatment conveys a set of rules about appropriate child-rearing practices. Consistent exposure to physically punitive disciplinary patterns may serve to sanction such behaviors so that they are viewed as normative for child-rearing. Likewise, due to the legitimacy accorded to physical punishment, inhibitions against using physical force generally are lessened. A recent experiment confirmed the relation between type of training and type of tactics used in a subsequent supervisory role (Gelfand, Hartmann, Lamb, Smith, Mahan, & Paul, 1974). Investigators found that a child disciplined by an adult with punitive tactics was more likely to use such tactics when given the chance to train another child.

This legitimation of violence in the form of physically punitive child-rearing may aid in understanding child abuse. Physical punishment (in severe forms, abuse) may be a deliberate and rational execution of well-ingrained patterns of behavior viewed by the parent as a reasonable and necessary aspect of appropriate child-rearing. Parents not only learn to use physically punitive tactics but also come to view these tactics as morally right and justified. In fact, they may say that physical punishment and even abuse are *necessary* to instill appropriate social and moral conduct (Steele & Pollock, 1968).

For these abusive families, physically punitive control tactics are legitimate techniques for preserving the family rule system. Often cooperation with authorities is minimal; law-enforcement agents and social service workers are viewed as interfering with parental rights to elect their own methods of discipline. There is limited sharing of values between the abusive family and the institutions of law or other community rule systems. Often guilt, remorse, or even recognition of social deviance, which may serve as inhibitors for future abusive attacks (Berkowitz, 1962), are lacking, thus increasing the probability of future abuse. In fact, adults may invoke the justification of a higher moral cause as a means of reducing dissonance for their norm violation.

Abuse is not always rational, deliberate, preplanned, or executed in the service of upholding a family moral code and "legal" control system. As Berkowitz argued regarding murder, "These violent outbursts are often too impulsive, too quick and involuntary to be greatly affected by the aggressor's belief as to what will be the outcome of their behavior, beyond the simple idea they will hurt their victim [1974, p. 65]." Prior child-rearing contributes to this scenario by providing the parent with a limited repertoire of child-care tactics. To the extent that physical punishment is the main control tactic, the general class of physically violent responses such as hitting will be well-rehearsed and highly available. A number of studies (e.g., Davitz, 1952) have shown that, under conditions of stress and frustration, predominant responses are likely to be emitted. Just as the availability of and prior experience with a gun make murder more likely under stress and anger, so previously experiencing and using violent child-rearing tactics make child abuse more likely.

*On the misuse of punishment.*   But to restrict the focus to child-rearing histories is too limited. Current situations must be studied to reveal the conditions that accelerate physical punishment to abusive levels. Classic studies on the antecedents of delinquency are instructive. Glueck and Glueck (1950) found that parents of delinquent boys were more "erratic" in their disciplinary practices than parents of nondelinquent boys. Other investigators (e.g., McCord, McCord, & Howard, 1961) noted that erratic disciplinary procedures correlated with high degrees of criminality. A strikingly similar pattern of inconsistent discipline is typical of abusive parents. Young (1964) reported that almost all abusive families (91–100%) were inconsistent in disciplining their children. By analyzing the consequences of such inconsistencies, the transformation of physical punishment into abuse becomes clear.

Laboratory studies of the effects of inconsistent punishment on children's aggression indicate that intermittent punishment administered by a single agent is less effective than consistent punishment (e.g., Parke & Deur, 1972). Nor is it simply intra-agent inconsistency that produces poor control. Stouwie (1972) and Parke and Sawin (1975b) found that inconsistency between two socializing agents leads to ineffective control of children's behavior. Inconsistent discipline also has long-term implications for social control. Deur and Parke (1970) found that boys who were inconsistently disciplined by occasionally being rewarded and at other times punished persisted in aggressive behavior longer than did boys who were treated consistently. The implication is clear: The socializing agent using inconsistent punishment meets resistance to future attempts to either extinguish deviant behavior or suppress it by consistently administered punishment.

Consideration of another outcome of inconsistent punishment may aid in understanding the punishment–abuse relationship: namely, the acceleration of low-intensity punitive responses into more intense and therefore potentially abusive responses. Since high-intensity punishment is more effective than low-intensity punishment (Parke, 1969), in the face of inconsistent handling socializing agents may accelerate the intensity of their punitive tactics. But if the punishment is erratic, only momentary control will be achieved, and a parent may resort to even more intense punishment on some future occasion. Abusive levels of punishment could develop out of such a parent–child interaction in a disciplinary context.

Patterson and colleagues have conceptualized a related type of interaction pattern wherein participants accelerate the exchange of aversive stimuli in the coercion process (Patterson & Cobb, 1971, 1973; Patterson & Reid, 1970). According to this paradigm, when one person presents an aversive stimulus, the second is likely to respond with an aversive stimulus if the initial aversive stimulus appears alterable. The aversive interchange continues escalating in intensity until one person withdraws the aversive stimulus; at this point, the other person withdraws as well. Although their work focused on peers and siblings as shapers of aggression, Patterson and Cobb spelled out the possible implications of their model for abuse:

In the case of mothers, it is hypothesized that there are many grown women with no past history of hitting, who are shaped by interactions with infants and children to initiate physical assaults. Presumably the shaping process is analogous to that provided by children, for children. The mother learns that hits terminate aversive child behavior. She may then be trained to display behavior of increasingly high amplitude as a function of contingencies supplied by children. We also suspect that many of the child homicides reported are in fact the outcome of such training programs. A young woman, unskilled in mothering, is trained by her own children to carry out assaults that result in bodily injury to her trainers [1971, p. 124].

Similarly Parke, Sawin, and Kreling (1974) found that responding to discipline by defying or ignoring an adult may accelerate the severity of adult treatment. A parent's success in inhibiting highly disruptive behaviors through the use of high-intensity tactics may serve to maintain these tactics.

Aggressive families base interaction on the exchange of aversive and noxious stimuli; their rates of exchange for positive events are much lower than those of nonaggressive families (Patterson, 1975). The rules governing family interaction in aggressive and abusive families are such that the probability of acceleration of aversive tactics to abusive levels is heightened. This evidence is strong support for the position that child abuse must be viewed from an interactive perspective. Clearly abuse develops not only as a result of parents' own prior experience but also through the interaction patterns parents evolve with their children.

*The child's role in abuse.* To understand child abuse, both the child and the parent need to be considered. With few exceptions (Milowe & Lourie, 1964; Parke & Collmer, 1975; Sameroff & Chandler, 1975), the child's role in eliciting abuse has received little attention, although investigators have pointed to the selectivity of abuse: Not all children are abused; even within a family usually only a single child is selected.

The child may contribute to abuse in a variety of ways. First, the child may have physical and behavioral characteristics that make abuse more likely. For example, hyperactivity may elicit abuse—of particular interest because of the relations between prematurity and later activity level patterns, and prematurity and abuse (Parke & Collmer, 1975; see also Steven-Long, 1973). Or, the child may develop behaviors through interaction with parents and peers that target him or her for abuse. Or, as a result of physical abuse, the child may develop behavior patterns that elicit more abuse even from those who may not have originally maltreated the child. As Bakan (1971, p. 109) noted, "the well taken care of child attracts positive reactions. The child who is abused and neglected becomes ugly in appearance and behavior and invites further abuse and neglect." In support of this speculation, Dion (1974) recently experimentally demonstrated that the degree of adult punitiveness is determined by the physical attractiveness of the child: An unattractive child receives more severe punishment than an attractive child.

While all children can contribute to their own abuse, the infant is often a target. The birth of an infant may be a stressful event affecting the relations of family members. Many tasks must be mastered including routine caretaking; also schedules and activities must be modified to accommodate another person (Bakan, 1971). In a unique longitudinal study Ryder (1973) found that women with a child, compared to those without, were less satisfied with their marriage and specifically reported that their husbands were paying insufficient attention to them. Special circumstances may make abusive reactions to the newborn more likely. For example, dissatisfactions are probably exaggerated when a child is the product of an unwanted pregnancy (see, e.g., Birrell & Birrell, 1968; Kempe, Silverman, Steele, Droegemueller, & Silver, 1962; Nurse, 1964).

Abusive patterns may also result from a mismatch in the modes of interaction preferred by the mother and her infant. For example, some babies resist being embraced,

hugged, and held tight (Schaffer & Emerson, 1964). This apparent genetic predisposition may be disruptive for mothers who prefer cuddly infants. Also, as Steele and Pollock (1968, p. 129) noted, "Some parents are disappointed when they have a placid child instead of a hoped-for more reactive, responsive baby. Other parents are equally distressed by having an active, somewhat aggressive baby who makes up his own mind about things when they had hoped for a very placid compliant infant." Current research aimed at isolating adaptations in parent–infant dyads should prove fruitful in the early identification of potential breakdowns in parent–infant interaction (Osofsky & Danzger, 1974; Parke & O'Leary, 1976; Parke & Sawin, 1975c).

*The role for the partner in child abuse.* Child abuse may be the outcome of parent–parent interaction. Particularly where strong norms limit husband–wife violence, the child may become a victim. Aggression may be directed toward the child too when extreme dominant–submissive patterns between the parents prevent a passive parent from directly expressing aggression toward the spouse (see Terr, 1970). Fenigstein and Buss (1974) recently provided evidence supporting the hypothesis of selective aggression against a weak victim: Angered adults were given the opportunity to deliver a mildly noxious stimulus to a confederate associated with an insulting experimenter *or* to aggress in a more intense manner against a nonassociated individual. Subjects preferred to display intense aggression rather than aggress against the victim most similar to the anger inducer. Analogously, a child as a weak victim sometimes serves as the target for anger elicited by a spouse.

The reaction of a partner or spouse may also contribute to abuse. Milgram (1974) found that in a situation in which adults made increasingly harmful aggressive responses to a victim, the presence of two supportive peers increased the subject's level of aggressiveness. But the presence of partners who refused to escalate aggressiveness served to lower the subject's aggressive behavior. Although abuse may seem more likely in single-parent homes because there is no partner to prevent serious acceleration of punishment, no simple prediction is possible without exploring the partner's attitudes. Nonreaction from a partner in situations involving serious harm may function as positive reinforcement or approval (Bandura, 1965). Clearly, the interaction patterns among all family members merit consideration.

## The Role of Community Support Systems in Child Abuse

If abuse is the outcome of mounting stress (Gil, 1970; Parke & Collmer, 1975), then the availability of supportive arrangements to provide periodic alleviations of sharing of responsibility for children may be important. This is particularly true where the extended family has been replaced by a self-contained nuclear family, often removed from its original community and established family ties (Bronfenbrenner, 1974). In times past, the extended family may have functioned in various ways to reduce the level of child abuse. The stresses of child care were often alleviated by other family members. The novice mother had an experienced model from whom to acquire mothering skills. At the same time an older caretaker could modify "inappropriate" tactics before escalation to abusive levels. With the demise of the extended family, these roles may be played by the informal network in the neighborhood and community or by formal support systems in law, health, and welfare. But members of a family isolated from both extended family and community contacts— informal and formal—have little opportunity to learn alternative resocialization strategies. Instead, they must rely on their own histories, untempered by the education and elaboration that stem from diverse experiences.

Using U.S. census data across 58 counties in New York State, Garbarino (1976) hypothesized that the rate of child abuse/ maltreatment is inversely related to the socioeconomic support system for the family in each county. Based on a multiple regression approach, which controlled for the intercorrelation among socioeconomic and demographic indices, Garbarino found that five indices, including employment and income levels for mothers and educational opportunities for both mothers and preschool children, accounted for 36 percent of the variance in child abuse across counties. His findings support a social-situational analysis of child abuse. While the data were derived from public agency sources that potentially overrepresent lower socioeconomic classes, the study nevertheless does suggest that environmental stress exacerbated by the unavailability of resources—even within lower-class groups—is related to child abuse.

While informal and formal support systems can be used in time of crises, unfortunately abusive families generally make poor use of such resources. Considerable data suggest that abusive parents are social isolates. Young (1964) reported that 95 percent of severe-abuse families and 83 percent of moderate-abuse families had no continuing relations outside the family. Friendships usually ended after a few weeks or months in a violent quarrel and bitterness; moreover, 85 percent of the abusive families did not participate in any organized groups. In Merrill's research (1962), 50 percent of the abusive families had no formal group association; 28 percent had only one group association—most frequently church. Using an anomie scale that measured distrust of society, retreat from it, and resulting isolation, Elmer (1967) found a difference between abusive and nonabusive mothers. Likewise, Lenoski (1974) detected self-imposed isolation; 89 percent of the abusive parents had unlisted telephone numbers in contrast to only 12 percent of the nonabusive parents. In addition, almost twice as many of the abusive families (81% versus 43%) preferred to resolve crises alone. Other evidence indicates that such isolation may not be entirely voluntary. Merrill (1962) reported that abusive families were accepted only moderately (36%) and minimally (47%) well by their communities. Schloesser (1964) too found that some families were actively rebuffed by the community.

The lack of social integration of abusive families may be a function of their high mobility. Few have nearby relatives or other roots in the community (Gil, 1970; Scholesser, 1964). The special point of mobility is the loss of the extended family, with a probable increase in psychosocial isolation (see also Giovannoni & Billingsley, 1970). Basically the extended family is just one more support system missing from abusive parents' lives: "Although certain natural forces may be conducive to making parents care for their children, nonetheless there must be adequate contextual supports for the parents in this enterprise. In the relative absence of social support, one may expect that contrary impulses arise, even if they are not always acted out [Bakan, 1971, pp. 89–90]."

## RESOCIALIZATION OF ABUSIVE FAMILIES

Control of child abuse through the resocialization of abusive families can be viewed in short- and long-term perspectives. Short-term control involves crisis intervention to prevent imminent cases of abuse. Telephone hot-lines, police intervention, crisis nurseries, and day-care dropoff centers are examples of short-term control. Temporary removal of the abused child from the home by the courts is yet another form of short-term control. But given the large number of abused children reported annually, neither removal nor foster-care placement is an economically feasible solution. Long-term control aims to restructure the family's interaction patterns that may cause abuse or modify the child's or the parent's attitudes, values, personality, and/or behaviors that are viewed as causative. The particular forms of long-term intervention and control vary with the theoretical orientation of the intervention agent. While some control tactics fo-

cus on changing the individual, other control programs aim to alter abuse rates by modifying social institutions and social conditions.

In this section, I examine strategies for controlling child abuse: (1) the role of the legal system, specifically the police and the courts; (2) changes in social structure and community support systems; (3) the potential of alternative family models; and (4) modification of interaction patterns of abusive families. My underlying assumption is that abusive patterns are learned and therefore can be modified.

### The Role of the Legal System: Police and Court Intervention

Child abuse is not only a sociopsychological problem but a legal one as well. "Every state now has criminal child neglect, abuse, or cruelty statutes [Mnookin, 1973, p. 629]," and legal machinery is often invoked in handling such cases. Police, prosecutors, and courts traditionally have been oriented to imposing criminal sanctions and intervening coercively in dealing with child abuse (Kempe & Helfer, 1972). Recently, however, there has been a marked skepticism among legal authorities and scholars (Delaney, 1972; Pitcher, 1972) about the utility of treating child abuse as a criminal offense. Revised goals as well as roles for professionals within the legal systems are evolving. In part, this shift is a multiply determined outcome of several factors: changing legal philosophy (Worsfold, 1974); limited success of the traditional adversary system in child-abuse cases (Mesch, 1971); and the potential benefits of alternative therapeutic resocialization programs.

*The police.* Although police are often the first formal authority to intervene in intrafamily conflict, little attention has been paid to their role in the prevention and control of child abuse and family violence. Parnas (1967) estimated that more police calls involve family conflict than all other types of criminal incidents. Police intervention often occurs before conflict has escalated to the abusive level, while medical authorities typically encounter the family only *after* the abusive incident. Unfortunately, police intervention itself frequently exaggerates rather than limits both individual violence (Toch, 1969) and collective aggression (Marx, 1970), perhaps due to serious differences in values between police and their clientele (Rokeach, Miller & Synder, Chap. 13) or to lack of specific training in handling familial violence (Bandura, 1973; Bard, 1971).

Bard's work provides evidence that police can function effectively in settling intrafamily disputes and thereby may prevent the escalation of violence to abusive levels. A special "Family Crisis Unit" was trained to handle family disputes through such techniques as modeling, role playing, lectures, and discussion groups. Bard (1971, p. 152) noted that, although "40% of injuries sustained by police occur when they are intervening in family disputes . . . the 18-man unit, exposed for more than would ordinarily be the case to this dangerous event, sustained only one minor injury" during the two-year project. The use of nonphysical tactics in interventions in family disputes, such as advice and mediation, not only defuses a short-term problem but also serves as a model of alternative ways of settling conflict.

The police officer's initial handling of the dispute affects later events. If an arrest is made, charging and labeling processes are activated that, in turn, may end up in a court hearing.[3] But if an arrest is not made, costly legal procedures can be avoided, and social service agency assistance can be invoked. Bard (1971) found that in the nontrained unit, family court was the referral choice in 95 percent of the cases, with no

_____
[3] A court hearing involves public disclosure of the family's mishandling of their child-care responsibilities. "Moreover, once the arrest has been made and criminal charges are pending, the parents are usually very uncooperative [Helfer & Kempe, 1974, p. 187]."

referrals to social and mental health agencies. In the trained (experimental) unit, 45 percent of the referrals are made to family court and 55 percent to social and mental health agencies. In addition, there were about 22 percent fewer arrests in the experimental unit. Bard concluded:

The lower rate of arrests in the experimental precinct is suggestive of the greater use of referral resources and of mediation. . . . It is well known that upon reaching the courts, and long after the heated dispute has cooled, most complaints of this type are dropped anyway. Sophisticated police intervention can provide immediate mediation service but can also serve as a preliminary screening mechanism for final resolution of family disharmony [1971, p. 160].

In sum, Bard's project shows that professionals within the legal system can effectively serve as facilitators of more constructive family functioning rather than merely as agents of law enforcement.

*The courts.* Most cases of child abuse fall within the jurisdiction of juvenile or family courts. The typical judicial solution has been removal of the child from the home and/or the imposition of criminal sanctions on the parent, but neither solution helps correct the abusive situation. Basically treating child abuse as criminal is aimed at punitive rather than rehabilitative goals, with generally poor results. For example, Pitcher reports:

Incarceration of a convicted abusive parent achieves only a temporary period of safety for a child-victim, at best, and prisons cannot be expected to improve parental caretaking abilities. At worst, this respite for the child is gained at the cost of the family's means of support or the potential for adequate future child care in the same family [1972, p. 244].

Courts can play a constructive role, however. Multiple alternatives that do not sacrifice due process guarantees and protections of the adversary system are available. The adversary system "must yield to or at least share with another system in which other disciplines also join in the fact finding and decision-making [Delaney, 1972, p. 193]." Specifically, the legal system can function as an authoritative partner in resocializing child abusers by (1) making parents aware of available social services and (2) facilitating and enforcing parental participation in the therapeutic programs established by other community agencies.

Increased sharing of decision-making responsibility will not alone improve the judicial treatment of child abusers. As noted earlier, child abuse is community defined. To the extent that judgments of abuse reflect middle-class community values of appropriate child-rearing, lower-class defendants may be unable to get an unbiased hearing (see also Mnookin, 1973). To protect against such unfairness, Rodham suggests:

One way to answer that complaint is to entrust the discretion . . . for evaluating a child's needs to persons representing the milieu in which a family lives. Boards composed of citizens . . . could make the initial decision regarding intervention or review judicial decisions. . . . Providing a check on judicial and bureaucratic discretion, this form of community involvement also might broaden the constituency of adults actively concerned about services for children. Without an increase in community involvement, the best drafted laws and most eloquent judicial opinions will merely recycle past disappointments [1973, p. 514].

Nor should participation in court decision making be limited to adults. Children need representation of their rights in legal contexts. Child advocates, such as the law guardian concept, which involves appointing an attorney to represent the interests of the child (Mesch, 1971), are important in gaining children's participation and in socializing both children and community to the elements of choice and competence, need and

interest (cf. Tapp & Levine, 1974). Children deserve a larger role in deciding among alternative solutions in child-abuse cases. In many court-adjudicated cases, the abused child is placed in a state-sponsored foster home—with little opportunity to express a preference. Although foster care is often justified in terms of a "best interests" argument, Mnookin (1973) argued that this solution is generally not in the child's best interests given the long-term negative effects of foster care on the developing child (Eisenberg, 1962; Parfit, 1967). Instead, he held that removal was appropriate only when the child could not be protected in the home. Increasing both community and child participation in the disposition of child-abuse cases should contribute to ensuring the integrity of the family unit and the rights of children and their parents. Such reforms would also curb the wide discretionary power of the court—a fundamental problem in the U.S. legal system (Mnookin, 1973, p. 630).

## Societal and Community Control of Child Abuse

The most consistent advocate of social changes as a solution to child abuse is Gil (1970, 1975), who emphasizes the importance of social support systems. He recommends comprehensive family planning programs and legal medical abortions—suggested by the finding that child abuse is more frequent in large families and with unwanted children. He also supports family-life education and counseling programs for both teenagers and adults to provide realistic information about the tasks and demands of marriage and child-rearing and to avoid the unrealistic expectations that abusive parents often have of children (see Steele & Pollock, 1968). Another of his suggestions has been incorporated into many child-abuse control programs: support services for mothers to relieve the stress of child care. Gil's underlying assumption is that "no mother should be expected to care for her children around the clock 365 days a year [1970, p. 147]." His recommendations offer considerable promise for the control of child abuse. They not only may serve to relieve the stress of child-care responsibilities but also may provide an opportunity for the child to learn new rules of social interaction from peers and other adults.

But more social services may not be sufficient. Publicity about institutional social support may be necessary as well. Often those most in need of social services do not know that government agencies are available. In a recent national survey of federal services, Kahn, Gutek, Barton, and Katz reported: "American bureaucracy apparently faces problems not only in helping people once they come in for service, but in getting them to come in at all. Among those who reported specific problems that the government might solve, many never found their way to the right agency and some had no idea an agency could help them [1975, p. 68]."

At the neighborhood level, various strategies can increase contacts among families. Groups such as Parents Anonymous can reduce the social isolation of abusive families. Hot-lines, modeled after the suicide emergency telephone lines, provide a valuable immediate resource. Other efforts include the Block Mothers' Program of St. Louis, Virginia Beach, and Des Moines, which are concerned about child abuse and runaways (*Parade,* June 22, 1975). Such programs could incorporate behavioral techniques aimed at modification of social isolation behavior through modeling of social skills (see Rimm & Masters, 1974). Further, programs within the community can implicitly and explicitly present rules for child care that offer alternatives for family governance and facilitate understanding the needs and rights of parents and child.

## Alternative Family Arrangements

New family life-styles may contribute to abuse reduction. Whitehurst (1974) has ar-gued that alternative family structures (i.e., families with more members than the traditional nuclear family), such as communes and group marriages, might reduce the potential for family violence. In addition to increased solidarity and the availability of others in crisis situations, Whitehurst asserted that most alternative families share norms of nonviolence. All these features should lead to lessened potential for violence. Although this nonviolence hypothesis remains untested, some support comes from earlier studies of the kibbutz (Rabin, 1965) and a recent study by Minturn, Gunnery, Holloway, and Peterson, which reported that commune residents in contrast to college students viewed their situations as "less competitive, more cooperative and less aggressive [1974, p. 494–495]."

Whitehurst offers the following warning: "[I]f we continue in conventional families to attempt to use outmoded legal and moral a priori answers to problems of life instead of rationally looking at the disparity of ends and means, we may well find more violence as a predicted outcome of family life [1974, p. 319]." To avoid such consequences, the rule structure and social control strategies within the nuclear family system need to be evaluated. Alternative family models may be instructive in that regard.

## Modification of Family Interaction Patterns

Intervention need not be restricted to changes at the cultural, legal, and community levels; techniques for modifying family interaction styles are needed as well. The basic assumption of this type of intervention program is that attitudes about physical punishment can change as a result of providing parents with alternative disciplinary techniques. Such intervention can be viewed as a resocialization process whereby parents acquire new child-rearing skills. The aim is to alter the rules governing interaction from a negative, coercive basis to a more consensual model in which the rights and responsibilities of all participants are recognized.

Programs for altering family interaction patterns have a two-level focus. First, the parents themselves who are using physically punitive tactics need a new repertoire of training strategies that are effective in child control and, therefore, can replace punitive methods. Second, through the use of new techniques, child behaviors that may be eliciting highly punitive parental reactions will be altered.

A variety of social control techniques avoid the negative consequences of physical punishment. Risley and Baer (1973) have reviewed these behavior modification techniques in detail. Extinction (Williams, 1959), reinforcement of incompatible responses (Brown & Elliott, 1965), time-out (Hawkins, Peterson, Schweid, & Bijou, 1966), and verbal reasoning (Parke, 1970, 1974) are effective for improving parental control of children's behavior. For example, a number of investigators have demonstrated the usefulness of the "time-out" procedure for modifying deviant child behaviors in home situations, and they have trained mothers to use these procedures (Hawkins, Peterson, Schweid, & Bijou, 1966).

All these techniques may be used by a therapist or change agent to reduce the child's deviant behavior that may be eliciting the punitive treatment. However, abusive behavior of parents may be more adequately modified through a program of parental retraining, perhaps using these same procedures in conjunction with modeling techniques (Bandura, 1969).

Patterson (1974) has developed a comprehensive program for the retraining of parents of aggressive children based on social learning principles, particularly operant conditioning concepts, in which the relation between parental reactions and deviant behavior is the focus. By making parents aware of such a relationship and by providing the opportunity to learn and rehearse alternative techniques for dealing with their children, the deviant behavior can be modified.

In this program parents are first required to study a programmed text on social learning-based child management techniques. They next are taught to carefully define, track, and record a series of targeted deviant and/or prosocial child behaviors. Then the parents work in a training group with two or three other sets of parents, where modeling and role playing are used as instructional techniques, usually for 8 to 12 weekly sessions. Where needed, training sessions are held in the home with the experimenters modeling the appropriate parenting skills. Finally, parents learn to build contracts that spell out what to do with particular behaviors at home and/or at school. Patterson combines these procedures with a set of classroom interventions.

Effectiveness of the program is assessed through careful observations by trained observers of the interaction patterns between the parents and the deviant child in the home situation. Study of 27 families in the program indicated that there was a significant decrease in deviant behavior across the treatment phase. Follow-up assessments revealed that noxious behavior increased for half the families during the month after the end of treatment; but the deviant behavior was reduced by providing families with a "booster shot" of about two hours of extra treatment. Most important, the results suggest that the effects induced by the training were relatively stable over one year. Finally, in contrast to long-term psychiatric therapy, this type of intervention program was relatively economical: Therapist contact time was 31.4 hours.

The success of this program clearly documents the feasibility of retraining parents to use nonpunitive techniques for effective child control. Part of the reason for the long-term stability of the changes is that as the child's behavior changes, the child may become a more attractive and valued family member and thus a less likely target for abuse. Patterson's work should serve as a model for future intervention attempts in terms of the careful assessment, programmatic intervention, and detailed documentation of outcomes. Further, this program illustrates the value of voluntary rehabilitation and nonpunitive procedures—in this case, for socializing children's deviant behaviors and resocializing abusive parent "offenders."

## EPILOGUE:
## THE RIGHTS OF CHILDREN

In the final analysis, child abuse must be viewed as inevitably intertwined with the broader issue of children's rights. Some (e.g., Zalba, 1971) have argued that the historical view of children as property has set the stage for child abuse. If so, control and decline of child abuse as a cultural phenomenon can only come about as rapidly as individuals in society reconceptualize and redefine the status and rights of children.

Overall, there has been a failure to appreciate the wide range of individual competence among children and the vast differences in the 18- or 20-year span of childhood (Rodham, 1973). Both the use of physical disciplinary tactics in controlling children and the limitations on children's rights are often justified in terms of children's limited cognitive abilities. But research over the past two decades has clearly shown that children can understand the sociolegal and moral basis of social rights at a much earlier age than generally had been assumed (Tapp & Kohlberg, Chap. 9; Tapp & Levine, 1974). Evidence also suggests that young children are responsive to nonphysical control tactics in the form of rationales (Parke, 1974). For example, 5-year-olds were effectively controlled by a prohibitory rationale based on property rights. In short, children can both understand and effectively use rationally based social rules to govern their own behavior well before adulthood or even before adolescence.

Justifying physical punishment as a control tactic in terms of the child's limited capacity for appreciating more humane cog-

nitively derived procedures is simply not tenable. A shift on the part of parents and other caretakers toward nonpunitive child-rearing tactics has implications beyond the possible reduction of child abuse. It is consistent with a more profound shift in thought and action concerning the rights of children, which suggests that the rights of children as individuals are not limited by their status but only by their capacity to participate competently in the formulation of social rules (Rawls, 1971; Worsfold, 1974). From this perspective, parents may not arbitrarily impose regulations and restrictions on children. Basically "children have a right to make just claims and adults must be responsive to these claims [Worsfold, 1974, p. 157]."

Moreover, children's rights should not be limited solely to family settings. Their rights within the legal system need to be recognized and guaranteed as well. As is evident from the discussion and research presented in this chapter, the child should be an active participant in the judicial process and in decision making. Further, children and adults both should be accorded the rights and responsibilities—benefits and burdens—that result from interaction between individuals and within institutions.

Too often it is easy to dismiss parental responsibility in the name of children's rights. Socialization involves a responsibility on the part of parents to give children a chance to learn the rules and norms of their society and culture and at the same time to realize their full social and cognitive potential. While it is most unlikely that physical punishment is either necessary or useful in this process, a shift away from physically punitive control tactics (wherever the setting) does not imply a shift to unsupervised freedom. Socialization implies control, but a view of the child as a self-respecting and self-determining human needs to be given primary recognition in evaluating the goals and types of regulation.

# CHAPTER 17

# The Socialization into Criminality
## On Becoming a Prisoner and a Guard[1]

—CRAIG HANEY and PHILIP G. ZIMBARDO

"Evil deeds are not necessarily the products of evil men." This statement directly contradicts a fundamental assumption in our legal and penal systems. It violates as well the premises of naive psychology often used to explain behavior. This chapter describes the social-psychological concept of "situational control" and examines its part in the criminal justice process. Institutional socialization, a protracted form of situational control, often co-opts individuals' goals and ideals in the service of situational ends. Tendencies to presume the rationality of institutional actions and to blame persons for their failure are mystifications that prevent us from perceiving the causes of social problems and aiming social change programs at the appropriate structural level. Nowhere is this obfuscation more complete than in the institution of prison. We argue that the institutional socialization in prison differs only in degree, not in kind, from that experienced by society's "at large" prisoners and guards. Social science research in institutions has a critical role for facilitating fundamental changes in these impersonal structures, for it is only when individuals understand the dynamics of their own social control that they can begin to create social institutions that promote justice, caring, and freedom.

A basic assumption of our criminal justice system—that the causes of behavior reside primarily within the individual—is most clearly reflected in what it regards as the most appropriate response to criminal behavior: apprehending and treating the individual lawbreaker. The system distributes punishment and treatment to those identified as having engaged in criminal behavior; it does not change environmental or situational conditions. As Wilkins wryly observed, "We even refer to a crime as being 'solved' when we have found someone who can be blamed for committing it [1973, p. 23]." Identifying criminal behavior as personal justifies the call for rehabilitation, the very concept of which presupposes some defect in the individual offender that can be corrected by incarceration. Whatever the specific form of rehabilitation (e.g., vocational training, psychotherapy, or merely increased knowledge of conditions of punishment), the implication is clear: Undesirable or lawbreaking behavior is to be reduced or eliminated by effecting change in individuals who perform it. The most vivid physical embodiment of this philosophy is the institution of prison.

## THE POWER OF SITUATIONS

A corollary of the view of person-as-cause is the belief that people engage in criminal conduct because of some special dispositions or traits. That some persons

[1] Work on this manuscript was aided by a Russell Sage Foundation Law and Social Science Award to Haney and an ONR grant to Zimbardo. The authors thank Roseanne Saussotte for her assistance in preparation of the manuscript.

commit crimes while presumably others do not is explained in terms of individual differences in the very nature of the people themselves. In essence, if criminal behavior is a function of personal defects, whether inborn or the result of conditioning, then the problem of crime and criminals is best addressed by acting directly on these dispositions. Such action may take the seemingly well-defined form of curing an individual's psychological disorder or the more ambiguous form of substituting moral strength and good character for weakness and turpitude. An extreme but logical extension of this approach is "preventive detention," whereby a hypothesized, underlying disposition provides sufficient justification for criminal sanction *in the absence of any criminal behavior.*

Explaining certain behaviors by imputing special characteristics to those who perform them is not limited simply to the criminal justice system. Psychologists have contributed much to this dispositional bias by emphasizing *personal* or trait explanations in their theories of human behavior. Moreover, psychiatrists and psychologists have provided lawyers, judges, and criminologists with conceptual and terminological tools to interpret deviant behavior "scientifically." Thus, criminal behavior is often explained by such phrases as "inability to delay gratification," "sociopathic personality," or "deficient super-ego."[2] Likewise, a number of "progressive" prison systems focus on making fundamental changes in prisoners' personalities through such psychological techniques as intensive psychotherapy and behavior modification (e.g., Mitford, 1973). A theory of behavior emphasizing personal dispositions implies a criminal justice system that attempts primarily to change individuals.

Yet the single important lesson to emerge from recent social-psychological research is the degree to which *situations* and *not personalities* control behavior. After careful scrutiny, the dispositional bias has been largely invalidated. All of us—laymen, psychologists, and judges—seem to have greatly *overestimated* the extent to which traits or dispositions determine behavior. Mischel (1968) systematically examined an extensive range of personality and trait measures and found them of little or no value in explaining and predicting individual behavior. Rather, he presented evidence that people tend to respond to relevant characteristics of the environment and rarely behave consistently across situations. He argued persuasively against the notion of any broad, underlying personality dimensions, including a generalized criminal tendency that might compel "immoral" behavior.[3]

Such research (see also Milgram, 1965, 1974) makes salient the tremendous potency of the environmental setting in the control of behavior. It suggests that the causes of even markedly deviant behavior are not to be found in continuing properties of the individuals who perform it, but reside instead in the characteristics of the situations in which the behavior occurs. The Milgram studies illustrate this principle dramatically. Under the guise of conducting experiments on the "effects of punishment on memory," Milgram (e.g., 1965) found that about two-

---

[2] When innate theories of behavior were less generally discredited and more politically feasible, "criminality" was explained in terms of the lawbreaker's "bad blood." A legacy of this belief is found in extant legislation: Three states still prohibit the marriage of a man with three felony convictions to a woman under the age of 45, and seven states authorize the sterilization of "habitual criminals" (see Bagdikian & Dash, 1972, p. 162).

[3] Mischel relied on the seminal research of Hartshorne and May (1928) on the moral behavior of children. Observing the specificity of children's behaviors in a variety of tempting situations, including the opportunity to cheat on tests, lie, and steal money, Hartshorne and May concluded that children simply do not have a generalized code of morals. Their findings parallel those of contemporary researchers who have found even extreme adult behaviors, like violence and aggression, to be a function of evoking and maintaining conditions of the situation (e.g., Bandura, 1973).

thirds of his laboratory subjects willingly behaved in ways *they* believed painful or harmful to others. Even though "victims" cried out in pain, feigned heart attacks, and literally begged for the study to be terminated, most subjects continued to obey and deliver what they believed to be high levels of electric shock. Such behavior may be regarded not only as cruel but felonious as well, demonstrating that under the proper circumstances many people will knowingly perform what amounts to serious violent crime merely at the urging of authority.

How are we to interpret these results? Few would argue that fully two-thirds of the population had criminal, even murderous, predispositions to such actions. Rather, the data speak to powerful situational forces present in the experimental paradigm and their ability to produce hitherto unexpected levels of deplorable behavior.

But the criminal justice system takes little formal account of situational forces as determinants of criminal behavior. Based on the premise of the individual as causal agent, its machinery is not designed to confront issues of "situational responsibility." The manifest purposes of its guilt-fastening process become even more ambiguous than at present if the acknowledged determinants of behavior are recognized as impersonal forces rather than as individuals. Provisions in the criminal law for situational elements to mitigate the seriousness of a crime (e.g., "passion and provocation" reduces murder to manslaughter) are generally reserved for those highly unusual situations where the individual's perceptual and reasoning processes are overwhelmed, precluding rational action—as in Justice Cardozo's "mind swept from its moorings [1931, p. 100]." While juries may take situational control factors implicitly into consideration, they most often recognize the effect of environmental contingencies despite, rather than because of, the dictates of the law (e.g., Kalven & Zeisel, 1966). The criminal law does not explicitly confront the issue of situational control in the more common and important

instance—when the accurate perception of situational elements and a rational response thereto leads ineluctably to what is defined as criminal behavior.

Legal doctrine and the machinery of criminal justice are often impervious to changing social and intellectual realities. Yet, in a world in which "the law" is increasingly regarded in secular rather than sacred terms, unquestioning obedience must yield to demands for justice and fairness. To be *just*, a legal system must at least begin with behavioral assumptions that are valid. As categories of behavior, crime and punishment are in one sense indistinguishable: They both inflict human pain and suffering. If the penal sanction is founded on false premises—a model of human beings recognized as pure "legal fiction"—the cloak of legitimacy that separates legal punishment from crime vanishes and the sanction of necessity becomes "criminal."

Criminality takes many guises. But we agree with Drekmeier (1971) that equating "evil with irrational violence deflects our attention from the highly calculated, indeed rational forms that evil may take [p. 200]." If we use the concept of situational control to understand such "rational evil," then we must look to the most potent of society's situations. There are few places where the forces of behavioral control are more extreme than in the institution of prison. Here is a kind of social crucible in which the dynamics of situational control are so concentrated that the behavioral reactions they catalyze may profoundly change, even denature, its dwellers. Yet the processes of change and control differ only in degree but not in kind from those common to more diverse environments.

## SOME GENERALIZATIONS ABOUT THE PROCESS OF INSTITUTIONAL SOCIALIZATION

Social institutions constitute a constant, prolonged "situation" for those living and working within them. Through the process of *institutional socialization,* the institution maintains and increases its protracted situational control. Understanding how a prison socializes people into the roles of "prisoner" or "guard" is advanced by considering certain features of adult socialization as it occurs in more diverse and familiar settings. We focus initially on the socialization processes most akin to becoming society's guards, since it is the guards who in turn become the "socializers" of prisoners.

## On the Banality of Evil

History has surely established the futility of seeking the sources of evil deeds exclusively in the nature of its performers. Even the greatest iniquity and inhumanity generally have been the products of unsettlingly "normal," average persons whose commonplace motives and relative naiveté were perverted in the service of evil purpose.

As comforting as the notion would be for us to maintain, belief in evil as the result of a few individuals of abject morality and deranged vision is simply not viable: The greatest malefaction has always required the participation of many and the tolerance of most (see, e.g., Opton, 1971). Even the ostensible leaders of corrupt and evil systems often fail to show the abnormality and deviance we assume produced their actions, as is dramatically documented in Arendt's study of Adolf Eichmann:

The trouble with Eichmann was precisely that so many were like him, and that the many were neither perverted nor sadistic, that they were, and still are, terribly and terrifyingly normal. From the viewpoint of our legal institutions and of our moral standards of judgment, this normality was much more terrifying than all the atrocities put together [1965, p. 276].

In our society the behavior of such "terrifyingly normal" persons is controlled most commonly (and effectively) in institutional settings. Thus we must look to the techniques by which institutions gain power and control over behavior, co-opting individual purpose to their own.

## Growing up Socialized

"Socialization" is a process of transformation. In an infant, this process transforms behavior initially controlled by biological exigencies and hedonistic principles into behavior governed by considerations of propriety: time, place, and occasion for eating; sleeping; and eliminating. Despite the effort, it is "well worth it" in the long run to have a socialized child whose behavior follows predictable and "civilized" conventions. With older children, socialization becomes a more pervasive indoctrination program with multiple goals: compliance with the laws and norms of the given society; conformity to the political, economic, and religious beliefs of the society; acceptance of ethical and moral values as guides to action and to learning the secrets of "making it"; and so forth. This second transformation is even more "worth it" to socializing agents because it insures the perpetuation of the status quo and (perforce) themselves.

Socialization is also a process of renunciation. Immediate rewards are foregone for future, more appropriate forms of gratification. This delayed pursuit of personal ends is thought to be "worth it" to the individual and *a fortiori* to society. But the precise terms of this hypothetical social contract are rarely, if ever, specified. Society justifies the imposition of terms in the name of general categories of traditional authority. Ideally, these categories are internalized by adulthood and become their own justification.

Commonly assumed to be the means by which egocentric, selfish, uncontrolled organisms become responsible, law-abiding adult citizens, socialization was thought to be self-limiting, ending in adulthood when presumably it was no longer necessary. But sociologists like Goffman (1959) and Garfinkel (1956) have shown that adults often continue to be transformed into even more socially approved and acceptable actors. Indeed, the practical necessity of being "properly socialized" is not diminished in adulthood: Individuals are economically dependent on institutions that can and do require conforming behavior. Unfortunately, as the moral force of traditional sources of socializing authority—church, flag, and family—wanes with nothing ennobling to fill its void, socialization becomes increasingly amoral. The values of the workplace—efficiency and productivity—owe no allegiance to moral restraint. As a primary goal of socialization, *obedience* may become free-floating and functionally autonomous. What was once achieved in the service of the highest social values may be obtained in the name of the less heroic, or none at all. *Professionalism*—the ability to perform competently any task, irrespective of personal values or belief—becomes an admired goal. Then individuals look not to authority, but seek mere *authorization* for their deeds.

Asked to describe the process by which he became involved in illegal behavior, convicted Watergate conspirator Jeb Magruder made the following comparison: "It's very typical in large corporations. Someone else is influential. He has an idea and he gets the idea approved. You're the one who has to carry it out. You don't agree with it, but it's important to satisfy the group consensus: 'It isn't that important and I might as well go along [Terkel, 1974, p. 67].' " With unsettling facility, the formula for "corporate success" may be adapted to the obstruction of justice or other equally ignoble ends.

In many cases, this final stage of socialization espouses values diametrically opposed to those revered and upheld in the transformations of the young. Practicality and cynicism are often the working principles that supplant potentiality and idealism—resignation to doing someone else's thing replaces the hope of doing one's own. To "not make trouble" and go unnoticed are the resocializing principles for which a sense of moral righteousness and individuality

must give way. Rubenstein, observing that a patrolman often must violate the law, lie, and steal as a part of his job, wrote that the police officer

knows that the only way [he] can be honest in the exacting sense required by his oath of office is to resign. [He] does not want to quit, so he makes little compromises. . . . He does things that are illegal, but he has no choice. He knows there are many dishonest policemen, but his rewards . . . are little more than the renewal of his right to continue in the job [1973, p. 401].

Thus, in order to merely stay "in the job," an officer must engage in exactly what the job (ostensibly) exists to prevent. Socialization often demands an alientation of values in the very name of the values renounced.

More insidious, the motives underlying participation in such activities may be the most common, mundane concerns: occupational security, advancement, peer approval, and the like. The properly socialized have been taught to value such motives. "Just doing my job," "following orders," and "being a team player" have in common the absence of passion and personal commitment. It is this that permits evil action in the absence of evil motive or will.

## The Psychology of Gradualism

In "Work and the Self," Hughes (1951) discussed the activities that constitute the "dirty part" of an occupation: "It may be dirty in one of several ways. It may be simply disgusting. It may be a symbol of degradation, something that wounds one's dignity. Finally, it may be dirty work in that it goes counter to the more heroic of our moral conceptions [p. 319]." "Becoming socialized" in institutional settings involves accustoming oneself to these varieties of "dirty work." In truly dehumanizing institutions work borrows elements from each of Hughes' categories, thereby insuring the degradation and compromise of the agents as well as the objects of their "institution-alization." However malleable prior sociali-zation may have rendered them, few are prepared for the "dirtiest" institutional tasks without additional training and experience.

Socialization in such institutional contexts is usually a graduated progression of activi-ties. Initial discontinuities between the self and the required tasks are generally minimal, and psychic effects are often experienced only as mild tension or unease. Since the process is persistent and one's exposure may be prolonged, the individual may move grad-ually toward the desired institutional goal without any severely traumatic or wrenching accommodations at all.

Crucial to this process is the absence of a definitive moral choice in which the indi-vidual is either ultimately compromised or self-affirmed. As Bettelheim observed:

[W]hen the state makes small inroad after small inroad, at which point is one to say: No more, even if it cost me my life? And pretty soon the many small inroads have sapped so much courage that one no longer has the nerve to take action . . . if action is delayed, the longer anxiety lasts and the more energy is spent on binding it, . . . the more a person is drained of vital energy and the less he feels capable of acting on his own [1960, p. 261].

It is the inability to react decisively to these "small inroads," to know when to resist even minor compromise, that makes us prey to this gradual yet seemingly relentless wearing down process.

Yet, essential to this socialization appears to be people's total unawareness of the power of the institutional setting to gain con-trol over them. Also, these individuals are generally unaware of the very process of socialization in which they are taking part. Tending to become submerged in the assumptions of the institution, individuals also becomes absorbed by what Gray (1973) called the "tyranny of the present." To the extent that those in the environment behave

similarly, perspective fades and one becomes unable to evaluate one's own behavior critically. No longer able to exercise the vigilance that might otherwise forestall or prevent situation co-optation, the individual will often accede where he or she might otherwise resist—not because of total in-sensitivity to situational pressures but be-cause the person lacks broader awareness of the pattern or direction of situational con-trol and of the final goals.

The force of the situation, the contingency of the moment, and the motive of the com-monplace come to govern ongoing behavior in institutional settings. Goffman (1959) claimed that persons may experience the dis-crepancy between institutional demands and their ideals: Individuals may constantly twist, turn, and squirm, even while allowing themselves to be carried along by the con-trolling definition of the situation. Yet, there is also much evidence to suggest that even the discontinuities between our self and our institutional role are transient.

Much social-psychological evidence indi-cates that the best way to change attitudes or beliefs is to get people to behave *as if* they believe in what they are doing (e.g., Bem, 1972). Contrary to general assump-tions, it appears that behavior is primary and attitudes and beliefs seem to change in consequence of it. While the parameters gov-erning this process are not all known, one dimension seems to be perceived freedom or choice. If individuals feel that they have freely chosen to engage in discrepant be-havior, then they are likely to alter their beliefs to make them consonant. Therefore, it is reasonable to predict that in institutional settings the more extensive and protracted people's involvement (again, particularly coercion), the more they will come to be-lieve in what they are doing.

Research by Haney and Collins (1971) and Collins and Hoyt (1972) has demon-strated that, when persons expect their counterattitudinal behavior to have serious negative consequences for others, they are more likely to change their private opinions to be consistent with those acts. This finding, too, augurs ill for the individual maintaining "self" while performing institutional roles that are dehumanizing or detrimental to others. When the "dirty work" becomes our own, then we have become truly "socialized": We believe we are acting from conscience, personal beliefs, and values. Then we are even more likely to strive to remake others in our own (new) image.

## The Presumption of Institutional Rationality

Institutional socialization is facilitated by a general tendency to grant social institutions a "presumption of rationality": We simply *assume* that institutional behavior is founded on rational grounds and considered purpose. This helps to explain why we allow institutions to prosper in our midst, tacitly if not enthusiastically condoning their behavior and conferring legitimacy on activities and purposes that would otherwise be more critically evaluated (see Drekmeier, 1971, p. 200). Since in our culture rationality is a sufficient justification for existence and continued functioning, by granting institutions the presumption of rational organization and aim, we can no longer analyze them critically. We rarely question the behavior of functionaries, but choose instead to focus on the objects or "targets" of their activity: We study students but not teachers, mental patients but not psychiatrists, and prisoners but not guards. Perhaps nowhere is a presumption of rationality granted more generously than with respect to the legal system.

Moreover, there is an illusion of permanence and inevitability that we attach to institutions. Since they are part of the "given" of everyday life, it is difficult to even imagine their nonexistence. We come to view them as the only viable response. Though they may no longer serve the purposes for which they were originally conceived, social institutions persist until other acceptable and similar (institutional) "solutions" are found. The empirical status of the popular maxim that "it's better than nothing" has rarely, if ever, been computed for most social institutions—we merely assume it to be true (see Rothman, 1971).

In one sense, then, an institution is not unlike a scientific concept or theory that tends to persist in spite of considerable disconfirming evidence until a replacement has been found (see Conant, 1947; Kuhn, 1962). The human mind, it appears, abhors an explanatory vacuum. Conant wrote that "a conceptual scheme is never discarded merely because of a few stubborn facts with which it cannot be reconciled; a concept is either modified or replaced by a better concept, never abandoned with nothing left to take its place [1947, p. 90]." Unfortunately, institutions that have outlived their usefulness often represent considerable human suffering and the proliferation rather than solution of social ills. And since the nature of an institutional "solution" contributes substantially to the very definition of the problem, reforms or supposedly innovative alternatives usually greatly resemble the original, so that "institutional change" masquerades for what are most often thinly disguised, rhetorical variations on "more of the same."

From wardens who run prisons to inmates who are locked involuntarily inside, most people agree that this institution has been an unqualified failure. Their critics argue that prisons accomplish very little more than the collective dehumanization and degradation of all who come in contact with them. Yet they persist. In part, they persist because we do not judge (nor are we generally capable of judging) institutions by the same standards that we judge people. That prisons accomplish virtually none of the purposes for which they supposedly exist, and that they engender palpably more harm than good, does not appear to matter—their nonexistence has become quite literally inconceivable.

## On Blaming Persons

Confronted with undeniable evidence that one of our presumably rational institutions has failed, we blame neither the institutions nor their policies; instead, we identify *individuals* as the source of failure. When institutions direct their agents into activities exceeding general limits of acceptability, we choose to view such events as infrequent anomalies or random perturbations in an otherwise smoothly functioning system. Similarly, when a social problem has proven refractory to an institutional program, the intractability is attributed to individuals, rather than to an inept or misguided policy.

The very definitions of most social problems are constructed with an inherent "person-bias": We are, for example, quite accustomed to hearing about children who "can't learn," less accustomed to hearing about teachers who "can't teach," and least of all used to hearing of school environments that "can't educate." If an educational problem is defined as a "failure to learn," then the relevant level of analysis becomes the individual student and problem solving will be focused accordingly. Behavior modifiers are consulted to instill motivation, correct "learning disabilities," or make changes to accommodate the individual to the system. Questions about the basic nature of curricula, teaching philosophies, and other *system-* or situation-oriented issues are simply ignored. We do not yet have a corps of behavior modifiers whose patients are social institutions.

Explanations of the deplorable conditions of the U.S. prison system and its uncontroverted failure similarly employ a person-blame orientation. Proponents of the prison status quo attribute the violence and disruption in prisons to the aggressive, psychopathic nature of the prisoner, while critics focus on prison brutality and repression as a function of the sadistic and insensitive guards and prison administrators. Blaming the failure of prison on persons diverts attention from the structure of the institution itself and from the complex social, economic, and political forces at the base of prison functioning. Rioting prisoners are identified and punished, others transferred to maximum security areas of different institutions, overzealous guards reprimanded, and corrupt officials suspended. But the institution itself continues fundamentally unchanged, its basic structure and assumption unexamined and unchallenged.[4]

---

[4] It was precisely the confrontation of this person–blame orientation that moved us to an unusual study of prison life. We felt that we could not truly understand the process of institutional socialization in prison by simply studying the conditions within existing prisons. Such naturalisitc observations necessarily confound the acute effects of the environment with the supposedly chronic characteristics of the inmate and staff populations. Only by populating a prison or prisonlike milieu with presumedly normal, healthy persons, could we learn about the effects of the prison environment per se. (A more detailed exposition of methodology and results appears in Haney, Banks, & Zimbardo, 1973; Zimbardo, Haney, Banks, & Jaffe, 1973).

To minimize the effects of preexisting dispositions, extensive interviewing and diagnostic testing were used to screen volunteer male college students. The 21 subjects who took part in the experiment were judged to be the most stable (physically and mentally) and mature. Half the subjects were randomly assigned to role-play prison guards in three-man shifts for 8 hours each day, while the others became prisoners and were incarcerated for nearly a full week, 24 hours a day. Neither group received any specific training in these roles.

Our intention was not to create a *literal* simulation of a U. S. prison but a functional representation of one. We first identified relevant conceptual variables through analyzing prison situations, then designed a setting in which these variables were made operational. No specific hypotheses were advanced other than the general one that assignment to the treatment of "guard" or "prisoner" would result in significantly different reactions on behavioral measures of interaction, emotional measures of mood state and pathology, attitudes toward self, and other indices of coping and adaptation. The research design then was a relatively simple one: It involved only a single treatment variable—the random assignment of either a "guard" or "prisoner" condition.

The prison was constructed in a 35-foot section of a basement corridor in Stanford's psychology building. The behavior of both groups of subjects was observed continuously. The contract was explicit that those assigned to be prisoners should expect to be under surveillance and to have some of their basic civil rights suspended during their imprisonment, excluding physical abuse. They were given no other information. The subjects assigned to be guards were introduced to the principal investigators, the "Superintendent" of the prison (P. G. Zimbardo), and an undergraduate, research assistant "Warden." The guards generally believed that the researchers were chiefly interested in the behavior of the prisoners. Their task was to maintain the reasonable degree of order within the prison needed for its effective functioning, although the specifics of how this might be done were not detailed. An explicit and categorical prohibition against the use of physical punishment or physical aggression was emphasized by the experimenters. With this single notable exception, however, the roles were relatively unstructured initially, requiring each "guard" to carry out activities necessary for interacting with a group of "prisoners" as well as with other "guards" and the "correctional staff."

Various procedures helped make the simulation realistic. With the cooperation of the local police department all the subjects assigned to the prisoner treatment were unexpectedly "arrested" at their residences. On arrival at the experimental prison, each prisoner was stripped, sprayed with a "delousing preparation" (a deodorant), and made to stand alone naked for awhile in the cell yard. When all the cells were occupied, the warden greeted the prisoners and read them the rules of the institution (developed by the guards and the warden). They were to be memorized and to be followed. Both guards and prisoners were fully uniformed.

The mundane reality of the prison was attested to by our prison consultant who had spent over 16 years in prison, as well as the priest who had been a prison chaplain and the public defender who were all brought into our simulated prison environment. Further, the depressed affect of the prisoners, the guards' willingness to work overtime for no additional pay, the spontaneous use of prison titles and I.D. numbers in nonrole-related situations all point to a high level of mundane realism.

The exploratory nature of this investigation led us to survey many behavioral and psychological manifestations of the prison experience on the guards and the prisoners. Data collection used the following sources: (1) *videotaping,* about 12 hours daily, regularly occurring events; (2) *audio recording,* over 30 hours of verbal interactions between guards and prisoners on the prison yard; (3) *rating scales,* mood adjective checklists and sociometric measures; (4) *individual difference scales,* selected dispositional indicators such as the *F*-scale of Authoritarian Personality and the Machiavellianism Scale; (5) *personal observations,* multiple measures including daily reports by the guards, informal diaries by the experimenters, and postexperimental questionnaires by all subjects.

The results of the experiment support many commonly held conceptions of prison life and validate anecdotal evidence supplied by articulate ex-convicts. Most crucial for the conclusions generated by this exploratory study is the consistency in the pattern of relations that emerge across a wide range of measuring instruments and different observers. The environment of arbitrary custody had great impact on the affective states of both guards and prisoners as well as on the interpersonal processes between and within those role-groups. In less than a week the behavior of the male subjects—highly representative of middle-class, Caucasian, U. S. society (17 to 30 years in age), average in intelligence and emotional stability—could be characterized as pathological and antisocial. The negative, antisocial reactions observed were clearly not the product of a collection of deviant personalities, but rather the result of an intrinsically pathological situation that could distort and rechannel the behavior of essentially normal individuals. As discussed in detail in this chapter, the "abnormality" lay clearly in the psychological nature of the situation and not in those who passed through it.

## A PHENOMENOLOGY OF IMPRISONMENT

Social science is designed to remove the individual bias of the observer and establish the basis for a consensually validated "reality." This analytical process itself is a biased translation from one reality to another. By describing the experience of dehumanization within a prison setting in traditional social-scientific terms (e.g., variables, factors, processes, interaction effects), one gains sufficient distance to deal with the phenomenon at a more comfortable intellectual level. But the very form and structure of such a "professional" approach to studying the experience itself contributes to the dehumanization it describes.

To minimize such academic dehumanization, in this section we summarize and present data from our prison simulation—as well as from extensive observations and conversations with prisoners and guards from real prisons—in four scenarios. Regardless of how it is described, institutional socialization reduces to an experiential level for its participants. It is this crucial dimension, so often neglected by social scientists, that we attempt here to understand.

### The Stanford Prison Experiment

. . . because it *was* a real prison to me. It was just a prison run by psychologists and not by the state, that's all.
—*A Stanford Prison "Inmate"*

SCENARIO I: It's my first day on the yard at Stanford Jail. My khaki uniform is just a size too big and there's too much starch in the shirt to make me feel comfortable wearing it. Sure feels weird to carry this big police billy club—must be a yard long and filled with a solid metal core. Of course, we've been told by the Superintendent not to use them as weapons, but carry them merely for "show." I hope the prisoners don't do anything stupid to force us to use them; *I* sure wouldn't want to get smashed with this thing. It's all just for the show we're putting on.

[After learning I've been accepted to be a guard here, diary entry reads: "As I am a pacifist and nonaggressive individual, I cannot see a time when I might maltreat other living things."]

[After our first group meeting with the other guards, a few of us went out to pick up the uniforms for the rest. Diary entry reads: "Buying uniforms at the end of the meeting confirms the gamelike atmosphere of this thing. I doubt whether many of us share the expectations of 'seriousness' that the experimenters seem to have."]

Well, here comes the last of the bunch. Police sure did their thing at the station. No rough stuff, mind you, but really efficient: fingerprinting, preparing the information file, hustling the prisoners from place to place, and finally leaving them blindfolded in the detention cell until we transferred them down here to our prison.

*"Take those dirty clothes off of him. This guy is going to infect the whole place with lice. Delouse him real good—he's not going to get a bath for a long time down here."*

*"Attention, all prisoners, the warden is here to greet you."*

As you probably already know, I'm your warden. All of you have shown that you are unable to function outside in the real world for one reason or another—that somehow you lack the responsibility of good citizens of this great country. We of this prison, your correctional staff, are going to help you learn what your responsibilities as citizens of this country are. Here are the rules. Sometime in the near future there will be a copy of the rules posted in each of the cells. If you follow all of these rules and keep your hands clean, repent for your misdeeds and show a proper attitude of penitence, you and I will get along just fine.

*"O.K., here they are. Rule Number One:*

*Prisoners must remain silent during rest periods, after lights are out, during meals, and whenever they are outside the prison yard. Two: Prisoners must eat at mealtimes and only at mealtimes. Three: Prisoners must not move, tamper, deface or damage walls, ceilings, windows, doors, or other prison property. . . . Eight: Prisoners must address the guards as 'Mr. Correctional Officer.' . . . Sixteen: Failure to obey any of the above rules may result in punishment."*

Here we go. My turn to do my scene. I feel sure that the prisoners will make fun of my appearance, and I evolve my first basic strategy—mainly not to smile at anything they say or do which could be admitting it's all only a game. At cell 3 I stop, and setting my voice hard and low say to 5486, *"What are you smiling at?"* "Nothing, Mr. Correctional Officer." "Well, see that you don't." As I walk off, I feel stupid.

*"So, 5704 wants a cigarette, does he? I don't smoke and I think smoking is a rotten habit. Don't you see the sign posted there? Smoking without permission. Even if you get a cigarette, you won't get any permission to smoke it, not on this shift. No smokes, no sympathy for your bad habits on this shift."*

*"That goes for you too, 1037—wipe that damned stupid grin off your ugly face."*

I am feeling empathetic toward 1037. He seems like a real nice guy, but I can't let him know, because it will be more difficult then to play my role convincingly. When it's all over, I can tell him I really like him, and I had to act this way because of my role. After all, a guard can't afford to get too friendly with a prisoner—it's not a fraternity house we're running.

Before we leave for the night, the captain of our shift and I can't resist taunting the prisoners with vivid descriptions of what we are going to do to our girlfriends when we see them tonight. They try to act as if we are not getting to them, but we can tell how envious they are.

*"Just because we're leaving, don't think we won't be thinking about you guys enjoying yourselves in your grubby little cells. I'm gonna think about nothing else the whole time I'm with my girl. Sleep tight—good dreams, men."*

\* \* \*

Those ding-dong guards on the morning shift must have been too soft to allow that rebellion to get started today. Can't believe that would have happened on our shift. I heard a lot of heavy stuff came down; they had to use fire extinguishers on the ringleaders to get them away from the cell doors they had barricaded. Then they really opened up on them—stripped them naked, stuck them into the hole, no privileges, toilet-bowl cleaning with bare hands, the whole trip. No wonder they seem so docile tonight.

That 5704 is the real trouble-maker of the lot. I can't stand him, he doesn't know how to take a joke. During the inspection, I went to cell 2 to mess up a bed he had made and he grabbed me, screaming that he had just made it, and he wasn't going to let me mess it up. He grabbed my throat, and although he was laughing I was pretty scared. I lashed out with my stick and hit him in the chin—although not very hard—and when I freed myself I became angry. I thought about getting back in the cell to have a go with him, since he attacked me when I wasn't ready.

The warden asks me to bring 5704 to the counseling office so the psychologist can discuss his negative attitude with him. I am surprised and angry that the psychologist rebukes me for handcuffing and blindfolding the prisoner before leaving the office, and I resentfully reply that it is both necessary security and *my* business anyway. It's easy for him to give orders from his safe easy-chair, to play Jesus Christ—he doesn't have to deal with these guys on their own terms hour after hour.

I am secretly delighted that 5704 does not have any visitors coming tonight. After warning the prisoners not to make any complaints about how we were treating them, unless they wanted the visit terminated fast, we finally bring in the first parents. I make sure I am one of the guards on the yard, because this is my first chance for the type of manipulative power that I find I really like here—being a very noticed figure with almost complete control over what is said or done. While the parents and prisoners sit in chairs, I sit on the end of the table dangling my feet and contradicting anything I feel like. This is more like it! This is the first part of this whole prison experiment I am really enjoying.

But this glow doesn't last too long after the last parent and friend leave and we have to get back to the boring routine of bringing the prisoners back and forth to the toilet, seeing that they don't make trouble, feeding them, and listening to their complaints. That 819 is obnoxious; he bears close watching. Although they are buckling under our force, and acting like sheep, or more like "cattle," I still keep thinking to myself, "I have to watch out for them in case they do try something. You never know." *I* sure wouldn't take all this shit so passively.

\* \* \*

Sure enough, today real trouble starts. We have a new prisoner to replace one of the ones who was released because they were acting as if they had a nervous breakdown. Personally, I think they were faking it and conned the big-shot psychologists. This new prisoner, 416, refuses to eat. That is a violation of Rule Two: "Prisoners must eat at mealtimes," and we are not going to have any of that kind of shit, not now when we have everything working so smoothly. He's so scrawny and scraggly, you'd think he'd be begging for seconds instead of refusing to eat any food. Obviously we have a trouble-maker on our hands.

If that's the way he wants it, that's the way he gets it. We throw him into the Hole ordering him to hold greasy sausages in each hand. After an hour, he still refuses. We have a crisis of authority; this rebellious conduct could undermine the complete control we have over the others. We decide to play on his loyalty to the other prisoners and tell the new one that all the others will be deprived of visitors if he does not eat his dinner. Prisoner 3096 gets furious—has been hanging on all week waiting for the ten-minute visit he could have with his girl-friend. He blows up—at 416—screaming at him, cursing him for being so selfish and making trouble for everyone. Still 416 refuses. We don't want to cut off visiting hours, but what can we do? I walk by and slam my stick into the Hole door. I am very angry at this prisoner for causing discomfort and trouble for the others. I decide to force-feed him, but he won't eat. I let the food slide down his face. I don't believe it is me doing it. I just hate him more for not eating.

We line up the prisoners and tell them that the fate of 416 is up to them. We guards do not want to be unreasonable. The prisoners are going to have to decide what should be done about this "problem," and we will abide by their decision. Should 416 be allowed to come out of solitary confinement or stay in that dark, cramped closet all night long? Those who vote for him to come out, even if he doesn't eat his sausage, will cast their vote by giving up their blankets and sleeping on the bare mattresses. Those who freely choose to teach the selfish bastard a lesson and have him stay in solitary all night can keep their blankets and call out loud and clear, so 416 can hear it.

As you might expect, the majority vote to punish that asshole trouble-maker. It's the only thing they do this whole week that staff can respect. They are on their way to becoming good prisoners! We are doing our job of rehabilitation real well.

SCENARIO II: I don't understand it, any of it! Nothing makes sense in here, and no one is concerned that nothing makes sense. Everybody has gone mad in this place, and they don't know it. No one person sees the change in him because the place and all the others are all made in the same way he is. No one questions all these arbitrary, inane rules. "You have to eat at mealtimes," even if you are not hungry or don't want to, "No talking allowed during meals," and any of a score of other rules. I can't tell whether the guards are more into this insanity than the prisoners or if it's the other way around. If you don't smile when that blond guard tells a dirty joke, you get punished. When he repeats it and you do smile, you get punished again for overreacting.

My buddies are acting like robots—servile, conforming, obedient robots—even anticipating what will be demanded and doing it before the order comes. "Sarge" is really in deep—he thinks he's beating the system by being the ultra-good, model prisoner, doing more than he has to. It's clear the guards dislike him for being so obedient and for seeming to enjoy their harrassment. The other prisoners are even more down on him for being such a nut. Whenever he overdoes something, that becomes the new standard for all the rest.

Maybe I'm reacting so adversely to this prison set-up just because I'm new. The others have gradually adjusted to the degradation, to the mental and physical abuse, and now they don't notice how far they've come. That 5704 was supposedly the ringleader of a rebellion they had here the other day. I can't believe it; the guards have him behaving like a trained seal, doing anything they ask, however servile or obscene—for a lousy cigarette. They discovered he's a cigarette addict, and they've used that to turn him into their toady. Maybe the rebellion itself is a fantasy trip all of the prisoners are on—never really happened. You need some fantasies to survive in here—there sure isn't much reality to hang your hat on.

I evolve my first basic strategy to get out of this place. I'll refuse to eat any of their food, pretend to get sick from lack of nourishment, and force them to release me. It's tough to do because I'm hungry already, but it's the only way out. Not one taste of their food, not one drop of water, no matter what.

The guards are really going out of their skulls now, just because I don't want to eat their lousy, greasy sausage. They don't care about *me*—why should they care whether or not I eat? They can't handle it—they start cursing, screaming at me, yelling that they're gonna cram the sausages up my ass. Into the Hole, sausages in each hand; out of the Hole, sausages still in each hand. I'm beginning to find new strength in my decision not to eat their food. I do not need their food to live, only their anger. As long as I choose to refuse to eat, I am free, I am still my own man. I am not imprisoned.

But it hurts me when the other prisoners start putting me down. I can understand why they're upset but it's not my fault. It's the stupid rules of the guards. What does my eating a sausage have to do with their visitors not being allowed in? It doesn't make sense to me, but it seems to make perfect sense to all of them.

I don't really mind the darkness of solitary, in fact, it's comforting. I doze off from time to time, awakened only by the deafening sound of a big billy club cracking down on the door to the Hole. I'm beginning to feel a little nauseous. The strategy is working. I'll be sick by tomorrow.

What's that they're saying? The prisoners have voted to keep me in here all night? I don't believe it! But the rule says that no prisoner will be kept in solitary confinement for more than one hour!

*"Violation of the rules." "You can't do that to me." "Goddammit, it's a violation of Prison Rules. . . ."*

*"John Wayne's" strained Texas drawl interrupts:*

The *guards* aren't doing anything to you—you're doing it to yourself. You started it, and your friends have voted in a true democratic election to finish it. So just get used to it—you're gonna be in there for a long time.

## Kind and Usual Punishment
## at San Quentin

The only way you really get to know San Quentin is through experience and time. Some of us take more time and must go through more experiences than others to accomplish this; some really never do get there.

*—Excerpt from San Quentin* Orientation Manual, 1970, p. 1.

SCENARIO III: You've heard the story ten times already from the old bulls, how that crazy nigger Jackson shot three officers and slit the throats of a couple of trusties before he got *his* trying to run the wall. That was a crazy thing to do! You wish you could remember more of the names of the other officers, especially the senior ones, but all in good time. What could make somebody murder officers and inmates indiscriminately and then try to jump a 20-foot wall manned by gunmen with their .357 Magnum, 30-30's, and enough fire power to shoot down a jet fighter? Prison sure must get to some of these guys!

Feeling pretty good in your new uniform. California Correctional Officer's patch neatly sewn on the shoulder and your C.C.O. badge on the military style hat. Hair cut maybe a little too short, though. Things run like clockwork here. It's a tight ship, if you sail it right. He said, "Remember, in case of trouble, blow your whistle and blow it loud."

Why should there be any trouble? I intend to be a good guard, to be fair, honest, and straight with the inmates. They've made a mistake, gotten caught, and we're here to help them get rehabilitated so it won't happen again. I'll bet a lot of them have a helluva story to tell. I might even get some good ideas for a little novel.

Slowly the cons shuffle into the yard. When most of the wall space fills, the others filter into clumps in the center of the yard. No one runs, no sudden movements of any kind, no loud talk, no laughter. It must feel good for them to have a chance to get out

of their cells to stretch, light up, talk to buddies. Wonder what they talk about? I'll walk around and let them get used to seeing me. We're all going to be here for a long time, I hope.

*"Did I hear you say 'fish bull'"?*
*"No sir, Mr. Correctional Officer."*

Better not to make eye contact with any of them, anyway. Where the hell are those other officers? Did they all go on a coffee break and leave me to take care of the store, all alone? Hmm, not very funny. No gun, no club, nothing but this goddamn little whistle between me and a knife in my back by any one of those nuts. They're all felons, you know, they've been through the mill; that's why they've dead-ended here at Q. We need more shake-downs and skin searches; it's too easy for them to conceal a home-made weapon.

They all look the same in those baggy green uniforms and expressionless faces They walk the same, stand the same, and act the same. Only difference is that there are the whites in one bunch, the blacks over there, and the Chicanos hovering around the South Wall. Shit, they *all* look like hardened killers to me. I wouldn't turn my back on any of these cons for a minute. Their stares don't mean a goddamn thing to me, nothing at all. I'm The Man here. I've got enough fire power backing me up to shoot their asses off to kingdom come. No filthy con is going to make me back down.

Just then, my senior officer appears. I know he's pleased by the way I handled the yard all alone.

*"Put Jones—A-24768 over there—in restraint gear; he's got a court appearance."*
*"Yes sir, but . . ."*
*"Move it out, this isn't a goddammed tea party you know!*
*"Yes, sir."*

How the hell should I know how to put this mess of chains on a con without any lessons? Why didn't they teach us how? Embarrassed, I have to ask the prisoner for help in putting him in the damn chains. One for their side

—or rather, one for the prisoners, and one for my so-called "fellow" guards, and none for me. If it's every man for himself here, then that's O.K. with me. I'll make it in spite of those officers with their fun-and-games-initiation rites for us newcomers. I can take it, and I can dish it out. They'll see.

Those animals better watch their asses too; they *are* animals, you know. They have to be, to survive here. They have to rely on primitive animal instincts because only the fittest survive in this jungle. Fortunately, they're caged. Maybe it's not such a good idea for them to be loose so long or so often in the yard. It would be simpler all around if we just kept them in their cells—they're used to it, probably prefer it. I heard some of these cons even call it "home." Imagine, calling a concrete box your "home!" They really get screwy from being here too long.

My neck is really tight—must be the cold. A good stiff drink when I get home is all I need to make me feel good as new again. God, this is a long day—can't wait to get home and get cleaned and relax. The place really makes you dirty and grimy. Bet the cons don't even notice it.

SCENARIO IV: Hi, kid! I'm Joey. I hope you've been enjoying the candies and the paperback I sent over. Sorry I couldn't get a detective story, but they were all out of them at the Commissary. Do you know how to use the headphones? You realize that you "fish," I mean first-timers here at Quentin, don't get no headsets for quite awhile. So you got no music to listen to on the house radio, and it can get awfully quiet and lonely up here in the "fish bowl" before you get put into the general population.

You'd be surprised how much I know about you—where you come from, your family, your rap, even where you have your appendix scar. Paid a whole carton of Luckies to look over your file, and now that I see you in the flesh, I'm glad I did. You certainly are worth it.

You see, kid, Quentin ain't like no other place you been in before. It's real dangerous here. Lots of racial stuff coming down. Guys get shanked for just looking the wrong way at some dude. Bulls putting the squeeze on to be a snitch. Lot of just plain mental cases running around in here too. You never know where to turn.

Unless you got yourself a friend . . . That's why I came to see you personally. Nice-looking kid like you is gonna be in real trouble in a place like this—an awful lot of animals in here. Can't blame them—some guys been here for most of their lives and never gonna see pussy or moonlight again. Me? Twelve years, assault with a deadly, Oakland traffic cop. Should be getting my date real soon now.

But we're getting off the point. I want you to consider me your friend. I want you should feel I will protect you from any mother here who tries to lay a hand on you. Don't want to brag, kid, but my clique runs the drug action in A-block. I can arrange it easy for you to be my cellmate—so we can spend a lot of time together getting to know one another real well. What do you say, wanna be Joey's kid?

No reason to go get yourself so upset. No rush. Take your time, think it over. Maybe you don't understand how important it is to have one good friend in here. You know no one escapes from anything in here. But I can understand where you're coming from —used to feel the same way once. But it's not a matter of whether or not you will— it's only a matter of *when*.

Be seein' ya around, kid!

## THE TECHNIQUES OF PRISON SOCIALIZATION

The dehumanization of imprisonment occurs at many levels, but the political is most basic. Presidents, governors, and other politicians may use prisons to gain votes by insuring concerned citizens that something is being done about crime. Since prisoners have no political lobby and do not form a legitimized constituency, they become mere pawns in political and economic power plays at various levels of bureaucracy. Although somewhat better organized, prison guards similarly exert little real political influence. As the tragedy at Attica indicated, the position of "prison guard" is not held in especially high esteem by society's decision-makers: Guards are an expendable commodity when it is their lives versus the "face-saving" of politicians and upper-echelon correctional administrators.

Legislators respond to public concern about crime by perfunctorily advocating imprisonment of more people, revocation of more paroles, or similar "get tough" platitudes. Since the public has been "educated" to believe that crime is due to the evil that lurks in the hearts of criminals (see Haney & Manzolati, 1976), they are comforted by promises of harsher and more intensive treatment. Such approaches deflect attention from the actual causes of crime. Even those legislators privately sympathetic to the plight of prisoners and guards are reluctant to take public stands, fearing negative reactions from their constituency.

To the extent that they figure at all in the decisions that affect their lives, members of prison society are depersonalized entities in someone else's calculus of political and economic gain. Decisions at this level, of course, must be translated into structures and procedures with operational consequences. Requiring a compatible vehicle for implementation, such a legally dehumanizing policy begins formally in the courtroom and ends unceremoniously in prison.

## The Ecology of Dehumanization

The physical structure of a prison conveys a direct, immediate, and constantly repeated message: This place is different from all others and is, therefore, unlike those where respectable, trustworthy people live. Locked steel gates, barbed wire on high walls, gun towers or tiers, and windowless cells all convey the invincibility of the law and the utter isolation of those inside. Garfinkel wrote, "The denounced person must be ritually separated from a place in the legitimate order, i.e., he must be defined as standing at a place opposed to it. He must be placed 'outside,' he must be made 'strange' [1956, p. 423]."

The interior design of the prison furthers dehumanization by minimizing the possibility for any privacy, except in solitary confinement. Mass eating in cafeterias, mass exercise in the yard, and animal-cage cells with bars instead of doors confirm the loss of autonomy and individual treatment. Prisoners must detach themselves psychologically —daydream or fantasize privacy—to be alone or be unseen though constantly watched by guards and other prisoners. Excessive control and surveillance have undesirable effects on those who *practice* it as well: The watchers come to believe in it as solely responsible for the proper behavior of those being watched (Bettelheim, 1960; Strickland, 1958). The guards convince themselves that their elaborate mechanisms of surveillance and control are effective and that prisoners are ready to disobey and revolt if procedures are relaxed—further alienating the two groups and engendering mutual suspicion and mistrust.[5]

---

[5] An example both of prison administrators' obsession with surveillance and their apparent ignorance of its accompanying social-psychological consequences is provided by a new maximum security unit in West Virginia. Designed as an "architectural method of controlling prisoners," its specifications exceed Orwellian proportions: large metal screens behind which guards remotely patrol the cellblock, an electronics system of serving food, and a closed-circuit television network through which the inmates receive visits. Among the violations that Acting Warden William Wallace specified as leading to up to six months' additional confinement in the unit was a "breach of trust" (*Freeworld Times,* 2(6), 1973).

In addition to little privacy and much control, the long corridors, barren cells, and drab-colored walls provide minimal sensory variation as do the monotonous daily routines of being processed for meals, for work, for relaxation, for everything. A San Quentin guard told us: "Men in total confinement and their 'protectors' play games to break the monotony. These games pass the time—create and stir an often boiling pot. The boiling pot then boils over, alleviating the pressure. Many men have been injured and some killed as a result of prison games."

## Anonymity

Prisons are designed to maximize anonymity. Uniforms categorize individuals as "guards" or "prisoners." Numbers may replace or become administratively more important than names. Uniqueness is further reduced by having new prisoners' hair shaved off, by insisting on standard hair lengths for prisoners and guards, and by having standard meals at standard times with standard tableware. Prisoners' sense of autonomy is lessened by restrictions on personal possessions and by unannounced cell and body searches. Inmates are punished for putting too much starch in their uniforms, for trying to look too good or too sharp or too different. (To some extent, individual guards appear to gain reflected strength from their identification as "guards" and may conceal personal fears and anxieties through anonymity. It is curious that the reflecting sunglasses used in our mock prison as part of an "anonymity manipulation" were worn out of personal preference by both the arresting city policemen in our study and many of the troopers at Attica.)

The need for uniqueness in an anonymous environment forces prisoners to clasify their world as "mine" and "not mine." Since they have so little personal territory, they must defend it (often with their lives) if they are to have any situational identity at all. A bar of soap or pencil becomes a precious possession that a prisoner is willing to fight

for if it is stolen or used by anyone else. They are his—and in a world of much that is not, what *is* his must be defended. Former Texas inmate Mike Middleton reported: "When you brush against a man, you had better apologize. If you don't, then the man is free to do what he wants to you. I have seen a shank put in a man's back for that."

## Rule Control

Rules are the backbone of all institutionalized approaches to managing people. Institutions vary only in how many rules they have and in how explicit and detailed they are. Imposing an impersonal, externalized structure on interpersonal relationships, they remove ambiguity from social interaction and make human conduct more predictable by reducing idiosyncratic reactions. They eliminate the need for personal justifications of a desired course of action: "It's the rule" is sufficient. Rules proliferate in institutional settings and come to have a life of their own, continuing even after their original purpose has been forgotten by the rule-enforcers. (Further, the functional autonomy of rules within *legal* institutions is compounded by the fact that these structures themselves exist in the service of an externalized and often antiquated rule system—the law.)

Rules can come to define reality for those who follow them. Since the *definition* of the situation frequently *is* the situation, violations and not rules are defined as the problem, no matter how unjust the latter may be. Becker wrote: "From the point of view of the well-socialized participant in the system, any tale told by those at the top intrinsically deserves to be regarded as the most creditable account obtainable [1970, p. 18]." When the guards in our simulated prison threatened to suspend visiting privileges unless a fasting prisoner ate his dinner, the other prisoners turned violently against *him*, not against the guards for their arbitrary rule. They had accepted the guards' definition of the situation and regarded the prisoner's defiance as blameworthy, rather than as a heroic, symbolic act to instill the courage they so desperately needed.

Coercive rules automatically force power relations on people: Someone must have power to enforce the rules, and someone must obey them. Those who obey often come to expect, and even respect, the structure that a rule-governed environment provides. In characterizing a good guard, many prisoners told us: "The guy who goes by the book, the one who is fair and who is a real 'professional' because he doesn't make exceptions. . . . his behavior is predictable by the prisoners because he, too, is controlled and dominated by the rules."

There are implicit consequences of obeying rules. Since rules are statements of permissible behavior, people go unnoticed (and unrewarded) when they do "what is expected." Mike Middleton said: "The only way to make it with the bosses is to withdraw into yourself, both mentally and physically —literally making yourself as small as possible. . . . They want you to make no waves in prison and they want you to make no waves when you get out." But if rule observance is expected and thus not rewarded, rule violation is always noticed and, consequently, punished. Thus, a social space encompassed by a network of explicit rules reduces the likelihood that influence will be exerted through reward or positive sanction, while increasing the likelihood that punishment strategies will be used.

## Emotional Expression and Suppression

Loss of the capacity to experience emotions and flattened emotional expression are taken as signs of major psychological disturbance. But rather than promoting a fuller, more normal expression of emotions among the inmates, prisons do the reverse: They create conditions that distort, inhibit, and suppress emotion. Emotions in institutional settings must be contained to the extent they represent spontaneous, impulsive, often unpredictable reactions. Charged

with the management of "deviant" individuals, institutions regard emotional expression as a source of potential danger that must be eliminated if it cannot be conveniently manipulated.

Institutional control of emotion may occur through explicit rules or be achieved indirectly by creating conditions in which inmates find it advantageous to suppress emotion. Those who show their emotions publicly reveal a vulnerability that may invite exploitation. In a prison environment, tender emotions may result in far more pain than pleasure. At the Rhode Island Correctional Institution, a prisoner told us that he "beat the system" after several years in solitary confinement. By learning "self-control," he "no longer feels anything for anybody." *Soledad Brother* George Jackson's letters proclaimed, "I have made some giant steps toward acquiring the things I personally will need . . . I have repressed all emotion [1970, p. 37]."

For the guards, emotional control begins with attempts at concealing fear in a working environment where they believe their lives to be always in danger. They must constantly affirm their fearlessness and toughness to prisoners and to each other. Fearful guards are seen as a threat to every other guard because (it is thought) they cannot be counted on in an emergency—an eventuality for which the guards are always preparing. Also, a guard who shows positive emotions toward the prisoners is suspected of being "wired up," taking graft, or being controlled by them in some way.

It is not surprising, then, that the basic advice given to "fish bulls" by the captain of the guards at San Quentin is to be "firm and fair but not friendly" with inmates. But not only must guards conceal their emotions from the inmates; they must also conceal them from each other. There is an implicit norm among correctional officers not to discuss their emotions and certainly not for the new men to tell the old bulls how they feel. Thus their intense feelings are likely to be displaced onto family and friends and also expressed as psychosomatic illness. There is much evidence that this is indeed the case—that considerable "silent suffering" occurs among officers who have not yet learned to detach their cognitive from their affective selves.

## Time Distortion

Prisons distort the conception of time. Imprisonment breaks the continuity of life by separating the imprisoned from their past, distancing the future (especially with an "indeterminate sentence"), and imposing a present-oriented framework. The endless routines and daily activities create seemingly undifferentiated time. All that matters is how much protection and power one has *now*. Where survival is primary, reliance on either the past or the future cannot be afforded.

This immediate time focus encourages overreaction to minor stimuli at the expense of planning for major events (such as what to do *after* parole). Events trivialize as they pass, further establishing the timelessness of prison and contributing to an atmosphere of unreality. The subtle manipulation of time sense alters fundamental aspects of thinking, feeling, and social interaction. "The time slips away from me. . . . the days, even the weeks, lapse into each other, endlessly into one another. Each day that comes and goes is exactly like the one that went before [Jackson, 1970, p. 110]."

## Force and Power

Prisons are best comprehended as variations on the themes of force and power. Disobedient prisoners soon learn that the guards have an arsenal of potent sanctions to use "legitimately" against them. Because prisoners have few, if any, officially recognized avenues of redress, those who have been wronged can *only* act "illegitimately" in retaliation and risk almost certain, harsher treatment when they do. In describing the social conditions that produce human aggression, Bandura is correct when he observes: "Maltreatment is most prevalent where marked imbalances of power exist [1973, p. 320]."

Since guards can commit acts against prisoners who have no officially sanctioned means to react, there is much opportunity for unbridled use of force. Rubenstein's observations on police parallel the situation of the prison guard: "Every policeman is faced at some point with the temptation to beat a prisoner. There is always someone who angers him or arouses fear in him that he seeks to eradicate by punishing the person who causes him to quiver. If his supervisors do not object, nothing can stop him [1973, p. 321]." And like the police (see Chevigny, 1969), prison guards can add legal insult to physical injury: Guard disciplinary reports, to which prisoners have no right of rebuttal, are most effective in extending prison sentences.

In this most unnatural human relationship, the use of force not only becomes more likely but takes on pathological characteristics as well. In the Stanford study, physical aggression and verbal harassment by guards increased steadily, despite the dramatic *decrease* of prisoner resistance. The exercise of power seemed to become self-perpetuating; acts of aggression appeared to acquire inherently rewarding properties and were no longer even quasi-rational responses to situational threats.

Guards' prison reputations are based on demonstrations of masculinity, uses of force, and past experience handling violent encounters. In the simulated prison, the most respected guards were those most sadistic in their treatment of prisoners and most forceful in responding to real or imagined affront. They became the leaders on each shift, and their aggression was modeled by others until their tough demeanor was adopted by nearly all.

Often at the mercy of guards' force and caprice, usually uninformed about the administrative decisions affecting them, prisoners soon learn that they cannot anticipate accurately the consequences of their actions. Videotapes of guard–prisoner interactions in our simulated prison showed that, when prisoners asked the guards a question, they were as likely to get harassed or abused as to receive an answer. This unpredictability in the environment also explains a more dramatic observation: By the end of the study, prisoners had simply *stopped behaving* and initiated almost no activity. They reacted in a totally passive manner, apparently manifesting the human analogue of the "learned helplessness" syndrome found by Seligman (1975) in arbitrarily shocked laboratory animals (see also Bettelheim, 1960).

We found that in such an environment, power comes to be vicariously modeled by prisoners; strength and forcefulness, admired and revered. On release, many prisoners essentially aspire to "guard" status and may demand absolute obedience from friends, relatives, and others around them. Intimate knowledge that one's unmitigated dominance is bought only at the expense of another's deprivation does not moderate this veneration of power. If they learn only one thing from the desperation of imprisonment, most prisoners learn to avoid interpersonal powerlessness at all costs.

Another consequence is that prisoners may come to depend on institutional regulations to order their daily lives. Although the initial adjustment is often uncomfortable, gradually the more benign, less confining rules add structure and regularity to life. Ironically, the prisoner is "freed" from the mundane, trivial contingencies occupying most of the people on the outside: Laundry, food, and so on are provided. Such dependency on structure may be debilitating when prisoners begin to live again where rules do not "regulate" so much of personal life. Those prisoners who do become socialized into total reliance on these enforced regularities may be unable to deal with the spontaneous contingencies of day-to-day existence. For the many who return to prison simply because they cannot make this transition, "perfect" adjustment to the institution has precluded *any* adjustment to the outside world.

Interestingly, the only personality dimension that related to differences in behavior in our mock prison was "authoritarianism." Those prisoners who adjusted best and remained longest were significantly higher on the F-scale of authoritarianism. Authoritarian personalities "fit" with the authoritarian structure of a prison in the very broadest sense: Believing that power underlies all human relations, they endure the harassment of prison life better because they are resigned to (and expect) the type of treatment they would administer if the power tables were turned. Prisoners with a more democratic orientation reject power as the basis for human relations and cannot accept the injustice of power domination under any circumstances. Those unwilling or unable to substitute authoritarianism for their more egalitarian world-view must endure the discomfort of the "maladapted," paying a costly psychic price for the possession of their humane and democratic sentiments.

There exists another, more insidious aspect of prisoner life. In denying the exercise of individual will and freedom of choice, prisons compromise the basic ingredient of human nature. In this totally controlled environment, *actors* become *reactors,* and individuals the mere processors of environmental inputs. Such conditions erode the individual's capacity for self-direction and ability to alter the impact of external forces. In a prison society, inmates lose not only their rights as citizens but also their power to choose and be responsible for their own choices. By systematically depriving the imprisoned of the opportunity for even trivial choices, prisons can debase and render meaningless their lives—that is the final act of dehumanization. "Beggars can't be choosers," society reminds the poor—and all others whom it has imprisoned.

## Dynamics of Desperation

Persons forced to endure pathological environments acquire seemingly pathological strategies for survival, something often overlooked by those who would describe prisoner "deviance" as "inherent" rather than "adaptive." To become "socialized" in such situations is often to accept the internally consistent illogic of events, to seek one's only joy in the baseness of the surroundings, and to manufacture meaning in the remotest corners of a limited universe in which there is little. Adjustment to the prison environment demands internalization of perspectives and values that contradict the alleged goals of the institution. Former Arkansas warden Tom Murton observed that to survive and be successful, the prisoner must learn "the ability to lie, cheat and manipulate others—and, if he does it skillfully enough, he will be paroled. He finds that he is conditioned—to reject any vestige of decency he brought to the prison with him [1973, p. 10]." Adaptation to prison life generates inversions of "normal" behavioral patterns. Under conditions of heterosexual deprivation an inverted code of sexual status evolves: Homosexuality becomes the necessary accoutrement of masculine power; on the outside, it is its antithesis. A former prison leader said, "My partners would have thought I was queer or something if I didn't have my stable of young white boys, since it was clear I was in a position to afford them."

Survival inside prison often demands behavior that perversely insures the continuation of the situational pathology. In trying to preserve some vestige of self-esteem in an environment systematically depriving them of it, prisoners create and impose distinctions among themselves. The infrastructure of prisoner culture creates an illusion of power and status within a group that has been rendered collectively powerless and devoid of status. Prisoner hierarchies, rigidly enforced, provide a mechanism by which some minimal sense of control and effectuality is preserved through mutual victimization (see, e.g., Flynn, 1972; Podgorecki, 1973). Their dehumanization is extended and made inescapable by the prisoners themselves—driven by circumstance to imprison one another further.

Such prisoner hierarchies are tolerated by the prison administration because the system depends on them for its operation (Lukacs, 1971, p. 257). Even under optimal conditions, guards are hopelessly outnumbered by prisoners, so the staff must find some means to prevent prisoners from organizing. Internecine prisoner conflict can be manipulated through strategies that pit one prison faction against another. Further, by allowing some individual prisoners to become moderately powerful at the expense of many others, the prison staff contributes to the collective impotence of the prisoner population as a whole. The illusion of power is permitted a few to avoid its becoming a reality for the many.

Prison guards, too, are controlled and degraded by the prison environment. Although they wield considerable power over individual prisoners, they have little freedom to make choices that might affect or improve their own working conditions. As an occupational group, prison guards have low status and are poorly paid, so it becomes especially important to maintain the degraded position of prisoners—if only to provide themselves a favorable contrast.

In response to prisoner hostility, guards behave in ways that generate even more hostility, making tension and fear increase and alternative ways of reacting less likely. Individual guards often learn from their early experience in prison that kindness and consideration are sometimes exploited by the prisoners. Prisoners may manipulate a helpful new guard—usually to the delight of other prisoners—until he "gets wise." Such exploitation by the prisoners is understandable in the total context of the treatment received from other guards. Most prisoners are suspicious of favors from guards, since they are often a ploy by which guards may make later claims or additional demands. Since it is incompatible with the prison infrastructure, genuine friendliness from guards cannot be relied on. Even among new, well-meaning guards, personal consideration and sensitivity to prisoner concerns are generally extinguished in a very short time, in part because of its reception by the prisoners.

Moreover, in the emotionally impoverished environment of prison, individual kindnesses have no easily interpretable meaning. Such behavior may be taken as a sign of weakness on the part of individual guards. In one sense, prisoners require guards to be tough: Toughness is the code by which they live; many have come to neither trust nor respect less. Within the confines of these normative expectations, it is nearly impossible for an individual guard to effect change, even at a personal level. It is not unreasonable, then, to speak of the way in which prisoners and guards "imprison" each other through inflexible negative expectations in an environment that makes prosocial behavior desirable, even necessary, to exploit.

Because they have been socialized to see each other exclusively as "enemy," guard and prisoner groups cannot appreciate the degree to which their individual plights are actually common ones. Perhaps no event more tragically symbolizes the functional equivalence of prison guards and inmates than the Attica massacre, where, to regain control of the prison, state troopers killed nearly as many guard hostages as they did prisoners. Yet, the friends and relatives of those killed, along with the guards who had not been taken hostage, believed so deeply that prisoners, and only prisoners, were the arch-enemies of guards that they simply *refused to believe* the coroner's report showing that the hostages had been killed by other guards and police. So strong was their need to avoid this lesson of mutuality that they were compelled literally to *deny* even the medical reports and physical evidence.

## THE SOCIALIZATION INTO CRIMINALITY: PRISON AS EMBLEM

The institution of prison, which rises as a symbol of the criminal law's devotion to the person-as-cause view of crime and corrections, stands also as a grim reminder of the consummate power of the situational control of behavior. Perhaps nowhere in society are humans more oppressively controlled by their environment than in prison. A more bitter irony, however, is that prisons, whose express purpose is to rehabilitate criminals and deter crime, actually make illegal behavior more likely. It is in this sense that one can begin to speak directly of a "socialization into criminality."

The physical as well as psychological survival of prisoners often depends on how well they have mastered the necessary "criminal" skills. As we have described, the inherently pathological constellation of social forces controlling behavior inside prison makes physical violence ever more likely, dishonesty and deceit often the very prerequisites for success. Whether they come to depend on an encompassing network of institutional procedure, learn to distrust others and to perceive everyone as potential "marks," or possess a burning hatred that motivates acts of recrimination against representatives of the system that placed them there, prison experience leads many prisoners inexorably toward crime when they are released. Another way in which the label "prisoner" has criminalizing consequences is that having been in prison insures the difficulty if not impossibility of finding acceptable work —making crime a likely, perhaps the only, way of surviving on the outside.[6]

---

[6] The U.S. Department of Justice reports that the median annual income of state prisoners *prior to their arrest* was $4639. This figure is actually inflated by the fact that those prisoners who reported *no* income were excluded from the calculations. See *Survey of Inmates of State Correctional Facilities 1974* (1976). An unpublished Library of Congress study prepared for Senator Burdick (D., N.D.) on the relationship between crime and unemployment claims that 80 percent of the changes in federal prison admissions and 78 percent of the changes in state prison admissions "could be statistically related to changes in unemployment." (See Jack Anderson's column, March 26, 1975.) Unemployment leads to crime, which leads to imprisonment, which virtually guarantees subsequent unemployment . . . and the circle goes unbroken.

It is not uncommon to hear of citizen outrage over defendants and convicts who have been treated "leniently" by the criminal justice system, only to commit subsequent crimes. But this excerpt from a letter by a state penitentiary inmate suggests the myopia and misdirection of such criticism:

Because of my refusal to let things die down and forget all that happened during my 37 months in solitary . . . I am the most hated prisoner in [this] penitentiary and called a "hard-core incorrigible." Maybe I am incorrigible, but if true, it's because I would rather die than to accept being treated as less than a human being. . . . But now I don't think I will be a thief when I am released. No, I'm not rehabilitated. It's just that I no longer think of becoming wealthy by stealing. I now only think of killing— killing those who have beaten me and treated me as if I were a dog. I hope and pray for the sake of my own soul and future life of freedom that I am able to overcome the bitterness and hatred which eats daily at my soul, but I know to overcome it will not be easy.

Rarely, if ever, do judges and parole boards face public anger over what is the common and more important counterexample to the charge of being "soft on criminals"—crimes committed as a result of being treated too harshly and too inhumanely by the system.

Conceptually, if not yet legally, prison actually constitutes a form of entrapment: It is a governmental "agency" that substantially increases the likelihood that certain people will engage in crime from which they would otherwise have refrained. Prison conditions induce prisoners to commit numerous crimes inside for which they have no "predisposition." Further, because rates of recidivism can be shown to vary directly as a function of time spent within prison, it follows that prisons are entrapping in their consequences. If, as Justice Stewart (*United States* v. *Russell,* 1973) has written, "[i]t is the Government's duty to prevent crime, not to promote it," clearly this duty is not being met. Not surprisingly, however, the law of entrapment still suffers from the same

person-as-cause bias that plagues the rest of the criminal justice system—it speaks not to the nature of governmentally created and maintained environments but monitors only the behavior of individual government agents. And the notion that some persons are continually "entrapped" by the conditions in which they must live continues to elude the criminal law.

Of course, many of the debilitating effects of prison would be transient if ex-convicts were released into "situations" on the outside that allowed them to prosper. Unfortunately, most re-enter the larger society under conditions scarcely less hostile than prison itself and identical to those which precipitated their original offense. Here is the irony and misdirection of "behavior modification" programs inside prisons: They violate their own most fundamental assumption, that behavior is a function of its eliciting and maintaining conditions. Prisoners are not "rehabilitated" because few are released into an environment in which prosocial, legal behavior is immediately adaptive. Thus, prisons are further "criminalizing" in that they divert our attention and resources away from the social structural changes needed to eliminate crime, and into person-centered treatment programs that have no hope of success.[7]

Guards too are criminalized by their prison socialization in the sense that they must become inured to the degradation and desperation of others. As Debs had pointed out, "The guard and the inmate cease to be human beings when they meet in prison. . . . The rules enforce this relation and absolutely forbid any intimacy with the human touch in between them [1927, p. 252]." There can be little doubt that such dehu-

---

[7] Indeed, one wonders if such diversions and misallocations are not the system's self-conscious *raison d'être*. Auditors from the General Accounting Office, for example, recently criticized New York and California for giving *too much*—not quite 30 percent—of their state anticrime funds to projects dealing with the underlying causes of crime! (See Weis & Milakovich, 1974, p. 31.)

manized interaction facilitates guard mal-treatment of their captives and may gener-alize to settings beyond the prison walls. Aside from becoming accustomed to and participating in cruelty, guards often behave in explicitly illegal ways (if the legal sanc-tion were applied here with the same rigor it is applied to certain others outside prison). The prevalence and availability of contra-band inside prisons clearly substantiate this "other" dimension to the guards' socializa-tion into criminality.

Cruelty and mistreatment, of course, can derive from personal hatred or animosity. Demeaning social roles, however, serve not only as a shelter for aggressive motives, but frequently act to *generate* such hostility and resentment. Many guards, themselves hav-ing relinquished personal autonomy and au-thentic aspiration, come to resent those prisoners who have effected an integration of self and purpose. One of the few acts of self-assertion available to them is to go be-yond the minimal demands of the role, vio-late the administration's halfhearted prohibi-tions on violence, and brutalize prisoners as an act of pseudo-selfhood. A social dynamic is thereby created in which specific instruc-tions are simply unnecessary to produce brutality—many guards will *want* to mistreat prisoners. Thus, the conspiracy is not one of explicit policy but of implicit situational frustration. Unlike the very first prison war-dens and administrators (who were often former ministers and men of religion), the upper echelons of today's correctional staffs are heavily populated with psychologists and "behavioral scientists." This raises interest-ing questions about the *legal responsibility* of prison systems for the harms they effect and implicit conspiracies they promote: How convincing can their plea of ignorance be to the charges against brutalizing conditions and depersonalizing procedures, when their managers hold advanced degrees in disci-plines that should have sensitized them to the human consequences of these forms of treatment?

Finally, we believe that prison socializa-tion is emblematic of the way "socialization into criminality" occurs in other levels and sectors of society. In form and effect, the situational control of prison provides a "model" of the processes by which one gen-erally becomes "criminal." Prisons may also promote rather than discourage violence by serving as behavioral models for potential aggressors—teaching them that some per-sons *deserve* to be punished and abused for what they do. Since the poor and powerless are most often and most visibly "repri-manded" by the criminal justice system, they are most likely to be the continuing victims of this lesson.

Crime is fundamentally the product of impoverished circumstances and the power imbalances that exist in society. It is part of the continuing conflict between the control-lers and the controlled. Brutalization of the impoverished by the agents of society's em-powered institutions is, as in prison, facili-tated by the dehumanization of both groups. Like prisoners, the poor become submerged in the dynamics of desperation: They tend to lose perspective inside their immediate situation and victimize those who can least afford it—each other. For many, crime be-comes not a choice, or even a necessary alternative, but rather a fact of life. As in prison, powerful socializing forces are pres-ent to instill in the poor the notion that the existing order—with themselves at the bot-tom—is the only legitimate one. Chronic powerlessness, the experience of being arbitrarily and totally subject to the sur-rounding circumstances, leads eventually to the feeling of hopelessness and for some a truly "learned helplessness" (see Seligman, 1975).

Just as in prison, victimization of the poor in society is implemented largely by persons who are themselves collectively powerless and have been reluctantly or unwittingly brought under the force of situational con-trol. Whether as objects or agents of insti-tutional purpose and the socioeconomic forces that dominate society, people are pre-vented by potent socialization processes from learning that what distinguishes pris-oner from guard, inside prison and beyond, is often the illusion of choice and power, not its reality.

## POSTSCRIPT ON CHOICE AND EVIL

Nearly everyone agrees that prisons are presently unmitigated failures. They do not effectively deter, for no positive relationship has ever been convincingly shown to exist between rates of imprisonment and the reduction of crime.[8] They do not rehabilitate. By all accounts, the longer persons are confined to prison the *more* likely they are to commit crime. Thus, we have argued that prison is an institution that not only fails to achieve its declared purposes but actually functions to contravene them. How can it be, then, that so many people continue to clamor for "better" and more of these so clearly harmful institutions?

Though they are pervaded by accident, error, and incompetence, prisons (and the criminal justice systems of which they are a part) are not random events—they do not just "happen." Rather, they are a product of the society in which they function. "As we begin to move from micro-situations and work up to macro-situations," Laing reminds us, "we find that the apparent irrationality of behavior on a small scale takes on a certain form of intelligibility when one sees it

---

[8] The evidence on general deterrence, such as it is, seems strikingly equivocal. Even when punitive sanctions were their most draconian, signs of their inefficacy abounded. Thus, while pickpockets were being publicly hanged on London's Tyburn Hill, other pickpockets were making their way through the crowd of spectators—picking their pockets. There are record numbers of people in prison. Yet, if we are to believe the government reports, the crime rate continues to grow. The United States—whose citizens rank "crime" as their foremost domestic problem—imprisons more people for longer sentences than any Western nation. In Holland there are about 24 prisoners per 100,000 population, whereas in the U.S. the rate is nearly *10 times that many*. Yet, there is no evidence that crime is rampant in the streets of Holland. Perhaps the Dutch are morally superior, or is there some other explanation?

in context [1968, p. 15]." The manifest irrationality of prison, too, becomes interpretable in context. Prisons punish a relatively narrow segment of the population—minorities and the poor—in "revolving door" fashion: The same people are caught, punished, released, only to be caught again. These people are held up to the rest of society as "lessons" of the adverse consequences of certain illegal acts. To the upper and middle classes who observe rather than provide this lesson, the system appears highly "cost efficient" for it localizes human sacrifice within a restricted group of (other) people. The poor not only provide most of the subjects for this object lesson in crime and punishment, but it is *they* who are most victimized by the temporary exiles of prison society. Consider this possibility: As taxpayers we subsidize the victimization of the poor (by the poor) in order merely to buttress an otherwise tenuous moral code, and to channel our overactive and overstimulated achievement and acquisitive drives into "legal," more socially acceptable directions. Moreover, by abdicating social-structural responsibility, prisons encourage us to ignore our own participation in the production of crime and to blame a certain restricted group of other people instead. The more localized the costs within the group, the more "effective" the subsidy, and the less grateful (or ashamed) we need to feel for their sacrifice —the more they obviously deserve what they get.

Our thesis has been that certain institutions, most notably prisons, constitute inherently pathological situations and are, by their very nature, evil. Only when people understand the potential of such situations to control their behavior and pervert their intentions can they acquire the vigilance and tenacity to resist them. Research in institutional settings must continue to document the excesses of institutional socialization in order to enhance people's capacity to resist institutional cooptation and to attain the awareness that precedes constructive institutional change.

Although we suggest that the concept of

the situational control of behavior be more fully recognized and integrated into the criminal law, we do not intend to propose the basis for a psychology of moral absolution. Rather, quite the opposite. When people are fully aware and informed about their choices, *and when they live in circumstances that offer genuine opportunity to choose otherwise,* then—and only then—can they be said to make truly "moral" decisions and only then can we begin to talk about the extent to which they should be held "responsible" for their actions. If we cannot provide awareness and opportunity to choose, how can we in fairness persist with the fiction of the responsible human being?

But it is not the concept of legal responsibility *per se* that is most troublesome, or even the realization that, as currently employed, it is pure legal fiction. Rather it is the cruel paradox that the people to whom it is most often and most harshly applied are precisely those for whom it is least applicable. They are the people whose social and material realities are most extreme and dehumanizing. In many ways the victims of the social structure are held most responsible for their own victimization. The poor and the powerless are the ones our criminal justice system holds accountable for illusory choices they never possessed. Thus, if we cannot eliminate the current concept of responsibility, let us *expand* it—expand it to include the responsibility of the rich for impoverishing the poor, the blame that belongs to the powerful for enervating the powerless, and the justice that is due the free for imprisoning the entrapped. If we cannot have fairness, let us at least have equality.

# CHAPTER 18

# Crime, Mental Illness, and Political Dissent[1]

## —DAVID LEVINE

The terms "crime," "mental illness," "social deviance," and "political dissent" are not scientifically useful and are becoming increasingly confused, so that scientific progress has stalled and much social and human injustice has taken place. Some research evidence and historical documentation are presented to support this view. The concepts of "threat to the community" and "danger" are suggested as more scientifically heuristic and socially just.

"Crime," "mental illness," and "political dissent" are labels for various forms of social deviance. These terms are so often confused that they have only limited scientific and social utility. Yet their application affects everyday judgments in both the legal and mental health systems. The use of such vague terms can aggravate injustice because of the substantial influence accorded to scientific and medical opinion by police, lawyers, judges, and politicians—perhaps especially when it meets their own needs. Thus this situation should not be dismissed as a basically intellectual or theoretical problem.

Each of these terms has generated a substantial amount of literature. Since 1960, for example, the label "mental illness" has been the center of renewed and heated controversy (e.g., Adams, 1964; Braginsky, Braginsky, & Ring, 1969; Ellis, 1967; Sarbin, 1967a, 1967b; Szasz, 1960). The most widely quoted critic of the concept is Szasz,

who claimed that the myth of mental illness permits ignoring the reality that the human condition ipso facto involves conflict, frustration, and distress and that maintenance of this myth supports a deceptive belief in magical solutions to human problems of living (Szasz, 1960, 1963). Likewise, Sarbin has been critical of the scientific status, linguistic logic, and social morality of the phrase "mental illness." Two very useful articles (Sarbin, 1967b; Sarbin & Mancuso, 1970) traced the historical roots of the term, analyzed the confusion that results from combining the words "mental" and "illness," and summarized data showing that, despite extensive programs of mental health education, "the public is not sympathetic toward persons who are labelled mentally ill. They . . . are willing to relegate them to a childlike, nonperson role [Sarbin & Mancuso, 1970, p. 168]."

Professionals in health-related fields are not immune from labeling deviant behavior or unhappiness as mental illness and recommending institutionalization for such conditions. About twenty years ago Cumming and Cumming (1956) found evidence that psychiatrically trained individuals were more

[1] I thank June Louin Tapp and Felice J. Levine for leading me to some of the ideas expressed in this chapter. Responsibility for errors in working out these ideas, however, belongs only to me.

likely than other adults to label patients' behaviors as symptoms of mental illness. Rosenhan's field study in 1973 suggested a similar conclusion about professionals' judgments of normal individuals who had infiltrated mental institutions. Another example of the dubious conclusions reached by some uses of the term "mental illness" is furnished by Rosenthal:

[I]f the same ratio (as found in Denmark) were to apply in this country, we would find more than sixty million people in the United States with some form of what we now call schizophrenic spectrum disorder . . . nine million people in the U. S. (with) a serious drinking problem . . . about one child in every twenty . . . thought to have a minimal brain dysfunction . . . one child in five between age ten and seventeen would one day appear before a juvenile court judge. . . . [1972, pp. 3–6].

Dohrenwend and Dohrenwend (1965), Ennis (1972), Goffman (1961, 1971), Hartung (1965), Kittrie (1972), and Spitzer and Denzin (1968) also documented the futility and injustice of continuing to label some people as "mentally ill."

The term "criminality" is as dysfunctional as the label "mental illness." Broadly speaking, crime is any behavior prohibited by "rules" of conduct called criminal statutes —from violent episodes (e.g., murder) and acts against property (e.g., burglary) to victimless behaviors (e.g., gambling) and white–collar transgressions (e.g., fraud). Perkins (1957, p. 5) noted: "A crime is any social harm defined and made punishable by law." Crime presents great difficulties for scientific study because it encompasses heterogeneous behaviors, many of them private and likely to be concealed, and because the definition changes according to place and time. The problem of identifying comparable crime categories not only affects historical and cross-cultural analyses, but also complicates understanding events occurring at the same time and in proximal locales. For example, in two cities with similar populations, Circourel found different rates of apprehending juveniles who had committed petty thefts and car thefts. This difference was due to discretionary judgments by police about using certain crime categories. Such problems led Wheeler to stress that the social definition of crime is "a result of three-way interaction between an offender, victims or citizens, and official agents [1967, p. 318]." Although the defining and the reporting of crimes are in theory distinct, in fact they overlap because of different tolerance levels for certain activities and different sentiments about the role of the legal system and the criminal justice process.

As with mental illness, how people feel about certain kinds of conduct influences their invoking the "crime" label. While some effects of criminal deviance-labeling have been considered (e.g., Becker, 1963; Erikson, 1966; Kitsuse, 1962; Schwartz & Skolnick, 1962), there has been little interest in defining criminal behavior. An exception is Megargee's effort to develop a definitional structure that can discriminate among individuals. His research revealed differences "in the psychodynamics, behavior patterns, and family backgrounds of different types of assaultive individuals [1973, p. 76]." But overall the situation has changed little since Allen pointed out: "[T]he question, what sorts of behavior should be declared criminal, is one to which the behavioral sciences might contribute vital insights. This they have largely failed to do, and we are poorer for it [1959, p. 228]."

The term "political dissent" is plagued by much the same confusion. In fact, in a society where tolerance of political diversity is integral to official morality, it is hard to identify what constitutes a departure from normative ideological standards. Political dissent can include such diverse activities as objecting to court decisions on school desegregation, engaging in war resistance, supporting the American Nazi Party, or taking part in espionage. While political dissent can be studied scientifically when it is public, it is more difficult to examine covert political activities aimed at changing governments by manipulation, force, or revolution. Therefore, in considering the relation between political deviance and the criminal justice and mental health systems, one may have to settle for impressionistic evidence (see also Meehl, Chap. 2; Webb, Campbell, Schwartz, & Sechrest, 1966).

The need for further understanding of the development and uses of the labels commonly applied to social deviance is clear. This chapter aims to explore how deviant behaviors are defined and classified and what society wishes to convey in affixing certain labels. To this end I first review the relations between crime and mental illness, between mental illness and political behavior, and between crime and political behavior. I then conclude by presenting some ideas designed to overcome the theoretical confusion and related social injustice surrounding these classifications of deviance.

## CRIME AND MENTAL ILLNESS

Confusion about the meaning of "mental illness" and "criminality" not only pervades penal institutions, mental institutions, and juvenile facilities but also affects judgments in schools and welfare systems. Problems related to the confusion of these two forms of social deviance are (1) reflected in the complex and overlapping relation between the criminal justice and mental health systems, (2) worsened by the differences between medical and legal perspectives, and (3) evident in rehabilitative approaches for persons in involuntary circumstances—both prisoner and patient.

### Overlap of Criminal Justice and Mental Health Systems

Whether the label "mental illness" or "criminality" is assigned—or which is assigned first—often relates to who has committed the behavior, who is evaluating it, and the social context of the evaluation (Shah, 1969, 1972). Since "mental illness" covers

a wide variety of activities considered to be "odd," some grossly maladaptive or undesirable law violation is apt from time to time to be considered in these terms. Such multiple labeling may reflect what Schur (1971) has observed as people's tendency to focus on "differentness." Despite any hard evidence that the mentally ill are any more dangerous than other groups (see also Shah, 1974), people seem to be comforted by a belief that violent acts are committed mostly by "sick" people and perhaps also by the belief that the mentally ill are likely to commit violent acts (Schur, 1971, p. 47).

The confusion is not limited to laymen, however. A leading international jurist at a symposium on the Mentally Abnormal Offender asked: "Is a mentally abnormal offender primarily an offender who is sick or a sick man who is an offender [de Reuck & Porter, 1968, p. 217]?" One suspects that the question stems from a preoccupation with administrative and organizational problems, rather than from an attempt to understand behavior. Rollins posed the issue more directly: "Should [the mentally abnormal offender] be treated for his mental illness or should he be punished for his offense [1969, p. 3]?" Of course, putting the question this way assumes that there is a difference between "treatment" and "punishment"—a questionable distinction considered below.

Empirical data demonstrate the ambiguity and fluidity of these labels. There is evidence that (1) people called "mentally ill" have committed crimes, and this commission is part of the reason why they are so labeled or hospitalized; (2) people who commit crimes are labeled "mentally ill" more often than people who do not; and (3) there is considerable movement of people between the criminal justice and mental health systems.

That the "mentally ill" are so labeled and hospitalized because of criminal behavior was verified by data I collected in a large public mental hospital in the United States (Levine, 1970). About 70 percent of the patients were there chiefly because they had committed a crime; their behavior before hospitalization was illegal, if one ignored the legal criterion of "intent." I also found a significant correlation between how much time the patient spent in the hospital and how much would have been spent in prison if, instead of having been hospitalized, the patient had been sent to prison. Similar data I collected in a large mental hospital in Great Britain showed the same association between time in the hospital and degree of criminality (Table 1).

A 30-year follow-up study of 524 child guidance clinic patients (Robins, 1966) provides useful information on the number of people in penal institutions who have been diagnosed (or considered) as mentally ill. During the follow-up period, these "deviant children" were arrested more often for more serious offenses, and imprisoned more often than a control group. Although the proportion arrested and imprisoned was greater for "sociopathic" children than for children referred to the clinic for other reasons, the arrest and imprisonment rate for these "others" was greater than for the nonclinic control. In addition, data from Great Britain suggest that the interchangeable and ambiguous use of these labels is increasing: The number of offenders referred for psychiatric examination according to prison department reports rose from 6366 in 1961 to 10,919 in 1966 (Rollins, 1969, p. 55).

Rollins also found evidence for what he called the "ping-pong" effect: Of a sample of 127 mentally abnormal offenders admitted to Horton Hospital during 1961 to 1962, about 50 percent had been in both mental hospitals and penal institutions. During a 2 to 4 year follow-up period, 58 percent committed new offenses; of these, about two-thirds were sent to prison or fined.

## Differences in Medical and Legal Perspectives

The data above document the overlap and probable confusion between mental illness and criminality labels. But to prove that there is overlap is only a first step. Somehow society must make decisions when confronted with criminal behavior by "mentally abnormal offenders." Determinations of civil commitment, mental incompetency, and criminal insanity fall within the jurisdiction of the legal system. Assume, for example, that Charles Starkweather (who killed 11 people in two days) had been found not guilty by reason of insanity, rather than found guilty and executed (see Coffey, 1974). Would society have been satisfied that, being found not guilty, he be released? Or should he be sent to a mental hospital and released upon the judgment of a single physician, who might or might not have had psychiatric training? Or consider the case of a man who during a brief, apparently psy-

**TABLE 1    Frequency of Various Crimes in Relation to Length of Hospitalization**

| | MALES AGED 20–50 WITHOUT BRAIN DAMAGE | | | |
| DAYS IN HOSPITAL | No crime (includes suicide attempts) | Crimes against property; assault | Assault and battery | TOTAL |
| --- | --- | --- | --- | --- |
| Less than 120 days | 9 | 5 | 1 | 15 |
| More than 120 days | 2 | 5 | 8 | 15 |
| Total | 11 | 10 | 9 | 30 |

*Chi-square = 13.4*
p < .001; C = .55

chotic, episode murders his wife in a bizarre manner, yet who is lucid the next morning and reports part of the homicide as if it were a dream. Does the community want him found not guilty and released?

On the other hand, shall we lock up "potential" murderers who have committed no crime—as some people argued after the University of Texas tower mass slayings, although ironically nothing in Whitman's history "square[d] with the image of a 'mad murderer' [Schur, 1971, p. 55]." Knowing the problems of predicting rare events (Meehl & Rosen, 1955; Megargee, 1970; SPSSI Newsletter, 1960) makes this hardly a reasonable solution, even if it were constitutional. But some such proposal is offered whenever an inexplicable crime occurs, and the difficulties seem to be forgotten.

From both mental health and legal perspectives, the practical problems are enormous. Some psychiatrists hold that psychiatric theory is concerned only with illness and health—that legality of behavior is irrelevant. But this position largely ignores the social context of behavior and the law's concern with responsibility. Szasz's (1960) view that mental illness is a myth and that all people must be held equally responsible would seem to blur some important distinctions. While the concept of *mental illness*, stemming from a deterministic philosophical and scientific framework, has largely ignored judging responsibility (Biggs, 1967), from a legal point of view the idea of a criminal act is intertwined with responsibility. The law does recognize the need to take into account a person's mental condition in establishing criminal liability—not only during the criminal act itself (*mens rea*) but also during criminal proceedings and dispositional determinations. The law wants to know the extent to which a person can be held responsible for his or her behavior, whether the legal proceedings can be understood, and so forth. Resolving this problem is hampered chiefly by the linguistic and philosophical difficulties encountered in trying to understand what is meant by the notions of "responsibility" and "understanding" (see, e.g., Hart, 1968).

At stake in defining legal responsibility and specifying rules for handling mental illness are basic issues of social justice. Yet conclusions may vary depending on whether psychological/psychiatric or legal perspectives are used. Shah (1969) concluded that the former set of "rules," rooted in a medical model, have led to overprediction so as not to err on the side of failing to detect disease; but legal rules are guided by traditional presumptions of innocence to protect individual rights and liberties. The pitfalls of overprediction have been well observed (Kozol, Boucher, & Garofalo, 1972; Monahan, 1975; Morris, 1974; Steadman & Keveles, 1972). Awareness of such problems implies not the belief that evaluating mental disorders be abandoned, but that it be made with caution and with sufficient due process safeguards and judicial review. As Shah concluded: "[V]ery meticulous care [must] be taken to use decision rules and burden-of-proof criteria that approximate *legal rules* and that carefully consider the consequences of such labeling [1969, pp. 31–32]."

### Rehabilitation for the Incarcerated

The confusion between mental illness and crime can lead to peculiar rehabilitation or treatment programs. Dispositions of mental incompetency, insanity, or defective delinquency often involve indeterminant confinement and involuntary treatment for the prisoner—both basically punitive, however well meaning the intent. As Rothman put it, "the concept of rehabilitation simply legitimates too much [1973, p. 24]." An illustration of the potential for abuse is supplied by events at an institution for defective delinquents in Jessup, Maryland (*Washington Daily News*, April 27, 1972):

Patuxent opened in 1955 to provide intensive psychiatric aid to rehabilitate men legally sane, but habitual law-breakers. Prisoners may be held there until the staff or a court finds them "cured" of "defective delinquent" or criminal tendencies—which may be never —regardless of how short a jail term an inmate may have received originally as a sentence. However, a panel of two Maryland Judges in November (1971) stated that the maximum security prison subjected inmates to such brutal and harsh treatment as a part of its "therapy" that it amounted to cruel and unusual punishment. . . . Judges Miller and Watts issued an 18-page ruling to stop inmate abuses and set up administrative regulations for the prison. . . . Patuxent has steadfastly resisted the court's order, refusing to make any but minor changes within the prison and fighting court-ordered changes by appealing parts of the two-judge ruling. . . . Records obtained by the Washington Daily News revealed that Patuxent, after 16 years and at a cost of more than $40 million dollars has pronounced "cured" only 97 inmates . . . of the 2,297 prisoners sent to Patuxent from 1955 to 1971. . . . Inmates testified that "negative reinforcement therapy" for breaking rules consisted of sometimes being placed strapped to a board by their ankles, wrists, neck and chest and left to lie in their own excrement for days on end in a cell devoid of light or any other human sound but their own [Bauer, 1972, p. 5].

And yet, in 1970 this institution was praised by a widely respected law professor and criminologist:

The Patuxent Institution in Maryland . . . provides treatment for psychologically disturbed and dangerous offenders. These institutions (Patuxent and Vacaville in California) are oases in the desert, of importance to the future treatment of that category of offender [Morris & Hawkins, 1970, p. 195].

Although coercive therapies and inadequate services whether in penal or mental institutions deny basic rights (see, e.g., Allen, 1959; Kittrie, 1972; Morris, 1974), in situations like Patuxent (of which there are many) the formal articulation of rehabilitative and therapeutic goals has resulted

in a reluctance by the courts to "second guess" and intervene. There is a tendency to refrain from examining the actual operations of custodial and correctional institutions (Rothman, 1973; Trotter, 1975a). Thus, social injustice is further reinforced.

## MENTAL ILLNESS AND POLITICAL BEHAVIOR

Whether or not an act is viewed as heroic, demented, bewitched, criminal, or sick has often been determined in relation to some subtle political end. When confronted with political dissidents, states can bring force to bear on individual persons by mobilizing the mental health system and legitimizing the control of human behavior under the cloak of rehabilitative goals. There have been no attempts to show by traditional scientific methodologies that diagnosis of mental illness may be determined by political expediency. By the nature of the hypothesis, it seems experimentally unverifiable; some aspects of society are not amenable to controlled manipulation. But that such politically oriented diagnosis has occurred time and again is uncontestable.

### Illustrative Events

An apt example is the case of Ezra Pound described by Szasz (1963) in the chapter, "Politics and Psychiatry: The Case of Mr. Ezra Pound." A more subtle form of psychiatric blackmail may have occurred when former U.S. Defense Secretary McNamara confirmed that a psychiatric examination was given to a Navy officer who discussed the 1964 Gulf of Tonkin incidents with Senator Fulbright. Although Mr. McNamara said the examination "can in no sense be viewed as an act of intimidation or reprisal" against the officer, he also said that "disclosure of the report's details would undoubtedly be harmful to the officer [International Herald Tribune, Feb. 28, 1968, p. 3]."

Examples abound. During the 1964 Presidential campaign of Barry Goldwater, some psychiatrists and psychologists willingly allowed their opinions about (and psychiatric diagnoses of) Goldwater to be made public. In addition, psychologist Clark (1971, p. 105) has asserted that "it would seem logical that a requirement imposed on all power-controlling leaders . . . would be that they accept and use the earliest perfected form of psychotechnological, biochemical intervention which would assure their positive use of power and reduce or block the possibility of their using power destructively."

In the U.S.S.R., there are reports of the use of mental hospitalization for the control of political dissenters. According to a document signed by 99 Soviet mathematicians, Alexander Yesenin-Vulpin, a scientist active in the protests against the Sinyavsky-Daniel trials, was taken "forcibly, without preliminary examination and without the consent of relatives and confined in Psychiatric Hospital No. 5 . . . [*Times* of London, March 13, 1968, p. 1]." As Allen emphasized, equating political and cultural dissent with mental disorder threatens basic political values and cannot be discounted "simply as typical excesses of a foreign totalitarian society [1974, p. 22]."

The case of Zhores A. Medvedev is perhaps the best documented and most widely known U.S.S.R. incident to date of mental institutionalization for political reasons (Medvedev & Medvedev, 1972; Stone, 1972a, 1972b). The Chief Psychiatrist of the U.S.S.R. Ministry of Health and Secretary of the Academy of Medical Sciences was reported to have said at a Ministry meeting that "obsessive reformist delusions" are a symptom of mental illness requiring hospitalization (Medvedev & Medvedev, 1972, p. 131). There was never any question of Medvedev's having any symptoms of psychological disorder or of his being of harm to himself or to others. His apartment was entered illegally, he was taken forcibly and placed in a mental hospital. He was released after three weeks because of constant pressure at the highest govern-

mental levels by his brother and many prominent scientists. Some time after his release, Medvedev's wife was shown her husband's diagnosis:

"Incipient schizophrenia" accompanied by "paranoid delusions of reforming society." The basic symptoms of the "illness". . . . "split personality, expressed in the need to combine scientific work in his field with publicist activities; an overestimation of his own personality, a deterioration in recent years of the quality of his scientific work, an exaggerated attention to detail in his publicist writings, lack of a sense of reality, poor adaptation to the social environment" [Medvedev & Medvedev, 1972, p. 175].

Impressions gleaned from history also support the notion that psychiatrists and rulers have made comfortable bedfellows. To illustrate, Dr. Samuel Cartwright claimed to have discovered a running-away disease (which he called "drapetomania") among slaves in the U.S. antebellum South (Swados, 1941). Another of his discoveries named "Dysaethesia Aethiopica" is in part described thus:

From the careless movements of the individuals affected with this complaint, they are apt to do much mischief, which appears as if intentional, but is mostly owing to the stupidity of mind and insensibility of the nerves induced by the disease. Thus, they break, waste, and destroy everything they handle—abuse horses and cattle—tear, burn, or rend their own clothing, and, paying no attention to the rights of property, steal from others to replace what they have destroyed. . . . They raise disturbances . . . without cause or motive, and seem to be insensible to pain when subjected to punishment. . . . The term "rascality" given to this disease by overseers, is founded on an erroneous hypothesis, and leads to incorrect empirical treatment, which seldom or never cures it [Bauer & Bauer, 1942, pp. 394–395].[2]

---

[2] I am grateful to Michael Randall for bringing these "diseases" to my attention.

Somewhat earlier in U.S. history, Dr. Benjamin Rush also invented a diagnosis:

Sharply contrasted with the good health of the patriots was the mental and physical breakdown experienced by those Americans who remained loyal to England. In many instances, they tended to suffer from hypochondriasis, which was popularly called the "protection fever" and which Rush termed *Revolutiana*. It was called "protection fever" because it appeared to rise from the excessive concern of the Loyalists for the protection of their persons and possessions. This basic cause was accentuated by such other factors as loss of power and influence, the suspension of the Established Church, changes in manners and diet as a result of inflation, and lastly the legal and extra-legal oppression to which the Loyalists were subjected [Rosen, 1968, p. 177].

Probably the most famous diagnosis of mental disorder complicated by political maneuvering is the case of King George III (Macalpine & Hunter, 1969). The major point of Macalpine and Hunter's book is that the king was suffering not from a "mental illness" but from porphyria, an inherited biochemical defect in which porphyrin (purple-red pigment contained in every cell of the body) formation and excretion are greatly increased with "widespread intoxication of all parts of the nervous system, peripheral and central [p. 173]." These authors detailed how psychological or behavioral aspects of the king's illness in 1788 were undoubtedly exacerbated by political events, by his relations with his children, by the conflicts among his physicians, and by the medical treatment (blistering, purging, blood-letting, confinement, use of the "strait-waistcoat") used to cure him.

It is obvious that the king's eldest son, the future George IV, had much to gain by having his father declared incompetent to rule on grounds of mental illness—a matter that did become a Parliamentary issue. Did the Prince of Wales (the future George IV) influence medical opinion to gain the throne? It is insufficient to write simply that

George III "fell into a depressed and violent insanity" or that "in February 1789, he regained his sanity [Watson, 1960, p. 305]." To what extent were the inconsistent medical reports (one doctor said the king was feverish, one not; one overestimated his confusion, one underestimated it) influenced by the political attitudes of the physicians? Although Macalpine and Hunter (1969) did not answer these questions, their careful delineation of events based on contemporary documents illustrates the close relation between mental illness and political events.

## Empirical Inferences

These reports—however well substantiated—are unsatisfying. At least two important questions remain: How common are situations in which political factors influence medical diagnoses? Can we delineate the political conditions under which this influence is most likely to occur?

The frequency with which political figures are "railroaded" into mental hospitals is probably very small. Yet, because of the enormous significance of these events when they occur, they need to be carefully studied. But, if one includes under this rubric "the politics of interpersonal relations" (e.g., the struggle for power in a family), it is likely that a careful analysis of admissions to mental hospitals will indicate that it occurs regularly. A study undertaken by Sarbin (1968) should furnish much relevant data.

Some inferences relevant to the conditions under which political considerations influence mental institutionalization may be furnished by cross-cultural data I have collected (Levine, 1972). The Opinions about Mental Illness Scale (OMI) (Cohen & Struening, 1962) was administered to samples of students, physicians, nurses, and police in Great Britain, Czechoslovakia, and West Germany. Although there were differences among occupational groups, the differences among countries were much more substantial. These data suggested that attitudes toward mental illness are part of a person's general orientation to social issues, rather than a narrow function of his concept of mental illness. Further, in a community climate characterized by an authoritarian social-political structure, we can expect to find authoritarian and socially restrictive attitudes toward the mentally ill.

These conclusions were based on a comparison of five factor scores derived from the OMI. But methodological problems remain: Since the OMI factors were based on U.S. samples, it is possible that the factors were not stable across cultures. The translations themselves might have affected the equivalency of items. To study this problem, responses to selected OMI items were compared among countries and occupations (Table 2). The same large differences emerged in this analysis as were seen in the analysis of factor scores. Further, since the words used varied by item, the stability of the differences suggested that the translations were satisfactory.

These cross-cultural differences in attitudes toward the mentally ill suggest a relation to the social-political structure. Also, political-legal socialization processes seem to account for attitudinal differences by generation. For example, German students were similar to British students in their attitudes; German physicians were similar to Czechoslovakian physicians. The German students socialized in post-World War II democratic West Germany had less authoritarian attitudes than their parents, socialized during the 1920s and 1930s. That this effect is not simply due to age differences seems to be indicated by the much smaller discrepancy between students and physicians in Czechoslovakia and Great Britain.

A major problem with this analysis concerns the need for a definition of "sociopolitical structure." What accounts for the cross-cultural differences? Later I present a theoretical model for understanding such issues. For purposes of this discussion, social-political structure refers to the manner in which power is distributed and exercised in a community. My assumption is that power is more centrally controlled and less widely distributed in Czechoslovakia than it is in Great Britain or West Germany and, further, that attempts at criticism of the government or redistribution of power in Czechoslovakia are more likely to be dealt with by force rather than by persuasion (e.g., the events of August 1968 when Russian tanks entered Czechoslovakia compared with a call for new elections in Great Britain or West Germany).

An essential theoretical question remains: If attitudes toward mental illness vary as a function of political-social structure, then does the use of mental hospitalization by the elite or powerful to quell political dissent correspondingly vary as a function of political-social structure? While this hypothesis requires testing, I expect such a relation. Since citizens in countries with an authoritarian political structure are more willing to agree with authoritarian opinions, the elite in these countries should find the public more willing to accept autocratic measures of any kind—including the use of mental hospitalization for political reasons. A major weakness in this argument is the lack of a demonstrated relationship between attitudes and behavior (Wicker, 1969). The opinions expressed on the OMI scale may not be related to how people would behave if confronted by the actual situation. Ultimately, the question comes down to the willingness of a people to express (overtly or covertly) political dissent, to act contrary to government when they feel they must, and the relation between these expressions of opinion and actual behavior—which leads to a discussion of crime and political dissent.

## CRIME AND POLITICAL BEHAVIOR

Since the criminal law deals with basic issues in the exercise of political (i.e., state) power vis-à-vis the individual, political objectives can often be achieved through its use—or nonuse. Ultimately, the relation of political justice and criminal justice rests on certain fundamental questions. What is the nature of liberty? What is the individual's

**TABLE 2    OMI Item Means by Occupation by Country**

| OMI ITEMS | STUDENTS | | | PHYSICIANS | | | NURSES | | POLICE | |
|---|---|---|---|---|---|---|---|---|---|---|
| | Ger. | Czech. | Brit. | Ger. | Czech. | Brit. | Czech. | Brit. | Ger. | Brit. |
| Subjects, N = | 79 | 114 | 117 | 80 | 103 | 181 | 116 | 188 | 136 | 98 |
| 1. Nervous breakdowns usually result when people work too hard. | 4.1 | 2.5 | 3.5 | 4.5 | 2.5 | 4.5 | 2.5 | 3.8 | 3.5 | 3.3 |
| F | | *43* | | | *101* | | | *56* | | *1* |
| 4. Although patients discharged from mental hospitals may seem all right they should not be allowed to marry. | 5.1 | 3.7 | 5.1 | 3.4 | 3.4 | 4.7 | 2.8 | 4.4 | 3.9 | 4.4 |
| F | | *49* | | | *37* | | | *98* | | *8* |
| 9. When a person has a problem or a worry, it is best not to think about it, but keep busy with more pleasant things. | 5.1 | 4.3 | 4.3 | 4.5 | 3.2 | 4.3 | 2.8 | 3.8 | 4.5 | 3.9 |
| F | | *11* | | | *24* | | | *23* | | *9* |
| 16. People would not become mentally ill if they avoided bad thoughts. | 5.5 | 4.7 | 5.2 | 5.4 | 4.1 | 5.1 | 4.0 | 5.1 | 4.6 | 5.0 |
| F | | *18* | | | *34* | | | *71* | | *7* |
| 22. Anyone who tries hard to better himself deserves the respect of others. | 2.0 | 1.8 | 2.3 | 1.6 | 1.5 | 2.2 | 1.7 | 2.0 | 1.7 | 2.0 |
| F | | *8* | | | *30* | | | *6* | | *8* |
| 28. Our mental hospitals seem more like prisons than like places where mentally ill people can be cared for. | 2.2 | 2.8 | 3.1 | 3.4 | 2.1 | 3.7 | 2.2 | 4.9 | 2.5 | 3.5 |
| F | | *10* | | | *53* | | | *267* | | *23* |
| 29. Anyone who is in a hospital for a mental illness should not be allowed to vote. | 3.6 | 3.5 | 3.5 | 3.0 | 3.0 | 4.0 | 3.3 | 4.4 | 2.7 | 3.0 |
| F | | *.3* | | | *16* | | | *35* | | *6* |

*Notes: Items scored from 1 to 6; 1 = strongly agree; 6 = strongly disagree.*
*Data are unavailable for German nurses and Czechoslovakian police.*
*Numbers underlined are the F's that reflect the statistical significance of the differences among the means involved.*
*The standard deviations (of the distributions on which these means are based) average 1.3 with a range of .65 to 1.72.*

relation to the state? Is liberty, as Judge Learned Hand said, "so much latitude as the powerful choose to accord the weak [cited in Mayer, 1969, p. 99]"? Or is it the "limits to the power which the ruler should be suffered to exercise over the community [Mill, 1955, p. 2]"? This moral dilemma need not be resolved here. It is enough to document the close relation—the ambiguity in fact—between crime and political dissent. Mayer traced the distinction between liberty and limits from Socrates to Mill and from the Nuremberg Trials to Woodstock: "At the very least we ought to be bold enough to live with the anguish of public discussion [1969, p. 15]."

Friedman (1970) and Allen (1974) have advanced such discussion. Friedman's article, "Political Power and Legal Legitimacy: A Short History of Political Trials," provided useful evidence on the relation between crime and political dissent. Analyzing such events as the prosecutions under the Alien and Sedition Acts (1798–1799), the trial of Susan B. Anthony (1873), and the Chicago Conspiracy trial (1969–1970), Friedman found ample documentation confirming that power, politics, and law are intertwined in complex ways. He concluded: "The decision to prosecute political outgroups or their leaders involved complicated political factors that have practically nothing to do with the even-handed upholding of law and order [1970, p. 165]."

Likewise, Allen (1974) cited many instances of government using the criminal justice process to undermine political dissent and subvert political justice. He cautioned, however, against rejecting the concept of political offense "as meaningless because of the abusive uses to which it has often been put [p. 40]." In fact, he underscored that "confusion" and "demoralization" stem from attending insufficiently to the definition and classification of terms like political crime, political trial, political prisoner (p. 41). Therefore, in his own work Allen proposed that political offenses be classified into two categories: (1) those explicitly involving political behaviors and interests (e.g., treason, internal subversion), and (2) those not political by definition (e.g., murder, arson) but reflecting the political motivations of the state (e.g., police, prosecutor). The second group of crimes is both the most controversial and liable to abuse.

## Definitional Confusion

The Calley case illustrates the confusion that results when politics, crime, and mental illness may all be involved. At the time of the trial and immediately afterward, we seemed to be dealing simply with the ambiguity between crime and political events. However, a UPI report appearing in the May 29, 1972, *Lincoln Journal* included the issue of mental illness:

Lt. William Calley became temporarily insane·under the stress of combat and could not have committed premeditated murder at My Lai, according to the *secret* data of a psychiatrist and two psychologists who examined him.

The psychiatrist wrote in the suppressed volume of data that a "killer instinct" clearly is part of Calley's "underlying psychotic and pre-psychotic state which he had before military service, during Vietnam and to this day."

The psychiatrist, Dr. Albert A. Laverne of New York . . . said he submitted all the reports to military authorities in 1971 and again several weeks ago.

UPI obtained a copy of Laverne's report and those of two psychologists, all of which are bound in a 150-page volume titled "suppressed evidence in the Lt. William Calley case."

Laverne's diagnosis went on to say "it is imperative to emphasize that if Calley is ever released to society, he should be under close medical and psychiatric surveillance for an unlimited period of time, during which he should be under psychiatric care and treatment [p. 2, emphasis added]."

Was Calley guilty of a crime? Was he innocent by reason of insanity? If innocent, is he now sane or insane? Did Calley's attorneys have access to the psychiatrist's report? To what extent were political decisions involved? Laverne believed that Calley should be under psychiatric care and treatment even if he objected. And if he did, what then? Forced submission to drug injection, or to electroconvulsive therapy, or to a lobotomy?

In retrospect, the Calley case raised key questions at the interface of criminality, mental illness, and political behavior. The psychiatric reports addressed the issue of Calley's legal responsibility. But note that such an issue is distinct from whether politically motivated criminal behaviors are— or should be—immune from prosecution. Allen considered the latter problem: "When politically motivated acts of extreme violence occur, a wise society does not confine itself to imposing penalties . . . but seeks in addition to locate the causes for such acts. . . . But a wise society does not recognize setoffs to murder [1974, p. 50]."

## Discretionary Abuses

In situations with political consequences, abuse can take the form of trumped-up charges and/or discriminatory enforcement (see also Allen, 1974; Friedman, 1970). Furthermore, such special procedures as electronic surveillance, instigation of crime, and preventive detention often have been "pursued with an enthusiasm bordering on fanaticism and rarely subjected to the test of whether they actually advance the purposes that presumably motivated their adoption in the first instance [Allen, 1974, pp. 67–68]." The events surrounding Watergate and the ultimate demise of the Nixon presidency provide apt illustrations.

As I noted earlier, it is clear that those in charge of the police, the governmental attorney's offices, and the courts determine what behaviors are labeled criminal. In any local jurisdiction, for example, the county attorney dismisses or brings charges depending on a host of factors. Police decisions on

arrest are also made on a discretionary basis. While discretionary powers are an integral and necessary part of the criminal justice system, greater responsibility, evaluation, and restraint are needed in dealing with political crimes and dissent. To show, however, that these law-enforcement and judicial decisions are influenced by political factors is difficult. The secrecy that surrounds much political and police activity does not allay the public's suspicions and does not make the task easier.

There is ample evidence that the police, government officials, and politicians are distrusted by the public and that police respond to this distrust by increased secrecy about their activities. In a recent study by Rotter and Stein (1971), politicians ranked 19th out of 20 occupations in degree of trust accorded them; the 20th was the "used-car salesman." Attitudes toward the police may depend on local conditions. A royal commission report on the British police stated that 83 percent of a sample of British voters had great respect for the police; only 1 percent indicated little or no respect (1962, p. 103). Unfortunately, the U.S. situation does not mirror that of Great Britain: Distrust and secrecy abound. According to a UPI report (*Lincoln Star*, June 21, 1972, p. 3), "[p]olice departments operate in comparative secrecy in the United States. . . . No major city has a civilian review board to check reports of . . . misconduct. Last month Robert Daley, New York deputy commissioner for public affairs, resigned. He claimed he was hampered in his efforts to end 'police secrecy.'" Westley (1970) reported that the police generally feel hated by the public and respond by protecting each other: 11 of 15 would not report another officer for stealing; 10 of 13 would be unwilling to testify against other officers; and 38 of 54 would not want their own sons to become policemen (see also Skolnick, 1966).

Citizens' concerns about repression and law-enforcement officials' apprehension about social unrest, crime, and conspiracy are an unfortunate by-product of what Allen

(1974, p. 75) termed the "war theory of law enforcement." In situations of power imbalance and at times of political or social crises great care must be exerted to avoid adopting a war psychology. Problems of bias, prejudice, and discretionary abuse are particularly evident in dealing with minority and impoverished groups. When Japanese-Americans were interned during World War II and their civil rights suspended, they became in a very real sense "political prisoners," though they engaged in neither political crimes nor political dissent.

Also in the United States, blacks are more often arrested, convicted, and sentenced for crimes; they are incarcerated for substantially longer terms (see, e.g., Schrag, 1971; Wolfgang, Figlio, & Sellin, 1972). The Report of the Commission on Civil Disorders characterized the pervasiveness of the deteriorated relationship (1968, p. 299):

In Newark, in Detroit, in Watts, in Harlem —in practically every city that has experienced racial disruption since the summer of 1964—abrasive relationships between police and Negroes and other minority groups have been a major source of grievance, tension, and, ultimately, disorder. . . .
    The policeman in the ghetto is a symbol not only of law, but of the entire system of law enforcement and criminal justice.

The commission's data strongly supported the assertion that the black community in the U.S. can be seen as an oppressed colony under white economic exploitation. Therefore, attempts to understand black crime, mental disorder, and political dissent must include economic and political considerations not necessarily relevant to understanding white deviant behavior (Fanon, 1963).

## REFORMULATION

The thesis of this chapter is that there has been imprecise use of and overlap in the terms "crime," "mental illness," and "political dissent" and that this conceptional confusion results in social injustice. My attempt to formulate a less ambiguous, more just model of social deviance draws heavily on the work of others, most importantly Sarbin (1967a, 1967b). The model makes no attempt to account for intrapsychic or imaginal processes, except as such processes have social impact. In this model the concept of "danger" is considered to be of central importance. Crime, mental illness, and political dissent share in common the attribute that they all may threaten the harmony of the community or of the state. The model focuses on the conditions under which social deviance is perceived as dangerous. Understanding these conditions is important because, when individual or societal perceptions of dangerousness emerge, social control mechanisms for handling deviance are likely to be activated.

### Postulates

I. Human beings are organized into communities (more or less structured groups of people) of varying sizes and varying degrees of complexity.
    A. All significant behavior occurs in a social context.
    B. Communities overlap, that is, a person is likely to be a member of several communities.
II. In order to survive, each community develops effective strategies of social organization.
    A. In complex communities, these strategies involve extensive legal systems; smaller or more primitive groups often fill this function with oral traditions and in a less formal manner.
    B. The social context—or simply, other people—are responsive to one another's nontrivial behavior. There is a wide-ranging set of explicit and implicit norms that circumscribe acceptable behavior.
    C. Groups lacking these strategies are transient; they do not survive.
III. An important aspect of the survival strategy of communities is the development

of differing roles for people in the community; some roles and some people have more power than others.

    A.  This distribution of power may take place by force (autocratically) or by persuasion (democratically).

    B.  Communities without role differentiation or without differential allocation of power do not survive.

## Corollaries

I. A situation/group/person is labeled dangerous when perceived as threatening the well-being or existence of the community.

    A.  People or groups with substantial power in a community are rarely seen as dangerous.

    B.  When a single person (rather than a community) is threatened, the likelihood of the label "danger" being employed depends on the power distributions of the people involved.

II. External dangers are those dangers that stem from forces other than members of the community.

    A.  A particular community may label a person as dangerous, while that person may label himself or herself not as a member of *that* community, but of a different one.

    B.  When it is possible for only one of two communities to survive, the situation is dangerous.

III. Internal dangers are those dangers caused by members of the community. Internal dangers may occur when there is an attempt to redistribute the power in a community. In such cases, the person with less power is labeled dangerous, especially if it is believed that such attempts at redistributing power do not conform to the community's rules.

## Implications

    All models by their very nature are oversimplified. Hopefully, however, a systematic specification of postulates and corollaries yields implications that are empirically verifiable.

    First, if danger is conceived in terms of a relationship between two people or between a person and a community, it is misleading to think of dangerousness solely as a personality trait residing within an individual. Empirical support for this statement was provided by Bowers (1973). Recommendations for a renewed effort to develop prediction tables for criminality or delinquency (e.g., Morris & Hawkins, 1970) are valuable, but attempts to predict who is dangerous can only be partially successful if the social context of behavior is ignored. Prediction tables developed without considering the interactions between persons and situations are likely to label persons as dangerous only because these people have been forced into dangerous situations (e.g., ghettos, prisons, mental hospitals). Thus the inferences from such calculations would be unjust.

    A second assumption is that crime, mental illness, and political dissent do not per se provide a basis for social control. The important distinction is between dangerous and nondangerous situations: to distinguish crimes that threaten or harm other people from victimless crimes, and to distinguish those "mental illnesses" that do not endanger other people, such as depression, anxiety, or inefficiency, from those that do threaten others. Probably most difficult is to distinguish political dissent that is not a "clear and present danger" to the community from political behavior that does present such a danger.

    Finally this model emphasizes the tension in relations based on power. A powerless person is a potential threat to a powerful person. When it appears that the powerless person may be taking steps to redistribute power, the threat becomes real, and the person with more power is likely to take steps to avert this danger. The protective steps that the powerful person takes may only increase the unequal distribution of power and thereby increase the tension. Also the powerful person may misperceive events. Sarbin has indicated (1967a, 1967b) that misperceptions may lead to "premature power displays" by government or people and that these displays may serve to increase the feelings of powerlessness of people lacking in power already. Accompanying this feeling of increased powerlessness is a degradation of one's status and a drive to overthrow the existing power differentials since there is so much less to lose. Hence, the dangerous individual or group may be dangerous only in response to events created by those in power. This circle of psychological events cannot last indefinitely and thus may account for violent uprisings—successful and unsuccessful. In fact, the model suggests that without a redefinition of power relationships, periodic and violent redistributions of power are inevitable.

## POSTSCRIPT

When this chapter was initially conceived and drafted, I was trying to understand and cope with the reports of a rising crime rate, the increasing alienation of young people, the criticism of our political and legal system by oppressed minorities (including patients in mental institutions), and the signs of extensive corruption in much of our national government. My perspective on these events was that of an academic clinical psychologist in a typical midwestern U.S. city—active in local mental health and criminal justice programs, but an observer of national and international affairs. My one year abroad (1967–1968) and some cross-national research were only the beginning of a global frame of reference. Nonetheless, subsequent events (e.g., Eagleton, Watergate and its cover-ups, Attica, Wounded Knee, Northern Ireland) and recent scholarship (e.g., Monahan, 1975; Morris, 1974; Shah, 1975; Steadman & Keveles, 1972) have generally supported the ideas I present and lead me to believe that the conceptual framework is a useful one.

It also has become clear, however, that substituting the concept of dangerousness for the concepts of crime, mental illness, and political dissent is only a very small step forward, and a step accompanied by enormous risks. Although considerations of dangerousness are important at almost every stage of the criminal justice system and mental health process, definitions of dangerousness have been circular, misguided, or irrelevant (Levine, 1975). However, the recommendations by Morris, Monahan, and others that the term not be used in legal decision making because it leads to unnecessary or unfair incarceration of people will be unacceptable to a public that wants to be protected from what it sees as increased violence. So it is that the delicate balancing of the public's desire for protection from danger and a just consideration for individual rights requires the wisdom and effort of social scientists, legal scholars, and politicians—as well as an alert citizenry.

# CHAPTER 19

# Why Criminal Law?
## Parameters for Evaluating Objectives and Response Alternatives

—*SAMUEL I. SHUMAN*

Criminal law is analyzed in terms of whether the problems and objectives it addresses are sufficiently precise to enable articulation and evaluation of solutions for handling deviance. This chapter presents a decision-making model that identifies and questions basic assumptions. The dichotomy between solutions to the crime problem that punish and those that rehabilitate is examined. Within this context, three contemporary solutions to deviance—institutionalization, conditioning, and biological reconstruction—are evaluated, and an alternative method within the framework of the law of torts is explored.

A recurrent theme in legal literature is the evaluation and comparison of various approaches for dealing with criminality (e.g., Ohlin, 1973; Quinny, 1969; Zimring & Hawkins, 1973). Basically criminal law is viewed as a valid response to deviance. The flaws in the response, and there are many, are presumed to lie in methods and response hierarchies. That some sort of criminal justice system must exist is neither addressed nor questioned. In this chapter I examine this basic assumption: Should a criminal justice system exist and does its performance justify the multiple costs entailed?

### EVALUATION PERSPECTIVE

At least five conditions determine whether a solution to a social problem is available and, if available, whether it is effective: (1) The problem must be defined with sufficient specificity that it is possible to identify a potential solution. (2) The objectives in effecting a solution must be sufficiently precise that they can be articulated understand-

ably. (3) The articulated objectives must be such that a decision procedure can be constructed for assessing the instrumental efficacy of alternative solutions. (4) To be implemented effectively, the decision procedure must be deemed adequate on scientific or other grounds in the community at the given time. (5) The strength of the social, moral, and political values underlying the objectives and solutions must be sufficiently understood that accurate judgments can be made about the probable community acceptance of alternatives.

Currently, these minimal conditions are not satisfied for the criminal deviance "problem." Instead, solutions are sought based on the simple notion that the criminal justice system is the primary social mechanism for handling those instances of deviant behavior defined as criminal. Although this statement of purpose is commonly accepted as sufficient, it is not useful for evaluating the system. It is ambiguous with reference to both defining criminal deviance and developing objectives for "dealing with" such behavior.

**239**

## PROBLEMS IN THE DEFINITION OF DEVIANCE

To label conduct as criminally deviant requires that there be norms, principles, and policies against which the conduct in question can be compared. Such norms, principles, and policies are almost exclusively "manufactured" (Hart, 1961) in modern industrialized societies. Manufactured norms are those that derive from the deliberate processes of the legal system (Diamond, 1973). Norms supplied by custom and religion are not manufactured—or at least not the way legal norms are. Customs grow, rather than being made; religions seem to emerge, rather than being invented. In contrast, the norms by which criminal deviance is identified are often the result of the most deliberate decisions made in the community (Shuman, 1963).

Since manufactured norms come from a more specific, temporally limited context than nonmanufactured norms, at least theoretically, it should be easier to articulate objectives clearly. The point is not that, if criminal deviance was defined only by sentiment and tradition, the social system would be incapable of functioning or would function in a way contrary to the community consensus. Rather, it is that, for complex, industrialized societies, appropriate mechanisms to respond to criminal deviance should be more difficult to identify, let alone evaluate, when the basis for the deviance labeling is not explicit in terms of source, time, and place.

### Restrictions on the Labeling Process

In some areas competing values limit the labeling process. For example, considerations of immunity and unenforceability discourage the creation of norms to regulate particular forms of behavior.

*Principles and policies, sometimes not manufactured, immunize certain realms of private and even public conduct from scrutiny, let alone standardization.* Charac-teristically in complex societies it is difficult to find convincing examples of overt conduct that, because of nonmanufactured principles or policies, are protected from regulation. In the United States it is generally believed that religious beliefs and political opinions are immune from regulation. Clearly, however, there are restrictions on both. The claim of protection on the grounds of religious belief or political opinion does not per se grant immunity for allegedly deviant conduct. The courts define what constitutes privileged religious or political opinion and within that domain immunize activity.

In illustrating immunized conduct, there are both difficult and relatively easy cases. Some First Amendment speech is protected by principles as well as a sequence of derivative norms (e.g., decisions by the Supreme Court). More difficult than speech that falls within the protection of the First Amendment is conduct, other than speech, that allegedly expresses a political sentiment (Shuman, 1971). Even more difficult is overt conduct that does not purport to express political or religious opinion but ought to be immune from standardization because it is not seriously harmful or offensive to others.

The following examples are arranged in descending certainty as to whether such immunity is likely to be granted:

1. The actor says in a public place, "Nixon was morally bankrupt and crooked as a dog's hind leg, and should not have been granted a pardon." Such conduct is almost certainly protected.

2. At a rally in support of former President Nixon, the actor appears with a large sign containing no letters or words, but only a hand in which the fist is clenched, with the middle finger pointing upward. This conduct expresses a political sentiment and almost certainly is protected, although it hardly qualifies for the speech protection of the First Amendment.

3. The actor "trespasses" at the draft board to protest the President's policies in a

foreign war. Although this behavior expresses a political opinion or sentiment, it probably is not protected.

4. Not intending to express political or religious opinion, but merely to express a life-style favoring "a return to nature," the actor regularly urinates in public places. While not seriously offensive to others, such conduct will probably not be protected, although police would do well to ignore the actor.

*Some overt conduct is immune from standardization because of the unenforceability of any manufactured norm.* Two considerations affect the efficacy of enforcement: (1) Some objectionable conduct is simply not suppressible, and (2) some conduct is suppressible only at a disproportionate price. Sexual conduct that is at least "statistically deviant,"; private drunkenness, and the private use of prurient materials are areas where considerations of enforcement efficacy have influenced decisions as to whether norms ought to be manufactured or retained. An even more dramatic illustration is the lack of norms for regulating conduct between parents and children. Apart from very recent norms concerned with child placement (see Goldstein, Freud, & Solnit, 1973), there are almost none that even purport to regulate the kind of conduct permissible by persons responsible for the care of minors.

The issue of enforceability is pivotal in the debate over "legislating morality" (Devlin, 1961, 1965; Dworkin, 1971; Hart, 1963). In regulating homosexuality, for example, one side argues that norms are very difficult to enforce. The rebuttal urges that the norms are sufficiently enforceable to warrant imposing a standard. The argument centers on whether the prevention of the objectionable deviance is important enough to warrant tolerating lower efficacy. Even assuming a general consensus as to the "evil" to be cured and the desirability of prevention or suppression, one might weigh whether the mechanism for suppression has

consequences more catastrophic than the unregulated behavior. A 24-hour TV monitoring system in all buildings might suppress consensual homosexuality between adults. However, the adverse effects on even traditional social relationships and the loss of privacy might make the price of suppression too high.

## Additional Limitations

Immunity and unenforceability are generally acknowledged as limiting the range of manufactured deviance norms. But there are additional issues.

*Should there be institutional management and response to deviance when a manufactured norm cannot be specified for labeling that behavior?* Such control without specific labeling does occur. In general, norms often purport to create standards, but the standards are not extricable from the norms. For example, sexual deviance is regarded as criminal and subject to institutional response even though there is no mechanism adequate for determining what constitutes such deviance (Schur, 1965, p. 78). An extreme case would be if the norms provided merely that no one shall be sexually deviant, and, if anyone is, he or she may be subject to criminal consequences. Should the manufactured norm be retained if there is no more specificity as to what constitutes deviance? The example given is extreme, but it is not atypical of much that obtains in criminal law (e.g., vagrancy and conspiracy laws).

*Should criminal law be constructued and maintained when the deviance affected reflects only relatively unimportant expectations about normal conduct?* Our deepest feelings about what it means to be human often cannot be reduced to the kind of language within which the criminal law establishment must function. Is that establishment still worth having if it must deal with less basic feelings? Might it not be better to dismantle the system, totally or in part, because what is capable of being handled is not worth the social and moral cost of keeping it? A system that spends most of its resources pulling drunks off the street or providing prostitutes with a day away from their clients may not be worth the costs (see, e.g., Kadish, 1967; Packer, 1968; Schur, 1965).

Even when we translate feelings into manageable language and develop enforceable norms, what we accomplish may still exceed the cost—even for most homicides. The most objectionable instances of homicide are killings for hire, not the "Saturday-night" killing after too much liquor. Yet killing for hire is the least amenable to detection. The Saturday-night killing, probably the least important, is the most difficult to prevent. If friends, acquaintances, and family members are "willing" to live where violent death is a possibility, is it worth maintaining a system to punish acts that could not have been prevented? Would the millions spent for punishing a few Saturday-night killers not be better spent in passing gun control legislation and in creating environments that would discourage resort to violence? If the best the criminal law system can do is deal with those cases where—because it is easy—we respond, then we must seriously examine our objectives and motivations.

## ARTICULATION OF OBJECTIVES

Given the present state of knowledge (Goldstein, 1974), I contend that we cannot state with sufficient specificity the basic "objectives" or "goals" for prevention or suppression of criminal deviance. Therefore, effective solutions can be neither identified nor evaluated. Nonetheless, societies do continue to function. Thus, we may have no choice but to pretend that we do know what we want to do and what might be worth doing. But in this pretense, if we choose to do anything, we must attempt only small tasks and be certain that we do no more than necessary.

The admonition against doing harm need not imply that action is never appropriate. Rather, it implies that trying to solve small problems may be more beneficial than tackling big ones. For example, assume a police department with a fixed budget. The department must either allocate funds for more motorcycles to increase mobility and reduce response time to call, or use the same funds to install a computer to improve the speedy deployment of police. For either solution, manageable objectives allow evaluation of alternatives within the hierarchy of values acceptable in the community. Deciding between computers and more motorcycles will not dispel the ignorance about the big "goals" in dealing with crime. But the consequences of that ignorance will be magnified if, in seeking the solution to the allocation of resources, we pretend to derive wisdom from ignorance. Neither computers nor motorcycles will make people better or more humane, but one or the other may reduce response time.

Often the wisest reaction to perceived deviance is to ignore any problem for which you do not have a good solution. An analogy to rearing children is appropriate. If parents react to their child's every objectionable act, family life would be ugly indeed, and children would view parents as jailers rather than as persons to respect and love. Also if social norms are created and enforced for all deviance susceptible to control, it would not be long before the system and its managers are viewed as enemies rather than as participants in a shared experience. A plea for diffidence, then, can be based both on our ignorance and on the belief that even where knowledge is available, refraining from creating and enforcing norms is often the wisest course.

This is not meant to imply that muggers, shoplifters, thieves, and so forth are to be ignored because we do not know how to deal with them effectively. Rather, we must accept that case-by-case judicial development of norms from general legislative policies and principles is inaccurate, short-sighted, and accidental. We should not delude ourselves into thinking that the way we deal with the crime problem now is optimal for solving problems or even that it constitutes a solution. Lack of specificity about goals may constitute a deprivation of substantive due process that no amount of procedural due process can cure even though the judicial model may be better than other alternatives (Allen, 1959; Packer, 1968).

One alternative is the substitution of a medical model for a judicial model (Kittrie, 1972; Szasz, 1961); that is, the proposition that deviance be treated as a health problem, biological or genetic, rather than as a problem to be dealt with by the legal machinery. In some ways the health model of deviance identification may be more dangerous and even more objectionable than the judicial model. In the health model, we hide our ignorance of deviance by regarding deviance as physical. At least with the judicial model, our deviance-labeling is overt (Shuman, 1974).

## INSTRUMENTAL EFFICACY
## OF ALTERNATIVE SOLUTIONS

Ignorance about what the crime problem is and what our goals are ought to discourage evaluating alternative solutions. Nonetheless, we continue to construct and maintain enormous institutions for "dealing" with persons "found" to be sufficiently deviant to deserve attention. Perhaps then we should consider other mechanisms for securing these objectives.

Apart from ignorance as to aims, a further difficulty in evaluating the efficacy of alternative solutions is the vagueness of the concepts of punishment and suffering (Benn, 1967; Morris, 1968). Often, a distinction is drawn between alternatives that punish and those that resocialize. But it is difficult to distinguish punishment components from alleged socialization or resocialization (rehabilitation) components. Almost any kind of punishment except, of course, capital punishment is expected to have some resocializing effect. Likewise, imposed re-

socialization involves elements of punishment. At times distinctions are premised on the motives or perceptions either of those initiating the action or the actual victims. Speaking about the Pennsylvania Dutch environment in which he was raised by his grandparents, Wolfgang writes:

I was never the object of physical punishment. . . . The technique of discipline was that of shunning and shaming in such a way that if I did anything that was viewed as a misbehavior . . . no member of the family would speak to me . . . I was excommunicated from the dialogue of the family and felt the enormous sense of guilt that was imposed upon me by the sheer silence. I found this very effective. I immediately wanted back into the circle of relationships [Snodgrass, 1972, p. 38].

Probably the most effective socializing mechanism, at least for the young, is the selective, deliberate use of rewards—particularly love, affection, and inclusion within the family or peer group. But even with socialization, the use of rewards and the withholding of "natural" rights to affection and group inclusion may constitute punishment. Although motives and perceptions are relevant, a requisite characteristic of punishment is the taking of *deliberate* action that results in the imposition or threat of *unwanted* suffering. Even where it is "natural" for the subject to suffer, it is still punishment if the suffering is unwanted. Thus, rehabilitative solutions when imposed and involuntary still include a punishing component.

The choice, then, is not between options that involve only socialization or only punishment. The issue is what kinds of games we ought to play with the *victims* identified as deviant. If every society must have its witches, do we achieve something better if, instead of indiscriminately burning witches, we do so discriminately, and if so, pursuant to which criteria? Further, what alternatives to witch-burning are worth considering—institutionalization, conditioning, or biological reconstruction (drugs, surgery, electrical stimulation, and so forth)?

## Control of Deviance by Institutionalization

Since at least the mid-nineteeth century, society has attempted to eliminate crime by locking up those labeled deviant both to protect society and to rehabilitate (Rothman, 1973). In part, apparent failure of this response modality reflects the fact that a *standardized* response to a *characteristic* situation is unlikely to produce anything worthwhile (Morris, 1974). Consider this example:

Prison cell number 1 is occupied by D1, who had no arrest record until convicted of killing his mother-in-law after a long-smoldering family quarrel. In cell 2 is warehoused D2, often linked to organized crime and arrested five times but never before convicted; he was convicted of bribing a public official. Cell 3 is home for D3 whose ghetto existence began at birth and whose drug history began at age 7. Now do D1, D2, and D3 all "suffer" equally or in the same way because they are locked up? Is their "suffering" equally unwanted? Is there some sense of punishment or resocialization that fits all three cases? Is incarceration, whether it is also equally punishment for all, used for each because it will obtain the same or different objectives? Is there some reason for having "chosen" incarceration rather than, or in addition to, conditioning or reconstruction (Feinberg, 1970)?

Uniform responses to conduct done with intentions as diverse as those of D1, D2, and D3 can only by chance have any benefit. The system's inability to accommodate the range of character and personality found among deviants (Kittrie, 1972; Rubington & Weinberg, 1973) is alone a good reason for restraint in initiating institutionalization. Is there any reason to believe D1's wife or children will benefit from his incarceration? Is there any reason to believe that D2 will be deterred from further crime? Is there any reason to believe that D3 will have his personality remade so that the influences of

ghetto life and drug involvement will be altered? The evidence is all to the contrary (Morris, 1974; Schulhofer, 1974).

Except for extremely brief emergency confinement, incarceration as now practiced is almost guaranteed to be dysfunctional (1) if there is any likelihood that D will be returned to society, and (2) if an identified objective is that D will return to society no more dangerous than he or she was before (Allen, 1959, 1964). Whether institutionalization is necessarily antithetical to resocialization is open. Although some styles of incarceration seem preferable to others in terms of making offenders no more dangerous upon release than before commitment (Morris, 1974; Ohlin, 1973), I know of no convincing evidence that this is an attractive way to rehabilitate. What is extraordinary is that while much has been invested in institutionalization, little attempt has been made to discover whether institutions achieve anything like what they are supposed to achieve (Schrag, 1971, p. 266).

Are there more efficacious solutions to the crime problem than incarceration, if one reasonable objective is that the defendant function in society at least no more dangerously than before commission of the offense? Even with this specifically articulated objective, there are enormous difficulties in evaluating incarceration as against conditioning or reconstruction. We know almost nothing about the relevant empirical questions. The dearth of research is due not to lack of interest, nor to ignorance about alternatives (e.g., fines, restitution programs, or occupational incentives). Rather, it may be that we really do not want to *know* that institutionalization does not work, both because people should suffer if they are bad, and because we would not know what to do if it is found that institutionalization is, in fact, counterproductive.

## Control of Deviance by Tinkering

"Tinkering" is altering an individual's personality and behavior by such methods as surgical reconstruction, drug therapy, electrical stimulation of the brain, and possibly some forms of operant conditioning. Probably any deliberate effort to resocialize may qualify as a kind of tinkering.

The belief that we ought not tinker has very ancient roots. While seldom made explicit, very powerful social, moral, and political prejudices reinforce the view that no effort should be made to deliberately "improve" what has been made by nature (or God). The "natural man" theory is sometimes formulated in terms such as "the sanctity of the mind," "the inviolability of the brain," or "the sacredness of the soul" (Skinner, 1971).

The "don't tinker" argument, however, suffers a deep inconsistency. Unlike other species, the human fetus is not left to survive through chance and natural selection. Instead, humans deliberately manipulate their environment, and nowhere is this more obvious than in the care exercised in the rearing (i.e., socialization) of babies. The human species does not just tinker, it tinkers massively. Humans are in large part the function of their own tinkering; if they stopped tinkering with themselves, they might well vanish as a species. Thus, the inconsistency in the "don't tinker" argument stems from the fact that what *is* natural about "man" is that to a large extent he is "man-made" (Skinner, 1971).

The relevant question is not whether we should "tinker," but how we should tinker when there are choices to be made. "Should we punish at all and, if so, how?" "Should we try to resocialize and, if so, how?" "Is conditioning or reconstruction an appropriate remedy and, if so, when?" Although deliberate tinkering might seem appropriate, we know so little about what we want to do that perhaps implementing the "don't tinker" myth ought to be indulged. At least it prevents less attractive alternatives.

*Conditioning.* Perhaps the most well-known proponent of conditioning techniques is B. F. Skinner (1948, 1953, 1971). According to Skinner, society justifies its use of punishment because it regards humans as free and autonomous and, consequently, responsible for what they do. Relying on an extreme behaviorism and a deeply entrenched environmentalism, Skinner defends tinkering as morally as well as efficaciously preferable to punishment. For him, tinkering means using scientific behavior technology and the mechanics of operant conditioning to attain an acceptable environment. Rejecting an autonomous-human-being hypothesis and attendant notions of responsibility, Skinner argues that individuals should be immune from punishment because their freedom to have chosen deviance is not politically or philosophically possible. Freedom carries with it a commitment to blame. At the heart of Skinner's view is the thesis that people should be absolved of the responsibility of being free and that by using operant conditioning their objectionable conduct will be prevented (see also Fuller, 1969b, pp. 163–165).

Skinner does not make a convincing case for conditioning, let alone reconstruction, as a preferable mechanism. On the contrary, none of Skinner's books offers any support for the argument that operant conditioning is better than institutionalization. This point must not be misunderstood: Operant conditioning may be effective for procuring defined objectives, but this "success" is no evidence whatsoever for the social or political philosophy that Skinner and other deterministic behaviorists construct. The fact that conditioning may work does not carry any implications as to the attractiveness or importance of values served or defeated by that "success."

The justification for conditioning is no better than that for incarceration. Both presume knowledge about objectives and means that we do not have. Both involve imposing an unwanted consequence as a result of having labeled someone deviant. If conditioning—although intended to alter or rehabilitate—requires the imposition of unwanted consequences, can it be something other than punishment? An important human right is the right to be unhealthy, even abnormal, even deviant. In light of that value, imposed conditioning is no more justified than imposed institutionalization.

*Reconstruction.* Whatever arguments apply against tinkering in general apply at least equally to tinkering by reconstruction. Modern reconstructive technologies offer unheard of and, until now, undreamed of possibilities for the human being to determine the biofeedback loop. Unlike institutionalization or conditioning, these technologies are potentially more exact, more permanent, and less expensive. Anyone who accepts the political or social system implications of extreme behaviorism should eagerly embrace these new possibilities. They should ask only, for example, whether a surgical intervention in the amygdala suppresses uncontrollable aggression or whether the new drug "Xeson" achieves chemical castration without adverse side-effects. If, however, one has the kind of concerns about behaviorist theory raised earlier, then these questions may be irrelevant, and the search for answers only a strategy clouding real issues.

This should not be construed to mean that reconstruction mechanisms are more objectionable than institutionalization or conditioning. It is often argued that the brain or "sex organs" are sacred or that surgery or chemotherapy may be irreversible, but I am unconvinced that these technologies are any more suspect than rehabilitating (or punishing) through incarceration and operant conditioning. Perhaps the one greater danger about reconstructive technologies is the easy substitution of the medical health-disease model for the deviance-control model. The ambiguity and vagueness of the concepts of health and disease, coupled with the territorial acquisitiveness of medicine, make it easy to compromise freedom, dignity, and even minimal autonomy in the name of anatomical or biological normalcy (Rothman, 1973; Shuman, 1975; Szasz, 1963).

**Overall Limitations**

We know very little about what deviance is and what we want to do about it, or how.

Unencumbered by knowledge, we travel fast and shoot off in any direction that at first blush offers hope for dealing with objectionable conduct. If criminologists, penologists, and others who purport to deal with deviance were instructed to "at least do no harm," we would have to ask whether deviance ought not be ignored unless the response can be shown to be less harmful—assuming we can define "harm." Since we cannot show that conditioning or restructuring is less harmful than institutionalization, and since we generally can show that incarceration as currently practiced is dysfunctional, it seems reasonable to ask whether we ought not decriminalize as much of the criminal law as possible.

Indeed, I suppose what I have been considering is whether the criminal justice system does not cost more than it is worth. If one of the basic purposes for having a legal system is to expand opportunities for human freedom and growth, then surely the criminal law is contrary to that higher goal unless it can be shown that, by labeling people as criminally deviant, freedom is enhanced for that individual or society as a whole. Neither demonstration has yet been made, nor has it yet been shown that institutionalizing, conditioning, or reconstructing people because they are criminally deviant is itself not more dangerous to society than permitting these allegedly dangerous people to be free of these involuntary mechanisms.

**TORTS: AN ALTERNATIVE TO CRIMINAL LAW**

Perhaps it is time to ask whether criminal law is worth having at all. Although this proposition may seem so untenable as to be dismissed outright, it is well to observe that the current trend toward decriminalization (Morris & Hawkins, 1970; Packer, 1968) would likewise have been unthinkable twenty years ago. It may be time to speculate carefully as to what life would be like if the only remedies available for deviance were those offered by the law of torts (see also Shuman, 1970, pp. 58–63).

Such a system of reparation without regard to the intentions of the actor and without a distinction between tort and crime is hardly a new idea. Indeed, Anglo-American and most continental legal systems grew and developed under just such a scheme up until about the fifteenth century. Under a system where expanded tort remedies replace most if not all of the criminal law, the need for punishment is not abandoned. I do not argue that society can survive without sanctions, but where the type of sanction is not efficacious or when the goal is less than indispensable, being humane demands more than indulging the instinct of an eye for an eye and so on.

The idea that tort remedies are more humane than criminal law remedies may be enhanced if we look at the source of society's right to judge or grade conduct. Almost every philosopher to have considered this question, at least since the eighteenth century (from Locke to Rawls), has ultimately urged some form of social contract theory, where members of society may reasonably expect an individual to obey the law because most agree to do so. Essentially grading compliance and punishing those that fall below grade (not complying) is based on the principle that reasonable expectations ought to be protected.

What is bothersome and indeed strange is that, despite the almost universal acceptance of the reasonable expectations theory, it makes so little sense within the context of contemporary life in the United States (if not elsewhere). We live in an urbanized, industrial society where learning experiences successfully insulate young people from authentic encounters with the dominant societal ethic. At best, a marginal commitment is encouraged. Yet we somehow expect the modern equivalents of the ancient taboos to be successfully transmitted. In pluralistic societies where the belief in open-ended value scales is regarded as a token of freedom and progress, why expect new generations to regard certain old expectations as reasonable?

We want young people to accept "our"

social system and its laws, yet we also want them not to overaccept; after all, look at what happened in Germany when *that* mistake was made. Is it any wonder that young people and ghetto people (black or white) tend to identify with subgroups where they can discover what they are supposed to be? If the obligation to satisfy the reasonable expectations of others begins with group membership, then by effectively denying membership we destroy the basis for the moral right to grade compliance. Occupying the same territory as "others" and even accepting the social values and laws of "others" do not imply intentionally choosing membership in a group.

The point here is that for many classes of deviants, society ought to be concerned (for its own sake and not out of charity) with enabling them to participate and function effectively in everyday life. For the civil protester, the homosexual, and other social "deviants," there is a basis for a claim to legitimacy even within traditional value schemes. In fact, it should be a reasonable expectation of the larger group that the kind of society worth having may require toleration of expanded classes of people unwilling to regard many of our expectations as reasonable.

If, then, some social deviants are necessary for a decent society and others are in no way deterrable, ought we not look for the most humane, least expensive way of discouraging such deviations that are too "criminal?" If so, are not tort remedies "bad" enough? Do we need to burn our witches— is it not enough to make them pay? Of course, the great danger here is that some witches will be judgment-proof and so, with immunity, they can commit crimes. But ought not the real task of a democratic society be to insure that no one is so poor that he or she can afford to be a criminal?

While a society without any crime may not be desirable, even if conceivable, it need not follow that a society must retain its criminal law. A crimeless society would be one where the process of social homogenization had effectively suffocated all the value pluralism that freedom connotes and makes possible, whereas a society without criminal law would be one where the social fabric was sufficiently resilient to tolerate the stress of deviants without requiring ego fortification by ritualistic sacrifices. A society without criminal law would be one where the price for real, universal freedom is never too high. In such a society, witches would not be burned, and even objectionable people would not be compelled to accept the "benefits" of incarceration, conditioning, or corrective social surgery.

# PART V

# *Decision Making in Legal Contexts*
## INTERSTITIAL BRIEF

*JUNE LOUIN TAPP*
*FELICE J. LEVINE*

A recurrent theme throughout this book is that law is a dynamic enterprise that evolves during the course of human activity. The making of decisions in legal contexts is not simply a function of the application or implementation of "black letter" law. Claims are pressed, choices made, and disputes settled because of interactions between personal variables (e.g., legal reasoning, prior experience, personality) and legal norms—both formal and informal, written and discretionary. The purpose of Part V is to illuminate the complexity of these decisional processes across judicial settings and in civil and criminal arenas. The primary emphasis of the preceding section was on the effects of situational/institutional variables on socialization and resocialization of the individual. In this final part, individual and institutional variables are again considered, but from the perspective of their reciprocal relationship in defining and shaping the nature of legal decision making.

In the tradition of an interactive conception of law (see Chaps. 3 and 15), Nimmer examines the impact of criminal justice reforms on the judicial process—from the filing of charges to ultimate disposition. Instead of evaluating impact in terms of whether a given reform achieves its policy objectives, the author considers in systemic terms the range of behavioral responses induced by a reform. Paralleling Zimring and Hawkins' chapter (Chap. 6) on the effect of legal threat on social change, Nimmer outlines how expectations, perceptions, and objectives between and among the participants in the judicial process (e.g., judge, prosecutor, defense attorney) affect accommodation to changes in the status quo—whether the reform is based on discretionary action, administrative rulemaking, statutory revisions, or case law. Beyond contributing insights about the introduction of reforms in the criminal justice system, Nimmer's chapter provides data-based support for the hypothesis that legal decision making is a function of a stable network of repeated interactions. In no way minimizing the role of formal law in the judicial process, this perspective shows that the definition and interpretation of formal law must be understood within the context of informal norms and routinized patterns of expectation.

A view of the judicial process as a balanced, continuous set of interactions clarifies the workings of the adversary system. As Nimmer points out, although formally the adversary model posits opposing interests competing to adjudicate issues and settle disputes, in reality conflicting parties and/or their counsels (defense and prosecution in criminal action, plaintiff and defendant in civil suit) share certain overlapping goals that often result in cooperation and accommodation. In many instances, these informal processes of exchange result in equitable outcomes for adversaries. For example, in studying the effect of revisions in sentencing statutes for heroin importation, Nimmer found that, even before the reform, sentencing practices arrived at through plea bargaining reflected the legal community's sense of justice. Of course, like formal regulations, informal practices are not always functional or adaptive to the involved parties.

In their chapter on "Legal Structures and Restoring Equity," Macaulay and Walster also consider the ongoing operations of the legal system. They focus on whether actual legal practices support dispute settlements at variance with the common-law goal of compensating victims for harm. Postulating that the legal system may socialize self-justification on the part of harmdoers in contrast to restitution, the authors analyze two exemplary cases—the automobile accident and welfare administration—to determine the role of law in the restoration of equitable relations. They report that actual practices (e.g., the time lapse between accident and court date, and the high cost of litigation) seem to foster a bargaining process that may not yield exact compensation. Applying theoretical formulations and empirically derived hypotheses from equity research, lawyer Macaulay and psychologist Walster conclude that the "norms" governing dispute resolution dilute incentives to make compensation and lead to the *fact* of institutionalized bargaining, rather than to the *goal* of equity. While bargaining and exchange can be desirable, these investigators maintain that present practices produce a "less-than-ideal bargaining system."

Evidently unintended norms, arising out of human interaction, may at times guide behavior in ways contrary to intended legal principles. Perhaps, as Zellman and Sears showed regarding free speech norms (Chap. 11), equity as a "rule of law" is socialized primarily as a slogan. Although, as Macaulay and Walster contend, a legal system cannot give limitless support to a principle without incurring operational conflicts (see also Friedman, Chap. 7), a system that supports a goal more strongly than it provides the means to achieve it can expect individuals to pay only lip service to that value. Therefore, to comprehend fully the dynamics of legal decision making, one must analyze both the actual operations of the legal system and the perceptions of the participants within it.

Haggard and Mentschikoff do just that in their consideration of decisional processes and the variables that affect the formal resolution of disputes in commercial arbitration. By focusing on the rendering of judgments in a quasi-judicial context, this lawyer-psychologist team explores the parameters of responsible decision making, that is, decisions by third parties with the authority to affect others. In their first offering, Haggard and Mentschikoff report the results of an *in situ* experiment conducted at the American Arbitration Association with 20 three-member panels of arbitrators who differed in occupations favoring the plaintiff or the defendant (pure or mixed groups). In analyzing their data, these researchers found that individuals made decisions and panels reached consensus through an essentially rational process. What an arbitrator identified as the central issue was the key factor determining awards. While affinity to one of the parties was important, it was far less critical than grasping the central issue and, in fact, was more likely to have an effect when the issues were not firmly determined in an arbitrator's mind. Thus, by empirical examination of the decision-making process, Haggard and Mentschikoff persuasively demonstrate that outcomes, which may have been construed as biased or based on "chance" factors, were in reality the result of a rational enterprise of comparing what ought to have occurred (in the dispute at hand) with what in fact happened.

Building upon their naturalistic experiments and field observations, lawyer Mentschikoff and psychologist Haggard in a second contribution elaborate an analytic model of the normative and personal factors operating in decision making and decision consensus. By detailing the interrelations among normative and personal factors, these investigators provide a set of working hypotheses on the nature of the decisional process. In brief, they posit five types of norms: The first two are substantive and fact-finding norms, which guide arbitrators' views of the conduct of the parties during the dispute; the last three are procedural, role, and status norms, which are used by the arbitrators to judge others and to determine their own behaviors. Further, the authors postulate that personal factors of affinity and communication affect the hearings and deliberations, but the impact of these variables in large part depends on the expertness of the arbitrators. According to Mentschikoff and Haggard, the arbitrators' expertise and prior experience are singularly important. While responsible decision making in adversary contexts is "predominantly a normative matter," expertness determines the availability and/or definition of norms and the extent of an arbitrator's influence. Given the apparent saliency of expertness, the reader is left to ponder the extent to which individual variables (e.g., skill, knowledge, legal orientation) shape legal norms and ultimately affect decision-making outcomes. This issue continues to pervade discussion of the jury, juror, and judge.

Focusing on jury decision making, the chapter by Kadish and Kadish addresses the relation between role conceptions and performance. In analyzing the role of courtroom decision-makers in achieving substantive and procedural justice, these legal scholars portray the law not as a separate system issuing pronouncements, but as a dynamic institution with built-in mechanisms for accommodating systematic and nonsystematic change. Their particular focus in this chapter is on the role of the criminal jury in rendering acquittal verdicts—a complex instance of nonsystematic change. To Kadish and Kadish, the jury system structures conflicted roles regarding powers, duties, and privileges to permit legitimate rule departures, that is, "legitimated interposition." As prescribed by the judge, the jury's function in criminal trials is to depart from unjust rules or from unjust application of these rules. Therefore, as Kadish and Kadish emphasize, it is false to interpret the juror role as simply "to hear and obey." Duty requires jurors to participate in the crucial process of assessing the underlying purpose and justice of rules; uncritical, blind obedience is antithetical to the juror function of creating as well as maintaining law.

In the context of the jury, one sees again the significance of assessing the relation between situational and individual variables. The extent to which jurors undertake legitimate departure to achieve just results and protection of rights should be related to their socialization into a role as law creator, rather than merely as law maintainer or lawbreaker. Perhaps the jury experience can also function to resocialize participants regarding conflict management and the distinction between absolute obligation and legitimate rule departure. If so, this role-taking opportunity, reminiscent of the procedures discussed in Parts III and IV, may have value beyond providing defendants with their rightful privilege to be judged by a community of peers.

Like claims of right pressed through the courts and administrative and statutory reforms discussed in previous chapters (e.g., Chaps. 7, 20), legitimate interposition is an important mechanism by which the legal system accommodates change. This rule departure in no way constitutes a rewriting of formal law. Underscoring the significance of looking at law as an interactive phenomenon, Kadish and Kadish point out that "[d]irectives of the legal system become rules, policies, and principles [only] through the manner of their use." In the courtroom context, accommodation to change occurs as a function not only of prescribed procedural norms but also of the judge's discretion. To illuminate the functional and dysfunctional aspects of discretionary mechanisms, conspiracy trials in the U.S. from Wounded Knee to Watergate bear conspicuous witness.

Kalven analyzes the 175 contempt citations issued in one of the first of these courtroom events to occur in recent history—the Chicago Conspiracy trial. Focusing on the viability of the courtroom, Kalven colorfully dissects how claims of right are pressed (see also Friedman, Chap. 7) and whether under any conditions participants in the trial forum can be relieved "of customary obligations to etiquette and relevance" (see Kadish & Kadish, Chap. 24). As with some subsequent political conspiracy cases, the defense attempted to use the trial as a forum for political protest; the alleged aim was to achieve social justice by using the courtroom in ways not officially intended. Kalven questions whether it is a legitimate expression of rights to enlarge the trial forum to a political one. As penetrating an issue is whether the courtroom under certain circumstances can demonstrate the flexibility to adapt to noncustomary activity. Can it accept a different style of deportment? Can it demonstrate as well some resiliency to accept political dissent? Kalven notes that discretionary departure, for example, by the judge to explain rulings could have offered the public a more positive socializing experience about law. Tolerance of departures from traditional courtroom behavior might have reduced unnecessary confrontation and provided the legal system—and the community generally —with a more just event. Instead, the values and role expectations of the participants in the trial seemed to clash and the ensuing conflict was unresolvable.

In political conspiracy trials, as in other adversary contexts examined in this volume, literal implementation of formal law can be as dysfunctional and liable to abuse as discretionary judgments. To reduce the occurrence of such problems, judicial decision making is guided by a norm stipulating that a verdict or judgment should be based on the merits of the presented evidence. As Mentschikoff and Haggard (Chap. 23) note, a corollary of this norm—in theory universally endorsed—is that those who decide must be impartial and must act responsibly. While procedural and decisional norms seek to insure that end, they too can be ignored, circumvented, or thwarted. As discussed by Davis, Bray, and Holt in analyzing studies of jury decision making, guilt-irrelevant or nonevidential factors (e.g., whether or not a defendant is rich or poor, black or white, attractive or not) can indeed affect verdicts. Yet, these authors simultaneously acknowledge that much of the support for this proposition derives from research data on verdicts rendered without (or prior to) any deliberation process.

In addition to building a model of the social decision process underlying a verdict, Davis, Bray, and Holt provide a critical and comprehensive examination of jury research in terms of theories that may be tested by or developed from empirical findings. They found many more efforts devoted to *juror* than *jury* behavior. Taking an explicitly psychological approach, the authors report bewildering, disorderly, and diverse findings, but little systematic theory. They therefore caution that few legal prescriptions should be drawn directly from such empirical studies. Illustratively, the Davis group discovered no generally "good" demographic predictor; deemed pretrial publicity data equivocal; and concluded that effects attributable to the order of presenting arguments were ambiguous. Such inconclusive findings warrant skepticism about "juror" research or theory. While "jury" research also suffered from methodological flaws, Davis et al. detected some orderly findings. For example, there is evidence that the judge's instructions about the law decidedly affect verdicts, supporting Kadish and Kadish's analysis of judges' impact on jurors' perceptions of the legitimacy of rule departure (Chap. 24) as well as Haggard and Mentschikoff's proposal that instructions about substantive and fact-finding norms might be introduced earlier in the proceedings (Chap. 22).

In reviewing the juror and jury research, Davis, Bray, and Holt unearth no theory specifically designed for jury deliberations and decision making. Aware of the serious methodological difficulties ranging from obtaining empirical data (e.g., courtroom access) to dealing with legal/ethical constraints (e.g., privacy and confidentiality rights), the authors recommend a social-decision-scheme model (SDS) of jury behavior to predict specific outcomes for normative or descriptive use. These statistical models have the capacity to deduce consequences not easily inferred from empirical data. The authors, however, acknowledge that the ultimate utility of such models depends on the number of parameters that can be estimated. A key need, of course, is to specify and measure variables relevant to the actual deliberation and decision-consensus process. Haggard and Mentschikoff have begun this work by identifying a network of factors that may significantly affect the intervening period between juror (arbitrator) decision and jury (panel) judgment.

Throughout the Davis, Bray, and Holt contribution, as well as the others in Part V, the necessity for examining actual practices and processes recurs. These chapters disclose that the complexities inherent in adversarial systems, whether in judicial or quasi-judicial settings, cannot be understood through a simple description of formal norms. People, whether legal professionals or private individuals, do not literally administer or enforce the "letter of the law." Law takes on its form or usage through an interactive process that is affected by values, judgments, demands, options, and expectations. In exploring legal decision making, the questions then include: To what extent and in what ways are participants aware that through their action or inaction they ultimately contribute to shaping legal norms? What in practice are the components of judiciousness and how, given the interrelationship of personal and social variables, can it best be achieved? Given the delicate balance between discretion and abuse in decision making, can legal socialization strategies facilitate the former while reducing the probability of the latter?

# CHAPTER 20

# The System Impact
# of Criminal Justice Reforms[1]

## —RAYMOND T. NIMMER

Most research about the impact of reforms on the criminal justice system assumes a limited, applied research perspective. This chapter adopts a broader approach: System impact is examined in terms of the effect of reforms on the behavior of individuals functioning within a major segment of the criminal justice system—the judicial process. This process is viewed as a complex set of overlapping interactions. Individual action is shaped by various informal norms, including norms that establish cooperative relationships among attorneys and judges and those that reinforce a system of bargaining and exchange as the dominant mode of case disposition. Implemented reforms are conceptualized as alterations within a stable environment that may or may not evoke behavioral change from individuals or groups involved in the judicial process. Two forms of reform stimuli —optional and mandatory—are discussed and the parameters of response analyzed.

Public criticism of the performance of the criminal justice system highlights a long-standing concern. Since the 1930s a diverse array of reform proposals has been advanced (e.g., President's Commission, 1967); however, there is little evidence to document significant improvement in system practice. Millions of dollars and hundreds of hours of analysis and discussion are spent yearly on criminal justice reform.

Yet, the system continues to operate, seemingly resistant or oblivious to change.

Amid cyclical flurries of reform activity and reform failure, there has been surprisingly little study of the impact of reform on the criminal justice system (i.e., system impact) as an independent phenomenon. Traditional assumptions about altering the behavior of individuals within the system still dominate: Discussion repeatedly centers on such topics as revision of statute or appellate case law, expansion of system resources, and training of police officers (Vorenberg & Vorenberg, 1973). To date, exploration of system impact has been done almost totally within the framework of evaluation research, with few efforts to relate specific experiences to general patterns (Glaser, 1974). In this chapter I examine the recurrent influences that shape the system impact of criminal justice reform.

[1] This chapter reflects an intermediate stage in my ongoing interest in the impact of criminal justice reforms on the behavior of functionaries within the legal system. Many observations and analyses presented here derive from impact studies that I conducted while at the American Bar Foundation. Throughout these studies, I was ably assisted by Patricia Ann Krauthaus and Terrence Gingle, who jointly served as Associate Project Directors. I extend my sincere appreciation to both.

## TERMINOLOGY

My basic postulate is that criminal justice reforms produce impacts in the system that can be both identified and predicted. "System impact" refers to any behavioral response induced by a reform stimulus. In evaluation studies of law reform, "impact" has been used differently than proposed here: Evaluation models identify the objectives of a reform and then measure the degree to which those objectives are reached (see, e.g., Feeley, 1973a; Mayo & Jones, 1964; Zimring, 1974).

Evaluation studies provide immediate feedback into policy-making processes relevant to a specific locale—feedback that can lead to immediate modification and improvement of the reform program. But this focus also creates its major limitation. The evaluation perspective concentrates on changes that define achievement or non-achievement of objectives. Impacts unrelated to policy goals are excluded or only tangentially discussed. In emphasizing immediate policy-relevant impact, the evaluation perspective fails to consider the links that are common to all situations in which change has been sought.

The view of impact taken here considers all responses to a reform as relevant and all instances of reform impact as conceptually related. It is not feasible, of course, to examine impact across all potentially affected groups and with respect to all behaviors. Yet, for understanding the stimulus-response pattern that characterizes system impact, all systemic behavioral changes produced by a reform are, initially at least, of equal importance (Feeley, 1973a; Wasby, 1970a, 1970b).

By "reform" I mean any planned change in the structures, rules of behavior, or resources under which the system functions. Within this definition, the reforms of the past 40 years cover a variety of substantive areas and formats that can be placed along a continuum based on the degree to which the reform involves the revision of rules of law. This continuum begins with highly informal adoptions of innovative practices in processing personal caseloads, moves through programs supported by federal grants and established by administrative rulemaking power (e.g., Nimmer, 1974a), and ends with statute and case-law revisions (e.g., Bases & McDonald, 1972; Oaks, 1970).

Many law-trained scholars, legislators, and reform entrepreneurs assume implicitly that reforms achieved by formal law revision (e.g., statutes and court decisions) are more effective than those premised on administrative rules or personal action. This assumption reflects a traditionalist view—that the formal law controls system behavior, subject to deviations that are labeled discretionary decisions (Black, 1972; Feeley, 1973b). For reasons that will become apparent, the traditional distinction between informal reforms and revisions of formal law is not warranted by current empirical evidence.

Conceptually, a reform can be construed as an alteration in the status quo—a stimulus that may or may not evoke a behavioral response within the system. The nature of the stimulus–response relationship will be affected both by characteristics of the reform (i.e., stimulus) and of the environment in which the reform is applied. Therefore, as a prelude to analyzing impact, it is first necessary to describe some aspects of the environment.

## JUDICIAL PROCESS

Since the criminal justice system involves a variety of actors and activities, system impact can best be analyzed initially by looking at a relatively homogenous subsystem. In this chapter, I consider the judicial process—the interval that begins when criminal charges are filed before a judicial officer and ends when those charges are disposed of in the trial court. This process is perhaps the most complex segment of the criminal justice system. It involves explicit interactions among at least the judge, prosecutors, and defense counsel and perhaps also witnesses, clerks, defendants, and to lesser extent correctional personnel.

The judicial process serves multiple functions. Among these are judging guilt or innocence, specifying bail conditions, and determining sentences to impose on guilty defendants. The policy objectives for each function are complex, ambiguous, and often conflicting. For example, the decision about guilt or innocence requires both a fact-finding inquiry into acts allegedly committed by the defendant and inquiries designed to monitor or regulate behavior of police and prosecutors (Oaks, 1970). Likewise, sentencing decisions simultaneously serve to punish and to rehabilitate, even though these objectives may be inherently inconsistent (Packer, 1968).

To accomplish these functions, the U.S. judicial process is formally set up as an adversary system that adjudicates issues under the binding guidance of statutory and other formal legal norms. In theory, defense and prosecuting attorneys, in representing competing positions, raise and illuminate relevant issues of law and fact that are then presented for decision to a judge or jury empowered to settle the dispute according to formal legal norms. In practice, however, this formal model only sporadically describes actual behavior. Instead, dominant patterns involve cooperation and accommodation—with informal norms being of equal or greater influence than the norms of the formal law (e.g., Blumberg, 1967b; Newman, 1956; Skolnick, 1967; Sudnow, 1965).

## Discretionary Decisions

The potency of these informal patterns derives from the broad discretionary latitude available to, and exercised by, participants. Discretion involves the ability to act on the basis of personal judgment, uncontrolled by prearticulated rules of law (Rosett, 1972; Rosett & Cressey, 1976). Discretionary decisions are repeatedly made by all participants and about most activities in the ju-

dicial process (see, e.g., Banfield & Anderson, 1967; Landes, 1974; Sudnow, 1965).

In part, the existence of discretionary power is a product of the policy concern that, while each case should be dealt with under standardized norms, each must also be handled in response to its unique characteristics. This calls for an interpretation of various aspects of each case by a decision-maker that requires personal judgments and therefore necessarily involves discretion (Remington & Rosenblum, 1960). In part, broad discretion also results from weak processes for enforcing the system's compliance with its norms (Feeley, 1973b). The only enforcement tools are the right to appeal or the right to file postconviction challenges, both generally available only to the defense and used only if deviation from a norm injures the defendant. Both are costly, time-consuming, reactive, and relatively infrequently used.

## Informal Group Norms

The action and reaction of each individual in a given context can be described in terms of three variables: (1) the perceived options available, (2) the tangible payoffs (incentives) attached to each option, and (3) the subjective value of the various incentives. The individual will choose the behavior option that appears likely to maximize positive and minimize negative payoffs. The judicial process is a complex set of overlapping interactions in which parties react both to prior actions of other parties and predictions of their response. Therefore, the tangible rewards and costs related to any behavioral option are seldom automatically or mechanically obtained. Payoffs require a filtering of the implicit or explicit demands, concessions, and expectations of other parties.

The network of interactions among individuals is shaped into standard, repetitive patterns due to various behavioral norms found in part in legislative, appellate court, or constitutional formulations. More important are the informal norms developed in repeated interactions among attorneys and judges (Blumberg, 1969; Sudnow, 1965; cf. Blau, 1955, 1956). These norms, often bearing little relation to formal legal norms, have potent effects on activities as diverse as setting bail and sentencing decisions.

In large criminal court systems a dominant norm sets up accommodative and cooperative relations between the principal participants, especially defense attorneys, prosecutors, and judges (Battle, 1971; Blumberg, 1967b; Platt, Schechter, & Tiffany, 1968; Skolnick, 1967). The cooperation affects all aspects of attorney behavior and includes, for example, mutual disclosure of case-relevant information, *pro forma* agreement to continuance requests, forebearance in contesting potentially relevant issues, and cooperative negotiation leading to nontrial disposition of cases.

The development of cooperative relationships is facilitated in the judicial process by the fact that the personal interests of defense and prosecuting attorneys as well as judges are often congruent or identical. All three, for example, are likely to want to minimize the amount of time spent on any single case (Blumberg, 1967a). Cooperative relationships develop through seeking similar objectives. Also, even when objectives are disparate, cooperation is often sought to obtain favorable discretionary decisions from the other decision-makers (Battle, 1971; Skolnick, 1967).

As with other informal norms, the norms favoring cooperation are unstated but are not unenforced. For example, a defense attorney's repeatedly aggressive adversary tactics may result in the withdrawal of cooperation and concession and, more generally, in a variety of actions by other participants that make more difficult the "deviant's" performance of his or her function (Blumberg, 1969, p. 284).

Another norm establishes the judicial process as a system of exchange, rather than adjudication (Cole, 1971; cf. also Blau, 1964; Homans, 1961). The items of ex-

change are the various aspects of case processing that are controllable by unilateral action. Chief among the exchanges are those that reduce questions about guilt or innocence from a matter for in-court adjudication to one of out-of-court plea negotiations involving questions both of guilt and of sentence. Typically the defense exchanges its right to contest guilt by demanding trial in return for prosecutor concessions with respect to the criminal charge and sentence characteristics sought in the resulting conviction (e.g., Newman, 1956, 1966).

These exchanges serve two important objectives. First, they result in efficient use of available time and resources. The reliance on barter and exchange reduces the need for time-consuming adjudications and substitutes a relatively efficient, informal setting (Blumberg, 1967b; Cole, 1971). Second, the exchanges reduce the risks. An adversary trial, for example, involves an ultimately unpredictable, "all-or-nothing" risk situation —either a verdict of innocence or of guilt with a sentence not moderated by prearranged concessions. Plea negotiation, however, allows participants to directly control and predict the result while eliminating the risk of the most undesirable outcome (Nagel & Neef, 1975).

Such exchange norms suggest a judicial process characterized by ongoing barter in each case filed. However, this effect is avoided by what might best be described as dispositional norms. Two such norms are of particular interest here:

**1.** Although formal doctrine assumes the defendant's innocence until guilt has been proven, the judicial process in large courts functions under an administrative presumption of guilt. This presumption grows out of the view of attorneys and judges that most persons arrested and charged with criminal violations have, in fact, committed some criminal offense (e.g., Blumberg, 1967a; Petersen, 1973, p. 90). The presumption, rebuttable rather than absolute, serves to deflect attention during plea negotiation from issues of guilt or innocence. Instead, the dominant issue in most cases is arriving at an appropriate sentence (Mather, 1974).

**2.** In many cases, guilty plea agreements are reached with little or no explicit negotiation; sentence and charge characteristics are determined by preexisting, informal norms called by Sudnow (1965) "normal crime" categories. Normal crimes, an outgrowth of the repetitive nature of criminal court caseloads, may be quite specific. They include elements that are not defined as relevant in the criminal code, but that have become relevant in practice as describing usual crime patterns and system response. For example, one normal crime might define a subcategory of auto theft as the taking of an auto from a parking lot, committed by a white high-school student, terminating in the recovery of the auto in unharmed condition, and normally disposed of by a guilty plea to "joyriding" and 1-year probation. Normal crimes both describe what dispositional responses have been appropriate in prior instances and serve to routinize the disposition of cases. Only contested is whether the offense sufficiently matches the normal category.

## SYSTEM IMPACT

In the abstract, the process by which system impact occurs can be readily described. A condition precedent to any systemic behavioral change is that the behavior of at least one participant in one case be modified as a result of a reform stimulus. This result can be achieved by sufficient manipulation of options, incentives, and/or subjective values. The manipulation must overcome the balance that would otherwise have prevailed (cf. Abelson & Rosenberg, 1958; Heider, 1958; Newcomb, 1953). The extent and direction of behavior change depends not only on the direction of the alteration in one party's behavior but also on the responses of other participants in a case and the extent to which the reform affects the individual's behavior with respect to actions beyond those dierctly altered by the reform.

Overall system impact is the sum of all such changes in individual cases. Varying attitudes, interpersonal relations, and case contexts add complexity to the aggregate analysis. While, for example, one defense attorney may react strongly to a benefit provided by an implemented reform, another defense attorney may be indifferent (e.g., Robertson & Teitelbaum, 1973).

Beyond these complexities, the judicial process itself has three elements that delimit and shape impact and tend to account for the absence of basic change in system behavior despite the recurrent implementation of reforms: First, many of the informal norms in judicial process are broad and diffuse. While some can be directly affected by a single reform stimulus (e.g., normal crime categories), no single reform is likely to affect much of the underlying support for most informal norms. An example are the norms of cooperation and exchange. Rather than being basically altered by a reform measure, these are more likely to serve as filters through which the reform is interpreted and its impact shaped.

Second, a reform seeks to produce behavior that deviates from existing patterns. In opting for that course of conduct, a person is affected by his or her willingness to deviate from current norms. Thus, stable patterns become their own justification (see Chap. 17).

Third, tangible payoffs are typically not automatic, but involve the responses of other participants. The motivations of other participants may be to dilute, restrict, or subvert reform impact, rather than enhance it. To the extent that there are such motivations, the capacity of a reform to offer "real" incentives and affect overall systemic behavior will be minimized.

This possibility is enhanced by the fact that preexisting practice reflects a balance of substantive interests and interpersonal power among the parties. Participants are likely to view this balance as desirable and to want to retain it. To achieve impact on one participant, a reform must offer results favorable to that participant, but this incentive implies an altering of the balance in a manner that may be aversive to some others.

The salience of these characteristics can be illuminated by a review of several studies. It is convenient to divide reforms into two categories: (1) reforms that are optional for individual cases based on an explicit decision by one or more participants, and (2) reforms that are mandatory.

## Optional Reforms

Although often viewed as mandatory, most criminal justice reforms are optional. Such reforms include the District of Columbia's preventive detention statute (Bases & McDonald, 1972), various pretrial diversion programs (Nimmer, 1974a), and Supreme Court rulings on the use of evidence obtained by police search-and-seizure practices (e.g., *Mapp* v. *Ohio*, 1961). To illustrate the impact of optional reforms, I examine search-and-seizure rules.

With respect to the Court rulings on the admissability of evidence, information obtained in violation of Constitutional norms cannot be used to convict. The rulings are enforced by adjudication into the facts of the underlying police activity. Adjudications occur, however, only if the defense raises the issue. Thus a defense decision initially determines system impact, affecting both the frequency of actual adjudications and the likelihood that judges or prosecutors will alter their behavior. When the defense does not explicitly raise the issue, the extent to which prosecutors and judges alter their behavior is a function of their interpretation of probable defense tactics.

The impact of such Court rulings on police behavior is unclear. But data do suggest that they have had substantial impact within crime categories in which evidence produced by search-and-seizure activity is commonly involved. Motions to exclude evidence obtained in violation of search-and-seizure rules occur in between 10 percent and 30 percent of all such cases filed

(Oaks, 1970; Spiotto, 1973)—indicating that this option significantly affects defense attorney behavior.

While the rulings speak solely to suppressing specific evidence, exclusion of evidence often leads to dismissal of charges (Oaks, 1970). In practice, such rulings can be sought with relatively little effort. Motions to exclude evidence can be easily prepared and are adjudicated during hearings that can be handled more expeditiously than typical trials. Equally important, an adverse ruling does not prevent the defense from continuing plea negotiations and achieving sentence concessions in exchange for waiving trial (Alschuler, 1968; Oaks, 1970).

Three additional patterns are noteworthy. First, a defense attorney may be reluctant to raise the issue unless certain of a successful adjudication, perhaps to save even a little time and also to be cooperative with the prosecutor (Alschuler, 1968; Battle, 1971). Second, prosecutors generally respond to a defense motion by offering an increased plea bargain concession. Although this may reflect in part a desire to avoid the hearing and the possibility of an undesirable outcome, it also reflects a response framed in terms of prevailing exchange norms. Likewise, defense acceptance of these norms often results in guilty plea bargains (Alschuler, 1968). Third, although use of the motion is relatively frequent in most locales, there is evidence to indicate that use rates (i.e., impact) correlate with variations in factors such as judicial willingness to grant such motions and the length of preparation and in-court time required to raise the issue (Neubauer, 1974).

Other illustrations of optional reforms can be found in the literature (e.g., Bases & McDonald, 1972; Robertson & Teitelbaum, 1973). While each reform might lead to multiple impacts, with optional reforms the issue initially focuses on use. It is clear that potential dismissal of charges is not in itself sufficient to stimulate use. Instead, the efforts needed to use the reform, the responses of other parties to these efforts, and the consistency with which the efforts yield desirable payoffs are determinative. For example, although one speedy trial statute mandates dismissal of cases when disposition does not occur within a specified time limit, the defense seldom invokes the provisions, and the statute has little effect in practice (Nimmer & Krauthaus, 1975). To qualify the case for dismissal, the defense attorney must engage in such deviant acts as resisting prosecution requests for delay. And the prosecutor may respond by withdrawing plea bargain offers and, where possible, proceeding to trial—often an unattractive result from the vantage of the defense.

From such illustrations flows the hypothesis that the impact of an optional reform will increase as participants—other than initiators—are increasingly favorable to its objectives and structural components. Participants antagonistic to a reform are not likely to respond in a manner that will enhance impact. Participants favorable to a reform may so act as to maximize its impact. This occasionally happens with optional reforms implemented by administrative rulemaking within the judicial process. Two recent studies of the omnibus hearing are exemplary (Nimmer, 1971, 1975).

The omnibus hearing is a procedural reform designed to concentrate informal disclosure of evidence, issue discussion, and plea negotiation into a period of two or three weeks after arraignment. Use is optional—at the discretion of both the prosecutor and the defense attorney. Procedurally, use commits both attorneys to an informal conference involving comprehensive information exchange and issue discussion as well as a court hearing at which the judge can monitor the process and perhaps dispose of some issues.

In the two courts studied, the omnibus hearing had widespread impact. It was used in between 70 and 80 percent of all cases filed, substantially increased disclosure, and altered the timing of guilty-plea dispositions. The high rate of use occurred in spite of what would appear to be relatively limited, tangible benefits and persuasive costs. For the defense, the benefits were disclosure of prosecution evidence and, in one court at least, elimination of formal motions to raise and adjudicate issues. However, since the hearing process was time consuming (30–60 minutes in court) and some disclosure was already available informally, the reform would not seem to be highly attractive. For the prosecution, tangible benefits were largely limited to promised certainty in scheduling court appearances, a potential increase of guilty-plea rates (which did not materialize), and time savings achieved by eliminating formal responses to motions. Offsetting these, the process was time consuming and forced the prosecutor to give information that otherwise would not have been released (Nimmer, 1974b).

In both courts, the effect of the incentives was augmented by the actions of the local, trial court judges (Nimmer, 1975, p. 45). Personally committed to the omnibus reform, the judges acted throughout to ensure full disclosure. Equally important, the aggressive advocacy of the local judges created an atmosphere in which using the reform and conforming to its disclosure and issue-discussion characteristics were construed as gestures of cooperation.

As I have indicated, use of the omnibus hearing and other optional reforms may have multiple impacts. But also note that with an optional reform, use itself is significant. Without use, an optional reform can do little to produce system alterations. And, unless use has been coerced, opting for the reform indicates that at least one participant desires the offered payoffs. Use of the reform in itself, however, does not necessarily ensure further impacts.

## Mandatory Reforms

In contrast to optional reforms, mandatory reforms, once set in motion, automatically apply to cases within their defined scope. Since use does not require an explicit decision, it does not imply that participants desire the changes contemplated by the reform, but rather that they comply with the mandatory characteristics of the process and have not elected to engage in circumventing acts.

Mandatory reforms, though sometimes implemented as administrative changes (e.g., trial court calendaring practices), most often involve legislative or appellate court rules (Nimmer, 1977). When such reforms are not endorsed, two avoidance patterns often appear: First, assuming that the reform does not alter significant parameters of prior practice, group decisions are likely to continue to follow old patterns, using only the terminology required by the reform. Second, reforms that do affect substantive parameters may produce efforts to avoid having cases fall into the defined scope of a reform (Alschuler, 1968; Rosett, 1972).

## MANDATORY REFORMS: A CASE STUDY

The case study reported here focuses on the system impact of a major reform of sentence statutes related to federal crimes involving the importation of heroin and marijuana in one federal district court.

### Case Study Site

Since it is near the Mexican border, the District Court for the Southern District of California (San Diego) processes the largest concentration of drug import violations in the federal system. Largely because of drug violations, the annual caseload in San Diego is over 2000 criminal cases. Before 1970 these cases were handled by two permanently assigned judges and a relatively small U.S. Attorney's staff; San Diego ranked consistently as the district court with the largest caseload per judge in the federal system. During 1970 three additional judges were assigned, relieving some of the caseload pressure.

The heavy caseload produces dispositional patterns in San Diego that are typical of large court systems. Extensive prosecutorial screening of complaints excludes many cases with apparently questionable evidence. Plea negotiation and other nonadjudicated modes of disposition are relied on heavily. Plea negotiation is based primarily on concessions in charges filed and prosecutors' recommendations on sentences.

### Data Base

Impact was examined by a before–after design focusing on disposition of marijuana and heroin importation cases. In some respects, this methodology is less than optimal (Campbell, 1969, 1971), but since disposition patterns in specific crime categories are not reported in court statistical reports, I had to collect data on sampled cases independently. As a result, multiple time-series analyses would have been prohibitive in terms of time and cost. (See also Lempert, 1966.)

Data were collected from random samples of drug cases filed during two 6-month periods: one beginning 12 months before and the other beginning 6 months after the reform. The prereform sample was 68 heroin and 136 marijuana cases; the postreform sample, 84 heroin and 116 marijuana cases. Data were collected from court docket sheets summarizing events during the processing of a case. The sheets included information on crime charged, types of disposition, crime convicted on, defendant bail status, number and type of defense motions filed, sentence characteristics, and overall elapsed time to disposition.

### Reform Characteristics

Before the reform, importation of drugs was covered by two provisions of the U.S. Code. Section 174 of Title 21 related to importation of drugs other than marijuana, providing:

Whoever fraudulently or knowingly imports or brings any narcotic drug into the United States or any territory under its control or jurisdiction, contrary to law, or receives, conceals, buys, sells . . . any such narcotic drug after being imported or brought in, knowing the same to have been imported or brought into the United States contrary to law, or conspires to commit any of such acts . . . shall be imprisoned not less than five or more than twenty years . . . [United States Code, 1964, p. 4325].

Section 176a applied to importing marijuana and provided a substantive definition and a sentencing structure (5–20 years) identical to that contained in Section 174.

A move toward the revision of this statutory scheme began in 1970, culminating in its repeal in 1971 and a new statutory framework (see Section 841, Title 21 of the United States Code, 1972, pp. 75–76). An extensive list of drugs was classified into several categories to which differential sentence consequences were attached. The revised statute, primarily affecting sentences, made few changes in the definition of the crime of drug importation—with the exception of creating federal offenses relating to possession of drugs. The 1971 reform produced major reductions in penalties for all drug offenses. Also new statutes drew a sharp distinction between crimes involving marijuana and heroin. The downward revision of the sentencing structure was greatest for marijuana (0–5 years in comparison to 0–15 years for heroin), with the new maximum sentence for marijuana equal to the minimum found in the old statute.

These statute reforms were mandatory. Assuming a pre-judicial decision to file charges of drug importation, the resulting case had to be filed under the reform statute. The sentencing provisions of the repealed statutes were no longer available for use.

Two hypotheses concerning the system impact of the reform are particularly relevant. First, the reform might reduce sentences imposed on persons charged with drug importation. Second, eliminating the relatively harsh sentences of the prior statutes might weaken the prosecutor's plea bargaining position and lead to defense counsel's willingness to contest charges by filing motions or demanding trial.

## Heroin Cases

*Sentencing impact.* To compare sentencing patterns, several methods were used. The first was an unweighted comparison of actual sentences. As Table 1 indicates, there was only a slight decrease in the average length of incarceration and probation terms following the reform. Neither change was statistically significant at the .05 level. A second method used a scale, developed by the Administrative Office of the United States Courts,[2] for the comparative weighting of sentences. Application of this scale to the data likewise revealed no statistically significant difference in imposed sentences (8.6 prereform; 8.1 postreform).

The absence of any change in sentences is explicable in terms of prior sentencing practices in the Southern District. Beyond the 20-year maximum sentence, the old statute had an apparently mandatory constraint—a 5-year minimum sentence that required incarceration. Under prior prac-

---

[2] The scale, adopted with respect to federal sentencing patterns, attaches a relative value to various sentences:

| Sentence | Value |
|---|---|
| Suspended sentence | 0 |
| Probation without supervision | 0 |
| Fine | 1 |
| Probation with supervision | |
| 1–12 months | 1 |
| 13–36 months | 2 |
| > 36 months | 4 |
| Imprisonment | |
| 1–6 months | 3 |
| 7–12 months | 5 |
| 13–24 months | 8 |
| 25–36 months | 10 |
| 37–48 months | 12 |
| 49–60 months | 14 |
| 61–120 months | 25 |

Adapted from Table 10 of the *Federal Offenders* (Administrative Office of the U.S. Courts, 1968, p. 35).

TABLE 1    **Mean Sentences for Heroin Convictions as a Function of Reform (in Months)**

| SENTENCE | PREREFORM | POSTREFORM |
|---|---|---|
| Incarceration | 42.2 (32)[b] | 40.2 (38) |
| Probation[a] | 40.1 (24) | 36.5 (32) |

[a]*Includes all cases in which no term of incarceration was imposed.*

[b]*Numbers in parentheses indicate number of convictions.*

tice, however, sentences at or above the 5-year minimum in the statute were infrequent, and sentences involving incarceration often were not imposed. These patterns were achieved through plea bargaining involving concessions in the charges on which a guilty plea was entered. As indicated in Table 1, sentences were well below 5 years. Before the reform, incarceration sentences ranged from 6 months to 7 years, while probation sentences ranged from 1 to 6 years. Sentences of 5 years or more occurred for only a third of all sentenced defendants, and only two sentences exceeded 5 years. Similarly, incarceration occurred for only 57 percent of all sentenced defendants.

Thus the reform only eliminated constraints that had already been abrogated and, in fact, formally established a sentencing structure no less severe than that in practice. The 15-year maximum, like the prior 20-year maximum, set an external limit not approached in routine cases. Presumably it was approached, if at all, only in atypical cases involving organized drug importation. The authorization to impose sentences between 0 and 5 years merely validated prior patterns.

In this context, the reform statute offered no incentive to alter prior sentencing practice. That it reflected a readjustment of legislative perceptions of appropriate sentence norms was, in itself, insufficient to cause an adjustment of the informal sentence norms. Under the new law, incarceration sentences ranged from 3 months to 7 years, while probation sentences ranged from 1 to 5 years. Both are virtually identical to prior

practice, as is the mean term of the actual sentences imposed (Table 1). Analogous to prereform patterns, slightly more than 30 percent of all sentenced defendants received a term of 5 years.

In addition, there was no significant change in the rate of incarceration terms imposed before and after the reform. Of the defendants sentenced, 57 percent were incarcerated under the old law as opposed to 54 percent under the new. There was, however, some indication that the reform altered sentencing at trial. Although the numbers are small, all trial defendants (10) sentenced under the old law were incarcerated for 5 years or more. Under the new statute, 2 of 12 defendants received probation and three defendants received incarceration terms under 5 years. The explanation for this effect is straightforward: The occurrence of a trial indicates that no concessions have been agreed to, and—as a result—judicial sentencing upon conviction is constrained by statutory terms. Therefore, in this limited context, the repeal of the 5-year minimum seemed to bring behavior change.

*Plea bargaining impact.* Plea bargaining under prior statutes involved the charge to which the plea would be entered, whether incarceration would be involved, and length of sentence. The reform produced what might be described as a procedural impact on plea bargaining. Under the old statute, 79 percent of all guilty pleas in cases originating under Section 174 involved a plea to a different statute with lesser sentence requirements (e.g., crimes involving tax payments with respect to the drugs). Under the new law, only 19 percent of all guilty pleas involved a charge reduction (e.g., to the crime of possession of drugs). Thus while it had been necessary to use another statute to obtain a sentence below 5 years, the new statute made this unnecessary. The few charge reductions under the new statute seemingly reflect a desire to avoid the label of drug importation, rather than a concern about sentence.

From one perspective, the plea bargaining process before the reform was heavily weighted against the defense. The old statute required relatively harsh sentences that could be avoided only by a successful trial defense or by agreeing to plead guilty to a lesser criminal charge. Thus the desire to avoid a severe sentence was a substantial incentive. In fact, one defense attorney described the preform practice as being devoid of negotiation—the defense was compelled to bargain by threat of a sentence.

With the deletion of the 5-year minimum, a substantial element of this compulsion was removed. Therefore, if the above view is accurate, the reform should have produced a change in disposition patterns. No significant change occurred (Table 2), however.

The stability of defense–prosecution interaction despite the reform is illustrated by other aspects of case processing. For example, under the old statute, the defense filed formal motions contesting matters such as the validity of search-and-seizure or confession evidence in 29 percent of all cases; under the new statute, similar motions were filed in 32 percent of all cases. Similarly,

the timing of guilty plea dispositions revealed no increased willingness of the defense to defer acceptance of prosecution plea bargain offers. In San Diego, most plea negotiation was conducted by the plea bargaining unit of the prosecutor's office. This unit controlled all cases until shortly after arraignment, at which time the case was transferred to the trial section of the prosecutor's office (Nimmer, 1971). Under the old statute, 61 percent of all guilty pleas were entered while the case was in the control of this unit; under the new statute, 66 percent were entered during that period. Finally, in both periods incarceration occurred in roughly 50 percent of all cases disposed of by a guilty plea; likewise, the mean length of incarceration sentences remained stable (34.1 months prereform; 36.8 months postreform).

As the absence of a substantive effect on plea bargaining suggests, cogent rationales supported prior practice. In part, these involved an apparent group view that the old sentences represented an appropriate balance of concerns. More important, prior practice had established a firm system of exchange. As indicated earlier, such exchange relationships are supported by a wide range of influences from joint interests in efficient use of time to a desire to influence the discretionary actions of other parties.

## Marijuana Cases

*Sentencing impact.* With the possible exception of cases that involve a conviction at trial, the heroin statute reform had only a

**TABLE 2  Disposition of Heroin Convictions as a Function of Reform (Percentages)**

| DISPOSITION | PREREFORM | POSTREFORM |
|-------------|-----------|------------|
| Guilty plea | 68 | 69 |
| Trial | 26 | 23 |
| Dismissal | 6 | 8 |
| (*N*) | (68) | (84) |

**TABLE 3**   **Mean Sentences for Marijuana Convictions as a Function of Reform (in Months)**

| SENTENCE | PREREFORM | POSTREFORM |
|----------|-----------|------------|
| Incarceration | 36.0 (60)[b] | 13.6 (34)* |
| Probation[a] | 36.3 (56) | 33.4 (60) |

[a]*Includes all cases in which no term of incarceration was imposed.*
[b]*Numbers in parentheses indicate number of cases.*
*p < .05

*pro forma* impact. The impact of the reform with respect to marijuana cases was somewhat more substantial. The data in Table 3 indicate a reduction of sentences following the implementation of the reform. The decrease in sentence length for incarceration is statistically significant at the .05 level. Likewise, there was a decrease in the frequency of incarceration sentences (52% of all sentences under the old law; 35% under the new). Finally, the decrease is also reflected in the weighted sentence scale of the Administrative Office of the U.S. Court (6.1 prereform; 4.5 postreform). This change in sentencing is related to the scope of the reform. The marijuana revision altered the formal sentence range from 5 to 20 years to 0 to 5 years. Even though actual sentencing patterns had been well below the prior statute's specifications, this extreme revision impinged on existing norms.

The prereform patterns for marijuana cases basically were similar to those in heroin cases. Incarceration sentences ranged from 1 month to 7 years, while probation sentences ranged from 1 to 7 years. Only 13 percent of all sentences were 5 years or more. Therefore, in reality the reform had a *direct* effect on only a small fraction of the sentences. Although postreform sentences in excess of 5 years were not prohibited, they could be obtained only after a trial conviction on more than one charge and then only if the trial judge imposed consecutive, not concurrent, sentences. Since consecutive sentences are rare (none were found) and only 5 percent of all marijuana cases involved

more than one count of illegal importation, the 5-year limit was operationally absolute.

As apparently occurred in the heroin cases, the marijuana statute reform seemed to produce a sentencing impact in trial cases. Under the prior statute, incarceration sentences of 5 years or more were imposed in all trial convictions (14), as all convictions were based on importation charges and, therefore, the 5-year minimum could not be avoided. Under the new statute, however, four of twelve trial convictions did not result in incarceration and five others involved incarceration terms of less than 5 years. The mean length of incarceration terms fell from 66.9 months (14 cases) to 23.3 months (8 cases).

*Plea bargaining impact.* The major impact of the reform was an indirect sentencing effect on plea bargaining practice. As with heroin cases, the reform also altered the form of plea bargains. Under the old statute, 92 percent of all guilty pleas involved a plea to charges other than the primary marijuana importation statute. Under the new law, only 30 percent involved a plea to such statutes (e.g., drug possession).

In contrast to heroin cases, the marijuana reform also led to effects in guilty plea sentencing. As a function of the reform, 5-year sentences were maximum, and incarceration was no longer guaranteed on trial conviction. Prereform, 45 percent of all plea bargain sentences involved incarceration of an average of 26.6 months. Postreform, incarceration occurred in only 30 percent of all guilty plea cases; the average was 10.6 months.

One could describe this change as resulting solely from a dilemma presented to the prosecutor. Although still wishing to obtain sentences at old levels, the prosecutor might recognize that the sentence differential would, if old levels were retained, be insufficient to induce guilty pleas at prior rates. Faced with the possibility of more frequent trials, prosecutors could adjust their plea bargaining offers accordingly. But while this explanation may account for the change in incarceration sentences under plea bargaining, it is also plausible that defense counsels, in exchanging the right to trial for a sentence concession, concurrently reevaluated and communicated their perception of an appropriate exchange to prosecutors.

The data suggest that reevaluation of the exchange was expeditiously reached: There was no discernable disruption of plea negotiation efficiency. As seen in Table 4, no significant change in guilty plea rates occurred. Similarly, the number of guilty plea agreements within the prosecutor's special unit did not decrease (60% of all guilty pleas under the old statute; 68% under the new). Also, defense motions contesting evidence and other issues were filed in about 25 percent of all cases both before and after the reform (25% prereform; 22% postreform).

These data suggest that the substantive change in guilty plea sentences was a by-product of the exchange system, that is, a result of mutual reevaluation rather than of one party initiating an action that produced a response from another. The reform altered one parameter—lowering the potential sentence on conviction by trial. The system accommodated this altered parameter by adjusting another—the concessions received in exchange for guilty pleas.

## CONCLUDING PERSPECTIVES

A basic premise of this chapter is that the system impact of reform within the criminal justice system can be delineated. The judicial process was described here in functional terms, emphasizing personal motivations and informal norms. This perspective toward the judicial process and, indeed, toward the entire legal system is essential to articulating a general model of system behavior. To the extent that reforms are seen as changes in formal rules of law, many crucial issues that impinge on impact are assumed to be irrelevant. But as my studies indicate, this view can lead to faulty inferences. The criminal justice system is determined by a network of complex influences and, thus, the relation of reform and impact is far less direct.

Two characteristics of the judicial process should be emphasized. First, it is an interactional system—a sequence of encounters between and among participants in a case. The processing of individual cases involves substantial, ongoing prediction of action and reaction to prior decision by *all* participants. Second, repeated interaction among attorneys and judges leads to the development of informal norms that shape behavior and, necessarily, affect system response to a reform stimulus.

**TABLE 4   Disposition of Marijuana Convictions as a Function of Reform (Percentages)**

| DISPOSITION | PREREFORM | POSTREFORM |
|---|---|---|
| Guilty plea | 75 | 74 |
| Trial | 18 | 16 |
| Dismissal | 8 | 10 |
| (*N*) | (136) | (116) |

While the distinction made here between optional and mandatory reforms has important operational implications, it is not dispositive for estimating the impact of reform. Reform structures must be considered in functional terms, rather than solely in terms of the policy objectives to which they are addressed. To wit, it is important to characterize reforms with reference not just to their *articulated* manipulation of rewards and costs but also to their *interpreted* manipulation of these variables. It is not simply that different individuals perceive events differently. Rather, given an interactional system, the response of any participant will be shaped both by what the reform plan articulates and by the actual character of the reform as it is interpreted by relevant others in the judicial process.

Despite the evident complexity of the task, available data indicate that an understanding of reform impact is possible to achieve. Generalized analysis of reform impact is of vital concern to those who want to understand major social institutions as well as those who are concerned with expediting change in criminal justice practices.

# CHAPTER 21

# Legal Structures and Restoring Equity[1]

## —STEWART MACAULAY and ELAINE WALSTER

Psychological research suggests that harmdoers respond in one of two ways after injuring another: They restore actual equity by compensating the victim, or they engage in defensive behavior that includes derogation of the victim, denial of responsibility for the act, or minimization of the victim's suffering. This chapter examines the factors tending to encourage or prevent individuals from voluntarily reestablishing equitable relations, and considers the extent to which current legal practices encourage or discourage the equitable resolution of legal disputes.

Individuals react in a variety of ways when they have injured another. Harmdoers sometimes make voluntary reparation to the victim or acquiesce when forced to make reparation. In other circumstances, they engage in defensive behavior to try to justify their harmdoing. They may insist that the victim deserves to suffer or may deny that he or she was really injured by their actions.

The victim of an injustice undoubtedly prefers to be compensated for suffering rather than have the suffering justified. Society, too, has a vested interest in encouraging disputants to reconcile their differences rather than rationalize their wrongdoing. In this chapter we examine factors that tend to encourage or prevent individuals from voluntarily reestablishing equitable relations and consider the extent to which current legal practices encourage or

discourage the equitable resolution of legal disputes.

## THEORETICAL BACKGROUND

Since this chapter focuses on the psychological impact that various legal procedures have on an individual, we define harmdoing in psychological terms: A harmdoing situation is one in which an *inequity* is produced in the relation between two persons. Our discussion will use conceptions of equity in human interaction advanced by Homans (1961), Adams (1965), and Walster, Berscheid, and Walster (1970, 1973).

## THE EQUITY FORMULATION

An equitable relationship has been defined as one in which a person's ratio of outcomes to inputs is equal to the other person's outcome/input ratio (Walster et al., 1973). *Inputs* are defined as the participant's contributions to the exchange, which are seen as entitling him or her to rewards or costs. The inputs a person contributes can be either assets entitling one to reward

[1] This research was supported in part by National Institute of Mental Health Grant MH-16661 and National Science Foundation Grants GS-2932 and GS-30822X. We would like to thank Dr. Jacqueline Macaulay and Professor Robert L. Rabin for their helpful comments.

or liabilities entitling one to punishment. In the employer-employee relationships with which Adams (1965) dealt, inputs were such contributions as skill, financial investments, education, and so on. But in social encounters quite different assets or liabilities are judged to be relevant inputs, since intent, fault, and negligence may be of primary importance. *Outcomes,* as defined by Walster et al. (1973) are the individual's "profits"— the positive or negative consequences of the relation with the other person. The person's total outcome from the relation is the sum of rewards obtained from the relation minus costs incurred.

Given this equity formulation, it is now possible to define harmdoing as the committing of an act that produces an inequitable relation between the members, such that the actor's outcome/input ratio becomes greater than that of the other member. The perpetrator is designated as a *harmdoer*; the member of the relation whose ratio has been reduced is a *victim*.

## THE PSYCHOLOGICAL CONSEQUENCES OF DOING HARM

Theorists assume that individuals experience distress after injuring others. This distress is variously labeled "guilt," "fear of retaliation," "dissonance," "empathy," or "conditioned anxiety." It seems to arise from two sources, both the products of early socialization.

When children harm others, they are sometimes punished. Soon the performance of harmful acts arouses conditioned anxiety (Aronfreed, 1970). Throughout life, harmdoing is often followed by punishment, and thus continues to generate conditioned anxiety. Such distress may have a cognitive component: The harmdoer may attribute distress to a fear that the victim, the victim's sympathizers, legal agencies, or even God will retaliate. Discomfort from this source is labeled *retaliation distress*.

Harmdoing may produce discomfort for another reason. In our society it is generally felt that one should be fair and equitable in dealing with others (see Fromm, 1956, on the pervasiveness of the "fairness" principle). Of course, not everyone internalizes exactly the same code to the same extent or follows it without deviation. Juvenile delinquents and people in the confidence game, for example, often seem to behave as if the exploitation of others were completely consistent with their self-concept. But evidence suggests that even deviants internalize norms of fairness. While they may violate the norms for financial or social gain, they experience such distress that they try to convince others that their actions were equitable. For example, some deviants argue that their victims' inputs are so negative that to exploit them is in fact to give them "what they deserve." (For anecdotal evidence see Goffman, 1952; Sykes & Matza, 1957.)

Doing a harmful act, then, should be inconsistent with a normal person's ethical principles and self-expectations. The distress that arises from such unethical or inconsistent acts, discussed by guilt theorists (Arnold, 1960; Maher, 1966) and cognitive dissonance theorists (Bramel, 1969), has been termed *self-concept distress*.

Presumably, retaliation distress and self-concept distress motivate a harmdoer to restore equity to the relationship with the victim.

## TECHNIQUES BY WHICH A HARMDOER REDUCES DISTRESS

### Restoration of Actual Equity

A harmdoer can restore equity to the relationship with the victim by voluntary compensation, a course viewed by cynics as relatively rare. But given the opportunity, a harmdoer will often exert considerable effort to make restitution. For example, large retailers often have a policy of "money cheerfully refunded" if a customer is not satisfied with a purchase. Such restitution attempts have been repeatedly documented

(Berscheid & Walster, 1967; Berscheid, Walster, & Barclay, 1969; Brock & Becker, 1966; Carlsmith & Gross, 1969; Freedman, Wallington, & Bless, 1967; Walster & Prestholdt, 1966; Walster, Walster, Abrahams, & Brown, 1966).

## Restoration of Psychological Equity

If a harmdoer is unable or unwilling to compensate the victim, distress can still be reduced by convincing the self (and perhaps others) that the inequitable act was in fact equitable. Individuals use several techniques in rationalizing harmful acts.

*Derogation of the victim.* That individuals often justify their cruelties by derogating their victims has long been apparent. Many studies have demonstrated this tendency (Berkowitz, 1962; Davidson, 1964; Glass, 1964; Sykes & Matza, 1957; Walster & Prestholdt, 1956). Davis & Jones (1960) found that subjects hired to humiliate others in a research project tended to convince themselves that the others in fact deserved to be ridiculed. Sykes & Matza (1957) found that juvenile delinquents often defend their victimization of others by arguing that the victims have traits that make them deserve punishment. Thus the victimizers could claim to be instruments of justice.

*Denial of responsibility for the act.* If harmdoers believe that it was not their behavior but rather the actions of someone or something else (e.g., fate) that caused the victim's suffering, then their relationship with the victim remains psychologically equitable. They often deny that the harm was their fault (Brock & Buss, 1962, 1964; Skyes & Matza, 1957). At the societal level the notion that another's suffering is not one's fault, that one does not owe the victim any reparation, is incorporated in formal legal rules.

*Minimization of the victim's suffering.* To the extent that harmdoers can deny that the victim was harmed, they can convince themselves that their relationship with the victim is still equitable. Sykes and Matza (1957) and Brock and Buss (1962) showed that harmdoers consistently underestimate how much harm they have done.

## PREDICTION OF A HARMDOER'S RESPONSE

The important question is which equity-restoring technique—compensation or justification—is a harmdoer likely to employ in various circumstances?

Logically, it seemed unlikely that harmdoers can restore equity by using both compensation and justification in concert. It should be difficult for harmdoers to convince themselves that the victim deserved to suffer or was not really injured, or that they were not at fault for the victim's suffering at the same time that fault is being acknowledged for the victim's undeserved suffering and an attempt is being made to assist the victim. Evidence supports the contention that compensation and justification are alternative rather than complementary ways in which harmdoers react to their victims (Lerner & Simmons, 1966; Webster & Prestholdt, 1966).

Although a harmdoer may care little whether equity is restored by compensating the victim or by rationalizing harmdoing, the victim and society both have vested interests in inducing the harmdoer to make restitution. A victim is naturally eager to secure compensation. Not only has he or she been deprived of material benefits. Also the victim may face the indignity of derogation plus the difficulty that the harmdoer, because of his or her derogation, may feel free to commit further injustices (Berscheid, Boye, & Darley, 1968). Society, as well, prefers that its citizens restore equity after committing injustices rather than engage in justifications that could end in shared bitterness.

How can society best move a harmdoer

to make restitution? In socializing children, parents and teachers can try to engender a greater commitment to maintaining equity. In addition, society can increase the likelihood of restitution by developing and strengthening social structures that facilitate it.

Several situational variables have been found experimentally to encourage individuals to make restitution to their victims. (For a partial list, see Walster et al., 1970.) Among those which the authors have found to be important determinants of a harmdoer's response are:

*Adequacy of available compensation.* If a harmdoer believes that he or she can make complete and exact restitution, voluntary compensation will be more likely than if the harmdoer believes that even his or her best efforts will be inadequate. Naturally enough, harmdoers are also reluctant to make excessive restitution.

*Cost of available compensation.* The harmdoer will be more likely to make complete restitution to the victim if it can be done at low psychological and material cost. Two factors affect the harmdoer's perceptions of the relative cost of compensation versus justification and thus willingness to compensate: (1) Once he or she has publicly defended the harmful act, admitting error becomes embarrassing (and psychologically costly). (2) If he or she will be in frequent contact with the victim, trying to rationalize the harmdoing may be dangerous (and costly).

## EFFECT OF THE LEGAL SYSTEM

Let us examine some of these variables in operation. To what extent do our legal structures support or socialize the goal of restitution and reconciliation? To what extent do they foster self-justification—that is, derogation, denial, and minimization—in the harmdoer? As a preliminary step one

can only rely on example and offer conclusions that are generally true.

## Support for Actual Equity or Support for Derogation and Rationalization

On its face, U.S. law supports compensation (if the harmdoer is at "fault" for causing the injury). The common law of torts, for example, consists of rules that say a wrongdoer must compensate the victim. In addition, the legal system has informal procedures that provide even more avenues to restitution. A police officer may decide not to arrest a shoplifter if the wrongdoer is not a professional thief and the stolen items are returned; a district attorney may decide not to prosecute if the amount embezzled is returned. These formal and informal procedures undoubtedly encourage wrongdoers to make compensation. But other rules and procedures also may discourage a harmdoer from making compensation and instead encourage him or her to justify the wrongdoing.

## Dilution of Incentive to Restore Equity

The automobile "accident" is a good example of how common-law civil litigation aimed at compensation may actually discourage participants from making exact compensation.

At the formal level, the relevant legal rules most commonly rest on some aspect of fault, requiring a determination of who did what under what circumstances (Rabin, 1969). The legal concept of fault is based, in part, on harmdoer intent or negligence. (Accidental harmdoing involves no "fault" in a legal sense.) The requirement of determining who is at fault may dilute the harmdoer's incentive to restore equity. Fault and fact often are unclear. Although the victim may have no question about the harmdoer's responsibility, judges, juries, and even the harmdoer may have great doubt. For example, the trier of fact must decide whether the defendant was driving at an appropriate speed for conditions and paying attention. But what is an appropriate speed in a residential neighborhood on an overcast afternoon? Can one who has the radio on and is talking to a passenger be said to be paying proper attention? While we can all agree that some conduct while driving a car involves fault and some does not, there are many situations where there is wide difference of opinion. If the harmdoer feels the victim is seeking excessive compensation, the rules resting on fault and fact often offer the harmdoer a chance to escape legal liability by contesting responsibility. Unwittingly the ambiguities in our concepts of fault may encourage denial and minimization instead of exact compensation.

In most states, substantive tort law also may encourage the harmdoer to derogate the victim. A victim who is contributorily negligent cannot recover from an injury partly caused by another's negligence. If the harmdoer can convince others that the victim was partly responsible for his or her own injury, the harmdoer can avoid having to make what would be viewed as an inequitably large settlement.

*Delay in judgment.* The time that often elapses between the accident and the possibility of compensating makes it easier for the harmdoer to deny fault. In time, memory dims and the harmdoer can more easily distort reality, consciously or unconsciously. Also, the harmdoer becomes more committed to resist pressures to compensate, which increases his or her motivation to put actions in a better and better light. Thus the process resulting from the need to establish fault predisposes the harmdoer to say, "I'm not really at fault. I really didn't cause the accident. I'm legally right, and if we went to court, I'd win."

*Costs of litigation.* The way the legal system and related social systems work may further dilute a wrongdoer's incentive to re-

store exact equity. (1) That litigants must pay high costs to bring and defend lawsuits and that courts are not adequately staffed to respond quickly predispose individuals to bargain rather than seek restoration of exact equity. Some injuries are so small as to fall beneath the economic barriers to litigation. The plaintiff's need for money today and an inability to wait for months or years for settlement may force a receptiveness to a settlement far below full compensation. In short, costs and delay join fault and fact to push for bargaining and compromise rather than reestablishment of equity. Given the chance to ignore some injuries and buy off others at a sharply discounted price, many harmdoers, the evidence suggests, deal with distress by strategies other than compensating the victim.

(2) Since such harms as those done by automobile accidents are predictable actuarially, another social institution—insurance—joins the legal system in resolving issues. Car drivers are given every incentive to buy insurance to ward off great financial liability for accidents. Practically, the thrust of insurance coverage is to avoid paying victims too much rather than to see to it that exact compensation is made. And to the insurance companies and insurance adjusters are added the plaintiff's attorneys, who specialize in personal injury litigation and negotiation with adjusters and often are paid a percentage of any recovery obtained.

This system of institutionalized bargaining is impersonal. Both the harmdoer and the injured usually are on the sidelines. The adjuster and the plaintiff's attorney play the game. This impersonality probably tends to dilute the harmdoer's sense of obligation to make full and adequate compensation. Possibly the harmdoer may think that an obligation to restore equity is met fully by referring the victim to the adjuster. Even if the harmdoer realizes that the victim is likely to be inadequately compensated, unpleasant confrontations can still be easily avoided. The defendant need only tell the plaintiff to call the insurance company. Rather than directly compensate, the harmdoer can delegate and derogate. In fact, if a harmdoer tries to help the victim obtain compensation from the insurance company, loss of rights under the policy may ensue. Insurers typically suggest that policyholders say and do no more than is necessary after an accident, and they must cooperate with the defense against the victim's claims.

Plaintiff, or plaintiff's attorney, then deals with an adjuster. The adjuster's primary goal is not to make exact compensation for the harm caused by the insured party but to obtain a settlement that minimizes the liability and total cost to the insurance company. Adjusters may compound the insured's harmdoing by unfair denials of responsibility, offers of inadequate settlement, or even spreading tales of fraudulent claims and dishonest plaintiff's attorneys.

Exact compensation rarely results from this bargaining between adjuster and plaintiff's attorney. Often the victim is inadequately compensated. Sometimes plaintiffs get settlements that exceed the harm caused because of their skill in manipulating the facts or because the insurer feels that it is cheaper to buy off the plaintiff than defend the claim. But such tactics do not reestablish equity; they simply convert the victim into a harmdoer of sorts. Bargaining thus tends to merge the extremes to the middle, giving those with good cases less than their loss and those with weak cases more than they would have received in court (Conrad, Morgan, Pratt, Voltz, & Brombaugh, 1964).

*Bargaining at expense of compensation.* While in theory common-law rules tend to emphasize compensation by a wrongdoer to a victim, in practice the process pushes toward bargaining. The tendency in the law is not to support the ideal of having the wrongdoer make good the harm done, but to support the best balance of self-interest possible between harmdoer and victim, in light of bargaining skill and position. Rather than develop the harmdoer's best motives,

the system tends to guard against the worst since the potential of litigation forces him or her to strike some bargain rather than ignore the victim's claim totally (Friedman & Macaulay, 1969).

Some might object that thus far we have focused on a socially trivial problem—automobile accident cases. One major index of the social importance of a problem is whether there are specialized structures to deal with it. It might be argued that traditional common law is only a backstop for problems not important enough to warrant the high cost of an administrative agency. In any case, our discussion is also relevant to other areas of law.

In some areas law has departed from the adversary, winner-take-all approach and has turned to experts—as in social service. Welfare workers prepare budgets for their clients based on some conception of client need. The situation could be viewed as one where the harm has been done by the social system and where the welfare worker is the agent of society charged with restoring equity in the particular case. But even welfare workers who accept this metaphorical view of welfare programs rarely can come close to achieving exact compensation because of limited resources, because of ideology about what welfare clients want or ought to do, and because generous levels of welfare are politically unacceptable. Thus, even in such agencies a type of bargaining often evolves. Officials carry out their tasks in certain ways and not others to gain support from the community and the legislature; a kind of tacit bargain is struck between these officials and the relevant public. Workers dealing with clients often tacitly bargain, too; funds needed to make up for such injuries as the lack of good schools are offered but at a price—the client must accept certain values and a dependent status. Here, too, the system in operation results in bargaining for partial restitution rather than full compensation. Attempts to force welfare agencies to conform to a due process model are beset with difficulties (Handler, 1967, 1969).

## Summary

We have argued here that social ideals and the formal rules of U.S. law state that harmdoers must compensate their victims, and that the actual operation of the legal system makes exact compensation unlikely and bargaining likely. Such bargained settlements, although failing to restore exact equity, still offer some support for the compensation value. That one might be sued and might lose is probably a major reason why many buy insurance to cover liability for injuries they may cause. Although the equity norm is met only indirectly and through bargains that may offer less than the real loss, insurance offers far more compensation to all those injured than would be available without it. Even the most well-intentioned harmdoer is limited by available resources. Given the choice of good intentions backed by little money or the bargain with an adjuster (typically producing some money in the bank), most victims would choose the latter. Indeed, it may be that some believe they are doing equity when they buy insurance and direct their victims to the adjuster. Insofar as harmdoers believe this, they are unlikely to commit further injustices based on derogation and rationalization. To this degree, the current system encourages "justice rather than justification."

Moreover, the norm of compensating one's victim may be given somewhat greater force if it is also a rule of law. Legal norms may—though indirectly and to a very limited extent—influence public perceptions of legitimacy (Berkowitz & Walker, 1967; Kaufman, 1970). The fact that equity is formally prescribed might motivate toward reconciliation some who would not voluntarily elect to do so.

Recently some barriers to using the legal system to gain compensation for some injuries have been lowered. Subsidized legal assistance programs offer people with lower incomes legal advice, help in bargaining, and trial representation. Test cases have been brought and some results favorable to lower-income people have been won. One would expect these test cases to influence future bargaining and change evaluations of the wisdom of initiating voluntary compensation.

Then, too, there is a trend to regulate certain kinds of harmdoers (particularly those whose practices affect consumers). Compelled compensation may eliminate some refusals to compensate victims. If manufacturers were required to provide new cars with service measured by certain standards, they could no longer refuse to make good harm done to buyers caused by the manufacturers' inadequacies. In this area derogation and rationalization by the manufacturers are the norm and compensation the exception; regulation, or the threat of it, may bring a significant change.

## EVALUATION OF THE SYSTEM

It is generally agreed that when one has done harm to another, one should do all one can to repair the injury. Even restricting this norm to cases involving fault, we have seen that the legal system offers only limited support for the goal of equity. The nature of its rules, the costs of using the system, and the limited power granted to experts produce a less-than-ideal bargaining system. There is an evident difference between society's strong support for a goal and its minimal support for the means of achieving it.

Just because it is desirable that harmdoers compensate those they injure does not mean that a legal system ought to pursue this goal at all costs. Society is often unwilling to pay the price to achieve a goal even though most of its members agree that it is important, particularly when resources are limited, when society is committed to competing goals, and when choices about allocations must be made. As long as resources are limited, it is difficult to conceive of a legal structure that would not support bargaining rather than exact equity restoration. Even if the state were to create an agency charged with seeing to it that harmdoers compensated their victims, more equitable compensation would not be guaranteed. Many would argue that public welfare does not have a very high priority; as a result the agency would find itself underfunded and understaffed. To save time and money, it would likely bargain for settlements so that something could be offered to all, or nearly all, victims.

Even if fairly adequate resources were allocated, some factors that support the bargaining system would remain. Most people would probably think that an accused harmdoer ought to be able to challenge the charge —"It was *not* my 1969 blue Ford that hit the victim." Few would advocate charging one person with the acts of others, excepting special circumstances, but most might cling to some view of fault—"While I was driving very carefully, the plaintiff ran out in front of my car from between two parked cars." Finally, most harmdoers would not be able to pay more than a fraction of the losses they cause. Thus, the agency would have only two alternatives: (1) it could leave losses uncompensated, or (2) it could turn to private or public compensators. But private insurers cannot be expected voluntarily to turn their full attention to doing equity at the cost of greater expense and less profit. Public compensators, too, would undoubtedly have real incentives to cut costs. Unless strong general social pressure developed for full compensation, public agencies charged with this burden would be likely to establish elaborate procedures to deal with cheating by victims and those claiming to be victims to please a cost-conscious public. In short, it is difficult to envision a legal system that would offer unqualified support for the equity goal. However, current efforts in several states with compensation programs may be illuminating in this regard.

Perhaps there are benefits from the indirect role the legal system plays in fostering bargaining. It has been suggested that cost barriers to litigation create socially desirable "reciprocal immunities," socializing people to be tolerant of the slight injuries of every-day life and fostering voluntary restitution. These barriers also inhibit the use of litigation as harassment or sport (Friedman, 1967). An injury must be seen as serious to justify invoking the elaborate litigation process. All these difficulties may tend to support adjustments that are less costly to almost all concerned. There are disincentives to heading to court before all other avenues are exhausted. If a bargain struck by the parties has advantages over a formal legal resolution where one party must be found "at fault," then we would not want to make the use of formal process too easy.

In conclusion, the U.S. legal system is likely to reflect ethically preferable goals: Harmdoers should compensate their victims rather than rationalize their harmdoing. For the most part, the legal system's basic rules reflect simple commonsense ideas of fault, choice, and status since legal norms do reflect the community sense of fairplay. Nonetheless, the legal system cannot act without monetary and social costs. Typically, legal questions involve deciding what costs one is willing to pay to achieve what proportion of what values.

Social science findings can bring much to a study of the legal system. They can broaden our picture of humanity (the subject of legal action and, hopefully, the beneficiary of it). They also can lead us to consider how the system works and can force us to look more at the consequences of legal action (or inaction) than legal scholars have done in the past. While findings about harmdoers and equity do not automatically dictate an appropriate legal response, they do suggest important issues concerning our largely unstudied legal system. The psychological equity formulation and the picture we have drawn of interchanges between the legal and insurance systems lead us, for example, to wonder to what extent this process frees automobile drivers from a sense of responsibility for the harm they may cause. One cannot know, of course, without further study.

# CHAPTER 22

# Responsible Decision Making in Dispute Settlement[1]

## —ERNEST A. HAGGARD and SOIA MENTSCHIKOFF

The setting of institutionalized commercial arbitration was used to study how individuals make decisions and how groups achieve decision consensus. Sixty arbitrators (30 manufacturers, 30 brokers) in 20 assorted three-member panels listened to a 45-minute recording of a dispute over the cancellation of a business contract, then deliberated until they settled the dispute. As hypothesized, the arbitrators' choice of the central issue in the dispute and how they perceived the evidence were the primary determinants of their decisions. Thus, although various nonrational factors were involved, the decisions were predominantly rational in terms of how the deciders viewed what the parties did, as compared with what they should have done, in the period that led to the dispute.

The term "responsible decision making" refers to those situations in which third parties have the authority and responsibility

[1] This research was supported by a grant from the Ford Foundation to the University of Chicago Law School and by a Research Career Award to the first author (No. K6-MH-9415) from the National Institute of Mental Health. J. Noble Braden and John Eastman of the American Arbitration Association made it possible for the research to be conducted at the AAA facilities in New York. Persons who assisted in the collection and analysis of the data include: Jean M. Allard, Sidney J. Blatt, Louise Corner, Joanne Holden, Philip W. Jackson, Frances A. Kareken, David Y. Klein, Raymond J. Kuby, Robert N. Navratil, Frank M. Potter, Richard R. Rosman, Hal M. Smith, Richard E. Stafford, and John H. Tarini. R. Darrell Bock, Kern M. Dickman, Merlin J. Foster, and Logan Green aided in the statistical analyses of the data. The research reported here was carried out between 1955 and 1959 under the direction of the first author (Haggard & Mentschikoff, 1960).

for making decisions that affect others. A typical consequence of responsible decision making is that the behavior of those affected by the decision—from one person to an entire society—will be changed or regulated in some important way.

The scope of responsible decision making is broad indeed. It includes most of the functions of government, and occurs also in a wide array of groups, from baseball umpires to dissertation committees to boards of business corporations. Given this range of situations, the conditions under which decisions are made can vary in numerous ways: Is the decision made by a single individual or by a group? If by a group, how large is it? Is it standing or ad hoc? Is the scope of decisions narrow or broad? Is special expertise required? Does the decision-making process require adherence to particular substantive and procedural rules? Is it expected that a particular decision will establish guidelines to be applied to future similar disputes? As these examples indicate, it is obviously not possible to study at one time all the parameters of this type of decision making.

Commercial arbitration is an ideal context in which to study responsible decision making. In some form it has no doubt existed since men first engaged in buying, selling, or exchanging goods and services (see, e.g., Bonn, 1970, 1972; Domke, 1968; Haggard & Mentschikoff, 1960; Jones, 1956, 1958; Lazarus et al., 1965; Mentschikoff, 1952, 1961; Smith, 1956), because disputes inevitably arise in connection with such transactions. Typically, one party claims that the other did not live up to some agreement about quality, quantity, or timing. If the parties do not resolve the issue themselves, they can informally ask a third party to settle the dispute; they can use the formal legal system (the courts) to obtain a decision; or they can use institutionalized arbitration machinery, such as the American Arbitration Association (AAA).

The AAA has several advantages for dispute settlement. It has facilities and procedures to assure that arbitration is conducted so that the decision is final and legally binding. It can also provide arbitrators who have expertise relevant to a wide range of business situations. Thus the AAA has the advantages of the formal legal system in settling disputes and reputedly can do so with greater speed, economy, and efficiency than the courts.

For a variety of reasons, commercial arbitration at the AAA is a particularly good setting for conducting research. (1) Because the deciders are experienced arbitrators, the decision-making process in an experimental setting is likely to correspond to that in an actual arbitration. (2) Because the AAA panel of available arbitrators includes persons with expertise in many substantive areas, researchers can study how those who know the customary business practices relevant to a dispute approach that dispute and reach a decision. (3) Because of the size of the AAA panel, it is possible to construct ad hoc groups of deciders who do not

know each other so that the decision-making process will not be contaminated by idiosyncratic procedures, norms, or roles that can develop in groups that meet repeatedly. (4) Because in the AAA three arbitrators usually are used when a dispute involves substantial sums of money, researchers can trace with relative ease how the arbitrators reach consensus as to what the proper decision should be.

## GENERAL PROCEDURE

The research reported here grew out of several preliminary phases. First, persons from the law and the behavioral sciences observed arbitrations at the AAA offices in Chicago and New York.[2] In all cases, we observed the hearings (where the parties—with or without legal counsel—presented their sides) and the deliberations (where arbitrators reached their decision). Second, we spelled out our impressions of how each arbitrator came to a decision and how and why each group of three did, or did not, achieve consensus. Third, we sketched a theoretical statement compatible both with our own observations and relevant theoretical statements (see, e.g., Aubert, 1969; Cardozo, 1921; Converse, 1968; Diesing, 1962; Eckhoff & Jacobson, 1960; Friedrich, 1964; Hamilton, 1932; Kalven & Zeisel, 1966; Kelley & Thibaut, 1969; Levi, 1963; Llewellyn, 1960; Michael & Adler, 1934; Peltason, Gluckman, Karlen, & Tannenhaus, 1968; Schaefer, 1956; Schubert, 1963, 1964, 1965; Simon, 1967). Two approaches were then used to test some aspects of our theory: (1) A modified tape of the hearings of a commercial dispute was presented to arbitrator panels to test the effect of certain conditions on decision making and consensus; (2) a series of complete arbitrations was recorded

---

[2] In addition to the authors, Jean M. Allard participated in this phase. For all the arbitration proceedings that were observed and tape-recorded, permission was given by the AAA, the arbitrators, the parties to the dispute, and their legal counsel.

to test aspects of the theory that could not be experimentally controlled. Some findings from the experiments are discussed in this chapter.

## ASPECTS OF A THEORY OF RESPONSIBLE DECISION MAKING

### The Role of Issues and Norms

Our theory assumes that to reach a rational decision, the decider must have clearly in mind the central issue (or issues) on which the decision will hinge. If the parties do not articulate and agree on the issue, it is up to the decider to determine it. Issue selection is central to rational decision making, since not everything that occurred or that is said during the hearing is of equal relevance to the dispute. Without knowing the issue, the decider cannot separate the relevant from the irrelevant. The issue selected thus serves (along with the appropriate norms) as a filter to screen the flow of material so that the decider can sift out and piece together whatever seems to be relevant.

The theory also assumes that the decider cannot rationally settle a dispute unless and until some reasonably coherent pictures of the *is* and the *ought* can be formed. For example, (1) what did the parties do to lead to the dispute, and (2) what should they have done under the circumstances.[3] To do this the decider must apply appropriate fact-find-

ing and substantive norms to the evidence. The fact-finding norms enable the decider to determine the inherent probability of the series of events that led to the dispute (including the likelihood that the parties are telling the truth) by relying on expectations of how individuals typically behave in such situations. The substantive norms enable the decider to determine what should, or should not, occur in particular classes of situations, which in turn indicate how behavior in those situations should be guided and hence may be judged.

It is also assumed that what the parties did and should have done that differ most obviously (as in the discrepancies between two partly overlapping geometric figures) should be more easily seen and remembered than what was essentially congruent. Thus, in comparing the dual pictures, the decider should focus on how the parties appear to have acted improperly.

Finally, it is assumed that, as the decider forms coherent pictures and can compare them, he or she can move through the steps that will determine the decision. Thus, if the decider can (1) determine the points of agreement or disagreement between the two pictures, it will be possible to (2) determine at what points and to what extent the behavior of each party coincides or is discrepant with what the decider believes each should have done. It will then be possible to (3) determine in what ways and to what extent each of the parties is in the right or wrong. When the decider reaches this point, (4) *essentially the decision has been reached—even though it may not have been articulated formally either privately or publicly.* In arbitrations involving business transactions, the decision usually is a "yes" or "no" answer to the plaintiff's claim and, if the answer is "yes," the amount to be awarded the plaintiff.

### The Role of Experience

The extent to which the decider can determine the central issue in a dispute and

---

[3] The formation of pictures of what *did* and what *should* have happened appears to follow laws of perceptual organization enumerated by Gestalt psychologists. The more coherent and developed the pictures, the more stable and resistant to change they become. Thus, as an individual's pictures become well articulated, internally consistent, and supported by relevant norms and evidence, the effect of new but incompatible evidence will tend to be minimized, and "missing" relevant evidence will tend to be filled in by the decider so that the pictures tend to maintain their coherence and remain convincing to the one who developed them.

apply the relevant fact-finding and sub-stantive norms is largely a function of background. Also, the more experience the decider has with situations similar to the dispute, the more this person is an "expert" with respect to such disputes. Degree of expertise tends to determine how the dispute is viewed, the ease with which it is handled, confidence in the decision, and hence its stability.

That a decider holds clearly articulated fact-finding and substantive norms does not indicate the nature of the norms or how they will be used. Insofar as individuals' experiences differ, it can be expected that they may hold different norms, apply them differently, and select different central issues —and so rationally may arrive at contradictory decisions.

Although responsible decisions tend to be made rationally, nonrational components are always present. One such component is because the decision involves other individuals. Besides viewing parties in terms of their actions, deciders also respond to them as persons. Thus, the more deciders see a similarity between themselves and one party in backgrounds, professional affiliations, value systems, and so forth, the more they tend to have an affinity to that party. Affinity usually includes more than just affective components: For example, familiarity with a party's business practices increases deciders' "understanding" of what the party is talking about and the party's motivations. Deciders' affinity to a party usually biases them in favor of that party.

Negative as well as positive affinities can develop (e.g., "I do not like thee, Dr. Fell."). Also, if deciders have a strong positive affinity to a party whose actions violate deciders' substantive norms, they may view that party's actions more harshly than if their affinity were minimal. But in any case, the factor of interpersonal affinity makes it difficult (if not impossible) for deciders to be completely impartial in their appraisal of the parties and their actions. (A more extensive description of our theoretical formulation is given in Chap. 23.)

## RESEARCH PROCEDURE

Our study sought to test certain aspects of our theory of how responsible decisions are made. To do this, we presented a taped dispute to arbitrators with varying occupational backgrounds. The dispute used was a modified version of the hearing from an arbitration recorded at the AAA. Changes were made to disguise the original dispute and modify the content so that arbitrators —depending on how they saw and evaluated the issues and evidence—could decide reasonably for either the plaintiff or the defendant.

### Summary of the Dispute

*Facts in the dispute.* Mr. Crane, the defendant, is a broker with sole rights to import closet rods manufactured in West Germany for sale in the United States. He signed a two-year contract with Mr. Temple, the plaintiff, giving him an exclusive distributorship (starting January 1) whereby Temple agreed to purchase a quota of 50,000 closet rod sets every 6 months and not to purchase and sell competing products. Crane had the right to cancel the contract on notice given 30 days before the expiration of any 6-month period in which Temple failed to meet the quota.

During the first 6 months ending June 30, Temple purchased 32,000 of the 50,000 quota. On June 20, Crane wrote a letter stating that he was not exercising his option to cancel as of May 31, but also that he did not waive any right to demand the purchase of the total 50,000 sets during the second half year, so that Temple was obliged to order at least 100,000 sets before the end of the year. Temple testified that Crane told him shortly thereafter to disregard the June 20 letter, that it was written to satisfy the manufacturer in Germany, and that he, Crane, was satisfied with Temple's performance. During the hearing Crane denied saying this.

Meanwhile, Temple had a part of the product manufactured in Japan. He testified that this purchase was only to establish the price for similar quality goods. The contract contained a clause forbidding Temple to purchase and sell closet rods other than those supplied by Crane. Temple did not sell any of these Japanese goods.

By November 1 Temple had ordered an additional 30,000 sets. Later that month Crane signed a contract with another distributor, and a few days after that he wrote to Temple cancelling the contract for failure to meet the quota and because of the Japanese purchase. Temple testified that he offered to tender a letter of credit for 19,000 additional sets immediately upon receiving the cancellation letter, but that Crane refused to accept his offer. Crane testified that he never actually refused the tender, since he had not received a letter of credit. Temple testified that he would have been willing to make any necessary additional purchases during December had Crane requested him to do so. It was undisputed that Crane made no such request of Temple and that Temple did not indicate to Crane his willingness to place such orders.

The plaintiff, Temple, claimed damages of $32,917.21 for improper cancellation. This amount included $5,982.87 of alleged out-of-pocket expenses ($1,686.62 of which was for contracted advertising costs for the month of December), $5,417.50 for alleged actual loss of profits, and $21,516.84 for expected loss of profits for the next year, based on his expectation of the same rate of sales.

*Issues in the dispute.* The issues include whether the contract between the parties should be interpreted as requiring Temple to purchase 50,000 closet rod sets each 6 months (as originally stipulated) or whether the original terms of the contract had been waived by the parties and, if so, by whom, in what way, and to what degree. In the event of waiver, various aspects of the parties' motivations and behavior, as presented in the tape, may be used as issues to decide the dispute.

## Research Hypotheses

Our theoretical formulation suggested a number of hypotheses regarding responsible decision making and decision consensus, four of which are discussed here. Two pertain to the decision-making process: (1) The decider's choice of the central issue in the dispute will tend to determine how relevant evidence is viewed and interpreted, including specific behaviors of the parties; these perceptions will, in turn, help to determine the ultimate decision in favor of one party. (2) The decider who feels an affinity to one party in a dispute will tend to find for that party. Two hypotheses pertain to the decision-consensus process: (3) The decider's arguments during the deliberations will not necessarily mirror a private view of the parties and their performance. (4) The decider who argues effectively during the deliberations will tend to emphasize which party and which actions are at fault more than which party performed adequately.

## Experimental Subjects and Conditions

The research setting was the American Arbitration Association offices in New York. We chose participants from the AAA Panel of approximately 5000 arbitrators in the area and used AAA facilities and hearing rooms. AAA arbitrators took part because of their commitment to the AAA as an institution and their interest in the subject. They were not otherwise compensated.

The 180 male arbitrators were randomly selected from specified occupational categories. Data from 30 brokers and 30 manufacturers are reported here. Brokers were chosen because they generally rely on contracts that are relatively standardized and not often modified or waived. Thus, it was thought, they would give major weight to the contract as written rather than as it might have been modified by the parties' conduct. Also, since Crane was essentially a broker, it was assumed that affinity might influence the brokers' views of the parties and the dispute. It was thus hypothesized that they would tend to decide in favor of Crane, the defendant. Manufacturers were chosen because their business was thought to involve some modifications or waivers of contracts in the course of performance. The manufacturers were not expected to emphasize the contract as written, but rather to emphasize its intent and the parties' motivations and behaviors. Thus, it was hypothesized that the manufacturers would tend to show a stronger tendency than the brokers to decide in favor of Temple, the plaintiff.

Each experimental panel had three arbitrators. There were four types of panels: two "pure"—all brokers or manufacturers; and two "mixed"—two from one occupation and one from the other. There were five panels of each type.

### Experimental Procedures

On arrival at the AAA offices, each panel selected a chairman and was told the general nature and purpose of the research. They were then given the documents pertinent to the dispute and listened to the 45-minute tape of the dispute. Immediately after hearing the tape, each arbitrator was asked privately to indicate the degree to which he favored the plantiff or the defendant (the pre-deliberation award). Then the arbitrators were asked to reach a decision as a panel in favor of either party. At the end of the deliberations any arbitrator who had not stated his dollar award was asked to do so (the post-deliberation award). The deliberations—which ran from five minutes to over an hour—were tape-recorded. At the end of the deliberations each arbitrator completed a 41-item questionnaire "as he would have filled it out just after hearing the tape."

### The Data

**1.** The *pre-deliberation award* question was asked each arbitrator privately just after the tape of the dispute had been heard. Responses were scaled from 1 (strongly pro-defendant) to 6 (strongly pro-plaintiff).
**2.** The *post-deliberation award* was based on each arbitrator's statement at the end of the deliberations of the dollar amount of the damages, if any, that he would award to the plaintiff. The amounts were categorized as being pro-defendant (1 = $0; 2 = $84) or pro-plaintiff (3 = $85 to $5000; 4 = $5001 to $10,000; 5 = $10,001 to $15,000; and 6 = over $15,000).

**3.** The *41-item questionnaire* measured, among other things, the arbitrators' views of the central and secondary issues in the dispute as well as their evaluations of the parties' character and performance.[4] Ratings ranged from 1 (strongly agree) to 6 (strongly disagree). The 15 items cited in this chapter are:

#### Central Issue Items:

Item 8. This dispute hinges primarily upon the interpretation of the contract (pro-defendant)

Item 18. The essential elements in this dispute have to do with the fact that *both* Mr. Crane and Mr. Temple waived provision of the contract (pro-plaintiff)

Item 20. This dispute involves primarily the evaluation of the motives and behavior of the parties (pro-plaintiff)

#### Evaluation of the Defendant (Crane)

Item 17. Mr. Crane is a good businessman whose behavior is essentially typical (pro-defendant)

Item 6. Mr. Crane appears to be evasive and unwilling to answer questions in a forthright manner, which casts doubt on his own credibility in this case (pro-plaintiff)

Item 26. Mr. Crane is a sharp businessman whom I would not be inclined to trust (pro-plaintiff)

---

[4] The 41 items were randomly ordered; the numbers here indicate their order in the questionnaire. "Pro-defendant" or "pro-plaintiff" after each item indicates the predicted award direction of the item if the arbitrator agreed with it. Other items deal with aspects of commercial arbitration as a decision-making procedure, the role of contracts in business dealings, and whether a contract's language or its intent is more important. For items not marked by an arbitrator, a score of 3 (tend to agree) or 4 (tend to disagree) was assigned randomly to avoid statistical complications of working with missing data.

### Evaluation of the Plaintiff (Temple)

Item 9.  Mr. Temple is a conscientious businessman who always tried to do the best he could with his product (pro-plaintiff)

Item 24.  It is unlikely that anyone would purchase an order the size of Mr. Temple's Japanese order without the intention of selling the merchandise (pro-defendant)

Item 37.  Mr. Temple seems basically untrustworthy (pro-defendant)

### Performance of the Defendant (Crane)

Item 1.  Mr. Crane had every right to sign a contract with a different company to handle the product since Mr. Temple was obviously behind in his orders (pro-defendant)

Item 3.  Mr. Temple was unjustly treated by Mr. Crane (pro-plaintiff)

Item 22.  Mr. Crane was trying to get out of the contract because he had a better deal with Midwest Furniture Wholesale Company (pro-plaintiff)

### Performance of the Plaintiff (Temple)

Item 12.  Mr. Temple is standing on a technicality to try to get money, which he doesn't deserve, from Mr. Crane (pro-defendant)

Item 23.  A correct interpretation of the "purchase and sale" issue indicates that Mr. Temple had no right to even purchase goods from Japan (pro-defendant)

Item 35.  Mr. Temple's offer to purchase during the first few days of December was substantially within the terms of the contract, and Mr. Crane was obliged to accept those orders (pro-plaintiff)

4. *Content analysis of the deliberations.*

The taped deliberations were transcribed and each "statement," that is, independent thought unit, was coded jointly by two law-trained assistants (see also Haggard, Baittle, & Isaacs, 1968). There were 40 mutually exclusive substantive categories (e.g., the performance of the parties) and 33 non-substantive categories (e.g., a wish to see and question parties). Each statement by each arbitrator was coded in only one of the 273 categories.

Not everything said by the arbitrators during the deliberations was useful. Of the 3599 statements made by 60 arbitrators before the group decision was reached, only 1213 dealt explicitly with the substantive aspects of the dispute—statements indicating the application of substantive norms to the evidence. Of the remaining 2386 nonsubstantive statements, however, only 26 were not relevant to the dispute.

## Data Analysis Procedures

Data were analyzed so that different groups of arbitrators could be compared. Two pairs of comparisons, already mentioned, are the occupation of the arbitrators and the composition of the panels. The arbitrators were compared also in terms of what they selected as the central issue and whether they changed their award.

*Issue selection groups.* The central issue in disputes involving a contract is whether or to what extent the conduct of the parties met the terms set forth in the contract. "The contract," however, may mean the written document, or as it may be interpreted in light of the parties' later actions. In the questionnaire the contract issue was addressed in item 8, "This dispute hinges primarily upon the interpretation of the contract," and item 18, "The essential elements in this dispute have to do with the fact that *both* Mr. Crane and Mr. Temple waived provisions of the contract." If an arbitrator took "contract" to mean the written document, then to agree with item 8 and disagree with item 18 would be to take a clear pro-defendant position—since Temple did not meet the quota of 50,000 sets during either half of the year. But if an arbitrator found that the terms of the contract had been waived or otherwise altered by the later conduct of the parties (e.g., Crane's failure to cancel by June 1), to agree with item 18 (and either to agree or disagree with item 8) would be to take a pro-plaintiff position.

If an arbitrator held that the contract had been waived, just acknowledging the existence of waiver would not be enough. To reach a decision, standards apart from the original contract must be used. Thus, item 20 was included, "This dispute involves primarily the evaluation of the motives and behavior of the parties." Agreement with this item and disagreement with items 8 and 18 would reject the contract as the central issue and, given the nature of this dispute, indicate a moderate pro-plaintiff position. For an arbitrator to agree with items 18 and 20 would be to take a strong pro-plaintiff position. Finally, for an arbitrator to agree or disagree with all three items suggests that the dispute or the central issue may not have been properly understood.

Three issue selection groups were formed on the basis of the response patterns of the 60 arbitrators: (1) 26 chose the written contract as the central issue (pro-Crane); (2) 14 chose waiver and/or the parties' motivation and behavior as the central issue (pro-Temple); and (3) 20 were equivocal as to the central issue.

*Decision stability groups.* During or after the deliberations, 18 shifters (from 15 of the 20 panels) changed their award from pro-defendant to pro-plaintiff, or vice versa. The 39 nonshifters did not thus change their award. (Many arbitrators did, of course, change from a strong to a moderate position, or vice versa; and 3 were not categorized since they said that they could not decide before the deliberation for either party.) Finally, by changing their awards,

16 shifters achieved decision consensus; whereas the other 2 were on 2 panels that remained in dissent.

## RESULTS

### Part I: Decision Making

Findings on decision making are based primarily on (1) the pre-deliberation award, (2) the post-deliberation award, and (3) responses to the questionnaire items.

*Hypothesis 1: The decider's choice of the central issue in the dispute will tend to determine how relevant evidence is viewed and interpreted, including specific behaviors of the parties; these perceptions will, in turn, help to determine the ultimate decision in favor of one party.* The importance of issue selection can be seen by comparing the responses of the 26 pro-contract and 14 pro-waiver arbitrators. On 9 of 12 items the views of the two issue groups differed at or beyond the customary level of statistical significance, $p = .05$ (see Table 1, col. 4). Only two performance items did not differentiate these groups: The arbitrators in both groups tended to be lukewarm regarding Temple's prowess as a businessman (item 9) and to disapprove of his Japanese purchase (item 23). Although their view of the Japanese purchase correlated at $p = .001$ with their evaluations of his credibility (item 24; $r = .52$) and his trustworthiness (item 37; $r = .46$), it did not correlate with their view of his conscientiousness as a businessman (item 9; $r = -.04$). Apparently the arbitrators tended to separate their evaluation of Temple's personal character from how they saw him as a businessman. Finally, as hypothesized, the two issue groups differed significantly with respect to their pre-deliberation ($p = .009$) and post-deliberation ($p = .002$) awards. These data thus indicate that meaningful, statistically significant relationships exist linking the arbitrators' choice of the central issue, their view of the parties and their performance, and their decision or award.

An examination of the correlation between responses to each central issue item and the other two issue items, the six evaluation items, the six performance items, and the two awards indicates that the presence or absence of waiver was the key central issue. Not only did waiver correlate beyond the .001 level with the other issue items (av. $r = .42$); it also correlated at the same level with 8 of 12 evaluation and performance items (av. $r = .41$). Note, too, that responses to the issue of waiver were related at the .0001 level to both pre-deliberation ($r = .54$) and post-deliberation ($r = .57$) awards. Responses to the other two issue items also were significantly related to their decisions, especially their final award ($p = .01$). These findings thus support the proposition that the decider's perception of the central issue in a dispute relates to his evaluation of the parties and their performance

and to his ultimate decision or award. However, separate factor analyses of the responses of the pro-defendant and pro-plaintiff arbitrators indicate that they also had formed general notions of which party was "the good guy" and which was "the bad guy" and that their awards were compatible with these notions.

*Hypothesis 2: The decider who feels an affinity to one party in a dispute will tend to find for that party.* As noted, the defendant, Crane, was a broker in that he acted as an agent to purchase closet rods for resale. The brokers who participated in this research were brokers in this sense or, like stock brokers, were agents who arranged transactions between buyers and sellers. Because of the assumed similarity of business practices and relationships it was hypothesized that brokers would tend to feel affinity to—and hence to find for—the defendant.

As indicated in Table 1, column 7, the

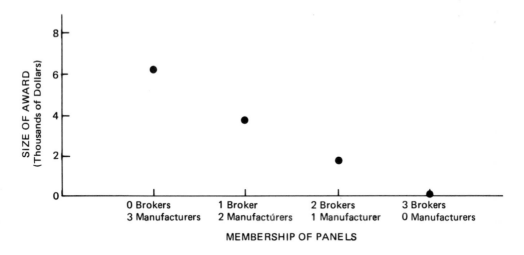

**Fig. 1.** Occupational membership of panels and the average award to the plaintiff. The average dollar amounts for the four panel types are, respectively, $6300, $3780, $1780, and $34 from the three-manufacturer to the three-broker panels.

**TABLE 1    Differences in Average Response to Questionnaire Items by Issue and Occupational Groups**

| QUESTIONNAIRE ITEMS | Pro-a | ISSUE SELECTION GROUPS | | | OCCUPATIONAL GROUPS | | | |
| --- | --- | --- | --- | --- | --- | --- | --- | --- |
| | | Contract (N = 26) | Waiver (N = 14) | Differences (p value)b | Brokers (N = 30) | Manufacturers (N = 30) | Differences (p values)b,c | |
| | (1) | (2) | (3) | (4) | (5) | (6) | (7) | (8) |
| *Central Issue* | | | | | | | | |
| 8. The contract as written | Def. | 1.6 | 4.5 | .0001d | 2.2 | 2.6 | .27 | .72 |
| 18. Waiver of the contract | Pl. | 4.9 | 2.6 | .0001d | 3.6 | 3.3 | .41 | .73 |
| 20. Motivation and behavior | Pl. | 3.4 | 2.8 | .21d | 3.0 | 2.8 | .67 | .83 |
| *Evaluation of Defendant* | | | | | | | | |
| 17. A good businessman | Def. | 2.5 | 3.7 | .0002 | 2.8 | 3.4 | .03 | .24 |
| 6. Credibility questioned | Pl. | 4.5 | 3.0 | .0003 | 4.1 | 3.1 | .002 | .01 |
| 26. Trustworthiness questioned | Pl. | 4.7 | 3.9 | .01 | 4.3 | 4.0 | .17 | .34 |
| *Evaluation of Plaintiff* | | | | | | | | |
| 9. A good businessman | Pl. | 3.5 | 3.0 | .18 | 3.3 | 3.1 | .65 | .88 |
| 24. Credibility questioned | Def. | 2.4 | 3.8 | .002 | 2.7 | 3.0 | .40 | .88 |
| 37. Trustworthiness questioned | Def. | 3.7 | 4.4 | .08 | 4.0 | 3.9 | .72 | .46 |
| *Performance of Defendant* | | | | | | | | |
| 1. New contract OK | Def. | 2.3 | 4.1 | .0003 | 2.9 | 3.8 | .03 | .26 |
| 3. Treated Temple unjustly | Pl. | 4.8 | 3.9 | .02 | 4.3 | 3.8 | .15 | .58 |
| 22. Cancellation (better deal) | Pl. | 4.0 | 3.1 | .04 | 3.6 | 3.2 | .21 | .69 |
| *Performance of Plaintiff* | | | | | | | | |
| 12. Standing on technicality | Def. | 2.8 | 3.8 | .02 | 3.3 | 3.3 | .93 | .19 |
| 23. Japanese purchase wrong | Def. | 2.6 | 2.9 | .62 | 2.6 | 2.7 | .72 | .91 |
| 35. Offer in December OK | Pl. | 4.2 | 3.1 | .02 | 3.9 | 3.0 | .02 | .11 |
| *The Awards* | | | | | | | | |
| Pre-deliberation | | 1.6 | 2.5 | .009 | 1.8 | 2.5 | .01 | .05 |
| Post-deliberation | | 1.5 | 2.9 | .002 | 1.9 | 2.8 | .01 | .24 |

*<sup>a</sup>The award direction of each item indicates which party is favored, depending on whether one agrees or disagrees with the item as stated.*

*<sup>b</sup>The p value designates the probability that a difference as large or larger would occur by chance (i.e., random fluctuations) alone if a large number of comparable samples were collected under the same experimental conditions. Thus, a p value of .01 (cf. item 26, col. 4) sometimes is read as "one chance in a hundred," and is the traditional level for calling a difference "highly significant." All p values are based on the conservative "two-tailed test."*

*<sup>c</sup>The p values in col. 7 are based on a direct comparison of occupational groups. The p values in col. 8 are based on a comparison between occupational groups after any effects due to panel type (pure, mixed) and final award (pro-defendant, pro-plaintiff) have been removed (cf. Bock, 1975; Bock & Haggard, 1968). Hence, for example, the change in the p value for post-deliberation award from .01 to .24.*

*<sup>d</sup>Criteria for determining composition of the two issue selection groups.*

brokers more than the manufacturers favored the defendant over the plaintiff on both their pre- and post-deliberation awards ($p = .01$). Also, as Figure 1 shows, the more brokers there were on a panel, the smaller the average amount awarded to the plaintiff. Furthermore, all 15 brokers who served on "pure" panels, but only 8 of 15 who served on "mixed" panels, found for the defendant ($p = .01$).

Were there corresponding differences in arbitrators' responses to the central issue, evaluation, and performance items? One would expect most brokers to be in the contract group and most manufacturers to be in the waiver and/or motivation and behavior group. This tendency, although present, was weak ($p = .25$). Likewise, one would expect brokers and manufacturers to differ on the evaluation and performance items, but they differed significantly on only 4 of 12 items (see Table 1, col. 7). That is, brokers more than manufacturers tended to assert that Crane was truthful, that he was a good businessman, that he was justified in contracting with a different company in November and in not accepting Temple's offer of additional orders early in December (items 6, 17, 1, and 35).

In a further analysis removing the effects of panel type and final award, only 1 of the 15 items in Table 1 continued to differentiate the two groups (see col. 8): On item 6, the brokers still showed a stronger tendency to affirm that Crane was telling the truth ($p = .01$). Furthermore, on one additional item dealing directly with affinity (item 10: "If I were to meet Mr. Crane I would not like him"), the brokers tended to disagree more than the manufacturers did ($p = .05$).

That the brokers showed a stronger tendency than the manufacturers to find for the defendant but not primarily on the basis of issues and performance suggests that affinity to the defendant influenced at least some brokers. Also, that the pro-defendant bias was more apparent for broker-only groups suggests that affinity may not always manifest itself. When one is expected to be impartial, a factor such as affinity to one party hardly substitutes for a well-articulated, issue-oriented approach to decision making and decision consensus.

**Part II: Decision Consensus**

Methodologically, the strength of the questionnaire lies in its ability to ensure coverage of key aspects of the dispute, but it offered no opportunity for the arbitrator to freely express any other views. Content analysis of the deliberations was designed to assess the arbitrator's freely-expressed views of the parties and their performance, the relation of his views to his decision, and his argument strategies while attempting to achieve decision consensus with colleagues.

*Hypothesis 3: The decider's arguments during the deliberations do not necessarily mirror a private view of the parties and their performance.* When arbitrators' private views regarding waiver, as expressed in responses to item 18, were correlated with public affirmations of waiver during the deliberations, the $r$ was found to be .30 ($p = .01$). A somewhat more broadly based method of comparing arbitrators' private and public views is to correlate their responses to selected questionnaire items with the net award direction of corresponding deliberation statements. Six topics—three on Crane's general performance, his contracting with a different company, and his cancelling of his contract with Temple; and three on Temple's general performance, his purchase of Japanese parts, and his offer to purchase additional closet rods early in December—were correlated with corresponding questionnaire items to "test" hypothesis 3. These six correlations ranged from .05 (Temple's general performance) to .58 (his Japanese purchase), with an average $r$ of .34, five of which were statistically significant ($p = .01$).

That five of six coefficients were significant is not relevant to hypothesis 3. What is relevant is the extent to which the correlations between the two sets of measures are less than 1.00, not whether they are greater than 0. If arbitrators' responses had corresponded in both direction and degree to the net award direction of their statements during the deliberations, the correlations would have approximated 1.00, and hypothesis 3 would be untenable. However, since an average $r$ of .34, or even an $r$ of .58, hardly approximates the limiting value of 1.00, hypothesis 3 is tenable.

Why arbitrators' public and private views of the dispute tend to differ is complex. One reason for the difference is that, in responding to the questionnaire, they did not have to take into account the other panel members' views as they did in the deliberations. Also, during the deliberations an arbitrator might not bother to state a point if a colleague already had done so, or the decider might introduce arguments to defend his private position or persuade another member to change his view and hence the award.

*Hypothesis 4: The decider who argues effectively during the deliberations will tend to emphasize which party and which actions are at fault more than which party performed adequately.* This hypothesis assumes that the decider's thinking is influenced not so much by similarities but by what is seen as discrepant between the *is* and the *ought*. The validity of this assumption may be attenuated in the case of decision consensus, where two or more persons who disagree initially try to reach agreement. If so, the fact that arbitrators in 15 of 20 panels began their deliberations in dissent can be expected to modify the hypothesized relation between the arbitrators' perceptions of the dispute and how they argued about it.

Dissent had several effects, one being that deliberations became more extensive. Arbitrators in the 15 dissenting panels averaged 75.5 statements as compared with 12.8 by those in the 5 unanimous panels ($p = .0001$) Dissent also increased the discrepancy between perceptions of the dispute (as indicated by questionnaire responses) and arguments during the deliberations, where an arbitrator has to consider colleagues' arguments and try to persuade others to change their views (if they differ) or to support them (if they agree). The data in Table 2 indicate that discrepant statements were often made: In fact, 60 percent of the pro-Crane and 39 percent of the pro-Temple nonshifters' statements were not compatible with their final award.

The data in Table 2 hardly provide strong or unequivocal support for hypothesis 4. Although the 13 pro-Temple nonshifters did

**TABLE 2    Selected Arbitrator Statements Regarding the Parties and Their Performance[a]**

| STATEMENTS[b] | 20 Pro-Crane Nonshifters | | | 13 Pro-Temple Nonshifters | | |
|---|---|---|---|---|---|---|
| | OK | Not OK | Total | OK | Not OK | Total |
| Re. Crane | 81 | 41 | 122 | 42 | 77 | 119 |
| Re. Temple | 116 | 24 | 140 | 57 | 43 | 100 |

[a]*The data include all nonshifters' statements coded in 116 of the content categories that pertain to (a) both parties' credibility and trustworthiness; (b) their general performance; (c) Crane's signing a new contract with a different company and his cancelling the one with Temple; and (d) Temple's Japanese purchase and his offer to order additional sets from Crane in December. All statement data (frequencies) were transformed to permit use of analysis of variance procedures.*

[b]*"OK" statements indicate approval of, and "Not OK" statements indicate disapproval of, the parties and/or their performance.*

make somewhat more anti-Crane than pro-Temple statements (77 vs. 57), the 26 pro-Crane nonshifters showed a strong tendency to make more statements that were pro-Crane than anti-Temple (81 vs. 24; $p = .001$) and even made more statements that were favorable to Temple than to Crane (116 vs. 81). Furthermore, the award direction of the arguments made by the 38 pro-Crane and 22 pro-Temple arbitrators did not differ appreciably with respect to the five areas that pertained to evaluations of Temple and his performance; in discussing Crane, however, they differed significantly (see Table 2, note a). In other words, the pro-Crane arbitrators' statements about Temple were not much less favorable than those of the pro-Temple arbitrators ($p$'s from .19 to .98), but the pro-Temple arbitrators' statements were significantly less favorable about Crane than those of the pro-Crane arbitrators ($p$'s from .05 to .004).

The differences in the argument tendencies of the two award groups may well stem from the central issues they chose and their perceptions of the parties and what they did. The pro-Temple arbitrators, not having a clear and simple issue, apparently had to argue that Crane had, for example, acted in bad faith and had not performed adequately, or at least not so well as Temple. But pro-Crane arbitrators, who identified the contract as the central issue, found it sufficient to observe that Temple had failed to meet its terms. These arbitrators thus could afford to make positive statements about Temple and his behavior since, in the final analysis, Temple had not lived up to the terms of the contract, which for them was decisive.

## DISCUSSION

In the research reported here arbitrators (brokers and manufacturers) met in assorted three-member panels to settle a dispute presented to them in a 45-minute tape recording. The fact that, overall, the award was split two-to-one in favor of the defendant, with three-fourths of the brokers and half of the manufacturers deciding thus, raises many questions regarding decision making and decision consensus.

*If all the arbitrators listened to the same dispute, and if they made their decisions rationally, why did their awards differ so much?* We have assumed that, in decision-making situations in which third parties have responsibility for dispute settlement, the decision tends to be made on rational grounds. As used here, rationality involves the decider's comparing personal pictures of the *is* and the *ought*. It does not specify what the *is* and the *ought* will be for any decider, hence what the consequent decision will be, or that others will consider it to be "right" or "wrong." On the contrary, in any given dispute, if the *is* and the *ought* differ significantly for any two deciders, their decisions will differ. It is therefore appropriate to qualify the assumption that all the arbitrators listened to the "same" dispute just because they listened to the same tape. To the extent that the arbitrators perceived differently the relevant issues, norms, and what the parties had done, it can be assumed that they listened to "different" disputes, which enabled them to arrive at different decisions.

It might seem that arbitrators' decisions were made largely on the basis of whim or sundry "chance" factors. But, as the data cited in connection with hypothesis 1 indicate, how the arbitrators viewed the central issue was significantly related to how they also viewed a variety of key aspects of the dispute and, consequently, to how they decided it.

Affinity appears to be an exception to the general tendency toward rational decisions. The data cited in connection with hypothesis 2 indicate that, for some brokers at least, affinity helped to shape their decision. But affinity appeared to predominate only when brokers met in pure panels. A second exception is that some arbitrators appear to have failed to understand the dispute, did not grasp the central issue, or could not apply the appropriate fact-finding and substantive norms to the evidence. These arbitrators often were equivocal in responding to items pertaining to parties and their performance, a tendency that characterized shifters more than nonshifters.

*What factors seemed to determine decision stability, as indicated by the characteristics of those arbitrators who held to their decision versus those who changed it during deliberations?* There is no simple answer. For example, it is likely that an arbitrator only tentatively pro-defendant before the deliberations who was assigned to a panel with two others who were strongly pro-defendant would be a nonshifter. But if the same arbitrator had been assigned to a panel with colleagues who held the contrary award position strongly and had greater experience and expertise relevant to the dispute, the decider almost certainly would have become a shifter.

Attempts were made to identify factors that differentiated shifters and nonshifters. We obtained measures of the arbitrators' personalities and characteristic modes of behavior in small group situations. For the sample of arbitrators reported in this chapter, such measures did not differentiate meaningfully between the two groups. Shifters and nonshifters did differ, however, in their questionnaire responses and in the relation of these responses to their final award: The nonshifters' responses were both more emphatic and more clearly related to their final award than were those of the shifters ($p = .01$).

*How did the arbitrators argue during the deliberations?* As has been noted, arbitrators in the dissent panels talked more than those in the unanimous panels. In addition, during deliberations pro-Crane arbitrators averaged 34.9 statements, whereas pro-Temple arbitrators averaged 102.9 statements ($p = .0001$). Similarly, panels deciding for Crane took less time to reach decisions than those that decided for Temple ($p = .002$). But there was no reason to expect significant differences between brokers and manufacturers, or shifters and nonshifters, on such measures and, indeed, none existed ($p = .59$ and .89, respectively).

Only a detailed sequential analysis of the statements made during each deliberation could describe adequately all the argument strategies.[5] Lacking such analysis, two points can be drawn from the data cited in connection with hypothesis 4: A surprisingly large proportion of arbitrators' arguments were incompatible with their award (see Table 2). Frequent argument strategies that made for this discrepancy include an arbitrator's conceding minor or lost points, sounding out a possible adversary's views, and trying to establish an alliance with another arbitrator in the hope of later inducing a change in views—at least enough to change the award. These data thus illustrate the importance of knowing the decider's private views in order to understand the purpose and meaning of the argument strategy. Further, the data also reveal some general characteristics of arbitrators' arguments. Most statements (about 90%) pertained to the parties' performance, two-thirds of which related to specific, rather than general, aspects of their behavior.

Why did the arbitrators prefer to argue in terms of specific actions of the parties? The fact that they argued in terms of what the parties did and ought to have done may not describe how they arrived at decisions so

---

[5] Insofar as it is not possible to replicate completely dispute-settlement situations, one must seek to grasp the uniqueness of the particular dispute. Llewellyn wrote: "The lawyer does not ask: How does an appellate tribunal arrive at *a* decision, *some* decision, *any* decision—in general . . . in perhaps three, even four or seven, cases out of ten? The lawyer asks, instead: How does *this* appellate tribunal arrive at the *particular and concrete answer* which it reaches *in the particular and concrete* case [1960, pp. 15–16]?" Methodologically, then, responsible decision making in dispute settlement typically uses the idiographic approach, whereas behavioral science uses (when possible) the nomothetic approach (see Allport, 1942, 1962; Holt, 1962). In the pursuit of understanding, the former relies on a subjective sense of certainty whereas the latter seeks to rely on an objectively defined estimate of probability.

much as how they justified them. Even the recordings of the deliberations do not reveal the mixture and sequence of rational and nonrational components that led to a decision. Thus, some arbitrators may have reached decisions initially on the basis of personal reactions to the parties but thought it neither proper nor expedient to express them. Perhaps the arbitrators displaced and disguised such reactions by focusing on specific aspects of the parties' behavior and by couching their arguments in terms of what the parties did and should have done.

*How are the findings of this research relevant to related decision-making situations?* Several characteristics that apply to dispute settlement in commercial arbitration provide a basis for generalizing from the findings of this research to other responsible decision-making situations. In addition to rationality, defined as a comparison of the *is* and the *ought,* responsible decision making typically involves also the importance of the decision, the competence and impartiality of the deciders, and the uncertainty of the final outcome.

*The importance of the decision.* In dispute settlement, the decision must be made so that normal relations can be resumed and maintained. For example, a baseball umpire settles any disputes that may arise between opposing team members, sees that the rules of the game are adhered to, and, if any rule infractions are detected, imposes appropriate penalties so that the game can proceed. Likewise, decisions that pertain to future events will determine the nature of individuals' or groups' activities: whether a scientist will be able to pursue his or her research interests with the requested support; whether additional facilities will increase the corporation's profits; or whether a particular regulation will facilitate international trade.

Usually, responsible decision making is not exposed to public view, often to protect the deciders and the interests they represent and/or the integrity of the decision-making process. Thus, there is relatively little sys-

tematic knowledge about, for example, how a jury deliberates or a board of directors makes its decisions. The data from this research indicate the extent to which those accustomed to making decisions that affect others take their task seriously. Although the arbitrators knew that the dispute before them was not "real," 99 percent of their statements during the deliberations pertained to the dispute. This may be due in part to the fact that the deliberations were being tape-recorded. While recording does tend to influence what· individuals say under such circumstances, its effect often is less than one might expect (Haggard, Hiken, & Isaacs, 1965).

*The competence of the deciders.* A decider's competence rests on relevant expertise— knowledge of the essential substantive and procedural aspects of the dispute and the ability to use this expertise effectively to reach a fair and just decision. For example, it is assumed that a jury member in a criminal trial can understand and evaluate the motives and behaviors of the person being tried and can compare them with the appropriate norms for acceptable behavior. Similarly, a scientist on a committee that awards research funds should be familiar with the substantive research area and be able to determine the quality of the proposed research and to predict the likelihood of the applicant's achievement of stated goals.[6]

On occasion the procedural aspects of the decision-making process may interfere with "good" decisions. As the decider appraises the evidence, he or she will focus on whatever seems to be meaningful and relevant to the central issue in the dispute as he or she understands it and dismiss evidence considered meaningless or irrelevant. The decider also will tend progressively to undervalue or even ignore evidence that does not "fit." If

---

[6] For a description of responsible decision making regarding the selection of applicants for support as research scientists, see Boothe, Rosenfeld, & Walker (1974, Appendix C).

he or she is unaware of the relevant issues and norms, the decider may, quite inadvertently, come to a conclusion that is not appropriate to the particular dispute. This theory thus suggests a reevaluation of the procedure in which the judge instructs the jurors only after they have heard the evidence, but before their deliberation, regarding the issue and norms that pertain to that trial.

*Impartiality of the deciders.* If a decider is to render a fair and just settlement, he or she should not be partial to one party at the expense of the other or be personally affected by the decision. Procedures have been developed to minimize bias by excluding those with known biases. Sometimes this procedure amounts to a random selection or balancing of the known biases of individual deciders in the hope that their combined biases will cancel each other out. Bias can also be minimized by requiring adherence to standardized procedural rules, as in the courts, where any new decisions must be justified in terms of precedent based on past decisions for disputes of a similar nature.

The goal of absolute impartiality is unattainable. Each decider brings to the decision-making situation a complete background, which of necessity influences selection of the central issue and determines what fact-finding and substantive norms are considered focal—or at least relevant—to the dispute. Also, decision may be influenced by positive or negative affinity to the parties (and possibly also to a colleague). The fact, however, that deciders cannot settle disputes between other persons with absolute impartiality does not mean that a decider will show a bias.

*The uncertainty of the outcome.* In most disputes between parties an out-of-court settlement is made, either because of a compromise solution or because one party is sufficiently in the right and the other sufficiently in the wrong that the outcome is sure. When the two parties bring their dispute to others

for settlement, it can be assumed that at least one of them believes more can be won by doing so. But when the dispute is settled by third parties, the disputants must accept some degree of uncertainty as to what the decision will be.

Uncertainty may exist as to the proper decision and the grounds on which it should be made.[7] Nevertheless, the fact and degree of uncertainty usually is not emphasized. It is inherent in the decision-making process, and emphasizing it would not be conducive to the disputants' acceptance of the decision.

It is possible to thwart the ideal of a fair and just trial by the introduction of bias, however subtle, as in the selection of the court and members of the jury. Examples of the vulnerability of the jury trial to such bias can be found in several recent trials—of Angela Davis (Hager, 1972), the "Harrisburg Seven" (Schulman, Shaver, Colman, Emrich, & Christie, 1973), the "Gainsville Eight" (Shaw, 1973), Mitchell and Stans (Arnold, 1974), and Joan Little (Tivnan, 1975). In one case the prosecution allegedly chose a court and locale that would favor a verdict of guilty (Schulman et al., 1973, p. 37), and in all of them the defense used sophisticated procedures to select jurors who felt a net positive (but not obvious) affinity to the ideological stance of the defendants, if not for the defendants themselves. The

---

[7] Schaefer wrote that "the judge who writes an opinion must be at least 51 per cent convinced in the direction of the result he reaches. But with the other judges of the court conviction may be less than 50 per cent, and the doubt will still go without expression, [1956, p. 5]." Llewellyn estimated that the outcome is fairly certain beforehand in about four-fifths of the cases that come before appellate courts, "but that there was no such certainty about the ground for the decision [1960, p. 25, note 16]." See also Cardozo (1921, pp. 149–150, 164–165) and his poignant observation: "I was much troubled in spirit, in my first years upon the bench, to find how trackless was the ocean on which I had embarked. I sought for certainty. I was oppressed and disheartened when I found that the quest for it was futile [p. 166]."

selection of pro-defendant jurors appears to have been sufficient to result in the rejection of all or most of the charges made by the prosecution. Thus, we find evidence that it is possible to influence the outcome of a jury trial by means of considerations that may be irrelevant to the case being tried.[8]

---

[8] As an example of presumed pro-prosecution bias (in the trial that included Fr. Berrigan): "Harrisburg . . . has three Republicans for every two Democrats; an unusually low proportion of Catholics and an unusually high proportion of fundamentalist religion sects; seven military installations and war-related industries; and an active Klu Klux Klan. Federal District Judge R. Dixon Herman, 60, a recent Nixon appointee, presided over the trial . . . [Schulman et al., 1973, p. 37]." For an example of presumed pro-defense bias (in the Angela Davis trial), Hager (1972, p. 3) observed: "On March 17, attorney Leo Branton, Jr. rose to tell the court: 'Your honor, the defense accepts

The delicate balance of forces that are seen to operate in a jury trial highlight the fact that an individual's fate can rest on the outcome of a decision reached by other persons. The importance of responsible decision making (of which dispute settlement is only one example) lies in more than its potential impact on individuals: The whole network of institutionalized rules that regulate the behavior of individuals and groups, and thus enable them to function in an orderly way, are based on such decisions.

the jury as presently constituted.' At that moment, her lawyers were all but certain the jurors they had selected would not find Angela Davis guilty of murder, kidnapping and conspiracy." After the trial was over, prosecutor A. W. Harris, Jr., observed: "We still feel we had the evidence for a conviction. But the jury never seemed to get the point [Hager, 1972, p. 22]."

# CHAPTER 23

# Decision Making and Decision Consensus in Commercial Arbitration

## —SOIA MENTSCHIKOFF and ERNEST A. HAGGARD

This chapter presents an empirically based conceptual view of decision making in commercial arbitration. Normative and interactional factors are defined and their respective roles identified. The decision-making and decision-consensus phases of this dispute-settlement context are examined from the perspectives of the expert and nonexpert arbitrator.

Between 1955 and 1960 a series of research studies on the institutional and decision-making aspects of commercial arbitration were undertaken under the direction of the first author.[1] Both authors observed decisional phenomena at the American Arbitration Association, formulated a general theory of decision making and decision consensus, and carried out experimental tests, as indicated in Chapter 22. This chapter deals with our theory as it applies to the commercial arbitration process.

## ARBITRATION: DEFINITIONS AND CONCEPTS[2]

Two factors play an important part in

[1] This research was supported by a grant from the Ford Foundation to the University of Chicago Law School.

[2] Arbitration process and procedure are not the same in all contexts but are affected by the institutional settings (trade association versus American Arbitration Association) and the subject matter of the disputes. See also Mentschikoff (1952, 1961).

arbitrators' settling disputes. The first, or normative, factor consists of standards arbitrators use (1) to judge the conduct of the parties at the time of the dispute and at the hearing, and (2) to regulate their own behavior at hearings and during deliberations. The second factor deals with the personal interactions of participants at the hearings and of arbitrators both at hearings and during deliberations.

### The Normative Factor

The term "norms" embraces two types of generalizations: (1) generalizations about the rightness or wrongness of particular behavior that can be used to judge and channel others' behavior or to guide one's own; and (2) generalizations about how people are likely to behave or things are likely to occur that can be used to predict behavior or assess the relative probability of the occurrence of past behavior.

These generalizations or norms can be readily illustrated. A norm of the second type could be: "If there is a shout of 'Fire' in a theater, people are likely to rush to the doors, and injury to some is likely to occur." The very statement of the norm carries with it a prediction. If it is reported that, when such a shout occurred in a theater, no one moved, the norm could be used to assess the probable accuracy of the statement. Or if it is reported only that there was a shout of "Fire," the hearer fills in the rest from this norm. Finally, the norm can be used to predicate a norm of the first type: "Shouting 'Fire' in a crowded theater is improper conduct." This norm in turn can be used either as a guide to oneself not to shout "Fire," or, if the holder of the norm is in an appropriate position, to serve as a basis for imposing a civil or criminal sanction.

For an individual, the origin of norms lies in learning the rules of what is and what is not acceptable and desirable behavior for a member of a family, society, or subcultural, economic, or occupational group. For a group, norms are relatively well-defined and stable standards that guide members in their performance of tasks. Norms, which are in people's minds and which also may be formalized into moral, legal, and other codes, pertain to all types of behavior in all types of situations (compare, e.g., Fuller, 1969b, pp. 123–125). They may take almost any form and for a given individual will to some extent be different from and to some extent similar to those held by other individuals, depending on learning and experience.

Norms differ along four major continua: *scope, generality, imperativeness,* and *explicitness.* "Scope" speaks to who holds a norm—from one individual to almost all members of a society. "Generality" deals with how many aspects of behavior the norm encompasses—from one to almost all. "Imperativeness" concerns how firmly the norm is held. And "explicitness" addresses the problem of how precisely, if at all, the norm is formulated—explicit and clear or implicit and diffuse.

The articulation of norms is a major function of the legal system. Such norms,

known as rules of law, delineate the standards by which behavior is to be judged or the direction in which such behavior is to be channeled. To the extent that such rules have maximal scope, limited generality, maximal imperativeness, and maximal explicitness, they tend to be universally observed and create few problems except when they conflict with other norms of equivalent status. Rules of law often, however, do not have all these characteristics, and much of the work of courts, legislatures, and administrative agencies is given over to the resulting problems. At the American Arbitration Association (AAA), some of the problems resulting from imprecise articulation or conflict in norms are not as acute as in the formal legal system, since arbitrators are under no pressure to lay down a rule for the future or to agree on the norms they apply if they can reach agreement on the result.

While the range of available norms is theoretically infinite, the norms used by AAA arbitrators in deciding commercial cases are relatively few and recurrent. The class of disputes is not very wide in terms of the possible range of disputes. Furthermore, the relatively few occupational and economic groups from which arbitrators are drawn are much alike compared to the population as a whole. And the task to be performed by the arbitrators is generally constant.

It is analytically useful to classify these norms into (1) those directly relevant to the conduct of parties at the time the dispute arose (always in the past)—substantive and fact-finding norms; and (2) those directly relevant to the conduct of hearings and to conduct during deliberation—procedural, role, and arbitrator status norms.

*Norms relating to conduct during the dispute.*

SUBSTANTIVE NORMS. "Substantive norms" are those used to judge the wrongness and rightness of the parties' conduct found by the arbitrators to have taken place at the time the dispute arose—what the legal system calls the substantive rules of law. There are two ways of expressing such rules and norms. One is simply to state that certain conduct is either proper or improper. The other, more typical of rules of law, is to state that, whenever a person under circumstances A, B, or C has done X, Y, or Z, then he or she is answerable to the state or to some person injured by such conduct. That the formal legal system pays little attention to norms whose violation is not followed by practical consequences[3] should not obscure the fact that a normative judgment as to the "goodness" and "badness" of particular kinds of behavior is implicit in all rules of law.

The major differences among arbitrators as to substantive norms seem to be a function of occupational group and economic status. Obviously no arbitrator can select a substantive norm of which he or she has no knowledge. For example, an arbitrator whose work experience has not permitted exposure to the variety of ways in which contracts may be interpreted usually has available a relatively limited set of relevant norms. An adequately trained lawyer will have had such exposure and knows perfectly well that contracts should sometimes be strictly interpreted and sometimes liberally interpreted to effect the purpose of the parties entering into the contract. In comparison, an arbitrator in an occupation where the terms of written agreements are carefully and precisely observed may be unable to conceive of a norm that would require or permit the contract language to be substantially ignored in the interest of doing equity. So, too, an arbitrator in an occupation where written terms are informally stated and subject to oral readjustment may find it difficult to believe that holding parties to the precise

_____

[3] Since substantive norms used by arbitrators do not necessarily carry statements of their consequence, there is always the subsidiary normative question in arbitration of what should be done about conduct of the parties that is judged improper under the substantive norm used.

terms originally stated in the written instrument is a proper norm if conditions have altered.

FACT-FINDING NORMS. Since arbitrators cannot know or find what the facts actually were, they must make a probability assessment as to what occurred. In making that assessment, they use available inherent probability and personal credibility norms.

Arbitrators use "inherent probability norms" to determine the likelihood that a transaction or conduct occurred as reported. An arbitrator who knows nothing about the situation or conduct in dispute will be unable to use this type of norm unless it is supplied by one of the parties or their counsel and is both understood and accepted. For example, if an academician were told that a humanities faculty member was to be paid $100,000 a year, the chances of this statement being accepted as accurate are, to put it mildly, remote. But an executive at a level where salaries were $100,000 to $250,000 a year with no knowledge of academic salaries might not be so incredulous. For inherent probability norms, as for substantive norms, an arbitrator's experience and learning greatly condition availability.

"Personal credibility norms" are used by arbitrators to determine whether a particular witness is telling the truth. Extreme cases of such norms are operative when a person says that members of an ethnic or religious group are not capable of telling the truth. Others find cues to truth or falsity in the witness's control of his or her hands or facial expressions. The point is not whether such norms are valid. Rather, it is that such norms do exist and are used to deal with testimony and evidence. In fact, when "inherent probability" norms are unavailable, these become the dominant norms for the determination of "the facts."

*Norms relating to the conduct of arbitration.*

PROCEDURAL NORMS. "Procedural norms" deal with the order of presentation, the admissibility of evidence, and the allocation of the burden of proof. These norms originate in arbitrators' concepts of their office and of the nature of the arbitration process. Concepts, however, may differ depending on the arbitrator's arbitration experience, learning, and occupational background. For example, most lawyers view arbitration as an extremely informal procedure compared to the courts, and, although they theoretically have available legal norms regulating matters of procedure and evidence, they are very articulate about not using them whenever the matter is brought specifically to their attention by counsel. When norms are not specifically called to their attention as legal, they tend to follow them, presumably because their conditioning makes following "normal." But lay arbitrators on the whole view arbitration as a fairly formal judicial proceeding and thus are much more prone to accept such procedural norms from the formal legal system as are brought to their attention.

All arbitrators hold as general procedural norms that hearings must be orderly and that parties should have a chance to be heard and to present evidence and argument. Arbitrators, however, differ on the procedural norms of issue posing and burden of proof. "Issue posing" is the focusing of the actual area of dispute by explicit statement. In no case is everything in dispute; there are typically large areas of agreement as to fact and substantive norm. Early issue posing depends on the arbitrator's concept of what constitutes an orderly hearing. Rather regularly arbitrators with arbitration experience and legal training try to get issues focused at the beginning of the case.

There are two facets to the "burden of proof" norm. First, one of the parties (i.e., the claimant) has the duty of presenting more evidence regarding what happened to "outweigh" the amount presented by the other. If both parties present an equal amount of evidence, the one carrying the burden of proof loses the case. Second, each factual condition of the substantive norm an arbitrator selects as most relevant must be supported by evidence. In the absence of such support, there is deemed to be a failure of proof with consequent loss to the party in whose favor the substantive norm otherwise ran but who also carried the burden of proof.

ROLE NORMS. The second set of norms concerns the arbitrator's conception of the role or office. The concept of role is extremely important in the formal legal system as well. Its importance is reflected not only in the common tendency to speak of certain situations as being best suited to a particular forum (e.g., judicial, legislative, administrative, political) rather than to another (see, e.g., Fuller, 1960, n.d.) but also in the recurrent controversy as to functions appropriate to Justices of the Supreme Court (see, e.g., Wechsler, 1958, 1961, 1965). The designation of particular matters as being suited to one forum rather than another reflects the speaker's view of the appropriate function of the deciders. The essential decisional processes are not significantly different except on this vital role aspect.

Individual arbitrators' role norms are determined by perceptions of the arbitration situations and judgments as to what the situation calls for in terms of their conduct and conduct toward them by others involved. The situation is conditioned by the nature of the arbitrator's task and by the place arbitration holds for him or her in relation to other dispute-settling machineries. Further, an arbitrator's personality structure produces additional normative statements about his or her proper conduct and, by reflection, the proper conduct of an arbitrator.

The situational aspect most alive to arbitrators is that *arbitration is neither a mediation nor a court procedure.* The proposition that arbitration is a more formal process than mediation or negotiation results in the creation of the procedural norms already discussed. The proposition that arbitration is not a court procedure produces potential corresponding normative statements that (1) arbitrators are not bound by legal rules of evidence and procedure, and (2) arbitrators are not bound by substantive legal rules.

The first proposition—not being bound by legal rules of evidence—has maximal scope among arbitrators (i.e., is endorsed by practically all arbitrators). Its existence does not mean, however, that arbitrators do not use such legal rules. The proposition is not phrased in terms of "must not use" but rather in terms of "are not bound" (i.e., not obligated to use).

The second proposition—relating to substantive legal rules—does not have the same scope as the first. Here is the first major source of difference in role norms among arbitrators. Many arbitrators believe they are bound by substantive rules of law. And even when an arbitrator does not feel so bound, a norm may in fact be used that duplicates one of the legal system's. But when an arbitrator does feel bound, it results in his or her rejecting norms perceived as different. An arbitrator who feels this way and also does not feel free to depart from such rules when justice requires is relatively rare. When this occurs, the arbitrator is reflecting a personally held image of the courts—an image far from accurate. Nonetheless, as a result the arbitrator proceeds in a "legalistic" fashion and arrives at a much more technical decision than would have been rendered in court (compare, e.g., Llewellyn, 1960).

Related to this situational aspect of arbitration are four task requirements that produce normative statements of importance for the arbitrator's role:

1. *The dispute to be decided is to be presented by the parties.* This means that arbitration is essentially an adversary procedure. In such a procedure it is the parties who control bringing the case, framing the issues, presenting the evidence and the argument, whereas in the investigatory system such control rests in the deciders.[4] That the dis-

pute is to be presented by the parties and therefore lies within their control produces the corresponding normative statements that (a) arbitrators must give the parties a full opportunity to be heard and to present their evidence and arguments, and (b) arbitrators must decide the dispute solely on the evidence and arguments presented.

The scope of the norm regarding the opportunity for a full hearing is again maximal. Since this proposition is also supported by the belief that arbitration is an informal procedure where parties should be permitted to present their case as they choose, including letting off hostility, this norm tends toward universality of application as well. Not that arbitrators permit any kind of excursus the parties wish to take; notions of relevance and the desire to avoid "unnecessary" detail or repetition are often applied.

The second proposition—that arbitrators must decide the dispute solely on the evidence and arguments presented by the parties—is not universally held. It is the second major source of difference as to role norms. The drive for the opposing norm (i.e., arbitrators must discover truth by making their own investigations) is usually buttressed by the view that arbitration is not a court procedure and that, unlike the courts, it is geared to the discovery of truth and not to a decision between rival contestants. That the validity of this image of the court system is open to grave doubt (compare, e.g., Llewellyn, 1960) does not lessen the impact of the image on those who hold it.

2. *The arbitrators must finally decide the dispute.* The potential corresponding normative statements are that (a) arbitrators must not mediate in an attempt to make the parties reach their own settlement, and (b) arbitrators must act judicially and not as compromisers in rendering awards. The first proposition is not of maximal scope, but its functioning is so carefully policed by AAA clerks that it attains maximal scope universally applied. The second proposition results in the third major source of difference

---

[4] This is not to say that any procedure is *wholly* adversary or investigatory. But any procedure partakes more of the one set than of the other, and arbitration like the formal court process is predominantly adversary. See also Llewellyn (1962, pp. 375–394).

among arbitrators. Those holding a compromise role argue that arbitration is not a court procedure. "Compromise," however, is always viewed by the Association as deviant behavior, and all institutional pressures tend toward a "judicial" (yes–no) attitude.

3. *Arbitrators are to decide the dispute on the merits.* This condition yields the corollaries that arbitrators (a) must act responsibly and (b) must be impartial. That is, they must select proper substantive norms and apply them to facts after having proceeded according to proper procedural and role norms. This norm of responsible action, as diffuse and implicit as it is, is of maximal scope and generality. Likewise, the proposition about impartiality is of maximal scope and is buttressed by legal sanctions. Although an arbitrator selected by a particular party may occasionally consider the appropriateness of a representative role, the implicit agreement among colleagues that he or she is not to so operate reinforces impartiality. Of course, all that impartiality can realistically mean is a willingness to listen with as open a mind as is humanly possible. We have not yet in either law or the social sciences fully explored what the extent of that openness is (but cf. Kalven, 1968; Kalven & Zeisel, 1961).

4. *The award rendered should be legally binding.* This norm supports ensuring a full opportunity to be heard with impartiality. In addition, if there is more than one arbitrator, it requires them to reach at least majority agreement and, if possible (and typically it is possible), unanimous agreement on the award itself. Under the laws of many states, unanimous decision is required for legal validity.

STATUS NORMS. Status norms predict and regulate the participants' interaction during the arbitration—arbitrators, parties, counsel and witnesses, and tribunal clerk or other administrative officer. For the arbitrator, the status norms are: (1) The parties should treat the arbitrators with respect and deference; (2) the parties should treat each other with courtesy; (3) the arbitrators should treat each other as equals; (4) the arbitrators should defer to the clerk or other administrative officer on matters of procedure and definition of task; and (5) the arbitrators should remain detached from the dispute to be settled, in the sense that their role is one of decider not disputant.

Individual arbitrators vary as to these norms, depending on personality structure and arbitration·experience, but the norms as phrased are typical. This does not mean that departures from the norms are not common. In fact, a hierarchy of status among arbitrators emerges early in the proceedings. Likewise, although parties and their counsel must maintain the appearance of respect and deference to arbitrators, a successful counsel tries to establish superior knowledge and integrity in comparison to both his or her counterpart and the arbitrators.

## The Personal Interaction Factor

In addition to the total complex of standards or norms that affect the processes of making decisions and reaching consensus, another complex of factors deals with the personal interactions of the participants at the hearings. These factors can be described along two major continua: affinity and communication.

### Affinity.

"Affinity" deals with the arbitrator's reaction to the person or the party; that is, the extent to which he or she likes and identifies with the party or reacts negatively (in terms of the party's prior or present behavior). The arbitrator's affinity to a party is affected by the congruence that the arbitrator perceives between himself or herself and the party in terms of occupation, social status affiliations, and personality structure (e.g., buyers tend to identify with buyers, Ivy Leaguers with Ivy Leaguers, extroverts with extroverts). Also important is the arbitrator's liking or disliking of the kind of person he or she perceives the party to be. Affinity is also related to the arbitrator's perception of the congruence between the party's behavior at the hearing and the arbitrator's individual status norms, procedural norms, and relevant role norms. Although individual arbitrators can and do vary in degree of affinity from highly positive to highly negative, most of them are relatively neutral. Their role as arbitrator tends to reinforce a neutral position.

*Communication.*

The effectiveness of the communication is of particular importance because arbitrators have no prior knowledge about the dispute they must resolve. Therefore, if either party fails to communicate effectively his or her version of the facts or arguments, an arbitrator must reach a decision without benefit of that perspective. In essence, if an arbitrator's attention is not specifically called to the relevance and importance of some piece of evidence, it may completely escape him or her or not be perceived as significant.

The relevance and importance of particular evidence can only be judged in relation to a substantive norm being urged as controlling over the dispute. Specific attention-calling to evidence requires articulation of the issue to be decided in a manner that clarifies both the substantive norm and any factual condition of that norm in dispute. Since attention span is limited, the issue should also be so stated as to focus rather than scatter attention. To the extent that the presenter succeeds in focusing attention, he or she has taken the first important step in communicating effectively. Needless to say, particular presenters vary enormously in terms of these two basic requirements of relevance and importance.

Finally, the factor of affinity bears an important relation to effective communication and is even more important to acceptance by an arbitrator of what is being communicated. If affinity to the presenter is negative, it is hard for an arbitrator to hear what is said. If affinity is positive, the arbitrator seeks to ensure that he or she understands. We

have all seen this in operation. When we converse with a person we dislike, we tend to hear only what confirms our dislike. When we converse with a person we like, we tend to listen carefully and sympathetically.

## ARBITRATION: THE MATRIX OF DISPUTE SETTLEMENT

Determining how these factors interrelate to result in the final decision requires a two-step analysis. Two quite different processes are involved: (1) the process by which an arbitrator arrives at a decision, however tentatively held, as to who is right and who is wrong—or "decison making"; and (2) the process by which the arbitrators arrive at an agreement on the award—or "decision consensus."

In both steps a major influence is the degree of expertise of the individual arbitrator. One kind of expertise has to do with the arbitrator's familiarity with the situation in dispute and thus depends largely on the arbitrator's prior work experiences. The second kind pertains to the conduct of arbitrations, which depends on the arbitrator's prior arbitration experience.

Expertise in either sense is important for both decision making and decision consensus. As previously indicated, the generality of a norm bears an important relation to its usefulness in handling a particular matter. An expert has available much more explicit norms than does a nonexpert. For example, a nonexpert in a particular situation may feel that the parties should behave "properly." An expert, however, would hold as a norm some such proposition as "a party should not proceed without at least ten days' notice to the other side since less than that is improper conduct." The expert may also be more familiar with what is being said and therefore can more easily concentrate on unique aspects in rendering a decision. Of course, experts are also more likely to have proper inherent probability norms at their disposal to settle issues of fact.

## Process of Decision Making

In determining how an arbitrator arrives at a decision, it is necessary to remember that his or her prime function, if the arbitrator is to act responsibly, requires applying a proper set of substantive norms to the facts that emerge as a result of using proper fact-finding norms. The other matters that have been described—procedural norms, role norms, status norms, and the interpersonal factors of affinity and communication—all tend to ease or make more complex this central function of the arbitrator. Performance of that function means that the arbitrator must select a relevant substantive norm and judge the facts as he or she sees them against that norm. There is a tendency both in legal literature and elsewhere to speak of finding the "facts" first and then judging the situation thus disclosed. This formulation of the process puts the cart before the horse. Until an arbitrator, however implicitly, has formed a substantive norm, he or she cannot listen effectively to the evidence presented. In other words, the answer to the problem, "How does an arbitrator find the facts?" starts not with the evidence but with the norms that one has available for listening to that evidence. This must be so since evidence is not all of equal relevance and importance, nor can it be used by a particular arbitrator in making a decision unless he or she is aware of it.

An arbitrator, like any other person, cannot hold in mind all of the things said by the parties, their counsel, and their witnesses. He or she must select some evidence as worthy of retention and disregard the rest. Obviously an arbitrator tries to retain all evidence he or she finds relevant and important. But, as noted earlier, relevance can only be determined in relation to some norms, and the norms that an arbitrator uses of necessity are those that are available. Available norms, therefore, operate as screens through which the presented evidence must pass. Even more important, an arbitrator who lacks his or her own relevant substantive norms and to whom the parties have not made one available sits in an impossible position: All is equally important; all cannot be held; chance determines what is held.

Since no arbitrator can listen to evidence at a hearing without having selected a substantive norm, it is important to consider the interaction between arbitrator and party in determining such a selection. The process differs significantly depending on whether the arbitrator is an expert regarding the situation in the dispute. The differences between expert and nonexpert are manifested in the speed, clarity, and stability with which the norm is selected and held and the relative weight of the interpersonal factors on that selection. Thus, the following section considers the process whereby an arbitrator arrives at a decision from the perspectives of both the nonexpert and the expert.

*Impact of initial communication.*

The initial selection of a substantive norm by each arbitrator at the hearing occurs under four types of situations: (1) The parties fail to communicate to the arbitrators their idea of the relevant substantive norm; (2) the parties both agree on the relevant substantive norm and manage to communicate that norm effectively to the arbitrators; (3) one of the parties effectively communicates his or her idea of the relevant substantive norm; the other fails to do so; and (4) the parties are not in agreement on the relevant substantive norm, but each effectively communicates a substantive norm and urges it as the most highly relevant.

Where the parties have failed to communicate relevant substantive norms, either explicitly or implicitly in stating the issue, the nonexpert arbitrator starts listening to the evidence with general and diffuse norms that are not effective screens. This occurs because the arbitrator does not have maximally relevant norms from prior experience and learning. The inadequacy of this screen usually makes the arbitrator uneasy—with the result that, shortly after hearings begin, he or she asks the parties what the dispute is about. The skill of the parties directly affects the usefulness of the communication that ensues.

The ideal statement of the issue would disclose (1) the nature of the dispute as one of fact or norm or both; (2) the precise area of disagreement; and (3) why, in terms of applicable substantive norms, that area of disagreement should be important or decisive. Since presenters at the AAA often fall far below this ideal model of communication, typically at the end of their statements the nonexpert is left with almost as diffuse a set of screens as before. The result is that the arbitrator continues to grope through a substantial part of the hearings and thus runs the danger of distorted perception or complete nonperception of the most relevant evidence. Also affinity to the parties tends to move negatively. If a presenter achieves effective communication, he or she makes the norms available to the arbitrator and moves the arbitrator toward positive affinity.

If the dispute is one of fact, with substantive norms implicitly or explicitly agreed on, the danger of distortion is less than if a dispute as to the appropriate substantive norm is also involved. If the dispute involves, or involves only, competing substantive norms, the arbitrator must select *one* norm as appropriate or find a new or different norm. If one party communicates a substantive norm and the other fails to communicate, the arbitrator tends to accept the norm communicated unless his or her affinity to the communicator is strongly adverse or the norm is contrary to his or her expertise. If the arbitrator moves toward rejection of the norm because of affinity, and not because knowledge or prior experience suggests its rejection on a cognitive level, he or she tends to participate in the hearings for the purpose of having the other party suggest an alternative norm or statement of issue. One case that was observed illustrates this point:

The parties were represented by attorneys of quite different skill. The arbitrators were nonexpert. The plaintiff's attorney, by far the more competent, had urged as the controlling substantive norm a "guarantee" by the defendant of adequate performance of the goods. The goods did not live up to the "guarantee." At least two arbitrators liked the young defendant, whereas they were neutral about the plaintiff, a more experienced person. They were reluctant to accept the reality of the existence of a guarantee of performance because they did not believe that the older, more experienced person would have relied on the younger's statements. Therefore, they began to try to ascertain whether the appropriate norm should require both the spoken words of guarantee and reliance. Of course, they did not make this potential alternative norm explicit. Counsel for the defendant did not perceive the significance of their line of participation. Plaintiff's counsel did perceive its significance and tried to shift the frame of reference to avoid any acceptance of an additional requirement of reliance. Since the defendant's counsel failed to urge this alternative norm, the arbitrators finally dropped the line of questioning. The result was that the arbitrators reluctantly found for the plaintiff, although they displayed strong positive affinity for the defendant by striking an item of damage that under normal circumstances would probably have been awarded. The vital thing here was the failure of defendant's counsel to make explicit and respectable for the arbitrators a substantive norm that would have permitted them to find for the defendant.

If both parties communicate conflicting substantive norms and urge them as maximally relevant to the dispute, the nonexpert arbitrator typically tries to reserve decision and hold both norms as screening devices. On the unconscious level, he or she retreats to more general norms and starts a process of attempting reconciliation. Typically this reservation of decision does not seem to operate, however, if the arbitrator's affinity to the parties is strong in either direction. In that situation he or she tends to select the competing norm compatible with positive affinity or contrary to negative affinity. The effectiveness of communication also affects the nonexpert's selection of substantive norms to use as screens during the hearings. What one does not understand cannot be used. Thus, the factor that operates most heavily in the nonexpert arbitrator's *initial* selection of norms is the interpersonal one of communication and affinity.

The expert's selection of norms to use as screens basically rests on the availability of substantive and inherent probability norms. Communication plays a different role. A short statement of the facts orients him or her and puts norms into operation. Beyond that, attempts at communication affect his or her judgment of the parties as competent or incompetent—aspects that go to assessing their relative trustworthiness. If the expert arbitrator has as a procedural norm that the issues should be delineated early in the proceedings, his or her reaction to the party's attempt to communicate that issue ultimately affects estimates of that party's competence. To the extent that the presentation of an issue presupposes a substantive or inherent probability norm incongruent with the expert's norms, the expert's affinity toward the presenter moves toward negativity (and vice versa). Because the expert arbitrator holds norms with a high degree of imperativeness, attempts to persuade him or her to shift norms are less likely to be successful. Further, to the extent that an expert arbitrator holds a role norm precluding active participation in the proceedings, the party urging incongruent substantive or inherent probability norms is at enormous disadvantage—since he or she does not realize the full difficulty of the task or the unfortunate affinity that is developing.

In sum, given inadequate initial communication, the nonexpert arbitrator often sits through hearings with general and diffuse substantive norms and virtually nonexistent inherent probability norms, whereas the expert arbitrator has fairly precise substantive and inherent probability norms available.

The nonexpert also holds norms with much less imperativeness and hence is more likely to shift them during the hearing and in the consensus process. Finally, the nonexpert is much more subject to factors related to affinity and to decisions based on personal credibility.

*Building net pictures.*

As the hearing progresses, each type of arbitrator constructs a net picture of what happened in the past—a net picture of "the facts." Here the expert arbitrator has a great advantage over the nonexpert. For the expert, inherent probability norms tend to supply and explain any gaps in the evidence. Not having such norms, the nonexpert has a less precise and definite net picture. The filling of gaps by the expert does not automatically mean that he or she uses them in deciding. If the expert holds the norms of being bound by the record, he or she asks questions to fill in the gaps and, in the absence of "fill in," follows the norm of being bound by the record, thus placing the compromise or judicial role norms and the burden of proof norms in central position.

As the hearings continue, arbitrators also form net judgments about the parties—judgments based both on affinity and on the congruence between the parties' reported behavior and the arbitrator's applicable substantive or inherent probability norms. Such judgments in large part reflect whether the party is perceived as trustworthy and competent. On the whole, this net picture is held with a high degree of imperativeness by the expert and a low degree of imperativeness by the nonexpert. The degree of imperativeness does not turn on any objective conclusions as to whether the arbitrator is in fact expert but on the arbitrator's self-perception as an expert or nonexpert.

*Formulating a decision.*

The final step in the formation of an individual's decision takes place as the parties sum up their presentations, if in fact they do. The absence of summation, a not-too-infrequent phenomenon, is particularly unhappy when one or more of the arbitrators is nonexpert. To the extent that in summation a party who is positively regarded communicates a total picture congruent with the arbitrator's own net picture, that net picture is reinforced and held with higher confidence than before. This is true for both the expert and nonexpert arbitrator. To the extent that in summation a party who is positively regarded communicates a total picture that departs from the arbitrator's individual picture, the nonexpert loses confidence in his or her own views and may even shift, whereas the expert loses little confidence in his or her picture but tends to move toward neutral affinity to that party.

This potential shift by a nonexpert is one important reason for summation. If the nonexpert's screens are such that only a diffuse picture has formed, summation is vital to providing a coherent picture of what happened. If the nonexpert feels a positive affinity to the person making the summation, he or she then acquires a relatively coherent base for his or her position on the merits—one usable in the consensus phase to support a decision. As is indicated later, an arbitrator who does not have a coherent picture of what must have happened is in a very poor position to support his or her decision in deliberations.

In sum, at the end of the presentation or hearing each arbitrator feels some kind of affinity to each party to the dispute, has arrived at a more or less coherent net picture of what happened, has a general reaction to the relative net trustworthiness of the parties, and, on the basis of these, has developed a net feel of who is wrong and who is right and to what extent. But there seem to be two distinct modes of arriving at this "net feel." For the expert, most important to producing a decision are substantive and inherent probability norms, with affinity, personal credibility, and effective communication being of relatively minor importance. For the nonexpert, the converse is true.

Furthermore, the expert's net picture is held with a relatively high degree of confidence or imperativeness, whereas the nonexpert's net picture is held with lower imperativeness except in the rare case where degree of affinity is highly positive or negative. The nonexpert, in other words, is the potential shifter in the decision-consensus process.

## Process of Decision Consensus

We come now to the process by which consensus is reached and the end product (i.e., the award) agreed on. At this point, the absence of institutional pressure to explain the award or decide a rule for the future minimizes the problems in reaching consensus. As with a jury, all that is required is agreement on the end product even though the participants disagree on the detailed picture of the facts or the applicable norms or both. These become important only if they result in differences as to whether the plaintiff or defendant shall prevail overall.

Although decision consensus is basically interactional, during the deliberations the normative factor is likewise important: In particular, role and status norms affect communication and operate to create positive or negative affinities among the arbitrators. Furthermore, the expertness of the arbitrator continues to shape the impact of both the normative and personal interaction factors.

*Initial differences in arbitrators' persuasiveness.*

Recall that, in principle, arbitrators perceive their status to be equal. From the start, though, there is an implicit and relatively subtle struggle for dominance. The first opportunity for change in equality can occur when the chair is selected. Arbitrators almost always choose the one who is different from the other two so that equality is preserved by establishing a balance of power. Occasionally, selection of the chair rests on a perception by the other two arbitrators not only that the third is different but also that the difference signifies a higher-status position or a differential expert position. The initial shift in equality that such selection represents is always tentative. The real shifts in status occur during the hearings.

Unless an arbitrator holds as a role norm that he or she may not and must not participate in the hearings, before deliberations an arbitrator almost always will have said or done something relative to the presentation of the case. Occasionally an arbitrator will also "think out loud" for the benefit of the parties so that argument may be directed to what he or she thinks. Such participation may raise or lower that arbitrator's status with the other arbitrators. To the extent that an arbitrator's participation reveals expertness or nonexpertness, it helps to establish whether the arbitrator should be given greater or lesser status during deliberations. As a result of the hearings, each arbitrator has already formed an opinion as to the relative expertness of the others.

Each arbitrator also has developed an affinity to each of the other arbitrators. This affinity factor, as in the case of the affinity relation with the parties, rests primarily on perceptions of congruity, particularly noticeable as to role norms. When two arbitrators hold the same role norm and the third has a divergent one, the two who agree tend to be more free and relaxed with each other. There is almost a "pairing."

At the beginning of the deliberations, then, each arbitrator has an opinion as to his or her position of expertness or competence in relation to each of the others. In other words, status norms have altered from those of equality to some kind of hierarchy. He or she also has developed an affinity to each of the other arbitrators. Since status position and affinity to the speaker are vital to acceptance of what is said, the relative persuasive powers of the arbitrators are fairly well set at the outset. They are enhanced or decreased by the effectiveness of communication.

*Impact of expertness on deliberations.*

In the actual deliberations, two other factors are of major importance: (1) the imperativeness with which the arbitrator persists in the belief about who is right and who is wrong; and (2) the effectiveness of each arbitrator's communication to the others. The importance of these factors in decision consensus is most perceptible when there is no initial unanimity among the arbitrators. Somebody has to shift to achieve consensus. The degree of imperativeness conditions the possibility of shift; the degree of effectiveness conditions the direction of shift.

As already indicated, the degree of imperativeness of substantive and fact-finding norms rests in large measure on the individual arbitrator's expertness, actual or thought by him or her to exist. An expert not only holds norms with a high degree of imperativeness but also has available norms that are much more specific and direct than those possessed by a nonexpert. The specific character of available norms plays an important part in the intensity with which they are held, because they relate directly rather than inferentially to the facts in the case.

An expert arbitrator's ability to state a position with conviction and in relatively precise terms helps his or her views to be more easily understood. If an arbitrator is recognized as more expert by the other arbitrators, he or she also speaks with a high degree of presumptive persuasive power. If the other arbitrators hold their net picture with a fair amount of tentativeness, they tend to be impressed both by the air of authority and the comparative precision. If the listening arbitrators also perceive the speaking arbitrator as an expert in the situation or as otherwise entitled to a superior-status position, the case is in effect over unless a listening arbitrator holds, with a high degree of intensity, a competing role or procedural norm.

To influence decisions, communication not only must be "effective" in the sense of being understood but also must be "accepted."

Acceptance involves the degree of an arbitrator's participation in the deliberations and the other arbitrators' perception of the kind of person he or she is. If the communicating arbitrator is perceived as an expert or otherwise a person of higher status, what he or she says has much more influence than what any of the other arbitrators say. Even if an expert says it only once, it is readily "accepted"—the most striking phenomenon to be observed in the deliberations. If, however, the communicating arbitrator is not perceived as an expert by the others and they themselves are equally nonexpert, then the more he or she talks, all other things being equal, the more influence that arbitrator has.

The quality of the nonexpert's statements also bears a relation to influence. If a nonexpert's communication is not effective or not oriented to the solution of the case, it is not "received" by the other arbitrators. That which is not received cannot be accepted. Small group research on the importance of the number and kind of statements in controlling decisions tends to show some validity in the consensus process (e.g., Bales, 1951; Hare, Borgatta, & Bales, 1956). But this aspect of interaction is regularly of far less importance in achieving acceptance than who is doing the communicating in terms of expertise.

In other words, in the interaction process the degree of influence depends, first, on the degree to which the speaker is perceived by the others as being a person whose words

are entitled to weight. Second, how an arbitrator states things and the number of times they are stated bears some relation to the acceptance of his or her statements by the other arbitrators. On the whole, arbitrators satisfy the requirements of "effective" communication; therefore, the problem is one of "acceptance" of communication.

## CONCLUSION

Overall, who the arbitrator is in terms of expertise and prior experience is the most important single factor in both the decisional and the consensus processes. *Who* he or she is determines the availability of both substantive and fact-finding norms, conditions the procedural and role norms that are held, and raises or lowers the degree of influence in interaction with other arbitrators. Furthermore, as in the courts, decision making and decision consensus are determined by normative standards—interpersonal dimensions have importance only as they help to supply and gain endorsement for the norms necessary to decision (Llewellyn, 1960).[5] In sum, responsible decision making in a context of adversary proceedings is predominantly a normative matter.

------

[5] The point is reinforced by Robert Bonn's subsequent research (1972) on disputes in the textile industry arbitrated through the American Arbitration Association from 1967 to 1968.

# CHAPTER 24

# The Institutionalization of Conflict
## Jury Acquittals

—*MORTIMER R. KADISH and SANFORD H. KADISH*

Legal systems, like other social systems, sometimes adjust to circumstances other than through explicit procedures for controlled change. A primary way is through the institutionalization of powers, rights, privileges, and duties that engender conflict for individuals who must reach decisions with respect to such powers, rights, privileges, and duties. A prime example is the jury role in acquittals. The obligation to defer to the court's instructions, while binding on the juror, exists side by side with a protected power and privilege to override that obligation. The result is the legitimated interposition of the juror's judgment between the consequences of the court's instructions and the fate of the defendant. There follows the possibility of a justified departure from rules by agents acting in role, a possibility that may serve social ends of major significance.

At least since the advent of legal realism in America and Europe it has become almost impossible to speak of the relationship between law and society without noting that law and society "'interact"; law "meets or ought to meet the needs of society"; law must be understood as "serving a social function"; society "influences" or "creates" law for its own purposes. Whatever such language means in detail, clearly the idea of a legal system standing apart from society, perhaps on pillars of natural law, and issuing pronouncements to society according to independently determined norms and principles of justice has been rejected. We would not, if we could, reverse jurisprudential direction. On the contrary, finding such "realistic" talk as right as it is vague, this chapter illustrates one way in which legal institutions, by virtue of their technical construction, may provide for the interaction of law and society. That way is through the distribution of legal powers, rights, duties, and privileges so that they conflict in their functioning and hence place a premium on the development of a justification for undertaking departures from the rules of the system itself.

Our aim is to explore and interpret that conflict as it might occur for the criminal jury in rendering a verdict of acquittal. We do not think that legal systems adjust to new circumstances, changing values, and emerging claims only by devising roles that confront those who enact them with conflict in rights, duties, powers, or privileges—that is, through the institutionalization of conflict. Nor do we believe it is necessarily the most important way; certainly, most people would think first of the explicit provisions incorporated into legal systems for judicial and statutory changes if they wished to show how the law adjusts to changing needs. Nevertheless, a case can be made that some legal systems at some points generate for their agents conflicts that introduce departures from the rules, and do so as modes of adjusting to change. We take the role of the criminal jury in the acquittal of defendants as a prototype case.

## THE CRIMINAL JURY AND ITS DEVELOPMENT

In an earlier day juries were held accountable for their mistakes and misjudgments and their verdicts given effect only so long as they were considered right. The earliest mode of control over jurors was the attaint: A party against whom the verdict went could invoke a larger jury to find the facts anew. If the larger jury found contrary to the first, it could attaint its members—which meant loss of lands, fine, or imprisonment—and reverse its judgment. Though attaints became obsolete in the fifteenth century, another means to control jury error took its place—judges assumed power to punish jurors for incorrect or corrupt verdicts. The practice was formalized in 1534 by a statute authorizing courts to punish jurors for giving "an untrue verdict against the King . . . contrary to good and pregnant evidence ministered to them [*Statutes at Large: Henry VIII*, p. 326]." In criminal cases, though the jury could be punished for an erroneous acquittal, the prisoner could not be, for new trials could not be ordered as they could in civil cases. This power was used from time to time (see Thayer, 1898, pp. 162–178) until the court of Common Pleas in 1670 (Bushell, 1670) repudiated the practice and discharged the jurors who had acquitted William Penn of unlawful assembly. Ordering a new trial was developed to control juries in civil cases; in criminal cases no comparable control evolved.

Since the late seventeenth century, the legal power of a jury in criminal cases has been substantial. They render a general verdict, that is, they respond with a general finding of guilty or innocent of the crime charged, both finding the facts and applying the law. The varieties of special pleading developed in civil cases by which questions of law were separated from those of fact were never extended to criminal proceedings. When criminal juries convict, a variety of checks and controls assure conformity with the law, including judicial power to set the verdict aside and grant a new trial. But where they acquit there are no such controls. The acquittal is a diktat, a "sovereign power [Devlin, 1956, p. 89]," for which stated reasons are neither expected nor permitted. The jurors may in no way be held accountable for their verdict, be made to explain it, or be questioned about it. The acquittal verdict is given final and conclusive legal effect, no matter how fully it may be shown that it was contrary to law.

What did this development mean for the legal authority of the criminal jury to acquit? What *is* the legal role of the jury with respect to the rules of the criminal law? These questions underlie a classic debate in English and U.S. law. From the end of the seventeenth century on, controversy continued over whether the jury in criminal cases had the right to determine the law as well as the facts, or if only the court could determine the law. The view that came to prevail was that the duty of the jury was to take the law strictly from the judge, notwithstanding the power to do otherwise. Behind this view stands the ideal of the rule of law, an ideal, it is reasoned, wholly incompatible with a jury's right to take law into its own hands (see, e.g., Justice Story in *United States* v. *Battiste*, 1835, pp. 243–244; Chief Justice Shaw in *Commonwealth* v. *Porter*, 1845, p. 280; Forsyth, 1852, p. 261). To recognize such freedom in a jury risks an intolerable uncertainty in the law as the law shifts from case to case depending on the chance makeup of the jury. Moreover, to do so invites any group of twelve persons to abrogate a duly enacted law on the basis of their own views of what the law should be. Protection against bad laws should not come through the nullification of democratically enacted legislation by any dozen jurors, but through the democratic processes for changing the law.

In recent years the rising moral repugnance to the Vietnam war and to the laws supporting it, such as the draft, led lawyers to renew the old claims by arguing that jurors should be told they are free to disregard the court's instructions and that lawyers should be permitted to state they should do so (*United States* v. *Moylan,* 1969; *United States* v. *Sisson,* 1968; Sax, 1968; Van Dyke, 1970). But the old tradition is apparently too long dead to be revived—the claims were flatly rejected. A standard, representative instruction on the jury's duty reads: "It is my duty to instruct you in the law that applies to this case and you must follow the law as I state it to you [California Jury Instructions, 1970, p. 2]."

But the triumph of the restrictive view of the jury's competence in the formulations of the courts by no means cleared the air of uncertainty concerning the jury role in acquittal. The setting and context in which the judge tells the jury what its duty is must also be considered if the conscientious juror is properly to understand what should and should not be done. And that setting and context often tend to cloud the clarity of the judge's conventional instructions to the jury.

### Power and Right

In criminal cases, the power to return a general verdict cannot be taken from the jury. It returns its verdict without stated reasons or justifications of any kind. If it finds the defendant not guilty, the acquittal must be given final and binding legal effect, no matter what may be thought or known about the jury's failure to follow the law. The jury is fully insulated from any accountability. In these circumstances Hamilton's argument has to be fairly faced:

All the cases agree that the jury have the *power* to decide the law as well as the fact; and if the law gives them the power, it gives them the *right* also. Power and right are convertible terms, when the law authorizes the doing of an act which shall be final, and

for the doing of which the agent is not responsible [*People* v. *Croswell,* 1804, p. 345].

He was not arguing that there should be no constraints on how the jury exercises its power. His point was that the legal right followed from the legal power (Goebel, 1964, pp. 828–829).

### The Courts and the Jury

The force of this proposition is enhanced by the courts' dealings with specific legal issues concerning the criminal jury. When a judge hears a criminal case without a jury and finds the defendant guilty of one charge and innocent of another where such a finding is illogical and inconsistent, the judgment of guilt is reversible, on the ground that there can be no confidence in the correctness of that judgment (see *United States* v. *Maybury,* 1959). But where a jury returns verdicts no less inconsistent and illogical, the guilty verdict is regarded as irreversible.

In civil cases tried before a jury the use of court-formulated special interrogatories to assist the jury's arriving at a general verdict logically and according to the court's legal instructions is long accepted. So is the special verdict, where the jury is instructed to return only a special written finding on each issue of fact, leaving it for the court to enter judgment in accord with the law as applied to the jury-found facts (see Rule 49 of the Federal Rules Civil Procedures, 1970). Both devices function to assure judgments in accord with the law. There is common-law authority for use of such devices in criminal cases as well, although the jury can always decline and insist on returning a general verdict (see *United States* v. *Ogull,* 1957). However, these devices have been even more rarely used in this country than in England, and current authority finds their use violative of the right to trial by jury.

In *United States* v. *Spock* (1969), the court reversed a conviction of conspiracy to counsel evasion of the draft. The trial court had put to the jury, in addition to the general issue of guilt or innocence, ten special questions calling for a yes or no answer. This was enough to require reversal of the conviction, even assuming the correctness of the questions proposed. The right to jury trial, the appellate court reasoned, would be meaningless if the jury were not free from judicial pressure. The prohibited directed verdict of guilty is the most direct of such pressures. But more indirect pressures, such as requiring a special verdict or using special interrogatories, are impermissible for the same reason. The court reasoned that these procedures infringed on the jury power to follow or not follow the instructions of the court. The controlling principle is that "the jury, as the conscience of the community, must be permitted to look at more than logic [*United States* v. *Spock,* 1969, p. 182]."

Also relevant is the basis on which the Supreme Court has held the right to trial by jury to be protected by the due process clause of the Fourteenth Amendment. In 1968, it recognized the jury's power to displace law by appeal to conscience as a characteristic so "fundamental to the American scheme of government" that a state violates due process of law in eliminating jury trial (*Duncan* v. *Louisiana,* 1968, p. 1444). Thus, the fundamental function of the jury is not only to guard against official departures from the rules of law, but also, on proper occasions, to depart from unjust rules or their unjust application.

### The Tradition of the Jury

The jury's obligations and freedoms are also determined by tradition. In landmark cases, particularly involving criminal libel and sedition, the jury invoked its power to nullify what were widely regarded as unjust laws. These actions are cited not as regrettable departures from the rule of law, but as historical and seminal acts, like Magna Carta and the Bill of Rights, by which the right to be free of unjust laws was asserted. Arguments supporting the fundamental value of the jury almost always rest on the nullifying function of criminal juries. As Dean Pound noted:

Jury lawlessness is the great corrective of law in its actual administration. The will of the state at large imposed on a reluctant community, the will of a majority imposed on a vigorous and determined minority, find the same obstacle in the local jury that formerly confronted kings and ministers [1910, p. 18].

### Jury Behavior

There is ample evidence of the tradition of jury nullification of unjust laws. The classic historical instances included the jury's refusal to convict in cases of criminal libel until the law was changed to give juries the authority to acquit through general verdicts (e.g., Fox's Libel Act in *Statutes at Large, George III,* 1792, Chap. 60), and the strategies of early English juries in avoiding capital punishment, such as finding against the evidence that only 39 shillings had been stolen when to find that more had been stolen meant a mandatory death sentence (Report of the Select Committee on Capital Punishment, 1930). We have witnessed the U.S. jury's systematic nullification of the Prohibition laws during the 1920s— "the most intense example of jury revolt in recent history [Kalven & Zeisel, 1966, p. 291]." Kalven and Zeisel's (1966) study demonstrated the more subtle use of power by contemporary U.S. juries. Of the 350,000 sample trials reported, about 19 percent were cases of jury acquittal and judge conviction. The authors determined that "jury sentiments on the law" were operative in 50 percent of all judge–jury disagreements. Of that 50 percent, twice as many disagreements were attributable to disagreements caused by a combination of facts and values than to values alone. This revealed "the salient role played by jury sentiments on the law in causing disagreements [Kalven & Zeisel, 1966, p. 115]." Further,

the jury does not often consciously and explicitly yield to sentiment in the teeth of the law. Rather it yields to sentiment in the apparent process of resolving doubts as to the evidence. The jury, therefore, is able to conduct its revolt from the law within the etiquette of resolving issue of fact [Kalven & Zeisel, 1966, p. 165].

"The revolt from the law," the authors noted, is a modest one. It manifests itself "as a moderate corrective against undue prosecutions for gambling, game and liquor violations and, to some extent, drunken driving [Kalven & Zeisel, 1966, p. 296]." Jurors reject particular rules of the criminal law that they feel inappropriate, such as the nice legal obstacles to the privilege of self-defense and the legal irrelevancy of contributory fault of the victim or how much the defendant had already suffered.

## INTERPRETING THE JURY'S ROLE

If jurors are obliged to do as they are told in the court instructions and if they may, nevertheless, do as they think best, how is the conscientious juror to understand his or her role? What is the juror to do in the jural role if following the court instructions would lead to a verdict that he or she is convinced ought to go otherwise?

The question appears puzzling on the common and not implausible assumption that the law must speak univocally to its agents and that a proper understanding of what the law requires of an agent in any one respect will reveal a single, consistent directive fixing the agent's duty and, so far as the law extends, leaving nothing up to the agent. Therefore, in order to interpret the jury's role in acquittals, we shall comment on each of the two possible positions which, making the assumption of the single, consistent directive, hold that the duty of the juror to comply with court instructions is

logically incompatible with the privilege to do as he or she thinks best, and that the legal system itself may have it one way or the other but not both. Then, we shall try to read the jury situation in acquittals on the hypothesis that the dilemma between duty and privilege is a false one for the legal system, and show how and in what sense.

### Interpretation 1: The Jury's Role Is to Follow the Court's Instructions

According to this first way of understanding the evidence, official formulations fully state the proper role of the jury: The jury reaches its general verdict by applying facts found in accord with the judge's legal instructions. Its sentiments concerning the law are of no consequence. Of no consequence also is its estimate of the force of any mitigating circumstance not comprehended in the law, or of its own view of the nature of the law if it differs from the judge's. The vaunted sovereignty of the jury thus is a matter of power, not of right. The jury *can* reach a perverse verdict of acquittal and get away with it, but that does not imply the right to reach such a verdict. When juries reach verdicts that run counter to the expressed instructions of courts, they usurp a discretion not theirs to exercise. That jury nullification has sometimes produced good results does not show that nullification is within its legal role.

The technique here is to acknowledge an inconsistency between jury power and jury duty to acquit, assume that the inconsistency cannot be, and then explain away the evidence that points to jury privilege. Yet why may one not discover in the scrupulous protection of jury power the institutionalizing of a sovereign right? There is nothing logically wrong with the finding of sovereignty. The question is how to construe the jury power to reach a perverse verdict of acquittal. Even in ordinary matters, when people are systematically protected not merely against incursions into their power to act as they think best, but also against any attempt to hold them accountable for alleged misuse of that power, they begin to believe that they have the right to act as they think best. If they are called to account for a wrong decision, they do not simply accept the criticism as arguable—they are outraged. Why would the adherents of Interpretation 1 not apply similar reasoning to juries were it not that they do not want it that way?

## Interpretation 2: The Jury's Role Is to Follow the Law-in-Action

One use of Pound's famous distinction (1910) between law-in-action and law-in-books is to make plausible the assumption of a single consistent directive defining the jury role in precisely the reverse sense of Interpretation 1. Thus it is held that the judge's instructions constitute only the formal law, and that the real law, the law-in-action, leaves it to the jury to follow these instructions only when so inclined. There is a real question as to what the law-in-action means. Sometimes it appears to mean that the law-in-action is what people in authority do, independent of any rule. That "law-in-action" lays no requirement on juries at all —whatever juries get away with is the law-in-action. At other times the distinction refers to the norms practiced in the community as distinguished from the norms "in the books" and disregarded in practice. It is in this second sense that we propose that the Realist distinction shores up a rule of competence for the jury: "Do as you think best; take or leave the court's instructions." Any jury that thought itself bound to the court's instructions would then have misunderstood its own role. The inconsistency between duty and privilege has been overcome; the duty is merely formal; the privilege is real in the law.

But even if Interpretation 2 should rest on a determination of what the real, not the apparent, norms of the law may be—how does one determine what the real norm is? We propose that there is no direct influence from the law-in-action to the real norm of

jury sovereignty postulated in Interpretation 2 without the addition of an independent preference for that condition. Interpretation 2, like Interpretation 1, needs a normative principle to select only one part of the evidence as determinative.

For the law-in-action to be the *law* in action, actual behavior must be able to count as a transgression even if the transgressor be an official. What actual behavior cannot violate can constitute no rule. Which class of behavior represents compliance with the actual norm and which a misguided attempt to follow merely fictitious ones—deferring to the judge's instructions or defying them? To ascribe to the jury a determinate role at all implies that the jury might deviate from the law-in-action. Why do the many instances of compliance with court instructions carry so much less weight in determining the law-in-action than the few instances of departure? Such questions are readily answerable only if one chooses one sort of jury behavior over another to determine what the law-in-action actually is. Behavior that fulfills allegedly valuable functions will satisfy the law-in-action, while behavior grounded on formal obligations that fulfill no such functions becomes a misguided attempt to satisfy the law-in-books.

Even if the jury's role *is* to follow the law-in-action and that law is determinable (by a proper judgment of value), much that legal practitioners consider law is systematically ignored. Jurors are obliged to swear to decide the case according to the law and the evidence. The judge *does* instruct the jurors in the applicable law and direct them to arrive at verdicts accordingly. Defense counsel may not argue to jurors that the law is other than as stated by the judge or that they should disregard it. At the very least, the jury does not have the right to invoke its own sentiments on what the law should be as does an official when the law delegates an explicit discretionary authority.

In short, the source of these oversimplifications is the notion that the law has to speak to the jury in one consistent voice. It requires arguing that, in considering whether to acquit, the jury either has an obligation to follow the court's instruction or has the power and a derivative right or privilege not to follow them. Either assumption leads covertly to introducing a normative principle, so that the notion of the single consistent directive can work.

## Interpretation 3: The Jury Role as a Conflicted Role

Logic does not prohibit interpreting the jury's role so that it both requires conformity to the court's instructions and extends a privilege to return a verdict of acquittal contrary to those instructions. What prohibits such an interpretation is only the notion of the single, consistent directive. Imagine a judge saying simultaneously, "Follow my instructions; it is your duty" and "Use your judgment." One could fairly conclude that such a judge did not know what he or she wanted; no guidance whatsoever could be conceived to come from the bench. And so it would be for the law as a whole if one conceived its directives and privileges to issue from the selfsame source, for the same subject and subject matter, in the same respect. Plainly, any single sovereign had better be consistent.

But if one does not confuse a theory of how legal judgments derive legitimacy with the structure of the law and its impact on persons enacting legally defined roles, the notion of a consistent directive of a single sovereign loses its apparent necessity. It is, after all, false that the judge says "Follow my instructions" and "Use your judgment." Only "Follow my instructions" is said. Other arrangements in the legal system convey a genuine privilege not to do so. A variety of claims and dispensations focus on the person in the jury box, who is instructed in the juror's role. Yet the juror need not do it and is protected against consequences of not doing so. The role is conflicted in the sense that there is conflict in the authoritative rules governing his or her competence in the role. Judgment

is thrust on the individual, not merely of the guilt or innocence of the defendant, but of the merit of the judge's instructions. The juror is told what the law is, authoritatively; he or she *is* obliged, and then told to reach a decision, totally alone, immune from consequence, the verdict of acquittal safe from overturning. The *juror* has become the final *judge* of whether or not to uphold his or her obligation.

How is that kind of role possible? How can the law distinguish a conflicted role such as the jury's from a role that is simply hung up, in the sense that the agents of that role have no way of deciding among the various voices that they hear?

First, all roles are set up to perform certain jobs for certain ends and in certain prescribed ways, according to certain procedures and constraints. The jury has been set up to reach judgments of guilt or innocence for the ends of criminal justice, according to certain procedures and constraints including the instructions of the court. This creates both conflicted roles *and* the possibility of a solution. While the means to secure the role's end bind those who seek the end in the role, the means may prevent the role agent from achieving the role's ends. But a solution is provided if the role has been set up, as has the jury role, to allow the role agent to consider the ends for which the constraints are accepted. So the conflicted role, in contrast to the hung-up role, makes available to the agent a system of ends that allows "judging" the applicability of his or her obligations and ensures acting accordingly.

Second, an obligation is not necessarily denied when it is held as something less than absolute. Therefore, we may say that the judge's instructions bind the jury and, at the same time, that the criminal jury can be required to judge the relevance of the obligation. Because the jury's role exacts from the conscientious juror the distinction between departing from an instruction because it seems preferable (thereby ceasing to treat the instruction as obligatory) and departing from it because there is "damn good reason" to do so (as determined by the role ends), the jury acquittal role retains the obligatory status of the instruction while permitting a departure from that instruction. For, in general, we recognize a constraint as obligatory upon us when we require not merely reason to defend our rule departures, but damn good reasons.

It may be objected that we can rid ourselves of the notion of a conflicted role and save the acquittal jury for a single consistent directive simply by recognizing the actual rule that defines a juror's role to be a conditional: "If you don't have good reason— 'damn good reason'—then do what the judge tells you!" This proposed conditional expresses the meaning of the struggle between jury freedom and judge's authority. To this idea we respond as follows:

The conditional is spurious if it intends to restate the conditions of a conflicted role as a single, consistent directive that in itself generates no conflict but is either obeyed or disobeyed. Privileges can always be stated to qualify obligations, but this diminishes neither the privilege nor the obligation. Any juror reading the above conditional would know immediately that he or she faces no less an obligation because it was not universally overriding—precisely that, it would be understood, was the point of "damned good reason." The same consequences would prevail. The choice whether to obey the instructions of the judge would have been thrown back upon the juror, who would not escape a judgment on what obligations are binding in the instant case; and he or she would still need to find reasons of overriding weight.

Further, "damn good reason" in the above conditional requires jury action on some ultimate norm or norms of the legal system or of morality. "Do as the judge tells you unless the consequence is serious injustice" is in no way the same as, "Assign applicants to windows according to last name unless the line exceeds ten persons." There is no routine for saying what "serious injustice"

means; that is why the juror in the conditional is told to consider whether a "serious injustice" may be done. If there were such a routine, very likely it would be provided and the case would become rather like the clerk's in determining window assignments. Also, the two sorts of conditionals are unalike because there can be no question of being pulled between assigning people by last names and the results of counting persons, as there can be between the demand to obey the court's authoritative instruction and the requirement to pursue the ultimate end of judgment, which is justice. Hence, it simply will not do to treat the introduction of an ultimate end into the deliberations as though one had introduced just another condition in a conditional directive for attaining some end, and thereby procured a directive that left the receiver of the law only the decision to comply or not.

In sum, then, the case for characterizing the role of the jury as conflicted turns on the following propositions: (1) Logical necessities do not prohibit such a role, nor does an easy reformulation make it disposable. (2) Conflicted roles like that of the jury perform distinct functions in the administration of justice. This characterization of the jury's role accommodates the apparently divergent themes presented by the evidence. It does not require that portions of the evidence be oversimplified or explained away.

So characterizing the role of the jury allows us to say the following: The duty of the jury is indeed to find the facts on the basis of the evidence and to issue a general verdict by applying those facts to the propositions of law given by the judge. This is the rule, and it imposes an obligation to comply. But it is not therefore an absolute and underlying obligation. Sometimes the jury's commonsense perceptions, considerations of fairness to the defendant, or appraisal of the law (in contrast to the judge's statement of it) are so weighty that they justify departure from the requirement that the jury defer to the judge's instructions. Some roles, that is, permit departures from the very rules that bind their agents when the agents are satisfied that there is not merely reason, but extremely good reason for doing so. They are capable of recognizing conflicts between role ends and the obligatory means regulating their achievement, and of making provision for resolving the conflict.

## LEGITIMATED INTERPOSITION AND THE INTERACTION OF LAW AND SOCIETY

We may use our analysis of the conflicted role of the jury to formulate a general conception for instances in which the official's role provides the possibility of justifying, under the law, departures from binding rules. In contrast to discretion, which denotes an explicitly delegated legal power to act according to an agent's best judgment within defined limits, and also to usurpation, which denotes an exercise of power in outright defiance of the legal system, we propose the concept of *legitimated interposition* to cover instances comparable to that of the jury when it acquits. According to Justice White:

[T]he essential feature of a jury obviously lies in the interposition between the accused and his accuser of the common-sense judgment of a group of laymen, and in the community participation and shared responsibility which results from the group's determination of guilt or innocence [*Williams* v. *Florida*, 1970, p. 1906].

The concept of legitimated interposition generalizes this phenomenon. Actions are legitimated for a role agent insofar as the role justifies taking such action. When a legal system offers an official the freedom to depart from a legal rule that might work counter to the ends of his or her role in the system, we say it legitimates the official's departure from the rule. It legitimates the interposition of one's own judgment that departure from the rule best serves the end.

For the most part, legal systems have been

conceived to work independently of any principles for adjusting rules to the requirements of agents' roles. But we believe it false that the only possible relation of agents is simply to hear and obey; therefore, we introduce *legitimated interposition* to discuss the properties of legal systems in relation to departures from rules.

## The Conditions of Legitimated Interposition

What characteristics of a working legal system support a view of the official's role that justifies the departure from a rule defining and limiting his or her competence? First, legitimated interposition requires that the official receive authority to effect legal consequences greater than that permitted by the rules defining his or her competence, and that the system recognize the exercise of this authority to produce those consequences with finality, either legally or practically. No effective legal recourse exists to test whether in exercising this authority the official complied with the rules. In addition, no other sanction can call the official to account for deviating from the rules of competence appropriate to the role. In short, a legal power is granted to effect legal consequences without recourse against either the action or the official.

Yet this is not and cannot be all if legitimation of a rule departure by an official is to have the force of a true justification. That an act and its agent are both unchallengeable may prove only the lamentable shortcomings of the system and confirm the truth of the famous dictum that all power tends to corrupt and absolute power absolutely. If there is to be legitimation, the system must make available to the agent who proposes to depart from a rule some set of ends that might truly justify the act of departure from a rule. Interposition must be shown to be the kind of act that on the whole has positive value for the legal system. For it is not the juror's vote contrary to the judge's instructions as a consequence of a bribe that is legitimated; it is the juror's vote as an essay, however mistaken, in the direction of justice. This condition, together with a power to effect legal consequences without recourse against the action or the official, establishes the presence of legitimated interposition.

But that this condition obtains is hardly self-evident. The relevant considerations are the extent to which a class of official deviation from rules is widely acknowledged, rationalized, and built on, serves purposes consonant with those of the legal system, and has become an integrally functioning instrument of the system. Yet when do the facts point that way? Involved in this determination is a reading of a complex and subtle interplay of rules, practices, and arrangements and of the underlying purposes achieved and missed. We have tried to show in the case of the jury what this might mean concretely.

## The Possibility of a Justified Rule Departure

At this point we must meet a possible objection, one not ostensibly aimed against the notion of a conflicted role (like the jury role in acquittals), but against the coherence of the idea of a legally justified departure from a legal rule. At issue is the desirability of *post hoc* explanations of legal phenomena. To answer a question about how a system secures its results, one states the characteristics of the results. The statute under which the defendant was penalized, having turned out to be unconstitutional, was never the "law." The court instruction was never "obligatory" in the process of the jury's decision because the decision that deviated from the instruction was sustained in the ways we discussed earlier.

The basic objection to such discourse is that it fails to describe how the agent confronts the rules in the process of deciding on an action. It obscures the decision the agent must make in an actual situation. For that reason it obscures what we may call "nonsystematic" change in accommodating

conflict. To be sure, legal change occurs, but always "systematically," within established channels by the exercise of delegated authority. The system expands; the system contracts, but expansion or contraction occurs by means (like the introduction or repeal of statutes) that are part of the manifest content of the system.

But as the jury acquittal illustrated, systems change also when lines of development in a complex institution, each representing different values, come into conflict under the stress of particular circumstances. If systems are not complete historically, it is not only because the dialectic of conflict propels incessant changes. More important here, systems may be incomplete because in consequence of the development of different lines of interest and value within the same institution, decision on which line shall be honored in particular cases must be thrown back upon individuals who receive only incomplete systematic guidance. So we speak of nonsystematic change through rule departures, and legitimated interposition constitutes a partial explanation of how, short of revolutionary abolition and institution of new legal systems, the legal system accommodates change.

There is another approach that would seem to deny us rule departures and hence cloud the accommodation to the conflict and incompleteness that characterize legal systems. One might say: You think you have found the legal system legitimating departures from its own rules when in fact you have found the legal system not legitimating *rule* departures but authorizing the deployment of different *principles* and *policies* to which different weights may be assigned.[1] Confrontation of conflicted demands is absorbed into entities called principles or policies, thus enhancing the authority of the legal system.

Our response is that there are no prin-

---

[1] Compare Dworkin's distinctions (1963, 1967) among rules, principles, and policies that might make such an objection possible.

ciples or policies in themselves. Directives of the legal system become rules, policies, or principles through the manner of their use. Their use does not follow from their nature, but their nature from their use. Generality, vagueness, and precision do not determine whether directives function as principles, policies, or rules. The critical determinant is how such directives function in a context of directives. When they work so that departures may be legitimated, then those directives tend to be adjudged principles and policies and not merely rules. Whether "Keep off the grass" is a policy or a rule depends on whether it exists in a complex of directives such that sometimes the obligation to keep off the lawn cannot be maintained simultaneously with other legally recognized obligations. Then, the fact accepted, it becomes a policy, to which we ascribe a certain weight.

## The Institutionalization of Conflict and the Values of Conflict Systems

Conflicts are institutionalized through the organization of systems of behavior that permit the legitimation of rule departures. That is what it means for the conflict to be institutionalized. For if, given conflict situations, there is no legitimation of the departure from rules, then, while the conflict nonetheless occurs, the resolution is driven underground as an illegal act. But legitimated interposition preserves the act of rule departure from falling outside the system.

How far can and does that institutionalization go? That question we have tried to deal with elsewhere (see Kadish & Kadish, 1973). Our submission here is that however restricted or extended the legitimation of rule departures may be under the present legal system, the study of those legitimations —where and how they occur, how they are restricted, and how advantageously they might be extended or restricted—constitutes an aspect of jurisprudence of considerable practical and theoretical profit to the student of legal systems, an aspect of jurisprudence that we call "the jurisprudence of lawbreaking."

An important consequence of the phenomenon of legitimation for the interaction of law and society is the installation of individuals as participants in the creation and administration of justice. A system that incorporates legitimated interposition generates a place for the exercise of individual judgment before the rules; and it extends such a place not simply in the sense of delegating specific discretion but with respect to the application and definition of those rules that define its discretion. In other words, such a system extends discretion to deviate from the rules, discretion not simply a violation (since it is legitimated), but not therefore a compliance. By the counterposition of duty to comply and privilege to depart, the legal system has generated freedom in a very fundamental respect: the freedom of people not simply subject to the law, but, always within limits, independent of the law and capable of using that law for the ultimate ends of the legal system. That consequence is itself a value, and makes possible adjustment to conditions that could not have been foreseen with any clarity and hence could not have been planned for in detail.

By the counterposition of duty and privilege a system also generates unpredictability, arbitrary action, and "justice" immune from planned social control. But what follows is not a need to decide between a system free of the possibility of legally justified rule departures or a system riddled with the possibility of such departures; what does follow is the challenge to create legal systems that under given conditions may attain the most salutary mix.

# CHAPTER 25

# "Please, Morris, Don't Make Trouble"
## Two Lessons in Courtroom Confrontation

*—HARRY KALVEN, JR.*

Taking courtroom etiquette and decorum as a complex instance of socialization, this chapter explores current challenges to the courtroom as the last citadel of etiquette by detailing two famous instances of courtroom confrontation: the Scopes trial in 1925, and the Conspiracy trial before Judge Hoffman in 1970. The chapter concludes with an assessment of the viability of the courtroom, given the recent styles of protest.

Gestures, times, and places of protest are diverse and difficult to analyze. The decade that began with the sit-in—1960—ended with the Chicago Conspiracy trial—1970. Words like "politicizing" and "confrontation" replaced older words like "civil disobedience" and "revolution." The Chicago trial in particular, because of its publicity, and perhaps also the abortive start of the Panther trial in New York generated a concern about the role and viability of the courtroom amid the newest styles of protest (Epstein, 1970; Hayden, 1970; Lucas, 1970).

There is in all this a novel but elusive topic. We can ask whether tactics of protest, which in the case of the civil rights movement went from the courts to the streets, have gone from the streets to the courts. We can ask about the resiliency of the trial process in the face of confrontation tactics. We can ask whether the trial process itself can be politicized, whether in the U.S. scheme of things it ever makes sense to talk about "political trials." We can ask whether there are circumstances under which political realities entitle participants in the trial

forum to certain privileges relieving them of customary obligations to etiquette and relevance. We can ask whether we have witnessed a breakdown in the socialization process that is reflected in trial procedures.

The problem is that there is no single rationale of protest to describe, analyze, and evaluate. The Chicago trial proves to have been an ambivalent instance of confrontation in operation. The challenge seems to reside in a denial that the trial forum and the political forum are as sharply separate and distinct as Anglo-American legal tradition has always made them. We are at least asked to reexamine our assumptions that the trial forum is sealed off from political currents with standards of etiquette and relevance all its own (Kalven, 1969, 1970).

I propose to look first at the Scopes trial of 1925 (*Scopes* v. *State,* 1927) and then at the Chicago trial[1] in quest of some preliminary observations on anatomy, effectiveness, propriety, and possible countermeas-

---

[1] For a partial transcription of the Chicago Seven trial, see Kalven and Clark (1970).

ures. These cases provide insight into the social discomfort caused by disrupting traditional modes of courtroom conduct, and test the acceptance of the courtroom as a nonviolent forum in which to press legitimate rights and interests.

## HISTORICAL BACKDROP:
## THE SCOPES TRIAL

Let us go to a very different place and time—to Dayton, Tennessee, and the trial in 1925 of John Thomas Scopes, a young school teacher, for violating the state statute entitled "An Act Prohibiting the Teaching of the Evolution Theory . . . ," which made it a misdemeanor "to teach any theory that denies the story of the Divine Creation of man as taught in the Bible, and to teach instead that man has descended from a lower order of animals." The Tennessee "Monkey Trial" has become a firm part of U.S. legend; its dramatic possibilities were realized in the successful play "Inherit the Wind."

At the end of a trial before a jury, Scopes was convicted and fined $100 by the court. On appeal the Tennessee Supreme Court upheld the statute, but upset the conviction on the technicality that fines over $50 were required by law to be set by the jury. The court did not, however, send the case back. "We are informed," the court observed, "that the plaintiff in error is no longer in the service of the state. . . . we think the peace and dignity of the state, which all criminal prosecutions are brought to redress, will be the better conserved by the entry of a nolle prosequi herein." It is not hard to hear the court uttering a deep sigh of relief as it dismissed the case.

On paper the Scopes case was a test of the statute, won by the statute (and repealed only in 1969). Yet the case was a milestone in the fight for intellectual freedom. The trial was a great victory for the defense because, by using confrontation, they appealed to the public outside the courtroom and ridiculed the law into oblivion. And the men who did it—Clarence Darrow, Dudley Field Malone, Arthur Garfield Hays—are regarded as heroes.

The defense in the Scopes case has been acclaimed for succeeding in turning the case into a circus. The defense offers distinguished witnesses, scientists, who were not allowed to testfy. The trial is moved from the courthouse to the lawn outside to accommodate the audience and the press. Since it is unbearably hot, permission is given to remove coats. At many points the record shows applause or laughter from the audience. At one point, after William Jennings Bryan has stated vigorously that the jury members were better experts on the Bible than any of the scholars the defense hoped to put on the stand, the record reads: "Voices in Audience: Amen." Said Darrow: "I hope the reporters got the Amens in the record." At another point there is a fuss about a large sign, reading "Read Your Bible," placed near the jury in the outside courtroom. Darrow objects that it is prejudicial in this case, and after some controversy, the court orders the sign down. At yet another point during his famous cross-examination of Bryan, there is applause for Bryan, and he notes to Darrow: "Those are the people whom you insult." Darrow rejoins: "You insult every man of science and learning in the world because he does not believe in your fool religion." The judge interposes, "I will not stand for that," but Darrow does not withdraw the remark, and a little later refers to "your fool ideas that no intelligent Christian on earth believes." Indeed, there is even a moment when Darrow is cited for contempt, although he apologizes the next morning and the matter is dropped.

There are two major factors that may account for the great difference in public response to the two trials. Whatever the strategy in the Scopes defense to ridicule the law and with it the religion of the local community, there is no resistance to the trial procedures, no disrespect for the judge or government counsel, and likewise no disrespect from them. Everyone is exceedingly cordial and polite and in the end the visitors thank the court and the bar for their hospitality. The trial judge, John T. Raulston, in turn makes a speech that seems incredibly remote from the tone of today, concluding:

I am glad to have had these gentlemen with us. This little talk of mine comes from my heart, gentlemen. I have had difficult problems to decide in this lawsuit, and I only pray to God that I have decided them right. If I have not, the higher court will find the mistake. But if I failed to decide them right, it was for want of legal learning and legal attainments, and not for the want of a disposition to do everybody justice. . . . We are glad to have you with us.

The second difference is what made the Scopes case so memorable—the appearance of William Jennings Bryan for the prosecution as the counterpoise to Clarence Darrow. The casting was perfect. The trial was made viable because Bryan was willing to be cross-examined by Darrow as an expert on the Bible and because the court permitted it as an informal and somewhat irregular procedure outside the presence of the jury. The result was to provide in the trial context a forum for debate over the essentially political issues of the trial without interfering unduly with the trial proper. It was almost as though the trial adjourned to permit debate of the political issues surrounding it. Thus, the pressure to enlarge the standard of relevance, a visible strain in Chicago, was greatly reduced in Dayton. The trouble with this insight about the Scopes case is that it is hard to see how it could work again. Imagine adjourning the Chicago trial for a few days while defendant David Dellinger and prosecutor Thomas Foran debated publicly such matters as racism, poverty, and the war in Vietnam.

## CONTEMPORARY FOCUS:
## THE CHICAGO CONSPIRACY TRIAL

We turn to the Chicago trial. At the conclusion of the trial, while the jury was de-

liberating, Judge Julius Hoffman, who had issued several prior warnings, called the defendants and their lawyers before him one at a time and read off a series of contempt specifications to them, adjudged them guilty of contempt, and sentenced them to periods ranging from 4 years to 2 months. His specifications were elaborate and detailed; 175 specific acts of contempt were cited. The transcript of that part of the trial provides a rational sample of the tactics deemed most offensive and disturbing to the trial process. It leaves two important impressions. First, the tactics of the defense varied widely and are complex to catalogue; second, there was no systematic strategy pursued steadily throughout the trial.

## Stratagems for Courtroom Unrest:
## A Quantitative Perspective

The judge's particularization of contempts provides a perspective on the ebb and flow of disruptions: One can plot the 175 citations on a calendar. The results are surprising.

There were, for example, stretches of the trial when few, if any, contempts arose. Thus, the 5 weeks from November 6 to December 10 showed 9 citations in all, 6 with penalties of less than 7 days. They fell on 5 of the days, and none of them involved lawyer William Kunstler or defendants Jerry Rubin, Tom Hayden, or John Froines. But events precipitated a rush of citable conduct. Thus, the troubles with defendant Bobby Seale peaked from October 28 to October 30 and during this 3-day interval 54 contempts occurred. Again, the 13-trial-day span between January 23 and February 7 accounted for another 48 contempts. Thus, 100 of the contempts occurred within 16 trial days of the 5-month trial. Indeed without the Seale episode, the trial proceeded from September 24 to January 8 relatively uneventfully; on some 50 trial days the judge found no conduct worth citing.

Somewhat the same impression holds for individual participants. Hayden and Rubin went through November and December without any conduct that Judge Hoffman cited as contumacious. Leonard Weinglass went from October 30 to January 13 without a contempt, and Kunstler had a 5-week span from October 30 to December 9.

I was impressed by the sense that the interruptions were in no sense random and that two or three triggering events, such as the handling of Seale and the revocation of Dellinger's bond, accounted for most of the troubles. The incidence of unrest seems not easily compatible with the notion that the defendants and counsel relentlessly and steadily pursued a single-minded strategy of disturbing the trial process.

### Stratagems for Courtroom Unrest: A Qualitative Perspective

The tactics also varied qualitatively. It is not clear that they ever reached the level of heckling, making it impossible to proceed. At one extreme were the one-line jokes at the expense of the judge, the witness, or the prosecutors. At the other extreme were efforts to turn the trial into a political forum at least briefly, as with the attempt to read the names of war dead. Occasionally, there was a gesture of sheer civil disobedience, as when in protest over Seale the defense refused for 4 days to rise for the judge. Ranging in between were two kinds of conduct: countless instances of caustic and at times insulting remarks about the fairness of the trial and the judge, and countless remarks that are simply "out of order" as in *Robert's Rules of Order*.

The heightened sense of interruption is perhaps attributable to five factors: (1) the gloss that the press insisted on placing on the events at the trial; (2) the theatrical posturing of the defense outside the trial forum; (3) the presence of the jury and the frequency with which the judge found it necessary to have the jury withdraw, thus producing a sense of crisis after crisis; (4) the presence of a "studio audience" that often interacted with the defense, producing applause or times when spectators were or-

dered removed; and (5) the judge's propensity to use *direct orders* to control the proceedings, escalating many minor incidents into relatively major ones.

### Dellinger as a Deportment Model

The defendants appear to have seen themselves as more strategically disruptive. David Dellinger's contempt "history" is instructive. He was given 32 citations, the largest number of any participant, and received sentences totaling over 25 months. Only 6 citations called for penalties of over 7 days; the remaining 26 were apparently regarded by Judge Hoffman as relatively minor—for 12 the sentence was 3 days or less. While Dellinger was more steadily disruptive from the judge's view than the others, he collected 9 of his citations in the 4 days when the Seale problem was at its height; he went through December and the first part of January with just 3 citations.

Dellinger's actions were of several kinds. On at least 5 occasions the controversy was over whether he had engaged in certain conduct in the courtroom; it had nothing to do with issues of the trial or with larger issues. Twice the dispute was over revocation of his bail. Four times the citation was for not rising for the judge as part of the Seale protest; at least 3 other times the event was directly connected with the Seale episode. Several times it was for laughing. Several times it was an angry outburst about a witness, as in his use of the epithet "bullshit," which caused the judge to revoke his bail, precipitating a major crisis. Several other instances involved a caustic remark about the fairness of a ruling by the judge. And once it was for rising to propose on behalf of the defense that the jury, which had been sequestered almost since the start of the trial, be allowed to go home for the Thanksgiving holiday. His tactics were never surreptitious; his stance was one of open defiance: "It was the defendant David Dellinger who made that statement," he said repeatedly.

It is from the rest of the occasions that the sense of "politicizing" arises. Thus, his first contempt on October 15 is for trying just before the resumption of the trial after lunch, to read the names of the Vietnamese war dead as part of the Moratorium Day activities and to ask for a moment of silence before a witness took the stand. Dellinger's move seems to me clearly out of order; the trial forum should not be enlarged to accommodate political protests. Conduct altogether unexceptionable almost anywhere else is inappropriate and irrelevant in the court. But the reaction of the judge and the prosecution to the gesture was equally inappropriate. Prosecutor Foran asked that the marshall take "that man" into custody; the court had the jury withdrawn and ordered Dellinger not to disrupt the proceedings. The judge turned to the court reporter: "I note for the record that his name is . . ." Dellinger interrupted: "David Dellinger is my name."

If Dellinger's move was made in cool anticipation that the judge and prosecution would over-react and furnish them with an incident, it is "'confrontation." But the move was made modestly before the trial had resumed, and the request for a moment of silence was polite. It was only the third week of the trial, and there had been virtually no disturbances thus far. Perhaps with a little resiliency and prudence by court and prosecutor this could not have been built up into an "incident." In any event if the objective was to make the court and prosecution look arbitrary and foolish, it is hard to say Dellinger did not succeed.

On several other occasions Dellinger made brief political speeches. Here are a few examples; they always arose after some triggering event. On December 15 a dispute arose over whether lawyer volunteer Stuart Ball laughed in court, and the judge ordered him removed. Dellinger interrupted to argue that Ball had not laughed. At the end of a lively exchange:

THE COURT (TO DELLINGER): Will you sit down?

DELLINGER: And you are very prejudiced

and unfair and I state that in open court. It is not a fair trial and you have no intention of giving us a fair trial and when I speak throughout the country, I say that you are the assistant prosecutor or maybe the chief prosecutor and it is true and the people of this country will come to learn that about you and about some other judges in this court.

[Disorder in the courtroom]

SPECTATOR: Right on, boys.

On January 12 after the court made an evidentiary ruling, Dellinger interrupted, "Oh, ridiculous," thereby generating another heated exchange, including:

THE COURT (TO THE REPORTER): Did you get all those remarks?

DELLINGER: I stand by them, too. You earned them. It really brings the whole system of justice under discredit when you act that way. What Mayor Daley and the police did for the electoral process in its present form you are now doing for the judicial process.

On January 23 after the judge again found it necessary to remove disorderly spectators after an extended controversy over a ruling, prosecutor Foran made a speech to the court in defense of traditional methods of trial that "have worked very well for two hundred years," and are "not going to change now for these people."

DELLINGER (RISING): Yes, kept the black people in slavery for two hundred years, and wiped out the Indians and kept the poor people in problems and started the war in Vietnam which is killing off at least a hundred Americans and a thousand Vietnamese every week and we are trying to stop it. (Dellinger ordered to sit down.) And that judge won't let that issue come into the trial, that's why we are here.

FORAN: Your Honor, in the American system there is a proper way to raise such issues and to correct them.

These vivid examples indicate a passionate refusal to abide by the traditional notions of what is relevant to the legal forum. They are simply speeches in the wrong place; they pose interesting issues about maintaining legal rather than political standards of etiquette and relevance. Ironically, the most interesting instance came only after the trial proper concluded and the judge was proceeding with the contempt citations. Dellinger spoke on his own behalf just after being sentenced for contempt:

> Now I want to point out first of all that the first two contempts cited against me concerned one, the moratorium action and, secondly, support of Bobby Seale, the war against Vietnam, the aggression against Vietnam, and racism in this country, the two issues that this country refuses to solve, refuses to take seriously.

Judge Hoffman admonished him to talk to the point, adding, "I don't want you to talk politics."

Dellinger replied:

> You see that's one of the reasons I have needed to stand up and speak anyway, because you have tried to keep what you call politics, which means the truth, out of this courtroom, just as the prosecution has.

When Judge Hoffman asked Dellinger to sit down, Dellinger made a speech about "good Germans" and "good Jews" and "the new generation of Americans who will not put up with tyranny." There was applause from the audience and efforts to remove some spectators. In a moment, the transcript tells us, there was "complete disorder in the courtroom," and the curtain came down on cries of "Tyrants, tyrants" and "Justice in America."

On the one hand, this episode can be viewed as a model of the new tactics in action. The speech goes outside trial relevance. As it escalates in rhetoric, the spectators react and coercive moves are made by the court with the final result "complete disorder in the courtroom." On the other hand, it did not come until the trial was over (after 5 long months) and the judge was delivering his contempt punishments. At trial's end Dellinger saw himself as having spoken out repeatedly to introduce political truth into the trial, although the contempt transcript would suggest that he did so only very infrequently and that the conduct, which so frequently upset the judge, was of a quite different order.

## EVALUATION OF COURTROOM ETIQUETTE

The phenomenon of courtroom confrontation, because it is so difficult to specify, is difficult to evaluate. The line between literal obstruction of the trial process and disrespect for it is not easy to draw. Nor can we be certain that we are observing a calculated strategy at work rather than spontaneous anger, misunderstanding about the kind of forum a court provides, or a "chemical" interaction of very different life-styles. One strong impression from the Chicago transcript is that we were watching a domestic comedy where the two parties cannot stand each other, cannot escape each other, and, above all, cannot let each other alone.

Perhaps we insist on more etiquette in the trial process than is indispensable for its functioning. A trial may be the last citadel of etiquette in a society that has lost some of its taste for etiquette; the Chicago trial may evidence not so much revolution as wretched manners. Perhaps too, our children have become more impatient than their parents. The tradition has been that a political trial was not readily possible in the United States. We have in the First, the Fifth, and the Fourteenth Amendments built-in protections against it. We have also had norms of polit-

play a somewhat different role in such ical freedom and freedom for dissent and standards of decency in criminal procedures that could be appealed to powerfully. The trial was never a final confrontation. Perhaps this apparatus of appeal is seen as too slow now for contemporary protest.

Many issues remain to be sorted out and reflected on. The concept of a political trial appears most unhelpful. When is a trial brought by the state political? The effort to disrupt a trial perceived as unfair seems no more the exercise of a privilege to protest and combat injustice than sustained heckling to disrupt a speech or meeting is an exercise of the privilege of free speech. But the use of the contempt sanction on the scale shown in Chicago in order to police trial decorum seems ugly and self-defeating.

Beyond having better judges, better prosecutors, and better laws, a few simple countermeasures come to mind. It is fairly clear that conspiracy charges invite disturbances; it remains to be seen whether a single defendant tried alone could have the audience, the resourcefulness, and the stamina. Further, excepting a conspiracy charge, it is not likely that the system will have to risk trials anywhere near as long as Chicago's. Obviously a 5-month trial invites troubles that a shorter trial would easily avoid. The Scopes trial lasted only 9 days; over 90 percent of all criminal trials last 4 days or less. And, although there may be questions about the constitutional right to a *public* trial,[2] it may not always have to be *so* public. At least, we might explore a format including the press and a limited number of spectators but excluding the "studio audience." It is fascinating to wonder how the Chicago trial would have gone had the audience not been there in the courtroom.

Then, too, one might ask the judge to

---

[2] Witness the Supreme Court decision in *Illinois* v. *Allen* (1970), in which the Court held that a disruptive defendant can be physically controlled as necessary to permit an orderly trial.

trials. The point is not so much that one control one's temper as that the judge realize that what is at stake is the image of justice being flashed to the world outside the courtroom, that one's "opponents" are engaging in baiting. This may require avoiding unnecessary confrontations, seasoning of legal responses with some political realism, and, perhaps, taking time to explain the rationale for rulings.

The new tactics may not endanger any considerable segment of the legal world. To be effective, there must be some resonance on the part of the public to such tactics; otherwise the defense will appear simply obstructive and perhaps mad. I am sanguine enough about the condition of society to suggest that there will not be many such occasions forthcoming. Not the least idiosyncrasy of the Chicago trial was that the conspiracy was predicated on the misadventures of the 1968 Democratic convention week.

Perhaps the best question such events bring to mind is why defendants in criminal trials, threatened by serious harm from the state, have in general over time continued to behave. Maybe it was patriotism or fear of the contempt sanction or the professional discipline of their counsel, but I suspect it was their perception of their own self-interest. The Anglo-American procedures, slowly won over the centuries, limit the society's use of power. It must be in the interest of the defendant now within the grasp of the state to cooperate in exploiting those limitations.

We may end then with a bittersweet Jewish story that has been haunting me over the past weeks. Two Jews are captured by an enemy and are ordered shot. As they stand in front of the firing squad, handkerchiefs are tied across their eyes. One Jew angrily tears off the blindfold shouting: "I won't have that dirty rag on my face." The other Jew nudges him and whispers: "Please, Morris, don't make trouble." A criminal trial is not a proceedings in front of a firing squad.

# CHAPTER 26

# The Empirical Study of Decision Processes in Juries

## A Critical Review[1]

—JAMES H. DAVIS, ROBERT M. BRAY, and ROBERT W. HOLT

This chapter provides a critical review of research on the jury. Substantially more research effort has been devoted to *juror* than jury behavior. Somewhat redressing this imbalance is a sizable body of theory applying directly to *jury* decision processes. The difficulty of obtaining empirical data, variability in research procedures, and ethical constraints underline the need for models useful for extrapolation and simulation. Few prescriptions for legal practice can or should be drawn directly from an empirical result on a one-to-one basis.

The legal process has long interested researchers concerned with social behavior (e.g., Marston, 1924; Weld & Roff, 1938), but in recent years there has been a substantial increase in research activity. The courtroom trial and the dynamics of the jury have proved to be particularly appealing for study, even though relatively few disputes come to trial and fewer yet are tried before juries. Nevertheless, data about jury functioning continue to accumulate.

This review concerns the *empirical* study of juries. We include only that research in which the investigator's intent or the experimental problem clearly dealt with jurors and/or juries. Even with this limitation, we found a bewildering array of investigations assessing many nuances of the trial or examining variables identified by analogy with courtroom practices.

Jury studies often reflect some feature of the court procedure that has been abstracted for closer empirical scrutiny. Settings, ranging from the laboratory to court records, have produced a vast body of findings but little systematic theory. The seeming disorderliness is only partly attributable to a lack of conceptual notions. Other factors include the social complexity of the courtroom, variation in legal practice from state to state, and dissimilarities among cases. Such obvious variation immediately suggests the value of a statistical or probabilistic outlook for jury phenomena. Yet both the law and those involved with it seem to reflect a "strictly deterministic" point of view. Perhaps strict determinism seems intuitively more in keeping with our traditional notions of justice. Such notions frown on the caprice implied by recognizing variation in the treatment of those brought before the law. But substantial variations seem unavoidable as long as laws and social institutions differ among jurisdictions, legal procedures change with time, and different individuals administer the law.

[1] This research was supported by research grants from the National Science Foundation, GS-40192X and SOC-7305697-01 to the first author, and a National Science Foundation Graduate Fellowship to the third author.

It thus seems prudent to avoid any imputation that principles inferred *directly* from an empirical study should guide legal practice and future legislation on a one-to-one basis. An alternative is to view empirical studies as "demonstrations" that may reveal that assumptions inherent in the law do not always hold or that the legal system sometimes works in a way other than that officially prescribed. For example, a jury may be assigned a particular decision rule or instructed to disregard certain evidence inadvertently placed before it. But data may show that sometimes a different rule is used or that "disregarded" evidence does influence verdicts. Obviously such findings may not generalize to different trial situations and may say little about needed changes even for cases essentially similar to the research setting. Also, there are likely to be gaps in knowledge that require some kind of theory not only for the needed interpolation, but also for extrapolation to areas not researched or even impossible to research empirically.

The utility of an organizing conceptual system is well illustrated in disentangling the relation of jurors' guilt preference to the jury's final verdict. Some variables relevant to groups may not be defined for individuals, and the important influences acting on the two may differ. Kalven and Zeisel (1966) have held that jurors have essentially "made up their minds" before deliberation; jury discussion serves mainly to meet the legal requirement of collective decision. This assertion underscores the importance of considering *both* jurors and juries. Moreover, there has been substantially more research addressed to juror than jury behavior, especially in experimental work, perhaps in part because of the enormous costs in subjects, time, and staff for conducting mock jury studies or perusing trial records.

We first examine research with individual jurors as the object. We then survey investigations where juries as task-oriented groups are the object. Finally, we summarize the most immediately applicable theories having juries as their primary concern.

## JUROR RESEARCH

That comparatively little empirical research has been performed with *actual* juries is understandable in light of the legal requirements of private deliberations and the like. Thus mock trials, in which jurors or juries respond to simulated case materials, have become a primary research vehicle. The mock trial permits both manipulation of important variables and replication of cases.

For convenience, studies have been grouped by principal content themes to emphasize similarities among experiments. But many differences remain, especially as to *dependent* variables—of guilt/innocence, sentence length, parole eligibility, and damage awards (civil cases). Assessment of guilt alone has been made on dichotomous guilty/not guilty scales, on $n$-point scales (e.g., 7-point) ranging from guilty to innocent, and on probability-of-guilt scales. Detailing all these nuances is not possible here; Table 1 identifies the type of scales used to assess guilt and other dependent variables included in the juror studies.

### Guilt-irrelevant Factors

A fundamental assumption in the judicial system is that jurors reach decisions regarding the defendant's guilt or innocence on the "facts" of the case, not on extraneous factors associated with a trial. Few experienced observers would agree without qualification. In fact, this assumption has been challenged by critics of the jury system (see Kalven & Zeisel, 1966; Simon, 1967), and studies have examined the impact of various nonevidential or "guilt-irrelevant" factors on decision making.

*Demographic variables and verdicts.* One class of variables considered irrelevant to a trial are the defendant's demographic characteristics. Whether one is rich or poor, black or white, should not affect a jury's decision according to the law. (See also a wide-ranging summary by Stephan, 1975.)

**TABLE 1  Juror Studies Classified by Dependent Variables and Form of Response**

| INVESTIGATORS | Guilt — Dichotomous Scale | Guilt — N-point Continuous Scale | Guilt — Probability Scale | Sentencing | Parole | Damage Awards |
|---|---|---|---|---|---|---|
| Becker, Hildum, & Bateman (1965) | | X | | | | |
| Boehm (1968) | X | | | | | |
| Bray (1974) | X | X | X | X | X | |
| Davis et al. (1975) | X | X | X | | | |
| East (1972) | X | | | X | | |
| Efran (1974) | | X | | X | X | |
| Fishman & Izzett (1974) | | X | | X | | |
| Gordon & Jacobs (1969) | X | | | | | |
| Griffitt & Jackson (1973) | | X | | X | X | |
| Hoiberg & Stires (1973) | | X | | | | |
| Izzett & Leginski (1974) | | X | | X | | |
| Jones & Aronson (1973) | | | | X | | |
| Jurow (1971) | X | | | | | |
| Kaplan & Kemmerick (1974) | | X | | X | | |
| Kirby & Lamberth (1974) | X | | | | | X |
| Landy & Aronson (1969) | | X | | X | | |
| Laughlin & Izzett (1973) | | | | X | | |
| Mitchell & Byrne (1973) | | X | | X | | |
| Mitchell & Byrne (1972) | | X | | X | X | |
| Myers & Kaplan (1976) | | X | | X | | |
| Nemeth & Sosis (1973) | | | | X | | |
| Richey & Fichter (1969) | | | | X | | |
| Rumsey & Castore (1974) | | | | X | | |
| Saks et al. (1974) | | | X | | | |
| Schmitt & Colligan (1974) | | X | | X | | |
| Sealy & Cornish (1973a) | X | | | | | |
| Sealy & Cornish (1973b) | X | | | | | |
| Sigall & Ostrove (1973) | | | | X | | |
| Simon (1970) | X | | X | | | |
| Simon (1966) | X | | | | | |
| Stone (1969) | X | | | | | |
| Sue et al. (1973) | X | | | X | | |
| Sue et al. (1974) | X | | | X | | |
| Thibaut et al. (1971) | | X | | | | |
| Walker et al. (1972) | | X | | | | |
| Weld & Roff (1938) | | X | | | | |
| Weld & Danzig (1940) | | X | | | | |

In one experiment, Gordon and Jacobs (1969) examined whether affluence (high or low) of the defendant, as inferred from residence cues, resulted in differential verdicts returned by mock jurors. A manipulation check showed that 72 percent of the subjects made correct inferences about the defendant's wealth from residence cues. With only these perceptive subjects in the analysis, no significant differences were found in the average verdicts of the two groups.

In contrast, defendant's race and type of crime have been found to produce differential sentences. Reviewing cases of 3644 inmates in a Texas prison for burglary, rape, or murder, Bullock (1961) reported racial differences in sentencing by actual juries. Blacks were given longer sentences than whites for burglary, while the opposite trend occurred for murder or rape of a same-race victim. But when these latter offenses involved an opposite-race victim, blacks once again received more severe penalties. While Bullock's study focused on only a single geographical region, a large number of actual cases with real juries was sampled, and thus the findings cannot be ignored. Unfortunately, Bullock gave no information about the composition of the juries.

*Liking and leniency.* From a legal standpoint, considerations of attraction to the defendant should be irrelevant to judgments of guilt or innocence. Nevertheless, several experiments have hypothesized that a well-liked defendant will receive more lenient treatment from jurors than one who is disliked. In most such research group interaction has not been permitted, although a few recent experiments have considered the effects of discussion.

*1. Effects without deliberation.* Using student mock jurors, Efran (1974) considered the defendant's physical attractiveness as a determinant of liking. Each subject was given a written case summary and a photograph of an attractive or unattractive defendant opposite in sex. The 8 photographs (2 males and 2 females in each attraction condition) had been previously rated for physical attractiveness. Jurors were asked to determine the degree of guilt and assign a sentence. The males judged the attractive defendants less guilty, gave more lenient prescriptions for punishments, and rated them as better liked than their unattractive counterparts. The author hypothesized that the lack of an effect for females resulted either from a weaker experimental manipulation of male attractiveness or from a tendency for females to be less responsive to physical attractiveness than males.

Character traits can also influence liking. Landy and Aronson (1969) used a written summary of a case involving negligent automobile homocide. Two experiments tested whether mock jurors' judgments were influenced by the character (attractive or unattractive) of the victim or of the defendant. The dependent variable was the length of defendant's prison sentence. The authors predicted that a *victim* with favorable character traits would provoke more severe sentences than one with unfavorable traits, while a *defendant* considered attractive would receive a lighter sentence than one considered unattractive. The experiments yielded the predicted effect for *defendant* attractiveness. The authors also concluded that the liking–leniency predictions held for *victim* attractiveness, but this latter assertion is questionable. Neither experiment by itself showed the effect for victim attractiveness. Only after pooling scores across the studies did an effect emerge, a research strategy debatable because of differences in samples and procedures in the two studies. Thus, conclusions about the influence of victim characteristics should be considered tentative, although leniency toward a *defendant* with a favorable character has been replicated in other experiments (Izzett & Leginski, 1974; Kaplin & Kemmerick, 1974; Mitchell & Byrne, 1972).

Nemeth and Sosis (1973) used the Landy-

Aronson case to assess the effects of defendant's attractiveness and race among two samples of college students (working-class conservatives or upper-middle class liberals). Since experimenter perceptions were used to distinguish between the two samples, it is not entirely clear what dimensions were actually involved. The results showed that conservative jurors gave more severe sentences to the unattractive defendant, but attractiveness did not influence the judgments of liberal jurors. Also, white defendants received significantly lighter sentences from liberal than conservative jurors, but there were no significant differences in sentences for black defendants. In addition, the attractive defendant was judged to be a lighter drinker and to feel more regret for the accident.

Another research technique has been to produce differential liking by manipulating attitude similarity between the defendant and jurors, a technique based on research by Byrne and associates, which consistently showed liking to increase with the proportion of attitudes held in common by two parties (Byrne, 1971). Griffitt and Jackson (1973) used this method in a study, again based on the Landy-Aronson case material. Manipulating similarity from a set of seven attitudes irrelevant to the trial, they found that mock jurors whose attitudes were similar to the defendant rated him as significantly more attractive, judged him to be slightly but significantly less guilty, gave him a shorter prison term (assuming guilt), and recommended shorter imprisonment before parole. Results consistent with these findings were also noted on several additional evaluative scales.

Mitchell and Byrne (1973) examined the effects of juror–defendant attitude similarity and juror authoritarianism on ratings of guilt and sentencing. Attitude similarity was manipulated on five topics irrelevant to a case concerning student theft of an examination, while authoritarianism was assessed on a 22-item $F$ scale. Their results showed an interaction between similarity and authoritarianism for both dependent variables, a contrast with the simple similarity effect reported by Griffitt and Jackson (1973). Only high authoritarians responded to the similarity information as a cue in making decisions about the defendant. Specifically, mock jurors who scored high on the $F$ scale rated a dissimilar defendant more guilty and imposed a more severe sentence than for a similar defendant, while those who scored low on the $F$ scale showed no significant differences.

These studies have generally supported the liking–leniency hypothesis. But great care must be taken in extrapolation because of the many differences among trials. Using a mock embezzlement case, Fishman and Izzett (1974) observed that a socially *attractive* defendant was sentenced more severely when he had low justification for his act (paying a personal debt) than when he had high justification (paying a large medical bill). Sentences for an *unattractive* defendant were not influenced by justification. Surprisingly, attractive defendants were judged more guilty than unattractive ones. Sigall and Ostrove (1973) noted another exception. In a mock trial when physical attractiveness was considered unrelated to the success of the crime (a burglary), an attractive defendant received more lenient treatment. But the opposite results were found when attractiveness was considered important to successful completion of the crime (a swindle).

From all these studies, one might conclude that the jury critics are correct in claiming that jurors are inappropriately influenced by "extralegal" factors. The studies discussed above suggest that a liked defendant will receive more lenient treatment than when disliked. This pattern may be examined from at least three conceptual approaches.

The first and most direct approach is the Byrne-Clore (1970) reinforcement model of attraction, which predicts that any stimulus associated with positive (negative) affect will be liked (disliked). Byrne (1971) has shown that a person who is liked will receive much more favorable judgments, such as approval of a loan or hiring, than one who is not liked. It is not surprising that mock jurors' judgments should be similarly influenced. The juror studies just reviewed are clearly compatible with the Byrne-Clore model. Common to these investigations is a manipulation of positive or negative affect toward the defendant, followed by assessing its influence on subsequent judgments. This differential liking for the defendant has been achieved in several ways, including manipulations of physical attractiveness, character traits, and attitude similarity to the jurors. But the influence of *affect* on jurors' judgments should not be interpreted as suggesting that trial information is unimportant. More appropriately, when trial-relevant information (evidence) is held constant, differing amounts of liking will influence individuals' judgments.

A second but related approach derives from research on impression formation. Impression formation models aim toward an accurate theoretical representation of subjects' combination of information to provide an overall coherent impression of the stimulus person—in our case, the defendant (cf. Anderson & Fishbein, 1965, on the additive model; Anderson, 1971, on the averaging model; and Wyer, 1973, on the conjunctive model). Regardless of how it is combined, one can argue that information rather than affect is the important element, since in these experiments all the manipulations provided additional information (either positive or negative) about the defendant (e.g., traits, social status, and attitudes). Jurors may reach different impressions after combining different kinds of information.

The third approach treats the judgment of guilt as a behavior and emphasizes the appropriate antecedent predictors of the behavior. Fishbein (1967) has proposed a model for predicting behavioral intentions —cognitions that are assumed to mediate overt behavior. Intentions, when properly selected, have shown a very high relation to overt behavior (Ajzen, 1967; Carlson, 1968;

Fishbein, 1966). According to the model, a person's intention ($I$) to perform a given act is a function of his or her attitude ($x$) toward doing it (as contrasted with attitude toward an object), personal beliefs ($y$) about whether others expect it, and motivation ($z$) to comply with others' expectations (cf. Ajzen, 1967; Fishbein, 1966). Other factors influence behavioral intentions only indirectly by affecting the weight, $c_1$ or $c_2$, respectively, of the attitudinal, $x$, or normative, $yz$, component in the expression $I = c_1x + c_2yz$. The relative importance of the two terms in predicting intentions are thought to vary according to the situation (Ajzen, 1967, 1971).

These three conceptual approaches are in sufficient contrast to be heuristically valuable in interpreting juror decision data. For example, it seems likely that attraction toward the defendant influences the behavior of finding the defendant guilty by changing the attitudinal component in the equation given above. It also seems likely that this component is the most important for individuals' judgments, while the normative component plays a minor role. The normative component probably has more importance, however, for the same judgments after a group interchange such as the deliberation process. If this assumption is correct, then results from studies using jurors only would be a poor analog of actual jury behavior. In any event, we hope that such conceptual approaches will be exploited further to determine their utility in accounting directly for juror and jury guilt decisions.

*2. Effects with deliberation.* The *juror* studies reviewed above have been criticized because of the absence of group discussion. Several other investigations permitting group discussion (but disallowing group decisions) have focused on the effect of discussion on subjects' judgments by comparing their prediscussion responses with those after discussion.

Izzett and Leginski (1974), using the Landy-Aronson case, assessed the effects of group discussion and defendant's character on mock jurors' verdicts. Subjects were asked to sentence either an attractive or unattractive defendant before and after 10 minutes of discussion about the reasons for their initial judgments. However, the 4- to 6-person groups were not asked to reach a group (jury) decision. Before discussion the unattractive defendant received a significantly more severe sentence than the attractive defendant. But after discussion, jurors who rated the unattractive defendant became significantly more lenient, in their judgments, while jurors who rated the attractive defendant did not change much. This pattern resulted in no significant differences between the attractive and unattractive conditions in post-discussion judgments. In short, discussion produced a leniency shift for the unattractive defendant that eliminated the initial differences in sentencing tendencies among jurors.

In Rumsey and Castore's (1974) study 3-person mock juries of the same sex deliberated to unanimous decisions, but the verdicts were not reported. In contrast to Izzett and Leginski's (1974) experiment, leniency effects were found for the attractive defendant *both* before and after discussion.

Laughlin & Izzett (1973) studied the effects of discussion when attraction was manipulated by juror–defendant attitude similarity. Mock jurors first sentenced a defendant in a euthanasia case who was similar or dissimilar to them on five attitudes irrelevant to the trial. Next, they discussed the case for 15 minutes in 6-person groups homogeneous in terms of the similarity manipulation; then they individually sentenced the defendant again. Interestingly, attitude similarity only produced a significant effect after discussion: A leniency shift emerged in the similar condition (i.e., sentences became significantly shorter). No significant change occurred for subjects in the dissimilar condition.

Myers and Kaplan (1976) also emphasized the importance of group discussion. In their experiment, mock jurors first made judgments of degree of guilt and length of sentence for eight traffic cases that varied in

implication of guilt (high or low). They then discussed half the cases (two high guilt, two low guilt) for 2½ minutes each in 6-person groups; finally, individual jurors again gave guilt and sentencing judgments. As predicted, deliberations polarized judgments. After discussion, the mean guilt judgment in low-guilt cases significantly dropped, while the opposite effect occurred for the high-guilt cases. In contrast, there was no significant change in decisions on those cases that were not discussed (control). Parallel results occurred for *sentencing* on the low-guilt cases, and—although not significantly—an expected trend toward severity was found for the high-guilt cases.

These last four studies emphasize the importance of the deliberation process but also raise questions about how it interacts with interpersonal attraction variables considered in some degree to be independent of the trial material. The common theme concerns some shifting in sentiment after discussion. But the exact conditions under which this occurs only for the well-liked defendant (Izzett & Leginski, 1974) or, more generally, across all treatments (cf. Myers & Kaplan, 1976; Rumsey & Castore, 1974) remains to be determined.

These seemingly contradictory findings might be reconciled by viewing the interaction processes of a task-oriented group as affecting a social decision scheme or rule for combining initial member preferences on some issue (e.g., defendant guilt) into a group decision (Davis, 1973). Whether shifts should result from group discussion depends both on the guilt-preference distribution describing the pool of individual jurors after the trial and the particular social decision scheme that characterizes the jury's interaction. Davis (1973) has shown that, when the initial *individual* distribution is skewed and a majority process is at work, the resulting distribution of *jury* verdicts exaggerates the nonuniformities in the individual distribution, under most conditions. This difference between group and individual distributions would, of course, be reflected in mean shift scores such as those noted in these studies.

That the groups merely discussed these cases without reaching a group decision does not necessarily rule out a social decision scheme explanation. Whether a group reaches a decision does not prevent jury members from recognizing the rule (norm) for doing so or from extrapolating what the decision would be. The processes invoked by discussion can, in principle, still be described by a decision scheme, the influence of which would be reflected in the individual post-deliberation mean scores. Thus, the use of different decision schemes by subjects in different experimental conditions is a plausible explanation of why shifts might occur in only some conditions of experiments (Izzett & Leginski, 1974; Laughlin & Izzett, 1973). In fact, Bray (1974) found that different decision schemes may have been in use within different experimental conditions.

Recall that for experiments studying the influence of irrelevant factors, discussion was introduced to determine whether the liking–leniency effect would persist in postdiscussion judgments. The more important issue, however, is whether irrelevant factors have an effect on jury decisions.

Bray (1974) used mock *juries* with interacting members and manipulated liking for the defendant by juror–defendant attitude similarity. In one of three attitude similarity conditions (similar, dissimilar, or control) all jurors listened to a 45-minute recording of a rape case. After the trial, they first gave guilt verdicts individually and then 6-person juries of the same sex deliberated to a group decision. For predeliberation ratings, the usual leniency effect occurred when the defendant held attitudes similiar to the jurors'. In addition, females favored conviction significantly more often than did males. When the decisions for *juries* were examined, however, no significant effects emerged. Analyses suggested that for attitude similarity the discrepancy between the findings for *jurors* and those for *juries* may have been due to differences in statistical power; there

was a substantially larger sample of jurors (504) than juries (84). Unfortunately, because of the rather weak similarity effect (i.e., small mean difference, though significant) among individuals, Bray could not address strongly the basic question of whether the liking–leniency effect will occur among juries. Considering that the trial presented via the tape recording was probably more vivid and engaging than the commonly used written case summary, this study raises questions about the extent to which attitude similarity has an influence on jurors' judgments.

Despite the findings for attitude similarity, sample size did not account for the juror–jury discrepancy for the sex variable in the Bray study. Further analysis showed that these individual–group differences were attributable to the social processes used by the groups. Even though male and female jurors gave significantly different guilt ratings by virtue of different social processes, the verdict distributions for the opposite-sex juries did not differ significantly. Whether similar results will occur for different case material awaits further investigation. At a minimum, however, the Bray experiment calls into question the practice of drawing inferences about *jury decisions based on data only from noninteracting jurors.*

## Juror Demographic Characteristics

Just as several investigations have studied jurors' characteristics in relation to the defendant's, so others have considered jurors' attributes independent of the defendant. Little consistency in the efficacy of demographic variables has been found across studies using different cases and even within the same experiment for different dependent variables. For example, sex differences in *guilt preferences* have been observed in some studies of mock jurors (cf. Bray, 1974; Davis, Kerr, Atkin, Holt, & Meek, 1975; East, 1972; Efran, 1974; Sealy & Cornish, 1973b; Sue, Smith, & Gilbert, 1974) but not in others (Griffitt & Jackson, 1973; Sealy &

Cornish, 1973a). When considering *sentencing* as the dependent variable, nearly all studies reported no statistically significant effects due to respondents' sex (Bray, 1974; East, 1972; Jones & Aronson, 1973; Landy & Aronson, 1969; Laughlin & Izzett, 1973; Sue, Smith & Gilbert, 1974). One study (Griffitt & Jackson, 1973) that did find a sex effect for the sentencing variable termed it a surprising result for which no explanation was posed.

Race and education are also obvious research targets. In mock trials involving pleas of insanity, Simon (1967) found that black jurors were more prone to acquit than whites and better-educated jurors were more likely to vote guilty than poorly educated jurors. Nonetheless, she was cautious about generalizations of such race and education effects. (See also Boone, 1973.)

Among adult mock jurors in Britain, Sealy and Cornish (1973b) assessed effects of sex, age, occupational status, education, and legal experience on individual jurors' verdicts for cases involving theft and rape. Even though there were scattered significant relations between some of these variables and decisions of guilt, the only consistent result across both trials was that younger jurors were more lenient in judgments of guilt. This effect, if consistently found, suggests an obvious restraint on generalizations from research with student jurors who often participate in mock jury trials in the U.S. One caution, however, must be noted. In the Sealy-Cornish study, the jurors deliberated in jury groups before giving individual judgments. If, as seems likely, jurors' judgments were influenced by group deliberations, it would not be surprising if they differed from similar judgments obtained before discussion.

The lack of consistent and robust relations between demographic variables and juror behavior is an unhappy outcome. Further, considering the many unique factors associated with any case (e.g., type of crime, defendant's prior record, seriousness of the charge, clarity of the evidence, competence of attorneys, and the dependent variables

studied), there seems to be little reason for optimism that such gross characteristics of individuals significantly aid in predicting juror/jury decisions.

## Attitudes, Values, and Guilt

It has long been believed that attitudes and behavior are closely linked. Trial lawyers, in selecting a jury by *voir dire* proceedings, believe that attitudes of jurors are critical in determining their responses to a trial. For example, in discussing jurors' occupations, Simon gave the following summary of opinion thought to be characteristic of trial lawyers:

As a rule, clergymen, school teachers, lawyers and wives of lawyers do not make desirable jurors. They are too often sought out for advice and tend to be too opinionated.

Retired businessmen are usually fair but disinclined to render wild verdicts. A reasonably well-educated laboring man is not to be despised. Generally railroad men and their wives are excellent jurors. They are solid, substantial citizens who work hard, are frugal in their personal living, yet have the opportunity to travel and to play more than their fellows [1967, pp. 103–104].

Noted trial lawyer Percy Foreman claimed: "The best defense in a murder case is the fact that the deceased should have been killed, regardless of how it happened [Smith, 1966, p. 96]." In one case that won acquittal, Foreman so effectively villified the victim that he felt "the jury was ready to dig up the deceased and shoot him all over again [p. 96]."

Recent literature summaries reveal little evidence for a close relation of attitudes and behavior (cf. Wicker, 1969). The relation of jurors' attitudes to their judgments of guilt shows a similar lack of correspondence. One part of Simon's work with cases involving claims of insanity (1967) examined the relation between a mock juror's attitudes toward a single object and his or her predeliberation verdict. She found no significant relation between them in three independent assessments that used attitudes toward the mentally ill, forms of sexual expression, and psychiatric interpretations of motivations and behavior.

There is some evidence that jurors' central or fundamental values affect their judgments. Becker, Hildum, and Bateman (1965) assessed whether religious values influenced mock jurors' verdicts on a "mercy killing." They hypothesized that jurors with a non-Catholic background would be more tolerant and hence less conviction prone than Catholics. This prediction was supported on guilt judgments taken both before and after jury deliberations. (Unfortunately the group verdicts were not reported.) Interestingly, the non-Catholics tended to be lenient even though they received a strict command to be severe, corroborating a frequent assertion that jurors do not follow the law but determine it.

Other studies have focused on authoritarianism and the liberal–conservative dimension of jurors. A general theme of these investigations is that the authoritarian juror is biased toward guilty verdicts, a notion of particular concern for cases involving the death penalty. Because all capital trial jurors must forswear scruples against the death penalty, it has been argued that such "death qualified" juries are inclined to be composed of politically conservative or authoritarian jurors.

To assess this last notion, Crosson (1967) tested real jurors (1) who had served in capital trials, and (2) who had served in noncapital criminal cases but professed scruples against the death penalty. The tests included Rokeach's Dogmatism Scale, Opinionation Scale, and Conservatism–Liberalism Scale, the Watson-Glaser Critical Thinking Test, and Seigal's Manifest Hostility Scale. The results showed that only the Conservatism–Liberalism Scale permitted one to discriminate between the two groups; the capital trial jurors were significantly more conservative. Due to the strong relation of the $F$ scale (authoritarianism) and the Conservatism–

Liberalism Scale (cf. Bray, 1974), the data supported the hypothesis that capital trial jurors tend to be high authoritarians.

Jurow (1971) studied whether jurors favorably disposed toward capital punishment were (1) more likely to convict than jurors opposed to it, and (2) more likely to be politically conservative, authoritarian, and punitive in assigning penalties. His subjects, industrial workers roughly comparable to many actual juror pools, gave guilty judgments in two mock trials. The predicted effect that capital trial jurors are conviction prone occurred in one trial but not in the other. The second hypothesis—that capital trial jurors tend to be politically conservative, authoritarian, and punitive—received strong support.

Boehm (1968) also dealt with the relation of authoritarianism and guilt judgments. Using two versions of a case in which the evidence either favored conviction or acquittal, she found that high-authoritarian students judged a defendant guilty more often than did anti-authoritarians. These results, however, are questionable because of conceptual and methodological problems related to the measurement of authoritarianism.

Three studies by Kirby and Lamberth (1974) concerned the development and use of an oral $F$ scale for juror selection. In the first study they developed a 9-item oral measure that correlated .82 with a 22-item, paper-and-pencil $F$ scale, which they tested in the second experiment, a mock courtroom trial. Twelve students over age 21 composed the jury in the jurybox, while 24 others composed two additional juries in the audience without regard to age. Subjects in the jurybox received the oral $F$ scale, while those in the audience completed the written $F$ scale. Based on a median split, jurors were classified within their own jury group as high or low authoritarians. After hearing a case involving a civil suit, jurors were asked to award damages. Only high authoritarians in the jurybox awarded damages. That the authoritarian jurors in the audience did not show similar responses was attributed to lack of subject involvement. But at least two rival explanations exist: Differences in the jurors' age and the relative degree of authoritarianism of the jurybox jurors compared to that of the audience jurors. The report contained insufficient information to assess the plausibility of these alternatives. If their conclusion about subject involvement is correct, however, the study suggests that high authoritarians are more punitive than low authoritarians.

In the third study, after deliberations each juror reported two verdicts: present sentiment about the defendant's guilt and what it had been before deliberations. Subjects also rated their perceived similarity to the defendant, although the dimensions for this rating were not reported. High authoritarians who perceived themselves as dissimilar to the defendant all found the defendant guilty; those who were similar all voted not guilty. Similarity did not have any effect on the verdicts of low authoritarians, but it was not clear whether these latter results were subjects' pre- or postdeliberation verdicts.

Mitchell and Byrne (1972) asked high- and low-authoritarian mock jurors to give ratings of guilt and recommend sentences for a defendant with a favorable or unfavorable character. In addition, the judge instructed them to either ignore or give special attention to this information. The results showed such a strong inclination toward guilt that the issue of whether authoritarians were more guilt prone than low authoritarians could not be addressed. For sentencing, however, high authoritarians were more lenient when the defendant's character was positive than when it was negative, despite the judge's instructions. Low authoritarians did not show any differences in sentences. In a second experiment, Mitchell and Byrne (1973) found that high authoritarians were both more guilt prone and punitive to a defendant with dissimilar attitudes. Again, these variables did not significantly influence judgments of low authoritarians.

A recent study by Bray (1974) found that high authoritarians gave longer sentences and time to parole but did *not* find the defendant guilty more often than low authoritarians. Further, he did not observe attitude similarity to interact with authoritarianism in subjects' ratings.

These studies suggest that judgments of punitiveness are consistently influenced (either independently or in combination with juror–defendant similarity) by juror authoritarianism. In all cases, the high authoritarians recommended more severe punishments. However, the claim that high authoritarians are more likely to reach a guilty verdict has only meager support. The study with the clearest results (Becker, Hildum, & Bateman, 1965) was in fact only suggestive; it dealt with religious values and did not directly compare high and low authoritarians. When considering the effect of authoritarianism alone, the only relevant study (Jurow, 1971) found mixed results, with high authoritarians judging the defendant guilty more often in one trial but not in the other. Of the three studies assessing the effect of similarity between the defendant and jurors, two (Kirby & Lamberth, 1974; Mitchell & Byrne, 1973) concluded that high authoritarians are more guilt prone only toward a dissimilar defendant, while the other study (Bray, 1974) found no indication that authoritarianism influenced guilt judgments. In summary then, it appears that for judgments of punitiveness high authoritarians tend to be more harsh than low authoritarians, but for judgments of guilt the influence of authoritarianism remains to be clarified. This conclusion, of course, only applies to individual jurors' judgments and only by implication addresses the influence of authoritarianism on jury verdicts.

## Effects of Judicial Instructions

During a trial jurors may be exposed to information that they are expected to disregard in reaching their final verdict. Indeed a function of the presiding judge is to instruct jurors about what information is relevant. Whether jurors follow these instructions has been the concern of several investigations.

It has been argued that in widely publicized cases it is impossible to impanel an unbiased jury since jurors will have made up their minds before hearing the evidence. (See Padawer-Singer & Barton, 1975, for a summary of pretrial publicity effects.) Simon (1966) found that "sensational" pretrial reporting influenced juror verdicts before the trial more than "conservative" publicity. But when the judge instructed jurors at the beginning of the trial to "lay aside any opinion that you may have formed about the case [p. 41]" and then heard the trial testimony, the differential effects vanished.

Kline and Jess (1966) also suggested that jurors are responsive to the judge's counsel to ignore pretrial information. In their study four mock *juries* heard a radio tape and read a newspaper account of facts surrounding the trial offense. While all the juries referred to this pretrial information in deliberating, three of them complied with the judge's instructions to ignore the information in their group decisions. Of course, with such a small sample, these results are merely suggestive.

It seems naive to assume that all jurors heed judges' instructions. Indeed, Mitchell and Byrne (1972) found that only the low authoritarians complied with the judge's instructions to ignore irrelevant information; high authoritarians let their judgments be influenced by legally inappropriate evidence.

More recent studies suggest that whether subjects disregard pretrial publicity depends more on the juror's sex and importance of the information than on the judge's instructions. Sue, Smith, and Gilbert (1974) found that regardless of instructions, when pretrial publicity provided very damaging but relevant evidence, female subjects judged a defendant guilty more often than males; for nondamaging irrelevant information, there were no sex differences in guilt ratings. The

same result has also been observed by Hoiberg and Stires (1973), but the fact that their trial concerned rape may explain the sex differences. Whether females tend to be influenced more than males by pretrial publicity remains to be clarified.

Even though they know that the judge will order it stricken from the record and will instruct the jury to disregard it, trial lawyers often introduce objectionable evidence they believe favorable to their client in the hope that jurors will nonetheless be influenced. Sue, Smith, and Caldwell (1973) presented mock jurors with either strong or weak evidence about a murder case. In the experimental conditions the jurors received other information ruled as admissible or inadmissible by the judge. The inadmissible evidence was influential only when the evidence for the case was weak. The judge's instructions to disregard inadmissible evidence were *not* followed when the admissible evidence was inconclusive but the inadmissible evidence was relevant and damaging.

In contrast, Sealy and Cornish (1973a) found that in two trials jurors followed the judge's instructions to ignore information about a defendant's previous convictions. When evidence of prior convictions on charges similar to the present offense was introduced, significantly more guilty verdicts were observed than when the judge ruled such evidence inadmissible. These results were obtained from adult mock jurors in Britain who had previously participated in jury deliberations. Since the Sue et al. experiment obtained judgments without any deliberaton, it is not clear whether the conflicting results of these studies are attributable to the discussion, the judge's instructions, or other differences inherent in the case material.

In summary, the effectiveness of the judge's instructions to disregard various bits of testimony is uncertain. Future research could effectively focus on clarifying whether male and female jurors differ in their susceptability to pretrial publicity and whether interacting juries heed a judge's counsel more closely than individual jurors.

Videotaped trial presentations suggest a way to avoid this problem altogether. As proposed by an Ohio judge (McCrystal, 1971, 1972), an entire trial would be videotaped and then edited by the presiding judge and attorneys before the jurors view it. Besides precluding objectionable information, this procedure could allow attorneys to alter the order in which their witnesses testify, thus presenting the strongest sequence of arguments for their clients. Videotaped trials might also help expedite cases, an attractive feature in view of crowded dockets.

But the empirical concern is whether verdicts from a videotaped presentation would be the same as those rendered in a "live" trial. Miller, Bender, Florence, and Nicholson (1974) arranged for 52 jurors (on their last day of jury service) to hear a case, staged by professional actors, concerning an automobile accident. The jurors were told that the large panel was being used for research on jury size and that the videotape equipment was being used to provide a trial record. Otherwise, the proceedings were conducted like a real trial until time for deliberations. At this point jurors completed a questionnaire that solicited their individual judgments of the defendant's negligence and a suggested damage award. One month later a comparable group of jurors viewed the videotape. The mode of presentation failed to produce significant differences in jurors' judgments, a finding supportive of the use of the video materials. Other research has begun to examine further the use of videotape in the courtroom (e.g., Miller, Bender, Boster, Florence, Fontes, Hocking, & Nicholson, 1975; Short, Florence, & Marsh, 1975; Williams, Farmer, Lee, Cundick, Howell, & Rooker, 1975).

## Order of Presentation and Information Integration

The long-standing controversy in psychology about the effect of order of presen-

tation in persuasive communications has perhaps its most practical application in the courtroom. Although the problem of order effects has been researched more generally in the attitude change literature, several studies have considered it specifically in the context of a jury trial.

Weld and Roff (1938) asked law students to make judgments on a 9-point guilt scale after each of 13 installments of testimony on a bigamy case. By varying the order of presenting the installments, they hoped to determine the importance of order and identify those facts most salient in determining the jurors' final opinions. Although no statistical analyses were reported, the data suggested that certain information had a critical impact on decisions and that the most recently heard evidence strongly influenced the final opinion. Weld and Danzig (1940) examined in a mock trial the influence of various bits of testimony on verdicts both for individual jurors and for three juries (12 males, 12 females, and 17 males and females). They did not vary the order of the evidential arguments, but for the particular order that was used, they concluded that recent arguments had the most influence on juror verdicts. Unfortunately, there were only three juries, and all three were declared hung after 30 minutes of deliberation.

In contrast, Stone (1969) failed to find significant differences in verdicts due to order of presentation. In his experiment either the prosecution or defense presented its case first, followed by the opposing side. Then mock jurors gave tentative verdicts; after a strong closing argument that favored the prosecution, they gave a final verdict. The results showed that the tentative verdict was an important predictor of the final verdict; the order of presentation had no significant effect.

Two investigations (Thibaut, Walker, & Lind, 1972; Walker, Thibaut, & Andreoli, 1972) studied the issue of argument presentation. As with Weld and Roff's research, mock jurors were asked to make judgments following installments of the facts. Walker, Thibaut, and Andreoli varied whether the prosecution or defense presented first and whether evidence was presented in a weak-to-strong sequence. For the former variable they found strong recency effects; for the latter they concluded that the weak-to-strong sequence was generally more effective. When Thibaut et al. tested the importance of presentation order in addition to assessing differences between an inquisitorial and adversary presentation, they once again found recency effects and also evidence favoring the adversary over the inquisitorial system. (See further Thibaut & Walker, 1975.)

Despite these trends toward recency effects, the evidence is far from complete. All these investigations required subjects to make periodic judgments throughout the experiment instead of a single judgment after all the evidence was presented. Byrne, Lamberth, Palmer, and London (1969) have suggested that this particular procedure may be more responsible for the findings of recency than the order of the arguments. Also, none of these studies considered order effects in connection with *deliberating juries*.

But Weld and Roff (1938) also wanted to know *how* information influences jurors' opinions. Since their early work, pertinent mathematical models have been developed that permit such information aggregation to be examined more precisely. Kaplan and Kemmerick (1974) used Anderson's (1971) model of information integration to aid in determining the extent to which mock jurors used evidential and nonevidential information (i.e., defendant characterization) in deciding guilt and appropriate sentences. For eight traffic felony cases, subjects heard either high or low incriminating evidence and received positive, neutral, negative, or no additional information about the defendant's character. The results suggested that jurors' final judgments were an additive function of both types of information. Since the defendant characterizations consisted of trait adjectives and the cases consisted of short summaries, future research could profitably examine whether Kaplan and Kemmerick's findings will occur with the increasingly complex stimuli to be encountered in studies more closely approaching an actual trial.

## Additional Juror Studies

A few issues have received only cursory attention and many important questions have yet to receive empirical consideration. Some research, too, has proved difficult to classify. This section considers these studies.

Lerner's (1965) "just world" hypothesis —that individuals get what they deserve and conversely deserve what they get—has a ready application to jury trials. Jones and Aronson (1973) made the counterintuitive extension "that if a disaster befalls an individual, more fault is attributed to that victim if he is a respectable person than if he is less respectable [p. 415]." Unrespectable people get their just reward. If a tragedy happens to a respectable person, some reasonable justification that can be attributed to the victim must be invented. Such justifications, said Jones and Aronson, result in attributions of "more responsibility (fault) to a victim the more respectable he is [1973, p. 416]." To test this hypothesis, they asked subjects to determine prison sentences and rate the extent to which a victim who was either married, a virgin, or divorced was at fault in a case of completed or attempted rape. The results confirmed the prediction that the respectable victim (i.e., married or virgin) was more at fault than the unrespectable victim (i.e., divorcee). In addition, when the victim was married, the defendant received a significantly longer prison term than when she was divorced.

The generality of the "just world" hypothesis is not entirely clear, however, as observed by Schmitt and Colligan (1974) using the Jones-Aronson case but in a setting more nearly in the mock trial tradition. Male or female subjects read a description of a rape in which either the victim or defendant was depicted as being attitudinally similar or dissimilar to themselves. Jurors then rated the victim's responsibility for the crime and sentenced the defendant. The "just world" prediction only held for male subjects, and there were no significant differences across conditions for defendant sentences. Clearly, additional research is needed to test further the empirical viability of the "just world" hypothesis.

Another issue that has received only fleeting attention concerns the meaning of the phrase "beyond a reasonable doubt." Simon (1970) and Simon and Mahan (1971) tried to quantify the meaning of this time-honored phrase. In the first study (Simon, 1970) mock jurors either gave dichotomous guilty/not guilty verdicts or rated probability of guilt on an 11-point scale. To determine the point on the probability scale that corresponded to the proportion of subjects voting for guilty (not guilty) on the dichotomous scale, Simon began with subjects selecting 100 percent probability of guilt and moved down the probability scale until the proportion of jurors voting guilty on the dichotomous scale had been reached. The results showed that jurors tended to vote guilty if they thought the probability of guilt was at least 74 percent. In a followup study, Simon and Mahan (1971) compared judgments of student jurors with those of actual jurors: Verdicts of student jurors favored the defendant more than those of actual jurors. In addition, both sets of jurors who estimated guilt on a probability scale and then on a dichotomous scale showed a pro-defendant bias; responses to the scales in the reverse order again showed students to be more lenient.

Simon and Mahan (1971) also asked judges, actual jurors, and student jurors to translate the phrases "beyond a reasonable doubt" (the standard used in criminal cases) and "by a preponderance of the evidence" (the standard applied in civil actions) into probability statements regarding guilt. For "reasonable doubt," there was close agreement among the respondents, with the majority of each group interpreting guilt at a probability of at least .86. But for "preponderance of evidence," judges were more lenient, interpreting a probability of .55 to mean guilty compared to about .75 for stu-

dents and actual jurors. Apparently the judges made a much sharper distinction between criminal and civil standards, a distinction they wrongly believed jurors make also. These data give an initial indication of what constitutes a reasonable doubt, although further research is needed to confirm and extend the findings. This research also argues that it is probably erroneous to conclude that the midpoint for an $n$-point degree-of-guilt scale represents the cutting point between sentiment for guilty and not guilty.

On another issue Vidmar (1972a) hypothesized that if the punitive consequences of a guilty vote were too severe, the juror would vote not guilty, even when believing the defendant had committed the crime. To test this idea, students were presented with a simulated version of a murder trial for which pretesting showed the preferred verdict to be either manslaughter or second-degree murder. The results confirmed the basic hypothesis. For example, subjects forced to choose between first-degree murder or not guilty chose not guilty significantly more often than those whose options included three levels of guilt and not guilty. Vidmar concluded that "under conditions of restricted alternatives, the more severe the degree of guilt associated with the least severe guilt alternative, the greater were the chances of obtaining a not guilty verdict [1972a, p. 215]."

Larntz (1975) presented an alternative interpretation of Vidmar's data. Using conditional probabilities, he obtained expected frequencies of verdicts for each experimental condition and then compared the expected frequencies to those obtained by a chi-square goodness-of-fit test. Larntz concluded that the data were explained by the model and hence not due to the psychological phenomena proposed by Vidmar. Although Larntz's approach is intriguing and worthy of extended investigation, his conclusion must be qualified because his conditional probability model "fits" Vidmar's data only marginally.

Finally, Saks, Werner, and Ostrom (1974)

examined whether jurors presume a defendant's innocence at the start of a trial as the law prescribes. They conceived the problem in terms of Anderson's (1971) information integration theory, and, by working "backward" from the final impression, they were able to estimate the initial impression. Based on subjects' rating of individual pieces of evidence, they concluded that their mock jurors generally presumed innocence as the law intends. The conception is intriguing, and it is hoped that further studies like it will follow.

## Summary and Conclusions: Research on Jurors

Results and conclusions from the studies with jurors should be qualified in several ways: (1) They are based mainly on studies using short case summaries as stimulus material. (2) They provide instances of influences on individuals but are not necessarily representative of *jury* functioning as their authors so often imply. (3) They are based on studies that rely heavily on student jurors, a population at least visibly different from that comprising most jury rolls.

The research on demographic variables has uncovered many isolated effects but no general patterns that facilitate prediction. But due to ease of study and "apparent" relevance of these variables (e.g., sex and race), they are likely to receive continued attention. The situational factors that probably interact with demographic variables dim optimism about their immediate usefulness. Their utility is further complicated by the variability of legal practice. It is plausible that demographic variables predictive in one jurisdiction may fail to aid in another.

A more positive assertion can be made about the relation of a juror's liking for the defendant and corresponding leniency in verdict. With few exceptions, studies where discussion among jurors was prohibited have shown that a better-liked defendant receives more lenient treatment for both judgments

of guilt and sentencing than one who is disliked. Where discussion was permitted, the leniency conclusion becomes highly tentative. This again illustrates the possible lack of correspondence between results from jurors and juries.

The claim that high-authoritarian jurors have a proclivity for guilty verdicts is basically unwarranted. What has been found is that juror authoritarianism (either independently or in combination with juror–defendant similarity) affects judgments of punitiveness such that high authoritarians were more severe.

On whether jurors follow judges' instructions to ignore pretrial publicity or inadmissible evidence, the data are equivocal. Definitive data resolving these questions should be welcomed by a legal profession concerned about the selection of biased juries. The use of videotape trials is one proposal to circumvent the problem of inadmissible evidence.

The research on order of presenting arguments also offers an ambiguous picture. The various procedures used in such studies have, no doubt, added to the general confusion. Investigations designed to resolve this problem should give careful attention to procedural nuances and must pursue the issue among interacting juries.

### JURY RESEARCH

In this section, we group jury studies in three classes: (1) studies aimed at the *deliberation* preceding the verdict that tend to emphasize interaction processes; (2) studies concerned mainly with the *verdict* reached by juries deliberating under various conditions, compositions, and so forth; (3) research in which court records, former jurors, or the like were polled in a search for statistical regularities. Studies falling in the last category tend to reflect actual cases and real juries to some degree, while research in the first two categories is more likely to use constructed case materials and mock juries.

Because of the difficulties in pursuing research questions that have a rather direct referent in the real world, many investigators have qualified their generalizations accordingly. Two common difficulties are inadequate sample size and the use of cases that so overwhelmingly favor either the prosecution or defense that jury deliberation has been severely curtailed. Table 2 offers a representative sample of jury studies.

## Jury Deliberation Processes

*Foreman selection and influence.* The foreman plays a unique role in the jury by virtue of having the duty to manage certain "housekeeping" functions and thus may have greater influence over the final verdict than other jurors. Several investigations have considered factors important in foreman selection, one of which is the juror's sex. A study by Strodtbeck, James, and Hawkins of mock jurors (from actual jury rolls) found that "only one fifth as many women were made foremen as would be expected by chance [1957, p. 715]." Gordon (1968) observed that 16 of 18 mock juries selected male foremen. Davis et al. (1975) reported that in 72 student juries 82 percent of those elected foremen were males, whereas 71 percent of all jurors were males.

Seating and conversation patterns of jurors during deliberation also affect choice of foremen. Strodtbeck and Hook (1961) found that 32 of 69 foremen were chosen from mock jurors occupying "end" positions at a rectangular table. Besides an end-of-the-table phenomenon, Gordon (1968) observed a tendency for mock jurors (both students and community adults) who began the conversation in the deliberation room to become foremen, an observation confirmed by Strodtbeck et al. (1957). Occupational status (proprietor, clerical, skilled, or labor) was also related to foreman selection: The higher the occupational status the more often foremen were chosen from that class. From these findings, one can deduce that a jury foreman is likely to be a male proprietor who begins conversation and sits at the end of the traditional rectangular table.

How much does the foreman influence the jury verdict? Simon (1967) found that foremen accounted for about 31 percent of the verbalizations during deliberations after a mock trial; according to Strodtbeck et al. (1957), the average participation rate was about 25 percent. Whether this additional participation serves to persuade other jurors or merely to regulate the proceedings is ambiguous. Strodtbeck et al. carried out a content analysis on foremen's verbalizations during deliberations and concluded that the foreman adopted a regulatory role, indicated by the taking of a more neutral position in the discussion than other high-participating jurors. In contrast, Bevan, Albert, Loiseaux, Mayfield, and Wright (1958) argued that the foreman was effectively persuasive in a case involving damage awards and adult mock jurors. In that study, however, the foremen were confederates of the experimenter who deliberately attempted to influence the jury verdict. While the study suggested that a foreman *can* influence the jury verdict, there is some question as to the incidence of persuasive acts that would routinely arise. A freely interacting "control" condition would have helped establish such a baseline.

*Juror participation.* An often-studied feature of group processes is the extent to which member jurors contribute to discussion. Some researchers have assessed characteristics of high participators; others have studied the formation of subgroups and factions during deliberations. Studies of juror participation have analyzed some of the same variables related to foreman selection; Strodtbeck et al. (1957) reported that jurors from high-status occupations tended to participate more than those from lower-status occupations.

Based on our calculations from Strodtbeck and Mann's (1956) data on mock jurors selected from actual jury rolls, males contributed on the average 61 percent of all verbal acts compared to 39 percent for females. In a similar study, James (1959) observed that the average male contributed 9 percent of the total verbalizations, while females contributed about 7 percent. Most recently Simon (1967) reported that in a similar sample males and females contributed about equally (7.5%) to the deliberations. There appears to be a modest trend away from male dominance in discussion. It is not clear whether this trend is due to sampling biases (after all, 1/12 = .083), nuances of the studies themselves, or a change in male–female roles.

Finally, educational level of jurors influences interaction rates. With James's mock jurors (1959) the better-educated persons participated more often and gave more attention to procedural matters than did the poorly educated. College-educated jurors showed an average participation rate of 13 percent compared to 4 percent for those with an eighth-grade background. In addition, the college and high-school groups emphasized court instructions, while the eighth-grade group focused on their personal experiences.

Also of interest is the formation of subgroups within the jury. In a study of 12-person mock juries, Forston (1968) found that a central work group of 5 to 7 high participators conducted the jury's work. Strodtbeck and Mann (1956), scrutinizing verbally active jurors by means of Bale's Interaction Process Analysis, found that their comments were best described as asking questions, giving orientation, and providing negative reactions to opposing opinions.

Hawkins (1962) studied size factions in mock juries and found that on the average interaction rates dropped from about 23 percent when the faction contained a single juror to 7 percent when it had from 7 to 11 members. That interaction rates changed with faction size is perhaps not too surprising. With more members the time for participation per individual will be reduced, given equal participation and a constant interaction period. However, no single explanation has proved acceptable in accounting for the relation between faction size and

participation (see, e.g., the reanalysis by Zeisel, 1963, of Hawkins' data). Beyond the Hawkins study there has been little assessment of the impact of factions on verdicts.

A related issue is whether significant changes in participation rates result when external factors such as jury size are varied. Kessler (1973) examined the participation rates of mock jurors in 6- and 12-member juries by dichotomizing them into totally "silent members" or "contributing members." Her results showed that for 6-member juries only 2 of the 48 participants were completely silent, while for 12-member juries 24 of the 96 jurors were silent. These data suggest the commonsense notion that jurors participate more in a small than in a large jury. However, Diamond (1974) and Diamond and Zeisel (1974) have questioned the appropriateness of Kessler's index of participation; Diamond has argued the proper index of juror participation would be one that *equated the expected proportion* of participation between the two jury sizes if each juror talked equally often. When she reanalyzed Kessler's data by modifying the participation ratios, she found that the 12-person jury minority member participated 24 percent more, on the average, than did the corresponding 6-person jury minority member. Clearly, various interaction indices may be constructed under various sets of assumptions. In the case at hand, other possible interpretations do not "favor" the 12-person jury as the agent of minority view expression. Perhaps the major lesson here is less a particular empirical result than a conceptual rediscovery: Various statistical treatments of data are usually possible, and some of these give different pictures. As much care is required for decisions in selecting analysis techniques as in collecting data.

In summary, studies of member participation suggest that (1) a central "work group" of jurors emerges that represents advocates both of conviction and of acquittal, (2) the verbal interaction of the work group is generally more task- and decision-oriented than that of the other jurors, and (3) high par-

**TABLE 2   Systematic Description of Selected Studies**

| Investigators | Population and Sample Size | Case Content and Origin | Trial Elements and Form | Independent Variables | Dependent Variables |
|---|---|---|---|---|---|
| Bevan et al. (1958) | $O$, $N_r = 88$<br>$N_y = 8$<br>$N = 12$ | AN(E) | O, T, C, J<br>(L) | S.D. = High vs. low prestige and high vs. low authoritarian, foreman | G-NG, $; SC |
| Broeder (1958) | $P$, $N_r = 360$<br>$N_y = 30$<br>$N = 12$ | AN(E) | O, T, C, J<br>(AT) | S.D. = High vs. low evidence, insurance reference, and jury decision rule | G-NG, $ |
| Hawkins (1962) | $P$, $N_r = 264$<br>$N_y = 22$<br>$N = 12$ | Not given | O, T, C, J<br>(AT) | S.D. = Size of faction in jury | V |
| Heimbach (1970) | $S$, $N_r = 64$<br>$N_y = 16$<br>$N = 4$ | AS, R(C) | T<br>(W) | S.D. = High vs. low evidence, confession vs. no confession, control vs. jurors | G-NG, Y |
| James (1959) | $P$, $N_r = 120, 240$<br>$N_y = 10, 20$<br>$N = 12$ | R(E) | O, T, C, J<br>(AT) | I.D. = Educational level, sex of juror | V |
| Kessler (1973) | $S$, $N_r = 144$<br>$N_y = 16$<br>$N = 6, 12$ | AN(E) | O, T, C, J<br>(VT) | S.D. = 6- vs. 12-member jury, pre- vs. postdeliberation verdicts | G-NG, V |
| Simon (1964) | $O$, $N_r = 51$<br>$N_y = 9$<br>$N = 5, 6$ | I(E) | O, T, C, J<br>(AT) | I.D. = Paranoids, depressives, and psychopaths.<br>S.D. = Homogeneous juries | G-NG |
| Simon (1967) | $N_r = 1176$<br>$N_y = 30, 68$<br>$N = 12$ | R, I(E) | O, T, C, J<br>(AT) | I.D. = Occupational, educational status; age, sex, religion, ethnicity.<br>S.D. = Case content, decision rule for insanity verdict | G-NG, V |
| Strodtbeck, James, & Hawkins (1957) | $P$, $N_r = 588$<br>$N_y = 49$<br>$N = 12$ | AN, C(E) | O, T, C, J<br>(AT) | I.D. = Sex of juror, occupational status of juror | V, SC |

| Strodtbeck & Mann (1956) | $P$, $N_r = 144$<br>$N_y = 12$<br>$N = 12$ | AN(E) | O, T, C, J (AT) | I.D. = Sex of juror, high vs. low participation, chosen vs. not chosen | V |
| --- | --- | --- | --- | --- | --- |
| Valenti & Downing (1975) | $S$, $N_r = 360$<br>$N_y = 40$<br>$N = 6, 12$ | AS(C) | T, J (AT) | S.D. = 6- vs. 12-member juries, high vs. low evidence | G-NG, V |
| Vidmar (1972) | $S$, $N_r = 44$<br>$N_y = 11$<br>$N = 4$ | M(P) | T, J (W) | I.D. = High vs. low dogmatism<br>S.D. = Homogeneous juries, pre-, post-, and group decisions | G-NG, Y |

Note:

Population and sample size:
P = Mock jurors from actual jury rolls
S = Student
O = Other adult

$N_r$ = Total number of jurors
$N_y$ = Total number of juries
$N$ = Number of jurors per jury

Case content and origin:
AN = Auto negligence
AS = Assault
I = Incest
M = Murder
R = Robbery

(E) = Edited
(P) = Paraphrased
(C) = Constructed

Trial elements and form:
O = Opening arguments
T = Testimony
C = Closing arguments
J = Judge's charge

(AT) = Audiotape
(L) = Live presentation
(VT) = Videotape
(W) = Written

Dependent variables:
G-NG = Verdict
Y = Number of years
$ = Amount of damages
SC = Sociometric choice
V = Verbal interaction measures

ticipators compose the work group and are most likely to possess higher levels of education and enjoy occupations of higher status. Although the effect of jury size on participation rates is largely unresolved, the size of a faction and the work group within that faction are clearly limited by the total number of jurors. Issues surrounding participation in deliberations will benefit from conceptual analyses and empirical data.

*Jury size and efficiency.* The right to a speedy trial is widely regarded as fundamental, but a jury trial may take longer than one before a judge. While the length of a jury trial is determined by many factors, the length of the deliberation is an important component. New interest in this question of trial efficiency has been kindled by the Supreme Court's decision (*Williams* v. *Florida,* 1970) that permits states to set jury sizes at some number less than the traditional twelve.

In comparing mock juries of 6- and 12-persons, Kessler (1973) reported a nonsignificant tendency for larger groups to require less deliberation time. Zeisel and Diamond (1974) have questioned these results on the grounds that some juries did not engage in "meaningful deliberations." Inspection of the predeliberation ballots showed that 10 of the 16 juries before discussion had reached the 5/6 majority vote required for a decision. The important difference in deliberation times was between juries initially possessing a sufficient majority to define a group decision (7–8 minutes) and those lacking this majority (36–38 minutes). For this latter group there were no significant differences in deliberation time between juries of different sizes, although size interacted with assigned rule. Unfortunately, this set contained only 6 juries, a number too small for confident inferences. In another investigation Davis et al. (1975) were also unable to conclude that a smaller jury expedited deliberation. In fact, neither the number of polls taken before the verdict nor the length of deliberations was influenced significantly by the size of the juries. Despite

the results of these two experiments, any interpretation that size is not significantly related to efficiency must be qualified; we will return to this qualification in later sections.

## Jury Verdicts

The function of a jury is to reach a decision—about guilt in criminal cases and for one of the contending parties in civil cases. Most of our discussion has implicitly assumed a criminal case, and this bias accurately reflects the relative frequency with which criminal and civil cases are the targets of empirical research. Our discussion of social process derives its importance from the role the jury plays in rendering verdicts.

*Jury size.* The number of jurors involved not only affects deliberation efficiency; it may influence the verdict itself. Available studies of juries of 6 and 12 (Davis et al., 1975; Kessler, 1973) did not find significant differences in decision outcomes. Thus, the empirical evidence, on the face of it, does not contradict the wisdom of the Supreme Court's decision relaxing jury size as mentioned earlier. But Davis et al. (1975) argued that differences in conviction rate due to jury size *should* in fact exist given any of several social decision rules (e.g., simple majority, otherwise equiprobability as inferred by Kalven & Zeisel, 1966; or the 2/3 majority, otherwise hung favored by Davis et al., 1975, for the mock trial they studied). The problem is that the *maximum difference possible* between juries of 6 and 12 is *only about 8 percent* for the simple majority social decision rule. Therefore, *very* large samples of exceptionally "noise-free" data would be required to pick up a difference of this magnitude. Valenti and Downing (1975) observed what seemed to be a different *pattern* to the distribution of conviction, hung, and acquittal as a function of group size. They reported a shift toward conviction for 6-person mock juries when the case was slanted toward conviction. The results are puzzling and require closer study, perhaps with larger samples including jury sizes other than 6 and 12.

*Rules and criteria for decisions.* Before deliberation, jury members receive instructions on the relevant law defining what is to be categorized as guilty/not guilty, insane/sane, and the like, depending on the case. Court-assigned social decision rules or social decision schemes (Davis, 1973) prescribe the proportion (e.g., unanimity, ¾ majority, or simple majority) of jurors who must favor a verdict to establish it as the jury's decision. The assigned social decision rule outlines neither the exact procedure the jury is to use nor the means of resolving the nonunanimities, nonmajorities, and so forth that may arise. In fact, a jury could be unanimous in agreeing on the verdict to be reported, but could have arrived at that decision by effectively obeying a rule such as simple majority.

Simon (1967) observed mock juries who heard prerecorded trials and had received instructions in the M'Naghten Rule, Durham Rule, or no rule at all relative to finding the defendant not guilty by reason of insanity. She found the criterion to be significantly associated with *individual jurors'* predeliberation judgments in both cases; the M'Naghten Rule led to more convictions than either the Durham Rule or no instructions. The sample in one case was too small for further conclusions, but juries in the other case who had been assigned the M'Naghten Rule rendered a significantly higher proportion of guilty verdicts than either of the other two conditions.

Kerr, Atkin, Stasser, Meek, Holt, and Davis (1976) found that jurors assigned a "harsh" criterion of reasonable doubt gave a significantly higher proportion of guilty judgments than did those assigned a milder criterion; this difference was larger yet in the corresponding mock *jury* conditions. But Sealy and Cornish (1973a), studying mock jurors instructed in three definitions of reasonable doubt, observed an effect from the criterion in only one of three defendants in

two cases. Thus, there is some evidence that the criterion as described in the judge's instructions on reasonable doubt has a decided influence on verdicts preferred by both jurors and juries. These results are perhaps more comforting than surprising. Nonetheless, adequate attention has not been given to the exact elements associated with the judge's instructions (e.g., style of delivery, nature of criteria, interaction with case type) that are effective.

Also the effects of court-assigned social decision schemes have not been adequately explored—although research is likely to increase due to a recent Supreme Court decision (*Johnson* v. *Louisiana,* 1972) allowing nonunanimous decision rules in state trials. Broeder (1958) concluded that "no significant difference in award level resulted between [mock] juries operating under the unanimity rule and juries operating under the ¾ majority rule [p. 754]." Davis et al. (1975) detected no significant differences in jury verdict distributions due to assignment of a unanimity or 2/3 majority rule. In their study the guilt of an alleged rapist was decided by both 6- and 12-member juries. Later, Davis, Kerr, Stasser, Meek, and Holt (in press) altered the same mock trial to *increase* predeliberation guilt preferences among individual jurors and observed that 6-person juries assigned a unanimity rule were "hung" significantly more often than those assigned a 2/3 majority rule. Bray (1974) also observed a trend for unanimity-assigned juries of 6 to be hung relative to similar juries assigned a 5/6 majority rule.

Overall, there may be some tendency for verdict distributions to reflect the assignment of social decision scheme or rule, but it is not strong. Clearly little satisfactory evidence is now at hand. Later we show that the effects of many social decision schemes are theoretically quite subtle and unlikely to be prominent in small samples and/or data sets containing much "noise." Thus, a decidedly important task is to determine the social decision scheme actually adopted, perhaps without complete awareness, by juries.

The rule assigned may be only one among many influences affecting the actual social decision rule or implicit social process. Even though jurors might correctly perceive the judge's assigned rule, they may unwittingly act more in accord with local norms than the law should the two be different.

Kalven and Zeisel (1966) reported that first ballot reconstructions suggest that an initial majority strongly determines the verdict unless there is an even split of guilty and not guilty members (6, 6), in which case the jury's verdict is as likely to be guilty as not guilty. Such a reconstruction is of course only an approximation and occurred prior to the Court's decision reducing the permissible jury size. Nevertheless, Davis et al. (1975) have concluded that a 2/3-majority, otherwise-hung plan permitted a close reconstruction of the verdict distributions from both 6- and 12-person mock juries. Bray (1974) has likewise found that his mock juries could be characterized better by a social decision scheme different than the one assigned and that the particular form of the rule most predictive of jury verdicts depended also on whether the jury was composed of all males or all females.

*Group composition.* Only a few studies have dealt with *jury* composition. Part of the difficulty may be due to serious problems with measurement, experimental control, and/or adequate sample sizes (especially of infrequent personality types). However, we suspect that there is no clear idea about how various *patterns* of juror types affect either interaction or verdicts. Simple monotonic relations between the total amount of a variable in a group and the verdict may not obtain. The crucial questions concern those compositions that emphasize various interpersonal patterns or "fits" among types of members. (See McGrath & Altman, 1966, for discussion of this "pattern hypothesis" relative to small group research.)

For example, Vidmar (1972b) composed some mock juries from subjects with homogeneously high scores on the Dogmatism Scale and others from subjects with homogeneously low scores. He found that, after deliberation, high-dogmatism juries recommended significantly longer sentences than low-dogmatism ones. Similarly, Simon (1964), working with mental patients, composed three homogeneous juries each of psychopaths, depressives, and paranoids. She found that the psychopaths were most lenient and the paranoids least lenient in the harshness of their verdicts. Obviously, the group composition question awaits clarification.

*Evidence.* It has been difficult even in *mock* trials to define important variables so that they may be manipulated in an orderly way. While a few studies of *jurors* have addressed the courtroom trial as a complex, persuasive communication setting with the attendant conceptual paraphernalia that this implies, little effort has been expended on similar studies with *juries.*

Broeder (1958) reported that a case with "somewhat doubtful" evidence produced lower average damage awards by mock juries than a case with "clear" evidence. Davis et al. (1975) observed that their version of an actual rape trial produced guilty decisions among 22 percent of the individual jurors, but not a single guilty verdict from juries. A later version of essentially the same mock trial (Davis et al., in press) used reputed newspaper articles to increase the prestige of the victim's husband, community status, and general respectability and to impugn the character of the defendant. These changes along with some additional incriminating evidence were sufficient to increase guilty judgments significantly over the earlier version among jurors (53%) and juries (41%) alike. The alterations in procedure were made for a purpose different from the study of evidential cues and thus do not illuminate the importance of any one change. But comparison of the two studies does demonstrate that student subjects hearing a mock trial are attentive and do respond to nuances of the case. Subtle differences between cases and trials plague confident inference in virtually all jury research, but present a special hazard to accurate generalizations in *mock* trials—since their results may also be affected by subject insincerity and inattentiveness.

The only direct study of evidential cues known to us is Heimbach's (1970), who reported that legally "strong" evidence significantly increases guilty verdicts relative to "weak" evidence. It is not, however, clear whether these judgments are from postdeliberation jurors or the juries themselves.

Juries can only deliberate using information recalled by jurors, but as yet there is little direct research on what kinds of information incline members and/or the jury to their decision.

## Survey Studies

Numerous summaries of various jury trial statistics constitute a valuable source of data in the same way that crime, divorce, or birth statistics are useful. Our discussion here is limited to studies of particular questions by aggregating data from court or other records or otherwise collecting data from actual courtroom trials.

*Jury size.* The Supreme Court decison (*Williams* v. *Florida,* 1970) that sparked new interest in the effects of jury size sent researchers to court records and to the mock trials mentioned earlier. Bermant and Coppock (1973) surveying 128 cases falling under the Workmen's Compensation Act, found that for 6- and 12-person juries 45 percent and 46 percent respectively favored the State Department of Labor and Industries over the plaintiff. The Institute of Judicial Administration (1972) found that for 391 civil cases, 58.0 percent of the 6-person juries and 57.3 percent of the 12-person juries decided for the plaintiff. Both studies concluded that the difference between 6- and 12-person juries was of no moment, an assertion challenged by Zeisel and Diamond (1974), who pointed out that cases in neither

study were randomly selected. Counsel had the option of demanding the larger size jury and apparently exercised this option more often for larger, more complex cases.

Mills (1973) surveyed 128 civil cases. His results showed that 61.5 percent of the 6- but only 52 percent of the 12-person juries rendered verdicts favoring the plaintiff. Unfortunately, between the empaneling of 12-person juries in 1969 and the 6-person juries in 1971, a change in procedure allowed insurance policy limits to be "discovered," which may have selectively biased settlements without a jury verdict—a confounding effect to be expected when aggregating actual trial results in this way.

Zeisel and Diamond (1974) cautioned against accepting the results of these survey studies at face value. We concur in counseling restraint in substituting smaller for larger juries and believe that there are a number of additional theoretical reasons, as mentioned earlier, to suspect subtle differences in verdicts due to jury size.

*Demographic variables.* Bronson (1970) in a survey of Colorado veniremen found that females and low-income persons were significantly more opposed to the death penalty than males and middle-to-higher income groups. However, neither educational level nor age was significantly associated with attitudes toward the death penalty. Reed (1965), surveying 158 former jurors, observed that a guilty vote was significantly and strongly associated with higher educational levels, higher social status, previous jury service, and a "North Louisiana and Southern U.S." birthplace. The age, marital status, religious preference, and church attendance of former jurors were not significantly related to their vote. Such information has some heuristic value, but it is difficult to judge its general importance until wider sampling with more consistent data-gathering techniques and the like have standardized the data base.

*Role playing and responsibility.* Variations in juries, cases, procedures, and so forth make constructing general principles diffi-cult. Moreover, the direct scrutiny of real juries at work is forbidden, though Kalven and Zeisel (1966) doubt that such intrusion would add much to our knowledge of jury psychology. One of the most persistent in-tuitions, however, is that a fundamental difference exists between mock and real juries. Even the most ardent role player seems unlikely to experience the sobering re-sponsibility that surely accompanies a ver-dict permitting a deprivation of liberty or treasure.

The notion that real juries might be more cautious in reaching guilty verdicts appears to have a measure of support from a study by Diamond and Zeisel (1974). Aggregating over 10 different courtroom trials, they found that only 50 percent of the real juries (whose members were selected in the usual way through *voir dire*) favored guilty, whereas 80 percent of the "challenged" juries (com-posed of jurors excused from the real juries during *voir dire*), 100 percent of the "Eng-lish" juries (composed of random selectees from the jury rolls without further exami-nation), and 90 percent of the presiding judges (privately) favored guilty. They at-tributed this significant association to the realism of the former's role (although all juries were otherwise treated as similarly as practicable by the court), and argued against the influence of composition per se. Never-theless, the real jury in fact differed from the others in composition as well as respon-sibility. The use of *two similarly composed* juries with one arbitrarily assigned the actual responsibility would disentangle this con-founding effect. But such a manipulation in a real trial seems improbable. At least as serious a question has to do with the lack of replication within the 10 trials.

## Summary and Conclusions: Research on Juries

Methodological problems arising in con-nection with a number of jury-related studies have provoked a substantial body of critical comment and reanalyses (e.g., Zeisel &

Diamond, 1974). More, not less, care is surely required for research with a fairly immediate potential for application.

Some orderly findings seem evident, how-ever. For example, factors associated with foreman selection, participation, and influ-ence have been well documented; how each relates to the decision process remains to be worked out. The same conceptual difficulty exists for relating member participation rates to verdicts. The jury is after all a task-oriented group, and its interaction processes are of interest primarily as they affect the verdict.

Jury behavior will almost certainly vary with time, geography, or subculture. For ex-ample, a comparison of studies separated in time showed that females relative to males increased their participation in deliberation from the earlier to later investigations. While the results may be due to a number of vari-ables changing concomitantly, we suspect that this effect is primarily related to the changing role of women in just such con-texts as juries. Likewise, the strong tendency for women to favor guilty verdicts and harsh sentences for alleged rapists might very well reflect concern with the currently high inci-dence of rape as well as the obvious differ-ential consequences to the sexes. Earlier studies, if available, might have shown a much milder judgment by women. What is needed, then, is to encourage longer per-spectives, dynamic theories, programmatic research, and—most of all—an appreciation that what is "real" is itself changing.

The inefficacy of individual difference variables, long lamented by small group re-searchers (e.g., McGrath & Altman, 1966), continues in jury research. Yet, demographic variables appeared to be more likely than personality variables to predict verdict pref-erences and participation. For all their in-adequacies (see, e.g., McGrath & Altman, 1966), group membership, educational level, and other demographic variables seem to offer the best hope. After all, it is this kind of public information that prosecution and defense lawyers seem to use, along with their implicit personality theories, in selecting jurors favorable to their side. In any single trial, even a slight edge in juror selection might provide a heavy later advantage to one contestant. Christie and Schulman (*Time*, 1974) have reportedly combined sociological "profile" information about a community with rater impressions of jurors' personality characteristics to identify jurors sympathetic to the defense (see also Schulman, Shaver, Colman, Emrich, & Christie, 1973).

Research on the effects of jury size and assigned decision rule has recently proved popular, partly due to Supreme Court decisions. As a body, the research lacks orderly variation in case type, adequate samples (a serious problem with jury research of *all* kinds), appreciation of geographical and cultural variation, and the like. These problems may be more easily corrected in future research because the size and rule variables are relatively well defined and have a clear (and important) existence independent of the research. The existence of theory especially sensitive to both factors is discussed more fully in the next section.

It appears that the inefficacy of jury size observed in numerous studies, and apparently supportive of Supreme Court decisions, must be questioned—on grounds both theoretical (e.g., Davis et al., 1975) and methodological (e.g., Zeisel & Diamond, 1974). Given the general majority effects of the jurors' initial preferences, only a small difference in verdicts between 6- and 12-person juries is possible, and these are unlikely to be detected by less than very large samples of relatively error-free data. Social interaction variables (e.g., total deliberation time) not very surprisingly have been more sensitive to variations in jury size and decision rule (e.g., under a unanimity criterion, juries of 12 have been observed to take significantly longer than those of 6 to reach a verdict).

## THEORIES OF JURY BEHAVIOR

The following discussion is concerned with theories that have juries as their primary focus or have been specifically applied or adapted to account for jury behavior.

No theory *specifically* designed or adapted for *juror* decision making could be found, although *jurors* have been the favored research target. This may result from the fact that many theories in social psychology are currently oriented toward individual cognitions, and specific juror applications may not have appeared to be a special case requiring additional theoretical work. (However, see Fried, Kaplan, & Klein, 1975, for a conceptual discussion of decision theory notions and *voir dire*.)

The stimulus for theoretical work on juries can probably be traced to changes in the law affecting court procedures, standards, and so forth (e.g., assigned decision rule and jury size). When confronted with such fundamental changes, it is natural to seek answers about possible logical consequences, given various conditions. Of course, such an aim benefits from a fairly explicit model that includes specific assumptions about social processes and provides for the definition of parameters in an unambiguous way.

## Two Outcomes: the Walbert Model

Walbert (1971) has advanced a relatively simple model to investigate the difference in verdicts between 6- and 12-member juries. Walbert assumed that a randomly drawn juror may be characterized by the probability, $P_G$, that a guilty verdict will be favored prior to deliberation,[2] otherwise not guilty with probability $P_{NG} = 1 - P_G$. He further assumed that jury deliberation will not alter jurors' preferences prior to the ballot decision and that a simple majority would determine the group verdict. Allowing only guilty or not guilty jury outcomes, his model used binomial probabilities to predict the probability of a guilty verdict in randomly formed groups of 6- and 12-members. In the special case when equal numbers of jurors favor each verdict, that is, (6, 6) or (3, 3) distributions of guilty/not guilty, he assumed

---

[2] The notation used throughout this section is sometimes slightly different from that in the original papers.

that the jury decision was as likely to be guilty as not guilty. The probability, $P_G$, of a jury reaching a guilty verdict is given in Table 3 for several values of the *juror* probability, $P_G$, and for juries of 6 and 12. There are some important systematic differences. Clearly, when $P_G < .50$, the jury of 6 is *more likely* to convict than one of 12. But when $P_G > .50$, the jury of 6 *is less likely* to convict than one of 12. If $P_G = .00, .50,$ or 1.00, there is no theoretical difference between the jury sizes in probability of a guilty verdict. Thus, the Court's decision allowing smaller juries (using the rationale that no size-based differences are to be expected) is false *if* the model is true.

Based on the research reviewed earlier, jury size has not been observed to produce detectable (statistically significant) effects in the nature of the jury decision. Most of this research has studied the verdict distribution of 6- and 12-person juries, and—as Table 3 reveals—the theoretical difference between them is quite small. Considering only the tabled values, the *largest difference* between the two jury sizes is .08. Since most jury studies used small samples, it is not surprising that they have failed to conclude that jury size influences verdicts. How large a sample of 6- and 12-person juries *would be required* for an absolute difference of at least .08 to be significant can be computed: Assuming an equal number of groups of each size and a Type I error of .05, 62 or more juries of *each* size are needed, result-

ing in $6(62) + 12(62) = 1116$ subjects. Thus, it would be difficult by current research practices to detect empirically a theoretical difference of only .08. But it would be equally difficult to ignore that technically a difference does exist between 6- and 12-person juries under Walbert's theoretical model. Human considerations require that in the long run we at least ponder *small but real* differences that would exist under the two different legal procedures. (See Lempert, 1975, for a discussion of the jury size issue and many of the related topics we engaged earlier.)

We are left, then, with the difficult question of where we wish to place the emphasis: (1) increase the probability, $P_G$, of the jury convicting when there is not much sentiment (small $P_G$) among jurors for it (implies juries of 6 persons); or (2) increase the probability of the jury convicting when the prevalent juror view (large $P_G$) is one of guilty (implies juries of 12 persons). (See also Feinberg, 1971, and Friedman, 1972, who discuss jury size and decision rule problems in terms of Type I and Type II errors.) We are confronting a logical problem at this point; data are not directly involved. For example, observe the curve family (from binomial expansions following Walbert's assumptions) shown in Figure 1. All curves pass through $P_G = .00, .50,$ and 1.00, but as jury size increases the steepness of the curve relating verdict probabilities to juror preferences increases. This pattern means that with

**TABLE 3**   **Probability of a Guilty Verdict in 6- and 12-Person Juries as a Function of Juror Guilt Preference under a Simple Majority Social Decision Scheme**

| Individual/Group Decisions | Probability of Guilty Verdict | | | | | | | | | | |
|---|---|---|---|---|---|---|---|---|---|---|---|
| Individual jurors | .00 | .10 | .20 | .30 | .40 | .50 | .60 | .70 | .80 | .90 | 1.00 |
| 6-member juries | .00 | .01 | .06 | .16 | .32 | .50 | .68 | .84 | .94 | .99 | 1.00 |
| 12-member juries | .00 | .00 | .01 | .08 | .25 | .50 | .75 | .92 | .99 | 1.00 | 1.00 |

Note: *This table is adapted from Walbert (1971). Hung juries were not allowed, and juries that were evenly split between guilty and not guilty were assumed as likely to render one verdict as the other.*

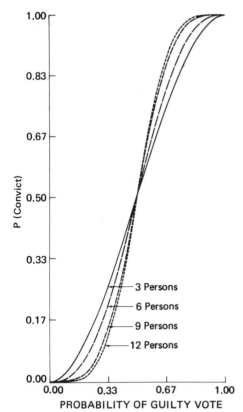

**Fig. 1.** Probability of a jury conviction ($P_G$) as a function of individual guilt performances ($P_G$) for several different group sizes ($r$) where we assume two outcomes (guilty and not guilty): that a simple majority is needed to convict, and that ties are as likely to result in conviction as acquittal.

(e.g., for some cases or some jurisdictions) operate on a social decision scheme (Davis, 1973) other than a simple majority (e.g., 2/3 or 3/4 majority). But the relaxation of the unanimity standard by the Supreme Court implied no important negative effect on the outcome expected from assigning a nonunanimous decision rule. The question of whether this judgment is empirically sound has stimulated studying assigned social decision schemes.

A simple binomial model can also be used to determine how the probability, $P_G$, that a jury reaches a guilty verdict is affected by various social decision schemes. Assuming two possible outcomes (guilty and not guilty), we calculated the probability, $P_G$, of a guilty verdict as a function of juror sentiment for guilt, $P_G$, under several different social decision schemes. The results (again logical consequences, not empirical observations) are displayed in Figure 2 for juries of size 12. Figure 2 reveals that variations in social decision schemes, like variations in group size, affect the jury verdict.

The rule assigned by the judge may be quite different from the *implicit* social decision scheme the jury actually follows. The implicit decision rule may be a function of local norms and could vary over time or place. The final ballot may itself not even reveal the actual social decision scheme, since jurors may arrive at unanimity by some plan (e.g., a majority rule) put into effect implicitly by "voice vote" during the deliberation. Kalven and Zeisel (1966) suggested this when they argued that the direct observation and analysis of discussion content may *not* be very informative since yielding to a majority might be cloaked in socially acceptable justifications.

## More than Two Outcomes—the Social Decision Scheme Model

The fact of hung juries forces one to consider more response options than two, at least for juries. Therefore, the use of multiple-alternative scales for juries might bear

increasing jury size the relative probability of conviction below .50 becomes progressively smaller, and above .50 progressively larger! Clearly, the jury size issue is logical and philosophical as well as empirical. Moreover, "bare" empirical data will not necessarily lead *directly* to reasonable solutions. Most of Walbert's work was in fact devoted to discussions about the plausibility of his model's assumptions rather than its consequences alone.

Any abstract formulation of a complex social process is likely to be to some degree an oversimplification. Juries may sometimes

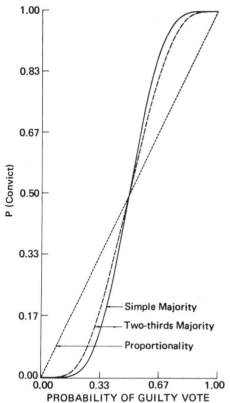

**Fig. 2.** Probability of a conviction ($P_G$) in 12-person juries as a function of individual juror preferences for guilt ($P_G$) assuming two alternatives (guilty and not guilty) under each of the following social decision schemes: (1) *simple majority*, where a simple majority of members must favor the verdict and ties are as likely to result in conviction as acquittal; (2) *2/3 majority*, where the verdict requires 2/3 of the members in support; otherwise the probability of an alternative being chosen is the proportion of members advocating that position; (3) *proportionality*, where the probability of an alternative being selected is the proportion of members favoring that verdict.

some scrutiny: A verdict of one among several possible judgments about the probability of guilt in light of confidence in the verdict might be more accurate or socially informative than the traditional dichotomy.

Unfortunately, the simple arguments based on the binomial expansion do not suf-

fice for the $n$-alternative case. Increasing the magnitude of the problem, too, is that the proportion of possible instances of simple or 2/3 majorities in a jury of fixed size, $r$, is smaller when the number of alternatives, $n$, is greater than 2. Likewise, the action of other kinds of social decision schemes in jury verdicts becomes more complex for $n > 2$. The reason is the very rapid increase in the number of distinguishable distributions, $m$, of verdict preferences that results from increases in $r$ (group size) and/or $n$ (number of alternatives) according to $m = \binom{n + r - 1}{r}$.

A rather general social decision scheme model (Davis, 1973) has been proposed for just such a problem, and includes the Walbert model as a special case.

The social decision scheme model has been applied to an illustrative reanalysis of some mock jury decision data (from Simon, 1967) and to recent experimental results (Bray, 1974; Davis et al., 1975). Given the probability, $P_j$, that a randomly chosen juror prefers the *j*th verdict alternative ($j = 1, 2, \ldots, n$) at the outset of interaction and an assumption about the social decision scheme in operation, the probability, $P_j$, of a jury deciding for the *j*th verdict ($j = 1, 2, \ldots, n$) may be caluculated. The calculations proceed by computing the (multinomial) probability, $\pi_i$, of each possible distribution of opinion in an $r$-person jury, and postmultiplying the vector of these probabilities, ($\pi_1, \pi_2, \ldots, \pi_m$) by the stochastic matrix, $D$, the entries, $[d_{ij}]$, of which are defined by the social decision scheme. The $m \times n$ matrix, $D$, covers all contingencies such that for the *i*th distribution of juror opinion in the group, the probability of the jury rendering the *j*th verdict is given by the $[d_{ij}]$. The result is the predicted distribution ($P_1$, $P_2, \ldots, P_n$) of juries favoring each of the $n$ possible verdict alternatives.

The discussions by Davis (1973), Davis et al. (1975), and Bray (1974) provide a more comprehensive description of these ideas, but some general notions will be discussed briefly. Suppose there are $n = 3$ verdict alternatives (e.g., three probabilities of guilt, or guilty, not guilty, and undecided) and $r = 6$ persons in the jury. The possible arrays of members are $m = \binom{n + r - 1}{r} = \binom{3 + 6 - 1}{6} = 28$. If the jury is operating on a simple majority plan, $10/28$ of these distributions can be shown to be nonmajorities (4 ties and 6 pluralities). Some subscheme must thus supplement the primary decision plan to give the full social decision scheme defining the $m \times n$ matrix $D$. The *probability*, $\pi_i$, of the $i$th distinguishable distribution is given by $\pi_i = [r_1, r_2, r_3]$ $P1^{r_1}P2^{r_2}P3^{r_3}$. Imagine that the individual verdict distribution is $p = (p_1, p_2, p_3) = (.20, .70, .10)$. As an example we calculate the probability of the 6-person jury having the internal verdict array $(2, 4, 0)$, for the three verdict alternatives respectively, as $\binom{6}{2,4,0}$ $(.20)^2 (.70)^4 = .14$. The other $\pi_i$, $i = 1, 2, \ldots, 27$, are calculated similarly to give $\pi = (\pi_1, \pi_2, \ldots, \pi_{28})$. We then calculate $\pi$. $D = (P_1, P_2, P_3)$, the predicted jury verdict distribution under the social decision scheme that defines the matrix $D$.

The social decision scheme model can be used to describe the verdict distributions in particular research contexts and explore, logically, jury verdict behavior when relevant empirical data cannot be obtained. The former use has been described earlier. We now illustrate the latter use with regard to (1) the character (shape, variability, or location) of the distribution of verdicts preferred *before deliberation by individual jurors* $(p_1, p_2, \ldots, p_n)$; (2) the kind of jury social decision scheme (e.g., simple majority, plurality); and (3) the size of the jury, $r = 2, 3, \ldots$. Although the number of alternatives the jury may choose in rendering its verdict has important implications in its own right, a fixed "verdict scale" of $n = 5$ alternatives has been selected for the following illustration. These alternatives should be considered mutually exclusive and exhaustive, similar to the assumptions of a

Likert scale. The verdict might be the selection of one alternative ranging, for example, from "not very likely to be guilty" to "very likely to be guilty" or from "guilty" through several degrees of indecision to "not guilty."

If we assume a simple majority social decision scheme, the effect of different *predeliberation juror distributions* $(p_1, p_2, \ldots, p_n)$ on *jury verdict distributions* may be seen in Figure 3. (When an initial majority did not exist, the probability of an alternative being chosen was the proportion of jurors advocating that position.) For each of two "input" distributions (symmetrical and skewed), the resulting jury verdict distribution $(P_1, P_2, \ldots, P_n)$ has been given for jury sizes, $r = 3, 6, 9,$ and 12. There is a general "sharpening" at the mode as we move up from individuals, but the progression is not regular in that the curve for $r = 9$ is higher at the mode than $r = 12$. Such "unexpected" reversals are not uncommon in combinatorics, and actual calculations such as are graphed in Figure 3 often reveal counterintuitive results.

Next, let juries be fixed at size $r = 12$, and let us assume four individual distributions across the verdict alternatives: *symmetrical, skewed, bimodal,* and *uniform.* Under these conditions, the effects of simple majority, 2/3 majority, plurality, and averaging social decision schemes were ascertained; the resulting theoretical distributions of jury verdicts are shown in Figure 4. Finally, the use of an averaging rule requires that we assume the five response alternatives to be an ordered set, and the "sub-scheme"—to deal with instances when the other primary rules could not apply—was proportionality.

The results shown in Figures 3 and 4 demonstrate that it is possible to deduce at least the logically expected effects of presumed social norms or prevailing social customs and the effects of proposed changes in legal procedures before trying them out. For example, under the simple assumptions made here, the results in Figure 3 suggest that the effect of increasing jury size is to increase peakedness at the mode, given that

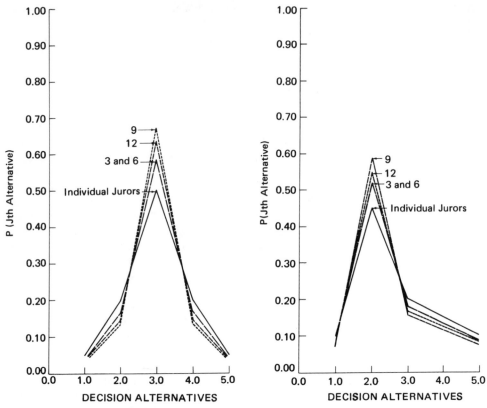

**Fig. 3.** Probability with which each verdict alternative is chosen by individual jurors and juries of $r = 3$, 6, 9, and 12. Such scales might refer to confidence in the verdict, probability of guilt, or other responses not limited to the traditional dichotomy. The effects of individual distribution shape are illustrated by the contrast between the two subfigures.

a simple majority is at work, and to suppress the less probable responses. Observe, however, that *the extent* of the size-induced changes is not so large as to be readily detected by empirical research.

Different social decision schemes, of course, can produce quite different jury verdict distributions, depending on the nature of the individual juror distribution. Figure 4 shows that majorities and pluralities will exaggerate nonuniformities found in juror distributions. Averaging will do likewise if the individual distribution is symmetrical; *but if skewed or bimodal* (Figures 4b and 4c), an averaging model will show a middling tendency for the resulting jury distri-

bution. This theoretical result has obvious application to cases such as those in which juries award civil damages. Among the models considered, averaging is the only one that predicts a jury–juror difference if the juror input is the uniform distribution. Clearly, whether juries follow the judge's decision rule or a process that leads to a different scheme, the study of various rules whereby preferences may be aggregated or combined is of considerable importance in assessing the likely effects of social change.

The social decision scheme model (including the special case of two alternatives) thus provides a convenient way of deducing specific outcomes under various assumptions about the ways juries operate. The model is very general and often permits formalizing theory for particular situations. The resulting predictions may be used normatively or descriptively as situations require.

## The Gelfand-Solomon Model

Gelfand and Solomon (1973, 1974) recently called attention to work by the famous probabilist Poisson (1837) who, among others (e.g., Condorcet, 1785; Cournot, 1938; LaPlace, 1886), used probability concepts for a study of the French legal system in the early nineteenth century—work largely unknown to behavioral scientists. In their clarification and extension of the Poisson model, Gelfand and Solomon demonstrated forcefully the value of a statistical model both in facilitating comparisons across time and cultures, and in deducing potential consequences not easily inferred from empirical findings alone.

Very briefly, the model defines two major parameters, $\theta$, the probability before the trial that the accused is guilty,[3] and $\mu$, the probability that a juror will not err in his or her vote (i.e., vote for the wrong verdict). The probability that an individual juror votes for conviction is $P_G = \theta\mu + (1-\theta)(1-\mu)$; that a jury of size $r$ (where $k$ out of $r$ jurors vote acquittal) will convict by a majority of *exactly* $M_{r,k}$ is $P_G(r,k) =$

$$\binom{r}{k} [\theta\mu^{r-k}(1-\mu)^k + (1-\theta)\mu^k(1-\mu)^{r-k}];$$ and by a majority of *at least* $M_{r,k}$ is $\Gamma_{r,k} = \Sigma_{j=0}^{k} P_G(r,j)$. In a further development, a three-parameter model was derived in which $\mu$ was replaced by $\mu_1$, and $\mu_2$, the respective probabilities that a juror will vote guilty given the accused is guilty and vote for acquittal given

the accused is innocent. (See Gelfand and Solomon, 1973, 1974, for the derivation of these and other important quantities.)

Under most conditions there are two differences between the Gelfand-Solomon model and the social decision scheme model discussed in the preceding section: (1) The probability, $P_G$, that a juror will vote guilty is not further defined in social decision scheme theory, but is a function of $\mu$ and $\theta$ in the Gelfand-Solomon model; and (2) the social decision processes examined under social decision scheme theory encompass a wide range of possibilities, but have been limited to a simple majority in the Gelfand-Solomon model.[4]

An important advantage of the Gelfand and Solomon approach is illustrated by the parameter $\theta$, the value of which might be interpreted as "a commentary on the legal system in the society which eventually brings an accused to trial as a result of arrest, arraignment and indictment [1973, p. 272]." Although $\theta$ does not make so much sense in a civil as criminal trial, it might reflect the "moral climate of the country, the criminal procedure employed, and the skill of the judiciary, including prosecutors and defense counsel [1973, p. 272]." Considered thus as summarizing substantial "cultural information," estimates of $\theta$ from different data sets permit interesting and highly economical comparisons that would otherwise require at best unwieldy manipulations of large data sets. Unfortunately, $\theta$ cannot be estimated directly, and its importance must be inferred by the behavior of estimative quantities that are a function of $\theta$, as well as of $\mu$ (e.g., $\Gamma_{r,k}$, the probability of conviction by a majority of at least $M_{r,k}$). While $\theta$ (the probability the accused is guilty before the trial) does not have a real referent in mock trials, $\mu$

---

[3] Gelfand and Solomon make the important point that a jury cannot know whether the accused is in fact guilty. Thus, they adopt the convention that their use of the term "guilty" will really mean legally "convictable" in light of the evidence.

---

[4] However, very recently Gelfand and Solomon (1975) have incorporated other plausible social decision processes into their model, greatly extending its usefulness.

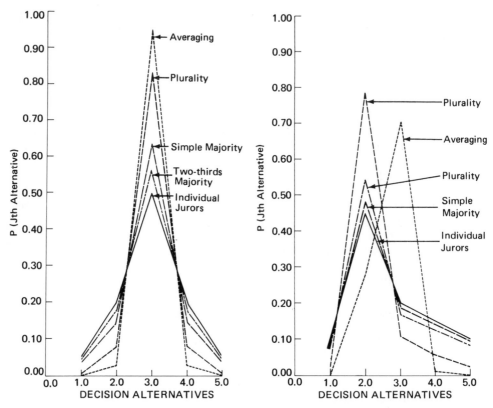

**Fig. 4.** The individual juror preference distribution is described by the solid curve. The broken curves are probability distributions expected for 12-person juries operating on the following social decision schemes: simple majority, 2/3 majority, plurality, and averaging. The four subfigures illustrate the effects on the jury verdict distribution of changes in the form of individual juror (input) distribution, again allowing five response alternatives.

(the probability the jury does not err) does have a sensible interpretation.

Gelfand and Solomon have used their model in two general ways: (1) to explore effects on the probability of conviction for 12-, $T(\mu, \theta)$, and 6-, $S(\mu, \theta)$, person juries from assuming various reasonable values of $\mu$ and $\theta$; and (2) to compare jury conviction data gathered in France, at two different times, with modern data gathered in the United States (Kalven & Zeisel, 1966) in terms of summarizing parameters, especially $\mu$ and $\theta$. Results pertaining to the first purpose are similar in spirit with those for a simple majority social decision scheme

model for two outcomes. Thus, the Gelfand-Solomon jury size results will not be discussed further, except to point out that, while the range of values they chose for $\mu$ and $\theta$ are themselves intuitively reasonable, upon calculating $P_G = \mu\theta + (1-\mu)(1-\theta)$, the resulting range of $P_G$ is rather small (viz., .21 to .79) for the illustrative purposes they had in mind (cf. Figure 1). However, the range of juror guilt preference in the region around $P_G = .50$ is very important, since a jury trial is unlikely to take place if the defendant is *very* likely to be judged innocent *or* guilty by a jury. This assumes that a jury is more likely to be used when there is some

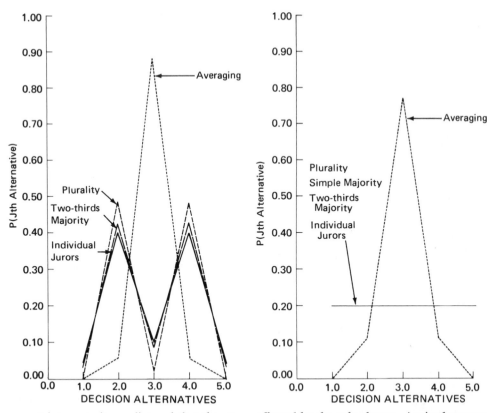

uncertainty as to its verdict and that the uncertainty is evident to participants, namely, when $P_G \simeq .50$.

Gelfand and Solomon's use of their model to compare different data sets by means of the parameters estimated from them is especially interesting. For example, they have drawn upon Poisson's earlier work to show that the estimated probability, $\hat{\Gamma}_{12,5}$, of a *conviction by at least a 7/12 majority* of French jury members was highly stable for the years 1825 to 1830—when the assigned social decision scheme (7/12) was constant. There is some variation in estimates, $\hat{\Gamma}_{12,5}$, using different estimation methods, but substantial consistency over years within a method (e.g., for one of these estimators, $\hat{\Gamma}_{12,5}$ is near .60 in each of the 6 years). When the law was changed to an 8/12 rule in the period 1831 to 1833, $\hat{\Gamma}_{12,4}$ was calculated and observed to be smaller than $\hat{\Gamma}_{12,5}$ accordingly for the years (1831-1833)

affected by the rule change. Again there was consistency within an estimation method, but the estimates of $\Gamma_{12,4}$ for the later period (i.e., 1831 to 1833) were generally *lower* than those of $\Gamma_{12,5}$ for the earlier period, suggesting that the 8/12 juries may have departed from their newly assigned rule to some degree. Thus, even if norms and customs are significantly altered by legal instructions, changes in norm-governed collective decision practices may lag behind.

Gelfand and Solomon have reported systematic variations in parameter estimates with type of crime; these results support the conjectures posed earlier about the relationship between the type of case and the particular social process underlying the verdict. For the years 1825 to 1830, the probability of a conviction was estimated to be somewhat higher for crimes against property than crimes against person.

A final set of results has been selected

from several of the Gelfand-Solomon (1973, 1974) tables (see Table 4). Results for the United States are based on representative data reported by Kalven and Zeisel (1966), and those for France are based on data from Poisson (1837). From Table 4 it appears that under the Gelfand-Solomon model the estimates for $\mu$ and $\theta$ are higher for the United States than French data. However, the Bayesian probability that the accused is guilty given conviction by a 7/12 majority does not differ much—it is very high in all categories. Within the French data, observe that the lower estimates come from juries hearing cases involving crimes against persons. It is perhaps not altogether chauvinistic to take some pleasure in observing that $\hat{\theta}$, the estimated probability before the trial that the accused is guilty, has a higher value for the twentieth-century U.S. than for nineteenth-century France. Similarly $\hat{\mu}$, the estimated probability that a juror will not err in voting is also higher for the U.S. After all, one would like to think there has been some progress both in bringing guilty defendants to trial and in improving the "accuracy" of a juror's vote.

In conclusion, Gelfand and Solomon emphasized that their empirical results are intended for illustrative purposes. But since it is unlikely that for various categories of potential interest the appropriate data will ever be available in sufficient detail, they suggested that further conceptual developments of this kind would be an important (and perhaps the only) way to proceed in the near future. The Gelfand-Solomon model is easily amended for future questions having to do, for example, with special populations not easily characterizable by a single parameter set.

### Summary and Conclusions: Theories of Jury Behavior

The amount of theoretical work outlined above is not large when viewed against the amount of empirical research on jurors and juries. Yet the formal character of these theories is an important asset. For example,

they can be used not only to predict and organize existing data but also to simulate interesting parameter values. The exploration and evaluation of planned procedural changes, along with the comparison of cultural and/or temporal variations, are among the important illustrations just discussed.

Unfortunately, neither of the major theories provides an account of individual verdict preferences. Supplemental theory is badly needed to organize the large amount of data on individual juror decision making and thus provide input, as it were, for current theories that emphasize the group rather than the individual level of behavior. Both models reflect a relatively static conception of the jury, although a collective decision of this sort incontestably involves dynamic processes. Gelfand and Solomon (1975) have recently adopted a more dynamic view, and Davis (1973) has suggested a state-to-state description to reflect the changing internal distributions of opinion.

### CONCLUSIONS

We believe that future research, to be suitably productive, might emphasize the *group* as an interacting system to a greater degree than in the past. In addition, more care must be given to methodological details than heretofore. The need for theory, however, is at least as important as the need for increased sophistication in research practice. While some theory exists that directly addresses the behavior of the jury, far too little conceptual work is now focused on the decision preferred by the individual juror, perhaps in part because the situations, case materials, subject population, and so forth have been too restricted or homogeneous to stimulate theory about individuals who are jurors. (See also the review of mock jury research by Gerbasi, Zuckerman, & Reis, in press.)

Finally, there is likely to be a rising concern about "realness." To some degree, laboratory studies using, for example, mock trials and mock jurors seem to lack face validity and other essential ingredients for

**TABLE 4   Estimates of Various Parameters from the Gelfand-Solomon Model of Jury Verdicts**

| Data Source/Type | Parameter Estimates[a] | | | Estimated Probability Accused Is Guilty, Given Conviction by Exactly 7/12[b] |
|---|---|---|---|---|
| | $\hat{\mu}$ | $\hat{\theta}$ | $\hat{P}_G$ | |
| French data | | | | |
|    Crimes against person | .68 | .54 | .51 | .95 |
|    Crimes against property | .78 | .67 | .60 | .99 |
|    Crimes overall | .75 | .64 | .57 | .99 |
| U.S. data | | | | |
| Crimes overall | .90 | .70 | .66 | .99 |

Note: *Data used were from nineteenth-century France and twentieth-century U.S. All entries were taken from Gelfand and Solomon Table 5 (1973) and Table 5 (1974), except* $\hat{P}_G$, *which we calculated. We also calculated the last entry in the right-hand column using their Eq. 3.6 (1973).*

[a] $\hat{\mu}$ *is the probability a juror will not err in his vote;* $\hat{\theta}$ *is the probability before the trial that the accused is guilty (i.e., legally convictable);* $\hat{P}_G = \mu\theta + (1-\mu)(1-\theta)$ *is the probability that an individual juror will vote for conviction* ($\gamma_{1,\theta}$ *in Gelfand-Solomon notation).*

[b] *Calculated from Bayes theorem for the 7/12 case, by the expression* $\theta\mu^2/[(1-\theta)(1-\mu)^2 + \theta\mu^2]$, *substituting appropriate estimates.*

direct application. Although a few studies used adult subjects from jury rolls, the basic experimental nature of the setting was not thereby dispelled. Even if one could directly study the actual jury deliberating and deciding, the lack of replication within a trial would seriously hamper confident inferences in application. Since we cannot conceive of meeting these objections and generating a data point for every conceivable jury-related question of interest, we argue the importance of theory to guide and shape decisions about the way the trial and its jury work, and how the situation might be changed in the social interest. Any data that improves our intuition or disciplines our adoption and use of such models would be valuable.

# PART VI

# Epilogue for Psychology and Law

JUNE LOUIN TAPP
FELICE J. LEVINE

The social ferment of the past 20 years has produced major transformations in cultural perceptions of the relation of persons to institutions in society. At the same time psychology has begun to consider its scientific and social responsibilities to study these transformations and other related phenomena in the law. Likewise, at a more fundamental level, psychologists and lawyers have begun to face their anxieties about their respective roles and responsibilities to pursue ethically sound, intellectually satisfying, and societally meaningful work. Reappraisals in law and in psychology, commingling with "rights" movements, have helped to accomplish in reality what have long been symbolic beliefs or myths about the legal system (e.g., due process rights, the rights to treatment of prisoner and patient, equal opportunity regardless of age, race, or sex).

The realms of inquiry outlined in this book illuminate these changes in society and point to new directions for research and reform. Demythologizing generates serious psycholegal questions: What is an individual? What is choice? What is compliance? What is the role of the court? What is rehabilitation or resocialization? What constitutes competence? What is the "rights" relationship between a psychologist *and* a patient, a guard *and* a prisoner, a parent *and* a child? These questions demand review of law as well as evaluation of institutional and individual relationships at legal and psychological levels. Likewise, ethical queries are also involved (e.g., see Boruch, 1974; Goldiamond, 1974; Tapp & Levine, 1974; Thibaut & Walker, 1975).

The explosion of law has done more than promote justice. It has clarified that the law is a mobility belt not solely for the "rights-deprived" but also for the "relevance-deprived": Psychologists had begun to experience frustration, futility, and doubt in the late 1960s and early 1970s, a period of insecurity for both science and society (cf. Buss, 1975; Elms, 1975; Gergen, 1973; Holden, 1971; McGuire, 1973). As a result some psychologists chose to act on or in the most potent "rule" or "norm" institution in the social structure—the law. Likewise, although the legal profession had "not changed as rapidly as the rhetoric [Marks, Leswing, & Fortinsky, 1972, p. 239]," lawyers were also questioning the adequacy of their role.

Simultaneous to certain lawyers embracing an expanded conception of advocacy in society (cf. Cahn & Cahn, 1970; Casper, 1972; Rosenthal, 1974; Tapp & Levine, 1974), they and others became increasingly interested in utilizing one of the new social sciences—psychology—to gain insights about human behavior in rule-governed settings.

### RULES FOR ROLES

Book in hand, the reader may again ask, "What is the role of psychology?" and "What is the role of law?" As cogently, what is the role of lawyer and the role of psychologist in specifying the nature of law and reconciling its functions with the nomotic urge and sense of justice singled out as distinctly human by philosophers (e.g., Fuller, 1969a; Rawls, 1971) and psychologists (e.g., Hogan & Henley, 1970; Lerner, 1975; Tapp & Levine, 1974). In this task, is each to function as scientist or technician? As theoretician or clinician? As academic or practitioner? Must the levels of communication or exchange remain distinct?

One answer is that psychologists and lawyers need not be viewed as discrete. This book should serve to dispel the myth of the dissociation between the two disciplines (Tapp, 1969, 1974, 1976). It is a fiction that remains primarily for those who require monolithic models or seek intellectual isolation. As revealed in the preceding chapters, the last few years have witnessed a crossing of concepts, a melding of methods, a reduction of defensive barriers, and an integration of levels of discourse and discovery. In short, the "limits" of the psychology–law interface are inextricably intermeshed. The basic issues in psychology and law can best be examined—as the readings herein suggest—by drawing on the analytic skills, empirical efforts, and commonsense experiences of both psychologists and lawyers. Some time ago, Cronbach and Meehl (1955) underscored the need for congruence in theoretical and methodological constructs. It is the coming together—the synthesis—of a mutually derived paradigm, devoid of patois, and congruent in both fields that can facilitate developing a new dialogue about the nature of law and the domain of psychology.

Second, the need for explanations beyond the first interaction that proceed with caution and clarity (cf. Buss, 1975; Cronbach, 1975; Elms, 1975; Gergen, 1973) can be realized most effectively by the push to ask and answer a question from the legal as well as the psychological side. As elaborated in the introduction to this volume, psychologists can help mobilize philosophical and legal constructs in ways unavailable to the traditional ethicist or jurisprudent. But psychologists need also to translate significant experiments (e.g., attribution and exchange theory *or* perception and cognition theory) as well as broad-scope studies into language available to the legal profession. For example, many criminal procedures suffer (e.g., the eyewitness identification process) precisely because the psychological "stuff" in perception or memory is simply not translated or projected into its social context (but see, e.g., Levine & Tapp, 1973). Similarly too, lawyers in various roles must recognize their educative, ethical, and experimental responsibilities both within and outside their discipline (see also Tapp, 1974). Lawyers are in a unique position to depict the substantive legal variables that, if investigated from a more pluralistic posture, could provide fresh insights. Clearly the lawyer-scholar who has embraced a research role must rely chiefly on the "soft" sciences including psychology. While the "soft" sciences, especially psychology, may be more anxiety producing particularly when *they* reject or query a "hard" science model (cf. Buss, 1975; Gergen, 1973; McGuire, 1973; Smith, 1973), lawyers can appreciate, utilize, and communicate to the citizenry the value of predictive probabilities without forsaking a healthy skepticism.

The informed guesses that are the first issue of empirical endeavors, while not establishing truth, reduce ignorance when appropriately understood. Psychologists and lawyers have already experienced the pain of failure. But both groups—mindful of their age and stage—should continue to commend the pursuit of psycholegal knowledge in the pursuit of social justice.

A third aspect of the relationship between psychology and law is that, while both fields may not be isomorphic in approach, they are both public in their pursuits. Among others, Freud and Fuller, some 60 or 70 years apart, addressed this attribute in describing their respective as well as mutual enterprises. Both fields are value-conscious and evidence-minded. Lawyers are concerned with value-laden concepts; psychologists increasingly acknowledge the value-laden aspects of their enterprise; both groups seek empirical solutions to value-laden problems. Since psycholegal activities cannot be undertaken "value-free," when psychological or legal assumptions are found wanting, they should be dismissed or reconceptualized. The problems chosen by psychologists and lawyers for study are frequently criteria setters. Therefore, where we choose, either solo or in concert, to put our energies is important.

Lastly, what is "true" for research and reform in law is certainly as "true" for psychology. More than one case is needed to demonstrate a point; more than one setting is needed to determine an antecedent; more than one method to unearth the reason. On balance, the criteria for research and reform whether by lawyers, psychologists, or both should be more alike than different. Such an approach to methodology and policy in assessing legal events is likely to produce a charge not merely "to stamp out crime (or poverty, or discrimination, or inflation)" but "to embark, wholeheartedly but skeptically, upon the social experiment to see whether or not it works [Meehl, 1970c, pp. 29–30]."

## RESEARCH POSSIBILITIES

Given such a stance, what are some exemplary areas in need of psycholegal research? The work to be done in rights is preeminent because understanding its social and legal aspects is basic to developing a sense of mutuality and of competence. To date, whether in law or psychology, the notion of rights has involved more rhetoric than research. Yet, comprehensive investigations need to be done on the theoretical and practical dimensions of rights by psychologists and lawyers. This work should encompass the legal and ethical, psychosocial and developmental viewpoints. It should also incorporate and aim to evaluate the perspectives of adults and children as well as individuals and institutions within and across cultures (e.g., parents' and children's conceptions of their rights; black and white rights in U.S. and non-U.S. settings).

A second major area for study coming to the fore is dispute settlement and decision making. Instead of defining the judicial process solely in terms of the courts, dispute handling in the legal system should be viewed functionally as a set of decisional processes from event (e.g., tort, crime) to ultimate disposition (e.g., plea bargaining, negotiated settlement, court awards). In each of these arenas, psychologists can offer insights about processing information. Many psychological constructs derived, for example, from equity research or small group studies could be operationalized. Psychologists can also "educate" lawyers about the mediating variables that may affect legal decision making (e.g., proximity, affinity, status). At the same time, lawyers can "educate" psychologists about specific conditions affecting disputes between individuals and between individuals and institutions.

Third, given the little evidence that any kind of treatment consistently moves anyone closer to "rehabilitation" or "resocialization," an important area for research and reform relates to criminal justice settings and alternatives to incarceration. For example, with the increased questioning of the rehabilitative ideal (see, e.g., Allen, 1959; Kittrie, 1972; Rothman, 1973), the role of the psychologist and the lawyer is under critical review. Some of the questions (ethical and legal) being posed demand an answer about the appropriate professional role toward a patient in *any* total institution. What is a psychologist's responsibility to society and to the individual? What is a lawyer's? Is the goal control or choice? Who is responsible in terms of protecting the rights of the individual and/or the rights of society? While these questions involve value determinations, they also raise empirical problems: The researcher must identify the behavioral assumptions underlying methods of deterrence and/or rehabilitation and implement paradigms that systematically measure impact.

A fourth area for study, slowly getting under way in more systematic fashion, is the relation between education and legal socialization. The school is a major "controlled" environment that can influence people's legal attitudes and actions. Therefore, empirical research in law should importantly direct its attention to the formal curricula in law-related education as well as to the impact of modes of governance in the school. An important part of this inquiry would include the professional education of lawyers. The socialization process from layperson to lawyer is crucial to understanding the role conceptions of the legal profession and the nature of professional services. Yet, there is reluctance to view the law school as a viable context for research and reform. Recently the American Bar Foundation commenced a research program in legal education under the joint direction of a social psychologist and a lawyer that should generate a data base and a set of working hypotheses for future investigation.

Finally, despite references and recommendations, the construct "justice" remains confounded in law and psychology (cf. Lerner, 1975). Whether one considers, for example, legal socialization and education, the judicial process with regard to jury decision making, or the effect of criminal justice contexts, the "word" across all settings in the past several years is "justice." Yet an examination of much psycholegal research discloses a need for greater clarification of the term epistemologically and empirically. Numerous references to such seminal scholars as philosopher Rawls, jurisprudent Fuller, or psychologist Piaget may all be necessary to "socialize" paradigms and practices, but alone they are not likely to be sufficient to assure congruent or valid results.

### RETROSPECTIVE RECAP

In this collection many issues pertinent to law, justice, and the individual in society have emerged. This foray should suggest common themes and future directions for research and practice. The range of issues at the nexus of psychology and law serves to underscore that the law is not simply a system of social control, the product of one institution, or the possession of one field. Further, problems related to law and order and justice in society are no longer solely the domain of the legal practitioner or the psychological clinician. The range of psychologists studying legal phenomena as well as the number of lawyers using psychological materials or themselves embracing research roles is multiplying. Changes in the nature of both professions are yet another indication of the theoretical and methodological, practical and policy shifts that have occurred. While these shifts may be a response to field and societal crises, the penetrating question is whether the psychology–law solution is sufficiently comprehensive to channel efforts constructively. Only the future—or the next forum of lawyers and psychologists—can attest to that.

In a sense we have only begun to explore the "circle" of law. Studies are needed that employ multiple methods and focus on individuals and institutions longitudinally and cross-culturally. The definition of the law as a dynamic, interactive institution must be operationalized by more studies that look at the law's effects continuously (e.g., time-series analyses, repeated observations). Further, as Triandis recommended for civil liberties research (1975), it is important to undertake studies that focus more on people's responses to events and the consequences of responses than on their responses to concepts. In the early phases of inquiry, social research often tends to inspect attitude and opinion (as revealed in some of the chapters in this book). In the long term, however, modes of investigation should be developed that are capable of measuring attitudes, actions, and interactions with validity.

In concluding the book, as editors and authors we continue to view it as a "beginning." There is much work to be done by psychologists and lawyers who have embarked on the social scientific examination of law. The work to date has been scattered and spread across a range of interests. This fragmentation, however, does not evidence failure. Scholarship and creativity necessitate the freedom to pursue varied analytic routes and intellectual demons in full recognition that even dead ends contribute to our understanding. While researchers should acknowledge the value of continuity and incremental learning, they must press for exploration that does not simultaneously stifle a broad-gauged approach to inquiry. In terms of the history of science, the past for psycholegal research has been relatively brief; therefore, persistence tempered with optimism and eclecticism is requisite.

For the moment, both law and psychology have seemingly become less parochial and do apparently seek interdisciplinary approaches. Although there are still enormous gaps—substantive and theoretical, methodological and empirical—together we *can* be more systematic, *are* more committed to documenting events descriptively, and *may* be more willing to ask questions from more than one perspective. This pluralistic framework means that both psychologists and lawyers can address a question in a number of ways and seek an answer in more than just one valid setting. Answering and asking the question in a number of ways should yield a pattern of congruences, if not "truth." Ultimately, such bits of information should be useful in promoting both science and society. We hope so.

# REFERENCES

Abelson, R. P. & Rosenberg, M. J. Symbolic psychologic: A model of attitudinal cognition. *Behavioral Science*, 1958, *3*, 1–13.

Adams, H. B. "Mental illness" or interpersonal behavior? *American Psychologist*, 1964, *19*, 191–197.

Adams, J. S. Inequity in social exchange. In L. Berkowitz (Ed.), *Advances in experimental social psychology* (Vol. 2). New York: Academic Press, 1965.

Adelson, J. The mystique of adolescence. *Psychiatry*, 1964, *27*, 1–5.

Adelson, J. What generation gap? *New York Times Magazine*, Jan. 18, 1970.

Adelson, J. The political imagination of the young adolescent. *Daedalus*, 1971, *100*, 1013–1050.

Adelson, J., Green, B., & O'Neil, R. P. The growth of the idea of law in adolescence. *Journal of Developmental Psychology*, 1969, *1*, 327–332.

Adelson, J. & O'Neil, R. P. The growth of political ideas in adolescence: The sense of community. *Journal of Personality and Social Psychology*, 1966, *4*, 295–306.

Adler, N. & Harrington, C. *The learning of political behavior.* Glenview, Ill.: Scott, Foresman, 1970.

Administrative Office of the U.S. Courts. *Federal offenders.* Washington, D.C.: United States Government Printing Office, 1968.

Adorno, T. W., Frenkel-Brunswik, E., Levinson, D. J., & Sanford, R. N. *The authoritarian personality.* New York: Harper & Row, 1950.

Ajzen, I. Attitudes, normative beliefs, and the prediction of behavior: An empirical investigation. Unpublished manuscript, University of Illinois, 1967.

Ajzen, I. Attitudinal versus normative messages: An investigation of the differential effects of persuasive communication on behavior. *Sociometry*, 1971, *34*, 263–280.

Allen, F. A. Criminal justice, legal values and the rehabilitative ideal. *Journal of Criminal Law, Criminology and Police Science*, 1959, *50*, 226–232.

Allen, F. A. *The borderland of criminal justice.* Chicago: University of Chicago Press, 1964.

Allen, F. A. *The crimes of politics: Political dimensions of criminal justice.* Cambridge, Mass.: Harvard University Press, 1974.

Allport, F. *Theories of perception and the concept of structures.* New York: Wiley, 1955.

Allport, G. W. The use of personal documents in psychological science. *Social Science Research Council Bulletin*, 1942, No. 49.

Allport, G. W. *Pattern and growth in personality.* New York: Holt, Rinehart and Winston, 1961.

Allport, G. W. The general and unique in psychological science. *Journal of Personality*, 1962, *30*, 405–422.

Almond, G. & Verba, S. *The civic culture.* Princeton, N.J.: Princeton University Press, 1963.

Alschuler, A. W. The prosecutor's role in plea bargaining. *University of Chicago Law Review*, 1968, *36*, 51–112.

American Bar Association Special Committee on Youth Education for Citizenship. *Directory of law-related educational activities* (Working Notes, No. 6, 2d ed.). Chicago: Author, 1974.

American Bar Association Special Committee on Youth Education for Citizenship. *Bibliography of law-related curriculum materials: Annotated* (Working Notes, No. 10, 2d ed.). Chicago: Author, 1976.

Andenaes, J. General prevention—Illusion or reality? *Journal of Criminal Law, Criminology and Police Science,* 1952, *43,* 176–198.

Andenaes, J. The general preventive effects of punishment. *University of Pennsylvania Law Review,* 1966, *114,* 949–983.

Andenaes, J. General prevention revisited: Research and policy implications. *Journal of Criminal Law and Criminology,* 1975, *66,* 338–365.

Anderson, L. R. & Fishbein, M. Prediction of attitude from the number, strength, and evaluative aspect of beliefs about the attitude object: A comparison of summation and congruity theories. *Journal of Personality and Social Psychology,* 1965, *2,* 437–443.

Anderson, N. H. Integration theory and attitude change. *Psychological Review,* 1971, *78,* 171–206.

Appel, J. B. & Peterson, N. J. What's wrong with punishment? *Journal of Criminal Law, Criminology and Police Science,* 1965, *56,* 450–453.

Arendt, H. *Eichmann in Jerusalem: A report on the banality of evil.* New York: Viking, 1965.

Arnold, M. How Mitchell-Stans jury reached acquittal verdict. *New York Times,* May 5, 1974, pp. 1, 41.

Arnold, M. B. *Emotion and personality. Psychological aspects* (Vol. I). *Neurological and physiological aspects* (Vol. II). New York: Columbia University Press, 1960.

Aronfreed, J. *Conduct and conscience: The socialization of internalized control over behavior.* New York: Academic Press, 1968.

Aronfreed, J. The socialization of altruistic and sympathetic behavior: Some theoretical and experimental analyses. In J. R. Macaulay & L. Berkowitz (Eds.), *Altruism and helping behavior.* New York: Academic, 1970.

Asch, S. E. *Social psychology.* Englewood Cliffs, N.J.: Prentice-Hall, 1952.

Aubert, V. Competition and dissensus: Two types of conflict and of conflict resolution. *Journal of Conflict Resolution,* 1963, *7,* 26–42.

Aubert, V. Some social functions of legislation. *Acta Sociologica,* 1966, *10,* 98–110.

Aubert, V. *Sociology of law.* Baltimore: Penguin Books, 1969.

Ayllon, T. & Azrin, N. *The token economy.* New York: Appleton-Century-Crofts, 1968.

Azrin, N. H. Effects of punishment intensity during variable-interval reinforcement. *Journal of the Experimental Analysis of Behavior,* 1960, *3,* 123–142.

Azrin, N. H. & Holz, W. C. Punishment. In W. K. Honig (Ed.), *Operant behavior: Areas of research and application.* New York: Appleton-Century-Crofts, 1966.

Babb, H. W. Petrazhitskii: Science of legal policy and theory of law. *Boston University Law Review,* 1937, *17,* 793–829.

Babb, H. W. Petrazhitskii: Theory of law. *Boston University Law Review,* 1938, *18,* 511–575.

Badia, P., Haber, A., & Runyon, R. P. (Eds.) *Research problems in psychology.* Reading, Mass.: Addison-Wesley, 1970.

Bagdikian, B. H. & Dash, L. *The shame of the prisons.* Washington Post National Report, 1972.

Bakan, D. The test of significance in psychological research. *Psychological Bulletin,* 1966, *66,* 423–437.

Bakan, D. *On method: Toward a reconstruction of psychological investigation.* San Francisco: Jossey-Bass, 1967.

Bakan, D. *Slaughter of the innocents.* San Francisco: Jossey-Bass, 1971.

Baldwin, J. M. *Social and ethical interpretations in mental development.* New York: Macmillan, 1906.

Bales, R. F. *Interaction process analysis.* Cambridge, Mass.: Addison-Wesley, 1951.

Bancroft, H. H. *Popular tribunals.* San Francisco: History Company, 1887.

Bandura, A. Influence of model's reinforcement contingencies on the acquisition of imitative responses. *Journal of Personality and Social Psychology,* 1965, *1,* 589–595.

Bandura, A. The role of modeling processes in personality development. In W. W. Hartup & L. Smothergill (Eds.), *The young child: Reviews of research.* Washington: National Association for the Education of Young Children, 1967.

Bandura, A. *Principles of behavioral modification.* New York: Holt, Rinehart and Winston, 1969.

Bandura, A. *Aggression: A social learning analysis.* Englewood Cliffs, N.J.: Prentice-Hall, 1973.

Bandura, A. & McDonald, F. J. Influence of social reinforcement and the behavior of models in shaping children's moral judgments. *Journal of Abnormal and Social Psychology,* 1963, *67,* 274–281.

Bandura, A. & Walters, R. H. *Social learning and personality development.* New York: Holt, Rinehart and Winston, 1963.

Banfield, E. The political implications of metropolitan growth. *Daedalus,* 1960, *90*(1), 61–78.

Banfield, L. & Anderson, C. D. Continuances in the Cook County criminal courts. *University of Chicago Law Review,* 1967, *35,* 259–316.

Barber, B. Resistance by scientists to scientific discovery. *Science,* 1961, *134,* 596–602.

Bard, M. The study and modification of intrafamilial violence. In J. L. Singer (Ed.), *The control of aggression and violence.* New York: Academic, 1971.

Barghoorn, F. C. *Politics in the U.S.S.R.* (2d ed.). Boston: Little, Brown, 1972.

Barnett, C. *The swordbearers: Supreme command in the First World War.* New York: Signet, 1965.

Barry, B. *Political argument.* New York: Humanities Press, 1965.

Barton, A. & Mendlovitz, S. The experience of injustice as a research problem. *Journal of Legal Education,* 1960, 13, 24–39.

Bases, N. & McDonald, W. F. *Preventive detention in the District of Columbia:*

*The first ten months.* New York: Georgetown University Law Institute, 1972.

Battle, J. In search of the adversary system—The cooperative practices of private criminal defense attorneys. *Texas Law Review*, 1971, *50*, 60–118.

Bauer, D. Patuxent brass: Possible contempt. *Washington Daily News*, April 27, 1972, p. 5.

Bauer, R. A. *The new man in Soviet psychology.* Cambridge, Mass.: Harvard University Press, 1952.

Bauer, R. A. & Bauer, H. Day to day resistance to slavery. *Journal of Negro History*, 1942, *27*, 388–419.

Bayley, D. H. & Mendelsohn, H. *Minorities and the police: Confrontations in America.* New York: Free Press, 1969.

Bazelon, D. L. Psychologists in corrections—Are they doing good for the offender or well for themselves? In S. Brodsky (Ed.), *Psychologists in the criminal justice system.* Urbana, Ill.: University of Illinois Press, 1973.

Beccaria, C. B. *An essay on crimes and punishment* (J. A. Farrar, Trans.). London: Chatto & Windus, 1880.

Beccaria, C. B. *On crimes and punishments* (H. Paclucci, Trans.). Indianapolis: Bobbs-Merrill, 1963.

Becker, H. S. *Outsiders: Studies in the sociology of deviance.* New York: Free Press, 1963.

Becker, H. S. Whose side are we on? In W. J. Filstead (Ed.), *Qualitative methodology: Firsthand involvement with the social world.* Chicago: Markham, 1970.

Becker, T. L., Hildum, D. C., & Bateman, K. The influence of jurors' values on their verdicts: A courts and politics experiment. *Southwestern Social Science Quarterly*, 1965, *45*, 130–140.

Bellak, L. & Antell, M. An intercultural study of aggressive behavior on children's playground. *American Journal of Orthopsychiatry*, 1974, *44*, 503–511.

Bem, D. J. *Beliefs, attitudes, and human affairs.* Monterey, Calif.: Brooks-Cole, 1972.

Benn, S. I. Punishment. In P. Edwards (Ed.), *The encyclopedia of philosophy* (Vol. 7). New York: Crowell Collier & Macmillan, 1967.

Bentham, J. *An introduction to the principles of morals and legislation.* Oxford: Clarendon Press, 1879.

Berg, N. E. & Mussen, P. The origins and development of concepts of justice. *Journal of Social Issues*, 1975, *31*(3), 183–201.

Berkowitz, L. *Aggression: A social psychological analysis.* New York: McGraw-Hill, 1962.

Berkowitz, L. *The development of motives and values in the child.* New York: Basic Books, 1964.

Berkowitz, L. & Walker, N. Laws and moral judgments. *Sociometry*, 1967, *30*, 410–422.

Berman, H. J. *Justice in the U.S.S.R.: An interpretation of Soviet law* (2d ed., Rev.). Cambridge, Mass.: Harvard University Press, 1963.

Berman, H. J. Reply to Tumanov. *Soviet Law and Government*, 1965, *4*(3), 11–16.

Berman, H. J. The educational role of the Soviet court. *International and*

*Comparative Law Quarterly*, 1972, *21*, 81–94.

Berman, H. J. *The interaction of law and religion*. Nashville, Tenn.: Abingdon, 1974.

Berman, H. J. & Quigley, J. B., Jr. (Eds. & Trans.) *Basic laws on the structure of the Soviet state*. Cambridge, Mass.: Harvard University Press, 1969.

Berman, H. J. & Spindler, J. W. Soviet comrades' courts. *Washington Law Review*, 1963, *38*, 842–910.

Berman, H. J. & Spindler, J. W. (Eds. & Trans.) *Soviet criminal law and criminal procedure: The RSFSR Codes*. Cambridge, Mass.: Harvard University Press, 1966.

Berman, H. J. & Spindler, J. W. (Eds. & Trans.) *Soviet criminal law and procedure: The RSFSR Codes* (2d ed.). Cambridge, Mass.: Harvard University Press, 1972.

Berman, J. The Cuban popular tribunals. *Columbia Law Review*, 1969, *69*, 1317–1354.

Bermant, G. & Coppock, R. Outcomes of six- and twelve-member jury trials: An analysis of 128 civil cases in the State of Washington. *Washington Law Review*, 1973, *48*, 593–596.

Bermant, G., Nemeth, C., & Vidmar, N. (Eds.) *Psychology and the law*. Lexington, Mass.: D. C. Heath, 1976.

Berscheid, E., Boye, D., & Darley, J. M. Effects of forced association upon voluntary choice to associate. *Journal of Personality and Social Psychology*, 1968, *8*, 13–19.

Berscheid, E. & Walster, E. When does a harm-doer compensate a victim? *Journal of Personality and Social Psychology*, 1967, *6*, 435–441.

Berscheid, E., Walster, E., & Barclay, A. Effect of time on tendency to compensate a victim. *Psychological Reports*, 1969, *25*, 431–436.

Bettelheim, B. *The informed heart: Autonomy in a mass age*. New York: Free Press, 1960.

Bevan, W., Albert, R. S., Loiseaux, P. R., Mayfield, P. N., & Wright, G. Jury behavior as a function of the prestige of the foreman and the nature of his leadership. *Journal of Public Law*, 1958, *7*, 419–449.

Biggs, J., Jr. *The guilty mind: Psychiatry and the law of homicide*. Baltimore: Johns Hopkins University Press, 1967.

Birrell, R. G. & Birrell, J. H. W. The maltreatment syndrome in children: A hospital survey. *Medical Journal of Australia*, 1968, *2*, 1023–1029.

Bishop, G. F. Presidential preferences and values in 1968. Unpublished manuscript, Michigan State University, 1969.

Black, D. J. The mobilization of law. *Journal of Legal Studies*, 1973, *2*, 125–149.

Black, D. J. The boundaries of legal sociology. *Yale Law Journal*, 1972, *81*, 1086–1100.

Black, D. J. & Reiss, A. J., Jr. Patterns of behavior in police and citizen transactions. *Studies of crime and law enforcement in major metropolitan areas*. Washington, D.C.: United States Government Printing Office, 1967.

Blatt, M. The effects of classroom discussion programs upon children's level of moral judgment. Unpublished doctoral dissertation, University of Chicago, 1969.

Blatt, M. & Kohlberg, L. The effects of a classroom discussion program upon the moral levels of preadolescents. *Merrill-Palmer Quarterly*, 1969.

Blau, P. M. *The dynamic of bureaucracy*. Chicago: University of Chicago Press, 1955.

Blau, P. M. *Bureaucracy in modern society*. New York: Random House, 1956.

Blau, P. M. *Exchange and power in social life*. New York: Wiley, 1964.

Blumberg, A. S. *Criminal justice*. Chicago: Quadrangle Books, 1967. (a)

Blumberg, A. S. The practice of law as a confidence game. *Law and Society Review*, 1967, *1*, 15–39. (b)

Blumberg, A. S. The criminal court as organization and communication system. In R. Quinney (Ed.), *Crime and justice in society*. Boston: Little, Brown, 1969.

Bock, R. D. *Multivariate statistical methods in behavioral research*. New York: McGraw-Hill, 1975.

Bock, R. D. & Haggard, E. A. The use of multivariate analysis of variance in behavioral research. In D. K. Whitla (Ed.), *Handbook of measurement and assessment in behavioral sciences*. Reading, Mass.: Addison-Wesley, 1968.

Boehm, V. Mr. Prejudice, Miss Sympathy and the authoritarian personality: An application of psychological measuring techniques to the problem of jury bias. *Wisconsin Law Review*, 1968, 734–750.

Bohannan, P. *Justice and judgment among the Tiv of Nigeria*. London: Oxford University Press, 1957.

Bonn, R. L. Commercial arbitration: A study in the regulation of interorganizational conflict. Unpublished doctoral dissertation, New York University, 1970.

Bonn, R. L. The predictability of nonlegalistic adjudication. *Law and Society Review*, 1972, *6*, 563–578.

Boone, J. S. The effects of race, arrogance and evidence on simulated jury decisions. *Dissertation Abstracts International*, Humanities, 1973, *33*, 7019A.

Boorstin, D. J. *The mysterious science of the law: An essay on Blackstone's Commentaries*. Cambridge, Mass.: Harvard University Press, 1941.

Boothe, B. E., Rosenfeld, A. H., & Walker, E. L. *Toward a science of psychiatry*. Monterey, Calif.: Brooks-Cole, 1974.

Boruch, R. F. *Costs, benefits and legal implications in social research*. Evanston, Ill.: Northwestern University Press, 1974.

Bowers, K. S. Situationism in psychology: An analysis and a critique. *Psychological Review*, 1973, *80*, 307–336.

Braginsky, B. M., Braginsky, D., & Ring, K. *Methods of madness: The mental hospital as a last resort*. New York: Holt, Rinehart and Winston, 1969.

Bramel, D. Interpersonal attraction, hostility, and perception. In J. Mills (Ed.), *Experimental social psychology*. New York: Macmillan, 1969.

Bray, R. M. Decision rules, attitude similarity, and jury decision making. Unpublished doctoral dissertation, University of Illinois, 1974.

Brim, O. G., Jr. & Wheeler, S. *Socialization after childhood*. New York: Wiley, 1966.

Broad, C. D. *Examination of McTaggart's philosophy*. Cambridge, Eng.: Cambridge University Press, 1933.

Brock, T. C. & Becker, L. A. Debriefing and susceptibility to subsequent experimental manipulations. *Journal of Experimental Social Psychology*, 1966, *2*, 314–323.

Brock, T. C. & Buss, A. H. Dissonance, aggression, and evaluation of pain. *Journal of Abnormal and Social Psychology*, 1962, *65*, 192–202.

Brock, T. C. & Buss, A. H. Effects of justification for aggression in communication with the victim on post-aggression dissonance. *Journal of Abnormal and Social Psychology*, 1964, *68*, 403–412.

Broeder, D. W. The University of Chicago jury project. *Nebraska Law Review*, 1958, *38*, 744–761.

Bronfenbrenner, U. Socialization and social class through time and space. In E. E. Maccoby, T. M. Newcomb, & E. L. Hartley (Eds.), *Readings in social psychology* (3d ed.). New York: Holt, Rinehart and Winston, 1958.

Bronfenbrenner, U. *Two worlds of childhood: U.S. and U.S.S.R.* New York: Russell Sage Foundation, 1970.

Bronfenbrenner, U. The origins of alienation. *Scientific American*, 1974, *213*(2), 53–57; 60–61.

Bronson, E. J. On the conviction proneness and representativeness of the death-qualified jury: An empirical study of Colorado veniremen. *University of Colorado Law Review,* 1970, *42*, 1–32.

Brown et al. *v.* Board of Education of Topeka et al. *United States Reports,* 1954, *347*, 483–496.

Brown, P. & Elliott, R. The control of aggression in a nursery school class. *Journal of Experimental Child Psychology*, 1965, *2*, 103–107.

Brown, R. M. *The South Carolina regulators*. Cambridge, Mass.: Harvard University Press, 1963.

Bruner, J. Social psychology and perception. In E. E. Maccoby, T. M. Newcomb, & E. L. Hartley (Eds.), *Readings in social psychology* (3d ed.). New York: Holt, Rinehart and Winston, 1958.

Buck *v.* Bell. *United States Reports,* 1927, *274*, 200–208.

Buergenthal, T. & Torney, J. V. *International human rights and international education*. Washington, D.C.: Department of State, United States National Commission for UNESCO, 1976.

Bullock, H. A. Significance of the racial factor in the length of prison sentences. *Journal of Criminal Law, Criminology and Police Science*, 1961, *52*, 411–417.

Burks, B. & Kelley, T. L. Statistical hazards in nature–nurture investigation. *Twenty-seventh yearbook of the National Society for the Study of Education, Nature and Nurture, Part I: Their influence upon intelligence*. Bloomington, Ind.: Public School Publishing, 1928.

Burt, C. The inheritance of mental ability. *American Psychologist,* 1958, *13*, 1–15.

Burt, C. The genetic determination of differences in intelligence: A study of monozygotic twins reared together and apart. *British Journal of Psychology*, 1966, *57*, 137–153.

Burt, C. The genetic determination of intelligence: A reply. *British Journal of Psychology*, 1967, *58*, 153–162.

Burtt, M. E. *Legal psychology*. Englewood Cliffs, N.J.: Prentice-Hall, 1931.

Bushell. *Howell's State Trials*, 1670, *6*, 999–1026.

Buss, A. R. The emerging field of the sociology of psychological knowledge. *American Psychologist*, 1975, *30*, 988–1002.

Byrne, D. Interpersonal attraction and attitude similarity. *Journal of Abnormal and Social Psychology*, 1961, *62*, 713–715.

Byrne, D. *The attraction paradigm*. New York: Academic Press, 1971.

Byrne, D. & Clore, G. L. A reinforcement model of evaluative responses. *Personality: An International Journal*, 1970, *1*, 103–128.

Byrne, D., Lamberth, J., Palmer, J., & London, O. Sequential effects as a function of explicit and implicit interpolated attraction responses. *Journal of Personality and Social Psychology*, 1969, *13*, 70–78.

Cahn, E. & Cahn, J. C. What price justice: The civilian perspective revisited. *Notre Dame Law Review*, 1966, *41*, 927–960.

Cahn, E. & Cahn, J. C. Power to the people or the profession?—The public interest in public interest law. *Yale Law Journal*, 1970, *79*, 1005–1048.

*California Jury Instructions*. St. Paul, Minn.: West, 1970.

Calvin, J. *Institutes of the Christian religion* (Bk. 2; J. Allen, Trans.). Philadelphia: Philip H. Micklin, 1816.

Cameron, M. O. *The booster and the snitch*. Glencoe, Ill.: Free Press, 1964.

Campbell, D. T. Reforms as experiments. *American Psychologist*, 1969, *24*, 409–429.

Campbell, D. T. Legal reforms as experiments. *Journal of Legal Education*, 1971, *23*, 217–239.

Campbell, D. T. Qualitative knowing in action research. Paper presented at the annual meeting of the American Psychological Association, New Orleans, 1974.

Campbell, D. T., Boruch, R. F., Schwartz, R. D., & Steinberg, J. Confidentiality preserving modes of access to files and to interfile exchange for useful statistical analysis. In A. M. Rivlin et al. (Eds.), *Protecting individual privacy in evaluation research*. Washington, D.C.: National Academy of Science and National Research Council, 1975.

Campbell, D. T. & Fiske, D. W. Convergent and discriminant validation by the multitrait–multimethod matrix. *Psychological Bulletin*, 1959, *56*, 81–105.

Campbell, D. T. & Ross, H. L. The Connecticut crackdown on speeding: Time-series data in quasi-experimental analysis. *Law and Society Review*, 1968, *3*, 33–53.

Cardozo, B. N. *The nature of the judicial process*. New Haven: Yale University Press, 1921.

Cardozo, B. N. *Law and literature and other essays and addresses*. New York: Harcourt Brace Jovanovich, 1931.

Carlin, J. E., Howard, J., & Messinger, S. L. *Civil justice and the poor: Issues for sociological research*. New York: Russell Sage Foundation, 1967.

Carlsmith, J. M. & Gross, A. E. Some effects of guilt on compliance. *Journal of Personality and Social Psychology*, 1969, *11*, 232–239.

Carlson, A. R. The relationships between a behavioral intention, attitude toward the behavior, and normative beliefs about the behavior. Unpublished doctoral dissertation, University of Illinois, 1968.

Carter, H. D. Twin similarities in occupational interests. *Journal of Educational Psychology*, 1932, *23*, 641–655.

Cartwright, D. & Zander, A. (Eds.) *Group dynamics: Research and theory* (2d ed.). New York: Harper & Row, 1960.

Casper, J. D. Lawyers in defense of liberty: Lawyers before the Supreme Court in civil liberties and civil rights cases, 1957–66. Unpublished doctoral dissertation, Yale University, 1970.

Casper, J. D. *Lawyers before the Warren Court: Civil liberties and civil rights, 1957–66.* Urbana, Ill.: University of Illinois Press, 1972.

Chein, I. There ought to be a law—But why? Paper presented at the annual meeting of the American Psychological Association, Chicago, 1975.

Chevigny, P. *Police power: Police abuses in New York City.* New York: Vintage Books, 1969.

Christie, R. & Schulman, J. Judging and jurors. *Time,* 1974, *103,* 60.

Chwast, J. Value conflicts in law enforcement. *Crime and Delinquency,* 1965, *11,* 151–161.

Cicourel, A. V. *The social organization of juvenile justice.* New York: Wiley, 1968.

Cicourel, A. V. Social class, family structure and the administration of juvenile justice. Unpublished manuscript, University of California at Riverside, n.d.

Clark, A. L. & Gibbs, J. P. Social control: A reformation. *Social Problems,* 1965, *12,* 398–415.

Clark, K. B. Problems of power and social change: Toward a relevant social psychology. *Journal of Social Issues,* 1965, *21,* 4–20.

Clark, K. B. The pathos of power: A psychological perspective. *American Psychologist,* 1971, *26,* 1047–1057.

Clausen, J. A. (Ed.) *Socialization and society.* Boston: Little, Brown, 1968.

Clinard, M. B. *The black market.* New York: Holt, Rinehart and Winston, 1952.

Cloward, R. A. & Ohlin, L. E. *Delinquency and opportunity.* Glencoe, Ill.: Free Press, 1960.

Coffey, M. Badlands revisited—A memoir of murderous days in Nebraska. *The Atlantic Monthly,* 1974, *234*(6), 70–81.

Cohen, J. The statistical power of abnormal-social psychological research: A review. *Journal of Abnormal and Social Psychology,* 1962, *65,* 145–153.

Cohen, J., Robson, R. A., & Bates, A. *Parental authority: The community and the law.* New Brunswick, N.J.: Rutgers University Press, 1958.

Cohen, J. & Struening, E. L. Opinions about mental illness in the personnel of two large mental hospitals. *Journal of Abnormal and Social Psychology,* 1962, *64,* 349–360.

Cole, G. F. Criminal justice as an exchange system. *Rutgers Camden Law Journal,* 1971, *3,* 18–31.

Cole, M. & Maltzman, I. (Eds.) *A handbook of contemporary Soviet psychology.* New York: Basic Books, 1969.

Coleman, J. S., Campbell, E. Q., & Hobson, C. J. *Equality of educational opportunity.* Washington, D.C.: United States Government Printing Office, 1966.

Collins, B. & Hoyt, M. Personal responsibility-for-consequences: An integration and extension of the "forced compliance" literature. *Journal of Experimental Social Psychology,* 1972, *8,* 558–593.

Commonwealth *v.* Porter. *Massachusetts Reports,* 1845, *51,* 263–287.

Conant, J. B. *On understanding science: An historical approach.* New Haven: Yale University Press, 1947.

Condorcet, le Marquis de. *Essai sur l'application de l'analyse à la probabilité des décisions rendues à la pluralité des voix.* Paris: Imprimerie Royale, 1785.

*Congressional Record.* 1970, *116*(121), July 17, 1970.

Conn, S. & Hippler, A. Paralegals in the bush. *UCLA-Alaska Law Review,* 1973, *3,* 85–102.

Conrad, A. F., Morgan, J. F., Pratt, R. W., Jr., Voltz, C. E., & Bombaugh, R. L. *Automobile accident costs and payments.* Ann Arbor: University of Michigan Press, 1964.

Converse, E. The war of all against all: A review of the *Journal of Conflict Resolution,* 1957–1968. *Journal of Conflict Resolution,* 1968, *12,* 471–532.

Converse, P. E. Attitudes and non-attitudes: Continuation of a dialogue. In E. R. Tufte (Ed.), *The quantitative analysis of social problems.* Reading, Mass.: Addison-Wesley, 1970.

Couch, A. & Keniston, K. Yeasayers and naysayers: Agreeing response set as a personality variable. *Journal of Abnormal and Social Psychology,* 1960, *60,* 151–174.

Cournot, A. A. Sur les applications du calcul des chances à la statistique judiciaire. *Journal des Mathématiques Pures et Appliqués,* 1838, *3,* 257–334.

Cowan, T. A. What law can do for social science. In W. M. Evan (Ed.), *Law and sociology: Exploratory essays.* New York: The Free Press of Glencoe, 1962.

Cowan, T. A. & Strickland, D. A. *The legal structure of a confined micro-society: A report on the cases of Penthouse II and III.* Space Sciences Laboratory Social Sciences Project, University of California at Berkeley, Internal Working Paper No. 34, 1965.

Cowles, J. T. Food-tokens as incentives for learning by chimpanzees. *Comparative Psychology Monographs,* 1937, *14,* 1–96.

Cressey, D. R. & Ward, D. A. *Delinquency, crime, and social process.* New York: Harper & Row, 1969.

Cronbach, L. J. Beyond the two disciplines of scientific psychology. *American Psychologist,* 1975, *30,* 116–127.

Cronbach, L. J. & Meehl, P. E. Construct validity in psychological tests. *Psychological Bulletin,* 1955, *52,* 281–302.

Crosson, R. F. An investigation into certain personality variables among capital trial jurors. *Dissertation Abstracts,* 1967, *27,* 3668B–3669B.

Cumming, E. & Cumming, J. Affective symbolism, social norms and mental illness. *Psychiatry,* 1956, *19,* 77–85.

Dahl, R. A. *Who governs?* New Haven: Yale University Press, 1961.

Danzig, R. Toward the creation of a complementary decentralized system of criminal justice. *Stanford Law Review,* 1973, *26,* 1–54.

Davidson, J. Cognitive familiarity and dissonance reduction. In L. Festinger (Ed.), *Conflict, decision, and dissonance.* Stanford, Calif.: Stanford Press, 1964.

Davis, J. H. Group decision and social interaction: A theory of social decision schemes. *Psychological Review,* 1973, *80,* 97–125.

Davis, J. H., Kerr, N. L., Atkin, R. S., Holt, R., & Meek, D. The decision processes of 6- and 12-person mock juries assigned unanimous and 2/3 majority rules. *Journal of Personality and Social Psychology,* 1975, *32,* 1–14.

Davis, J. H., Kerr, N. L., Stasser, G., Meek, D., & Holt, R. W. Victim consequences, sentence severity, and decision processes in mock jurors. In *Organizational behavior and human performance,* in press.

Davis, K. E. & Jones, E. E. Changes in interpersonal perception as a means of reducing cognitive dissonance. *Journal of Abnormal and Social Psychology,* 1960, *61,* 402–410.

Davitz, J. R. The effects of previous training on postfrustration behavior. *Journal of Abnormal and Social Psychology,* 1952, *47,* 309–315.

Dawson, R. E. & Prewitt, K. *Political socialization.* Boston: Little, Brown, 1969.

Debs, E. V. *Walls and bars.* Chicago: Socialist Party, 1927.

Decree of the Central Committee of the Communist Party of the Soviet Union. On measures for further development of legal science and improvement of legal education in the country. *Kommunist,* 1964, *12,* 70–74.

Delaney, J. J. The battered child and the law. In C. H. Kempe & R. E. Helfer (Eds.), *Helping the battered child and his family.* New York: Lippincott, 1972.

Dempsey, J. C. Isolations of the police officer. Unpublished manuscript, Colorado State University, 1967.

DePalma, D. J. & Foley, J. M. (Eds.) *Moral development: Current theory and research.* Hillsdale, N.J.: Lawrence Erlbaum Associates, 1975.

DeReuck, A. V. S. & Porter, R. (Eds.) *The mentally abnormal offender.* London: Churchill Ltd., 1968.

Deur, J. L. & Parke, R. D. The effects of inconsistent punishment on aggression in children. *Developmental Psychology,* 1970, *2,* 403–411.

Deutsch, K. W. *The nerves of government: Models of political communication and control.* New York: The Free Press of Glencoe, 1963.

Deutsch, M. Equity, equality, and need: What determines which value will be used as the basis of distributive justice? *Journal of Social Issues,* 1975, *31*(3), 137–149.

Devlin, P. A. *Trial by jury.* London: Stevens, 1956.

Devlin, P. A. *Law and morals.* London: Oxford University Press, 1961.

Devlin, P. A. *The enforcement of morals.* London: Oxford University Press, 1965.

Dewey, J. *Moral principles in education.* Boston: Houghton Mifflin, 1909.

Dewey, J. *How we think.* Boston: Heath, 1910.

Dewey, J. *Democracy and education: An introduction to the philosophy of education.* New York: Macmillan, 1916.

Dewey, J. Experience and conduct. In C. Murchison (Ed.), *Psychologies of 1930.* Worcester, Mass.: Clark University Press, 1930.

Dewey, J. *On education: Selected writings* (R. Archambault, Ed.). New York: Modern Library, 1964.

Dewey, J. & Tufts, J. H. *Ethics.* New York: Holt, Rinehart and Winston, 1932.

Diamond, A. S. *Evolution of law and order.* Westport, Conn.: Greenwood Press, 1973.

Diamond, S. S. A jury experiment reanalyzed. *University of Michigan Journal of Law Reform,* 1974, *7,* 520–532.

Diamond, S. S. & Zeisel, H. A courtroom experiment on juror selection and decision making. Paper presented at the annual meeting of the American Psychological Association, New Orleans, 1974.

Dicey, A. B. *Lectures on the relation between law and public opinion in England during the nineteenth century.* London: Macmillan, 1905.

Diesing, P. *Reason in society.* Urbana, Ill. University of Illinois Press, 1962.

Dion, K. K. Children's physical attractiveness and sex as determinants of adult punitiveness. *Developmental Psychology,* 1974, *10,* 772–778.

Dodd, D. J. Police mentality and behavior. *Issues in Criminology,* 1967, *3*(1), 47–67.

Dohrenwend, B. P. & Dohrenwend, B. S. The problem of validity in field studies of psychological disorder. *Journal of Abnormal and Social Psychology,* 1965, *70,* 52–60.

Dollard, J., Doob, L. W., Miller, N. E., Mowrer, O. H., & Sears, R. R. *Frustration and aggression.* New Haven: Yale University Press, 1939.

Domke, M. *The law and practice of commercial arbitration.* Mundelein, Ill.: Callaghan, 1968.

Drekmeier, C. Knowledge as virtue, knowledge as power. In N. Sanford & C. Comstock (Eds.), *Sanction for evil.* San Francisco: Jossey-Bass, 1971.

Dror, Y. Law and social change. *Tulane Law Review,* 1959, *33,* 787–802.

Dulov, A. V. *Sudebnaia psikhologiia* [Judicial psychology]. Minsk: Vysheishaia Shkola, 1970.

Duncan *v.* State of Louisiana. *Supreme Court Reporter,* 1968, *88,* 1444–1472.

Durkheim, E. *The rules of sociological method* (8th ed.; S. Solovay & J. Mueller, Trans.). Chicago: University of Chicago Press, 1938.

Durkheim, E. *Sociology and philosophy* (D. F. Popcock, Trans.). New York: Free Press, 1953.

Dworkin, G. Paternalism. In R. A. Wasserstrom (Ed.), *Morality and the law.* Belmont, Calif.: Wadsworth, 1971.

Dworkin, R. M. Judicial discretion. *Journal of Philosophy,* 1963, *60,* 624–641.

Dworkin, R. M. The model of rules. *University of Chicago Law Review,* 1967, *35,* 14–46.

East, M. E. The effects of the sex of the defendant, the sex of the subject-juror, and the family status of the defendant on judicial decision. Unpublished manuscript, Purdue University, 1972.

Easton, D. & Dennis, J. *Children in the political system: Origins of political legitimacy.* New York: McGraw-Hill, 1969.

Eckhoff, T. & Jacobsen, K. D. *Rationality and responsibility in administrative and judicial decision-making.* Copenhagen: Munksgaard, 1960.

Efran, M. G. The effect of physical appearance on the judgment of guilt, interpersonal attraction, and severity of recommended punishment in a simulated jury task. *Journal of Research in Personality,* 1974, *8,* 45–54.

Eisenberg, L. The sins of the fathers: Urban decay and social pathology. *American Journal of Orthopsychiatry,* 1962, *32,* 14.

Ekelof, P. O. *Straffet, skadestandet och vitet.* Leipzig: Harrassowitz, 1942.

Elkind, D. Adolescent cognitive development. In J. F. Adams (Ed.), *Understanding adolescence.* Boston: Allyn & Bacon, 1968.

Ellis, A. Should some people be labeled mentally ill? *Journal of Consulting Psychology,* 1967, *31,* 435–446.

Ellsworth, P. C. & Levy, R. J. Legislative reform of child custody adjudication: An effort to rely on social science data in formulating legal policies. *Law and Society Review,* 1969, *4,* 167–233.

Elmer, E. *Children in jeopardy: A study of abused minors and their families.* Pittsburgh: University of Pittsburgh Press, 1967.

Elms, A. C. The crisis of confidence in social psychology. *American Psychologist,* 1975, *30,* 967–976.

Elston, R. C. & Gottesman, I. I. The analysis of quantitative inheritance simultaneously from twin and family data. *American Journal of Human Genetics,* 1968, *20,* 512–521.

Ennis, B. J. *Prisoners of psychiatry: Mental patients, psychiatrists, and the law.* New York: Harcourt Brace Jovanovich, 1972.

Epstein, J. *The great conspiracy trial.* New York: Random House, 1970.

Epstein, R. Development of conceptions of rules in young children. Unpublished manuscript, University of Chicago, 1965.

Erikson, E. Identity and the life cycle. *Psychological Issues,* 1959, *1* (Whole Monograph 1).

Erikson, E. The golden rule and cycle of life. In R. White (Ed.), *The study of lives.* New York: Atherton Press, 1963.

Erikson, K. T. *Wayward Puritans.* New York: Wiley, 1966.

Erlanger, H. S. Jury research in America: Its past and future. *Law and Society Review,* 1970, *4,* 345–370.

Erlanger, H. S. Social class differences in parents' use of physical punishment. In S. K. Steinmetz & M. S. Straus (Eds.), *Violence in the family.* New York: Dodd, Mead, 1974.

Erlenmeyer-Kimling, L. & Jarvik, L. F. Genetics and intelligence: A review. *Science,* 1963, *142,* 1477–1479.

Erskine, G. The polls: Textbook knowledge. *Public Opinion Quarterly,* 1963, *27,* 133–141.

Estes, W. K. An experimental study of punishment. *Psychological Monographs,* 1944, *57* (Whole No. 263).

Etzioni, A. Science threatens jury system. *St. Paul Sunday Pioneer Press,* June 2, 1974, 1; 5. (Reprinted from *Washington Post.*)

Fanon, F. *The wretched of the earth.* New York: Grove Press, 1963.

*Federal Rules of Civil Procedure.* St. Paul, Minn.: West, 1970.

Feeley, M. M. Power, impact and the Supreme Court. In T. L. Becker & M. M. Feeley (Eds.), *The impact of Supreme Court decisions.* New York: Oxford University Press, 1973. (a)

Feeley, M. M. Two models of the criminal justice system: An organizational perspective. *Law and Society Review,* 1973, *7,* 407–425. (b)

Feifer, G. *Justice in Moscow.* New York: Simon & Schuster, 1964.

Feigl, H. & Meehl, P. E. The determinism-freedom and body mind problems. In P. A. Schilpp (Ed.), *The philosophy of Sir Karl Popper* (Vol. 1). La Salle, Ill.: Open Court Publishing, 1974.

Feinberg, J. The expressive function of punishment. *The Monist,* 1965, *49,* 397–423.

Feinberg, J. Crime, clutchability, and individuated treatment. In *Doing and deserving: Essays in the theory of responsibility.* Princeton, N.J.: Princeton University Press, 1970.

Feinberg, W. E. Teaching the type I and type II errors: The judicial process. *The American Statistician,* 1971, *25*(3), 30–32.

Felstiner, W. L. F. Influences of social organization on dispute processing. *Law and Society Review,* 1974, *9,* 63–94.

Fenigstein, A. & Buss, A. H. Association and affect as determinants of displaced aggression. *Journal of Research in Personality,* 1974, *7,* 306–313.

Festinger, L. *A theory of cognitive dissonance.* Evanston, Ill.: Row, Peterson, 1957.

Fishbein, M. Sexual behavior and propositional control. Paper presented to Psychonomic Society, 1966.

Fishbein, M. Attitude and the prediction of behavior. In M. Fishbein (Ed.), *Readings in attitude theory and measurement.* New York: Wiley, 1967.

Fishkin, J., Keniston, K., & McKinnon, C. Moral reasoning and political ideology. *Journal of Personality and Social Psychology,* 1973, *27,* 109–119.

Fishman, L. & Izzett, R. R. The influence of a defendant's attractiveness and justification for his act on the sentencing tendencies of subject-jurors. Paper presented at the annual meeting of the Midwestern Psychological Association, Chicago, 1974.

Flavell, J. *The developmental psychology of Jean Piaget.* Princeton, N.J.: Van Nostrand, 1963.

Flavell, J. An analysis of cognitive-developmental sequences. *Genetic Psychology Monographs,* 1972, *86,* 279–350.

Flavell, J., Botkin, P. T., & Fry, C. L. *The development of role-taking and communication skills in children.* New York: Wiley, 1968.

Flynn, E. E. Sources of collective violence in correctional institutions. In *Prevention of violence in correctional institutions.* Washington, D.C.: Law Enforcement Assistance Administration, Criminal Justice Monograph, 1972.

Forster, M. C. A study of father–son resemblance in vocational interests and personality traits. Unpublished doctoral dissertation, University of Minnesota, 1931.

Forston, R. F. The decision-making process in the American civil jury: A comparative methodological investigation. Unpublished doctoral dissertation, University of Minnesota, 1968.

Forsyth, W. *History of trial by jury.* London: Parker & Sons, 1852.

Franck, T. M. The new development: Can American law and legal institutions help developing countries? *Wisconsin Law Review,* 1972, 767–801.

Frank, J. *Law and the modern mind.* New York: Brentano's, 1930.

Freedman, D. A. & Freedman, N. Behavioral differences between Chinese-American and European-American newborns. *Nature,* 1969, *224,* 1227.

Freedman, J. L., Wallington, S. A., & Bless, E. Compliance without pressure: The effect of guilt. *Journal of Personality and Social Psychology,* 1967, *7,* 117–124.

French, J. R. P., Jr. & Raven, B. The bases of social power. In D. Cartwright

(Ed.), *Studies in social power.* Ann Arbor: University of Michigan, 1959.

Freud, A. *The ego and mechanisms of defense.* New York: International Universities Press, 1936.

Freud, S. Psycho-analysis and ascertaining of truth in courts of law. In *Clinical papers and papers on technique, collected papers* (Vol. 2). New York: Basic Books, 1959.

Freund, P. A. *On law and justice.* Cambridge, Mass.: Belknap Press of Harvard University Press, 1968.

Fried, M., Kaplan, K. J., & Klein, K. W. Juror selection: An analysis of voir dire. In R. J. Simon (Ed.), *The jury system in America: A critical overview.* Beverly Hills, Calif.: Sage, 1975.

Friedman, H. Trial by jury: Criteria for convictions, jury size and type I and type II errors. *The American Statistician,* 1972, *26,* 21–23.

Friedman, L. Political power and legal legitimacy: A short history of political trials. *The Antioch Review,* 1970, *30,* 157–170.

Friedman, L. M. Legal rules and the process of social change. *Stanford Law Review,* 1967, *19,* 786–840.

Friedman, L. M. Legal culture and social development. *Law and Society Review,* 1969, *4,* 29–44. (a)

Friedman, L. M. Social welfare legislation, an introduction. *Stanford Law Review,* 1969, *21,* 217–247. (b)

Friedman, L. M. *The legal system.* New York. Russell Sage Foundation, 1975.

Friedman, L. M. & Macaulay, S. *Law and the behavioral sciences.* Indianapolis: Bobbs-Merrill, 1969.

Friedrich, C. J. (Ed.) *Rational decision: Nomos VII.* N. Y.: Atherton, 1964.

Fromm, E. *The art of loving.* New York: Harper & Row, 1956.

Fuller, J. L. & Thompson, W. R. *Behavior genetics.* New York: Wiley, 1960.

Fuller, L. L. Adjudication and the rule of law. *Proceedings of the American Society of International Law,* 1960, 1–8.

Fuller, L. L. Human interaction and the law. *The American Journal of Jurisprudence,* 1969, *14,* 1–36. (a)

Fuller, L. L. *The morality of law* (Rev. ed.). New Haven: Yale University Press, 1969. (b)

Fuller, L. L. Two principles of human association. In J. R. Pennock & J. W. Chapman (Eds.), *Voluntary associations: Nomos XI.* New York: Atherton, 1969. (c)

Fuller, L. L. The forms and limits of adjudication. Unpublished manuscript, Harvard University, no date.

Gallatin, J. & Adelson, J. Individual rights and the public good: A cross-national study of adolescence. *Comparative Political Studies,* 1970, *2,* 226–244.

Garbarino, J. A preliminary study of some ecological correlates of child abuse: The impact of socio-economic stress on mothers. *Child Development,* 1976, *47,* 178–185.

Garfinkle, H. Conditions of successful degradation ceremonies. *American Journal of Sociology,* 1956, *61,* 420–424.

Gavrilov, O. A. O problemakh sovetskoi sudebnoi psikhologii [On problems of Soviet judicial psychology]. *Voprosy Psikhologii [Problems of Psychology],* 1965, *6,* 136–147.

Geis, G. & Monahan, J. The social ecology of violence. In T. Lickona (Ed.), *Moral development and behavior: Theory, research, and social issues.* New York: Holt, Rinehart and Winston, 1976.

Gelfand, A. E. & Solomon, H. A study of Poisson's models for jury verdicts in criminal and civil trials. *Journal of the American Statistical Association,* 1973, *68,* 271–278.

Gelfand, A. E. & Solomon, H. Modeling jury verdicts in the American legal system. *Journal of the American Statistical Association,* 1974, *69,* 32–37.

Gelfand, A. E. & Solomon, H. Analyzing the decision-making process of the American jury. *Journal of the American Statistical Association,* 1975, *70,* 305–310.

Gelfand, D. M., Hartmann, D. P., Lamb, A. K., Smith, C. L., Mahan, M. A., & Paul, S. C. The effects of adult models and described alternatives on children's choice of behavior management techniques. *Child Development,* 1974, *45,* 585–593.

Gelles, R. J. Child abuse as psychopathology: A sociological critique and reformulation. *American Journal of Orthopsychiatry,* 1973, *43,* 611–621.

Gelles, R. J. The social construction of child abuse. *American Journal of Orthopsychiatry,* 1975, *45,* 363–371.

Gerbasi, K. C., Zuckerman, M., & Reis, H. T. Justice needs a new blindfold: A review of mock jury research. *Psychological Bulletin,* in press.

Gerbner, G. The violence profile: Some indicators of the trends in and the symbolic structure of network television drama 1967–1970. Unpublished manuscript, University of Pennsylvania, 1972.

Gergen, K. J. Social psychology as history. *Journal of Personality and Social Psychology,* 1973, *26,* 309–320.

Germann, A. C., Day, F. D., & Gallati, R. R. J. *An introduction to law enforcement,* 1962. (Quoted after J. D. Lohmann in *Federal Probation,* 1967, *31*(4), 22–30.)

Gibbs, J. L., Jr. The Kpelle Moot: A therapeutic model for the informal settlement of disputes. *Africa,* 1963, *33,* 1–11.

Gibbs, J. P. Definitions of law and empirical questions. *Law and Society Review,* 1968, *2,* 429–446.

Gil, D. G. *Violence against children: Physical child abuse in the United States.* Cambridge, Mass.: Harvard University Press, 1970.

Gil, D. G. Unraveling child abuse. *American Journal of Orthopsychiatry,* 1975, *45,* 346–356.

Giovannoni, J. M. & Billingsley, A. Child neglect among the poor: A study of parental adequacy in families of three ethnic groups. *Child Welfare,* 1970, *49,* 196–204.

*and delinquency programs.* Rockville, Md.: National Institute of Mental

Glaser, D. *Routinizing evaluation: Getting feedback on effectiveness of crime* Health, Center for Crime and Delinquency, 1974.

Glass, D. C. Changes in liking as a means of reducing cognitive discrepancies between self-esteem and aggression. *Journal of Personality,* 1964, *32,* 520–549.

Glass, G. V. Analysis of data on the Connecticut speeding crackdown as a time-series quasi-experiment. *Law and Society Review,* 1968, *3,* 55–76.

Glidewell, J. C. New psychosocial competence, social change, and tension management. In J. W. Carter, Jr. (Ed.), *Research contributions from psychology to community mental health.* New York: Behavioral Publications, 1968.

Glidewell, J. C. A social psychology of mental health. In S. E. Golann & C. Eisdorfer (Eds.), *Handbook of community mental health.* New York: Appleton-Century-Crofts, 1972.

Gluckman, M. *The judicial process among the Barotse of Northern Rhodesia.* Manchester: Manchester University Press, 1955.

Glueck, S. & Glueck, E. *Unraveling juvenile delinquency.* Cambridge, Mass.: Harvard University Press, 1950.

Goebel, J., Jr. (Ed.) *The law practice of Alexander Hamilton* (Vol. 1). New York: Columbia University Press, 1964.

Goffman, E. On cooling the mark out. *Psychiatry: Journal for the Study of Interpersonal Processes,* 1952, *15,* 451–463.

Goffman, E. *The presentation of self in everyday life.* New York: Doubleday, 1959.

Goffman, E. *Asylums: Essays on the social situation of mental patients and other inmates.* Garden City, N.Y.: Doubleday, 1961.

Goffman, E. *Relations in public: Microstudies of the public order.* New York: Basic Books, 1971.

Goldiamond, I. Toward a constructional approach to social problems: Ethical and constitutional issues raised by applied behavior analysis. *Behaviorism,* 1974, *2,* 1–84.

Goldman, N. *The differential selection of juvenile offenders for court appearance.* New York: National Research and Information Center, National Council on Crime and Delinquency, 1963.

Goldstein, J., Freud, A., & Solnit, A. *Beyond the best interests of the child.* New York: Macmillan, 1973.

Goldstein, M. Brain research and violent behavior. *Archives of Neurology,* 1974, *30,* 1–35.

Goode, W. J. Force and violence in the family. *Journal of Marriage and the Family,* 1971, *33,* 624–636.

Gordon, R. I. A study in forensic psychology: Petit jury verdicts as a function of the number of jury members. Unpublished doctoral dissertation, University of Oklahoma, 1968.

Gordon, R. I. & Jacobs, P. D. Forensic psychology: Perception of guilt and income. *Perceptual and Motor Skills,* 1969, *28,* 143–146.

Gorecki, J. Divorce in Poland: A socio-legal study. *Acta Sociologica,* 1966, *10,* 68–80.

Gorecki, J. (Ed.) *Sociology and jurisprudence of Leon Petrazycki.* Urbana, Ill.: University of Illinois Press, 1975.

Gottesman, I. I. Genetic aspects of intelligent behavior. In N. Ellis (Ed.), *Handbook of mental deficiency.* New York: McGraw-Hill, 1963.

Gottesman, I. I. Biogenetics of race and class. In M. Deutsch, I. Katz, & A. R. Jensen (Eds.), *Social class, race and psychological development.* New York: Holt, Rinehart and Winston, 1968. (a)

Gottesman, I. I. A sampler of human behavior genetics. In T. Dobzhansky, M. K. Hecht, & W. C. Steere (Eds.), *Evolutionary biology* (Vol. 2). New York: Appleton-Century-Crofts, 1968. (b)

Gray, J. G. *The warriors: Reflections on men in battle.* New York: Harper & Row, 1973.

Gray, W. & Stults, R. (Eds. & Trans.) *RSFSR Civil Code, 1964.* Ann Arbor: University of Michigan Press, 1965.

Greenstein, F. I. *Children and politics.* New Haven: Yale University Press, 1965.

Grierson, P. J. *The silent trade.* Clifton, N.J.: Kelley, 1903.

Griffitt, W. & Jackson, T. Simulated jury decisions: The influence of jury–defendant attitude similarity–dissimilarity. *Social Behavior and Personality,* 1973, *1,* 1–7.

Gulliver, P. H. *Social control in an African society.* Boston: Boston University Press, 1963.

Guthrie, C. R. Law enforcement and the juvenile: A study of police interaction with delinquents. Unpublished doctoral dissertation, University of Southern California, 1963.

Guttman, L. An outline of the statistical theory of prediction. In P. Horst (Ed.), *The prediction of personal adjustment, SSRC Bulletin, No. 48.* New York: Social Science Research Council, 1941.

Haan, N., Smith, M. B., & Block, J. Moral reasoning of young adults: Political-social behavior, family background and personality correlates. *Journal of Personality and Social Psychology,* 1968, *10,* 183–201.

Hager, P. Five factors noted in Angela Davis innocent verdict. *Los Angeles Times,* June 6, 1972, Part 1, pp. 3; 22.

Haggard, E. A., Baittle, M. R., & Isaacs, K. S. The diagnostic interview as a data collection instrument. In M. J. Feldman (Ed.), *Studies in psychotherapy and behavioral change. Research in individual psychotherapy* (Vol. I). Buffalo, N.Y.: State University of New York at Buffalo, 1968.

Haggard, E. A., Hiken, J. R., & Isaacs, K. S. Some effects of recording and filming on the psychotherapeutic process. *Psychiatry,* 1965, *28,* 169–191.

Haggard, E. A. & Mentschikoff, S. Responsible decision making and decision consensus: An experimental analysis of a case in commercial arbitration. Unpublished manuscript, University of Chicago Law School, 1960.

Hamilton, W. H. Judicial process. In E. R. A. Seligman (Ed.), *Encyclopedia of the social sciences* (Vol. 8). New York: Macmillan, 1932.

Handler, J. F. Justice for the welfare recipient: Fair hearings in AFDC—the Wisconsin experience. *The Social Service Review,* 1967, *43,* 12–34.

Handler, J. F. Controlling official behavior in welfare administration. *California Law Review,* 1969, *54,* 479–510.

Haney, C., Banks, C., & Zimbardo, P. Interpersonal dynamics in a simulated prison. *International Journal of Criminology and Penology,* 1973, *1,* 69–97.

Haney, C. & Collins, B. Forced compliance and the anticipated consequences of counterattitudinal behavior. Unpublished manuscript, Stanford University, 1971.

Haney, C. & Manzolati, J. Television criminology: Network illusions of criminal justice realities. Unpublished manuscript, Stanford University, 1976.

Harding, J., Proshansky, H., Kutner, B., & Chein, I. Prejudice and ethnic relations. In G. Lindzey & E. Aronson (Eds.), *The handbook of social psychology* (Vol. 5, 2d ed.). Reading, Mass.: Addison-Wesley, 1969.

Hare, A. P., Borgatta, E. F., & Bales, R. F. *Small groups: Studies in social interaction* (Rev. ed.). New York: Knopf, 1965.

Hare, R. M. *The language of morals.* New York: Oxford University Press, 1952.

Hart, H. L. A. *The concept of law.* London: Clarendon Press of Oxford University Press, 1961.

Hart, H. L. A. *Law, liberty, and morality.* Stanford, Calif.: Stanford University Press, 1963.

Hart, H. L. A. *Punishment and responsibility: Essays in the philosophy of law.* New York: Oxford University Press, 1968.

Hartshorne, H. & May, M. *Studies in the nature of character. Studies in deceit* (Vol. I). New York: Macmillan, 1928.

Hartung, F. E. *Crime, law and society.* Detroit: Wayne State University Press, 1965.

Hawkins, C. H. Interaction rates of jurors aligned in factions. *American Sociological Review,* 1962, *27,* 689–691.

Hawkins, G. Punishment and deterrence: The educative, moralizing and habituative effects. *Wisconsin Law Review,* 1969, 550–565.

Hawkins, R. P., Peterson, R. F., Schweid, E., & Bijou, S. W. Behavior therapy in the home: Amelioration of problem parent–child relations with the parent in the therapeutic role. *Journal of Experimental Child Psychology,* 1966, *4,* 99–107.

Hayden, T. *Trial.* New York: Holt, Rinehart and Winston, 1970.

Healy, W. *Honesty: A study of the causes and treatment of dishonesty among children.* Indianapolis: Bobbs-Merrill, 1915.

Heider, F. *The psychology of interpersonal relations.* New York: Wiley, 1958.

Heimbach, J. T. Social psychology in the jury room: The effects of evidence, confession, and group interaction in sentencing. Paper presented at the annual meeting of the Midwestern Psychological Association, Cincinnati, 1970.

Helfer, R. E. & Kempe, C. H. *The battered child* (2d ed.). Chicago: University of Chicago Press, 1974.

Herbert, M. J. & Harsh, C. M. Observational learning by cats. *Journal of Comparative Psychology,* 1944, *37,* 81–95.

Hess, R. D. Political socialization in the schools. *Harvard Educational Review,* 1968, *38,* 528–536.

Hess, R. D. & Easton, D. The child's changing image of the President. *Public Opinion Quarterly,* 1960, *24,* 632–644.

Hess, R. D. & Tapp, J. L. *Authority, rules, and aggression: A cross-national study of the socialization of children into compliance systems: Part I.* Washington, D.C.: United States Department of Health, Education & Welfare, 1969.

Hess, R. D. & Torney, J. V. *The development of political attitudes in children.* Chicago: Aldine, 1967.

Hetherington, E. M. & Frankie, G. Effects of parental dominance, warmth and conflict on imitation in children. *Journal of Personality and Social Psychology,* 1967, *6,* 119–125.

Hirsch, J. (Ed.) *Behavior genetics analysis.* New York: McGraw-Hill, 1967.

Hirschi, T. *Causes of delinquency.* Berkeley, Calif.: University of California Press, 1969.

Hobson *v.* Hansen. *Federal Supplement,* 1967, *269,* 401–519.

Hoffman, M. L. & Saltzstein, H. D. Parent discipline and the child's moral development. *Journal of Personality and Social Psychology,* 1967, *5,* 45–57.

Hogan, R. A dimension of moral judgment. *Journal of Consulting and Clinical Psychology,* 1970, *35,* 205–212.

Hogan, R. Legal socialization. In G. Bermant, C. Nemeth, & N. Vidmar (Eds.), *Psychology and the law.* Lexington, Mass.: Heath, 1976.

Hogan, R. & Henley, N. Nomotics: The science of human rule systems. *Law and Society Review,* 1970, *5,* 135–146.

Hogben, L. *The relationship of probability, credibility, and error: An examination of the contemporary crisis in statistical theory from a behaviorist viewpoint.* New York: Norton, 1958.

Hoiberg, B. C. & Stires, L. K. Effects of pretrial publicity and juror traits on the guilt attributions of simulated jurors. *Journal of Applied Social Psychology,* 1973, *3,* 267–275.

Holden, C. Psychologists beset by feelings of futility, self-doubt. *Science,* 1971, *173,* 1111.

Holt, R. R. Individuality and generality in the psychology of personality. *Journal of Personality,* 1962, *30,* 377–404.

Homans, G. C. *Social behavior: Its elementary forms.* New York: Harcourt Brace Jovanovich, 1961.

Honig, W. K. (Ed.) *Operant behavior: Areas of research and application.* New York: Appleton-Century-Crofts, 1966.

Honzik, M. P. Developmental studies of parent–child resemblance in intelligence. *Child Development,* 1957, *28,* 215–228.

Hovland, C. I., Harvey, O. J., & Sherif, M. Assimilation and contrast effects in reactions to communication and attitude change. *Journal of Abnormal and Social Psychology,* 1957, *55,* 244–252.

Hoyt, E. E. *Primitive trade.* Clifton, N.J.: Kelley, 1926.

Hyman, H. *Political socialization.* Glencoe, Ill.: Free Press, 1959.

Hughes, E. Work and the self. In J. Rohrer & M. Sherif (Eds.), *Social psychology at the crossroads.* New York: Harper & Row, 1951.

Hutchins, R. M. & Slesinger, D. Legal psychology. *Psychological Review,* 1929, *36,* 13–26.

Illinois *v.* Allen. *Supreme Court Reporter,* 1970, *397,* 337–357.

Inhelder, B. & Piaget, J. *The growth of logical thinking from childhood to adolescence.* New York: Basic Books, 1958.

Institute of Judicial Administration. *A Comparison of Six- and Twelve-Member Juries in New Jersey Superior and County Courts.* New York: Author, 1972.

International News Service *v.* Associated Press. *United States Reports,* 1918, *248,* 215–267.

Izzett, R. & Leginski, W. Group discussion and the influence of defendant characteristics in a simulated jury setting. *Journal of Social Psychology,* 1974, *93,* 271–279.

Jackson, D. N. Multimethod factor analysis in the evaluation of convergent and discriminant validity. *Psychological Bulletin,* 1969, *72,* 30–49.

Jackson, G. *Soledad brother: The prison letters of George Jackson.* New York: Bantam Books, 1970.

Jacob, P. E. *Changing values in college: An exploratory study of the impact of college teaching.* New York: Harper & Row, 1957.

James, R. M. Status and competence of jurors. *The American Journal of Sociology,* 1959, *64,* 563–570.

Jeffery, C. R. Criminal behavior and learning theory. *Journal of Criminal Law, Criminology and Police Science,* 1965, *56,* 295–300.

Jenkins, J. J. & Paterson, D. G. (Eds.) *Studies in individual differences: The search for intelligence.* New York: Appleton-Century-Crofts, 1961.

Jennings, M. K. & Niemi, R. G. Patterns of political learning. *Harvard Educational Review,* 1968, *38,* 443–467. (a)

Jennings, M. K. & Niemi, R. G. The transmission of political values from parent to child. *American Political Science Review,* 1968, *62,* 169–184. (b)

Jennings, M. K. & Niemi, R. G. *The political character of adolescence: The influence of families and schools.* Princeton, N.J.: Princeton University Press, 1974.

John, E. R., Chesler, P., Bartlett, F., & Victor, I. Observational learning in cats. *Science,* 1969, *159,* 1489–1491.

Johnson *v.* Louisiana. *United States Supreme Court Reports* (Lawyers' Edition), 1972, *32,* 152–183.

Jones, C. & Aronson, E. Attribution of fault to a rape victim as a function of respectability of the victim. *Journal of Personality and Social Psychology,* 1973, *26,* 415–419.

Jones, W. C. Three centuries of commercial arbitration in New York: A brief survey. *Washington University Law Quarterly,* 1956, 193–221.

Jones, W. C. An inquiry into the history of the adjudication of mercantile disputes in Great Britain and the United States. *University of Chicago Law Review,* 1958, *25,* 445–464.

Jurow, G. L. New data on the effect of a "death-qualified" jury on the guilt determination process. *Harvard Law Review,* 1971, *84,* 567–611.

Kadish, M. R. & Kadish, S. H. *Discretion to disobey: A study of lawful departures from legal rules.* Stanford, Calif.: Stanford University Press, 1973.

Kadish, S. H. The crisis of overcriminalization. *The Annals of the American Academy of Political and Social Science,* 1967, *374,* 157–170.

Kahn, R. L., Gutek, B. A., Barton, E., & Katz, D. Americans love their bureaucrats. *Psychology Today,* 1975, *9*(1), 66–71.

Kalven, H., Jr. The quest for the middle range: Empirical inquiry and legal policy. In G. C. Hazard (Ed.), *The American assembly.* Englewood Cliffs, N.J.: Prentice-Hall, 1968.

Kalven, H., Jr. The image of justice: Reflections on the Chicago conspiracy trial. *New Republic,* 1969, *161*(19), 20–23.

Kalven, H., Jr. Chicago howler: There was no conspiracy. *New Republic,* 1970, *162*(10), 21–23.

Kalven, H., Jr. & Clark, R. (Intro.) *Contempt: Transcript of the contempt citations, sentences and responses of the Chicago conspiracy.* Chicago: Swallow Press, 1970.

Kalven, H., Jr. & Zeisel, H. Law, science and humanism. In J. Huxley (Ed.), *The humanist frame.* New York: Harper & Row, 1961.

Kalven, H., Jr. & Zeisel, H. *The American jury.* Boston: Little, Brown, 1966.

Kant, I. *Fundamental principles of the metaphysics of morals.* New York: Liberal Arts Press, 1949.

Kaplan, M. R. & Kemmerick, G. D. Juror judgment as information integration: Combining evidential and nonevidential information. *Journal of Personality and Social Psychology,* 1974, *30,* 493–499.

Karst, K. L. & Clement, N. C. Legal institutions and development: Lessons from the Mexican Ejido. *UCLA Law Review,* 1969, *16,* 281–303.

Kaufman, H. Legality and harmfulness. In J. R. Macaulay & L. Berkowitz (Eds.), *Altruism and helping behavior.* New York: Academic Press, 1970.

Kay, H. H. The family and kinship system of illegitimate children in California law. *American Anthropologist,* 1965, *67*(6), 57–81.

Kechekyan, S. F. Social progress and law. *Transactions of the Third World Congress of Sociology,* 1956, *6,* 42–51.

Kelley, C. *Crime in the United States—1972.* Washington, D.C.: United States Government Printing Office, 1973.

Kelley, H. H. The process of causal attribution. *American Psychologist,* 1973, *28,* 107–128.

Kelley, H. H. & Thibaut, J. W. Group problem solving. In G. Lindzey & E. Aronson (Eds.), *Handbook of social psychology* (Vol. 4, 2d ed.). Reading, Mass.: Addison-Wesley, 1969.

Kelman, H. C. Compliance, identification, and internalization: Three processes of attitude change. *Journal of Conflict Resolution,* 1958, *2,* 51–60.

Kelman, H. C. The social consequences of social research: A new social issue. *Journal of Social Issues,* 1965, *21*(3), 21–40.

Kelman, H. C. *A time to speak: On human values and social research.* San Francisco: Jossey-Bass, 1968.

Kelman, H. C. Patterns of personal involvement in the national system: A social-psychological analysis of political legitimacy. In J. N. Rosenau (Ed.), *International politics and foreign policy* (2d ed.). New York: Free Press, 1969.

Kempe, C. H. & Helfer, R. E. *Helping the battered child and his family.* Philadelphia: Lippincott, 1972.

Kempe, C. H., Silverman, F. N., Steele, B. B., Droegemueller, W., & Silver, H. K. The battered child syndrome. *Journal of the American Medical Association,* 1962, *181,* 17–24.

Kennedy, D. B. & Kerber, A. *Resocialization: An American experiment.* New York: Behavioral Publications, 1973.

Kenny, C. S. *Outlines of criminal law* (15th ed.). Cambridge, Eng.: Cambridge University Press, 1936.

Kerr, N. L., Atkin, R. S., Stasser, G., Meek, D., Holt, R. W., & Davis, J. H. Guilt beyond a reasonable doubt: Effects of concept definition and assigned decision rule on the judgments of mock jurors. *Journal of Personality and Social Psychology,* 1976, *34,* 282–294.

Kessler, J. B. An empirical study of six- and twelve-member jury decision-making processes. *University of Michigan Journal of Law Reform*, 1973, *6*, 712–734.

Key, V. O., Jr. *Public opinion and American democracy*. New York: Knopf, 1961.

Kinberg, O. *Basic problems of criminology*. Copenhagen: Levin & Munksgaard, 1935.

Kiralfy, A. K. R. (Trans.) *The Civil Code and the Code of Civil Procedure of the R.S.F.S.R., 1964. Law in Eastern Europe* (Vol. 11). Atlantic Highlands, N.J.: Humanities, 1966.

Kirby, D. A. & Lamberth, J. The lawyers' dilemma: The behavior of authoritarian jurors. Paper presented at the annual meeting of the Midwestern Psychological Association, Chicago, 1974.

Kitsuse, J. Social reactions to deviance behavior. *Social Problems*, 1962, *9*, 247–256.

Kittrie, N. N. *The right to be different: Deviance and enforced therapy*. Baltimore: Johns Hopkins Press, 1972.

Kleiman, A. Children's views on rules-laws, justice, and conditions for compliance. Unpublished manuscript, University of Chicago, 1967.

Klette, H. Nagra resultat fran tre rattfylleriundersokningar jamforda med trafiknykterhetskommittens lagforslag. *Nordisk Tidsskrift for Kriminalvidenskab*, 1964, 119–135.

Kline, F. G. & Jess, P. H. Prejudicial publicity: Its effect on law school mock juries. *Journalism Quarterly*, 1966, *43*, 113–116.

Knutson, J. N. (Ed.) *Handbook of political psychology*. San Francisco: Jossey-Bass, 1973.

Kohlberg, L. The development of modes of moral thinking and choice in the years ten to sixteen. Unpublished doctoral dissertation, University of Chicago, 1958.

Kohlberg, L. The development of children's orientations toward a moral order: I. Sequence in the development of moral thought. *Vita Humana*, 1963, *6*, 11–33. (a)

Kohlberg, L. Moral development and identification. In H. W. Stevenson (Ed.), *Child psychology: The sixty-second yearbook of the National Society for the Study of Education*. Chicago: University of Chicago Press, 1963. (b)

Kohlberg, L. Development of moral character and moral ideology. In M. L. Hoffman (Ed.), *Review of child development research* (Vol. 1). New York: Russell Sage Foundation, 1964.

Kohlberg, L. The child as a moral philosopher. *Psychology Today*, 1968, *2*(4), 24–31. (a)

Kohlberg, L. Moral development. In D. E. Sills (Ed.), *International encyclopedia of the social sciences*. New York: Macmillan, 1968. (b)

Kohlberg, L. Stage and sequence: The cognitive-developmental approach to socialization. In D. A. Goslin (Ed.), *Handbook of socialization theory and research*. Chicago: Rand McNally, 1969.

Kohlberg, L. From is to ought: How to commit the naturalistic fallacy and get away with it in the study of moral development. In T. Mischel (Ed.), *Cognitive development and epistemology*. New York: Academic Press, 1971.

Kohlberg, L. & Kramer, R. Continuities and discontinuities in childhood and adult moral development. *Human Development,* 1969, *12,* 93–120.

Kohlberg, L. & Lockwood, A. Cognitive-developmental psychology and political education: Progress in the sixties. Paper presented at the Social Sciences Consortium Convention, Boulder, Colorado, 1970.

Kohlberg, L., Scharf, P., & Hickey, J. Justice structure of the prison. *Prison Journal,* 1971, *51,* 3–14.

Kohlberg, L. & Turiel, E. Moral development and moral education. In G. S. Lesser (Ed.), *Psychology and educational practice.* Glenview, Ill.: Scott, Foresman, 1971.

Kohlberg, L. & Turiel, E. (Eds.) *Research in moralization: The cognitive developmental approach.* New York: Holt, Rinehart and Winston, in prep.

Korsch, B., Christian, J., Gozzi, E., & Carlson, P. Infant care and punishment: A pilot study. *American Journal of Public Health,* 1965, *55,* 1880–1888.

Kovalev, A. G. Vazimovliianie liudei v protsesse obscheniia i formirovanie obshchestvennoi psikhologii [The mutual influence of people in the process of social intercourse and the formation of social psychology]. In A. I. Gertsena (Ed.), *Voprosy psikhologii lichnosti i obshchestvennoi psikhologii [Problems of personal and social psychology].* Leningrad: Izdatel'stvo Leningradskogo Universiteta, 1964.

Kovalev, A. G. *Psikhologii lichnosti [Psychology of the person].* Moscow: Prosveshchenie, 1965.

Kozol, H. L., Boucher, R. J., & Garofalo, R. F. The diagnosis and treatment of dangerousness. *Crime and Delinquency,* 1972, *18,* 371–392.

Kramer, R. Moral development in young adulthood. Unpublished doctoral dissertation, University of Chicago, 1968.

Kuhn, T. S. *The structure of scientific revolutions.* Chicago: University of Chicago Press, 1962.

Kurtines, W. & Grief, E. B. The development of moral thought: Review and evaluation of Kohlberg's approach. *Psychological Bulletin,* 1974, *81,* 453–470.

Kutchinsky, B. Sociological aspects of deviance and criminality. *Collected Studies in Criminological Research, IX: Perception of Deviance and Criminality,* 1972, *9* (Whole Issue).

Kutchinsky, B. "The legal consciousness": A survey of research on knowledge and opinion about law. In A. Podgorecki, W. Kaupen, J. Van Houtte, P. Vinke, & B. Kutchinsky, *Knowledge and opinion about law.* London: Martin Robertson, 1973.

LaCrosse, J. & Kohlberg, L. The predictability of adult mental health from childhood behavior and status. In B. Wolman (Ed.), *Handbook of psychopathology.* New York: McGraw-Hill, 1969.

Laing, R. D. The obvious. In D. Cooper (Ed.), *To free a generation: The dialectics of liberation.* London: The Institute of Phenomenological Studies, 1968.

Lambert, W. E. & Klineberg, O. *Children's views of foreign peoples.* New York: Appleton-Century-Crofts, 1967.

Landes, W. M. Legality and reality: Some evidence on criminal procedure. *Journal of Legal Studies,* 1974, *3,* 287–337.

Landy, D. & Aronson, E. The influence of the character of the criminal and his victim on the decisions of simulated jurors. *Journal of Experimental Social Psychology,* 1969, *5,* 141–152.

Lane, R. E. *Political life: Why people get involved in politics.* Glencoe, Ill.: Free Press, 1959.

Lane, R. E. *Political ideology: Why the American common man believes what he does.* New York: Free Press, 1962.

Langer, J. *Theories of development.* New York: Holt, Rinehart and Winston, 1969.

Langton, K. P. (Ed.) *Political socialization.* New York: Oxford University Press, 1969.

Langton, K. P. & Jennings, M. K. Political socialization and the high school civics curriculum in the United States. *American Political Science Review,* 1968, *62,* 852–867.

LaPlace, le Marquis de. Essai philosophique sur les probabilités. Introduction to *Théorie Analytique des Probabilités, Oeuvres Completès de LaPlace.* Paris: Gauthier-Villars, 1886.

Larntz, K. Reanalysis of Vidmar's data on the effect of decision alternatives on verdicts of simulated jurors. *Journal of Personality and Social Psychology,* 1975, *31,* 123–125.

Laughlin, E. R. & Izzett, R. R. Deliberation and sentencing by attitudinally homogeneous juries. Paper presented at the annual meeting of the Midwestern Psychological Association, Chicago, 1973.

Laurence, J. E. White socialization: Black reality. *Psychiatry,* 1970, *33,* 174–194.

Laurence, J. E. & Scoble, H. M. Ideology and consensus among children of the metropolitan socioeconomic elite. *Western Political Quarterly,* 1969, *22,* 151–162.

Lazarus, S., Bray, J. J., Jr., Carter, L. L., Collins, K. H., Giedt, B. A., Holton, R. V., Jr., Matthews, P. D., & Willard, G. C. *Resolving business disputes.* New York: American Management Association, 1965.

Lempert, R. Strategies of research design in the legal impact study: The control of plausible rival hypotheses. *Law and Society Review,* 1966, *1,* 111–132.

Lempert, R. O. Uncovering "nondiscernible" differences: Empirical research and the jury-size cases. *Michigan Law Review,* 1975, *73,* 644–708.

Lenoski, E. F. Translating injury data into preventive and health care services —Physical child abuse. Unpublished manuscript, University of Southern California, 1974.

Leontiev, A., Luria, A. R., & Smirnov, A. (Eds.) *Psychological research in the U.S.S.R.* (Vol. 1). Moscow: Progress, 1966.

Lerner, M. J. Evaluation of performance as a function of performer's reward and attractiveness. *Journal of Personality and Social Psychology,* 1965, *1,* 355–360.

Lerner, M. J. (Ed.) The justice motive in social behavior. *Journal of Social Issues,* 1975, *31*(3) (Whole Issue).

Lerner, M. S. & Simmons, C. H. Observer's reaction to the "innocent victim": Compassion or rejection? *Journal of Personality and Social Psychology,* 1966, *4,* 203–210.

Levi, E. H. *An introduction to legal reasoning.* Chicago: University of Chicago

Press, 1963.

Lévi-Strauss, C. *Structural anthropology.* Garden City, N.Y.: Doubleday Anchor Books, 1967.

Levine, D. Criminal behavior and mental institutionalization. *Journal of Clinical Psychology,* 1970, *26,* 179–184.

Levine, D. A cross-national study of attitudes toward mental illness. *Journal of Abnormal Psychology,* 1972, *80,* 111–114.

Levine, D. The concept of dangerousness—Criticism and compromise. Paper presented at the National Criminology Conference, University of Cambridge, England, 1975.

Levine, F. J. & Preston, E. Community resource orientation among low income groups. *Wisconsin Law Review,* 1970, 80–113.

Levine, F. J. & Tapp, J. L. The psychology of criminal identification: The gap from Wade to Kirby. *University of Pennsylvania Law Review,* 1973, *121,* 1079–1131.

Levy, R. I. On getting angry in the Society Islands. In W. Caudill & T. Y. Lin (Eds.), *Mental health research in Asia & the Pacific.* Honolulu: East-West Center Press, 1969.

Levy-Bruhl, H. *Sociologie du droit* (2d ed.). Paris: Presses Universitaires de France, 1964.

Lewin, K. *A dynamic theory of personality.* New York: McGraw-Hill, 1935.

Lewin, K. *Resolving social conflicts: Selected papers on group dynamics.* New York: Harper & Row, 1948.

Lewin, K. *Field theory in social science: Selected theoretical papers.* New York: Harper & Row, 1951.

Lickona, T. (Ed.) *Moral development and behavior: Theory, research, and social issues.* New York: Holt, Rinehart and Winston, 1976.

Liebert, R. M., Neale, J. M., & Davidson, E. S. *The early window: Effects of television on children and youth.* New York: Pergamon, 1973.

Light, R. J. Abused and neglected children in America: A study of alternative policies. *Harvard Educational Review,* 1973, *43,* 556–598.

Lindesmith, A. R. *The addict and the law.* Bloomington, Ind.: Indiana University Press, 1965.

Lipset, S. M. Why cops hate liberals—And vice versa. *Atlantic,* 1969, *223*(3), 76–83.

Litt, E. Civic education, community norms, and political indoctrination. *American Sociological Review,* 1963, *28,* 69–75.

Livermore, J. *Minnesota evidence: Minnesota practice manual 22.* Minneapolis: University of Minnesota General Extension Division, 1968.

Livermore, J. M., Malmquist, C. P., & Meehl, P. E. On the justifications for civil commitment. *University of Pennsylvania Law Review,* 1968, *117,* 75–96.

Livermore, J. M. & Meehl, P. E. The virtues of M'Naghten. *Minnesota Law Review,* 1967, *51,* 789–856.

Llewellyn, K. N. *The common law tradition: Deciding appeals.* Boston: Little, Brown, 1960.

Llewellyn, K. N. *Jurisprudence: Realism in theory and practice.* Chicago: University of Chicago Press, 1962.

Llewellyn, K. N. & Hoebel, E. A. *The Cheyenne way: Conflict and case law in primitive jurisprudence.* Norman, Okla.: University of Oklahoma Press, 1941.

Loevinger, J. Objective tests as instruments of psychological theory. *Psychological Reports,* 1957 (Whole Monograph Supplement 9).

Lucas, J. A. *The barnyard epithet and other obscenities.* New York: Harper & Row, 1970.

Lukacs, G. Legality and illegality. In *History of class consciousness.* Cambridge, Mass.: Massachusetts Institute of Technology Press, 1971.

Lundstedt, V. *Principinledning.* Uppsala: Lundquistska Bokhandeln, 1920.

Lundstedt, V. *Tillfragan om ratten och samhallet.* Uppsala: Lundquistska Bokhandeln, 1921.

Lykken, D. T. Statistical significance in psychological research. *Psychological Bulletin,* 1968, *70,* 151–159.

Lynn, D. B. *Parental and sex role identification: A theoretical formulation.* Berkeley, Calif.: McCutchan, 1969.

Macaulay, S. Non-contractual relations in business: A preliminary study. *American Sociological Review,* 1963, *28,* 55–67.

Maccoby, E. E. The development of moral values and behavior in childhood. In J. A. Clausen (Ed.), *Socialization and society.* Boston: Little, Brown, 1968.

Maher, B. A. *Principles of psychopathology: An experimental approach.* New York: McGraw-Hill, 1966.

Malcalpine, I. & Hunter, R. *George III and the mad-business.* New York: Random House, 1969.

Manosevitz, M., Lindzey, G., & Thiessen, D. *Behavioral genetics: Methods and research.* New York: Appleton-Century-Crofts, 1969.

Mapp *v.* Ohio. *United States Reports,* 1961, *367,* 643–686.

Marks, F. R., Leswing, K., & Fortinsky, B. A. *The lawyer, the public, and professional responsibility.* Chicago: American Bar Foundation, 1972.

Marshall, J. *Law and psychology in conflict.* Indianapolis: Bobbs-Merrill, 1966.

Marston, W. M. Studies in testimony. *Journal of Criminal Law and Criminology,* 1924, *15,* 5–31.

Marx, G. T. Civil disorders and the agents of social control. *Journal of Social Issues,* 1970, *26*(1), 19–58.

Massell, G. J. Law as an instrument of revolutionary change in a traditional milieu: The case of Soviet Central Asia. *Law and Society Review,* 1967, *2,* 179–228.

Mather, L. M. Some determinants of the method of case disposition: Decision-making by public defenders in Los Angeles. *Law and Society Review,* 1974, *8,* 187–216.

Matza, D. *Delinquency and drift.* New York: Wiley, 1964.

Maxwell, A. E. *Analysing qualitative data.* London: Methuen, 1961.

Mayer, H. *Das Strafrecht des deutschen volkes.* Stuttgart: Enke, 1936.

Mayer, H. *Strafrecht, allgemeiner teil.* Stuttgart: Kohlhammer, 1953.

Mayer, M. *On liberty: Man v. the State.* Santa Barbara, Calif.: Center for the Study of Democratic Institutions, 1969.

Mayo, L. H. & Jones, E. M. Legal-policy decision process: Alternative thinking and the predictive function. *George Washington Law Review,* 1964, *33,* 318–456.

McCarty, D. G. *Psychology for the lawyer.* New York: Prentice-Hall, 1929.

McClosky, H. Conservatism and personality. *American Political Science Review,* 1958, *52,* 27–45.

McClosky, H. Consensus and ideology in American politics. *American Political Science Review,* 1964, *58,* 361–382.

McCord, J., McCord, J., & Thurber, E. Some effects of paternal absence on male children. *Journal of Abnormal and Social Psychology,* 1962, *64,* 361–369.

McCord, W., McCord, J., & Howard, A. Familial correlates of aggression in non-delinquent male children. *Journal of Abnormal and Social Psychology,* 1961, *62,* 79–93.

McCormick, C. T. *Handbook of the law of evidence.* St. Paul, Minn.: West, 1954.

McCrystal, J. L. Video tape trials. *The Ohio Bar,* 1971, *44,* 639–642.

McCrystal, J. L. Ohio's first videotape trial. *The Ohio Bar,* 1972, *45,* 1–4.

McDougall, W. *An introduction to social psychology.* London: Methuen, 1908.

McGrath, J. E. & Altman, I. *Small group research: A synthesis and critique of the field.* New York: Holt, Rinehart and Winston, 1966.

McGuire, W. J. The nature of attitudes and attitude change. In G. Lindzey & E. Aronson (Eds.), *The handbook of social psychology* (Vol. 3, 2d ed.). Reading, Mass.: Addison-Wesley, 1969.

McGuire, W. J. The yin and yang of progress in social psychology: Seven koan. *Journal of Personality and Social Psychology,* 1973, *26,* 446–456.

McNamara, J. H. Uncertainties in police work: The relevance of police recruits' background and training. In D. J. Bordua (Ed.), *The police: Six sociological essays.* New York: Wiley, 1967.

Mead, G. H. *Mind, self, and society: From the standpoint of a social behaviorist.* Chicago: University of Chicago Press, 1934.

Mead, M. *Sex and temperament in three savage tribes.* New York: Morrow, 1935.

Medvedev, R. A. & Medvedev, Z. *A question of madness.* New York: Knopf, 1971.

Meehl, P. E. *Clinical versus statistical prediction: A theoretical analysis and a review of the evidence.* Minneapolis: University of Minnesota Press, 1954.

Meehl, P. E. Theory-testing in psychology and physics: A methodological paradox. *Philosophy of Science,* 1967, *34,* 103–115.

Meehl, P. E. Letter in "Input." *Psychology Today,* 1969, *3*(6), 4.

Meehl, P. E. Nuisance variables and the ex post facto design. In M. Radner & S. Winokur (Eds.), *Minnesota studies in philosophy of science* (Vol. 4). Minneapolis: University of Minnesota Press, 1970. (a)

Meehl, P. E. Psychological determinism and human rationality: A psychologist's reaction to Sir Karl Popper's "Of Clouds and Clocks." In M. Radner & S. Winokur (Eds.), *Minnesota studies in philosophy of science* (Vol. 4). Minneapolis: University of Minnesota Press, 1970. (b)

Meehl, P. E. Psychology and the criminal law. *University of Richmond Law Review,* 1970, *5,* 1–30. (c)

Meehl, P. E. High school yearbooks: A reply to Schwarz. *Journal of Abnormal Psychology,* 1971, *77,* 143–148.

Meehl, P. E. Specific genetic etiology, psychodynamics, and therapeutic nihilism. *International Journal of Mental Health,* 1972, *1,* 10–27.

Meehl, P. E. & Rosen, A. Antecedent probability and the efficiency of psychometric signs, patterns, or cutting scores. *Psychological Bulletin,* 1955, *52,* 194–216.

Megargee, E. I. The prediction of violence with psychological tests. In C. Spielberger (Ed.), *Current topics in clinical and community psychology.* New York: Academic Press, 1970.

Megargee, E. I. The heuristic value of the concept of social deviance for psychology. *Representative Research in Social Psychology,* 1973, *4,* 67–81.

Megargee, E. I. & Hokanson, J. E. (Eds.) *The dynamics of aggression.* New York: Harper & Row, 1970.

Mentschikoff, S. The significance of arbitration—A preliminary inquiry. In R. Kramer (Ed.), *Commercial arbitration: Part II, Law and contemporary problems,* 1952, *17,* 698–710.

Mentschikoff, S. Commercial arbitration. *Columbia Law Review,* 1961, *61,* 846–869.

Merelman, R. M. The development of political ideology: A framework for the analysis of political socialization. *American Political Science Review,* 1969, *63,* 750–767.

Merelman, R. M. The development of policy thinking in adolescence. *American Political Science Review,* 1971, *65,* 1033–1047.

Merrill, E. J. *Protecting the battered child.* Denver, Colo.: American Humane Association, 1962.

Merryman, J. H. & Vigoriti, V. When courts collide: Constitution and cassation in Italy. *American Journal of Comparative Law,* 1967, *15,* 665–686.

Mesch, M. The role of the attorney. In A. Glazier (Ed.), *Child abuse: A community challenge.* Buffalo, N.Y.: Henry Stewart, 1971.

Michael, J. & Adler, M. J. The trial of an issue of fact. *Columbia Law Review,* 1934, *34,* 1224–1306.

Michelman, F. I. In pursuit of constitutional welfare rights: One view of Rawls' theory of justice. *University of Pennsylvania Law Review,* 1973, *121,* 962–1019.

Milgram, S. Behavioral study of obedience. *Journal of Abnormal and Social Psychology,* 1963, *67,* 371–378.

Milgram, S. Some conditions of obedience and disobedience to authority. *Human Relations,* 1965, *18,* 57–76.

Milgram, S. *Obedience to authority: An experimental view.* New York: Harper & Row, 1974.

Mill, J. S. *On liberty.* Chicago: Henry Regnery, Gateway Edition, 1955.

Miller, G., Bender, D., Florence, T., & Nicholson, H. Real versus reel: What's the verdict? *Journal of Communication,* 1974, *24,* 99–111.

Miller, G. R., Bender, D. C., Boster, F., Florence, B. T., Fontes, N., Hocking, J., & Nicholson, H. The effects of videotape testimony in jury trials:

Studies on juror decision making, information retention, and emotional arousal. *Brigham Young University Law Review,* 1975, *2,* 331–373.

Miller, M. G. Socialization and the compliance system: An attitudinal study of adolescents, teachers, and police. Unpublished doctoral dissertation, Michigan State University, 1971.

Miller, N. E. & Dollard, J. *Social learning and imitation.* New Haven: Yale University Press, 1941.

Mills, L. R. Six-member and twelve-member juries: An empirical study of trial results. *University of Michigan Journal of Law Reform,* 1973, *6,* 671–711.

Milowe, I. & Lourie, R. The child's role in the battered child syndrome. *Society for Pediatric Research,* 1964, *65,* 1079–1081.

Minturn, L., Gunnery, K., Holloway, M., & Peterson, C. The peaceful communities. In J. de Wit & W. W. Hartup (Eds.), *Determinants and origins of aggressive behavior.* The Hague: Mouton, 1974.

Minturn, L. & Lambert, W. W. *Mothers of six cultures.* New York: Wiley, 1964.

Minturn, L. & Tapp, J. L. *Authority, rules, and aggression: A cross-national study of children's judgments of the justice of aggressive confrontations: Part II.* Washington, D.C. United States Department of Health, Education & Welfare, 1970.

Mischel, W. *Personality and assessment.* New York: Wiley, 1968.

Mitchell, H. E. & Byrne, D. Minimizing the influence of irrelevant factors in the courtroom: The defendant's character, judges' instruction, and authoritarianism. Paper presented at the annual meeting of the Midwestern Psychological Association, Cleveland, 1972.

Mitchell, H. E. & Byrne, D. The defendant's dilemma: Effects of jurors' attitudes and authoritarian judicial decisions. *Journal of Personality and Social Psychology,* 1973, *25,* 123–129.

Mitford, J. *Kind and usual punishment.* New York: Knopf, 1973.

Mnookin, R. H. Foster care: In whose best interests? *Harvard Educational Review,* 1973, *43,* 599–638.

Monahan, J. The prediction of violence. In J. Monahan (Ed.), *Community mental health and the criminal justice system.* New York: Pergamon, 1975.

Moore, U. & Callahan, C. C. Law and learning theory: A study in legal control. *Yale Law Journal,* 1943, *53,* 1–136.

Morris, H. Persons and punishment. *The Monist,* 1968, *52,* 475–501.

Morris, N. The future of imprisonment. Chicago: University of Chicago Press, 1974.

Morris, N. & Hawkins, G. *The honest politician's guide to crime control.* Chicago: University of Chicago Press, 1970.

Morrison, D. E. & Henkel, R. E. (Eds.) *The significance test controversy.* Chicago: Aldine, 1970.

Morton, J. D. *The function of criminal law.* Toronto: Canadian Broadcasting Corporation, 1962.

Munsterberg, H. *On the witness stand: Essays on psychology and crime.* New York: Clark, Boardman, 1908.

Murphy, W. F. Courts as small groups. *Harvard Law Review*, 1966, *79*, 1565–1572.

Murton, T. The dilemma of prison reform: The traditional prison model. *The Freeworld Times*, August–September, 1973, pp. 10–11.

Myers, D. G. & Kaplan, M. F. Group-induced polarization in simulated juries. *Personality and Social Psychology Bulletin*, 1976, *2*, 63–66.

Nader, L. Styles of court procedure: To make the balance. In L. Nader (Ed.), *Law in culture and society*. Chicago: Aldine, 1969.

Nader, L. Forums for justice: A cross-cultural perspective. *Journal of Social Issues*, 1975, *31*(3), 151–170.

Nader, L. & Metzger, D. Conflict resolution in two Mexican communities. *American Anthropologist*, 1963, *65*, 584–592.

Nader, L. & Yngvesson, B. On studying the ethnography of law and its consequences. In J. J. Honigmann (Ed.), *Handbook of social and cultural anthropology*. Chicago: Rand McNally, 1973.

Nagel, S. S. & Neef, M. G. Decision theory, equilibrium models, and plea bargaining. Paper presented at the Law and Society Conference, Buffalo, New York, 1975.

Nemeth, C. & Sosis, R. H. A simulated jury: Characteristics of the defendant and the jurors. *Journal of Social Psychology*, 1973, *90*, 221–229.

Neubauer, D. W. *Criminal justice in middle America*. Morristown, N.J.: General Learning Press, 1974.

Newcomb, T. M. An approach to the study of communicative acts. *Psychological Review*, 1953, *60*, 393–404.

Newcomb, T. M. *The acquaintance process*. New York: Holt, Rinehart and Winston, 1961.

Newman, D. J. Plea guilty for considerations: A study of bargain justice. *Journal of Criminal Law, Criminology and Police Science*, 1956, *46*, 780–790.

Newman, D. J. *Conviction: The determination of guilt or innocence without trial*. Boston: Little, Brown, 1966.

Newman, K. J. Punishment and the breakdown of the legal order: The experience in East Pakistan. In C. J. Friedrich (Ed.), *Responsibility: Nomos III*. New York: Liberal Arts, 1960.

Nichols, R. C. The resemblance of twins in personality and interests. *National Merit Scholarship Reports*, 1966, *2* (Whole No. 8).

Niederhoffer, A. *Behind the shield: The police in urban society*. Garden City, N.Y.: Doubleday, 1967.

Niem, T. C. & Collard, R. Parental discipline of aggressive behaviors in four-year old Chinese and American children. Paper presented at the Annual Meeting of the American Psychological Association, Washington, D. C., 1971.

Nimmer, R. T. *The omnibus hearing: An experiment in relieving inefficiency, unfairness and judicial delay*. Chicago: American Bar Foundation, 1971.

Nimmer, R. T. *Diversion: The search for alternative forms of prosecution*. Chicago: American Bar Foundation, 1974. (a)

Nimmer, R. T. Judicial reform: Informal processes and competing effects. In H. Jacob (Ed.), *The potential for reform of criminal justice*. Beverly Hills,

Calif.: Sage Publications, 1974. (b)

Nimmer, R. T. *Prosecutor disclosure and judicial reform.* Chicago: American Bar Foundation, 1975.

Nimmer, R. T. *The system impact of criminal justice reforms: A case study and preliminary concepts.* Chicago: American Bar Foundation, 1977, in press.

Nimmer, R. T. & Krauthaus, P. A. The impact of speedy trial statutes: A joint policy perspective. Unpublished manuscript, American Bar Foundation, 1975.

Nonet, P. *Administrative justice: Advocacy and change in a government agency.* New York: Russell Sage Foundation, 1969.

Nordland, F. Allmennprevensjon og disiplin i oppdragelsen [General prevention and discipline in upbringing]. *Nordisk Tidsskrift for kriminalvidenskab,* 1966, 220–237.

Nurse, S. M. Familial patterns of parents who abuse their children. *Smith College Studies in Social Work,* 1964, *35,* 11–25.

Oaks, D. H. Studying the exclusionary rule in search and seizure. *University of Chicago Law Review,* 1970, *37,* 665–757.

Ohlin, L. E. (Ed.) *Prisoners in America.* Englewood Cliffs, N.J.: Prentice-Hall, 1973.

Opton, E. M., Jr. It never happened and besides they deserved it. In N. Sanford & C. Comstock (Eds.), *Sanctions for evil.* San Francisco: Jossey-Bass, 1971.

Osofsky, J. D. & Danzger, B. Relationships between neonatal characteristics and mother–infant interaction. *Developmental Psychology,* 1974, *10,* 124–130.

Packer, H. L. *The limits of the criminal sanction.* Stanford, Calif.: Stanford University Press, 1968.

Padawer-Singer, A. M. & Barton, A. H. The impact of pretrial publicity on jurors' verdicts. In R. J. Simon (Ed.), *The jury system in America: A critical overview.* Beverly Hills, Calif.: Sage, 1975.

Palmer, S. *The violent society.* New Haven: College & University Press, 1972.

Parfit, J. (Ed.) *The community's children: Long-term substitute care: A guide for the intelligent layman.* New York: Humanities Press, 1967.

Parke, R. D. Effectiveness of punishment as an interaction of intensity, timing, agent nurturance, and cognitive structuring. *Child Development,* 1969, *40,* 213–235.

Parke, R. D. The role of punishment in the socialization process. In R. A. Hoppe, G. A. Milton, & E. C. Simmel (Eds.), *Early experiences and the process of socialization.* New York: Academic Press, 1970.

Parke, R. D. Rules, roles and resistance to deviation in children: Explorations in punishment, discipline and self control. In A. Pick (Ed.), *Minnesota symposia on child psychology* (Vol. 8). Minneapolis: University of Minnesota Press, 1974.

Parke, R. D. & Collmer, C. W. Child abuse: An interdisciplinary analysis. In E. M. Hetherington (Ed.), *Review of child development research* (Vol. 5). Chicago: University of Chicago Press, 1975.

Parke, R. D. & Deur, J. L. Schedule of punishment and inhibition of aggression in children. *Developmental Psychology,* 1972, *7,* 266–269.

Parke, R. D. & O'Leary, S. Family interaction in the newborn period: Some findings, some observations, and some unresolved issues. In K. Riegel & J. Meacham (Eds.), *The developing individual in a changing world. Social and environmental issues* (Vol. 2). The Hague: Mouton, 1976.

Parke, R. D. & Sawin, D. B. *Aggression: Causes and controls.* Homewood, Ill.: Learning Systems, 1975. (a)

Parke, R. D. & Sawin, D. B. The effects of inter-agent inconsistent discipline on aggression in children. Unpublished manuscript, Fels Research Institute, 1975. (b)

Parke, R. D. & Sawin, D. B. Infant characteristics and behavior as elicitors of maternal and paternal responsivity in the newborn period. Paper presented at the Biennial Meeting of the Society for Research in Child Development, Denver, Colorado, 1975. (c)

Parke, R. D., Sawin, D. B., & Kreling, B. The effect of child feedback on adult disciplinary choices. Unpublished manuscript, Fels Research Institute, 1974.

Parnas, R. I. The police response to the domestic disturbance. *Wisconsin Law Review,* 1967, 914–960.

Patterson, G. R. Interventions for boys with conduct problems: Multiple settings, treatments and criteria. *Journal of Consulting and Clinical Psychology,* 1974, *42,* 471–481.

Patterson, G. R. The aggressive child: Victim and architect of a coercive system. In L. A. Hamerlynck, E. J. Mash, & L. C. Handy (Eds.), *Behavior modification and families.* New York: Brunner/Mazel, 1975.

Patterson, G. R. & Cobb, J. A. A dyadic analysis of "aggressive" behavior. In J. P. Hill (Ed.), *Minnesota symposia on child psychology* (Vol. 5). Minneapolis: University of Minnesota Press, 1971.

Patterson, G. R. & Cobb, J. A. Stimulus control for classes of noxious behavior. In J. F. Knutson (Ed.), *The control of aggression: Implications from basic research.* Chicago: Aldine, 1973.

Patterson, G. R. & Reid, J. B. Reciprocity and coercion: Two facets of social systems. In C. Newunger & J. Michael (Eds.), *Behavior modification in clinical psychology.* New York: Appleton-Century-Crofts, 1970.

Pavlov, I. P. *Experimental psychology and other essays.* New York: Philosophical Library, 1957.

Peltason, J. W., Gluckman, M., Karlen, D., & Tannenhaus, J. Judicial process. In Davil L. Sills (Ed.), *International encyclopedia of the social sciences* (Vol. 8). New York: Macmillan, 1968.

Penner, L., Homant, R., & Rokeach, M. Comparison of rank-order and paired comparison methods for measuring value systems. *Perceptual and Motor Skills,* 1968, *27,* 417–418.

People v. Croswell. *Johnson's Cases.* 1804, *3,* 336–413.

Pepitone, A. Social psychological perspectives in crime and punishment. Paper presented at the annual meeting of the American Psychological Association, Chicago, 1975.

Perkins, R. M. *Criminal law* (2d ed.). Mineola, N.Y.: Foundation Press, 1969.

Perkins, R. M. *Criminal law.* Brooklyn, N.Y.: Foundation Press, 1957.

Petersen, T. K. The Dade County pretrial intervention project: Formalization of the diversion function and its impact upon the criminal justice system. *University of Miami Law Review,* 1973, *28,* 86–114.

Petrazhitskii, L. J. *Law and morality* (H. W. Babb, Trans.). Cambridge, Mass.: Harvard University Press, 1955.

Pfiffner, J. M. *The function of the police in a democratic society.* Los Angeles: Civic Center Campus, Center for Training and Career Development, University of Southern California, 1967.

Piaget, J. *Judgment and reasoning in the child.* London: Routledge & Kegan Paul, 1928.

Piaget, J. *The child's conception of the world.* London: Routledge & Kegan Paul, 1929.

Piaget, J. *The moral judgment of the child.* New York: Kegan Paul, Trench, Trubner, 1932.

Piaget, J. *The psychology of intelligence.* London: Routledge & Kegan Paul, 1947.

Piaget, J. *Science of education and the psychology of the child.* New York: Orion Press, 1970.

Piaget, J. & Inhelder, B. *The psychology of the child.* New York: Basic Books, 1969.

Pick, A. The games experimenters play: A review of methods and concepts of cross-cultural studies of cognition and development. Unpublished manuscript, University of Minnesota, 1974.

Piliavin, I. & Briar, S. Police encounters with juveniles. *American Journal of Sociology,* 1964, *70,* 206–214.

Pinkney, A. *The American way of violence.* New York: Random House, 1972.

Pinson, K. S. *Modern Germany: History and civilization* (2d ed.). New York: Macmillan, 1954.

Pitcher, R. A. The police. In C. H. Kempe & R. E. Helfer (Eds.), *Helping the battered child and his family.* Philadelphia: Lippincott, 1972.

Platt, A., Schechter, H., & Tiffany, P. In defense of youth: A case of the public defender in juvenile court. *Indiana Law Journal,* 1968, *43,* 619–640.

Pock, J. C. *Attitudes toward civil liberties among high school seniors.* Cooperative Research Project No. 5–8167, Reed College, Portland, Oregon, 1967.

Podgorecki, A. Double life in Polish prisons. Unpublished report, Center for Advanced Study in the Behavioral Sciences, 1973.

Poisson, S. D. Récherches sur la probabilité des jugements en matière criminelle et en matière civile. *Precedées des régles generales du calcul des probabilités.* Paris: Bachelier, Imprimeur-Libraire, 1837.

Pospisil, L. Legal levels and multiplicity of legal systems in human societies. *Journal of Conflict Resolution,* 1967, *11,* 2–26.

Pospisil, L. The ethnology of law. *Addison-Wesley Modular Publication,* 1972, No. 12.

Pound, R. Law in books and law in action. *American Law Review,* 1910, *44,* 12–36.

Pound, R. *Jurisprudence* (Vol. 1). St. Paul, Minn.: West, 1959.

Preiss, J. J. & Ehrlich, H. J. *An examination of role theory: The case of the state police.* Lincoln, Nebr.: University of Nebraska Press, 1966.

President's Commission on Law Enforcement and Administration of Justice.

*The challenge of crime in a free society.* Washington, D.C.: United States Government Printing Office, 1967.

Prothro, J. W. & Grigg, C. W. Fundamental principles of democracy: Bases of agreement and disagreement. *Journal of Politics,* 1960, *22,* 276–294.

Quinney, R. (Ed.) *Crime and justice in society.* Boston: Little, Brown, 1969.

Rabin, A. I. *Growing up in the kibbutz.* New York: Springer, 1965.

Rabin, R. L. Some thoughts on tort law from a sociopolitical perspective. *Wisconsin Law Review,* 1969, 51–81.

Rahmani, L. *Soviet psychology: Philosophical, theoretical, and experimental issues.* New York: International Universities Press, 1973.

Rappoport, L. & Kren, G. What is a social issue? *American Psychologist,* 1975, *30,* 838–841.

Rawls, J. Two concepts of rules. *Philosophical Review,* 1955, *64,* 3–32.

Rawls, J. The justification of civil disobedience. In H. Bedau (Ed.), *Civil disobedience: Theory and practice.* Indianapolis: Pegasus, 1969.

Rawls, J. *A theory of justice.* Cambridge, Mass.: Belknap Press of Harvard University Press, 1971.

Reed, E. W. & Reed, S. C. *Mental retardation: A family study.* Philadelphia: Saunders, 1965.

Reed, J. P. Jury deliberations, voting, and verdict trends. *The Southwestern Social Science Quarterly,* 1965, *45,* 361–370.

Reiss, A. J., Jr. Career orientations, job satisfaction, and the assessment of law enforcement problems by police officers. *Studies of crime and law enforcement in major metropolitan areas.* Washington, D.C.: United States Government Printing Office, 1967.

Remington, F. J. & Rosenblum, V. G. The criminal law and the legislative process. *University of Illinois Law Forum,* 1960, 481–499.

Remmers, H. H. & Franklin, R. D. Sweet land of liberty. In R. S. Sigel (Ed.), *Learning about politics: A reader in political socialization.* New York: Random House, 1970.

*Report of the National Advisory Commission on Civil Disorders.* New York: The New York Times Company, Bantam Books, 1968.

*Report of the Select Committee on Capital Punishment (House of Commons).* London: Her Majesty's Stationery Office, 1930.

Rest, J. R. Developmental psychology as a guide to value education: A review of "Kohlbergian" programs. *Review of Educational Research,* 1974, *44,* 241–259.

Rest, J. R. New approaches in the assessment of moral judgment. In T. Lickona (Ed.), *Moral development and behavior: Theory, research, and social issues.* New York: Holt, Rinehart and Winston, 1976.

Rest, J. R., Turiel, E., & Kohlberg, L. Level of moral development as a determinant of preference and comprehension of moral judgment made by others. *Journal of Personality,* 1969, *37,* 225–252.

Reynolds, P. D. *Value dilemmas associated with the development and application of social science: A report submitted to the International Social Science Council of UNESCO.* Paris: UNESCO, 1975.

Richard, W. L. Faculty regulations of American law schools. *Cleveland-Marshall Law Review,* 1964, *13,* 581–585.

Richey, M. H. & Fichter, J. J. Sex differences in moralism and punitiveness.

*Psychonomic Science,* 1969, *16,* 185–186.

Riesman, D. Some observations on law and psychology. *University of Chicago Law Review,* 1951, *19,* 30–44.

Rimm, D. C. & Masters, J. C. *Behavior therapy: Techniques and empirical findings.* New York: Academic Press, 1974.

Risley, T. R. & Baer, D. M. Operant behavior modification: The deliberate development of behavior. In B. M. Caldwell & H. N. Ricciuti (Eds.), *Review of child development research* (Vol. 3). Chicago: University of Chicago Press, 1973.

Roberts, R. C. Some concepts and methods in quantitative genetics. In J. Hirsch (Ed.), *Behavior-genetic analysis.* New York: McGraw-Hill, 1967.

Robertson, J. A. & Teitelbaum, P. Optimizing legal impact: A case study in search of a theory. *Wisconsin Law Review,* 1973, 665–726.

Robins, L. N. *Deviant children grown up.* Baltimore: Williams & Wilkins, 1966.

Robinson, D. N. (Ed.) *Heredity and achievement.* New York: Oxford University Press, 1970.

Rodgers, H. R., Jr. & Taylor, G. Pre-adult attitudes toward legal compliance and the law. *Social Science Quarterly,* 1970, *51,* 539–551.

Rodham, H. Children under the law. *Harvard Educational Review,* 1973, *43,* 487–514.

Rodnick, E. *Postwar Germans.* New Haven: Yale University Press, 1948.

Rokeach, M. *Beliefs, attitudes, and values: A theory of organization and change.* San Francisco: Jossey-Bass, 1968. (a)

Rokeach, M. A theory of organization and change within value–attitude systems. *Journal of Social Issues,* 1968, *24*(1), 13–33. (b)

Rokeach, M. Religious values and social compassion. *Review of Religious Research,* 1969, *11,* 24–38. (a)

Rokeach, M. Value systems in religion. *Review of Religious Research,* 1969, *11,* 3–23. (b)

Rokeach, M. Faith, hope and bigotry. *Psychology Today,* 1970, *3*(11), 33–37.

Rokeach, M. The measurement of values and value systems. In G. Abcarian & J. W. Soule (Eds.), *Social psychology and political behavior.* Columbus, Ohio: Merrill, 1971.

Rokeach, M. *The nature of human values.* New York: Free Press, 1973.

Rokeach, M. & Mezei, L. Race and shared belief as factors in social choice. *Science,* 1966, *151,* 167–172.

Rokeach, M. & Parker, S. Values as social indicators of poverty and race relations. *The Annals of the American Academy of Political and Social Science,* 1970(388), 97–111.

Rollins, H. R. *The mentally abnormal offender and the law.* London: Pergamon, 1969.

Rosen, G. *Madness in society.* New York: Harper & Row, 1968.

Rosenhan, D. On being sane in insane places. *Science,* 1973, *179,* 250–258.

Rosenthal, D. Genetic factors in mental disorder. Paper presented at the Medical Genetics Symposium of the 1972 annual meeting of National Academy of Sciences, Washington, D.C., 1972.

Rosenthal, D. E. *Lawyer and client: Who's in charge?* New York: Russell Sage Foundation, 1974.

Rosett, A. Discretion, severity and legality in criminal justice. *Southern California Law Review,* 1972, *46,* 12–50.

Rosett, A. & Cressey, D. R. *Justice by consent: Plea bargains in the American courthouse.* Philadelphia: Lippincott, 1976.

Ross, H. L., Campbell, D. T., & Glass, G. V. The British crackdown on drinking and driving: A successful legal reform. Laboratory of Educational Research Paper No. 29, University of Colorado, May 1969.

Ross, M. & DiTecco, D. An attributional analysis of moral judgments. *Journal of Social Issues,* 1975, *31*(3), 91–109.

Rothman, D. J. *The discovery of the asylum: Social order and disorder in the new republic.* Boston: Little, Brown, 1971.

Rothman, D. J. Decarcerating prisoners and patients. *Civil Liberties Review,* 1973, *1*(1), 8–30.

Rotter, J. B. & Stein, D. K. Public attitudes toward the trustworthiness, and altruism of twenty selected occupations. *Journal of Applied Social Psychology,* 1971, *1,* 334–343.

*Royal Commission on the Police 1962: Final Report.* London: Her Majesty's Stationery Office, 1962.

Rozeboom, W. W. The fallacy of the null-hypothesis significance test. *Psychological Bulletin,* 1960, *57,* 416–428.

Rubin, Z. & Peplau, L. A. Who believes in a just world? *Journal of Social Issues,* 1975, *31*(3), 65–89.

Rubington, E. & Weinberg, M. (Eds.) *Deviance: The interactionist perspective* (2d ed.). New York: Macmillan, 1973.

Rubinstein, J. *City police.* New York: Farrar, Straus, 1973.

Rumsey, M. G. & Castore, C. H. The effect of group discussion on juror sentencing. Paper presented at the annual meeting of the Midwestern Psychological Association, Chicago, 1974.

Rush, G. B. Status consistency and right-wing extremism. *American Sociological Review,* 1967, *32,* 86–92.

Ryder, R. G. Longitudinal data relating marriage satisfaction and having a child. *Journal of Marriage and the Family,* 1973, *35,* 604–606.

Saks, M. J., Werner, C. M., & Ostrom, T. M. The presumption of innocence and the American juror. Unpublished manuscript, Boston College, 1974.

Sameroff, A. J. & Chandler, M. J. Perinatal risk and the continuum of caretaking casualty. In F. D. Horowitz, E. M. Hetherington, S. Scarr-Salapatek, & G. Siegel (Eds.), *Review of child development research* (Vol. 4). Chicago: University of Chicago Press, 1975.

Sarbin, T. R. The dangerous individual: An outcome of social identity transformation. *British Journal of Criminology,* 1967, *7,* 285–295. (a)

Sarbin, T. R. On the futility of the proposition that some people should be labelled "mentally ill." *Journal of Consulting Psychology,* 1967, *31,* 447–453. (b)

Sarbin, T. R. Notes on the transformation of social identity. In L. M. Roberts, N. S. Greenfield, & M. H. Miller (Eds.), *Comprehensive mental health: The challenge of evaluation.* Madison: University of Wisconsin Press, 1968.

Sarbin, T. R. & Mancuso, J. C. Failure of a moral enterprise: Attitudes of the public toward mental illness. *Journal of Consulting and Clinical Psychol-*

*ogy*, 1970, *35*, 159–174.

Sax, J. Conscience and anarchy: The prosecution of war resisters. *Yale Review*, 1968, *52*, 481–494.

Schaefer, W. V. *Precedent and policy*. Chicago: University of Chicago Press, 1956.

Schaffer, H. R. & Emerson, P. E. Patterns of response to physical contact in early human development. *Journal of Child Psychology and Psychiatry*, 1964, *5*, 1–13.

Schloesser, P. The abused child. *Bulletin of Menninger Clinic*, 1964, *28*, 260.

Schmitt, N. & Colligan, M. Influence of attitudinal similarity to a defendant and victim on guilt attribution by simulated jurors. Paper presented at the annual meeting of the Midwestern Psychological Association, Chicago, 1974.

Schrag, C. *Crime and justice: American style*. Rockville, Md.: National Institute of Mental Health, Center for Crime and Delinquency, 1971.

Schubert, G. (Ed.) *Judicial decision-making*. New York: Free Press, 1963.

Schubert, G. *Judicial behavior: A reader in theory and research*. Chicago: Rand McNally, 1964.

Schubert, G. *The judicial mind*. Evanston, Ill.: Northwestern University Press, 1965.

Schulhofer, S. J. Harm and punishment: A critique of emphasis on the results of conduct in the criminal law. *University of Pennsylvania Law Review*, 1974, *122*, 1497–1607.

Schulman, J., Shaver, P., Colman, R., Emrich, B., & Christie, R. Recipe for a jury. *Psychology Today*, 1973, *6*(12), 37–44; 77–84.

Schur, E. M. *Crimes without victims*. Englewood Cliffs, N.J.: Prentice-Hall, 1965.

Schur, E. M. *Labeling deviant behavior: Its sociological implications*. New York: Harper & Row, 1971.

Schwartz, R. D. & Orleans, S. On legal sanctions. *University of Chicago Law Review*, 1967, *34*, 274–300.

Schwartz, R. D. & Skolnick, J. Two studies of legal stigma. *Social Problems*, 1962, *10*, 133–142.

Schwilck, G. L. & Meade, E. J., Jr. Foreword. In Danforth & Ford Foundations, *The school and the democratic environment*. New York: Columbia University Press, 1970.

Schwitzgebel, R. K. Ethical and legal aspects of behavioral instrumentation. *Behaviour Therapy*, 1970, *1*, 498–509.

Scopes *v*. State. *South Western Reporter*, 1927, *289*, 363–370.

Scriven, M. Methods of reasoning and justification in social science and law. *Journal of Legal Education*, 1971, *23*, 189–199.

Sealy, A. P. & Cornish, W. R. Juries and the rules of evidence. *Criminal Law Review*, 1973, April, 208–223. (a)

Sealy, A. P. & Cornish, W. R. Jurors and their verdicts. *Modern Law Review*, 1973, *36*, 496–508. (b)

Sears, D. O. Political behavior. In G. Lindzey & E. Aronson (Eds.), *Handbook of social psychology* (Vol. 5, 2d ed.). Reading, Mass.: Addison-Wesley, 1969.

Sears, D. O. Political socialization: Part I: Attachment to the system. In F. I.

Greenstein & N. W. Polsby (Eds.), *Handbook of political science: Theoretical aspects of micropolitics* (Vol. 3). Reading, Mass.: Addison-Wesley, 1974.

Sears, P. S. *The effect of classroom conditions on the strength of achievement motive and work output on elementary school children.* Final Report, United States Cooperative Research Project No. 873, 1963.

Seligman, M. *Helplessness: On depression, development, and death.* San Francisco: Freeman, 1975.

Selman, R. & Damon, W. The necessity (but insufficiency) of social perspective taking for conceptions of justice at three early levels. In D. J. DePalma & J. M. Foley (Eds.), *Moral development: Current theory and research.* Hillsdale, N.J.: Lawrence Erlbaum Associates, 1975.

Selvin, H. C. & Hagstrom, W. O. Determinants of support for civil liberties. *British Journal of Sociology,* 1960, *11*, 51–73.

Selznick, P. *Law, society, and industrial justice.* New York: Russell Sage Foundation, 1969.

Shah, S. A. Crime and mental illness: Some problems in defining and labeling deviant behavior. *Mental Hygiene,* 1969, *53*(1), 21–33.

Shah, S. A. The criminal justice system. In S. E. Golann & C. Eisdorfer (Eds.), *Handbook of community mental health.* New York: Appleton-Century-Crofts, 1972.

Shah, S. A. Some interactions of law and mental health in the handling of social deviance. *Catholic University Law Review,* 1974, *23*, 674–719.

Shah, S. A. Dangerousness and civil commitment of the mentally ill: Some public considerations. *American Journal of Psychiatry,* 1975, *132*, 501–505.

Shapley, D. Jury selection: Social scientists gamble in an already loaded game. *Science,* 1974, *185,* 1033–1034; 1071.

Shaw, R. D., Jr. Conspiracy trial—Arsenal of evidence a dud. *Miami Herald,* September 2, 1973, pp. 1A; 5A.

Sheppard, D. *The 1967 drink and driving campaign: A survey among drivers.* Road Research Laboratory Report LR 230, 1968.

Sherif, M. *The psychology of social norms.* New York: Harper & Row, 1966.

Shields, J. *Monozygotic twins brought up apart and brought up together.* London: Oxford University Press, 1962.

Short, E. H., Florence, B. T., & Marsh, M. A. An assessment of videotape in the criminal courts. *Brigham Young University Law Review,* 1975, *2,* 423–465.

Shuman, S. I. *Legal positivism.* Detroit: Wayne State University Press, 1963.

Shuman, S. I. Responsibility and punishment: Why criminal law? *American Journal of Jurisprudence,* 1970, *15,* 25–63.

Shuman, S. I. Social policy and direct action as freedom of expression. In *Law and Disorder.* Detroit: Wayne State University Press, 1971.

Shuman, S. I. Psychosurgery: Legal, moral and philosophical issues. In F. J. Ayd, Jr. (Ed.), *Medical, moral and legal issues in mental health care.* Baltimore: Williams & Wilkins, 1974.

Sidel, R. *Women and child care in China.* New York: Hill & Wang, 1972.

Siegel, S. *Nonparametric statistics.* New York: McGraw-Hill, 1956.

Sigall, H. & Ostrove, N. Effects of the physical attractiveness of the defendant and nature of the crime on juridic judgment. Paper presented at the annual meeting of the American Psychological Association, Montreal, 1973.

Sigel, I. How intelligence tests limit understanding of intelligence. *Merrill-Palmer Quarterly*, 1963, *9*, 39–56.

Silberman, C. *Crisis in the classroom.* New York: Random House, 1970.

Simon, R. J. Mental patients as jurors. *Human Organization*, 1964, *22*, 276–282.

Simon, R. J. Murder, juries, and the press. *Trans-action*, 1966, *3*(4), 40–42.

Simon, R. J. *The jury and the defense of insanity.* Boston: Little, Brown, 1967.

Simon, R. "Beyond a reasonable doubt"—An experimental attempt at quantification. *Journal of Applied Behavioral Science*, 1970, *6*, 203–209.

Simon, R. & Mahan, L. Quantifying burdens of proof: A view from the bench, the jury and the classroom. *Law and Society Review*, 1971, *5*, 319–330.

Simpson, E. L. Teachers of justice: A preliminary report of politico-legal socialization. Paper presented at the annual meeting of the American Psychological Association, Montreal, 1973.

Singer, B. F. Psychological studies of punishment. *California Law Review,* 1970, *58*, 405–443.

Skinner *v.* Oklahoma. *United States Reports*, 1942, *316*, 535–547.

Skinner, B. F. *The behavior of organisms.* New York: Appleton-Century-Crofts, 1938.

Skinner, B. F. *Walden two.* New York: Macmillan, 1948.

Skinner, B. F. *Science and human behavior.* New York: Macmillan, 1953.

Skinner, B. F. *Cumulative record.* New York: Appleton-Century-Crofts, 1961.

Skinner, B. F. *The technology of teaching.* New York: Appleton-Century-Crofts, 1968.

Skinner, B. F. *Contingencies of reinforcement: A theoretical analysis.* New York: Appleton-Century-Crofts, 1969.

Skinner, B. F. *Beyond freedom and dignity.* New York: Knopf, 1971.

Skolnick, J. H. *Justice without trial: Law enforcement in democratic society.* New York: Wiley, 1966.

Skolnick, J. H. Social control in the adversary system. *Journal of Conflict Resolution*, 1967, *11*, 52–70.

Smigel, E. O. *The Wall Street lawyer: Professional organization man?* Bloomington, Ind.: Indiana University Press, 1969.

Smith, A. B., Locke, B., & Walker, W. T. Authoritarianism in college and noncollege oriented police. *Journal of Criminal Law, Criminology and Police Science*, 1967, *58*, 128–132.

Smith, D. N. Man and law in urban Africa: A role for customary courts in the urbanization process. *American Journal of Comparative Law*, 1972, *20*, 223–246.

Smith, H. Commercial arbitration at the American Arbitration Association. *Arbitration Journal*, 1956, *11*, 3–20.

Smith, M. Percy Foreman: Top trial lawyer. *Life*, 1966, *60*(13), 92–101.

Smith, M. B. Is psychology relevant to new priorities? *American Psychologist*, 1973, *28*, 463–471.

Snodgrass, J. Dialogue with Marvin Wolfgang. *Issues in Criminology*, 1972, *7*, 37–58.

Snyder, E. C. The Supreme Court as a small group. *Social Forces*, 1958, *36*, 232–238.

Society for the Psychological Study of Social Issues. Council statement dated January 31, 1960 on the New York City Youth Board Report: An experiment in predicting juvenile delinquency. *SPSSI Newsletter*, April 1960.

Spiotto, J. E. Search and seizure: An empirical study of the exclusionary rule and its alternatives. *Journal of Legal Studies*, 1973, *2*, 243–278.

Spitzer, S. P. & Denzin, N. *The mental patient: Studies in the sociology of deviance.* New York: McGraw-Hill, 1968.

Stanford Law Review. *Symposium on law and psychology.* 1974, *26*, 1243–1490 (Whole Issue).

Stark, R. *Police riots: Collective violence and law enforcement.* Belmont, Calif.: Wadsworth, 1972.

Stark, R. & McEvoy, J. Middle class violence. *Psychology Today*, 1970, *4*(6), 52–54; 110–112.

*Statutes at Large: George III.* 1792, *37*, 627–628.

*Statutes at Large: Henry VIII.* 1534, *4*, 326–327.

Staub, E. To rear a prosocial child: Reasoning, learning by doing, and learning by teaching others. In D. J. DePalma & J. M. Foley (Eds.), *Moral development: Current theory and research.* Hillsdale, N.J.: Lawrence Erlbaum Associates, 1975.

Steadman, H. J. & Keveles, G. The community adjustment and criminal activity of the Baxstrom patients: 1966–70. *American Journal of Psychiatry*, 1972, *129*, 304–310.

Steele, B. F. & Pollock, D. A psychiatric study of parents who abuse infants and small children. In R. E. Helfer & C. H. Kempe (Eds.), *The battered child* (2d ed.). Chicago: University of Chicago Press, 1968.

Stein, A. H. & Freidrich, L. K. Impact of television on children and youth. In E. M. Hetherington (Ed.), *Review of child development research* (Vol. 5). Chicago: University of Chicago Press, 1975.

Stein, D. D., Hardyck, J. A., & Smith, M. B. Race and belief: An open and shut case. *Journal of Personality and Social Psychology*, 1965, *1*, 281–289.

Steinmetz, S. K. Intra-familial patterns of conflict resolution: United States and Canadian comparisons. Paper presented at the annual meeting of the Society for the Study of Social Problems, Montreal, Canada, 1974. (a)

Steinmetz, S. K. Normal families and family violence: The training ground for abuse. Paper presented at National Institute of Health Research Conference on Child Abuse and Neglect, Bethesda, Maryland, 1974. (b)

Steinmetz, S. K. Occupational environment in relation to physical punishment and dogmatism. In S. K. Steinmetz & M. A. Straus (Eds.), *Violence in the family.* New York: Dodd, Mead, 1974. (c)

Stephan, C. Selective characteristics of jurors and litigants: Their influences on juries' verdicts. In R. J. Simon (Ed.), *The jury system in America: A critical overview.* Beverly Hills, Calif.: Sage, 1975.

Stephen, J. F. *A history of the criminal law of England* (Vol. 2). London: Macmillan, 1883.

Stern, W. *Beitrage zur psychologie der aussage.* Leipzig: Verlag Barth, 1903.

Stevens-Long, J. The effect of behavioral context on some aspects of adult disciplinary practice and affect. *Child Development*, 1973, *44*, 476–484.

Stevenson, H. W. Reflections on the China visit. *Society for Research in Child Development Newsletter*, Fall 1974.

Stjernquist, P. How are changes in social behaviour developed by means of legislation? In *Legal essays: A tribute to Frede Castberg on the occasion of his 70th birthday, 4 July 1963*. Oslo: Universitets-forlaget, 1963.

Stone, I. F. Betrayal by psychiatry. *The New York Review of Books*, February 10, 1972, *18*(2), 7–14. (a)

Stone, I. F. Can Russia change? *The New York Review of Books*, February 24, 1972, *18*(3), 14–23. (b)

Stone, J. *Legal system and lawyers' reasonings*. Stanford, Calif.: Stanford University Press, 1964.

Stone, V. A. A primacy effect in decision making by jurors. *Journal of Communication*, 1969, *19*, 239–247.

Stouffer, S. A. *Communism, conformity, and civil liberties*. New York: Doubleday, 1955.

Stouwie, R. J. An experimental study of adult dominance and warmth, conflicting verbal instructions, and children's moral behavior. *Child Development*, 1972, *43*, 959–972.

Straus, M. A. Some social antecedents of physical punishment: A linkage theory interpretation. *Journal of Marriage and the Family*, 1971, *33*, 658–663.

Strickland, L. H. Surveillance and trust. *Journal of Personality*, 1958, *26*, 200–215.

Strodtbeck, F. L. & Hook, L. H. The social dimensions of a twelve-man jury table. *Sociometry*, 1961, *24*, 397–415.

Strodtbeck, F. L., James, R. M., & Hawkins, C. Social status in jury deliberations. *American Sociological Review*, 1957, *22*, 713–719.

Strodtbeck, F. L. & Mann, R. D. Sex role differentiation in jury deliberations. *Sociometry*, 1956, *19*, 3–11.

Strong, E. K., Jr. *Vocational interests of men and women*. Stanford, Calif.: Stanford University Press, 1943.

Strong, E. K., Jr. Interests of fathers and sons. *Journal of Applied Psychology*, 1957, *41*, 284–292.

Study Commision on University Governance, University of California, Berkeley. *The culture of the university: Governance and education*. San Francisco: Jossey-Bass, 1968.

Sudnow, D. Normal crimes: Sociological features of the penal code in a public defender office. *Social Problems*, 1965, *12*, 255–276.

Sue, S., Smith, R. E., & Caldwell, C. Effects of inadmissible evidence on the decisions of simulated jurors: A moral dilemma. *Journal of Applied Social Psychology*, 1973, *3*, 344–353.

Sue, S., Smith, R. E., & Gilbert, R. Biasing effects of pretrial publicity on judicial decision. Unpublished manuscript, University of Washington, cited in *Psychology Today*, 1974, *7*(12), 86–90.

Sullivan, H. S. *The interpersonal theory of psychiatry*. New York: Norton, 1953.

Sumner, W. G. *Folkways*. Boston: Ginn, 1906.

*Survey of Inmates of State Correctional Facilities 1974, Advance Report.* Washington, D.C.: United States Department of Justice, 1976.

Swados, F. Negro health on the antebellum plantations. *Bulletin of the History of Medicine,* 1941, *10,* 462.

Sykes, G. M. & Matza, D. Techniques of neutralization: A theory of delinquency. *American Sociological Review,* 1957, *22,* 664–670.

Szasz, T. S. The myth of mental illness. *American Psychologist,* 1960, *15,* 113–118.

Szasz, T. S. *The myth of mental illness.* New York: Hoeber-Harper, 1961.

Szasz, T. S. *Law, liberty, and psychiatry: An inquiry into the social uses of mental health practices.* New York: Macmillan, 1963.

Taft, D. R. *Criminology.* New York: Macmillan, 1942.

Tajfel, H. Social and cultural factors in perception. In G. Lindzey & E. Aronson (Eds.), *Handbook of social psychology* (Vol. 3, 2d ed.). Reading, Mass.: Addison-Wesley, 1969.

Tapp, J. L. Psychology and the law: The dilemma. *Psychology Today,* 1969, *2*(9), 16–22.

Tapp, J. L. A child's garden of law and order. *Psychology Today,* 1970, *4*(7), 29–31; 62–64. (a)

Tapp, J. L. Cross-national perspectives. In L. Minturn & J. L. Tapp, *Authority, rules and aggression: A cross-national study of children's judgments of the justice of aggressive confrontations. Part II.* Washington, D.C.: United States Department of Health, Education & Welfare, 1970. (b)

Tapp, J. L. What rule? What role?: Reacting to Polier's *Rule of law and role of psychiatry. UCLA Law Review,* 1970, *17,* 1333–1344. (c)

Tapp, J. L. Reflections. *Journal of Social Issues,* 1971, *27*(2), 1–16. (a)

Tapp, J. L. (Ed.) Socialization, the law, and society. *Journal of Social Issues,* 1971, *27*(2) (Whole Issue). (b)

Tapp, J. L. *Cross-cultural and developmental dimensions of a jurisprudence of youth.* Law and Society Center, University of California, Berkeley, Working Paper No. 5, 1973.

Tapp, J. L. The psychological limits of legality. In J. R. Pennock & J. W. Chapman (Eds.), *The limits of law: Nomos XV.* New York: Lieber-Atherton, 1974.

Tapp, J. L. Psychology and the law: A first recital. Paper presented at the annual meeting of the American Psychology-Law Society, Chicago, 1975.

Tapp, J. L. Psychology and the law: An overture. In M. R. Rosenzweig & L. W. Porter (Eds.), *Annual review of psychology* (Vol. 27). Palo Alto, Calif.: Annual Reviews, 1976.

Tapp, J. L., Kelman, H. C., Triandis, H. C., Wrightsman, L. S., & Coelho, G. V. Continuing concerns in cross-cultural ethics: A report. *International Journal of Psychology,* 1974, *9,* 231–249.

Tapp, J. L. & Levine, F. J. Persuasion to virtue: A preliminary statement. *Law and Society Review,* 1970, *4,* 565–582.

Tapp, J. L. & Levine, F. J. The jurisprudence of youth. Unpublished manuscript, American Bar Foundation, 1971.

Tapp, J. L. & Levine, F. J. Compliance from kindergarten to college: A speculative research note. *Journal of Youth and Adolescence,* 1972, *1,* 233-249.

Tapp, J. L. & Levine, F. J. Mismatch: The game of legal socialization. Paper presented at the annual meeting of the American Psychological Association, Montreal, 1973.

Tapp, J. L. & Levine, F. J. Legal socialization: Strategies for an ethical legality. *Stanford Law Review*, 1974, *27*, 1–72.

Taubman, J. Law and sociology in the control of small groups. *University of Toronto Law Review*, 1959, *13*, 23–33.

Terkel, S. *Working: People talk about what they do all day and how they feel about what they do*. New York: Pantheon, 1974.

Terman, L. M. & Miles, C. C. *Sex and personality studies in masculinity and femininity*. New York: McGraw-Hill, 1936.

Terr, L. C. A family study of child abuse. *American Journal of Psychiatry*, 1970, *127*, 665–671.

Thayer, J. B. *A preliminary treatise on evidence at the common law*. Boston: Little, Brown, 1898.

Thibaut, J. & Walker, L. *Procedural justice: A psychological analysis*. Hillsdale, N.J.: Lawrence Erlbaum Associates, 1975.

Thibaut, J., Walker, L., & Lind, J. Adversary presentation and bias in legal decision-making. *Harvard Law Review*, 1972, *86*, 386–401.

Thompson, W. R. Some problems in the genetic study of personality and intelligence. In J. Hirsch (Ed.), *Behavior-genetic analysis*. New York: McGraw-Hill, 1967.

Thyrén, J. C. W. *Straffrattens allmanna grunder* [The foundations of criminal law]. Lund: Gleerupska Universitets Bokhandelen, 1970.

Timasheff, N. Petrazhitskii's philosophy of law. In P. Sayre (Ed.), *Interpretations of modern legal philosophies*. New York: Oxford University Press, 1947.

Tivnan, E. Jury by trial. *The New York Times Magazine*, November 16, 1975, Section 6, pp. 30–31; 54; 56; 58; 60; 64; 68; 70.

Toby, J. Is punishment necessary? *Journal of Criminal Law, Criminology and Police Science*, 1964, *55*, 334–335.

Toch, H. (Ed.) *Legal and criminal psychology*. New York: Holt, Rinehart and Winston, 1961.

Toch, H. H. Psychological consequences of the police role. *Police*, 1965, *10*(1), 22–25.

Toch, H. *Violent men: An inquiry into the psychology of violence*. Chicago: Aldine, 1969.

Torney, J. V., Hess, R. D., & Easton, D. The child's idealization of authority. Paper presented at the annual meeting of the American Psychological Association, St. Louis, Missouri, September 1962.

Torney, J. V., Openheim, A. N., & Farnen, R. F. *Civic education in ten countries: An empirical study*. New York: Wiley International, 1975.

Tracy, J. J. & Cross, H. J. Antecedents of shift in moral judgment. *Journal of Personality and Social Psychology*, 1973, *26*, 238–244.

Triandis, H. C. Research directions suggested by the ACLU. *Journal of Social Issues*, 1975, *31*(2), 165–181.

Tribe, L. H. An ounce of detention: Preventive justice in the world of John Mitchell. *Virginia Law Review*, 1970, *56*, 371–407.

Trotter, S. Patuxent: "Therapeutic" prison faces test. *American Psychological Association Monitor*, 1975, *6*(5), 1; 4; 12. (a)

Trotter, S. Token economy program perverted by prison officials. *American Psychological Association Monitor*, 1975, *6*, 10. (b)

Truman, D. B. *The governmental process.* New York: Knopf, 1963.

Tumanov, V. A. Failure to understand or unwillingness to understand? *Soviet Law and Government*, 1965, *4*(3), 3–10. Originally published in Russian in *Sovetskoe Gosudarstvo i Pravo*, 1965, No. 8, 64–72.

Turiel, E. An experimental analysis of developmental stages in the child's moral judgment. Unpublished doctoral dissertation, Yale University, 1964.

Turiel, E. An experimental test of the sequentiality of developmental stages in the child's moral judgment. *Journal of Personality and Social Psychology*, 1966, *3*, 611–618.

Turiel, E. Stage transition in moral development. In R. M. W. Travers (Ed.), *Second handbook of research on teaching.* Chicago: Rand McNally, 1973.

Turiel, E. Conflict and transition in adolescent moral development. *Child Development*, 1974, *45*, 14–29.

Turiel, E. The development of social concepts: Mores, customs, and conventions. In D. J. DePalma & J. M. Foley (Eds.), *Moral development: Current theory and research.* Hillsdale, N.J.: Lawrence Erlbaum Associates, 1975.

Turiel, E., Kohlberg, L., & Edwards, C. P. Development of moral judgment in Turkish village and urban children. In L. Kohlberg & E. Turiel (Eds.), *Research in moralization: The cognitive developmental approach.* New York: Holt, Rinehart and Winston, in prep.

*Uniform Commercial Code.* St. Paul, Minn.: West, 1970.

*United States Code.* Washington, D.C.: United States Government Printing Office, 1964.

*United States Code.* St. Paul, Minn.: West, 1972.

United States *v.* Battiste. *Sumner's United States Circuit Court Reports*, 1835, *2*, 240–251.

United States *v.* Butler. *United States Reports*, 1936, *297*, 1–88.

United States *v.* Maybury. *Federal Reporter* (2d Series). 1959, *274*, 899–908.

United States *v.* Moylan. *Federal Reporter* (2d Series). 1969, 417, 1002–1009.

United States *v.* Ogull. *Federal Supplement*, 1957, *149*, 272–279.

United States *v.* Russell. *United States Reports*, 1973, *411*, 423–450.

United States *v.* Sisson. *Federal Supplement*, 1968, *294*, 520–524.

United States *v.* Spock. *Federal Reporter* (2d Series). 1969, *416*, 165–194.

Valenti, A. C. & Downing, L. L. Differential effects of jury size on verdicts following deliberation as a function of the apparent guilt of a defendant. *Journal of Personality and Social Psychology*, 1975, *32*, 655–663.

Valentine, A. *Vigilante justice.* New York: Reynal, 1956.

Van Dyke, J. M. The jury as a political institution. *The Center Magazine*, 1970, *3*(2), 17–26.

Vandenberg, S. G. The nature and nurture of intelligence. In D. C. Glass (Ed.), *Genetics.* New York: Rockefeller University Press, 1968.

Vandenberg, S. G. & Kelly, L. Hereditary components in vocational preferences. *Acta Geneticae Medicae et Gemellologiae*, 1964, *13*, 266–274.

Vandenberg, S. G. & Stafford, R. E. Hereditary influences on vocational preferences as shown by scores of twins on the Minnesota Vocational Interest Inventory. *Journal of Applied Psychology*, 1967, *51*, 17–19.

Viano, E. C. Attitudes towards child abuse among American professionals. Paper presented at the biennial meeting of the International Society for Research on Aggression, Toronto, Canada, 1974.

Vidmar, N. Effects of decision alternatives on the verdicts and social perceptions of simulated jurors. *Journal of Personality and Social Psychology,* 1972, *22,* 211–218. (a)

Vidmar, N. Group-induced shifts in simulated jury decisions. Paper presented at the annual meeting of the Midwestern Psychological Association, Cleveland, 1972. (b)

Vorenberg, E. W. & Vorenberg, J. Early diversion from the criminal justice system: Practice in search of a theory. In L. E. Ohlin (Ed.), *Prisoners in America.* Englewood Cliffs, N.J.: Prentice-Hall, 1973.

Vygotsky, L. S. *Thought and language* (E. Hanfmann & G. Vakar, Trans.). Cambridge, Mass.: M.I.T. Press, 1962.

Vygotsky, L. S. Development of the higher mental functions. In A. Leontiev, A. R. Luria, & A. Smirnov (Eds.), *Psychological research in the U.S.S.R.* Moscow: Progress, 1966.

Walbert, D. F. The effect of jury size on the probability of conviction: An evaluation of Williams *v.* Florida. *Case Western Reserve Law Review,* 1971, *22,* 529–554.

Walker, L., Thibaut, J., & Adreoli, V. Order of presentation at trial. *Yale Law Journal,* 1972, *82,* 216–226.

Walker, N. Morality and the criminal law. *Howard Journal of Penology and Crime Prevention,* 1964, *11,* 209–219.

Walker, N. & Argyle, M. Does the law affect moral judgments? *British Journal of Criminology,* 1964, *4,* 570–581.

Waller, J. H. Achievement and social mobility: Relationships among IQ score, education, and occupation in two generations. *American Journal of Human Genetics,* 1971, *18,* 252–259.

Walster, E., Berscheid, E., & Walster, G. W. The exploited: Justice or justification? In J. R. Macaulay & L. Berkowitz (Eds.), *Altruism and helping behavior.* New York: Academic Press, 1970.

Walster, E., Berscheid, E., & Walster, G. W. New directions in equity research. *Journal of Personality and Social Psychology,* 1973, *25,* 151–176.

Walster, E. & Prestholdt, P. The effect of misjudging another: Overcompensation or dissonance reduction? *Journal of Experimental Social Psychology,* 1966, *2,* 85–97.

Walster, E., Walster, G. W., Abrahams, D., & Brown, Z. The effect on liking of underrating or overrating another. *Journal of Experimental Social Psychology,* 1966, *2,* 70–84.

Walters, R. H. & Parke, R. D. Social motivation, dependency and susceptibility to social influence. In L. Berkowitz (Ed.), *Advances in experimental social psychology.* New York: Academic Press, 1964.

Wasby, S. L. *The impact of the U.S. Supreme Court: Some perspectives.* Homewood, Ill.: Dorsey Press, 1970. (a)

Wasby, S. L. The Supreme Court's impact: Some problems of conceptualization and measurement. *Law and Society Review,* 1970, *5,* 41–60. (b)

Watson, J. B. Psychology as the behaviorist views it. *Psychological Review,* 1913, *20,* 158–177.

Watson, J. S. *The reign of George III, 1760–1815*. Oxford: Oxford University Press, 1960.

Watson, N. A. An application of social-psychological research to police work: Police–community relations. Unpublished doctoral dissertation, American University, 1967.

Webb, E. J., Campbell, D. T., Schwartz, R. D., & Sechrest, L. *Unobtrusive measures: Nonreactive research in the social sciences*. Chicago: Rand McNally, 1966.

Wechsler, H. Toward neutral principles of constitutional law. *Harvard Law Review*, 1958, *73*, 1–35.

Wechsler, H. *Principles, politics, and fundamental law: Selected essays*. Cambridge, Mass.: Harvard University Press, 1961.

Wechsler, H. The courts and the Constitution. *Columbia Law Review,* 1965, *65*, 1001–1014.

Weick, K. Social psychology in an era of social change. *American Psychologist,* 1969, *24,* 990–998.

Weiss, K. & Milakovich, M. E. Political misuses of crime rates. *Society,* 1974, *11*(5), 27–33.

Weld, H. P. & Danzig, E. R. A study of the way in which a verdict is reached by a jury. *American Journal of Psychology,* 1940, *53,* 518–536.

Weld, H. P. & Roff, M. A study in the formation of opinion based on legal evidence. *American Journal of Psychology,* 1938, *51,* 609–623.

Westin, A. F. Responding to rebels with a cause. In Danforth & Ford Foundations, *The school and the democratic environment*. New York: Columbia University Press, 1970.

Westley, W. A. The police: A sociological study of law, custom and morality. Unpublished doctoral dissertation, University of Chicago, 1951.

Westley, W. A. *Violence and the police: A sociological study of law, custom, and morality*. Cambridge, Mass.: M.I.T. Press, 1970.

Wexler, D. B. Token and taboo: Behavior modification, token economies, and the law. *Behaviorism,* 1973, *1,* 1–24. (Reprinted from *California Law Review,* 1973, *61,* 81–109.)

Weyrauch, W. O. An anthropological study of the legal profession: Erwin O. Smigel, *The Wall Street lawyer. University of Pennsylvania Law Review,* 1965, *113,* 478–484.

Weyrauch, W. O. *The law of a small group: A report on the Berkeley penthouse experiments with emphasis on penthouse V*. Space Sciences Laboratory Social Sciences Project, University of California, Berkeley, Internal Working Paper No. 54, 1967.

Weyrauch, W. O. Law in isolation: The penthouse astronauts. *Trans-action,* 1968, *5*(7), 39–46.

Weyrauch, W. O. Governance within institutions. *Stanford Law Review,* 1969, *22,* 141–153.

Wheeler, S. Criminal statistics: A reformulation of the problem. *Journal of Criminal Law, Criminology and Police Science,* 1967, *58,* 317–324.

Whipple, G. M. The observer as reporter: A survey of the "psychology of testimony." *Psychological Bulletin,* 1909, *6,* 153–170.

Whipple, G. M. (Ed.) Intelligence: Its nature and nurture. *Thirty-ninth yearbook of the National Society for the Study of Education* (Vols. 1 & 2).

Bloomington, Ill.: Public School Publishing, 1940.

Whitehurst, R. N. Alternative family structures and violence reduction. In S. K. Steinmetz & M. A. Straus (Eds.), *Violence in the family*. New York: Dodd, Mead, 1974.

Whittaker, D. & Watts, W. A. Personality characteristics of a nonconformist youth subculture: A study of the Berkeley nonstudent. *Journal of Social Issues*, 1969, *25*(2), 65–89.

Wicker, A. W. Attitudes versus actions: The relationship of verbal and overt behavioral responses to attitude objects. *Journal of Social Issues*, 1969, *25*(4), 41–78.

Wilkins, L. Crime and criminal justice at the turn of the century. *The Annals of the American Academy of Political and Social Science*, 1973(408), 13–29.

Williams *v.* Florida. *Supreme Court Reporter*, 1970, *90*, 1893–1914.

Williams, C. D. The elimination of tantrum behavior by extinction procedures. *Journal of Abnormal and Social Psychology*, 1959, *59*, 269.

Williams, G. R., Farmer, L. C., Lee, R. E., Cundick, B. P., Howell, R. J., & Rooker, C. K. Juror perceptions of trial testimony as a function of the method of presentation: A comparison of live, color video, black-and-white video, audio, and transcript presentations. *Brigham Young University Law Review*, 1975, *2*, 375–421.

Wilson, J. Q. The police and their problems: A theory. *Public Policy*, 1963, *12*, 189–216.

Wilson, J. Q. Police morale, reform, and citizen respect: The Chicago case. In D. J. Bordua (Ed.), *The police: Six sociological essays*. New York: Wiley, 1967.

Wilson, J. Q. *Varieties of police behavior: The management of law and order in eight communities*. Cambridge, Mass.: Harvard University Press, 1968.

Wolf, R. P. (Ed.) *The rule of law*. New York: Simon & Schuster, 1971.

Wolfgang, M. E., Figlio, R. M., & Sellin, T. *Delinquency in a birth cohort*. Chicago: University of Chicago Press, 1972.

Worsfold, V. L. A philosophical justification for children's rights. *Harvard Educational Review*, 1974, *44*, 142–157.

Wyer, R. S., Jr. Category ratings as "subjective expected values": Implications for attitude formation and change. *Psychological Review*, 1973, *80*, 446–467.

Yngvesson, B. & Hennessey, P. Small claims, complex disputes: A review of the small claims literature. *Law and Society Review*, 1975, *9*, 219–274.

Young, L. *Wednesday's children: A study of child neglect and abuse*. New York: McGraw-Hill, 1964.

Zaitsev, E. & Poltorak, A. *The Soviet bar*. Moscow: Foreign Languages Pub., 1959.

Zalba, S. Battered children. *Trans-action*, 1971, *8*(9–10), 58–61.

Zeisel, H. What determines the amount of argument per juror? *American Sociological Review*, 1963, *28*, 279.

Zeisel, H. & Diamond, S. S. Convincing empirical evidence on the six-member jury. *University of Chicago Law Review*, 1974, *41*, 281–295.

Zigler, E. Metatheoretical issues in developmental psychology. In M. H. Marx (Ed.), *Theories in contemporary psychology*. New York: Macmillan, 1963.

Zimbardo, P. G., Haney, C., Banks, C., & Jaffe, D. The mind is a formidable jailer: A Pirandellian prison. *New York Times Magazine,* April 8, 1973.

Zimring, F. E. Measuring the impact of pretrial diversion from the criminal justice system. *University of Chicago Law Review,* 1974, *41,* 224–241.

Zimring, F. E. & Hawkins, G. J. *Deterrence: The legal threat in crime control.* Chicago: University of Chicago Press, 1973.

# BIOGRAPHICAL SKETCHES

**JOSEPH ADELSON** is Professor of Psychology at the University of Michigan and Director of its Psychological Clinic. He is co-author with Elizabeth Douvan of *The Adolescent Experience*. He is currently writing a book with Judith Gallatin on adolescent political thought, and editing the *Handbook of Adolescent Psychology*.

**JOHANNES ANDENAES** is Professor of Law at the University of Oslo, Norway. Formerly Dean of the Law School and President of the University, Professor Andenaes was President of the Norwegian Association of Criminalists and is a member of the Commission of Criminal Law Reform. He has been Visiting Professor at the University of Pennsylvania and the University of Minnesota as well as Visiting Scholar at the University of Chicago. His book *The General Part of the Criminal Law of Norway* is the only European textbook on criminal law that has been translated into English. Most recently he published the book *Punishment and Deterrence*. His various articles on deterrence are widely read and acclaimed in this country by legal and social science scholars alike.

**HAROLD J. BERMAN** is James Barr Ames Professor of Law at Harvard Law School, where he has taught since 1948. He has been a member of the Executive Committee of the Russian Research Center of Harvard University since 1952. He is the author of 17 books and over 150 articles, dealing with a wide range of subjects including comparative law, legal history, legal philosophy, and sociology of law as well as the law of international trade. His books include *Justice in the U.S.S.R.: An Interpretation of Soviet Law, Soviet Criminal Law and Procedure: The RSFSR Codes, The Nature and Functions of Law*, and *The Interaction of Law and Religion*. He is at present working on a multivolume study of the Western legal tradition and its relation to the great revolutions of Western history.

**ROBERT M. BRAY** received his PhD from the University of Illinois in 1974 and is presently Assistant Professor of Psychology at the University of Kentucky. His broad research interests concern small-group functioning, interpersonal perception and attraction, and the relationship of attitudes and behavior. Currently he is investigating decision-making processes among mock juries and studying the role of "extra-legal" influences on those decisions.

**JAMES H. DAVIS** received his PhD from Michigan State University and is currently Professor of Psychology at the University of Illinois. In addition to numerous articles on small-group problem solving and group decision making, he is author of *Group Performance*. His research has primarily been concerned with formal theories of basic social processes associated with collective behavior.

**PAUL A. FREUND** is Carl M. Loeb University Professor Emeritus at Harvard University. Having received his LLB and SJD from the Harvard Law School, he joined the faculty in 1939 after clerking for the late Justice Louis D. Brandeis

**419**

and serving the government as an attorney. An expert in constitutional law and legal process, his books include *The Supreme Court of the United States, On Law and Justice, Constitutional Law: Cases and Other Problems* (with Arthur Sutherland, Mark Howe, and Ernest Brown), and *Experimentation with Human Subjects* (editor). In addition, he is an author in and editor-in-chief of the multivolume *History of the Supreme Court of the United States*. A member and past President of the American Academy of Arts and Sciences, he also has been a Fellow at the Center for Advanced Study in Behavioral Sciences, and in 1975 was the Jefferson Lecturer appointed by the National Endowment for the Humanities.

**LAWRENCE M. FRIEDMAN** is Marion Rice Kirkwood Professor of Law at Stanford University. He received his JD and LLM from the University of Chicago. In addition to numerous articles in scholarly journals, he is the author of *Contract Law in America: A Social and Economic Case Study, Government and Slum Housing: A Century of Frustration, A History of American Law*, and most recently *The Legal System: A Social Science Perspective*. He is co-editor with Stewart Macaulay of *Law and the Behavioral Sciences*. His main fields of specialization are American legal history, sociology of law, and social welfare legislation. He is a Trustee of the Law and Society Association. During 1974–1975, he was a Fellow at the Center for Advanced Study in the Behavioral Sciences.

**LON L. FULLER** is Professor Emeritus at Harvard University School of Law, where he was Carter Professor of General Jurisprudence until 1973. An internationally regarded figure in the fields of jurisprudence, arbitration, adjudication, and sociology and law, he is on the Executive Board of the International Association of Philosophy of Law and Social Philosophy. In addition to numerous articles in scholarly books and journals, he is author of *The Law in Quest of Itself, Anatomy of the Law, Legal Fictions,* and *The Morality of Law*.

**JUDITH GALLATIN** is Associate Professor of Psychology at Eastern Michigan University. In addition to many articles in scholarly journals, she is author of *Adolescence and Individuality: A Conceptual Approach to Adolescent Psychology* and has contributed chapters to two other books, *Comparative Human Rights* and *Understanding Adolescence*. She served as Project Director for a comprehensive study of the development of political thinking during adolescence and is currently collaborating on a book in this area with Joseph Adelson. In addition, she is writing a book on abnormal psychology.

**ERNEST A. HAGGARD,** Professor of Psychology in the Department of Psychiatry at the University of Illinois and holder of a Research Career Award from the National Institute of Mental Health, received his PhD from Harvard University. Although his research and theoretical writings cover a variety of substantive areas, they are characterized by two central interests: research methodology and the importance of the historical and situational contexts in the understanding of behavior. As Co-Director of the Center for Interdisciplinary Study at the University of Miami School of Law, he is continuing and extending his research interests in the decision-making process.

**CRAIG HANEY** received his PhD in experimental social psychology from Stanford University, where he is currently a Russell Sage Foundation Resident in Law and Social Science. His research concerns the interrelatedness of self and social control processes, and the dehumanizing effects of institutionalization. In addition to his work with Philip Zimbardo on the psychology of imprisonment and prison reform, he is interested in the uses and abuses of psychology in law, the behavioral control of behavior controllers, and ideology in the criminal justice process.

**GORDON HAWKINS** is Associate Professor of Criminology at Sydney University Law School and a member of the Australian Law Reform Commission. Since 1967 he frequently has been engaged as a Research Fellow at the Center for Studies in Criminal Justice at the University of Chicago. He received his BA at the University of Wales in 1950 and spent three years as a Research Fellow in Philosophy at Balliol College, Oxford. He has been Governor of an English prison, served in the Indian Army, and was Assistant Principal, U.K. Prison Staff College. Having widely published articles in various legal, sociological, and criminological journals, he also is co-author of *The Honest Politician's Guide to Crime Control* (with Norval Morris), *Letter to the President on Crime Control* (with Norval Morris), and *Deterrence: The Legal Threat in Crime Control* (with Franklin Zimring) as well as author of *The Prison: Policy and Practice* and *Beyond Reasonable Doubt*.

**ROBERT W. HOLT** is presently a graduate student in the PhD program at the University of Illinois, Department of Psychology, Division of Social Psychology. He received his BA from the University of Illinois in 1970, spent the years from 1970–1972 in the U.S. Army as a psychiatric medic–social worker, entered the graduate program in social psychology at the University of Illinois in 1972, received his MA degree in 1975, and is presently working on a PhD degree. He has engaged in a series of mock jury experiments under the direction of James H. Davis. His current interests include research in interpersonal attraction prior to social interaction.

**MORTIMER R. KADISH** is Professor of Philosophy at Case Western Reserve University. Educator and philosopher, he received his PhD from Columbia University. In addition to many articles in professional journals, he is author of *Point of Honor* and *Reason and Controversy in the Arts* as well as co-author with Sanford Kadish of *Discretion to Disobey: A Study of Lawful Departures from Legal Rules*.

**SANFORD H. KADISH,** lawyer and educator, is Dean and Morrison Professor of Law at the University of California at Berkeley. He has served as President of the American Association of University Professors, Reporter for the California Legislative Penal Code Revision Project, a member of the California Council on Criminal Justice, and Consultant to the President's Crime Commission. He received his LLB from Columbia University. He is co-author of *Criminal Law and its Processes* (with Monrad Paulsen) and *Discretion to Disobey: A Study of Lawful Departures from Legal Rules* (with Mortimer Kadish), as well as numerous articles appearing in law reviews and scholarly journals.

**HARRY KALVEN, JR.** (1914–1974) was Harry A. Bigelow Professor of Law at the University of Chicago, where he had taught since 1945. A nationally renowned legal scholar, he specialized in torts and constitutional law with special focus on problems of the First Amendment. Commencing in 1955 in collaboration with Hans Zeisel, he directed the school's large-scale interdisciplinary study of the jury system, which culminated in the publication of Zeisel, Kalven, and Buchholz's *Delay in the Court*, and Kalven and Zeisel's *American Jury*. In addition, he wrote *The Negro and The First Amendment* and was co-author of the *The Uneasy Case for Progressive Taxation* (with Walter Blum), *Public Law Perspectives on a Private Law Problem* (with Walter Blum), and *Cases and Materials in Torts* (with Charles Gregory). He was a Fellow of the American Academy of Arts and Sciences and a Guggenheim Fellow for 1970–1971.

**LAWRENCE KOHLBERG,** Professor of Education and Social Psychology at Harvard University, received his PhD from the University of Chicago. Author of numerous articles in professional journals and books in the areas of cognitive development, development of sex-role attitudes, and moral development and education, much of his work has been directed toward developing a universal schema of moral development. He is co-author with Elliot Turiel of the forthcoming *Research in Socialization: The Cognitive Developmental Approach.*

**DAVID LEVINE** (1928–1976) was Professor of Psychology at the University of Nebraska. He received his PhD in clinical psychology from New York University in 1953, followed by four years with the Veterans Administration —two in clinical work and two in research. Joining the faculty at Nebraska in 1957, he first served as Director of the Psychological Clinic, then Director of the Clinical Training Program, and ultimately Chairperson of the Department from 1968–1974. During 1974–1975, he was a Visiting Fellow at the Institute of Criminology, University of Cambridge. His research interests included analysis of misapplications of mathematical models in psychological research and practice, the sociopolitical context of behavior, and the relation between law and psychology. At the time of his death, he was working on a book on the psycholegal analysis of the term "dangerousness."

**FELICE J. LEVINE** is a Research Social Scientist at the American Bar Foundation and Co-Director of its Research Program in Legal Education and Professionalization. In addition, she is currently directing two studies on childhood and the law and one on the impact of a criminal diversion counseling program. Each of these efforts aims to illuminate how individuals, through the life cycle, interact with systems of law and how the nature of sociolegal contexts affects human behavior. Her various articles in social science and law review journals reflect these basic interests in socialization, values, and social behaviors. She is presently on the Board of Trustees of the Law and Society Association and Chair of its Publications Committee.

**STEWART MACAULAY** is Professor of Law at the University of Wisconsin. While on leave in 1970–1971, he served as Director of the International Legal Center's Law Program in Santiago, Chile. His interest in the integration of social science and law began with his study of the marginal role of contract law in transactions between corporations, published in the *American Sociological Review* in 1963. Subsequently, he studied the attempts of organized automobile dealers to affect their relationships with manufacturers by appeals to the legal system. His book *Law and the Balance of Power* reports the relatively important impact of congressional hearings and mediation systems that arose in response to the passage of statutes and the relatively insignificant contribution of formal proceedings under those statutes won by the dealers' lobbying. With Lawrence Friedman he co-authored *Law and the Behavioral Sciences* and a second edition of this work that was published in 1977. He participated in the Russell Sage Foundation Law and Sociology program at the University of Wisconsin and was a Fellow at the Center for Advanced Study in the Behavioral Sciences.

**PAUL E. MEEHL** took his BA and PhD (1945) at the University of Minnesota. While mainly a clinical psychologist (and engaged in part-time private practice of psychotherapy), he has also published research in learning theory, animal behavior, and philosophy of science. A Diplomate (Clinical) of the American Board of Professional Psychology, he is a past President of the American Psychological Association (1962) and a recipient of its Distinguished Scientific Contributor Award. He is the author of *Clinical versus Statistical Prediction: A Theoretical Analysis and a Review of the Evidence, Psychodiagnosis: Selected Papers, Atlas for the Clinical Use of the MMPI* (with Starke Hathaway), *Modern Learning Theory* (with William Estes and others), and numerous articles. His current research interests are taxonomic statistics, behavior genetics, and forensic psychology. At the University of Minnesota he is Regents' Professor of Psychology, Adjunct Professor of Law, Professor of Health Care Psychology in the Medical School, and Professor in the Minnesota Center for Philosophy of Science.

**SOIA MENTSCHIKOFF** is Dean of the University of Miami School of Law. She received her LLB from Columbia University. From 1944–1951 she served as Associate Chief Reporter for the Uniform Commercial Code. Her primary areas of interest are jurisprudence, commercial law, arbitration, international transactions, and international law. She is author of *Commercial Transactions: Cases and Materials* and *Unification of Private International Law* (with Nicholas Katzenbach). A past President of the Association of American Law Schools, she is a member of the American Academy of Arts and Sciences, a life member of the American Law Institute, a member of the Permanent Editorial Board for the Uniform Commercial Code, and on the Board of Trustees of the Rand Corporation.

**MARTIN G. MILLER** received his PhD in social science at Michigan State University. He is presently Director of the Systems Research Unit of the Iowa Youth Services System, Office of the Governor, and Associate Professor of Sociology at Iowa State University. Formerly, he was Assistant Director and Instructor at the National Center on Police and Community Relations, School of Criminal Justice, Michigan State University. His interests include program evaluation, community-based youth services systems, the criminal and juvenile justice system, police and community relations, police and youth interrelationships, the sociology of deviance and compliance, and political socialization.

**RAYMOND T. NIMMER** is an Assistant Professor of Law at Bates College of Law, University of Houston. He is a graduate of Valparaiso University School of Law where he received his JD degree with distinction in 1968. His involvement in empirical studies of law-related topics began in 1968 while he was a Research Attorney at the American Bar Foundation. In addition to various articles appearing in law review and social science publications, his books include *Two Million Unnecessary Arrests; The Omnibus Hearing: An Experiment in Relieving Inefficiency, Unfairness and Judicial Delay; Diversion: The Search for Alternative Forms of Prosecution; Prosecutor Disclosure and Judicial Reform; and The System Impact of Criminal Justice Reforms.* He served as a consultant to the Courts Task Force of the National Commission on Criminal Justice Standards and Goals.

**ROSS D. PARKE** is Professor of Psychology and Chair, Division of Developmental Psychology at the University of Illinois at Champaign. He received his PhD from the University of Waterloo and has previously held positions at the University of Wisconsin and the Fels Research Institute. His main interests include socialization of aggression and self-control and the role of the father in early infancy. He is editor of *Readings in Social Development* and *Recent Trends in Social Learning Theory* and recently co-authored *Child Psychology: A Contemporary Viewpoint* with E. Mavis Hetherington. He is an associate editor of *Child Development.*

**MILTON ROKEACH,** born in Hrubieszow, Poland, received his PhD in social psychology from the University of California at Berkeley. He is Professor of Sociology and Psychology at Washington State University in Pullman. He is the author of *The Open and Closed Mind, The Three Christs of Ypsilanti,* and *Beliefs, Attitudes, and Values.* Most recently he published *The Nature of Human Values,* which is about the organization of values, the measurement of values, long-term changes in values, and the long-term cognitive and behavioral consequences of such changes. His current research interests include value therapy, the ethics of value change, the conceptualization and measurement of value conflict, and the conceptualization and measurement of institutional values.

**DAVID O. SEARS** is Professor of Psychology and Political Science at the University of California at Los Angeles. He received his PhD in social psychology from Yale University. The author of articles on ghetto riots and experimental studies of attitude change and selective exposure, he also wrote the chapters on political socialization and political behavior in the *Handbook of Political Science* and the *Handbook of Social Psychology,* respectively. He is a co-author of *Public Opinion* (with Robert Lane), *Social Psychology* (with Jonathan Freedman and Merrill Carlsmith), and *Politics of Violence: The New Urban Blacks and the Watts Riot* (with John McConahay).

**SAMUEL I. SHUMAN** is Professor of Law and Psychiatry at Wayne State University. He received his PhD from the University of Pennsylvania, his JD from the University of Michigan, and his SJD from Harvard University. In addition to writing numerous articles for scholarly journals, he is author of *Legal Positivism: Its Scope and Limitations* and *Psychosurgery and the Medical Control of Violence: Autonomy vs. Deviance* (in press), as well as editor of *Law and Disorder: The Legitimation of Direct Action as an Instrument of Social Policy*, and *The Future of Federalism.* He is also co-editor with Norbert West of *American Law: An Introductory Survey of Some Principles, Cases and Text.* His numerous professional activities include serving on the Editorial Board of the American Journal of Jurisprudence, and President (1976–1978) of the American Section of the International Association of Philosophy of Law and Social Philosophy.

**JOHN A. SNYDER** is Research Fellow in Interdisciplinary Social Science at Michigan State University. He was formerly a Research Assistant with the National Center on Police and Community Relations at Michigan State University and presently is the Evaluation Coordinator at the Michigan Office of Criminal Justice Programs. His research work includes managing the Model Evaluation Program of the State of Michigan and creating training programs for criminal justice agencies.

**JUNE LOUIN TAPP,** formerly Professor of Psychology and Criminal Justice Studies at the University of Minnesota, is now Professor of Psychology and Provost of Revelle College, University of California at San Diego. She received her PhD in 1963 from Syracuse University; in 1974 she received its Distinguished Alumna Award. Her research interests focus on social and political psychology, legal socialization, and the relationship of personality to ideology and legality from cross-cultural perspectives. She was on the SPSSI Council from 1972–1976, founded its Committee on Socialization and the Law, and is President-elect for 1977–1978. Author of numerous articles for behavioral science and legal journals, she is co-author of *Ambivalent America: A Psycho-Political Dialogue* (with Fred Krinsky).

**JUDITH V. TORNEY** is an Associate Professor in the Department of Psychology at the University of Illinois at Chicago Circle. She received her PhD from the Committee on Human Development, University of Chicago, where she was an Associate Project Director on the study of political socialization reported here. She is co-author of *The Development of Political Attitudes in Children* (with Robert D. Hess), *Civic Education in Ten Countries* (with A. N. Oppenheim and Russell Farnen), and *International Human Rights and International Education* (with Thomas Buergenthal). Her interests include research in the socialization of children to international and intercultural orientations, as well as international human rights education.

**ELAINE WALSTER** is an experimental social psychologist. She received her PhD in psychology at Stanford University and is currently Professor of Psychology and Sociology at the University of Wisconsin. Her research has focused on developing and testing equity theory and on discovering antecedents of romantic attraction. Having published widely in scholarly books and journals, she is co-author with Ellen Berscheid of *Interpersonal Attraction*.

**WALTER O. WEYRAUCH** is Professor of Law at the University of Florida. He received legal training in Germany and in the United States, including the DrJur from the University of Frankfurt (thesis: *The Psychological and Ethical Elements of Guilt*) and the JSD from Yale University. He has been Visiting Professor of Political Science at the University of California in Berkeley and Visiting Professor of Law at the University of Frankfurt. He authored *The Personality of Lawyers* (also revised in a German edition, *Zum Gesellschaftsbild des Juristen*) and contributed to H. Freeman, *Legal Interviewing and Counseling*. He is listed in *Who's Who in America*.

**GAIL L. ZELLMAN** is a social psychologist at the Rand Corporation. She obtained her PhD in social psychology at the University of California at Los Angeles, and was most recently at Michigan State University. She has done research on political socialization, women and politics, and aging.

**PHILIP G. ZIMBARDO** is Professor of Psychology at Stanford University, where he conducts research on a variety of social-psychological issues related to the social and cognitive control of human behavior. He is the author of *The Cognitive Control of Motivation: The Consequences of Choice and Dissonance, Influencing Attitudes and Changing Behavior* (with Ebbe Ebbesen and Christina Maslach), *Psychology and Life*, and *Shyness: What It Is, What to Do about It*. His interest in psychological aspects of law and law enforcement emerged during graduate school at Yale University when he researched the area of police interrogation techniques and admissibility of "coerced" confessions under the tutelage of Abraham Goldstein, Professor of Law. He is currently active in trying to encourage reform of the prison system, raise consciousness about prison conditions, and understand the social psychology of the legal justice system. A slide show of the Stanford Prison experiment that he developed has been effectively presented at hundreds of schools, ACLU groups, as well as at a Senate subcommittee hearing and as evidence in a class action trial.

**FRANKLIN ZIMRING** is Professor of Law and Director of the Center for Studies in Criminal Justice at the University of Chicago. He received his JD from the University of Chicago in 1967. He is co-author of *Firearms and Violence in American Life* (with George Newton) and *Deterrence: The Legal Threat in Crime Control* (with Gordon Hawkins). He also authored the National Institute of Mental Health monograph *Perspectives on Deterrence*.

# NAME INDEX

# SUBJECT INDEX